APPLIED SPECIALTIES IN PSYCHOLOGY

Contributing Authors

Elizabeth M. Altmaier
Virginia D. C. Bennett
Douglas K. Candland
Bruce R. Fretz
Sol L. Garfield
Mark R. Ginsberg
Thomas L. Hafemeister
William C. Howell
Mary Jansen
Charles A. Kiesler
Richard R. Kilburg
Richard J. Lutz
Susan M. Markle
Elizabeth Meid
Merle E. Meyer
Bruce D. Sales
William Schofield
Sharon Shueman
Laurence Siegel
Charles D. Spielberger
David E. Stenmark
Ralph B. Taylor

Applied Specialties in Psychology

Edited by

Elizabeth M. Altmaier
The University of Iowa

Merle E. Meyer
University of Florida

Random House   New York

Distributed exclusively by

Lawrence Erlbaum Associates, Inc., Publishers

Hillsdale, New Jersey, and London

First Edition
987654321

Cover design and background photo by: Nadja Furlan-Lorbek
Digitized photo by: Thomas Porett/Photo Researchers

Library of Congress Cataloging in Publication Data
Main entry under title:

Applied specialties in psychology.

Includes bibliographies and index.
1. Psychology—Vocational guidance. 2. Psychology, Applied—Vocational guidance. I. Altmaier, Elizabeth M. II. Meyer, Merle E. [DNLM: 1. Psychology, Applied. BF636 A652]
BF76.A64 1985 150'.23 84-23420
ISBN 0-394-35060-X

Manufactured in the United States of America

PREFACE

The discipline of psychology is a broad one, encompassing such diverse areas as basic research on human and animal physiology; applied research on the effectiveness of various treatment strategies; and applications of therapy, consultation, and counseling. Just as the field of psychology, from a scientific perspective, has greatly advanced in recent years, so has the field of applied psychology. Psychology as an applied profession exists by means of various specialties—where each specialty builds a body of knowledge and develops a set of skills and techniques, both of which are used to solve practical human problems. The purpose of *Applied Specialties in Psychology* is to provide a comprehensive review of the profession by considering each of its defined specialties and by viewing the specialties within the larger context of psychology as a whole.

We have attempted to provide a balanced mixture of information concerning the theory and research base of each specialty; highlight the activities performed by a psychologist in each specialty; and focus on areas of application across themes of populations, settings, and services. We realize that some students will have an extensive background in psychology while others may have only an introductory course. We have therefore attempted to discuss both research and applications in clear language and at the same time to include information essential to understanding both the development and evaluation of the applications.

The text is organized in five units so that students will be introduced to more traditional specialties first and then progress to more innovative specialties. The first unit contains the specialties of clinical psychology, counseling psychology, community psychology, and health psychology. In recent years, psychology has broadened its focus to include the promotion of physical as well as mental health. Nonetheless, these specialties emphasize the traditional roles of applied psychology in diagnosis, counseling, psychotherapy, and consultation.

The second unit discusses the traditional and innovative specialties contained in educational settings: school psychology, instructional psychology, and the teaching of psychology. Perhaps the first "applied psychologist" was Lightner Witmer, to whom school psychology and clinical psychology owe a historical debt. The chapters in this unit take psychology from Witmer's earliest clinic to the current use of computers in school settings. Given the importance society places on education and the recent emphasis on increasing educational quality, the work of psychology in educational settings is likely to broaden in the future.

While the traditional view of psychology's applications may emphasize health promotion, another view of the applied role of psychology emphasizes resolution of problems connected with employment. Historically, psychologists have been interested in assisting individuals to find satisfactory employment and to achieve optimal performance on the job. The chapters in the third unit—industrial and organizational psychology, engineering psychology, and consumer psychology—share the business world setting. These specialties have a common concern with the effective application of research findings and the contribution of research to the specialty's knowledge base.

Unit four contains specialties that all fit in a recent area of application for psychology—the "public domain." This unit includes chapters on environmental psychology, law and psychology, and psychology and public policy. These three specialties are perhaps the newest for psychology, and present unique challenges to the field.

The last unit contains a chapter that discusses issues related to the practice of psychology in the United States and also provides a full context for the preceding chapters on specific specialties.

A text as complete and complex as this one could not have been written by one or two persons. We therefore greatly appreciate the efforts of our contributing authors, each of whom was chosen for being a recognized "expert" in his or her specialty. This text would not have been possible without their contributions. We also wish to thank a number of colleagues who provided criticism and suggestions for the text: Steven D. Brown, University of Minnesota; Sara E. Snodgrass, Skidmore College; Joy Stapp, American Psychological Association; and Dawn R. Van Velzen and Valerie S. Tarico, University of Iowa. Reta Litton and Ginny Travis assisted by patiently typing and retyping parts of the manuscript, and we appreciate their efforts. We would also like to thank Jack Beckwith and our publisher's staff for their assistance with this project. Lastly, we wish to acknowledge the enthusiastic support of Stuart Johnson and Merryl Sloan, our editors during the book's development.

Psychology as a field is evolving and developing. This characteristic lends excitement as well as frustration to the work of conducting research and using research findings to solve human problems. Much of the steady progress of applied psychology is owed to those who have labored at this venture before us. We both worked as colleagues with such a person, an outstanding scholar, clinician, and historian to whom the field of applied psychology owes a great debt—Robert I. Watson, Sr. It is to his memory that we dedicate this book.

July 9, 1984   E.M.A.
                                                                           M.E.M.

CONTRIBUTORS

Lauren B. Alloy, Department of Psychology, Northwestern University, Evanston, Ill.

Elizabeth M. Altmaier, College of Education, The University of Iowa, Iowa City, Iowa

Kathryn Anthony, Department of Psychology, California State Polytechnic University, Pomona, Calif.

James Bell, Department of Psychology, Howard Community College, Columbia, Md.

Virginia D. C. Bennett, Graduate School of Professional Psychology, Rutgers University, Busch Campus, New Brunswick, N.J.

Douglas K. Candland, Department of Psychology, Bucknell University, Lewisberg, Penn.

Loren J. Chapman, Department of Psychology, University of Wisconsin, Madison, Wis.

Bruce R. Fretz, Department of Psychology, University of Maryland, College Park, Md.

Sol L. Garfield, Department of Psychology, Washington University, St. Louis, Mo.

Mark R. Ginsberg, American Psychological Association, Washington, D.C.

Thomas L. Hafemeister, Department of Psychology and College of Law, University of Nebraska—Lincoln, Lincoln, Neb.

William C. Howell, Department of Psychology, Rice University, Houston, Tex.

Mary Jansen, American Psychological Association, Washington, D.C.

Charles A. Kiesler, Department of Psychology, Carnegie-Mellon University, Pittsburgh, Penn.

Richard Kilburg, American Psychological Association, Washington, D.C.

Irwin Jay Knopf, Department of Psychology, Emory University, Atlanta, Ga.

Richard J. Lutz, Department of Marketing, University of Florida, Gainesville, Fla.

Susan M. Markle, Office of Instructional Resources, University of Illinois, Chicago Circle, Chicago, Ill.

Len McCord, West Des Moines High School, Des Moines, Iowa

Elizabeth Meid, American Psychological Association, Washington, D.C.

Merle E. Meyer, Department of Psychology, University of Florida, Gainesville, Fla.

Ben B. Morgan, Jr., Department of Psychology, Old Dominion University, Norfolk, Va.

Bruce D. Sales, Department of Psychology, University of Arizona, Tucson, Ariz.

William Schofield, Division of Health Care Psychology, University of Minnesota, Minneapolis, Minn.

Sharon Shueman, American Psychological Association, Washington, D.C.

Laurence Siegel, Department of Psychology, Louisiana State University, Baton Rouge, La.

Robert Sommer, Department of Psychology, University of California, Davis, Calif.

Charles D. Spielberger, Department of Psychology, University of South Florida, Tampa, Fla.

David E. Stenmark, Department of Psychology, University of South Florida, Tampa, Fla.

Scott I. Tannenbaum, Department of Psychology, Old Dominion University, Norfolk, Va.

Ralph B. Taylor, Center for Metropolitan Planning and Research, Johns Hopkins University, Baltimore, Md.

CONTENTS

APPLIED SPECIALTIES IN PSYCHOLOGY

MERLE E. MEYER AND

ELIZABETH M. ALTMAIER

INTRODUCTION

■ PSYCHOLOGY AS A SCIENCE AND A PROFESSION

Psychology can be defined in two ways. First, psychology is the science of behavior and, some might add, mental processes and human experiences. Psychology is taught as a scientific discipline at colleges and universities where its practitioners, as is the case with many sciences, place emphasis upon teaching and research. The second way that psychology can be defined is as an *applied profession*, where each "specialty" area of psychology has a body of knowledge and a set of skills and techniques, both of which are used to solve human problems. The primary purpose of this book is to impart information about psychology, and its various applied specialties, as a profession.

Like other scientific disciplines, psychology began as a branch of philosophy and then went on to establish itself as one of the natural sciences. Over the course of its scientific development, psychology also evolved a number of applied specialty areas. This evolution has resulted in the broadening or redefining of psychology to include applied specialties. The American Psychological Association (APA) states that

> As a scholarly discipline, psychology represents a major field of study in academic settings, with emphasis on the communication and explanation of principles and theories of behavior.
>
> As a science, it is a focus of research through which investigators collect, quantify, analyze, and interpret data describing animal and human behavior, thus shedding light on the causes and dynamics of behavior patterns.
>
> As a profession, psychology involves the practical application of knowledge, skills, and techniques for the solution or prevention of individual or social problems; the professional role provides an opportunity for the psychologist to develop

1

further his/her understanding of human behavior and thus to contribute to the science of psychology (American Psychological Association, 1975).

The applied specialties in psychology grew out of a long history of both basic and applied research as well as the delivery of psychological services. Typically, a specialty area began as a foundation of basic scientific knowledge with an informal network of persons working on related problems and evolved to a formal structure, with a defined body of basic and applied research, a set of prescribed skills, and a description of specific responsibilities related to the specialty and its practitioners.

Affiliations of psychologists

In the beginning of this chapter, we said that psychology could be defined in two ways, as a science and as an applied profession. Another way to describe or define psychology would be to ask the 75,000 to 85,000 persons calling themselves psychologists to indicate their primary scientific and/or applied specialty and their primary employment setting. By this procedure, about one-third of all psychologists would describe themselves as experimental psychologists. This designation would include those psychologists who work within the basic research specialties of learning and memory, cognition, sensation and perception, biopsychology, social and personality psychology, developmental psychology, quantitative psychology, and/or general psychology. The majority of experimental psychologists teach and do research within college and university settings; however, some are employed in other settings: hospitals, consulting organizations, business and industry, and governmental agencies (Stapp & Fulcher, 1981, 1982).

The other two-thirds of all psychologists would describe themselves as applied psychologists; they would likely designate their primary specialty as either clinical, counseling, community, industrial/organizational, education/school, engineering, environmental, law, health, consumer, or public policy psychology. Like their experimental colleagues, some applied psychologists teach and do research at colleges and universities. The growing majority, however, work in hospitals, clinics, and schools; have independent or group practices; or consult with business and industry or governmental agencies. Stapp and Fulcher (1981) estimate that, of the persons holding doctorate degrees in psychology, approximately 43% work within an academic setting; 5% in public school systems; 24% in clinics, hospitals, community mental health centers, and counseling centers; 15% in private practice; and 13% in business, government, research organizations, and industry.

Some recent trends

While the distribution of psychologists' primary affiliations is about one-third experimental and two-thirds applied, this distribution has only recently emerged. During the 1960s and early 1970s, there was a rapid increase in the number of doctorates granted in science and engineering and in education and humanities. Recently, as Figure 1.1 illustrates, there has been a decrease in the number of earned doctorates in science, engineering, and humanities from the peak years of the 1970s. The life sciences and psychology have not followed

FIGURE 1.1   The number of doctorate degrees granted within various fields from 1960 to 1982.

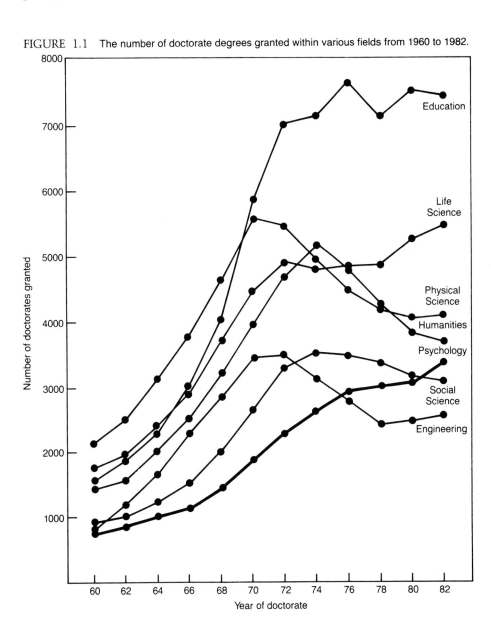

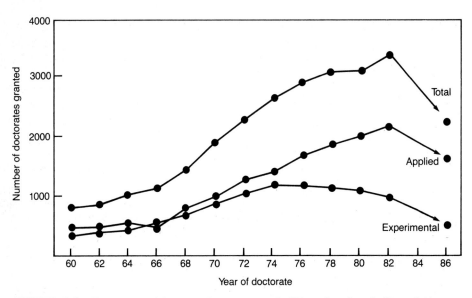

FIGURE 1.2   The number of doctorate degrees granted within various "applied" specialties (clinical, counseling, educational, school, industrial, other) and within various "experimental" specialties (developmental, learning, cognitive, social, personality, biopsychology, quantitative, general) from 1960 to 1982 and projected to 1986.

this decreasing trend; these areas have shown a continuous increase in the number of doctorate recipients over the past twenty years (Syverson, 1982).

As Figure 1.2 shows, the year 1970 was pivotal. At that time, the number of doctorate recipients in applied psychology began to increase and pull away from the number earning experimental psychology doctorates. Since 1970, the total increase in doctoral recipients in psychology has been primarily a function of the increase in applied psychology doctorates; this increase, in turn, has been a function of the increase within the applied specialties of clinical and counseling psychology, as illustrated in Figure 1.3.

While recent historical trends are interesting and important, the major concern of many undergraduates is in the future of experimental and applied psychology as a profession. Each of the following chapters makes some projection of change within each specific applied specialty, but we will make some "guesses" across psychology in general. Based upon the 1982 graduate enrollments, the total number of doctorate recipients is projected to drop substantially by 1986 to about 2,200. The number of clinical and counseling psychology doctorates will be approximately at the 1970s level, but the numbers in experimental will plummet to the level of the 1960s (see Figure 1.2) (Stapp, 1983).

Since the mid-1970s there has been a general decline in the percentage of recent doctorate recipients employed in academic settings. We will assume that the relationship between academic and nonacademic employment is consistent with this trend (despite some variations among certain experimental areas year to year). Various professional and federal agencies project that, through the 1980s and well into the 1990s, there will be zero growth in the number of academic positions, but while the number of positions may not increase, there will be many faculty replacements because of retirements. Since there will be a sharp increase in the demand for psychologists in every applied specialty that "delivers service" through the 1990s, one possible growth area in academics may be teaching in those professional areas of demand. For example, there are now high demands for professors in consumer behavior; this demand may be because business and industry have and will continue to draw persons at the master's degree level from the graduate schools to industrial employment, thus significantly reducing the number of persons in the doctorate programs for teaching the next generation.

FIGURE 1.3   The number of doctorate degrees granted within applied specialties of psychology from 1960 to 1982.

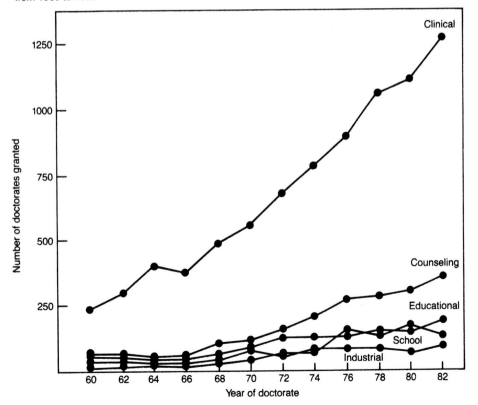

As a robust and adaptive discipline, psychology will continue to have new or modified applied specialties. These will evolve out of societal needs, governmental policies or commitments, and other factors. For example, during the early 1980s, psychology participated in an accelerated debate regarding federal support for research and clinical training in mental health, a debate that will shape graduate training in the future whatever its outcome. During this same time period, various state legislatures began to appropriate funding for quality improvement in public education, again an event that will influence related psychological specialties. Escalating health-care costs may force our society to turn toward prevention rather than the attempt to "cure" the diseased. These dynamics and a host of other factors will shape, expand, and modify applied specialties in psychology over the next few decades.

■ RESEARCH SCIENTIST–PRACTITIONER

We would like to give you a context for the chapters that follow by describing a continuum between the research scientist and the practitioner. On one end of this continuum, the *research scientist* is identified by a commitment to seeking answers to "basic" and/or "applied" research questions. Basic psychological research emphasizes the definition, quantification, and classification of psychological phenomena. Basic research, therefore, consists of formulating statements of empirical relationships (laws) as well as theoretical relationships (theories and models) among psychological phenomena. Applied research tends to center upon obtaining answers and solutions to individual or societal problems and testing the implementation of these solutions. Whether basic or applied, the research scientist is committed to developing new knowledge through research.

At the other end of this continuum, the *practitioner* is an applied psychologist who is committed to the delivery of psychological services. The practitioner's relationship to research is that of a consumer, utilizing findings generated by research scientists to develop increasingly effective solutions. Each applied specialty in psychology is typically associated with four general classifications that distinguish it from the other specialties. Each specialty and its practitioners are related to certain *problem areas*, such as mental health, physical health, or education. Also, each specialty is related to certain groups of *persons*, such as the physically ill. Each specialty is defined by various *services* that are rendered, such as psychotherapy, teaching, or consultation. Lastly, each specialty practices in certain *settings*, such as clinics, hospitals, or governmental agencies. The psychologist practitioner is a recognized specialist in an applied area of psychology who has completed a professional training program, understands the specialty's knowledge base, possesses its skills and technologies, and can deliver services for particular problems, to certain populations, and in certain settings.

It may be obvious that psychologists can at one time be involved in basic research and at another time center their interests on applied research, while all the time be delivering psychological services as a professional practitioner. For this reason, graduate training programs in applied specialties place an emphasis on research competence. Those programs that follow a scientist–practitioner model attempt to train psychologists within the specialty as both research scientists and as practitioners. Other training programs or models may place less emphasis on training in research and more emphasis on the delivery of services.

■ TRAINING IN PSYCHOLOGY

In most professions, the use of the title associated with the profession allows an observer to determine what kind of training that professional has had. For example, we know that an "attorney" has completed three years of law school. We also know that a "physician" has completed four years of medical school, three years of internship and residency, and perhaps additional years in fellowship status. However, the term "psychologist" is not associated with a particular kind or length of training. While several of the chapters that follow will discuss training in psychology, we would like to introduce you to some important aspects of training.

Levels of training

Historically, a "psychologist" has been a professional with a doctoral degree (usually Ph.D.). However, there are many practicing psychologists who have earned a master's degree only. Recently, the American Psychological Association has taken the stand that calling oneself a psychologist should mean that one has earned the doctoral degree.

> The title "professional psychologist" has been used so widely and by persons with such a wide variety of training and experience that it does not provide the information the public deserves. As a consequence, the APA takes a position and makes it a part of its policy that the use of the title "professional psychologist," and its variations such as "clinical psychologist," "counseling psychologist," "school psychologist," and "industrial psychologist" are reserved for those who have completed a doctoral training program in psychology in a university, college, or professional school of psychology that is APA or regionally accredited. The APA further takes the position and makes a part of its policy that only those who have completed a doctoral training program in professional psychology in a university, college, or professional school of psychology that is APA or regionally accredited are qualified independently to provide unsupervised direct delivery of professional services including preventive, assessment, and therapeutic services (APA, 1977a).

While the American Psychological Association has been working to restrict the use of the term "psychologist" to persons with doctoral level training, many training programs have been developed that terminate with a master's degree. This conflict has been particularly sharp in certain specialty areas, such as school psychology. Chapter 6 on School Psychology presents further information on the use of the designation "school psychologist" by master's level persons. A key issue in the conflict of doctoral versus master's degrees is that of independent practice. While persons with bachelor's and master's degrees can perform many valuable functions in psychological service settings, the APA has taken the position that independent practice (work that is unsupervised) requires a doctoral degree.

As will become apparent in the following chapters, some specialty areas in psychology have very specific training methods or models associated with them. For example, a student in a clinical psychology doctoral training program usually takes four to five years of course work and supervised practicum and internship experience to complete a Ph.D. During this time, students take basic psychology courses as well as advanced sequences of courses to learn skills related to practice (such as assessment and psychotherapy). Students receive research training, including courses in research design and statistics and the completion of a master's thesis and a doctoral dissertation. Finally, students receive training in the actual practice of psychology, beginning at the practicum level (where students see clients under closely supervised conditions) progressing to the internship level (where students work in a service setting for one year under supervision). This particular training program has often been referred to as the *scientist–professional model*, where the student is expected to be competent in both the science of psychology and the practice of psychology.

There are other specialty areas in psychology where training is not as easily defined. For example, Chapter 14, Psychology and Public Policy, discusses the interdisciplinary training necessary in order to function as a psychologist who analyzes public policy. Requirements include preparatory course work in political science, economics, anthropology, and so on. Chapter 11 on Consumer Psychology discusses a training approach in which the student may complete the doctoral degree in a psychology department with a consumer psychology program or in a business school. In this type of program, course work in economics, business, management, and so on would be undertaken. Finally, there are specialty areas where training models are currently evolving. Chapter 5, Psychology and Health, discusses the development of a training curriculum for health psychologists.

Because there are many avenues of training in applied psychology, the American Psychological Association (1977b) in its Standards for Providers of Psychological Services has specified a minimally acceptable *level* for the provider of services.

All persons providing psychological services shall meet minimally acceptable levels of training and experience, which are consistent and appropriate with the functions they perform. However, final responsibility and accountability for services provided must rest with psychologists who have earned a doctoral degree in a program that is primarily psychological at a regionally accredited university or professional school.

This principle speaks to the need for any psychologist in any specialty to have completed work at the doctoral level in order to function independently. The exact nature of that work may be determined by standard models of training, by evolving models of training, or by the person himself or herself, depending upon the specialty.

Graduate education

The American Psychological Association accredits doctoral training programs in clinical, counseling, and school psychology, as well as combined professional–scientific programs; the APA also accredits professional psychology internships. The purpose of accreditation is to assure students, as well as the general public, that accredited programs meet minimal criteria for training. These criteria (Committee on Accreditation, APA, 1980) relate to the institutional setting, the faculty, the students, the facilities, the curriculum, and training procedures. For example, one requirement for accreditation is that the doctoral training program must be clearly and publicly identified as a psychology program wherever it is administratively housed. The "wherever administratively housed" aspect of this criterion allows programs to be accredited that are not in psychology departments. Some counseling psychology programs are in colleges of education, and some clinical psychology programs are in colleges of medicine. It does not matter for accreditation where the program resides, as long as the program is clearly labeled a psychology program.

Another accreditation criterion has to do with curriculum. Students must demonstrate competence in four major areas of basic psychology. The first is *biological bases of behavior*; course work in this area would include physiological psychology, neuropsychology, comparative psychology, and psychopharmacology. The second area is that of *cognitive/affective bases of behavior*. Students demonstrating competence in this area would take courses in motivation, learning, memory, perception, emotion, and thinking. *Social bases of behavior* is the third area; course work in social psychology, cultural and ethnic processes, and group dynamics would meet this requirement. Last, competence in *individual differences* must be demonstrated; relevant course work would be in personality theory, human development, individual differences, and psychopathology. Students also receive course work in ethics, statistics and research methodologies, measurement, and the history of psychology.

What do the accreditation criteria mean for graduate education? While there is no such thing as a "typical" program in professional psychology, accreditation criteria have resulted in a certain degree of standardization. Table 1.1 presents a sample four-year program of study for an average counseling psy-

TABLE 1.1   **Four-Year Counseling Psychology Program**

	Fall semester	Spring semester
Year 1	Social psychology Measurement Theories of counseling I Counseling skills I Research seminar	Statistics I Theories of counseling II Counseling skills II Vocational psychology Research seminar
Year 2	Statistics II Research methodology I Psychopathology Practicum	Statistics III Research methodology II Cognitive psychology Practicum
Year 3	Group therapy Professional ethics Physiological psychology Practicum	Theories of supervision Psychology of teaching History and systems of psychology Practicum
Year 4	Internship, dissertation	Internship, dissertation

chology student. As you can see in Table 1.1, the student takes theory and research courses, practices under supervision, learns and performs research, and completes a full-year internship. Beginning courses, such as counseling skills, are followed by more advanced courses, such as supervision. Additionally, continual enrollment in practicum allows the student to gradually integrate theory and research into practice.

The American Psychological Association is currently considering whether all psychology programs, not just those in certain applied specialties, should undergo evaluation through a *designation* process (Task Force on Education and Credentialing, 1983). This process would

> articulate the criteria that specify the corpus of knowledge that is common to all . . . psychology programs and the administrative structure under which that body of knowledge is transmitted to students. (p. II-1)

While such a designation system would be voluntary on the part of psychology programs, the Task Force recommended the use of a designation system for all psychology programs to assist in defining the nature of graduate education for the profession of psychology.

Over the years, psychologists have engaged in considerable discussion regarding the type of training needed to function effectively as a psychologist. As we have mentioned in this chapter, discussion has occurred concerning whether training should be at the master's or doctoral level, and concerning what the content of graduate education should be. There have been several major national conferences held regarding this issue. For example, training in clinical psychology was first discussed at The Boulder Conference, Boulder, Colorado, 1949 (Raimy, 1950). This conference endorsed the scientist–professional model of training, presented earlier in this chapter. A similar endorsement for training counseling psychologists was the result of the Northwestern Conference in 1951 (APA, 1952), the first conference on counseling psychology training. The Stanford Conference in 1955 (Strother, 1956) emphasized preparing psychologists for roles in community mental health, although such preparation would still be within the scientist–professional model.

While other conferences were also held, perhaps the most important recent conference on graduate education was held in Vail, Colorado in 1973 (Korman, 1976). This conference was the first to endorse a primarily *professional* model of training. This model, in contrast to the scientist–professional model, emphasizes preparation in necessary skills for applied work as opposed to preparation balancing both research and practice. This training model also endorsed the notion of a career lattice, where psychologists might enter training at different points in their professional career (i.e., after working several years with a master's degree). Professional schools of psychology, located outside of traditional university systems, were initiated based on these and other aspects of the Vail conference.

■ CREDENTIALING, CERTIFICATION, AND LICENSURE

As several of the chapters in this book will discuss, the practice of psychology has become increasingly regulated by state psychological associations, state licensure boards, and federal and state laws. For example, the title "psychologist" has come to be used to indicate a person with a doctoral degree. Additionally, many states have enacted legislation to restrict the practice of psychology to those persons considered fully qualified. Chapter 13 presents a discussion of the interface of law and psychology, and Chapter 15 presents a full discussion of licensure and certification. By way of introduction, the term *licensure* refers to laws that are designed to limit the practice of psychology and the self-identification as a psychologist to those persons who meet particular criteria. *Certification* refers to laws designed to restrict only the use of the title.

Licensure is a legal process meant to achieve certain objectives (Fretz & Mills, 1980). First, licensure protects the public by setting minimal standards of competence for practitioners. Therefore, a consumer using a licensed psychologist would be confident that the psychologist had had certain kinds of training and had demonstrated a certain level of competence. When a client selects a psychologist, he or she may be going through a crisis where making a decision is difficult; licensure allows the consumer to make some judgment of a professional's qualifications. Second, licensure is meant to establish professional standards for practice. Because the licensure process involves clearly developed criteria and standards, it is assumed that practitioners will become increasingly competent as they work toward meeting these standards. A related aspect is that licensure upgrades the profession of psychology by forcing all practitioners to meet certain minimal requirements. Last, licensure is meant to assist in defining the profession. Particularly as licensure allows practitioners to define specialty areas, the scope of the profession of psychology becomes more clearly defined.

Currently, all fifty states have licensure regulations. Each state has its own set of procedures to obtain licensure. Because of this diversity, the American Association of State Psychology Boards (AASPB) was founded in 1961 to assist in coordinating standards and procedures across states. The AASPB developed a professional examination for psychology in 1964, and every state now uses the Examination for Professional Practice in Psychology (EPPP). Additionally, AASPB and APA worked together to draft model guidelines for state legislation (APA, 1978).

■ PROFESSIONAL ETHICS

Applied psychology involves a great variety of activities practiced in many contexts and settings. Whereas some of this practice may be regulated by state laws, much of what a psychologist does is governed by his or her own professional judgment. Therefore, as does every profession, psychology has formulated ethical principles to assist the individual psychologist in making decisions of integrity and sound judgment. McGowan and Schmidt (1962) noted that ethical codes serve several purposes, both for the individual and across the profession of psychology. First, ethical codes provide principles to use in conflict areas. Second, they define the nature of the relationship that should exist between a professional psychologist and his or her client, whether that client is a person, a family, or a company. At a broader level, a code of ethics assures the profession that common standards of practice are followed. An ethical code also gives the public an assurance that psychologists will demonstrate adherence to certain societal expectations.

Box 1.1 presents the ten basic ethical principles of psychologists (APA, 1981). The American Psychological Association has also published more detailed ethical principles having to do with research (APA, 1982) and with the use of psychological tests (APA, 1974). As you can see, the ethical principles provide neither specific answers nor do they solve individual problems. But the principles, and the elaborative material on each principle, will guide the professional in making the best choices possible in his or her practice.

B O X 1.1   ETHICAL PRINCIPLES OF PSYCHOLOGISTS

1. Responsibility: In providing services, psychologists maintain the highest standards of their profession. They accept responsibility for the consequences of their acts and make every effort to ensure that their services are used appropriately.

2. Competence: The maintenance of high standards of competence is a responsibility shared by all psychologists in the interest of the public and the profession as a whole. Psychologists recognize the boundaries of their competence and the limitations of their techniques. They only provide services and only use techniques for which they are qualified by training and experience. In those areas in which recognized standards do not yet exist, psychologists take whatever precautions are necessary to protect the welfare of their clients. They maintain knowledge of current scientific and professional information related to the services they render.

3. Moral and Legal Standards: Psychologists' moral and ethical standards of behavior are a personal matter to the same degree as they are for any other citizen, except as these may compromise the fulfillment of their professional responsibilities or reduce the public trust in psychology and psychologists. Regarding their own behavior, psychologists are sensitive to prevailing community standards and to the possible impact that conformity to or deviation from these standards may have upon the quality of their performance as psychologists. Psychologists are also aware of the possible impact of their public behavior upon the ability of colleagues to perform their professional duties.

4. Public Statements: Public statements, announcements of services, advertising, and promotional activities of psychologists serve the purpose of helping the public make informed judgments and choices. Psychologists represent accurately and objectively their professional qualifications, affiliations, and functions, as well as those of the institutions or organizations with which they or the statements may be associated. In public statements providing psychological information or professional opinions or providing information about the availability of psychological products, publications, and services, psychologists base their statements on scientifically acceptable psychological findings and techniques with full recognition of the limits and uncertainties of such evidence.

5. Confidentiality: Psychologists have a primary obligation to respect the confidentiality of information obtained from persons in the course of their work as psychologists. They reveal such information to others only with the consent of the person or the person's legal representative, except in those unusual circumstances in which not to do so would result in clear danger to the person or to others. Where appropriate, psychologists inform their clients of the legal limits of confidentiality.

6. Welfare of the Consumer: Psychologists respect the integrity and protect the welfare of the people and groups with whom they work. When conflicts of interest arise between clients and psychologists' employing institutions, psychologists clarify the nature and direction of their loyalties and responsibilities and keep all parties informed of their commitments. Psychologists fully inform consumers as to the purpose and nature of

BOX 1.1 *(Continued)*

an evaluative, treatment, educational, or training procedure, and they freely acknowledge that clients, students, or participants in research have freedom of choice with regard to participation.

7. Professional Relationships: Psychologists act with due regard for the needs, special competencies, and obligations of their colleagues in psychology and other professions. They respect the prerogatives and obligations of the institutions or organizations with which these other colleagues are associated.

8. Assessment Techniques: In the development, publication, and utilization of psychological assessment techniques, psychologists make every effort to promote the welfare and best interests of the client. They guard against the misuse of assessment results. They respect the client's right to know the results, the interpretations made, and the bases for their conclusions and recommendations. Psychologists make every effort to maintain the security of tests and other assessment techniques within limits of legal mandates. They strive to ensure the appropriate use of assessment techniques by others.

9. Research with Human Participants: The decision to undertake research rests upon a considered judgment by the individual psychologist about how best to contribute to psychological science and human welfare. Having made the decision to conduct research, the psychologist considers alternative directions in which research energies and resources might be invested. On the basis of this consideration, the psychologist carries out the investigation with respect and concern for the dignity and welfare of the people who participate and with cognizance of federal and state regulations and professional standards governing the conduct of research with human participants.

10. Care and Use of Animals: An investigator of animal behavior strives to advance understanding of basic behavioral principles and/or to contribute to the improvement of human health and welfare. In seeking these ends, the investigator ensures the welfare of animals and treats them humanely. Laws and regulations notwithstanding, an animal's immediate protection depends upon the scientist's own conscience.

NOTE: From "Ethical Principles of Psychologists" by the American Psychological Association, 1981, *American Psychologist, 36,* 633–638. Reprinted by permission.

■ CONCLUSION

We have certain goals for you as you read each of these chapters. First, we want you to be familiar with the history of applied psychology as it has guided the development of each of the applied specialties. Second, we want you to understand the scope of the knowledge base that each specialty works from. While there obviously is considerable overlap among these knowledge bases, especially among specialties whose problem areas, populations, services, or settings are similar, each specialty does contribute via research to a knowledge base and draws from this knowledge base when developing applications. Third, we hope that you will become excited about the many activities performed within each specialty. It is easy to have a narrow view of the activities of different kinds of psychologists; the chapters to follow should widen your perspective on the work of applied psychologists within each specialty. Last, we hope that you will gain an appreciation of the role of psychology within society and the challenges and problems that being a psychologist entails.

While we have provided a structure for considering specialties, namely examining problem areas, populations, services, and settings, we want to warn you that this structure is not always easily applied to each specialty. Some specialties emphasize applications of psychological knowledge. Some specialties concentrate on applied research, and some specialties consider evaluation as a primary activity. Thus, we cannot provide you with a clear definition of an "applied specialty" that will be perfect for each of these specialties to follow. Nonetheless, this diversity can be and is an exciting aspect of the field of psychology. You can be an applied psychologist and also be a researcher, a practitioner, a scientist–practitioner, and so on. Such is the varied nature of applied psychology.

□ □ □ □ □ □ □ □ □

□ □ □ □ □ □ □ □ □

□ □ □ □ □ □ □ □ □

□ □ □ □ □ □ □ □ □

UNIT I   PSYCHOLOGY APPLIED TO
            PROMOTE INDIVIDUAL HEALTH

Most people's conceptualization of applied psychology
focuses on activities related to mental health. That this
conceptualization is widely held is not surprising, since
the applied psychological specialties dealing with mental health are the most traditional specialties, namely
those of clinical psychology and counseling psychology.
In recent years, psychology has broadened its focus to
include the promotion of physical as well as mental
health; nonetheless the traditional role of applied psychology has been in assessment, counseling, and psychotherapy.

      This unit contains four chapters detailing psycholo-
gy's role in the promotion of individual health. As you
read these chapters, you will notice that there are many
similarities among these health-related specialties.
First, they all include assessment activities to clarify the
nature of the problem being dealt with and to formulate
treatment plans. Second, they involve intervention on
the part of the applied psychologist to remediate the
problem, to prevent future problems, and/or to help the
individual develop coping skills to deal with the problem
in the future. Third, they emphasize applied psychology's focus on health, both physical and mental. While
health can be defined in many ways, and indeed is differently defined according to the specialty, the specialties described in this unit are those whose goal is the
improvement of individuals' lives, including physical

health, work adjustment, interpersonal relationships, and feelings about oneself.

While there certainly are similarities among the specialties to be discussed in this unit, there are also very clear differences. First of all, each specialty has evolved via a different history. Since the current appearance of the specialty is determined by its historical development, each chapter reviews the history of its own specialty. Second, each specialty emphasizes different client populations. There is considerable overlap among these specialties, but the traditionally emphasized fields of endeavor are as follows: for clinical psychology, people who have severe personality disorders; for counseling psychology, people with problems of adjustment; for community psychology, people whose mental health is impaired by community systems; for health psychology, people who are at risk for or are actually experiencing physical illness. Last, in spite of their overlap, each of the specialties discussed in this unit enjoys a considerable amount of pride in its own individuality. Training programs for these specialties are different, divisional memberships within the American Psychological Association are different, and students' professional identities as a "clinical psychologist," "counseling psychologist," "community psychologist," or "health psychologist" are unique and special.

SOL L. GARFIELD

CLINICAL PSYCHOLOGY

■ INTRODUCTION

Clinical psychology is the most popular specialty within the field of psychology. In the years 1979 and 1980, approximately 35% of all students receiving their doctoral degrees in psychology were clinical psychology students (Stapp & Fulcher, 1982). There are several reasons why so many students select clinical psychology as their choice of career. First, it is a "helping" profession, and many students desire a career that will provide them with an opportunity to help their fellow human beings. Second, there is a certain attraction or appeal to working with people who need help. Movies, television shows, magazine articles, and the "typical" case histories presented in textbooks on abnormal psychology make clinical psychology appear to be a rather glamorous field, potentially more so than it actually is. A final aspect of clinical psychology, mentioned by a number of prospective graduate students, is the diversity of activities engaged in by clinical psychologists. Individuals can select from a large number of activities and can participate in more than one. Clinical psychologists engage in research, therapy, and training; within each of the broad areas, there are many different types of activities.

This chapter will introduce the reader to the field of clinical psychology. After offering a definition of clinical psychology and differentiating clinical psychology from other related fields, a brief account of the historical development of the field will be presented. More recent developments in clinical psychology will then be emphasized, with particular attention to the roles, activities, work settings, theoretical orientations, and training programs that characterize the field today. I will close this chapter with a discussion of important current issues, both professional and scientific.

Clinical psychology is that specialty area within psychology that is concerned broadly with the study and treatment of disturbed or maladaptive behavior. Specifically, clinical psychologists are involved with the study, diagnosis and assessment, therapeutic modification, and prevention of personality and behavioral problems. Although the broad area of personality problems and adjustment defines the area of specialization of clinical psychologists within the field of psychology, it should be pointed out that this is not the exclusive domain of clinical psychologists. Other professional disciplines are also concerned with such problems and with areas that overlap those of the clinical psychologist. Psychiatry, for example, is a specialty area within medicine that focuses on nervous disorders and "mental illness." Other professions, such as psychiatric social work and psychiatric nursing, also are participants in this area. Besides these more traditional mental health professions, there are overlapping professions in the area of human adjustment services, such as pastoral counseling. In addition, within psychology there are specialties, such as counseling psychology, that work with adjustment difficulties of relatively more "normal" people and with cases of less severe pathology than the clinical psychologist. Over time, however, such distinctions have tended to become blurred. Thus clinical psychologists may treat relatively mild cases of maladjustment and counseling psychologists may work with seriously disturbed individuals. Despite this overlap, clinical psychology maintains a major emphasis on the treatment of pathology.

Clinical psychology in the United States has undergone numerous changes as it has developed and grown, particularly in the last forty years. During this time, the functions, activities, and roles of the clinical psychologist have also undergone modification and change. Consequently, before discussing the present functions and activities of the clinical psychologist, it is worthwhile to understand the historical developments that have led to the current status and popularity of clinical psychology.

■ HISTORICAL DEVELOPMENT

As a specialty in psychology, clinical psychology has been influenced and shaped by many factors, both inside and outside of psychology. Perhaps most important, clinical psychology has been influenced by academic experimental psychology. This influence was particularly strong in the early development of clinical psychology. In more recent times, influences from other sources have played a role in its development.

Lightner Witmer and his contribution

The founder or father of clinical psychology in the United States was Lightner Witmer, a remarkable and innovative psychologist who during his lifetime never received the recognition due him. Witmer received his Ph.D. degree in psychology under Wilhelm Wundt in Leipzig in 1892 and subsequently was appointed director of the Laboratory of Psychology at the University of Pennsylvania. In 1896, he founded the first psychological clinic in this country and also offered the first course titled "Clinical Psychology." Although the term clinical psychology was used earlier in France, it was used essentially by psychiatrists. It was Witmer, however, trained in experimental psychology, who applied this designation to a special area within the field of psychology.

A few of Witmer's other contributions should be mentioned briefly. Besides founding the first psychological clinic, he utilized a hospital, which he felt was essential for the detailed observation and study of the cases referred to him. Interestingly enough, it was the case of a "bad speller" that Witmer credits with starting him off on his involvement with clinical work. Most of Witmer's work was with children referred to him from schools within the Philadelphia area. He used the services of consulting physicians to evaluate sensory and physical aspects of the cases referred to him. The cases were quite diverse, ranging from school difficulties and suspected mental retardation to speech difficulties and behavioral disturbance.

Witmer was clearly an outstanding pioneer. He taught the first course called clinical psychology, he founded the first psychological clinic in this country, he founded and edited the first clinical psychology journal for a period of 29 years, and he was one of the first psychologists to use tests of mental ability. Because of these many contributions, it is surprising that his influence on the field of clinical psychology was limited in his day. There appear to be two major reasons for this. First, Witmer's interests with school problems and mental retardation are different from those of the school guidance movement (i.e., behavioral, social, and personality difficulties), which appeared a decade or so later (Shakow, 1938; Watson, 1953). Second, at the time of Witmer's work, the field of psychology was not well established. In some cases, psychology was not even a separate department within universities and clinical psychology as a program was not well defined. In view of these aspects of the history of clinical psychology, it seems reasonable to view Witmer as an innovative individual who was ahead of his time and whose outstanding contributions to clinical psychology were only recognized at a later date.

The influence of psychological tests

Another significant influence with a more direct and pronounced effect on the development of clinical psychology was the construction of the Binet-Simon Scale of Intelligence. The French psychologist, Alfred Binet, working with his colleague, Théodore Simon, developed the first feasible intelligence test as a means of identifying retarded or slow learners in the Parisian schools. The conceptual basis for the scale appears deceptively simple today, but was of great importance. Essentially, Binet introduced the concept of mental age. Various test items were given to children of various ages and those items that could be solved by children at the various ages were classified as such. For example, an item that can be performed successfully by most five year olds, but is too difficult for most four year olds, is indicative of a mental age of five years. Such a performance constitutes normal mental development for the average five year old. On the other hand, if a three year old performs this item, one could say that the child has a mental age of five years—at least on the basis of this item. Binet and Simon did not rely on a single item. By collecting a number of items calibrated at different age levels, they could administer an entire set of items, give certain mental age values for each item completed, and secure one total mental age for each subject. After much preliminary work, they published the mental age scale in 1905 and revised it in 1908. Chapter 6 presents further information on the development of this scale.

The appearance of the Binet-Simon Scale was an important event in the history of clinical psychology. Henry Goddard, an American clinical psychologist working in the area of mental retardation, brought the scale to the United States and translated it into English. In 1916, Lewis Terman of Stanford University published a revision of this scale (now known as the Stanford-Binet) that became the most widely used individual test of intelligence in this country for many years. Other psychologists also developed a variety of psychological tests for appraising various psychological functions. The use of such tests by the U.S. Army in the First World War led to an expansion in the use of psychological tests in various areas of applied psychology. The activities of clinical psychologists became largely identified with the administration and interpretation of psychological tests, particularly with the Stanford Revision of the Binet-Simon Scale. The psychologist's contribution to the evaluation of clinical cases was seen as the objective and quantitative appraisal of psychological functions, and during the 1920s and through the 1930s, clinical psychology was identified largely with the administration of the Stanford-Binet (Louttit, 1939). Special courses were provided to train psychologists in the administration of this scale and, later, in the administration of the various Wechsler Scales developed to evaluate the intelligence of adults.

Other early developments

Although the development of psychological tests was of great importance, there were other influences on the later development of clinical psychology that also deserve mention. The beginning of the mental hygiene movement, which was largely fostered by Clifford Beers after he experienced a period of hospitalization for his own mental disturbance, was one such influence. Beers's account of his hospitalization in the book *A Mind that Found Itself*, first published in 1908, focused attention on the great need for more humane treatment of those who suffer from severe mental disorder (Beers, 1948).

A related development was the establishment of child guidance clinics. The initial emphasis for such clinics was on the prevention of later disturbance by focusing attention on the early problems of children. The first child guidance clinic was established in Chicago in 1909, with the psychiatrist, William Healy, as its first director. Shortly thereafter a psychologist was hired to work at the clinic. Only a small number of other clinics were established in the next few years, but then the growth of such clinics progressed steadily. The pattern of the "clinical team," consisting of a psychiatrist, psychologist, and psychiatric social worker, was established in the child guidance clinic and, with some variation, has continued in many clinical settings. Psychological testing became the clinical psychologist's main professional function; however, other duties such as educational and vocational guidance, remedial work with school problems, and counseling were also undertaken. See Box 2.1 for a brief explanation of child therapy today.

A last influence of potential importance was the appearance of the psychoanalytic school in the late 19th and early 20th centuries (Freud, 1938). Sigmund Freud, the founder and key figure of this development, is well known to most readers. Freud, trained as a neuropsychiatrist, became increasingly impressed with the possibility that the symptoms of many patients were not due to some type of physical cause. Rather, he came to the view that certain experiences that caused conflicts in the individual were repressed or kept out of awareness. These thoughts, images, and feelings, although unconscious, exerted a dynamic influence and were responsible for the neurotic disturbances or symptoms of the individual.

Although the psychodynamic views of Freud were not well received at first, particularly the view that sexual and aggressive strivings were at the root of many difficulties, eventually his theories became exceedingly influential. Freud's emphasis on psychological causation was an important antidote to the prevailing emphasis on organic sources of personality disorder, and psychological factors were accorded greater importance than they had been before Freud. Freud provided the first truly comprehensive theory of personality as well as a psychological method of therapy.

All of the above influences contributed in different ways to the gradual development of clinical psychology. Witmer provided a name for the new specialty and a training model, Binet contributed what for many years was the main tool of the clinical psychologist, the child guidance movement provided a professional role for the psychologist, the mental hygiene movement focused on the need for humane care and treatment, and psychoanalysis provided a theory and treatment orientation that was essentially psychological.

The Second World War and its aftermath

Despite the events mentioned above, clinical psychology developed quite slowly. Treatment facilities for the emotionally disturbed were limited, there were relatively few jobs for clinical psychologists, and there were no specific training programs for clinical psychologists. Training, which was primarily academic, was criticized as not being adequate for the training of clinicians (Lout-

BOX 2.1   CHILD THERAPY

IRWIN JAY KNOPF

Most people are familiar with the surface characteristics of psychotherapy with adults from the frequent portrayals of the process in books, films, and other media. One stereotype depicts the patient lying on a couch speaking whatever comes into mind or reporting his or her most recent dreams to the analyst. Another popular picture of psychotherapy shows the patient and therapist in a face-to-face confidential talk session. Obviously, these highly verbal forms of psychotherapy cannot be very effective with those who are limited in their expressive language development, such as young children. If verbal communication or interaction is not a fruitful therapeutic avenue for children, then what is?

Play therapy has many variations as it is practiced today, although it was introduced as an alternative treatment method to psychoanalysis for preadolescent children by Freud's daughter, Anna, and another distinguished child analyst, Melanie Klein (Knopf, 1984). Play was viewed as the natural communication medium of young children, and a useful substitute for words through which children could safely express their inner fantasy life and reveal their basic conflicts and problems. Since children like to play, it was reasoned further that play would facilitate rapport between the child and the therapist, and make the treatment session relatively interesting and non-threatening.

Psychoanalytically oriented play therapy involves both free and structured play activities wherein the child is either free to choose from the available toys, games, or play materials (clay, crayons, paints, etc.) or the choice of play is made by the therapist (i.e., a doll house with doll figures representing family members). Often, therapy begins with free play, which is intended to allow the child to display conflicts or problems that are unconscious. Later, structure is introduced to the form and content of the play session by the therapist to

---

tit, 1939; Shakow, 1938). Furthermore, the role of the clinical psychologist was largely limited to the administration of psychological tests. The arrival of the Second World War and the events following it changed the situation dramatically and transformed the specialty of clinical psychology.

As the war continued, there was a large increase in the number of psychiatric casualties and an inadequate number of psychiatrists to care for these individuals. In order to alleviate this problem, clinical psychologists were called upon to help. In 1944, the U.S. Army directly commissioned clinical psychologists and an army training school for clinical psychologists was set up. As a result, several hundred psychologists received clinical training and experience working with a variety of disturbed soldiers. Furthermore, many of the clinical psychologists engaged in a variety of clinical activities including an expanded diagnostic role and psychotherapy.

When the war was over, the Veterans Administration (V.A.) was faced with the staggering task of providing services for the large number of disabled veter-

enable the child to act out the conflicts identified earlier as well as to strengthen coping skills by helping the child to be aware of his or her experiences and feelings. Still later, the therapist interprets these experiences and feelings in order to increase the child's awareness of, and ability to deal with, the sources of anxiety that are interfering with the child's functioning.

Another form of treatment appropriate for children, which has been based on research findings, is behavior therapy or behavior modification. This approach includes a variety of techniques that are derived from learning principles and that are designed to either increase or decrease the occurrence of a target behavior. Techniques may be combined to increase a desired behavior while decreasing or eliminating an undesired behavior. For any technique, the therapist needs to assess the rate of the occurrence of the target behavior (establish a base rate) and specify the conditions that influence the occurrence of the behavior. In addition, the construction of a specific treatment plan requires that the therapist evaluate the responses the child is capable of, the range of stimuli that is processed by the child, and the particular stimuli that influence the occurrence of the target behavior. As early as 1924, Jones (Jones, 1924a, b) showed that a learned fear response (to a furry rabbit) could be eliminated in a young child by pairing an experience incompatible or contradictory to the fear (eating a favorite food) with the gradual presentation of the rabbit (the fear-evoking stimulus). Lovaas and his associates (Lovaas, Freitag, Gold, & Kassorla, 1965) used strong punishment to eliminate self-destructive and mutilating behaviors of severely psychotic children. An additional example is the work of Patterson and colleagues (Patterson, Jones, Whittier, & Wright, 1965) who used techniques of positive reward and reinforcement to decrease the unwanted behaviors of hyperactivity and social unresponsiveness among psychotic children. In general, behavior therapy has demonstrated a great deal of promise as a set of treatment methods applicable to a wide variety of abnormal behaviors among children and adolescents.

ans. The medical and psychiatric services were greatly expanded and modified. The Veterans Administration also took over the Army model of the clinical psychologist and established attractive positions for clinical psychologists. However, the number of clinical psychologists available for such employment was still inadequate to meet the needs of the V.A. Consequently, working with a number of cooperating universities, the V.A. undertook a large-scale and innovative program of clinical training. Doctoral students at these universities who desired to participate in this program spent approximately half of their time at V.A. hospitals and clinics, and the other half at the university. In addition to receiving a stipend from the V.A., which allowed them to pursue graduate study, these trainees received supervised training and clinical experience at the V.A. This program was quite successful and grew until over 700 psychology trainees were in the program each year.

In addition to the V.A., federal support for training mental health professionals was provided by the National Institute of Mental Health. Fellowships for graduate students as well as grants to the training universities were provided. The latter allowed university psychology departments to hire clinical faculty and related personnel. Such support contributed greatly to the expansion of clinical psychology and to its increased importance as a mental health profession.

Training and related developments

As has been indicated, clinical psychology received increasing recognition after the war, which was accompanied by a strong demand for the services of clinical psychologists. However, there were no formally organized programs of training in clinical psychology, and the existing opportunities for training were considered inadequate. Particularly lacking was any provision for supervised experience with clients or patients in an actual clinical setting. It was evident, therefore, that more adequate programs of clinical training would have to be developed. A Committee on Training in Clinical Psychology was appointed within the American Psychological Association (APA) and published its report in 1947 (APA, Committee on Training in Clinical Psychology, 1947). This report contained a number of specific recommendations that were later adopted. Among the important recommendations were the following:

1. The clinical psychologist was to be trained at the Ph.D. level, and thus was to receive training in research.
2. The clinical psychologist was to be a psychologist first, and a clinician second. This was to emphasize that the clinical psychologist was not merely a technician, but was familiar with the basic field of psychology.
3. Six primary areas of study were to be emphasized:
    a) general psychology,
    b) the psychodynamics of behavior,
    c) diagnostic methods,
    d) research methods,
    e) disciplines related to clinical psychology,
    f) therapy.
4. A one-year clinical internship, usually to be taken in the third year of graduate study, was to be a required part of the program.

Two years later, a national conference on training in clinical psychology was held in Boulder, Colorado. The recommendations of this conference for the most part followed the suggested guidelines of the Committee on Clinical Training (Raimy, 1950). The *Boulder Model*, as it came to be called, emphasized a scientist–practitioner model of the clinical psychologist. The clinical psychologist was to be a unique professional, trained in a graduate school of a university in both research and practice competencies. Enthusiasm for this model of clinical psychology training was strong, and the model remained as the only model for about twenty years, at which time other models were introduced. We will discuss these more recent models later in the chapter.

At this time, there was a great deal of activity on the part of American psychologists regarding professional concerns. The American Board of Professional Psychology was set up to examine candidates and to certify a high level of competence in three psychological specialties, including clinical psychology. These examinations included the actual clinical appraisal of a patient as well as more formal tests of professional and scientific knowledge. The model was that of the specialty boards in medicine. In addition, increasing concerns about professional practice led to the publication of a set of ethical standards in 1953, which have been periodically revised since then (APA, 1967, 1981).

Thus, within a short time following the close of the Second World War, numerous and significant changes and innovations took place, probably more than in any comparable period of time in the history of clinical psychology. There was a strong demand for the services of clinical psychologists, new and well-paid positions were available, organized training programs and internships were developed, federal support for training was provided, ethical codes were prepared, specialty boards appeared, and the field expanded rapidly. There were also changes that took place with regard to the functions and activities of the clinical psychologist.

■ PROFESSIONAL FUNCTIONS AND ACTIVITIES

As indicated earlier, psychological testing was a significant part of clinical psychology and it continued to be such during the war and in the immediate postwar period. However, clinical psychologists began to participate more actively in other activities, as well as taking on a somewhat different diagnostic role. In contrast to the earlier emphasis on objective test scores, the new diagnostic testing was more "clinical" in nature and utilized personality theory, specifically psychodynamic theory, as a frame of reference. In this newer approach, the psychologist used a battery of tests that featured the projective tests of personality. The best known of the latter types of tests are the Rorschach Test, composed of ten inkblots, and the Thematic Apperception Test, consisting of a set of pictures. These tests played an important part in the post-war activities of clinical psychologists, and are still among the most widely used clinical tests (Garfield & Kurtz, 1973; Wade & Baker, 1977).

Projective tests differ from the usual psychological tests in a number of ways. First, they are based on an essentially psychoanalytic construct, *projection*. Because such unstructured stimuli as ink blots are used and the client is asked to respond by stating what the ink blots look like or suggest, it is hypothesized that the client projects something of his or her personality in the responses made. In essence, the meanings given to the various ink blots or segments are provided by the client. Furthermore, unlike interview questions or items on personality questionnaires, the client is supposedly unaware of the significance of the responses made. Because of this, it was hypothesized that the responses of the client, when interpreted by the clinician utilizing psycho-dynamic theory, would reveal the client's underlying unconscious motives and conflicts.

The projective tests also differed from traditional psychological tests in relying on the subjective interpretation of the clinician to score the client's answers. Therefore, there were no normative (comparative among clients) data available on most of these tests. Also, information on their reliability and valid-ity was scanty. Nevertheless, adopting a pattern set by psychologists at the Menninger Foundation (Rapaport, Gill, & Schafer, 1945), clinical psychologists relied on a battery of tests that included mental tests as well as projective tests of personality. This testing was viewed as their important contribution to the diagnostic appraisal of the patient, and, in the 1940s and early 1950s, was the primary activity of the clinical psychologist. This type of diagnostic testing was viewed as a complicated clinical activity that required the observation, theoret-ical knowledge, and interpretive skills of the psychologist. It was decidedly dif-ferent from the less complex testing role of the psychologist in the pre-war period and it tended to be regarded highly by many of the psychologists' psychi-atric colleagues who referred the cases for psychological evaluation.

The views toward this type of diagnostic psychological testing and the psy-chologist's involvement with it gradually changed. By 1960, according to a sur-vey of clinical psychologists, diagnostic testing had been superceded by psycho-therapy as the activity in which psychologists spent the greatest portion of their time (E. L. Kelly, 1961). At this time, psychotherapy had become the most engaged-in activity of clinical psychologists. There are several reasons for the shift in emphasis from testing to psychotherapy. One is that the extensive bat-tery of tests used by psychologists was a very time-consuming activity. It might require as many as 10 to 15 hours or more to give the tests and then to score, interpret, and write up the results. This was an expensive undertaking. In addi-tion, the interpretations of the psychologist were sometimes challenged by col-leagues as being inconsistent with other clinical findings, and there were a number of studies that questioned the validity of the test interpretations (Gar-field, 1983). Finally, psychologists were very much interested in participating in psychotherapy. They did not want to be mere diagnostic testers with other professionals responsible for providing treatment. Furthermore, since psycho-therapy is a psychological form of treatment, psychologists feel that they are particularly equipped by their training to perform such functions.

Two more recent trends in terms of clinical testing also should be men-tioned. One concerns the increasing use of computerized scoring and interpre-tation of personality questionnaires. Probably the most popular personality scale of this type is the Minnesota Multiphasic Personality Inventory, usually referred to as the MMPI (Hathaway & McKinley, 1951). Originally constructed to aid in the diagnostic appraisal of psychiatric patients, it has become widely used as a means of more general personality appraisal. The MMPI consists of 550 items or statements to which the individual responds by indicating a "yes" or "no" answer to each statement as it pertains to that individual. The answer sheet is then scored by a computer and a profile of scores on the various scales of the test secured. Descriptions of many personality characteristics have been provided by a number of clinicians for selected profiles. Thus, the computer also is able to print out a complete personality description for the individual. However, many clinical psychologists prefer not to use this approach and instead rely on their own interpretation of the MMPI as well as other tests.

Another development has been the construction of more adequate and specialized tests for appraising possible brain dysfunction. Probably the best known test of this kind is the Halstead-Reitan battery of neuropsychological tests (Reitan, 1966). This is a comprehensive and time-consuming battery of a variety of tests including an earlier version of the Wechsler Adult Intelligence Scale, tests of abstract reasoning, and tests of sensory-perceptual functions. Rather elaborate equipment is required and the test tends to be used by clinical psychologists specializing in neuropsychology. Box 2.2 discusses some of the difficulties in diagnosing schizophrenia.

Thus, although diagnostic testing remains an essential function of the clinical psychologist, and practically all graduate students receive academic and practicum training in the clinical uses of psychological tests, the relative importance of this function has declined since the immediate post-war years. The amount of time spent on diagnostic activities based on a survey of 855 clinical psychologists in the mid-1970s is shown in Table 2.1 (Garfield & Kurtz, 1976). As is evident there, diagnostic and assessment activities were the fourth most frequently engaged-in activity, accounting for just under 10 percent of the total work time of the sample surveyed. It should also be pointed out that diagnostic and assessment activities may include clinical interviews and behavioral assessments as well as testing. Psychotherapy, on the other hand, is clearly the major activity of clinical psychologists and, if we combine individual and group psychotherapy with behavior modification, over 31 percent of the psychologist's time is devoted to such pursuits.

Before discussing the therapeutic activities of the clinical psychologist in more detail, it may be well to comment further on the activities listed in Table 2.1. Some of the activities in which clinical psychologists engage occur in a few settings while others take place in many settings. Thus, teaching, the second most frequently engaged-in activity, occurs mainly in academic institutions as does research and scholarly writing. Administration can take place in any type of setting—hospitals, clinics, universities, medical schools. Community consultation, in which the psychologist consults with a variety of community agencies and groups, probably occurs most frequently in community mental

B O X 2.2   SCHIZOPHRENIA

LOREN J. CHAPMAN

Schizophrenia is the central enigma of psychopathology. The cause or causes of schizophrenia are only slightly understood. This statement is almost true by definition because
patients are called schizophrenic if they show various psychotic symptoms that cannot be
attributed to the presence of a known organic disorder.

One common schizophrenic symptom is a severe disorder of thought, which is for the
most part inferred from disordered speech. In the early stages of the disorder, patients'
thoughts seem merely vague and rambling. In more developed cases, the thoughts
become disconnected and disorderly, sometimes to the point of chaos and incoherence.
Words are used in unusual ways and given private meanings. Sometimes the patients
even invent new words, which are called *neologisms.* Often the flow of ideas seems to be
directed by associative connection rather than by the demands of logic, and speech
seems to be used with an apparent disregard of any goal of communicating with other
people. Patients who exhibit this verbal chaos often complain that they are unable to focus
their attention and are easily distracted.

Another schizophrenic symptom is social withdrawal and apathy. The patients lose
interest in other people, in their own appearance, and in the usual activities of life. Hence
they become unable to carry out their responsibilities, take care of themselves, or maintain
social relationships. Emotionally, patients become flat and inappropriate. They show little
emotional response to topics that usually arouse feeling or they show inappropriate emotional response, such as laughing or weeping for no apparent reason.

Delusions (false beliefs) and hallucinations (false perceptions) are also prominent
symptoms in schizophrenia. The content of delusions is highly varied but is frequently
grandiose or concerned with religion, sex, or health. The delusions are often bizarre, that
is, are absurd and physically impossible. For example, many patients complain that their
thoughts, feelings, or actions are not their own or that they are controlled by other people
or forces. These are called "passivity experiences." The hallucinations are most often auditory. The messages from hallucinated voices are often related to delusional ideas.

The boundaries of the diagnostic category of schizophrenia are controversial. There
exist several competing diagnostic systems that differ primarily in the kinds of symptoms
that are believed to indicate schizophrenia. Currently, the most widely used diagnostic system in the United States is that of the American Psychiatric Association's *Diagnostic and
Statistical Manual of Mental Disorders* (third edition) or DSM-III. According to DSM-III, a
patient is considered schizophrenic only if he or she exhibits at least one of a list of psychotic symptoms similar to those described above, and if the psychotic symptoms are
more prominent in the illness than symptoms of depression or mania, and if the patient has
declined from a previously higher level of functioning and has shown either psychotic
symptoms or symptoms of developing disorder for at least six months.

Diagnostic systems such as DSM-III are useful for specifying the pattern of psychotic
symptoms but do not define clinical entities that are as distinct from one another as are
most physical diseases. Most researchers believe that schizophrenia has diverse causes
and consists of several distinct disorders that have not yet been identified.

BOX 2.2 *(Continued)*

Symptoms like those of schizophrenia often result from a known organic disorder, such as a metabolic disorder or a brain tumor or a drug. Patients with such known organic disorders are not usually called schizophrenic. Nevertheless, there is considerable evidence that at least some schizophrenia has organic symptoms that are less well understood. Recently developed computerized tomographic x-ray techniques show clearly that some of the more chronic schizophrenics have enlarged ventricles of the brain. Also, at least some schizophrenia has a substantial genetic component although transmission does not follow any simple Mendelian pattern. Between 25 and 75 percent of the monozygotic twins of schizophrenics are themselves schizophrenic. The fact that this concordance rate falls short of 100% shows that environmental influences also are important. The nature of these environmental contributions to the disorder is unclear. Speculations range from viral infection and early brain injuries to destructive family relationships.

health centers, but is not limited to such settings. University faculty and even individuals in private practice may act as community consultants. With regard to psychotherapy, clinical psychologists in almost any setting are likely to be engaged to some extent in this activity, although the amount of time devoted to it would vary with the functions of the individual involved.

Psychotherapy, although neither synonymous with clinical psychology nor an exclusive function of clinical psychologists, nevertheless is a primary and

T A B L E 2.1   **Percentage of Time Devoted to Designated Activities**

Activity	Percent of time
Individual psychotherapy	25.07
Group psychotherapy	4.35
Behavior modification	2.00
Diagnosis and assessment	9.79
Community consultation	5.23
Teaching	13.82
Clinical supervision	7.78
Research	7.04
Research supervision	2.71
Sensitivity group	.40
Scholarly writing	3.77
Administration	13.21
Other	4.82
Total	99.99%

From "Clinical Psychologists in the 1970's" by S. L. Garfield and R. M. Kurtz, *American Psychologist*, 1976, *31*, 1–9. Copyright © 1976 by the American Psychological Association. Reprinted by permission.

favored activity of this professional group. However, it is important to note that although psychotherapy is discussed as if it were one specific and identified type of therapeutic activity, it is actually a very broad category. There are literally hundreds of varieties of psychotherapy (Herink, 1980). There are individual therapies, group therapies, family therapies, marital therapies, and child therapies, and within each of these broad categories there are also many separate varieties deriving from different theoretical orientations.

■ PSYCHOTHERAPY: SOME THEORETICAL APPROACHES

In the two decades following the Second World War, the most influential theoretical view was undoubtedly that of psychoanalysis and its psychodynamic offshoots. As was mentioned in the discussion of projective techniques, diagnostic as well as therapeutic activities were very much influenced by this theoretical orientation. Psychoanalytic theory emphasized unconscious motivating forces as the most important in explaining both normal and abnormal behavior. Freud finally developed psychoanalysis as a method for treating neurotic disorders. In order to effect a "cure" or help the patient, the unconscious conflicts had to be brought into the patient's awareness. However, this had to be done gradually, for facing this conflictual material was very threatening to the individual, and if forced to do so too quickly, the patient might break off treatment or get worse. Consequently the process had to be a gradual one. To accomplish this goal, Freud had the patient lie on a couch away from the gaze of the analyst, and "free associate," or say whatever came to his or her mind. It was thought that by this means, the train of associations would gradually lead to the unconscious material; with the help of the therapist's interpretations, the repressed material would be brought forth and the patient's problems resolved. In this process, the therapist was relatively passive, particularly in the early stages of therapy, with the focus being on the free associations of the patient.

Early in the development of psychoanalysis, there were evidences of theoretical differences among some of Freud's followers. Adler, Jung, Horney, and Sullivan, among others, prepared their own theoretical views and forms of therapy (Hall & Lindzey, 1978). Although many of these individuals still accepted the view of unconscious factors as important in personality disorders, they differed in other ways. As a result there were a number of different psychodynamic approaches to psychotherapy. Other individuals also developed different therapeutic approaches and procedures so that the varieties of psychotherapy increased (Garfield, 1980). We will only mention a few here to illustrate the diversity of approaches.

Probably the earliest psychologist to describe a specific type of psychotherapy was Carl Rogers (1942). Rogers was dissatisfied with the psychoanalytic approach, and developed what he first called non-directive therapy and later referred to as client-centered therapy. Rogers reacted negatively to the "expert" role of the therapist and instead emphasized the potential for change inherent in the client. He came to believe that if the therapist possessed and communicated certain qualities, the client would make significant change (Rogers, 1957). Three such attributes were emphasized: the ability to be empathic, to communicate nonpossessive warmth to the client, and to be a genuine person (Truax & Carkhuff, 1967). Client-centered therapy is presented in more detail in Chapter 3 on Counseling Psychology.

Another important development that differed noticeably from both psychoanalysis and client-centered therapy was that of behavior therapy. This approach to therapy stemmed more directly from attempts to apply the principles of learning derived from experimental psychology. Some of the earliest experiments (Jones 1924; Watson & Rayner, 1920) reported the formation of fears using conditioning techniques based on animal research. Over the next thirty years, there were a few publications that dealt with the application of conditioning principles to such problems as bedwetting and alcoholism. However, the time apparently was not propitious for radical departures from conventional therapies. In 1958, a psychiatrist from South Africa, Joseph Wolpe, published a book entitled *Psychotherapy by Reciprocal Inhibition*, and behavior therapy began to attract attention. Since that time it has become an important approach to psychotherapy and behavior change.

As indicated, behavior therapists tend to utilize theories of learning as well as other views from experimental psychology upon which to base their therapeutic procedures. Wolpe, for example, relied greatly on principles of classical conditioning and hypothesized that if an individual could be helped to attain a state that was antagonistic to an undesirable one such as anxiety, the former would inhibit the latter. Thus, in treating cases of specific fears, the patient was taught relaxation exercises and then, while relaxed, was asked to visualize the fearful stimuli, beginning with the least troublesome and working up to the most fearful one. This procedure, known as *systematic desensitization*, was shown to have positive results. Another method of treating such cases is to employ models who can approach the fearful stimulus without fear and without negative consequences, or to have the client approach the fearful object in stages under the guidance of the therapist and without harm occurring. If this approach takes place, the conditioned fear response can be gradually extinguished.

Behavior therapy has expanded greatly and a variety of procedures have been developed and applied to a diversity of clinical problems ranging from a lack of assertiveness to the autistic and withdrawn behavior of very seriously disturbed individuals. Operant conditioning principles have been applied in mental hospital settings as well as in schools and the home (Kazdin, 1978). Utilizing principles of reinforcement, ward personnel, teachers, and parents have been taught to reward positive behaviors, but not negative ones. Although this may seem very obvious or simple, it does appear true that many parents and teachers give more attention to the child when misbehavior occurs and little attention when good behavior is demonstrated.

More recently, a variety of therapeutic approaches have appeared that stress the improtance of cognitions. Therapists of this persuasion emphasize that faulty or distorted cognitions lead to anxiety, depressions, and related negative feelings. It is what the person believes or perceives that influences behavior and feelings. Consequently, if such irrational thoughts can be changed

---

B O X 2.3   DEPRESSION: SADDER BUT WISER?

LAUREN B. ALLOY

It is common knowledge that depressed people view themselves and their experiences negatively. According to Beck's cognitive model of depression (Beck, 1967, 1976), these negative evaluations are the core symptom and cause of depression and stem from de-pressives' "systematic bias gainst the self." While it is well known that depressed people's self-perceptions are negatice in content, the unique aspect of Beck's model is that it hypothesizes that these negative self-perceptions are produced by specific logical errors in interpreting reality. That is, depressed people are seen as making inferences about the self and the world that are unrealistic, extreme, and illogical; whereas normal, nondepressed individuals are viewed as rational information processors who are logical, realistic, and who do not exhibit systematic biases in their perceptions. Similarly, the learned helpless-ness theory of depression (Abramson, Seligman, & Teasdale, 1978; Seligman, 1975) also focuses on distortion in depressives' inferences. According to this theory, depressed indi-viduals are characterized by the generalized expectation that desired outcomes are uncon-trollable. This expectation produces the cognitive, motivational, and affective symptoms of depression and biases depressives' perception of control so that they consistently under-estimate their personal control over events.

Recently, however, a striking paradox has come to the attention of depression researchers. Although the cognitive theories of depression emphasize distortion in depres-sive inference, a growing body of research suggests that depressed people's perceptions and inferences are actually more accurate or realistic than those of nondepressed people. For example, Alloy and Abramson (1979) found that depressed individuals' judgments of their personal control are quite accurate both in situations in which objectively they do exert control as well as in situations in which they do not exert control. In contrast, nonde-pressed individuals succumb to systematic illusions about their personal control over out-comes. Nondepressives exhibit an "illusion of control" and overestimate their impact on objectively uncontrollable outcomes that are associated with success (e.g., winning money) and an exhibit an "illusion of no control" and underestimate their impact on controll-able outcomes that are associated with failure (e.g., losing money). Similarly, Lewinsohn,

in a positive direction, the behaviors and feelings will also be changed. Albert Ellis (1962), for example, has called his approach *rational-emotive therapy* and emphasizes the significance of unrealistic expectations and irrational thoughts in creating personal discomfort. Other cognitive therapists have examined the importance of cognition in cases of depression where individuals take a negative view of themselves, their current situation, and the future (see Box 2.3) (Beck, 1976). Again, changing cognitions is an important aspect of such therapies. Currently, there is a fusion of cognitive and behavioral approaches (Ken-

---

Mischel, Chaplain, and Barton (1980) found that nondepressed psychiatric patients and normal controls rate their social competence more positively than do objective observers, whereas depressed patients' self-ratings are in agreement with observers' ratings of them. Interestingly, depressives' realism in perceptions and judgments may be specific to the self. Although they judge their own control accurately, depressives overestimate other people's control over positive outcomes that are, in fact, uncontrollable (Martin, Abramson, & Alloy, 1984). Clinicians such as Beck assume that depressives' unfavorable comparisons of themselves to others reflect distortions in self-perception and greater objectivity in perceptions of others. Ironically, depressives appear to perceive themselves realistically while it is their overly positive judgments about others that may be in error.

What is the causal direction of the association between depression and realism in judging personal control? Perhaps the state of depression itself causes people to assess their impact on events accurately. Alternatively, those people who tend to judge their control over outcomes accurately may be more vulnerable to depressive states than people who systematically misjudge the efficacy of their responses. As a first step in investigating the direction of the relationship between depression and accuracy in judging personal control, Alloy, Abramson, and Viscusi (1981) induced depressed mood in naturally nondepressed students and elated mood in naturally depressed students and assessed the impact of these transient mood states on students' susceptibility to the illusion of control. They found that the mood inductions were successful in reversing subjects' typical judgments of control. Depressed students made temporarily elated showed illusions of control normally observed in nondepressed individuals, whereas nondepressed students made temporarily depressed gave accurate judgments of control of the kind normally observed in depressed individuals.

A final issue concerns the relative adaptiveness of optimistic cognitive distortions versus realism. The nondepressive tendency to view oneself as having control over positive outcomes but not over negative outcomes may have several functional behavioral and affective consequences: the maintenance or enhancement of self-esteem; relative invulnerability to depressive reactions in the face of stress; and increased behavioral persistence. It is ironic from the standpoint of the cognitive theories of depression, but maladaptive symptoms of depression such as low self-esteem, negative affect, and decreased persistence may be consequences of the relative *absence* of optimistic, nondepressive biases and distortions rather than of the presence of pessimistic, depressive cognitive biases.

---

dall & Hollon, 1979). A cognitive-behavioral treatment goal is the client acquisition of *coping skills* for use in present as well as future troublesome situations.

A strong emphasis of behavior therapy is that of objectively evaluating
treatment outcomes. Perhaps more than any other orientation, it has stressed
the clear appraisal of therapeutic results, although Rogers and his follow-
dynamic therapists have tended not to be research oriented and have carried
out little systematic research evaluating the effectiveness of their forms of therapy. There are several other differences between behavior therapy and dynamic
therapies. Behavior therapists, in general, are not concerned with early childhood experiences, do not attempt to uncover unconscious thoughts or feelings,
do not use projective techniques, and do not take a passive role in therapy.

Besides the therapeutic systems described here, there are several others
used with individual therapy. There are also many types of encounter, sensitivity, marathon, and growth groups offered by a variety of individuals, including
clinical psychologists, which appeal to individuals in search of self-enhance-
ment, as well as to individuals with personal problems. One may well ask,
therefore, "How does the clinical psychologist select the type of therapy that is
best?" There is no clear answer to this query and, undoubtedly, there are different reasons for different individuals. Some may be influenced by the theoretical
orientation of their training program, some by their internship experience or
their later experience, some by their own personal therapy, some by their reading, and others by still different factors.

Finally, it can be added that despite the proliferation of therapeutic schools
and the influence of these schools, the largest number of clinical psychologists
designate themselves as *eclectic* (Garfield & Kurtz, 1976). This means that
they do not identify themselves with any particular school, but attempt to
combine features of two or more orientations (Garfield & Kurtz, 1977). Thus,
even though they may consider themselves as eclectic, such therapists may
vary widely among themselves with regard to the actual procedures used in
therapy.

■ WORK SETTINGS

At the present time, clinical psychologists function in a variety of settings. The
primary settings in which the majority of clinical psychologists are employed
are indicated in Table 2.2 from Garfield and Kurtz's (1976) data base of 855 psychologists. In terms of specific designations, private practice and university
psychology departments account for over 44 percent of the sample surveyed.
The rest are distributed in a variety of medical or mental health installations.
The category of "other" included public school systems, juvenile correction
centers, rehabilitation centers, state departments of health, and the federal gov-

T A B L E 2.2   **Primary Institutional Affiliations**

Primary affiliation	Number	Percent
None	10	1.17
Mental hospital	72	8.42
General hospital	51	5.97
Outpatient clinic	44	5.15
Community mental health center	64	7.48
Medical school	68	7.95
Private practice	199	23.27
University psychology department	188	21.99
University, other	60	7.02
Other	99	11.58
Total	855	100.00%

From "Clinical Psychologists in the 1970's" by S. L. Garfield and R. M. Kurtz, *American Psychologist*, 1976, *31*, 1–9. Copyright © 1976 by the American Psychological Association. Reprinted by permission.

ernment. Some clinicians work primarily with children and some with severely disturbed institutionalized patients, whereas others are engaged primarily with alcoholics or mental retardates. The largest number of clinicians probably see some range of patients. A few are engaged in research almost exclusively, whereas about half of the group are engaged in some part-time private practice in addition to their other employment.

Clinical psychologists consequently have a variety of work settings and professional opportunities open to them. Depending upon the interests of the individual psychologist and the opportunities available at a given time, the individual may specialize in one specific activity or engage in a variety of activities. In most small clinical settings, as well as many larger ones, the clinical psychologist is usually called upon to provide a variety of services including diagnostic assessment, individual and group therapy, and community consultation and education. In larger settings there may be more specialization. If the clinical agency is engaged in training, the psychologist may also be called upon for clinical supervision and some limited instruction. In a medical school, the psychologist may participate in instructing nurses, medical students, psychiatric residents, and clinical psychology interns, besides engaging in research and clinical activities. Psychologists in academic clinical training programs will usually provide clinical and research supervision to the graduate students and may even see a small number of clients for diagnosis or therapy in addition to their formal teaching and research.

It is relatively more difficult to secure employment in some clinical settings than others. At the present time, positions in university clinical training programs are scarce and very competitive, with an emphasis on the research potential of the candidate. Positions in medical schools are also comparable in these respects. Jobs in clinical settings are less competitive, particularly in smaller and more rural communities.

■ CURRENT ISSUES

Thus far, the reader has been introduced to the historical development of clinical psychology, the functions and orientations of clinical psychologists, and settings where such psychologists perform their professional functions. Before we conclude this chapter, we will discuss some of the issues that currently exist in the field and some possible future trends.

Issues in training

As was noted earlier, in 1949 the Boulder model of the scientist–practitioner was recommended as the model for all clinical psychologists and appropriate guidelines suggested. This model held sway for over twenty years, but there were various dissatisfactions voiced from time to time. A number of graduates, precisely how many is difficult to say, stated that the clinical-practical aspects of training were inadequate and that the more traditional academic concerns were given greater priority by the faculty. Although a later survey of clinical psychologists in the mid-1970s did not support this stated degree of dissatisfaction (Garfield & Kurtz, 1976), steps were initiated to introduce new types of more professionally oriented programs. The University of Illinois began a Doctor of Psychology (Psy.D.) program alongside its Ph.D. program in 1968. In this new program, four years in length, the dissertation requirement was omitted and additional practical training substituted (Peterson, 1968). Obviously, this was a radical departure from the traditional model.*

An even more radical departure at about the same time was the start of the first professional school of clinical psychology in California (Pottharst, 1970). This was an independent school started by members of the state psychological association and was not affiliated with any university. It was staffed largely by part-time faculty who tended to be primarily clinical practitioners. A training conference held at Vail, Colorado, in 1973 under the auspices of the APA gave some sanction to the setting up of more professionally oriented programs as alternatives to the traditional scientist–practitioner model.

Since that time the number of such new programs has grown rather markedly, and at the present time we have independent professional schools awarding either the Ph.D. or Psy.D. degree, a few professional schools of psychology in university settings, some Psy.D. programs in a few universities, and Ph.D. or Psy.D. programs in a small number of medical schools. Thus, in a relatively

---

*This program was recently discontinued.

short time, a great diversity among the programs training clinical psychologists has come about.

Although it is too early to evaluate adequately these new programs, some potential problems appear likely. While there is diversity in type of program, there is also diversity in the quality of the program. For example, it is doubtful if most or even some of the independent professional schools can match university resources. There have also been questions about the relative value and commitment of part-time versus full-time faculty. In addition, concerns have been voiced concerning the practically total dependence of the independent professional schools on students' tuition for operating expenses.

Finally, some clinical psychologists have wondered about the impact of different models of training on the identity and unity of the field. Previously there was one model, there was a shared system of values, and a distinctive uniqueness characterized the field. Furthermore, the research function was one that gave clinical psychologists considerable visibility in the mental health field. For example, in the area of research on psychotherapy, clinical psychologists have been preeminent and their contribution acknowledged. How these new developments in training will affect the future of clinical psychology remains to be seen.

Professional issues

At the beginning of the post-war period there were few states that had any legislation regulating the title or practice of psychology. Thus, there was nothing to keep anyone from calling himself or herself a psychologist, even if the person had little or no training in psychology. People seeking professional help might engage the services of such "psychologists" and in some instances be harmed by inadequate psychological service. Consequently, psychologists worked to get the appropriate legislation passed that would prevent such practices and ensure certain minimal standards for the title or practice of psychology.

Getting legislation passed in the state legislatures was not an easy task. Some groups, particularly medical groups, frequently opposed such legislation and succeeded in blocking it. By the late 1970s, such legislation was finally secured in all fifty states. The jubilation over this event, however, was short lived. Something new, called the *sunset procedure*, recently made its appearance. This refers to a procedure that automatically lets a law expire unless the existing law is reenacted or a new law passed (Cohen & Goldman, 1980). In three states, the legislature sunset the psychology practice legislation (although such legislation was reenacted). Chapter 15 presents a fuller discussion on the legislative regulation of the practice of psychology.

The efficacy of psychological treatments

Another issue that has existed for at least thirty years, but which has attracted more widespread attention of late, concerns the effectiveness of psychotherapy. Because psychotherapy is the major professional activity of clinical psychologists, and since much of the research evaluating the outcomes secured by means of psychotherapy has been performed by clinical psychologists, it is no surprise that this is a very significant issue. Furthermore, what was once primarily a scientific and professional issue has become in recent years a political-social issue.

A good starting point for discussing this controversy is an article published in 1952 by the British psychologist, Hans Eysenck. In this article, Eysenck reviewed the results of 24 studies reporting results on the outcome of psychotherapy, and concluded that there were no adequate data to support the efficacy of psychotherapy. Psychoanalysis was found to be no better, if as good, as so-called eclectic psychotherapy, and neither type could exceed, and hardly even match, the results of patients who had not received formal psychotherapy. On the basis of such an evaluation, Eysenck recommended that psychologists not be trained in such dubious procedures.

As might be anticipated, Eysenck's rather dismal appraisal of psychotherapy outcome stirred up a strong reaction. He was criticized for a number of reasons. First, he may have used inadequate comparison patient groups (control groups). He also combined different types of patients and therapists into larger groupings. In later papers, Eysenck offered additional appraisals of outcome in psychotherapy based on studies conducted with better methodologies. In these appraisals, he came to similar negative conclusions about psychotherapy although he did report a more positive evaluation of behavior therapy (Eysenck, 1961, 1966).

A number of clinical psychologists attempted to respond to the critical evaluations of Eysenck by conducting their own reviews of the literature on outcome in psychotherapy. Meltzoff and Kornreich (1970) in their review criticized Eysenck for not including a number of published studies that they found that generally reported positive results for psychotherapy. They analyzed the results from 101 research studies and stated that 80 percent favored psychotherapy over the control condition. Shortly thereafter, several other psychologists also published their views of the outcome literature. Bergin (1971) and later, Bergin and Lambert (1978) reanalyzed some of the original data on psychoanalytic therapy that Eysenck had used in his first report and took exception to the appraisals made by Eysenck. One can argue as to which interpretation is the more correct, but it is clear that research data can be interpreted in more than one way. Bergin also disagreed with Eysenck's estimate of the percentage of individuals who improve spontaneously without therapy. Eysenck's estimate was an improvement rate of approximately 65 percent, which was about the same as the improvement rate for psychotherapy. Bergin and Lambert (1978) in their later estimate, offered a so-called spontaneous improvement rate of about 43 percent. Thus, psychotherapy had a moderately positive effect, but achieved results somewhat more quickly than no therapy.

Another group of investigators reviewed the results of a number of studies that met certain research criteria (Luborsky, Singer, & Luborsky, 1975). The results again favored psychotherapy over no psychotherapy by approximately a ratio of 60 to 40. These authors also reported that in their review they found no therapy that was consistently superior to other forms. Comparable comments were also made by Meltzoff and Kornreich (1970) and by Bergin and Lambert (1978).

Recently, a new statistical procedure for analyzing the results of many research studies, *meta-analysis*, has been applied to the existing research literature on outcome in psychotherapy (Smith & Glass, 1977; Smith, Glass, & Miller, 1980). By means of this procedure a large number of studies can be combined and evaluated in an objective manner. In the most comprehensive report, 475 studies dealing with outcomes in psychotherapy were evaluated and the average effect of psychotherapy computed (Smith, Glass, & Miller, 1980). According to the authors, 85 percent of those who received psychotherapy were judged to secure outcome evaluations that exceeded the average appraisal of the control subjects. This was interpreted as clearly indicating the effectiveness of psychotherapy.

The appraisals by Smith and her colleagues, while greeted with approval by many psychotherapists, have also received criticism (Eysenck, 1978; Gallo, 1978; Rachman & Wilson, 1980). Among the latter were such problems as the use of therapists who were still in training, many unpublished studies, a very young group of clients in many of the studies who were largely college undergraduate volunteers, and a limited sample of clinical problems. For such reasons, questions were raised about the applicability of the results to actual clinical situations and clinical populations. It can also be mentioned that Rachman and Wilson (1980) in their review of the literature on outcome in psychotherapy came to somewhat different conclusions than the other reviewers, except for Eysenck. They found no adequate evidence to support the efficacy of psychoanalysis, only weak evidence favoring psychotherapy more generally, but evidence supporting the value of behavior therapy. They were also particularly critical of the results obtained by Smith and Glass (1977), which found no important differences between the different forms of psychotherapy evaluated. Thus, among the reviewers of the research literature on psychotherapy, there is still no unanimity concerning its effectiveness.

The research on psychotherapy has had a wider audience in recent years than it had in the past. Psychotherapy has become a much more popular treatment and has been given various kinds of publicity in the press and other media. Paperback books on a variety of psychological topics and appealing to various audiences are very apparent in campus and other bookstores. With that kind of popularity, psychotherapy has entered a broader domain of interest.

Criticism of psychotherapy has come from popular writers, psychologists, and congressional committees, sparked in part by the matter of health insurance payments for psychotherapy and the possibility of national health insurance. The issue of the effectiveness of psychotherapy thus has become a public and fiscal issue. In the public domain, several writers have published strong attacks on the efficacy of psychotherapy (Gross, 1978; Tennov, 1975). Additionally, finance committees of various legislative bodies have expressed their interest in this matter, for the potential underwriting by insurance companies of expensive but noneffective treatments is a serious concern (Marshall, 1980).

Consequently, the effectiveness of psychotherapy is a complicated issue with many implications. Professionally, as the primary treatment modality of clinical psychologists, its importance is very obvious. A profession based on ineffective procedures could not long endure. On a scientific level, the matter is also of great importance. The scientific part of clinical psychology should be able to conduct the required research and come up with some creditable conclusions. However, there are many different types of psychotherapy and they have been used with a diverse range of disorders. To evaluate adequately all of these possible combinations of therapies and disorders with fully trained and competent therapists and with appropriate measures of outcome is a tremendous task. The National Institute of Mental Health, for example, has been coordinating a study in three mental health centers in which two forms of psychotherapy and an antidepressant medication (imipramine) are being compared in the treatment of moderately severe cases of depression. The first phase of the project requires several years and the cost is estimated to be 3.4 million dollars—for just two forms of psychotherapy and one category of disorder. To evaluate all of the forms of psychotherapy over the range of disorders where it has been used would be a lengthy and unbelievably expensive undertaking.

Evaluating psychotherapy thus presents many problems for the researcher in this area. Apart from the diversity that exists among the psychotherapeutic approaches, one must also consider the variation among therapists, clients, and the types of measures used to evaluate outcome. In the past, evaluations of outcome were based solely on the ratings or judgments of the therapist. Since therapists are not completely uninvolved or objective observers of the therapy they have conducted, such appraisals have been found wanting. The ratings of outcome by clients or patients, or by objective clinicians uninvolved in the therapy, have also been used. The fact that different groups of raters do not always agree has led more recently to an emphasis on securing several different measures of outcome. Tests also have been used to evaluate the patient's status before and after treatment. Thus, a sound program of evaluation might include all of the above-mentioned measures as well as actual behavioral or performance measures (Garfield, 1980). The planning and conducting of an effective research project to evaluate the outcomes of psychotherapy, therefore, is a rather complex and expensive undertaking.

Currently, the issue of the effectiveness of psychotherapy remains unresolved, although the bulk of the evidence does indicate modestly positive outcome in about two-thirds of the cases studied. This type of conclusion, however, has to be viewed tentatively, for as we have emphasized, we need to be able to specify the type of therapy to be administered by what type of therapist for designated types of problems. Although a small number of clients appear to show rather marked improvement, we cannot yet identify the factors responsible for such improvement.

■ CONCLUSION

Clinical psychology from a very small start near the turn of the century has grown, slowly at first, and then more rapidly during the past forty years to become the most popular area of psychology. During this latter period the field has been greatly transformed by a number of significant developments. The diagnostic function was broadened, organized training programs emphasizing practical clinical training were developed, standards for training and professional behavior were formulated, legislation for practice was enacted, psychologists became immersed in psychotherapy of various kinds, and the number of clinical psychologists increased rapidly. Job opportunities expanded and a significant number of clinical psychologists went into private practice.

In the past few years, some of the forces stimulating the growth of clinical psychology have diminished or been curtailed. A significant decrease in federal support for clinical training, an increase in the supply of clinical psychologists, and a decrease in job opportunities, related in part to economic recession, have been among the changes that have occurred. How long such trends will continue is impossible to say. Professional schools of psychology and less scientifically oriented programs of training have also appeared in large numbers during the past decade. We also noted the possible impact of sunset legislation on the certification and licensing of psychologists and issues concerning the effectiveness of psychotherapy. All of these are important developments whose impact on the future of clinical psychology will have to be appraised. What we can say with some assurance is that clinical psychology has been a changing and dynamic field that has overcome many problems in the past and faces many new challenges in the future. Based on its history, we can expect clinical psychologists to face the challenges and to move ahead with a desire to improve its practices and procedures in order that society be well served.

■ SUGGESTED READINGS

Garfield, S. L. (1983). *Clinical psychology: The study of personality and behavior* (2nd ed.). Hawthorne, NY: Aldine.

> This is a textbook on clinical psychology that provides the reader with a comprehensive description of the field. Included are a brief history of clinical psychology, descriptions of various assessment and treatment procedures, and a discussion of training opportunity and current professional issues. It would be suitable for the advanced undergraduate student.

Garfield, S. L. (1980). *Psychotherapy: An eclectic approach.* NY: Wiley.

This book describes an eclectic orientation to psychotherapy. The client, the therapist, the psychotherapeutic process, problems in psychotherapy, and research on the effectiveness of psychotherapy are discussed.

Garfield, S. L., & Kurtz, R. M. (1976). Clinical psychologists in the 1970's. *American Psychologist, 31*, 1–9.

This article reports on a survey of 855 clinical psychologists, including amount of time devoted to various professional activities, theoretical orientation, and attitudes toward training.

Hall, C. S., & Lindzey, G. (1978). *Theories of personality* (3rd ed.). NY: Wiley.

This is a well-known text that provides descriptions of a number of important theories of personality. It would be suitable for an advanced undergraduate student.

Herink, R. (Ed.). (1980). *The psychotherapy handbook: The A to Z guide to more than 250 different therapies in use today.* NY: New American Library.

Brief descriptions of over 250 therapies are provided either by the founder of the therapy system or by an exponent of the particular form of therapy.

BRUCE R. FRETZ
COUNSELING PSYCHOLOGY

■ INTRODUCTION

Dr. A works in a university counseling center. He sees about 15 clients each week, in individual sessions, for personal problems like loneliness, anxiety, and motivation to study, and indecision about choice of major and first career. He conducts weekly group therapy sessions for students with personal problems and a couples communication skills program each semester. He also provides training for those students who volunteer to work with the crisis telephone line.

Dr. B works for a major automobile company in their employee assistance program. Her regular weekly appointments include employee and supervisors (and sometimes their families as well) for personal problems that are affecting their work productivity. Additionally, she provides assessment and counseling for those employees who wish to consider other positions in the company, helping them to decide whether they have the interests, abilities, and personality attributes necessary to be successful and satisfied in alternative careers. She also provides training for managers on how to improve supervisor-supervisee relationships.

Dr. C is the director of psychological services in Axel House, a residential facility in the community for those who have been previously hospitalized in mental institutions and are not yet ready for fully independent living. She provides a broad range of individual and group counseling services and training of the paraprofessional and custodial staff to improve their relationships with residents.

Dr. D is employed as a counseling psychologist in a Veterans Administration General Medical–Surgical hospital to run treatment programs for addicted patients (both substance abusers such as alcoholics and drug addicts as well as compulsive gamblers). He also counsels cancer patients and their families and trains nursing personnel to cope with the difficult job of caring for dying patients.

What do these four psychologists have in common? Despite their very different roles, they are all counseling psychologists. The major part of this chapter is devoted to helping you understand the shared perspectives and varied contributions of the expanding group of professionals who call themselves counseling psychologists. In a later part of the chapter, we will review even more varied roles and places of employment of counseling psychologists. Finally, we will discuss how the profession will be changing in the decade ahead, bringing the unique perspective of counseling psychology to the other professional settings into which counseling psychologists have moved in the last ten years.

In a time when specialties within psychology seem to have fewer and fewer boundaries, you may have many questions about the relationships among various applied psychological specialties. Before focusing on the unique contributions and perspectives of counseling psychology, we will examine the history of psychology in general and counseling psychology specifically.

■ HISTORICAL DEVELOPMENT

As Chapter 2 has related, both of the World Wars greatly increased the number of applied psychologists. The war-time experiences helped psychologists see the usefulness of a blending of both research and applications in understanding phenomena as diverse as starvation in prisoner-of-war camps to the development of psychological tests for the selection of effective pilots. Many young psychologists, trained initially in basic research in learning during the 1930s, emerged from World War II as "applied" psychologists, some with tremendous amounts of experience and new interests in test development and personnel selection and others in psychological treatment of battle fatigue and related problems. To deal with this new diversity of interests among psychologists, the American Psychological Association (APA) established a division structure whereby psychologists with common interests would have opportunities to focus their attention on specific areas yet still at the same time be part of the larger body of psychologists in America.

The formmal origins of counseling psychology can be dated back to the mid-1940s. At that time a number of the psychologists returning from World War II, having been involved in the development and use of psychological tests in military settings began using these skills with the thousands of veterans who had postponed their education during World War II and were now entering colleges and universities. Since clinical psychologists at the time were oriented primarily towards treating institutionalized persons with severe personality disturbances and since consulting psybhologists were located mostly in industrial settings and not engaged in any counseling or therapeutic type efforts, a small group of psychologists led by John Darley and E. G. Williamson proposed in 1946 that a new division be developed. The by-laws of the division stated that its purposes were "To extend the techniques and methods of psychology to counseling and guidance activities in vocational, personal, educational, and group adjustments, . . . encountered in educational institutions" (Whiteley, 1980, p. 29). Nearly 500 APA members immediately joined the division. In 1955, the division was officially re-titled "Counseling Psychology." Now with over 2500 members it remains one of the larger divisions within APA.

Most counseling psychologists think of their official beginning as the 1951 Northwestern Conference that was held to prepare statements on doctoral training of counseling psychologists. The Veterans Administration was a major financial supporter of this conference. Veterans Administration (VA) Hospitals, along with university counseling centers, have been major training and employment locations of counseling psychologists. A journal of theory and research, the *Journal of Counseling Psychology*, was begun in 1954 by researchers in counseling psychology. The journal proved to be so successful that it was incorporated by the American Psychological Association in the early 1960s as one of their publications. The journal has been popular with students when they are free to select readings in whatever psychology journal they wish (Carskadon, 1978). In 1969 another journal, *The Counseling Psychologist*, was begun. In contrast to the usual research article format of journals, this journal usually presents one major treatise in each issue, followed by several brief critical analyses by prominent scholars and practitioners. Topics have ranged from client-centered therapy to counseling women to assertiveness training.

The Greyston Conference, held in 1964 (Thompson & Super, 1964), reviewed the development of the profession and updated its standards for training and research. Both it and the prior Northwestern conference chose, as the preferred training model, the scientist–professional model. This model emphasizes both scientific and professional aspects of training in counseling psychology so that persons can be trained not only in how to do counseling but how to identify the need for, and develop and evaluate, better theories and procedures for the psychological well-being of all persons.

While the preceding paragraphs have briefly described the formal history of the profession of counseling psychology, understanding the changing and expanding nature of the profession during the past thirty years and the ideological foundation built during this time requires a broader perspective than dates and places.

Looking at the changing nature of society in the United States during the first half of the twentieth century can help one understand how, by the 1950s, a profession like counseling psychology could grow so quickly. As the industrial revolution led to more and more technical refinements in the work place, job selection and job training became increasingly important aspects of life in this country. In the early part of this century, psychologists involved in the development of aptitude and ability tests began to collaborate with persons working to assist the post-school adjustment of boys and girls. Much of this work, pioneered by Frank Parsons (1909), has been cited the world over for its contributions to helping persons choose careers suited to their abilities and preferences.

Large-scale unemployment in the 1930s made job selection even more salient. At the same time, what was becoming increasingly clear to psychologists assisting persons in career adjustment was that having the right abilities did not necessarily guarantee that one would be either successful or satisfied. Increasing recognition was given to the psychological adjustment factors and emotional aspects of individuals, as well as to their measured abilities, in choosing and planning careers. The now well-demonstrated relationship of career adjustment to psychological adjustment was regularly being observed by these psychologists.

This combination of psychological tests, career guidance principles, and emotional adjustment considerations blossomed in post-World War II universities when thousands of veterans were trying to make the adjustment from war to peacetime as well as the adjustments of establishing or renewing family relationships, returning to educational settings, and choosing a life's work. Not surprisingly, at many colleges and universities, previously existing "testing centers" developed an additional service called the "counseling center." In these new centers, assessment of abilities was not abandoned but rather served as a starting point for understanding the combination of abilities, interests, and values in relation to effective adjustment, both personal and vocational.

A hallmark of counseling psychology by the 1940s and 1950s was this clear emphasis on identifying and developing personal and social resources and helping the individual make more effective use of them. This emphasis, in contrast to a focus on weaknesses and pathology, has remained constant in the profession over the years and still underlies the work of counseling psychologists.

This emphasis on strengths led counseling psychologists to pay special attention to persons in transitions, such as adjusting to college or adjusting to parenting or adjusting to divorce and remarriage. Psychologists have found that in times of transition, persons are ready to look at themselves and to learn how they can better cope with life's stresses. Just as counseling psychologists learned that work adjustment was often improved by including therapeutic counseling along with assessment of abilities, interests, and values, they also learned that in order for clients to use the coping strengths they possessed or were learning, therapeutic counseling was often required. Therefore, along with an emphasis on aiding psychological development through the enhancement of strengths, counseling psychologists began to provide personal therapeutic counseling to their clients.

Since the late 1950s, counseling psychologists have been increasingly involved in therapeutic counseling. Smith's (1982) review of trends in counseling and psychotherapy identifies the tremendous impact Carl Rogers' client-centered, psychological growth-oriented therapy has had. Therefore, skills in psychotherapy as well as in developmental and preventive interventions have become a major part of the profession. This development has highlighted the overlapping interests of counseling and clinical psychologists. Within this common area of interest, counseling psychologists have completed some major research identifying the basic ingredients in therapeutic relationships and specifying the best methods of training effective counselors and therapists.

Looking back over this history of counseling psychology, it is evident that counseling psychologists have three distinct, although not mutually exclusive, purposes: "One is to help persons who are presently experiencing difficulty. This is the *remedial* or rehabilitative role. Another is to anticipate, circumvent, and, if possible, forestall difficulties which may arise in the future. This is the *preventive* role. A third role is to help individuals to plan, obtain, and derive maximum benefits from kinds of experiences which will enable them to discover and develop their potentialities. This is the educative and *developmental* role" (Jordaan, 1968, p. 1). The research activities of counseling psychologists provide the theoretical and data-based (empirical) foundations for the development and evaluation of techniques and theories for each of these purposes. Many of the counseling psychologists who conduct such research are also involved in teaching future counseling psychologists. These teacher–researchers provide training and continue to analyze and study our professional understanding of counseling to determine which problems remain poorly helped by our services.

The special contributions counseling psychologists make are based primarily on years of research and intervention experience in several focused areas of psychological development and adjustment. The next section reviews the accomplishments of these major foci of the profession. The areas first covered deal with the most remedial work, progressing then to the more developmental and preventive aspects of the work of counseling psychologists.

■ FOCAL AREAS OF RESEARCH AND INTERVENTION

Therapeutic counseling

While counseling psychology has emphasized from its beginning the development of both preventive and educational services, continued requests for remedial counseling to assist with unmet adjustment problems has maintained therapeutic counseling, or psychotherapy, as a major service and research activity of counseling psychologists. Research articles on the process and outcomes of therapeutic counseling outnumber any other topical area of articles published in the *Journal of Counseling Psychology.* Moreover, some 60 percent of new counseling psychologists begin their professional careers in health service settings such as counseling centers, community mental health centers, and hospitals (Banikiotes, 1980).

What do counseling psychologists do as therapeutic counselors? A full answer to this question would require an entire book in itself. Depending on how one counts, there may be as many as 300 different models of counseling. Counseling psychologists use one or more of these models in at least part of their work. These various approaches to counseling have been developed by a broad variety of psychologists, physicians, and other mental health personnel primarily during the middle decades of this century. Some theories, like Freud's, grew out of clinical practice; others, like Jung's, developed primarily from personality theories; and still others, like behavioral counseling, came from basic research on psychological processes.

In earlier decades, it was assumed that good psychologists adopted a single theoretical position and treated all clients within that particular model. Starting in the 1950s, research by both counseling and clinical psychologists began to show that effective therapists used a variety of techniques: the more experienced they were, the more they resembled each other (using many theories) rather than using any one theory (Fiedler, 1950). More recently, Smith and Glass (1977) have shown that most types of therapies have some effectiveness; all things considered, no one type is more effective than others. D. Smith (1982) also has identified a current trend among counseling and clinical psychologists toward an eclectic combination of therapies as compared to exclusive use of any one school of therapy.

Before reviewing counseling psychologists' research in psychotherapy, it may be useful to discuss briefly the major theoretical foundations of the therapeutic work of counseling psychologists (other sections will include theoretical foundations in areas other than psychotherapy). The theory of Carl Rogers (1942, 1951) historically has been most influential for counseling psychologists' research and practice. There was, in the 1940s, a particularly good "fit" between Rogers' growth-oriented views of counseling and therapy and the spirit of the then-young profession of counseling psychology. The major elaborations of Rogers' theory came from his work with college students, the same group that was the focus of the work of most counseling psychologists at that time. His work was seen as a welcome alternative to what then was the only other well-known theoretical school—psychoanalysis and its neo-analytical derivations, all with varying degrees of greater attention to psychopathology than to psychological health. It should, therefore, not be surprising that Smith (1982) found Rogers the most influential psychotherapist, followed by Albert Ellis and Sigmund Freud, as rated by contemporary counseling and clinical psychologists.

Since the 1950s, the therapy research of counseling psychologists has focused on identifying the basic ingredients and stages in counseling that make it more likely that we can help a broad range of clients with diverse problems. This focus was a direct outgrowth of Rogers' concept that certain conditions were necessary in order for effective counseling to occur. Despite the many accomplishments that have been made, we are still decades away from having a specific procedure for a given problem, like increasing red light exposure for 43 seconds a day for a plant with specific growth deficiencies. In fact, many psychologists argue that we will never be able to get that specific in helping human beings with their complex, ever-changing problems. However, we must recognize that twenty years ago, just as many psychologists felt that we would never have a brief, effective treatment for phobias. In fact, some psychologists then believed that phobias could not be treated. Yet, there is now strong evidence that several behavior therapies, among them systematic desensitization and participant modeling, are effective in treating phobias (Rosen, 1976).

Counseling process ▪ Research focusing on the counseling process has extended from the early beginnings of the profession right through to the present time. In the 1940s, Carl Rogers and Frances Robinson at The Ohio State University began to use the then-new technology of audio recording to record counseling sessions in order to provide data for analysis. Robinson and his doctoral students in counseling psychology were some of the first to describe and categorize counselor techniques. These included conveying acceptance of the client as a unique person (acceptance), helping the client specify the parts of his or her problem (clarification), and making the meaning of a client's statements clear to him or her (interpretation) (Robinson, 1950).

An important early discovery in this line of research was that moving too quickly to solve a client's problem was a bad counseling strategy. Not only did this strategy fail to be effective, it is also important from a philosophical perspective that clients be the ones who play a major role in developing the solution to the problem. The counselor's help is critical, of course, but if clients feel that they play a significant role in developing the solution, they are more likely to try it out, evaluate it, and, most importantly, apply it in future situations. Counseling psychologists are much more gratified to have clients say "You helped me see . . . " than to have clients say "You solved my problem." The ultimate goal is to have the client take responsibility for his or her own behavior; counseling is not "finished" until this goal is accomplished.

Counseling psychologists more recently have worked to determine the conditions that are essential for the successful initiation of therapeutic relationships. Two major theories have been developed: empathy as a necessary and sufficient condition for counseling (Rogers, 1957) and social influence as a major aspect of the process of counseling.

Most of the research on empathy is based on the work of Truax and Carkhuff (1967) who were originally associated with Carl Rogers' research on the effectiveness of client-centered therapy. They published studies that demonstrated that clients were most helped when the counselor provided accurate empathy, nonpossessive warmth, and genuineness. These concepts have been repeatedly investigated in the last couple of decades, with the concept of empathy receiving the greatest attention.

The term *empathy* has had a fascinating history (see Barrett-Lennard, 1981). For counseling psychology, the focus has been on empathically understanding the client: "It is an active process of desiring to know the full present and changing awareness of another person, of reaching out to receive his communication and meaning and translating his words and signs to experienced meaning that matches at least those aspects of awareness that are most important to him at the moment" (Barrett-Lennard, 1962, p. 3).

Specific examples of nonempathic versus empathic responses are provided here, adapted from Egan (1982):

Client: I have a vague feeling that I could do something more with my life. I'm successful enough by ordinary standards, but what does that mean? It's about time I took a good look at my values because I have the feeling I'm not really living up to them.

Counselor: (unempathic) Why do you think you aren't more successful?

Counselor: (empathic) You have some gnawing doubts about the quality of your life—especially your value system.

Client: I've been to other counselors and nothing has ever really happened. I don't even know why I'm trying again. But things are so bad that I guess something has to be done, so I'm trying it all over again.

Counselor: (unempathic) Good counselors are hard to find.

Counselor: (empathic) You're uneasy because you're not at all sure this is going to work, but you feel you have to try something.

Rogers (1951) postulated that empathy was one of the most critical ingredients of effective counseling. Counseling psychologists have given empathy considerable attention in the past twenty years in both practice and research. Trainers of counselors have developed more refined training models to help people become empathic. Perhaps the most widely cited and used empathy training models are those of Carkhuff (1969) and Egan (1982). Both of these books serve as texts in numerous courses to train persons in helping skills, whether the trainees are peer counselors, such as fellow college students or fellow alcoholics, or professional counselors, such as social workers, psychiatrists, clinical psychologists, and counseling psychologists.

How to measure empathy and to determine whether it is as important for counseling as Rogers suggested has been the major focus of empathy research.

The most concise summary that can be made, at present, of theory and research on the nature and importance of empathy is that the results are controversial. The findings of the 1960s indicating that empathy was indeed a necessary and sufficient quality for good counseling have not been consistently replicated. In fact, Parloff, Waskow, and Wolfe (1978) concluded that there was some evidence that good therapy could occur without the presence of empathy, and that the presence of empathy did not guarantee good therapy would take place. However, they cited empathy as one variable that needs continued attention in future psychotherapy research, suggesting that its real importance may be found in the complex relationship that exists among a therapist, his or her client, and his or her techniques. Barrett-Lennard's (1981) refinement of the concept of empathy in terms of various phases in counseling relationships provides the basis for continued theorizing and research on how to determine the contribution of empathy to the therapeutic process.

In this brief overview of the research on empathy, we have seen the practical and research developments of a concept that most therapists and counselors regard as crucial. An entirely different theoretical perspective on counseling is provided by a model emphasizing counseling as an interpersonal (social) influence process. In this model, with very different research techniques, counseling psychologists have focused on the basic conditions in counseling relationships, particularly the initial stages of the relationships. Strong (1968) introduced an interpersonal influence model of counseling that has proved to be the forerunner of an extensive body of research. Indeed, his article has recently been identified as one of the emerging classics in the field (Heesacker, Heppner, & Rogers, 1982). His basic conception may be paraphrased as follows. When counselors are working with clients, they are trying to help the client achieve a change in behavior, attitudes, or values. Social psychology has intensively investigated influence and persuasion techniques. Can social psychology explain the process of counseling as a special form of influence? Strong's belief that counseling is an interpersonal influence process has had tremendous impact on investigators in many fields of psychology (Strong, 1978).

By 1980, there were some seventy studies of counseling as a social influence process. Corrigan, Dell, Lewis, and Schmidt (1980) reviewed these studies and concluded that the social influence model is an accurate reflection of counseling process. Just as social psychologists have found that leaders are listened to and followed more closely when they are regarded as highly credible and an acknowledged authority, research results suggest that when clients see their counselors as highly credible (e.g., having higher degrees, being more experienced), clients are more apt to change their opinions to conform with those of the counselor. Additionally, counselors have influence when clients view them as attractive; this condition occurs when clients believe that counselors have had experiences similar to those of clients. Finally, counselors are more influential when they are seen as trustworthy, when the client believes that the counselor is acting in the client's best interest.

The vast majority of these studies on social influence have been *analogue studies*; that is, these studies did not use actual clients and counselors but rather students and other potential clients listening to or viewing tapes of counselors and then rating the degree to which these counselors affected their attitudes and beliefs. However, some research on social influence theory has been accomplished in actual counseling settings. For example, Zamostny, Corrigan, and Eggert (1981) have shown that nearly 48 percent of the variance in clients' satisfaction with their initial interview could be attributed to the perceived expertness, attractiveness, and trustworthiness of the counselor.

In summary, this social influence model has proved to be particularly powerful in explaining clients' initial impressions of counseling. Yet to be determined is how much social influence theory can explain later stages in the counseling process. As Corrigan et al. (1980) noted, the intriguing question is whether or not everyday influence processes, such as those used in salesmanship, legal trials, and politics, can give us a new perspective on understanding the counseling process. While the analogy of counseling to business and legal procedures is an anathema to many, the research thus far certainly suggests the potential fruitfulness of research and theoretical developments of this kind. There is obviously much to be gained by counseling psychologists paying continued attention to the methodology and findings of experimental social psychology.

Other research on the counseling process focuses on the specific language and categories of counselors' responses to clients. Measuring and determining the effects of categories of responses (e.g., clarifications, reflections, and interpretations) at various stages of counseling (Hill, 1978), especially when combined with the technology of computerized language analysis systems (Meara, Pepinsky, Shannon, & Murray, 1981), has the promise of moving us closer to a stronger scientific basis for our field. Twenty years ago we could not offer systematic training for basic skills in counseling because we did not know what those skills were. Perhaps ten years from now we might be able to provide systematic skills for later phases of counseling as well, making counseling more effective and easier to teach.

Counseling outcome ▪ There is yet another major type of investigation of counseling, that of the evaluation of its effects. Such research is usually referred to as *outcome research* in counseling. Both counseling and clinical psychologists, as well as psychiatrists, have been involved in an increasing amount of such research in the last decades. There has been much controversy about the effectiveness of counseling and psychotherapy. The most-cited summary of that literature is the meta-analysis of Smith, Glass, and Miller (1980). After a review of several hundred studies of the effectiveness of counseling and psychotherapy, including over 25,000 clients, they were able to conclude that, on the average, clients who received counseling were better off than 85 percent of those who had not received counseling.

Determining how effective counseling is has proved easier said than done. Whom does one ask? If a client is satisfied, does that constitute successful counseling? Actually, the vast majority of clients are very satisfied with counseling. Do we ask other people who know or observe the client whether or not clients have changed? When we do that, evidence is less clear-cut that counseling has had an impact. In order to make reasonable conclusions about the effectiveness of counseling, one needs to know a variety of research methodologies and appropriate statistical analyses (Bergin & Lambert, 1978; Garfield & Bergin, 1978; Gelso & Johnson, 1983).

Progress in demonstrating the effectiveness of counseling has been frustratingly slow. There is now increasing controversy as to whether or not new scientific models of studying counseling are needed in order to have major breakthroughs in this area (Harmon, 1982). Good counseling psychologists are always asking, "How well am I doing for my clients?" "Are there other treatment procedures that would be more effective with this particular client?" We also need to ask, "What research methodologies can best help us answer these questions?" These are the continuing challenges for counseling psychologists' theoretical and empirical research on how therapeutic counseling works.

Educational development

In this focal area of research, as well as in the next section on career development, both the remedial and developmental aspects of counseling psychology are readily apparent. Although you have grown up in a era when the prevailing concept has been that anyone can learn a great deal given the right educational environment, it was only a few generations ago that people believed that some students were naturally smart, others naturally dumb, with not much to do for the dumb ones.

During the 1930s, several counseling psychologists focused their research on students who were supposedly bright, but were not succeeding academically. What kinds of interventions could be made to help these students? One of the major differences that was shown to exist between students with very different college performance records, but similar intelligence levels, was the nature of their reading and study skills. Frances P. Robinson therefore developed what is now a widely used reading and study skill technique, the SQ3R method (survey, question, read, recite, review) (Robinson & Hall, 1941). As referenced in Robinson's latest edition (1970), a long series of studies has repeatedly demonstrated that using effective study habits (like time schedules) and good study skills (like the SQ3R) lead to significant improvements in academic performance.

Heffernan and Richards (1981) have recently shown that students trained in study skills and in techniques to isolate themselves from interpersonal distraction had a great improvement in grades. Research such as their study stimulated colleges with well-developed student services to provide a study-skills center, often administered by a counseling psychologist. The staff in such a center may be advanced undergraduate or graduate students who have been trained in the specific techniques of educational skills counseling. As can be seen from the many research articles in the *Journal of Counseling Psychology* dealing with study skills training, this area continues to be an important one for counseling psychologists.

The interests of counseling psychologists in helping able students who encounter significant academic difficulties has led in more recent years to the development of workshops in topics such as note-taking and writing term papers. Why, you might ask, are counseling psychologists involved in these kinds of workshops? Aren't they for English teachers to do? What counseling psychologists have seen as a result of helping many clients who have trouble with various steps in writing is that it is psychological factors, not "English" skills, that often get in the way of performing what the English teacher may well have already taught the client. For example, how many of you find yourself in this situation when you have a paper to write? "Every time I sit down to write, nothing comes out." Or, "Well, I wrote an outline, but then I wrote another outline, and then another outline." Counseling psychologists, often in conjunction with writing specialists, design programs to help people get past these "writer's blocks." In each of these interventions, the counseling psychologist's primary role has been the development of the program, often applying much of the knowledge we have gained from behavior modification programs (see later section in this chapter).

A well-researched contribution by counseling psychologists to educational development has been the specification of treatments to reduce test anxiety. The basic underlying concept for most treatments is what is known as systematic desensitization, that is learning how to relax even in the presence of cues for anxiety. A structured training program first teaches basic relaxation skills. Then the client is asked to arrange a hierarchy of very mild anxiety-provoking thoughts or images to very high anxiety-provoking thoughts or images. A final step is practicing, for several sessions, how to relax first when visualizing a mild anxiety-provoking image, and, once the client has mastered relaxing to that stimulus, up the hierarchy to more anxiety-provoking images.

Counseling psychologists have been developing and evaluating test anxiety programs since the 1960s (Osterhouse, 1972). This research has repeatedly shown that test anxiety treatments (based on desensitization) result in less test anxiety than learning study skills alone or having no treatment at all. For example, Deffenbacher and Michaels (1981) conducted an after-treatment and a 15-month follow-up assessment of students who had received anxiety management training and self-control desensitization. This study reported that students receiving treatment, compared to those not receiving treatment, reported less anxiety about tests and tended to have slightly higher psychology grades. At the 15-month follow-up assessment, students receiving treatment continued to feel less anxious about taking tests and showed less anxiety about other problematic areas in their lives than did students who had not received training.

Some research attention has also been given to less demanding techniques for reducing test anxiety. Altmaier and Woodward (1981) have shown that watching video tapes of desensitization sessions, without actually receiving the treatment oneself, could result in lower test anxiety than receiving study skills training alone or receiving no treatment. Many counseling centers now offer programs for test anxiety reduction based on these and other research results.

Career development

Both the remedial and developmental aspects of counseling psychology are also seen in counseling psychologists' work in the area of vocational counseling, or to use the preferred broader term, *career development*. While such work constitutes less of the actual services of counseling psychologists than counseling for emotional-social problems, it is the area for which counseling psychologists have their greatest distinction. As reviewed earlier in this chapter, the profession developed primarily after World War II by assisting thousands of veterans in preparing for and choosing careers. Thus, counseling psychologists were the ones who developed the assessment and intervention methods to help people make these choices. From these experiences, several counseling psychologists devoted their entire professional careers to articulating theoretical models and establishing research programs; these have led to effective and comprehensive approaches to vocational assessment and intervention. Descriptions of the major approaches may be found in Osipow (1983) and Crites (1981). Crites' earlier book (1969) remains a classic in describing the full range of theory and research in vocational psychology. Two of the theoretical models developed by counseling psychologists have had at least an indirect, if not direct, impact on all students and young adults in this country in the last twenty years. These two theories are briefly described in the next few paragraphs, followed by a description of the range of, and effects of, career counseling strategies.

Holland's theory of career choice is currently the best known and most widely used model of career choice. His theory represents a culmination of many years of research on occupational environments and personality characteristics of workers. Holland's theory (1973) is often considered a *type theory* since he proposes that all work environments can be categorized into one of six groups of types: realistic (for example, printers, truck drivers), investigative (biologists, mathematicians), social (social workers, teachers), conventional (secretaries, bank tellers), enterprising (salesmen, managers), and artistic (reporters, musicians). Holland also believed that people can be categorized into one of six same-named type groups: realistic, investigative, social, conventional, enterprising, and artistic. When people work in occupational environments that match their personality style (for example, a social person in a social occupational environment), then they will be the most satisfied and productive. Holland also observed that people tend to view the vocational world in terms of occupational stereotypes. "Holland hypothesized that where the individual possesses little knowledge about a particular vocation, the resulting stereotype is revealing, much in the manner a projective test presumably exposes personality dynamics" (Osipow, 1983, p. 82). Holland developed a measure in which a person could project his or her preferred life style, the Vocational Preference Inventory (Holland, 1965). The use of that instrument has provided data for developing and testing Holland's theory, subsequently leading to the development of The Self-Directed Search (Holland, 1974), a self-administered career counseling inventory.

Super's (1942) self-concept theory of career development is the other most easily identified outstanding theoretical contribution in vocational development. Like Holland, Super developed his theory after years of empirical research in career psychology. Super acknowledges that he was strongly influenced by both the self-theory of Carl Rogers as well as the work of developmental psychologists in the 1920s and 1930s. Super's theory (1942), while much more complex than Holland's, is basically quite straightforward. He postulated that one chooses to enter the occupation that is seen as most likely to permit self-expression and most likely to fulfill one's self-concept. A developmental emphasis is reflected in the proposition that the particular career-oriented behaviors a person engages in at any point in time are a function of a person's life stage and career stage. Vocational decision making during adolescence is, according to Super's theory, of a different form and style than are decisions made during late middle-age.

Super's work has led directly to the concept of *career maturity*, a concept that has been studied extensively in the last two decades (Crites, 1978; Westbrook & Parry-Hill, 1973). The development of measures of career maturity has allowed counselors to assess whether an adolescent or adult is considering the appropriate kinds of information and has the necessary decision-making skills for his or her life stage. Such assessments have the potential for being extremely useful to the career counselor in identifying information or skill deficiencies of the client.

Another lasting and major contribution of Super's work emerged from his career pattern studies. Super began, in the early 1950s, to study the career attitudes and behaviors of boys then in junior high school. He has conducted a longitudinal study now spanning several decades, with the follow up of these men at age 36 currently being prepared for publication. Even by the early 1960s, when these young men were then in their twenties, it was apparent that their early career success and satisfaction were not predicted by their having made an early career decision. Rather, the data suggested that students who were oriented toward learning about the world of work and making assessments of their own interests and skills during the junior high years were the ones who were able to make the best starts in careers. These data have been critical in helping change a persistent feature in Western educational systems: encouraging early career decision making, in fact, having to make decisions by age 12 or 13 that would put a student in particular high school tracks such that a change of mind could set one back several years. Super's data contributed significantly to the development of more flexible patterns of high school education and less pressured career exploration and decision making. The concept of career education occurring throughout life as opposed to at a single decision point is based on Super's theory.

In reviewing both Holland's and Super's theoretical contributions, we have identified the two theories from counseling psychology that have had the largest impact on the greatest number of persons in contemporary society. Almost every school student is now exposed to some sort of career assessment and education, both of which have been strongly influenced by Super's and/or Holland's theoretical developments. Elaboration of their work continues, especially as applied to adults, as more and more employers include career development as part of their services (see later section in this chapter). The achievement of a satisfying and productive career is, as both Super and Holland have noted, a life-long process that can be facilitated by an understanding of the attitudes, skills, and knowledge that one needs in various stages of life or environmental studies for making appropriate decisions.

From the two major theoretical models, we shift attention to career counseling—what is it like; is it worthwhile?

Career counseling in the past few decades has taken on many forms, from an entire multi-grade classroom curriculum to a series of individual counseling sessions to a computer-assisted programmed instruction format. While some counseling psychologists question whether the more structured options should be called "counseling" (many prefer the more generic term "interventions"), in recent years, data have accumulated showing that this immense variety of interventions has consistent positive effects. Spokane and Oliver (1983) reviewed studies of career counseling in the same way Smith and Glass reviewed psychotherapy studies. Their analysis indicated that persons who receive career counseling were better off than 81 percent of those who had not. (Recall that the figure was 85 percent for psychotherapy studies).

Surprising to the researchers is the fact that the effects of these interventions have not differed as much as the length of treatment would suggest; one hour programs have, at times, yielded results similar to semester-long courses. A recent review by Holland, Magoon, and Spokane (1981) concluded that positive effects are obtained when career counseling includes the following components: (1) exposure to occupational information; (2) opportunity to reflect on and rehearse some vocational aspirations; (3) assistance in designing and organizing information about self, the world of work, and their relationships; and

(4) social support or reinforcement from counselors or group members to help make specific plans. Related to this last point is the fact that there is some evidence in both of the reviews cited above that group career counseling may be more effective than individual career counseling, probably because of the importance of the support and reinforcement from fellow group members. Equally important, some of these data suggest that almost everyone planning or making career choices, not only as young persons but throughout adulthood, can benefit from self-administered materials like The Self-Directed Search (Holland, 1974) or a self-help book like What Color Is Your Parachute? (Bolles, 1978). However, for persons who are very indecisive about their careers, there is increasing evidence that all of these techniques work less well. We have yet to discover what treatments work best for such persons (Fretz & Leong, 1982a). Do they need individual counseling for patterns of indecisiveness or behavioral programs for raising self-esteem? Questions like these are part of our current challenge.

Career counseling is more varied in form than is psychotherapy. Programs may be highly structured to very unstructured, may be individualized or conducted in large groups, may be every bit as personalized as psychotherapy or may be as impersonal as being in a classroom full of computer terminals. Computer technology is especially valuable in career counseling for its capacity to store huge amounts of information and yet display only the particular pieces of world-of-work or self-assessment information needed by a given individual. Consequently, counseling psychologists working with career counseling have been on the leading edge of computer technology applied to counseling efforts.

As has been shown in the preceding paragraphs, the work of counseling psychologists in the field of career development has assisted not only persons greatly troubled by the career decisions they face, but also individuals struggling with choices affecting personal fulfillment in terms of interests, abilities, and competencies. The importance of satisfactory career adjustment to overall life adjustment has long been recognized. Freud noted explicitly that the goal of psychoanalysis was to help persons become productive and satisfied in both their love and work relationships. Data continues to accumulate indicating the significant relationships of work adjustment and general mental health (Fretz & Leong, 1982b).

Facilitating normal development

The three areas of practice and research reviewed so far have focused on the remedial and developmental roles of counseling psychologists. In this last area of facilitating normal development, the primary thrust is in conducting research and implementing treatment programs pertinent to the developmental and preventive roles of counseling psychologists. The developmental role refers to teaching skills that make dealing with the everyday problems of life less disruptive; the preventive part refers to helping clients make changes in their personal and interpersonal environments that will minimize the occurrence of problems.

Counseling psychologists, being located primarily in universities, have focused most of their developmental studies on college students. Psychologists were able to observe that college students, both those who did not come to counseling centers as well as those who did, went through major changes during their college years. What were the differences between those that changed without encountering lots of problems versus those who needed the help of the counselor? Could we be more helpful to persons in difficulty if we had a better understanding of how college students developed and changed? Attempts to understand psychological development during the college years have been numerous (e.g., Chickering, 1969; Yamamoto, 1968).

Research continues on how to help college students attain the greatest amount of personal growth from their college years (Whiteley, 1982). Knefelkamp, Widick, and Parker (1978) have reviewed the various models of college student development that emerged by the 1960s and 1970s. Each of these models has generated a variety of research projects, each lending some support to the usefulness of each model. Some theories are of the psychosocial type, focusing on the interaction of the developing person and the social environment. These theories are similar to Erikson's (1963) lifespan developmental theory with its developmental tasks for eight stages of life. The work of Chickering (1969) is an example of such a model where he specifies that the goal for college years includes mastering the tasks of achieving competence, managing emotions, becoming autonomous, establishing identity, freeing interpersonal relationships, clarifying purposes, and developing integrity.

A completely different approach is represented in a cognitive developmental theory of college student development. Perry (1970) has suggested stages of cognitive development for the college years, each stage representing a qualitatively different way of thinking about the nature of knowledge. At the least developed level is dualistic or dichotomist thinking. Someone who thinks dualistically believes something is either right or wrong, and prefers that someone else tell him or her what is right. Life at this stage is comfortable in many ways—no hard decisions to make. Dualism gives way, in the Perry model, to two stages of multiplicity, where the individual sees that a number of factors affect how a decision can be made. This is the stage where students will question their dualistic ways of thinking but still be oriented to what others say—a stage that makes one quite susceptible to the influence of others. If more cognitive development occurs, students move into the two stages of relativism, using their own thoughts and decision-making skills to form a solution to questions of concern to themselves. The most cognitively mature students not only make decisions that incorporate a whole range of information, they also begin to feel a personal commitment to themselves. New information and new decisions can be integrated into their values and into who they are as persons.

Knefelkamp and her colleagues have proposed that courses which are arranged to take into account college students' cognitive functioning will be more effective; that is, students who are taught with the methodology suited to their cognitive level will learn more than if mismatched. Initial research supports this proposition (Knefelkamp & Slepitza, 1976; Touchton, Wertheimer, & Cornfeld, 1977).

Finally, there are typology theories of college student development, probably best represented by Heath (1964) in his readable book, *The Reasonable Adventurer.* He classified students on two dimensions: *ego functioning,* which refers to maturity level, and *personality temperament* style. He found that students at various levels of ego functioning and temperament would show maturity, throughout the college years, in quite different ways.

In summary, there have been a number of theoretical approaches, none of which have been entirely satisfactory, for explaining how and why some college students make significant gains during their college years while others do not. All investigators in this area have shared in studying one of the major transition periods in American life: the college years.

As the focus in our society shifts from a youth orientation to one emphasizing the mature adult years, counseling psychologists too are beginning to study the normal development of people beyond the college years, on into the middle and elderly age spans. You may be familiar with psychological viewpoints about the stages that persons go through in childhood (Piaget, 1952) and adulthood (Levinson, Darrow, Klien, Levinson, & McKee, 1978). While these stage theories are still debated, what is clear is that many persons go through transition periods during their lives, all of which have the common effect of challenging old and comfortable ways of functioning. People are often left frustrated, anxious, and inflicted with self-doubts; they are then less able to use those skills that they do have. Some researchers have argued that competence is the key concept in resolving these transition stages (White, 1973). Other researchers have hypothesized that it is one's belief in one's own competence, one's sense of self-efficacy, that is more critical (Bandura, 1977). Counseling psychologists are now studying middle-aged and older adults to develop models that can be scientifically tested of how transitions are most successfully resolved.

Outreach ▪ From studies of normal development, it seems clear that everyone encounters stress and transition in life. While most individuals do not require the assistance of mental health professionals to survive these periods, statistics indicate that these stresses cause great personal disruptions for many who are not in psychological treatment. Are there broad sets of skills and strategies that could be taught to these individuals, making them more effective and satisfied with their lives? Counseling psychologists have, for the past three decades, researched several approaches for identifying such skills. In recent years, most attention has been on three areas: communication skills, behavioral self-management skills, and stress management skills. Programs in all three of these areas are usually offered to the "general public" (as compared to "clients"), whether that is a university campus or a local community. The only prerequisite for taking part is that people wish to learn skills to help themselves live more productive lives. These kinds of programs are often referred to as *outreach* programs. The concept of outreach means direct services to non-client populations with the aim of helping these people develop skills to make life less frustrating and more productive (Drum & Knott, 1977).

Looking first at communication skill groups, you might ask what psychologists have to do with communication skills. Think, however, about the everyday problems that revolve around talking with each other: husband–wife, parent–adolescent, supervisor–employee. The study of the basic steps in training counselors made it obvious to many counseling psychologists that the same skills that were needed to start working with a client were the skills that we need in relationships to make other people feel listened to and respected. Using structured communication skills programs like Microcounseling (Ivey, 1971), Human Relations Training (Carkhuff, 1969, 1972), and Interpersonal Process Recall (Kagan & Krathwohl, 1967), counseling psychologists have been able to help participants achieve more satisfying marriages, fewer roommate changes in college settings, fewer expulsions in junior high school, fewer problems of racial conflict, and better warden–inmate relationships. Each program involves four to forty or more hours, depending on the background of the participants and how much improvement in communication skills is desired. A few of the titles of the sections of these programs give you a flavor of what topics might be covered: attending behavior, effective listening skills, exploration skills (helping the person to talk freely about concerns), responding to feelings and emotions, and problem-solving strategies.

During the last two decades, other counseling psychologists have developed applications of Skinner's (1953) behavioral principles of psychology, especially self-management applications, given our profession's focus on helping individuals aid their own personal development. In self-management, you decide what behavior you want to change, and choose from various techniques for changing it (Thoresen & Mahoney, 1974; Williams & Long, 1975). Psychologists have demonstrated that self-control is a skill, not something someone "has" or "doesn't have." What most of us are lacking, and often learn only by experience, are the techniques by which we can exercise that control. Behavioral psychology has provided that technology for us. What we need to learn is to identify the specific behaviors we want to change, to monitor them both before and after we begin our own self-management program, and to follow specific steps to increase our chances that we can be successful in changing those behaviors. Common sense often misguides us here, suggesting, for example, that we should start with a problem that is most important to us or start with a behavior we need to stop. As described in the books already cited, psychologists have been able to show that those "common sense" ideas are wrong ones. Greater success in changing behavior comes if small problems that are not the most important and that require an increase in a behavior rather than a decrease in a behavior are used as initial goals.

More recently psychologists—counseling as well as clinical and industrial psychologists—have given attention to aiding development through stress management techniques. As Thoresen (1980) noted, stress is a major factor not only in the creation of psychological health problems but also physical health problems. Programs have been designed that help people learn to identify stresses in their environment and to manage their stress responses (e.g., Davis, McKay, & Eshelman, 1980). Chapter 5 presents more information about research and treatment aspects of stress reduction.

Outreach programs can respond to important social problems as well as help college students become more competent in dealing with everyday minor problems. Schinke, Blythe, and Gilchrist (1981) provided urban high school sophomores with a structured training program for prevention of adolescent pregnancy. The program included contraceptive information, steps for solving problems and for practicing communication of decisions about sexual behavior. A six-month follow-up showed that the young women and men who participated in the training groups had better attitudes toward family planning and were practicing more effective contraception than were the young people in the control conditions.

In another setting, Brown (1980) combined a number of the structured programs of relaxation, anxiety management, social skills, and self-reinforcement procedures. He offered them as a thirty-hour program to residents of the community served by a community mental health center. The participants were compared to other community residents who were in more traditional group-counseling programs focused on personal problems and anxiety, but including no structured skills training. At the completion of the instruction, and three months later, the group receiving the combined structured programs had lower levels of anxiety and fear and higher levels of assertion. Such results give promise of, and lay the foundation for, more extensive studies of the preventive contributions of outreach programs.

Consultation ▪ A second aspect of facilitating normal development is the prevention of psychological problems. Are there psychological equivalents to immunization shots and good health habits that will minimize the occurrences of psychological dysfunction? Can we find ways to change individuals and/or environments that will result in fewer than the usual 10–15 percent of college students needing counseling services? Counseling psychologists working in this area share overlapping roles with organizational psychologists in business settings and with community psychologists in community mental health centers. Although there are many types of psychological prevention activities, counseling psychologists have mostly utilized consultation roles. *Consultation*, as used by psychologists, has been defined by Gallessich (1982) as indirect services to clients, that is, the psychological consultant assists an agency with its work-related concerns rather than working directly with individual clients.

Somewhat ironically, counseling psychologists usually become involved as consultants because someone in an agency becomes concerned that "some people" have a problem and asks the psychologist to "help those people." An example is that every semester at registration time, there are some students who become so frustrated over procedures that they disrupt the process, harass secretaries, steal credit slips, and so forth. Another example is the expulsion rate in high schools. A third example is the vandalism rate in university dormitories. Traditionally, when psychologists were presented with problem situations, they focused their attention on the individuals involved. What can be done about students who are disrupting the registration process? How can we help students being expelled? What can we do with students who are vandalizing the dormitories?

A more contemporary approach by psychologists is to assess the organization or environment in which the problem is occurring and determine whether there are ways in which changes could be made in that environment to reduce the number of such problems. Rather than asking what is "wrong" with the person, the question becomes the degree to which the environment is causing the problem. Are there ways of improving the registration process to reduce frustrations? Could changes in teacher–student relationships lead to fewer expulsions? Could changes in dormitory design lead to less vandalism? For each problem situation, the possibilities of organizational policy changes are examined as an alternative to trying to "treat" the people who are involved. The goals of such activities are to make the persons, organization, and community more effective in its operations and to reduce the stress for staff and consumers/citizens alike. Achievement of this goal decreases the number of problems for all concerned; moreover, the psychologist, in one intervention, has helped a large number of persons both for now and in the future, if the organizational change is maintained.

Since every such problem is really quite different, it is hard to make many generalizations about consultation beyond saying that one must approach the parties involved in the conflict situation with all the exploratory and listening skills we referred to above, as well as a great deal of patience for exploring and planning alternatives and trying out new possibilities. Gallesich (1982) provides well-illustrated descriptions of the various steps for consultation: preliminary exploration, contracting, entry, building working relationships, data gathering, diagnoses, intervention, evaluation and termination. Her examples are drawn largely from public service programs such as probation offices, day care centers, planned parenthood, and the Peace Corps. Katz and Kahn (1978) provide similar perspectives for consultation in more traditional business organizations.

■ WHERE DO COUNSELING PSYCHOLOGISTS WORK?

Surveys in recent years (Banikiotes, 1977, 1980) indicate that about two-thirds of new doctoral-level counseling psychologists enter direct service positions; that is, they provide counseling or consultation to clients. About one-third of this group enter university counseling centers, another third are in community mental health services, and the other third are distributed across services ranging from hospitals to substance abuse centers to rehabilitation centers. About 25 percent of all new doctoral-level graduates in counseling psychology enter primarily academic teaching and research careers, either in university centers or medical schools.

These data are in contrast to a long history of surveys (Pallone, 1980) that indicate that over 50 percent of all counseling psychologists are employed in university settings. The difference appears to be in the generation of counseling psychologists being surveyed. The latter group of studies focused on counseling psychologists of all ages. Banikiotes's surveys were of doctoral-level counseling psychologists graduating during the late 1970s. The differences are understandable. During the 1950s and 1960s, the most rapidly expanding parts of our population were the school- and college-age groups. Additionally, after World War II, schools and colleges increased their commitment to providing general psychological and career and educational development services. At that time there was no possibility of providing doctoral-level counseling psychologists for all of those services. The vast majority of service providers were those holding master's degrees. A large proportion of doctoral-level counseling psychologists were offered faculty appointments at universities to teach in master's degree programs which, in turn, provided the counselors for many settings. Over 400 master's programs in counseling existed by the early 1970s.

The decade of the 1970s, of course, brought a radical change in demographics, with sharp decreases in the number of students in public schools. Training programs for M.A. counselors no longer needed expansion; many counseling centers soon had their desired complement of doctoral-level staff. The growth in the 1970s was largely in community mental health centers, a kind of center that was almost nonexistent prior to the late 1960s. Therefore, even though the surveys reviewed by Pallone and Banikiotes cover different groups, it is likely that Banikiotes's data does foretell a changing distribution of settings in which counseling psychologists work, with a decreasing percentage employed in university settings. However, it should be noted that while it will be a decreasing percentage of placements, it is and will remain probably one of the largest single categories of employment. There are over 200 counseling centers in universities throughout this country, many with staffs of ten to twenty counseling psychologists.

At the beginning of this chapter there were four brief descriptions of diverse positions held by counseling psychologists. Even that diversity includes only a fraction of the many varied positions held by counseling psychologists. Counseling psychologists with good mathematical backgrounds are highly valued by industrial and defense agencies that are giving considerable attention to the use of computer systems to provide both psychological assessment and career assessment and counseling for their thousands of employees. As described in the next section on emerging areas of research and practice for counseling psychologists, there is an increasing number of opportunities for positions in hospitals, in cross-cultural counseling, and in industrial settings. Other opportunities are related to the provision of consultation services as described in an earlier section. Those particular skills have allowed many counseling psychologists to move into part-time or full-time consultation with school boards, police departments, churches, and other civic organizations; these counseling psychologists utilize the specialty's traditional skills for the more effective running of the organization as well as the training of personnel such as police officers, teachers, and others in communication and relationship skills.

For counseling psychologists who wish to teach and conduct research as well as provide counseling services, there remain many opportunities for appointments as faculty members in counseling psychology programs. In the last five years, there has been a 50 percent increase in the number of APA-approved doctoral training programs in counseling psychology. These and other programs have not been able to find a sufficient number of counseling psychologists interested in and qualified for faculty positions.

The same skills that prepare counseling psychologists for their developmental and consultation roles also make them prime candidates for administrative positions. A very large number of counseling psychologists have moved on to positions such as vice president for student affairs and chief psychologist in community mental health centers or in Veterans Administration Hospitals. In fact, within the Veterans Administration system, the number of chiefs from counseling psychology backgrounds is much greater than the proportion of counseling to clinical psychologists in the total VA system.

Private practice has, up until now, included only a small percentage of counseling psychologists, although it should be noted that nearly 40 percent of all counseling psychologists have a part-time private practice. Banikiotes's data suggest that a greater percentage of counseling psychologists will be choosing that route: his data from 1976 to 1979 showed an increase of 4.5–7.8 percent of new doctoral students entering full-time private practice.

The increasing number of employment positions in community mental health centers during the 1970s will continue in most places only if there is continued federal funding for community mental health centers, a process that has suddenly stopped short in the early 1980s. What the future counseling or clinical psychologist must keep in mind is that the kinds of job opportunities will be directly affected by the nature of funding. As long as health insurance programs continue their present level of mental health benefits, private practice will remain an attractive option since the client is sometimes paying, directly, as little as 20 percent of the cost. However, when mental health benefits are significantly cut back, there will be a corresponding reduction in the number of people going into private practice and an increase in those going to community mental health centers. In brief, the location of service provision of the therapeutically oriented, as compared to the developmental and consultative, services of counseling psychologists is greatly affected by the source of the funds being used to pay for such services.

■ COUNSELING PSYCHOLOGY IN THE FUTURE

There are at least three emerging areas of research and practice that are now receiving increased attention by counseling psychologists: cultural diversity and cross-cultural counseling, behavioral medicine and counseling in health settings, and counseling in industry. In the profession's recent reviews of itself (see Suggested Readings), recommendations were made that would support the further development of these emerging areas. The addition of these three emerging areas to the four still vital and viable focal areas previously reviewed provides a challenging breadth of opportunities for the counseling psychologist of the future.

Cultural diversity and cross-cultural counseling

The increase in social consciousness of the late 1960s and early 1970s regarding the effects of sexism and racism led to the recognition that most theories of development and intervention had dealt primarily with the study of white middle-class males. Are theories of normal personality, of career and educational development, and of counseling applicable to women and to Blacks, Asian-Americans, Hispanics, and Native Americans? Are the interest, personality, and ability measures used by counseling psychologists valid for these groups? Counseling psychologists have recently entered this latter area of research. What can be concluded at this point is that any psychologist about to use a test or standard counseling approach with anyone other than white males should check carefully for research determining its appropriateness for that person. Some tests and models have proved to be as valid with a culturally diverse person as with a white male, but other tests and models have not.

Counseling psychologists have been in the forefront of developing sex-fair measures of interest in order that women not continue to be channeled only into traditional career choices such as nursing, teaching, and clerical work. The kind of research leading to the development of sex-fair interest measures (e.g., Zunker, 1981) is now being conducted with Blacks and Asian-Americans to determine whether changes in assessment and intervention strategies are needed in order to highlight a broader range of career opportunities for ethnic groups. A question that needs to be answered is whether patterns of underrepresentation of certain ethnic groups in certain professions are an accurate reflection of skills and interests or are a function of how our educational and psychological assessments reflect current social stereotypes.

What about counseling interventions with the culturally diverse, whether for remedial or developmental purposes? Are there special sensitivities counselors need when working with someone of a different cultural background? As with assessment issues, research on counseling women has been much more extensive than counseling with ethnic minorities. The Committee on Women of the Division of Counseling Psychology in the American Psychological Association was the first group to develop a set of Principles Concerning Counseling/Therapy of Women. Many other groups of psychologists have now adopted the guidelines that should be followed by anyone working with female clients.

We are just now beginning to see the development of models (Sue et al., 1982) that are focused on the different kinds of considerations and interventions that are needed for counseling ethnic minorities. The need for such models is already all too well known. Ethnic minorities have typically had few counseling services offered them. For many ethnic groups, seeking counseling remains much more a stigma than it is for white middle-class persons. Add to this the difficulties many counselors have in establishing rapport with someone of a very different background, and it is not surprising to find that ethnic minorities both begin counseling less often and drop out of the counseling more often than others. Sladen (1982) has demonstrated Blacks give better ratings to counselors and clients matched on race and socioeconomic status; however, LaFramboise and Dixon (1981) found American Indians rated both Indian and white counselors as trustworthy. Much additional research needs to be conducted to determine which variables are affected by which ethnic differences. These data are all the more compelling when one realizes that, in this country, ethnic minorities are the most likely to have had poor educational training and restricted job opportunities leading to greater psychological stress.

The research now underway by counseling psychologists will help establish guidelines and models that can lead to more effective counseling for minorities and to the creation of psychological environments that are less stressful for culturally different persons.

Behavioral medicine

The functions of counseling psychologists in other than psychiatric hospitals have grown very slowly in the last few decades. However, in recent years there has been a great increase in the number of psychologists working with physicians and other physical health care specialists (Stone, Cohen, & Adler, 1979). Traditionally, psychological services in a hospital included only diagnosis of psychopathology and assessment for rehabilitation potential. The role of psychologists in hospitals has rapidly expanded in the last decade as is clear in Chapter 5 on Psychology and Health.

Physicians now frequently refer patients to psychologists for anxiety and depression that occur along with their diseases or injuries; others are referred because their adjustment to their disabilities is tenuous. Still other patients need support and coping skills in view of an acute health crisis or life-threatening condition. May (1977) describes several cases referred to a counseling psychologist. First, a recently diagnosed leukemia patient will not cooperate with a treatment plan. Second, a leg amputee refuses to learn to walk with a prosthesis. Third, a man with chronic lung disease must assume a housekeeper role while his wife works outside the home. He questions his masculinity and has sexual problems. A counseling psychologist can help these cases as well as many others. Additionally, counseling psychologists are active in the training of physicians in helping skills and communication skills (Kagen, 1979).

Reviewing the kinds of problems referred to the psychologist, one can see that a broad range of assessment and intervention skills is needed. Fortunately, the counseling psychologists' skills in exploring feelings, developing supportive relationships, and carefully planning changes in behavior are often just the combination that bring about change for each of these problem areas. Larger roles may be developing for counseling psychologists in this area based on the work of Thoresen (1980) who postulates that the most-needed contribution from psychologists at this time is to help persons develop more healthy lifestyles resulting in better physical health and an increased life span.

Counseling in industry

New developments in counseling in hospitals and industry represent a change in settings more than a change in roles. There have been a few counseling psychologists in hospital and industrial settings for the past few decades. The change now is in the rapid increase in the number of opportunities in both of these settings and the possibilities for providing, within a single company or single hospital, a more comprehensive range of services.

A full range of opportunities within industrial settings for counseling psychologists has been elaborated by Toomer (1982). Counseling as well as clinical psychologists play a major role in many of the employee-assistance programs that are developing in industry to provide direct therapeutic services for employees with personal adjustment problems such as alcoholism, depression, and marital and family conflicts. Additionally, counseling psychologists in such settings may engage in consultation with managers and/or employees concerning employee relationships and communication skills. A growing number of companies are interested in providing outreach and prevention services in the interest of improving employee satisfaction and commitment to the company. Such programs might include structured groups, such as described in an earlier part of this chapter, focused on self-esteem enhancement, assertiveness, relaxation, and stress management.

A final area of development in industrial settings is well suited to one of counseling psychologists' unique skills: career development for all stages of adulthood. In such a service, there may be opportunities for current employees to have assessment and counseling regarding how they might move to other positions within the company in order to be more satisfied and feel a sense of advancement. Others might seek counseling on how to obtain education to become technologically updated, and finally, as retirement approaches, how to plan effectively for retirement. Additionally, as noted by Levinson et al. (1978), many adults enter a stage in life where they question their own usefulness, meaning in life, and satisfaction in employment. Previously successful employees could well move into long periods of stagnation unless they receive some counseling assistance in working through these issues. All of these services are important contributions to employees' well-being, and companies have found the career development services useful in helping keep their good employees. When for reasons of reductions in force or no-longer-needed skills employees need to be let go, the company gains at least a modicum of good will if it helps the employee find other positions, a process commonly called outplacement.

In their interactions within industry, counseling psychologists have increased their overlap with industrial/organizational psychologists and are giving more attention to employee adjustment problems such as turnover, job satisfaction, absenteeism, performance. *The Journal of Vocational Behavior* provides numerous samples of the common interests of both of these kinds of psychologists in helping employees be more satisfied and productive and helping companies and organizations to be more efficient and effective. One exciting frontier in this collaboration is sorting out how much attention needs to be given to helping individuals adjust to an organization as compared to how much organizations should change to accommodate individuals.

■ CONCLUSION

Recall that the hallmark of training in counseling psychology is to acquire the knowledge and skills to formulate and implement research and service projects that respond to contemporary social issues. Looking over the present and emerging areas of practice and research in counseling psychology, you can see many challenges that need our attention. The list that ends this chapter is but one of many that counseling psychologists could develop. Consider it simply as one counseling psychologist's invitation to a growing profession that finds its own satisfaction in contributing to the knowledge and skills that enhance the quality of life for all persons.

Can social influence theory explain the relative efficiency of time-limited therapy as compared to long-term therapy?

Can anxiety treatment programs significantly reduce minority students' withdrawal rate from colleges?

Can counseling center programs be developed to assist the pervasively indecisive person?

Can a set of psychological coping skills be identified and taught to all college students that reduces the number of mental health crises they encounter in adulthood?

Can white counselors be trained so that their minority clients can benefit from counseling as much as nonminority clients do?

Can hospital counseling programs be developed that help patients take the greater responsibility for post-treatment recovery that many physicians believe is necessary?

Can comprehensive career development services in industrial settings improve quality of work performance as well as employee satisfaction?

Responses to these and similar questions are the challenges to be met by counseling psychologists in the remaining years of the twentieth century.

■ SUGGESTED READINGS

Egan, G. (1982). *The skilled helper* (2nd ed.). Monterey, CA: Brooks/Cole.

This book is probably the most widely-used skills training book. Egan describes and illustrates a three-stage model of helping. He identifies typical pitfalls and misapplications of the various parts of each stage. Beginning chapters provide the basic philosophy and prerequisites for using his model. This book is suitable for students at the advanced undergraduate level.

Kagan, N. (Ed.) (1982). The next decade. *The Counseling Psychologist, 10* (2), 7–84.

This issue contains the reports of four committees commissioned by Division 17 (Counseling Psychology) of APA. These committees on training, employment, research, and definition make recommendations for future development in each of these areas.

Patterson, C. H. (1980). *Theories of counseling and psychotherapy* (3rd ed.). New York: Harper & Row.

This textbook comprehensively details fifteen theoretical viewpoints directly applicable to the work of counseling psychologists. The range of theories encompasses psychoanalysis to behavior therapy to existentialism. Each chapter includes a critique of the theory's contributions and limitations. Students with prior course work in personality theory will find this text understandable and interesting.

Rogers, C. R. (1975). Empathic: An unappreciated way of being. *The Counseling Psychologist, 5* (2), 2–10.

In this special issue of *The Counseling Psychologist,* Carl Rogers discusses the usefulness of the concept of empathy and reviews relevant research findings.

Zunker, B. C. (1981). *Career counseling: Applied concepts of life planning.* Monterey, CA: Brooks/Cole.

This comprehensive textbook for career counseling provides a good introduction to the various knowledge domains. Major sections cover concepts, methods, programs for special populations, career search strategies, and occupational classification systems. This book would be interesting to the average undergraduate.

CHARLES D. SPIELBERGER

AND DAVID E. STENMARK

COMMUNITY PSYCHOLOGY

■ INTRODUCTION

The stresses encountered in modern industrial societies place many new and different demands on the human condition, and significant advances in psychological theory, research and practice are needed in order to help people cope with an everchanging world. Community psychology is an emerging field that provides a relatively new frontier for the study of human behavior. The goals of community psychology are broadly concerned with clarifying the complex interrelationships between individuals and their social environment, and with the discovery and implementation of more effective ways for coping with the stresses of modern life.

Recognition of the need for psychologists to get involved in community affairs is of relatively recent origin. Prior to World War II, most psychologists worked in university settings, and were concerned primarily with teaching and laboratory research. Psychologists associated with mental hospitals, child guidance clinics, and other community agencies were few in number and their responsibilities were generally limited to administering and interpreting psychological tests.

The current emphasis on community involvement seems to stem, in part, from the many complex social problems that confront our society and the belief that psychologists can contribute to their solution. Rising crime rates, juvenile delinquency, alcohol and drug abuse, racial conflict, and a veritable revolution in sexual practices are but a few of the many sources of stress that have tremendous influence on individuals, their relationships with one another, and the social groups to which they belong.

The rapid growth of community psychology has been stimulated by a growing recognition of the importance of environmental stressors in contributing to pressing social problems, as well as their impact on mental health and emotional disorders, and by wide-spread dissatisfaction with the limitations of traditional clinical approaches to mental health problems. The past twenty-five years have witnessed a tremendous expansion in training programs that prepare psychologists for public service work, and in the employment of psychologists in a variety of community settings. As an academic discipline, psychology is justifiably proud of its scientific roots and its resistance to the styles and fads of the marketplace. But, psychologists who are seriously concerned with human problems have come to believe that theories of behavior based largely on studies of laboratory animals, college sophomores, and psychiatric patients must be tested in a wider context. More and more, the value of psychological theory is being judged in terms of its predictive potential in community settings.

In this chapter, we describe the origins, evolution, and development of community psychology as an area of specialization within the broader field of applied psychology. Since community psychology is most meaningfully defined by the theoretical conceptions that guide research and practice in this field, we will consider in some detail what we consider to be the three major theoretical models, along with applications of these models in practice and research. We will also describe some of the settings in which community psychologists typically work and the specific psychological skills they must have in order to successfully carry out their duties. Finally, we touch briefly on the education and training of community psychologists, and offer some advice for the serious student who may wish to pursue a career in this exciting new field.

■ HISTORICAL DEVELOPMENT

The community mental health movement arose out of a growing awareness that some individuals behave in a deviant or abnormal fashion because they are unwilling or unable to comply with contemporary traditions, moral standards, and acceptable codes of behavior. Many different approaches have been applied by governments, religious groups, and community agencies to severely punish, incarcerate, hide, or separate these individuals from the mainstream of society. Except for isolated pockets of enlightened and supportive care occasionally provided by courageous individuals such as Pinel (see Selling, 1943) and groups such as the Gheel Shrine in Belgium (Karnosh & Zucker, 1945), persons experiencing psychological disorders were ostracized and hidden from public view.

The two World Wars brought clearly into public awareness the psychologically devastating experience of combat stress. Together with separation from the social support systems of home and family, war experiences visibly changed and altered hundreds of thousands of people who had previously appeared "normal." Since psychiatrists, psychologists, and other allied professionals had entered the armed forces on both sides of the confrontation, and had assisted in screening military personnel prior to enlistment and combat, there could be little doubt that war experiences played a causative role in the psychological impairment of many veterans. Explanations that attributed mental illness to the presence of demons or the forces of evil, to neurological and biological deficiencies, or to other simplistic causes were no longer acceptable to the professional community or the public.

As Chapter 2 indicated, immediately following World War II urgent demands to provide care for thousands of military psychiatric casualties stimulated the development of graduate training programs in clinical psychology. Aided by financial support from the Veterans Administration (VA) and the National Institute of Mental Health, doctoral programs in clinical psychology were established at a number of major universities. Most of these programs adopted the scientist–professional model for graduate education in clinical psychology. In addition to a broad general education in the field of psychology, this model emphasized intensive professional training in psychodiagnosis and psychotherapy (Raimy, 1950).

During the decade 1946–1955, clinical and counseling psychology were concerned primarily with the diagnosis and treatment of intrapsychic phenomena. The goals of psychodiagnosis were to determine how personality deficiencies and repressed (unconscious) motives caused deviant behavior. The goals of treatment were to modify the personality structure of patients through appropriate therapeutic procedures so that patients could resolve their personal problems or learn to live with them more successfully. By 1955, however, many psychologists were recognizing that mental health involved something more than the absence of mental illness. It was also becoming apparent that preoccupation with the mentally ill was preventing psychologists from giving needed attention to a full range of community mental health problems.

Community mental health

The treatment of psychologically impaired individuals in mental hospitals predestined them to long-term institutional care, personal dependency, and hopelessness. Moreover, since the involvement of family and friends in treatment was generally not practical in centralized VA and state hospitals, community support systems were not utilized to stimulate and facilitate beneficial behavioral change. During the 1950s and early 1960s, research by clinical and social psychologists, psychiatrists, and cultural anthropologists pointed to the greater effectiveness of community-based as opposed to hospital treatment. Social scientists, politicians and the general public have also become increasingly aware that the best way to solve social problems was to keep them from occurring— the proverbial "ounce of prevention." It should be noted that this view was not entirely altruistic and idealistic: Community mental health was potentially less expensive than hospital care in terms of the financial costs as well as human suffering.

Recognizing the inherent limitations in traditional conceptions of mental illness and its treatment, the Education and Training Board of the American Psychological Association convened a conference in 1955 on Psychology and Mental Health (Strother, 1956). In the conference keynote address, Robert H. Felix, then Director of the National Institute of Mental Health, challenged psychology to embrace non-clinical community-oriented approaches to mental health problems:

> To what extent can non-clinical approaches actually produce changes in people that represent improvement in their mental health? This is the question that constantly bedevils those of us who want to develop public health programs in the mental health field. Each of us knows that there is no justification to attempt to handle all the psychological problems of all people on a treatment basis. It is unlikely that we could ever produce enough therapists to meet this objective. Consequently, we talk about mental health education, child rearing practices, mental health in the schools, and the contribution of other agencies to mental health and prevention (Felix, 1956, pp. 7–8).

Increasing concern about mental illness and mounting evidence of unmet community mental health needs led the United States Congress to pass the Mental Health Study Act of 1955, establishing the Joint Commission on Mental Illness and Health. Nationwide studies carried out under the sponsorship of the Joint Commission have profoundly influenced the development of community psychology. These studies showed that: (1) the nations's mental health manpower resources were severely limited (Albee, 1959); (2) mental health services for children and for racial and ethnic minority groups were lacking (Robinson, DeMarche, & Wagle, 1960); and (3) mental health services were typically not accessible at times of major crises and only minimally available to the poor (Gurin, Veroff, & Feld, 1960). The final report of the Joint Commission (Ewalt, 1961) recommended that new mental health facilities be established in community settings, that educational and consultative services be greatly expanded, and that research and preventive efforts be intensified.

These recommendations were subsequently embodied in the "New Frontier" legislative programs of John F. Kennedy, the first American president to deliver a message to Congress specifically related to the mental health of the nation. In response to this message, Congress passed the Mental Health Facilities Act of 1963, which provided funds for the construction of comprehensive community mental health centers throughout the nation. Subsequent federal legislation provided support for professional staff as well. Responsibility for the treatment of the mentally ill, as well as the arena in which treatment would take place, was thus moved from the mental hospital to the community, with the goal of overcoming the many major shortcomings of the traditional mental hospital.

Bloom (1977) enumerated several inadequacies of the traditional mental hospital systems. First of all, mental hospitals have erred in being divorced from the communities in which their patients live. In a related vein, mental hospitals have not provided an organized system of services that meets the mental health needs of the community in which the hospital is located. In terms of patient care, mental hospitals have been almost exclusively focused on the treatment of psychopathology, and have failed to devote adequate resources to activities that might prevent certain forms of psychopathology. In emphasizing long-term individual therapy, therapeutic strategies that might be helpful to greater number of patients were not developed. Finally, mental hospitals have not reached out to the community with an organized system of services. They also failed to develop effective liaison relationships with other caretaking agencies in the community, and were not able to coordinate adequately with other services or nontraditional sources of personnel.

The advent of community mental health centers, especially in the deprived areas of cities, has resulted in drastically changed concepts about psychotherapy and other helping procedures. The poor do not distinguish between social pathology and psychopathology, nor do they appreciate the attempts of the mental health professions to make such distinctions. While Medicare and Medicaid have provided new approaches to the delivery of medical services to the poor, and documented the need for even fuller medical coverage, these programs have also placed tremendous strains on existing medical resources.

Other New Frontier legislation led to the founding of the Peace Corps in which psychologists have played an active role. The Kennedy years also brought a greater awareness of the problems of poverty and cultural deprivation, and prepared the way for President Johnson's Great Society legislation that created community action programs such as Head Start, Upward Bound, day care, VISTA, and the Neighborhood Youth Corps. Thus, the decade 1955–1965, which began with Felix's challenge for psychology to embrace a community-oriented public health approach, ended with the enactment of broad-ranged social legislation that provided funds for community-action programs.

The beginnings of community psychology

During the 1950s and 1960s, shortages in professional personnel led an increasing number of clinical psychologists to invest significant portions of their time in consulting with community care-givers (e.g., ministers, public health nurses, welfare workers, school personnel) about mental health problems, rather than in working directly with individual clients or patients. Mental health consultation reflected a significant departure from the traditional clinical role of the mental health professions and an important new dimension for mental health practice.

Concerns with community mental health have subsequently evolved into a broader conception that recognizes that the community itself must be examined as a social system (Bennett, Anderson, Cooper, Hassol, Klein, & Rosenblum, 1966). It is no longer sufficient to deal only with the mental health problems of individuals who are casualties of the system. Many events have contributed to a shift in focus from community mental health to community psychology and the increasing involvement of psychologists in community affairs. While a detailed review of these events is beyond the scope of this chapter, we might note the general malaise of the cities, the impact of civil rights legislation, and growing concerns with problems of population.

Recent developments in the community make it necessary to look at old problems in different contexts and to seek new solutions. For example, violence in the streets has always been with us, but its recent increase and the forms of its manifestation have challenged traditional methods of law enforcement. Relationships between the police, the laws they are called upon to enforce, and the citizens they serve have never been more strained. Consequently, the need for communities to develop new standards and better internal controls has never been greater. The establishment of the Office of Economic Opportunity during the Johnson years to conduct the War on Poverty has also resulted in a variety of community-based action programs such as day care and Head Start, which cannot operate in a vacuum; active participation by the families and by the communities of the children who are served is required.

The complex new roles that are being assumed by community psychologists have been described by various terms such as mental health consultant, participant-conceptualizer, social-systems evaluators, social engineers or change agents, and the like (Cowen, 1970; Spielberger & Iscoe, 1970, 1972). As mental health *consultants*, community psychologists assist other community care-givers in handling the emotional problems of their clients, as will be described below. The community psychologist as *participant–conceptualizer* helps community leaders and care-givers analyze and clarify social and mental health problems in terms of social systems variables. As *social engineers* or change agents, community psychologists attempt to solve the problems they have helped to clarify, either by working directly on the problems themselves or by training others. In *program evaluation*, the community psychologist examines the specific processes and outcomes of a particular intervention in order to determine its value or success in achieving predetermined objectives (Bloom, 1972; Spielberger, Piacente, & Hobfoll, 1976).

Given the diversity and wide range of professional activities in which community psychologists are engaged, a simple definition of this field is not possible. Clearly community psychology does not imply a homogeneous group of psychologists with a unified body of knowledge and an established set of professional procedures. It may be viewed as a general orientation or movement within applied psychology that reflects a significant shift from the treatment of emotional disorders to their prevention. As Scribner (1968, p. 4) has cogently observed, "Community psychology represents the bringing together of various kinds of psychologists who have some concern with the broad question of 'man in society.' " Community psychology also implies a strong commitment to the promotion of positive mental health, and to the creation of environments that will be more conducive to human growth and development and harmonious human relations.

The optimistic *Zeitgeist* (or spirit) in the 1960s stimulated the formulation of three major theoretical models that now shape community psychology's social problem solving efforts: (1) the community mental health model; (2) the social-environmental ecology model; and (3) the social action model.

■ MODELS FOR COMMUNITY PSYCHOLOGY: CONCEPTIONS THAT GUIDE THEORY, RESEARCH AND PRACTICE

Seymour Sarason, a founder and leading contributor to community psychology, has often said that the way a problem is defined will determine and limit the universe of alternative solutions. Psychologists, like most people, tend to define problems in terms of the frames of reference accumulated from their own training and professional experience. Since community psychology has evolved primarily from clinical psychology, and many community psychologists were originally trained as clinicians, it is not surprising that the prevention of emotional disorders and the promotion of mental health are the primary concerns of most community psychologists.

Historically, community psychology developed during the 1960s in an era of unprecedented social consciousness and support for community-oriented social programs financed by the federal government. At the center of this sociopolitical context was the widespread belief that neighborhoods and community groups, by working together, could resolve systemic social problems. Through concerted and cooperative social action, it was assumed that the quality of life could be improved and that people could become the architects of their own destiny.

In science, the term "model" denotes an organized and integrated set of theoretical concepts and empirical relationships that have been firmly established by replicated research findings. A model must meet the test of providing accurate predictions about events or outcomes when sufficient information about antecedent conditions is given. According to this definition, there are, today, no well-established models in community psychology. Our use of this term is intended to catalog, in a preliminary way, the rapidly growing body of research knowledge and practical experience. The three models that are described below provide a tentative theoretical framework for organizing rudiments of interrelated theory, research, and practice of community psychology.

To better appreciate the need for models in community psychology, let us examine the rapid growth in the knowledge base reflected in published research in the 1960s and 1970s. In the mid-1960s, Stenmark, Taulbee, and Wright (1967) compiled a comprehensive annotated bibliography of 860 research studies relating to community mental health, broadly defined. A similar bibliography, which focuses more narrowly on research in community psychology from 1970 to 1980, is currently being compiled by Stenmark, Walfish, Kinder, and Aubuchon. Thus far, more than 3000 references have been identified for the decade of the 1970s.

The dramatic increase in the number of research publications in community psychology over the past decade has been facilitated by the establishment of new journals, the publication of books concerned with research and practical applications of community psychology, and the expansion of master's and doctoral training programs in community psychology. We have witnessed an explosion in education and training and in the knowledge base of community psychology over the past decade. Unfortunately, the replication of earlier research findings, which is essential for theory building, model development, and a meaningful synthesis of this information, lags woefully behind the vigorous efforts of the researchers. This state of affairs results, in part, from the infancy of the field. It also reflects the fact that communty psychologists are doggedly action-oriented, and perhaps somewhat less inclined toward research.

In the following sections, we describe and compare the three major community psychology models. Representative examples of professional practice and research applications are also presented to illustrate each model.

The community mental health model

For proponents of the community mental health model, the major concern is the prevention of mental disorders and the promotion of positive mental health. While these goals seem relatively straightforward, in actuality they require dealing with a host of ubiquitous forces in the social and physical environments that influence mental health. Indeed, one of the major problems in implementing the community mental health model is that virtually every human endeavor and environmental event falls within the purview of its definition.

Congruent with the view that community psychology may be defined in terms of what community psychologists *do*, contemporary definitions of the community mental health model have evolved along functional lines. The boundaries for this model are determined, in part, by its heritage and close affiliation with clinical psychology. There are also strong historical ties with developmental and social psychology. Proponents of the community mental health model engage in research and in applied interventions that are directed toward changing the knowledge, attitudes, and behaviors of individuals, small groups (e.g., families), neighborhoods, and communities. The allocation of professional time and resources are generally invested in working with impaired individuals and, to a lesser extent, with persons assumed to be at high risk of future impairment.

In contrast to more clinically oriented treatment approaches, a greater proportion of effort and resources are expended for consultation, crisis intervention, and short-term treatment with impaired or deviant individuals and their families. Although strongly espoused by this model, less energy and resources are typically expended in providing mental health education and in the prevention of mental disorders.

The community mental health model differs from the other two community psychology models in two important respects. First, the focus of the intervention is primarily on individuals and small groups, as contrasted with, for example, large organizations and social institutions. Secondly, although originally established to emphasize the prevention of mental health impairment, in practice the emphasis has been on secondary and tertiary preventive interventions rather than on primary prevention. *Primary prevention* refers to efforts to reduce the number of new cases of a disorder, either by changing the environment or by strengthening the ability of individuals to cope with various sources of environmental stress. *Secondary prevention* refers to the early identification and effective treatment of emotional problems or symptoms of mild forms of a mental disorder before it becomes disabling. *Tertiary prevention* involves rehabilitation and reintegration into the community of persons who have recovered from a mental illness in order to prevent *recidivism*, that is, a recurrence (relapse) of the original disorder.

Most community psychologists were educated in academic programs with a strong emphasis on clinical psychology, and have had clinical/medical psychology internship training experiences. As a consequence of their training, community psychologists who follow the community mental health model have greater knowledge and skill in the treatment of mental disorders than those who subscribe to other models. Typically, their professional activities are designed to facilitate the development of skills among their clients for more effective coping with life stresses. Such professional activities would include crisis intervention and brief psychotherapy, consultation, training paraprofessionals and caregivers from other disciplines (e.g., ministers, nurses), and education of the lay public.

To illustrate how community psychologists work within the context of the community mental health model, let us examine more closely one of the most important roles prescribed by this model. *Mental health consultation* refers to "a helping process, an educational process, and a growth process achieved through interpersonal relationships" (Rieman, 1963, p. 85). Through mental health consultation, the community psychologist helps other key community workers (e.g., teachers, police officers, public health nurses) become more sensitive to the needs of their clients, and more comfortable and effective in their relationships with them.

The general goal of mental health consultation is to assist care-givers in handling the problems of their clients with greater effectiveness, and in making appropriate referrals to qualified specialists when this is required (Spielberger &

Iscoe, 1970). In essence, mental health consultation provides a mechanism whereby community psychologists work with other community care-givers in helping them to utilize mental health principles more fully in their own work. It should be noted, however, that consultants do not attempt to teach the caregivers with whom they work professional techniques such as psychological testing, psychotherapy, or behavior modification, which require extensive training and supervised experience.

In practice, mental health consultation has been concerned primarily with interactions between a consultant and a single consultee (Caplan, 1964). Typically, a relationship is established when a consultee requests assistance with a problem that has been stimulated by one of his or her clients. The consultant then arranges to meet with the consultee to discuss the client's problem and the consultee–client relationship. When restrictions on the consultant's time make it impractical to render on-call response to individual consultee crises, group consultation procedures have proved effective (Altrocchi, Spielberger, & Eisdorfer, 1965; Spielberger, 1967).

In addition to expertise in consultation techniques, the psychologist who functions as a mental health consultant must have a comprehensive understanding of social and developmental psychology, personality, and psychopathology and other forms of social deviance. In order to be able to use this information in clarifying specific problems, consultants must also have interpersonal skills that permit them to develop helping relationships with caregivers. Through mental health consultation, the community psychologist can reach a much greater number of persons who need psychological assistance than would be possible in working with individual clients or patients.

To illustrate the professional activities of a community psychologist working as a mental health consultant, we will consider a problem involving a delinquent youth who has been apprehended for vandalism. Initially, the consulting psychologist can help the juvenile court judge and the probation officer to understand the motivational and environmental factors that may have contributed to the youth's delinquent behavior. For example, the consultant might assist the juvenile court judge and the probation officer to distinguish between antisocial behavior, which reflects a character disorder or emotional disturbance, and dissocial or "gang" behavior, which generally indicates adherence to a different set of social norms. In this action, the consultant's role would be to clarify basic concepts and core problems in juvenile delinquency. The consultant might also provide the court officials with information about available community resources so these can be more fully utilized in dealing with the problem. He or she might also help them make the referral arrangements for psychological testing and/or treatment if this is considered necessary or desirable.

The social-environmental ecology model

The social-environmental ecology model in community psychology is less well defined and has more permeable "turf" boundaries than the community mental health model, and it is more likely to have proponents with academically diverse and hybrid interdisciplinary training and experience. In addition to psychology, fields such as sociology, anthropology, political science, criminal justice, engineering, epidemiology and public health contribute to the knowledge and practice base for this model. Community psychologists who subscribe to the social-environmental ecology model also generally tend to be more research-oriented than those who follow the community mental health and social action models.

The goals of the social-environmental ecology model are even broader and more ambitious than the community mental health model. The social-environmental ecology model provides a framework for addressing the entire spectrum of social and environmental problems encountered in the delivery of almost all forms of human services. Specific interventions and professional activities guided by this model can be designed to modify, redirect and change a wide variety of attitudes and behaviors in a manner that not only minimizes suffering and psychological impairment, but also enhances human potential and productivity and the quality of life.

The social-environmental ecology model is vitally concerned with research and with data-based decision making. The community interventions guided by this model are often designed to influence complex social systems, large oganizations, and entire communities. The impact of interventions and research programs generated by the model, as far as individual behavior is concerned, are indirect, but any intervention that is effective in changing the social and physical environment is likely to have profound effects on the behavior of individuals.

A specific, relatively simple example of an application of the social-environmental ecology model may help to clarify how modifications in the social and/or physical environment can markedly influence human behavior. In the mid-1970s, the United States and most of the free world experienced a crisis in obtaining oil. Many people with restricted availability of fuel to heat their homes and gasoline for their automobiles were either not convinced of the veracity of the issue or were insufficiently motivated to modify their consumption of natural fuels voluntarily. Despite mass media campaigns directed at encouraging fuel-saving activities, such as car-pooling or using public transportation, most people persisted in their habits of driving to work alone.

In an effort to modify the solitary driving behaviors of individuals, some cities designated certain freeway traffic lanes as high-speed express lanes, which could be used only when car-pooling. In other cities, tolls on roads and bridges were eliminated for energy-saving, car-pooling citizens. Mass media programs, the creation of "express lanes", and the elimination of tolls are examples of interventions designed to modify attitudes and behaviors regarding car-pooling. Although only minor modifications in the social and physical environment were involved, these changes were successful in altering the behavior of many individuals in the desired direction.

Many examples of applications of the social-environmental ecology model can be found in the research literature on environmental health. Chapter 12 on Environmental Psychology also presents examples. The content of specific studies ranges from research on community nuisances, such as controlling dog litter in urban communities (Jason, Zolik, & Matese, 1979), to major life-threatening catastrophes, for example, the pollution of the Love Canal (Levine, 1982).

The social action model

Although community psychologists are often called upon as experts in the field of mental health, they make it clear to those who seek their assistance that emotional disorders indicate problems in the social system as well as instances of individual deviance. For example, the term "juvenile delinquency" does not denote a set of symptoms that exist in isolation, but rather behaviors that occur within a social context. Consequently, the basic structure of the social system that produces the problem may require modification along with the behaviors of deviant individuals within the system.

Throughout the course of history, humans have obtained food, built cities, waged war, conquered disease, and journeyed into space by means of organized social action. In general terms, social action may be defined as the collective, focused efforts of groups of individuals directed at some common set of goals. Consistent with this definition, the social action model in community psychology has the following goals and objectives: (1) to mobilize community resources for effecting beneficial change in the attitudes and behaviors of individuals and groups, and in the structure of organizations, communities, and institutions by constructive, educative interventions; (2) to stimulate knowledgeable involvement and control of social actions by the constituents and consumers who will be most influenced by these actions; and, (3) in bringing about social change, to maintain a steadfast commitment to recognizing the rights of the individual in the context of cultural pluralism.

The major tasks of community psychologists engaged in social action include a variety of approaches. Community psychologists can conduct evaluative research on important aspects of contemporary life, such as developing quality of life indicators. The development and evaluation of mass media campaigns is another important task. Examples are persuading people to avoid injury in automobile accidents by using seatbelts, or persuading citizens to obtain immunization against communicable diseases to improve community health. Community psychologists also engage in social policy analysis: an example might be conducting public opinion surveys of community attitudes regarding the legal age for purchasing alcoholic beverages. As might be expected, community psychologists consult with and lobby legislators concerning laws and public policies. Last, community psychologists both plan and develop social action programs by serving on state planning commissions for mental health programs, organizing community programs for the prevention of alcohol and drug abuse, and so on.

Proponents of the social action model may also be concerned with developing technology and implementing programs for pervasive and sweeping social and environmental changes that contribute to the empowerment of individual rights and the enhancement of the quality of life. Ideally, social action should proceed from the grass roots, beginning at the local community level. The appropriate role for the community psychologist in these programs is to facilitate the efforts of concerned citizens. In striving toward this goal, the community psychologist participates in conceptualizing and designing ethical social interventions, and in developing assessment procedures based on the best available data for evaluating these interventions. It should be noted, however, that interventions generated by the social action model have a greater potential for misjudgment and the misdirection of resources than the community psychology models previously described. Clearly, social action is not a suitable arena for the superficial thinker or for the timid or the impulsive psychologist.

Community psychologists are far from agreement on the proper role for psychologists in social action programs. Given the current limitations in the knowledge base, the absence of integrative theoretical models, and reliance on psychometrically weak measurement tools, many academic psychologists sincerely believe that the role of psychology should be restricted to scientific research. They argue that it is premature for psychologists to engage in social action that might compromise the scientific integrity of the discipline and result in political repercussions that impair the flow of resources for scientific research. Even the strongest proponents of the social action model recognize its inherent problems. Community psychologists must be sensitive to the dangers associated with social interventions that are not based on adequate theory and methodology. They must also be sensitive to prevailing customs and moral and legal authority.

In community social action interventions, ethical, moral and legal issues are frequently intertwined and difficult to separate. Even when these issues can be clearly articulated, there is often disagreement with regard to their implications. The community psychologist who follows the social action model must, therefore, be concerned about three related but distinctive aspects of the interventions in which he or she participates: role clarity, morality and professional ethics, and accountability or "truth in advertising."

Questions relating to *role clarity* arise in all interventions and research activities in which community psychologists are involved as observers, conceptualizers, or participants. Role conflict is inevitable if the psychologist is expected to participate in social actions while endeavoring to report his or her observations accurately and maintain professional objectivity and emotional detachment. The complex interplay of role clarity with moral, ethical, and legal issues can be seen in the dilemma faced by a community psychologist who was called upon by the Tennessee Valley Authority (TVA) for consultation regarding possible resistance to the construction of a nuclear power plant.

The psychologist was asked to design and implement a social action intervention to modify the attitudes and behaviors of the residents of a specific geographic area so that they would be more inclined to accept and welcome the construction of a nuclear generator in their home community. Additional electrical energy was needed; clearly, the request was not illegal, nor did it represent an obvious violation of moral or ethical codes. However, the impetus for the consultation request came from a survey of the residents of the community who were the potential targets of the proposed intervention, which revealed that they were opposed to the plant construction. Accordingly, the community psychologist should have strong moral reservations about participating in this project, apart from any personal concerns or opposition he or she might have to the particular use of nuclear energy.

The final basis on which a community social action program must be judged is the accountability or legitimacy of the intervention. The ultimate criterion of accountability for a particular community intervention rests on the answer to the question, "Who asked for it?" (Stenmark, 1981). To answer this question requires clarification of the origins or motivation for a particular social action program. As a case in point, consider the issues involved in adding fluoride to the water supply of a city in order to prevent dental cavities. While there is substantial evidence that such programs are effective, there is also a legitimate basis for the fears expressed by citizens of some communities with regard to possible adverse effects as yet unknown of this form of treatment. Should the community psychologist participate in a social action program designed to change the attitudes of those who oppose fluoridation? In the final analysis, the community psychologist must ascertain that indigenous members of a community in substantial numbers have requested and support the development of a particular community intervention.

■ WORK SETTINGS AND SKILLS OF THE COMMUNITY PSYCHOLOGIST

Where do community psychologists work? What kinds of functions do they perform? What abilities and skills are required for them to be successful? We have already seen that community psychologists work in a variety of settings and that the tasks they perform depend to some extent on the particular model of community psychology to which they subscribe. Some representative work settings associated with each of the three conceptual models are discussed below.

Community psychologists who work within a community mental health model are often found in community mental health centers. Additionally, they may work in preschools and public school systems, where they function within the school as a community. Also, community mental health model psychologists may be found in alcohol/drug treatment centers, military mental health units, and human service agencies. Because of their involvement with policy planning and implementation, community psychologists who operate out of a social-environmental ecology model are often working on urban planning commissions, departments of transportation, human engineering departments of business and industry, and consulting with state human service agencies. Last, those community psychologists working out of a social action model often are found in state and federal lobby organizations, as consultants to community action groups and national policy groups, and as researchers for congressional representatives.

It should be noted that there is no one-to-one correspondence between work settings and models for research and practice in community psychology. Although the work place will determine, in part, the nature of the community psychologist's duties, the same psychologist may engage in a wide range of professional activities, many of which are prescribed by different models. Given the rapid growth of community psychology and the constantly changing nature of this field, it is difficult to determine the proportion of community psychologists who follow each of the major models. The best available information on where community psychologists work and what they do is reflected in the results of several recent surveys of the work settings and professional practices of community psychologists.

Work settings and professional practice

Educational background and employment settings of community psychologists were examined in a recent study by Bachman, Smith, and Jason (1981). These researchers analyzed the reponses of members of the American Psychological Association who labeled themselves as "community psychologists" on questionnaires mailed to all APA members in 1974 and 1978. The percentages of community psychologists reporting primary employment in various work settings during the years of the survey are presented in Table 4-1.

Clearly, the largest number of community psychologists worked in human service settings, which included hospitals, community mental health clinics, and private practice. The next largest number was employed in universities, colleges and professional schools, and a substantial number were working in government agencies. This survey also revealed that most community psychologists were originally trained as clinical or counseling psychologists, and that more than 75 percent of the survey respondents had doctoral degrees.

In order to determine the extent to which the services performed by community psychologists were unique, Bachman et al. (1981) compared responses of community psychologists to the 1978 APA questionnaire with those of a group of "human services" psychologists who reported they performed com-

T A B L E 4.1   **Employment Settings for Community Psychologists in 1974 and 1978***

Work settings	Year of survey	
	1974	**1978**
Human services	50%	46%
Universities	23%	29%
Government agencies	13%	12%
Nongovernment organizations	3%	2%
Other†	11%	11%

* Based on survey data reported by Bachman, Smith, and Jason. (1981).

† This category included primary and secondary schools, business and industry. The percentage of community psychologists employed in any one of these work settings was less than 1%.

munity psychology functions, but who described themselves primarily as clinical, counseling, school, or social psychologists. Table 4-2 gives the percentage
of each group who reported that they performed each specified professional
activity.

A larger percentage of the community psychologists, as compared with the
human services psychologists, was involved in the more traditional profes-

T A B L E 4.2   **Unique Professional Functions Performed by Community Psychologists***

Professional activities	Human services (percent)	Community psychologist (percent)
Community psychology	47	53
Community mental health	55	45
Family	80	20
Crisis	67	33
Day hospital	75	25
Mental health services	48	52
Community mental health consultation	59	41
Community mental health service planning	36	64
Community mental health administration	55	45
Community development	33	67
Personnel training	59	41
Social policy analysis	40	60
Social program planning	42	58
Research and training	36	64
Counselor of education	95	5

* Adapted from Bachman, S., Smith, T., & Jason, L. A. (1981) with the permission of the *American Journal of
Community Psychology* and Plenum Publishing Corp.

sional activities such as community planning, community development, and social policy analysis. In contrast, the human services psychologists were more often engaged in the traditional community mental health activities of crisis intervention, working with families, day hospital programs, community mental health consultation, and personnel training. There was, however, a substantial overlap in the activities and functions of the two groups of psychologists, which is undoubtedly related to the fact that the majority of community psychologists were originally trained as clinicians or counselors.

Skotko (1980) has also investigated the amount of time spent by community psychologists in various professional activities. He sent questionnaires to a large random sample of the members of the APA Division of Community Psychology, which currently numbers approximately 2000 psychologists, and asked them to report the amount of time they devoted to various professional activities during the previous year. The results of this survey are shown in Table 4-3.

That community psychologists continue to invest the greatest percentage of their time (29%) in clinical and counseling activities is again consistent with the fact that most community psychologists were trained in these areas. Community psychologists also devote a great deal of time to administration (25%) and teaching (22%), which is consistent with the fact that 51 percent of the members of the APA Division of Community Psychology work in academic institutions, as compared to only 29 percent of the APA members who labeled themselves as community psychologists in Bachman's 1978 survey. The very large standard deviations for each type of work listed in Table 4.3 indicate the tremendous variability in the professional activities of community psychologists. While some community psychologists spend a great deal of time on particular work tasks, others devote little or no time to that activity.

T A B L E 4.3   **Average Percentage of Time Spent in Various Professional Activities by Members of the APA Division of Community Psychology***

Type of activity	Average % time	Standard deviation
Clinical/counseling	29	26.48
Administration	25	26.66
Teaching	22	23.97
Program evaluation	10	16.24
Organizational development (consultation)	8	13.17
Community development/social change	6	11.85
Basic research	3	10.09
School systems (consultation)	2	9.27

* Adapted from Skotko (1980) with the permission of the *American Journal of Community Psychology* and Plenum Publishing Corp.

The vast majority of community psychologists, in both university and community work settings, spend their time in professional activities that correspond most closely to the community mental health model. The fact that community psychologists devote only a small percentage of time to the types of activities prescribed by the social-environmental ecology and social action models may reflect a time lag between the development of these models and the creation of jobs that enable psychologists to carry out the functions associated with them. It seems likely that the amount of time community psychologists spend in the type of professional activities prescribed by the social-environmental ecology and social action models has increased since Skotko's questionnaires were mailed to psychologists who were members of the APA Division of Community Psychology in 1978.

Professional skills and competencies of community psychologists

What kinds of skills do community psychologists need to carry out the unique functions of their work? Several years ago one of the writers (D. E. Stenmark) posed this question to graduate students enrolled in a seminar in community psychology. The students were given a bibliography of approximately 3000 published studies describing research considered to be related to community psychology. They were asked to carefully review these studies and identify the particular skills judged to be essential for the community psychologist to do the work that was described. Each study was examined by at least two graduate students.

The lists of research and applied community psychology intervention skills that were identified as essential by the students were collated, the nature of each skill was clarified, and redundant items were eliminated. From a cursory review of these essential skills, which are listed alphabetically in Table 4.4, it is apparent that no single community psychologist could be expected to have expertise in all of these areas. Moreover, no single academic program or agency involved in training community psychologists could possibly offer the diverse range of training experiences required to prepare a student to develop proficiency in all of these skills.

The skills listed in Table 4.4 were used by Walfish, Polifka and Stenmark (1984) in a study of skill acquisition. Directors of a number of master's and doctoral-level community psychology training programs were asked to distribute the list of skills given in Table 4.4 to recent graduates of their programs. The graduates were requested to rate themselves on each skill in terms of their perceived competence at the time they received their degrees from their respective programs. A rating of 1 was assigned if the graduate felt "very incompetent;" a rating of 6 was given if the graduate felt "very competent."

The competence ratings of graduates of M.A. and Ph.D. programs are reported in Table 4.4. In general, the recent graduates rated themselves as moderately competent in most of the skills. They rated themselves highest with

T A B L E 4.4   **Mean Skill Competency Ratings for Skill Areas for Community Psychologists for the Total Sample and for M.A. and Ph.D. Graduates***

Skill area	Total		M.A.		Ph.D.	
	$\overline{X}$	S.D.	$\overline{X}$	S.D.	$\overline{X}$	S.D.
Administration	3.63	1.48	3.55	1.49	3.75	2.48
Basic research	4.57	1.25	4.40	1.26	4.81	1.20
Case-centered consultation	3.68	1.50	3.77	1.37	3.55	1.70
Community organization	3.84	1.53	3.83	1.49	3.87	1.61
Crisis intervention	3.62	1.62	4.04	1.46	2.97	1.63‡
Empowerment	2.94	1.61	2.90	1.50	3.00	1.78
Enhancing citizen participation	3.45	1.44	3.45	1.65	3.45	1.39
Environmental design	2.53	1.45	2.48	1.43	2.61	1.50
Epidemiology	2.74	1.48	2.67	1.26	2.84	1.77
Field research	4.42	1.42	4.02	1.41	4.97	1.26‡
Grant writing	3.61	1.81	3.13	1.74	4.31	1.70‡
Group process	3.61	1.81	4.21	1.14	4.40	1.40
Mental health education	3.53	1.46	3.80	1.36	3.10	1.52†
Mental health interventions in industry	2.51	1.32	2.60	1.26	2.38	1.43
Needs assessment	4.30	1.32	4.43	1.28	4.13	1.39
Paraprofessional training	3.60	1.62	3.74	1.64	3.39	1.61
Primary prevention	3.83	1.51	4.00	1.40	3.58	1.65
Secondary prevention	3.75	1.36	3.82	1.28	3.63	1.59
Tertiary prevention	3.56	1.35	3.70	1.28	3.33	1.45
Program-centered consultation	3.91	1.48	3.64	1.42	4.31	1.49†
Program evaluation	4.51	1.32	4.23	1.36	4.91	1.08†
Program planning	4.28	1.25	4.11	1.22	4.53	0.92
Research supervision	3.50	1.63	3.23	1.53	3.90	1.76
Resource development	3.75	1.48	3.81	1.51	3.66	1.47
Social network development	3.58	1.57	3.60	1.51	3.55	1.68
Social policy analysis	3.25	1.56	2.96	1.49	3.71	1.57†
Teaching	3.95	1.40	4.19	1.31	3.59	1.46

*1 = Very incompetent; 6 = Very competent
† $p < .05$
‡ $p < .01$

regard to self-assessed competency on research and data-oriented activities such as program evaluation, and felt least competent with regard to working with people in their natural environment, for example, empowerment and mental health interventions in industry.

As might be expected, the doctoral-level graduates rated themselves overall as somewhat more competent than the graduates of the M.A. programs and these differences were significant for field research, grant writing, program-centered consultation, program evaluation, and social policy analysis. Surprisingly, the graduates of the M.A. programs rated themselves as substantially more competent in crisis intervention than the doctoral program graduates.

■ TRAINING IN COMMUNITY PSYCHOLOGY

What are the academic foundations and field training experiences that are needed to prepare community psychologists to function in the many new roles that are being created for them by society's needs? Given the complexity of community psychology, it must draw upon the resources of many different areas within psychology as well as other disciplines for its basic knowledge.

Content of academic training

Theoretical conceptions and research findings from abnormal, developmental, and social psychology; personality; perception; and learning are of particular relevance for community psychology, but utilization of knowledge from these fields often requires new integrations. Many current techniques and methods used in clinical, counseling, industrial, and school psychology are also of undeniable value to community psychologists, but these techniques generally require modification and refinement when applied in a broader community context.

For psychologists to function effectively in community settings, they must also borrow from fields such as sociology, anthropology, social psychiatry, epidemiology, economics, political science, social work, and urban planning. Community psychologists require a basic understanding of community organization if they are to work effectively with care-givers and community leaders as mental health consultants, and such knowledge is especially important for those who are called upon to intervene in complex social systems as change agents.

Training in research methodology germane to the problems of community psychology is also required. For example, courses in demographic and epidemiological methods, biometrics, attitude measurement, and survey research are often more useful than traditional courses in small-sample inferential statistics and analysis of variance. Community psychologists who carry out research on social system problems require knowledge of computer methods for multivariate analysis and for the simulation of complex social processes. In addition, the community psychologist needs to have some understanding of the major research methods of the other social science disciplines.

To prepare community psychology graduate students to work effectively in community settings, it is essential to expose them to a broad range of every-day problems in the natural environments in which these problems occur. Confrontations with problems at the scene of the action is called for, not merely academic discussions of these problems in the classroom. Since the field settings in which psychologists are trained profoundly influence the skills they develop and their attitudes toward their professional work, it has been necessary for community psychology training programs to place their students in nontraditional community agencies in addition to mental health settings.

There is great diversity among the models for training in community psychology and in the nature of individual training programs, but there are also important commonalities among community psychology programs (Spielberger & Iscoe, 1977). There is agreement, for example, on the desirability of moving away from a mental illness model and focusing instead on broader social-system problems that relate to the enhancement of coping skills and competencies. There is also a strong preference for indirect services, such as working with community agencies and institutions, rather than working directly with individual clients. Finally, there is substantial agreement with regard to the importance of maintaining a solid academic base for community psychology to facilitate the integration of theory, field work, and research.

Admission to graduate training

In order to pursue an exciting, challenging, and rewarding career in community psychology, the serious student must seek advanced academic training. The obvious first step is to gain admission to graduate school, which, as a matter of fact, is not an event, but rather a process that requires a great deal of planning and preparation. These preparatory activities are briefly reviewed here, but a more comprehensive understanding may be obtained from relevant publications that describe various training programs, and by consultation with knowledgeable faculty at your college or university.

Within psychology, courses in developmental, social, personality, and abnormal psychology provide the essential foundations for community psychology. In addition, we suggest that students obtain a broad base in the sciences and humanities, including courses in anthropology, political science, mass communication, sociology, and community organization. In addition to formal course work, aspiring community psychologists should obtain supervision and training in applied community settings, and should avail themselves of intense involvement with faculty members in directed research. Such experiences help students to articulate their future professional career goals, while also providing an experiential basis for a more comprehensive understanding of their academic training. Finally, it is important to become familiar with the research literature as found in community psychology journals. This is a habit to be cultivated that will serve you well in your future career.

Perhaps no single decision will have greater impact on your professional career as much as your choice of a graduate program. In addition to discussing graduate programs with your own faculty, we recommend that you obtain a copy of the latest edition of a reference book, entitled *Graduate Study in Psychology*, which is available from the American Psychological Association, 1200 Seventeenth Street, N.W., Washington, D.C. 20036. This book provides complete, up-to-date descriptions of all APA-approved master's and Ph.D. level training programs. It also describes admissions requirements and procedures for each program, and gives pertinent information about available financial assistance.

In *Graduate Study in Psychology*, community psychology programs are currently listed under headings that reflect their primary conceptual focus. These index headings include the following: clinical/community psychology (12 programs listed); community psychology (20 programs); community agency counseling (3 programs); and community/clinical (7 programs). In addition, one or more programs are indexed under the following headings: community development and planning; community mental health; community organizational psychology; rural community psychology; community/school-psychology; school/community psychology; and school/community/clinical psychology. Social ecology, transactional ecology, and environmental psychology programs also have substantial community psychology content. Since each program is listed only once in the index, all of these headings should be individually reviewed.

Although it is more difficult to gain admission to doctoral programs than those at the master's level, we strongly urge the aspiring community psychologist to enter a Ph.D. training program, if possible. Training at the doctoral level is generally required for a research career in community psychology and for advancement to senior administrative positions. There are, however, many excellent master's level programs and, as was previously noted, graduates of these programs may have greater competence in selected skill areas. In order to increase the probability of being accepted for graduate training, most applicants should include both doctoral-level and master's-level programs in the list of institutions to which they apply.

■ CONCLUSION

It is likely that community psychology will have a growing role in the years to come. The emphasis on providing patients with treatments in non-restrictive environments will dictate a shift from institutionalization to community care. Other roles for community psychologists based on the social action model and the social-environmental ecology model are being developed. As in other specialty areas emphasizing individual and group mental health enhancement, community psychology will be in the forefront of the development of innovative approaches.

■ SUGGESTED READINGS

Bachman, S., Smith, T., & Jason, L. A. (1981). Characteristics of community psychologists in 1974 and 1978. *American Journal of Community Psychology, 9,* 283–291.

This brief article analyzes the professional activities of community psychologists and the work settings in which they are employed. The services performed by community psychologists are compared with those of other "human services" providers, and information about the training of community psychologists is also reported.

Bloom, B. L. (1977). *Community mental health: A general introduction.* Monterey, CA: Brooks/Cole Publishing Company.

Written as a textbook for upper-division undergraduate courses in psychology, psychiatric nursing, social work, and public health, this volume provides a comprehensive overview of the fields of community mental health and community psychology. Important applications of community psychology such as crisis intervention, mental-health consultation, and preventive intervention are reviewed in historical perspective.

Mann, P. A. (1978). *Community psychology: Concepts and applications.* New York: The Free Press.

This basic textbook on community psychology provides a concise yet comprehensive overview of the specialty area. The author reviews the history of community psychology, explores its roots in the community mental health movement, and critically examines four major models or approaches to research and practice. Specific issues and problems in the practice of community psychology are also examined.

Skotko, V. P. (1980). Professional activities and the perceptions of needs and opportunities for community psychologists. *American Journal of Community Psychology, 8,* 709–714.

The author analyzes the amount of time community psychologists actually devote to various professional activities. Views of community psychologists regarding current needs and opportunities in this specialty field are also examined. In reviewing this article, students are encouraged to examine recent issues of the *American Journal of Community Psychology* to better understand and gain perspective with regard to the theoretical issues and research problems on which community psychologists are presently working.

WILLIAM SCHOFIELD   # PSYCHOLOGY AND HEALTH

■ INTRODUCTION

There are many definitions of psychology, of varying degrees of complexity, but they all encompass the basic concept that psychology is the *study of behavior*. As a branch of psychology, health psychology concerns the study of those behaviors that are significant determiners of health or illness, the loss of health. As the goal of all science is understanding, with understanding measured by the ability to predict and control, health psychology is concerned with understanding the behavior of persons that undergirds positive total health or predisposes to illness. The validity of the knowledge and methods developed or applied by health psychologists is measured by their ability to help individuals (or groups) to maintain health, to reduce or refrain from health threatening behaviors, and to cope effectively with the consequences of illness.

As is true for other fields of applied psychology described in this volume, health psychology finds its foundations in a number of the fields of basic scientific psychology. Among these are the research fields of experimental psychology, psychometrics, physiological psychology, developmental psychology, psychology of personality, social psychology, educational psychology, psychopharmacology, and neuropsychology. In terms of applied fields of professional psychology, health psychology is closely related to clinical psychology (see Chapter 2) and counseling psychology (see Chapter 3).

Because of the diversity of basic psychological fields relevant to the practice of health psychology and the variety of health settings in which psychologists are employed, sometimes as researchers and sometimes as clinicians, question can be raised as to whether health psychology is a meaningfully distinct field of applied psychology or only a useful rubric to serve organization and communication purposes. With a formal, organizational history of less than five years (see the following section), the definition of health psychology is still in process of formulation. As a beginning, Matarazzo (1980) offered this definition:

> Health Psychology is the aggregate of specific educational, scientific, and professional contributions of the discipline of psychology to the promotion and maintenance of health, the prevention and treatment of illness, and the identification of etiologic and diagnostic correlates of health, illness and related dysfunction.

The definition recognizes the potential for psychology to make contributions to problems of health and illness over and beyond those specifically of *mental* health and *mental* illness. Respecting the significant contributions of psychology to promotion of mental health and treatment and prevention of mental illness, the field of health psychology is directed primarily to issues of physical health and illness.

With regard to organizational development of interest groups, health psychology must be contrasted with *medical psychology* and *behavioral medicine.* Although in Great Britain, medical psychology is essentially synonymous with psychiatry, in the United States it refers to the application of psychological principles and procedures in the study and management of physical illness. Accordingly, its focus is narrower than that of health psychology. Medical psychologists are found almost exclusively in medical hospitals and clinics and are typically more involved in research than in clinical activity.

Behavioral medicine is an interdisciplinary enterprise that seeks to apply behavioral science to the study and treatment of physical illness (Benson, 1980). It has been defined (Schwartz & Weiss, 1978) as "The interdisciplinary field concerned with the development and integration of behavioral and biomedical science, knowledge, and techniques relevant to health and illness and the application of this knowledge and these techniques to prevention, diagnosis, treatment and rehabilitation." Thus, behavioral medicine incorporates many disciplines other than psychology although the focus area of physical illness is similar.

■ HISTORICAL DEVELOPMENT

Applied psychology

From the founding of psychology as a distinct branch of scientific inquiry, whether measured from the establishment of Wilhelm Wundt's laboratory in Lepzig in 1879 or the beginning of William James's formal Harvard laboratory in 1882, until nearly mid-century, psychology was predominantly an academic discipline. Psychologists were primarily teachers and the full-time research psychologist was rare. Psychologists carried on their work, with very few exceptions, as college and university faculty members. Factors of convenience and limitations of research funding made the accessible and compliant sophomore and the white rat primary subjects for investigation.

The research efforts of the early American psychologists carried the seeds of what would develop later into widespread applications; among these were the development of theory and methods of psychometrics, studies of the processes of learning, the study of individual differences, and psychophysiological investigations, especially of sensory processes.

World War I afforded a critical opportunity for the young science of psychology to find application. Of particular note were the development of group tests of intellectual ability and the design of measures of emotional stability—both of these applied and validated in the large scale screening of military personnel.

The period between World War I and World War II witnessed extensive growth in the application of psychological techniques and tools to human problems. The "testing movement" was established and psychologists were employed increasingly in clinics, schools, hospitals, and other social agencies. The work of these psychologists was oriented largely around problems of diagnosis and correction; these represented the first battalion of "clinical" psychologists. In the same period there were developments in aptitude testing and vocational interest measurement that provided tools for guiding individuals toward positive adjustment; the authors and employees of these instruments were the vanguard of "counseling" psychologists. Together these embryonic developments in "clinical" and "counseling" psychology, the number of psychologists identified with them, and the concern of these psychologists for issues of training and standards led to the founding in 1937 of the American Association for Applied Psychology.

World War II brought a second national call and opportunity for applied psychology. Experimental psychologists, measurement experts, test developers, educational specialists, psychophysiologists and many others found challenges for their expertise in the varied needs of our armed forces. Their experiences and discoveries as military psychologists had a significant impact on their research when they returned to civilian life.

The most enduring and highly visible impact of World War II was in the field of clinical psychology (see Chapter 2). The massive dislocations and disruptions in the lives not only of service men and women but of their families led to recognition by the federal government of the need to provide for the immediate training of a significantly increased number of mental health professionals. The war experiences had brought recognition of the critical contribution of psychologists in managing the emotional disorders associated with military service and they were subsequently acknowledged in the plans for nationally subsidized training in psychology as a primary mental health profession (Schofield, 1982).

The evolution of health psychology

Many events, legislative actions, political pressures, and social needs have provided the impetus for the emergence of a new health profession—health psychology. The established profession of clinical psychology provided a major organizational base out of which health psychology has evolved.

Several factors have influenced clinical psychology to expand its area of interest beyond the boundaries of mental illness and beyond concern with diagnosis and treatment of psychiatric disorders. In the 1960s, clinical psychology, with the support of the American Psychological Association, waged a progressively successful campaign to be fully recognized as an autonomous *mental* health profession whose services should be provided for and reimbursable under all comprehensive medical or health insurance policies. In addition to achieving recognition by many of the major underwriters of comprehensive medical insurance, psychologists were successful in gaining recognition as service providers under a variety of federal programs (e.g., Civilian Health and Medical Program of the Uniformed Services, the Community Mental Health Centers regulations, and the Health Maintenance Organization legislation) (see Kiesler, 1979).

These developments occurred during a period when there was vigorous debate on the need for and specifics of a program for National Health Insurance. The debate arose out of recognition of the spiralling costs of health care and the nature of the primary sources of death and disability in our population. Epidemiological studies suggested that there were significant psychosocial factors (e.g., smoking behavior) associated with major illnesses. Psychological studies began to report the role of personality variables and response to stress as factors in susceptibility to certain illnesses, e.g., coronary heart disease. The planning for National Health Insurance and the findings from "life-style" studies coalesced with a growing public concern for maintenance of health to a new focus and emphasis on prevention.

In 1968, the APA commissioned a major study and report on the role of psychology in the delivery of health services (Schofield, 1969). This essay argued that psychology was identifiable as both a *health service* and a *health profession* and concluded:

> . . . by self-identification, by service and research, by legislation, by insured coverage of professional fees, by federally legislated provision for leadership in comprehensive health centers, and in teaching of other health professionals—psychologists clearly are invested in the health enterprise and play a significant role in the delivery of health-related services. They are doing this in sufficient numbers and with sufficient competence to have achieved recognition and acceptance among the allied health professions (Schofield, 1969, p. 571).

The essay pointed up the as-yet mostly unrealized potential for nearly all fields of psychology to contribute to an improved level of national health and outlined areas for psychological research that had thus far been neglected by psychologists.

As a follow-up on this overview of psychology's actual and potential role in the nation's health, in 1973 the APA established a Task Force on Health Research. This task force compiled a roster of some 500 psychologists active in health-related research outside of the area of mental illness, stimulated the interest of several federal health agencies in supporting behavioral research into facets of physical illness, and facilitated communication among psychologists who were investigating psychological variables in health and illness behavior. The final report of the task force, recognizing *health psychology* as a newly emerging, comprehensive field for applied psychology observed:

> There is probably no specialty field within psychology that cannot contribute to the discovery of behavior variables crucial to a full understanding of susceptibility to physical illness, adaptation to such illness, and prophylactically motivated behaviors. The areas open to psychological investigation range from health care practices and health care delivery systems to the management of acute and chronic illness and to the psychology of medication and pain (APA Task Force, 1976, p. 272).

By 1979, the foregoing activities had stimulated the awareness of a sufficient number of psychologists to support the establishment of a new interest group within APA—The Division of Health Psychology, with a membership of over 1300 psychologists. This event and the publication in 1982 of the first issue of the Division's official organ, the journal *Health Psychology*, establishes the reality of health psychology as a new branch of applied psychology.

The rapidly growing interest in the behavioral aspects of illness are further expressed in the founding of two other organizations, both in 1978. The Academy of Behavioral Medicine Research, under the sponsorship of the National Academy of Sciences, restricts membership to established behavioral scientists who are active researchers on behavioral problems. The Society of Behavioral Medicine is a multidisciplinary organization that facilitates communication among behavioral scientists, and psychologists in particular, whose research focuses on the application of behavioral modification techniques to the management of physical disorders.

Psychology—A bridge between knowledge and action

The last two decades have brought impressive gains in the scientific understanding of the causes, courses, correction, containment, and consequences of many major illnesses. Modern communication media have made this knowledge readily available to the general public. In some instances, this has given the individual a new sense of control over (and, ideally, a sense of responsibility for) his or her health or susceptibility to illness. Thus, research establishing the connection of cigarette smoking with development of lung cancer, the broad public dispersal of this information, and focussed campaigns to reduce the number of smokers have achieved some success. However, there remain many individuals who resist such efforts and many others who are unsuccessful in efforts to change their smoking behavior. Here is a specific behavior that expresses the interaction of attitudes, values, motives, habit strength, and psychological addiction. Clearly it is a prime area for psychological study and for development and testing of psychological methods to achieve and maintain behavioral changes (Wright, 1976).

Medical research has established the significant relationship between obesity and susceptibility to life-threatening illnesses such as heart attack. Again, we see obesity as a function of behaviors that are multidetermined by a variety of psychological variables. It is a research task for the health psychologist to determine on which element or complex of elements to focus his or her intervention efforts.

In approaching these important areas of health behavior the psychologist is trained to be ever aware of the range of individual differences—differences in values, in expectancies, in attitudes, in general morale—as all of these impinge upon the readiness of the individual to behave in health-promoting or health-threatening ways. The health psychologist is essentially, as researcher or clinician, a builder of a bridge between established medical facts and the proper incorporation of those facts by the individual in his or her daily behavior.

■ THE HEALTH CARE PSYCHOLOGIST

The graduate education of psychologists who are actively identified with problems of health and illness is highly diverse. It is a consequence of this diversity in education and training that health care psychologists occupy a variety of roles and are found in many different work settings.

There are three primary roles represented in the work of the health psychologist—teacher, investigator, and intervenor. Although some psychologists invest their efforts exclusively in one of these roles, this is the exception rather than the rule. There is a general tendency to model oneself after one's teachers. Since the majority of graduate level teachers of psychology engage in a variety of activities, combining their teaching with work as researchers, consultants, or clinicians, there follows a natural tendency for their students to expect and seek multidimensional roles for themselves. This trend is strengthened by the fact that, at present, the area of health psychology affords only limited opportunities for a psychologist to be hired as a full-time teacher or full-time investigator or full-time clinician. The fact that both the modeling process and the circumstances of the employment market dictate multiple roles for the majority of health psychologists has advantages for this new and growing enterprise of applied psychology. Teaching is enriched when the instructor can bring to the discussion of general themes and principles specific and concrete examples drawn directly from his or her experiences as a consultant or researcher. The clinician who also has teaching responsibilities is compelled and has time to keep abreast of the relevant literature of the field to a degree that is often difficult for the full-time clinician. The clinician who is actively engaged in research has opportunity for early field tests of the relevance of research findings. In turn, the experiences of direct clinical service can provide observations and hypotheses to be explored in research.

Teacher

The health psychologist in the role of teacher finds employment primarily in three settings—medical schools, nursing schools, and schools of public health.

The medical schools of the United States have a long history of including psychologists as members of their teaching faculty. The last twenty-five years have seen a steady increase in the number of medical school psychologists (Nathan, Lubin, Matarazzo, & Perseley, 1979). With this increase has come a slight shift in the medical school departments with which they are identified. While psychologists formerly were almost exclusively appointed in departments of psychiatry, in recent years an increasing number of psychologists have been appointed in other departments; notable among the latter are departments of pediatrics, physical medicine and rehabilitation, neurology, and family practice or community medicine. This as-yet modest expansion in the departmental affiliations of medical school psychologists beyond the discipline of psychiatry has been accompanied by shifts in their primary responsibilities, especially as clinicians; most notably they are increasingly active as consultants as well as rendering direct service in managing the psychological problems of a variety of patients.

In the role of medical school teachers, psychologists find a major opportunity for contributing, albeit indirectly, to the delivery of health care services. As instructors of both undergraduate medical students as well as residents in specialty training, they seek to sensitize these future clinicians to the importance of recognizing the psychology of the patient. It is the psychology of the individual that determines his or her reaction to physical symptoms. It is the psychology of the individual that determines how soon or how late he or she will seek professional help. It is the psychology of the patient that largely determines how clearly medical information is understood and how cooperative the patient will be with prescribed regimens of therapy. Medical schools have increasingly recognized the importance of sensitizing future physicians to the importance of psychosocial factors in understanding and caring for patients. This concern has resulted in the provision of behavioral science courses in the pre-clinical curriculum and the inclusion of a section on behavioral science in the National Board examination. Psychologists have played a major role in these developments.

While psychologists have been employed in smaller numbers in schools of nursing, their role has been similar to that in medical schools. As has been true also of medical school psychologists, those in nursing schools have contributed significantly to research studies designed to predict student success and to appraise personality variables related to choice of nursing specialties. The curricula of nursing schools have given increased attention to instruction in behavioral science as the professional nurse has become increasingly responsible not only for management of the physical treatment of patients but for attending to the psychological needs of the patient (Napoletano, 1981; Shepherd, Durham, & Foot, 1976). Psychologists have had a prominent role in introducing nurses to the principles of behavior modification as an important method in helping patients to cope with aspects of illness or handicap (Barnard, 1980; Closurdo, 1975). For the psychiatric nurse and in the newly developing field of the nurse practitioner, basic instruction in human psychology is of great importance (Hallam, 1975; Lurie, 1981). In recent years a number of experienced nurses have earned graduate degrees in fields of psychology. As members of nursing school faculties, they play a prominent role as health psychologists in the instruction of student nurses. Many of these nurse-psychologists are active researchers, applying the methods of psychology to the study of behavioral aspects of physical illness.

Psychologists on the faculties of schools of public health occupy a special role. Schools of public health may be contrasted with the other health professional schools, medicine and nursing, by a distinct difference of purpose. While medical and nursing schools have the primary goal of training clinicians or practitioners, i.e., direct service providers, the aim of schools of public health is primarily to train professionals whose focus is on disease prevention and health promotion through epidemiological study and programs of community education. The research activities of public health schools have been prominent in establishing the significant relationship between certain behaviors (e.g., smoking, drinking, over-eating) and susceptibility to major illness. These research findings in turn have provided impetus for training health educators in the design of preventive programs and programs to encourage positive health practice. The success of such endeavors rests heavily on the psychology of the individual citizen and the response to broad social messages. Psychologists' expertise in the areas of motivation, attitude measurement and attitude change, and responsiveness to group pressure have made them valuable members of public health faculties. Nearly all schools of public health have psychologists on their faculties and many of the schools have departments of behavioral science (Matthews & Avis, 1982).

Finally, mention should be made of those psychologists who are primarily full-time teachers in academic departments. Regardless of whether their specialty is in physiological, social, cognitive, or some other field of psychology, the basic principles and methods they transmit have potential relevance for the field of health psychology. Most directly, those academic psychologists who are specialists in clinical psychology have shown increasing awareness of the relevance of their expertise for broad issues of health and illness; many identify actively with the field of health psychology.

Researcher

The formal definition of health psychology (given at the beginning of this chapter) implies the areas of research in which health psychologists are active: (1) the search for psychological variables that may have a causal role in certain illnesses, or may be determiners of health-oriented behaviors; (2) the development of specific programs to encourage and reinforce behaviors that reduce the risk of certain illnesses and promote positive health; and (3) the clinical application of psychological principles to improve the total treatment program in certain illnesses. These three dimensions represent the primary research interests of health psychologists. There is a "second line" of research that is secondary only in time—this is evaluation research. A significant number of health psychologists specialize in program evaluation; they design studies and analyze data to test out the applicability and effectiveness of treatment procedures discovered by front-line investigation.

Health psychology research conceives the person as a fully integrated bio-psycho-social organism (Engel, 1977). Biologically, there is an inherited constitution by which the individual receives a matrix of factors that make for a highly specific basic resistance and basic susceptibility to certain forms of illness. The period of infancy and childhood exposes the individual to factors (e.g., nutrition) that may enhance basic resistance or increase basic susceptibility. Still later, as a learning organism, the individual acquires or fails to acquire behaviors (e.g., dental care) that will influence subsequent health. Still later he or she is variously exposed to social pressures (e.g., to conform, to achieve, to be a jogger) that influence the adoption of behaviors that may improve health or predispose to illness. With this developmental history there is also the acquisition of certain attitudes (e.g., excessive concern about minor symptoms, distrust of physicians, over-valuing of body image) that may lead to behaviors that affect the individual's health status.

A focal concept that has received great attention from both physicians and psychologists is that of *stress*. Stress is variously defined, depending on the investigator's primary interest, as a psychological state (temporary) or a psychological condition (chronic); there is general agreement, however, that it results from an interaction of the impingement on the organism of external variables (stressors) and how the individual interprets his or her environment (appraisal). There is also agreement that stress, particularly if it is persistent, may increase the likelihood of specific physical disorders or may generate a broad likelihood of a variety of illnesses, depending upon the individual's specific pre-existing susceptibility (Lazarus, 1966; Selye, 1976).

These general conceptions—of the individual as an integrated biopsychoso-
cial organism with a particular developmental history, and of stress as a causal
factor in illness—have provided a large domain for psychological investigations
(Wright, 1977). A few illustrative lines of research will be reviewed briefly.

Coronary heart disease ▪ Coronary heart disease is a major health problem and
has been the primary cause of U.S. deaths since the 1940s (Levy & Moskowitz,
1982). For many years, the clinical literature of medicine had recorded the
anecdotal observations of physicians who as acute observers had noted certain
psychological characteristics of patients with coronary heart disease (CHD).
There was a growing consensus that such patients typically revealed a pattern
of being chronically in a state of psychological tension. As part of a large-scale
epidemiological study of coronary patients, two physicians set about to make
standardized interview observations of CHD patients to determine if they
could define behaviors that characterized these patients and differentiated
them from other patients and from normal comparison subjects (Rosenman &
Friedman, 1960). In addition to observation of characteristic speech patterns
(e.g., tendency to anticipate the interviewer's words), objective measures were
recorded of such behavior as hand-clenching and inspiration-expiration patterns. These measures were also obtained while the subjects listened to two
autotaped messages that differed markedly in interest of content and pace of
delivery. Optimal combinations of some of these measures, some behavioral
and some physiological, were found to identify 95 percent of those patients to
whom the "Pattern A" label was applied. None of the normal comparisons and
none of the patients with functional cardiovascular disease revealed the characteristic pattern. Their clinical observations led these investigators to characterize the Pattern A persons (labeled "Type A" in subsequent investigations) as
revealing a high level of competitiveness, a strong desire for recognition
through achievement, a tendency toward involvement in many responsibilities
with deadlines, and a "propensity to accelerate the pace of living." Of medical
significance was the finding that Type A's showed higher serum cholesterol
levels and faster blood clotting times—factors with distinct implications for
development of heart disease.

With this ground-breaking identification of the Type A personality and its
relation to coronary illness, it became immediately desirable to develop methodology for identification of Type A's that would be more objective and less
cumbersome, time consuming, and expensive than the laboratory interviews
and physiological monitoring and, hence, more widely applicable than the original procedures of Rosenman and Friedman. These investigators collaborated
with a psychologist, making their criterion patient samples available, so that
the psychologist could develop a standardized self-report form (Jenkins, Rosenman, & Friedman, 1967). Jenkins developed a large set of questions with a mul-

tiple-choice response format. Examples of the type of questionnaire items, paraphrased, are

Have you ever been told that you walk too fast?

_____ Very often
_____ Occasionally
_____ Never

Do you arise and leave your bed at the same time every day, even on weekends and holidays?

_____ Always
_____ Occasionally
_____ Never

Using appropriate psychometric procedures, Jenkins identified those items and responses that reliably differentiated the Type A subjects from Type B's (subjects characterized by an absence of the clinical and laboratory indices of the Type A's). These items were grouped into sub-scales (for A and B respectively) for scoring purposes, and the validity of these scales was then examined by validation studies with new criterion samples. In its published form, the Jenkins Activity Schedule consists of 52 items, in multiple-choice format, as a self-administered questionnaire that can be machine scored.

This research program has several significant implications for health psychology, both in application and theory. Of immediate and clinical importance is the provision of a practical method for identification of persons whose lifestyle, personal tempo, and motivational structure may have direct relevance to their current or future health, and in particular to their susceptibility to coronary heart disease. The Type A traits appear to be stable, long-standing personal characteristics. If longitudinal research clearly establishes that such variables are causally linked via psychophysiological and biochemical functions to medical precursors of heart disease, the potential value of early markers is tremendous inasmuch as they provide a feasible method for population screening and efforts at early intervention. At an applied level, the concept of the Type A personality with an implication of possible constitutional factors and life-long habit patterns raises a challenge to the ability of psychological principles to be applied toward effective behavior change. The history of the Type A concept and its broad exploration is an excellent example of the potential gains to be derived from the collaboration of physicians and psychologists.

As a distinct personality "syndrome," the Type A concept is of interest to personality theorists as well. Further differentiation and clarification of the dimensions of Type A is desirable as well as defining its interrelationship with other personality measures. Type A's do not express any psychopathology as measured by the Minnesota Multiphasic Personality Inventory (MMPI), although they show greater "femininity" than non-A's. They score high on the Activity, Impulsivity, and Dominance Scales of the Thurstone Temperament Schedule. Contrasted with non-A's, Type A subjects express greater dissatisfaction with their marriages and their personal achievements; they value respect and recognition more than affection. From a psychodynamic viewpoint, these findings suggest that the excessive activity orientation of Type A's may be a response to an underlying passivity and desire for dependence (Keegan, Sinha, Merriman, & Shipley, 1979).

Matthews (1982) provides an overview of a wide variety of explorations of correlates of the Type A personality. Early in the research on Type A, there was identification of a contrasting personality, labeled Type B. Type B's are characterized not only by absence of the behavioral and attitudinal definers of Type A, but by a separate constellation of attributes that are perceptibly different in their connotations from those attributed to Type A's. (Accordingly, the Jenkins Activity Schedule provides scores on separate "A" and "B" scales.) Much subsequent research has been directed at further delineation of variables that differentiate Type A and Type B persons. Comparisons have been made on physiological as well as behavioral variables. The finding that when under anesthesia for surgery A's record higher blood pressure readings than B's can be compared with the finding that B's outperform A's in tasks calling for slow, careful responses.

Given the apparent susceptibility of Type A's for CHD, and the fact that we now have appropriate screening methods for early identification of people "at risk" for CHD, the question then becomes the choice of intervention treatment. Should it be primarily medical (regimens of diet, exercise, weight control, and drugs) or primarily psychological (efforts to alter the habitual behavior patterns and value structures)? Even where the intervention chosen is essentially medical, the requirement that the patient be consistent and cooperative (compliant) entails elements of motivation and restructuring of habits—distinctly psychological matters.

Hypertension ▪ The traits manifested by Type A personalities indicate that they are in a more or less chronic state of "stress." Programs of therapeutic intervention to reduce coronary risk in identified Type A's have been generally aimed at stress reduction. Similarly, the treatment of hypertension (high blood pressure) has involved teams of psychologists and physicians in studies of the efficacy of teaching relaxation techniques to hypertensive patients. Definite hypertension (measured in millimeters of mercury by the common pressure cuff technique) is generally defined as systolic pressure of 160 or greater and diastolic pressure of 95 or greater. It is estimated that as many as 35 million North Americans are hypertensive. Because hypertensives are at very high risk for development of serious heart problems, and because of the relative inexpensiveness of screening the general population for hypertension, this condition represents a public health condition with great potential for programs of intervention to reduce risk and, accordingly, to lower the incidence of acute and chronic heart problems. Such potential is seriously limited by the fact that the majority of hypertensives are unaware of the condition because they are without symptoms to arouse their concern. Thus, even when "caught" by a public health screening program, the fact that they are without symptoms (pain, discomfort, reduced capacity) acts to lower their motivation to conscientiously engage in any prescribed behavior to lower their blood pressure. This reduced motivation is also important in considering maintaining long-term changes among patients who do participate in short-term intervention programs.

Psychologists play an important role both in the design of studies and in the development of procedures when patients are to be taught specific procedures for reducing psychophysiological stress and achieving a state of relaxation. Methods to induce relaxation have a long history that has included periods when particular techniques, such as those of hypnosis or transcendental meditation (TM), have had extensive utilization. Basically all methods involve teaching the subject how to achieve a state of progressively deep relaxation. In a typical study, patients (diagnosed hypertensives) and various comparison subjects are introduced to the experimental situation. This is frequently a soundproofed, air-conditioned room with a comfortable chair. One or more sensory devices (a plethysmograph to record blood pressure, electrodes to record muscle tension, etc.) are attached to the subject and their purpose explained. A nonexperimental period of several minutes follows to allow the patient to adapt to the room and situation. During this period, *baseline*, pre-intervention measures of the criterial variable, blood pressure, are recorded. When these have become stable, the investigator begins instruction to the patient designed to achieve and maintain a state of general relaxation. Blood pressures are recorded either continuously or periodically at the end of the training session. At the end of the training period, the subject may be given specific instructions to practice the relaxation procedure at home for one or more periods each day. Most studies provide for a number of training sessions in the laboratory spread over several weeks. At the end of the training series, provision is made for follow-up readings of the subjects' blood pressure at intervals of several weeks and/or months. Experimental control groups may be composed of hypertensives who are receiving medication alone, medication plus relaxation training, or general, supportive psychotherapy. Ideally, the critical pre- and post-treatment measures of blood pressure are obtained by the subject's personal physician in the usual clinical setting.

The general findings from such studies is that training in relaxation can bring about clear lowering of blood pressure and that such decreases can be maintained for as long as a year after treatment. Such changes are rarely great enough to move the patient from hypertensive to normotensive states and are usually less than the results achieved by medication. The fact that medication has serious side effects for some patients and that a combination of medication with relaxation produces better results than either alone means that there is a continuing role for this method of psychological intervention. Psychologists are challenged to discover optimal methods of teaching the relaxation response and, perhaps of even greater importance, methods of assuring that patients will continue to practice relaxation after both the training trials and the follow-up contacts are over.

Biofeedback ▪ A specific methodology that has arisen out of studies in psychophysiology and has been applied to a variety of physical ailments is that of biofeedback (Blanchard & Epstein, 1978; Orne, 1979; Schwartz, 1979). This method is based on the electrical wave activity that is generated by both the central and autonomic nervous systems. Brain waves (measured by EEG), autonomic activity as reflected in the sweat gland-response (measured by GSR), and muscle activity (measured by EMG), can be recorded and "fed back" to the subject as direct data (auditory, visual, or both) on his or her functioning. Similarly, heart beat, pulse rate, and blood preassure can be monitored continuously and reported to the subject. With such recording and suitable instruction a subject is able to learn to control functions (e.g., blood pressure) that are not usually under voluntary control. The technique has been used to enhance an individual's capacity to achieve and maintain relaxation, to reduce tension (e.g., in tension-related headaches, such as migraine) (Friar & Beatty, 1976), to reduce blood pressure in cases of hypertension (Blanchard, Miller, Haynes, & Wicker, 1979), or to increase blood pressure in cases of orthostatic hypotension (Dworkin, 1982). All of these procedures essentially involve the subject's learning to gain control of biological function through the medium of operational (conditioned) learning (Hume, 1977; Shapiro, 1979). A variation of the above is represented in the development of electronic monitoring devices to assist patients in the correction of serious postural defects (Dworkin, 1982). For example, if a subject is given direct, current information on his or her heart rate and can observe its increases and decreases, he or she can learn adaptive responses of a subtle nature that produce those changes.

Putting this in the context of the relaxation method to reduce blood pressure, when the subject has direct information on the fluctuation in pressure related to the degree of relaxation, the learning of relaxation responses is facilitated. It then becomes an interesting research problem to tease out how much of any change in a function such as blood pressure is attributable to biofeedback and how much to relaxation. The issue is complicated by the fact that the usual laboratory set-up to conduct biofeedback study involves conditions (e.g., soundproof room, comfortable chair, etc.) likely to induce significant degree of relaxation.

In an illustrative study, matched groups of hypertensive patients were treated respectively by (1) biofeedback of blood pressure (BP) data via video screen, (2) biofeedback of muscle tension (measured by EMG) data via variable tone, and (3) instructions to induce relaxation (Blanchard, et al., 1979). The EMG (muscle tension feedback) treatment did not result in decreases in blood pressure. While the BP (blood pressure) group changes were not of significant magnitude, these changes were maintained in a four-month follow-up. In contrast to both of these groups, the relaxation group significantly lowered their systolic blood pressure over the treatment period, but did not maintain this change in the four-month follow-up period.

The absence of consistent replication of findings in biofeedback research, especially in the area of hypertension studies, illustrates the difficulty of having subjects in different groups who are comparable. A failure to control, or match, on personality variables (such as Type A, or anxiety levels) may be an important factor. A consistent finding is that within-sample variance (individual to individual variation within a group) is larger than between-group differences in response to treatment. This, coupled with the finding that some individuals achieve highly significant responses to biofeedback training, keeps psychologists in vigorous pursuit of the promise of this method, and of clarification of its unique contribution as contrasted with the effects of relaxation. The rather general finding that positive effects dissipate over time appears to be related to the problem of non-reinforcement over the post-training period and suggests the need to program "booster" sessions.

Life events • In contrast to research focused on a particular illness, such as hypertension, the studies of Holmes and Rahe (1967) have generated numerous investigations of general susceptibility to illness as a function of changes in the individual's life situation. It is assumed that major "events" require the individual to adjust, that each adjustment entails some degree of stress, and that the greater the frequency of "events" in a given period the lesser the individual's general resistance and the greater his or her susceptibility to illness. A range of studies, varying in whether the target is general decrease in health status or development of specific symptomatology, have explored the utility of the "life event-life stress" concept as a determiner of illness (Healy et al., 1981; Johnson & Sarason, 1978; Lehrer, 1980; Toves, Schill, & Ramanalah, 1981). This line of research involves questions concerning the validity and reliability of retrospective reports, the determination of appropriate weighing of "positive" versus "negative" life experiences, and the determination of how long the prodromal (pre-illness) period may be to determine causal relationships. The methodological issues involved in this research have received critical attention (Cleary, 1980; Rabkin & Streuning, 1976; Zeiss, 1980).

While the "life event" researchers have given general support to the hypothesis that positive and negative experiences influence susceptibility to physical illness, the actual magnitude of the correlation between scores on "life event" scales and subsequent health status have generally been quite low. Noting the finding of a significant relationship between event–stress measures and complications of pregnancy only in a subsample of women whose psychological support systems were deficient, Johnson and Sarason (1978) postulated that the usual finding of low correlations between occurrence of stressful events and later illness could result from failure to explore the role of other variables (mediators). To test this hypothesis, they administered four questionnaires (scales) to a sample of university student volunteers. These four were (1) a "life experiences" inventory; (2) a scale to measure psychological depression; (3) a measure of anxiety; and (4) a measure of "locus of control." The last is a concept developed by Julian Rotter (1966) that describes a basic personality trait, namely, a stable, persistent readiness of each individual to view himself or herself either as responsible for the good and bad things experienced (i.e. to have an "internal" locus of control), or by contrast, to characteristically view both positive and negative experiences as the result of outside forces and chance (i.e. to have an "external" locus of control).

Johnson and Sarason found a significant relationship between the extent of negative (undesirable, unpleasant) recent experiences reported by their subjects and the degree of anxiety and depression the subject reported only for those who indicated an external locus of control. In other words, the reasonable expectation that negative events should be followed by depression or anxiety holds true only for those individuals who believe that they do not have control over their lives. This study, illustrative of the role of mediating variables, also exemplifies the subtleties and complexity of research into the relationship of intrapsychic factors (such as attitudes and values) and behavioral responses.

Smoking ▪ The health psychology research represented in "Type A" personality studies and studies of "life events" focus on somewhat general or complex risk factors. They may be contrasted with research directed to attempts to change highly specific behaviors which increase susceptibility to serious illness.

Ever since the widespread publication in 1964 of findings that cigarette smoking was linked to lung cancer and other associated life-threatening illnesses, health educators and the medical profession at large has sought to decrease the number of persons who are addicted to tobacco (Department of Health, Education and Welfare, 1979). All the major media have carried messages to discourage non-smokers from taking up the practice and to encourage habitual smokers to stop. This educational effort has met with some degree of success. However, there is a very large number of smokers with motivation to stop who have found it very difficult or impossible to cease. Inasmuch as smoking represents an overt pattern of behavior that is under conscious control, it represents a special challenge to health psychologists. Research has been directed at the development of techniques that apply the principles of learning (behavior modification) and of social psychology (group pressure). It has sought to modify smoking behavior (reduce or eliminate) by providing systematic aversive stimulation (punishments) for smoking, or systematic reward for non-smoking, or a combination of both (Paxton, 1981; Pomerleau, 1980: Poole, Sanson-Fisher, & German, 1981). Research has also investigated the effects of such programs conducted on a group basis so that the individual is both encouraged and pressured by the group for his or for her efforts (McFall, 1978). Completion of such treatment programs is sometimes assured by a contract that requires a monetary deposit that is "earned back" by the participants as he or she attends sessions and achieves certain goals.

An example of the use of aversive stimulation in a conditioning paradigm is the rapid-smoking technique. In this procedure the smoker is exposed to a series of trials in which he or she smokes while inhaling normally but under instruction to inhale at regular and very brief intervals (e.g., every 5 or 6 seconds). A point of unpleasant "satiation" is reached, and following brief rest there may be additional trials during each experimental session. The goal is for the total behavior pattern of smoking (extracting a cigarette, lighting up, etc.) to become the conditioned stimulus for a negative experience (unpleasant sensory and physiological states) with a consequent diminution of the frequency of smoking between sessions, toward a goal of total abstinence. Early studies with this technique reported as many as 60 percent of subjects to be abstinent as long as six months following the treatment program. In some studies, the rapid-smoking technique has been compared as a solo procedure and in combination with other interventions to determine their relative efficacy. For example, Poole et al. (1981) compared the rapid-smoking technique (RST) above with RST combined with relaxation training and with RST plus relaxation plus contingency contracting (an initial monetary deposit by the subject, refundable upon completion of the program and follow-up). The different therapy programs did not have reliably different outcomes. At the conclusion of the therapy programs, two-thirds of all the subjects had ceased smoking. However, at the 12-month follow-up, only one-third of the subjects were still abstinent.

Paxton (1981) undertook an analysis of the variables in contingency contracting in relation to smoking programs, noting that such programs have had somewhat superior results as measured by the number of subjects who are abstinent at the time of follow-up. The essence of contingency contracting is to assure a sufficient level of motivation of the smoker so that all treatment sessions will be followed and intermediate goals obtained. Paxton required a standard start-of-treatment deposit of $100 of all subjects but, with matched groups, varied the amount of delay before refund payments were begun, the amount refunded per payment, and the frequency of repayment. While the groups were not markedly different in percentage abstinent at conclusion of the treatment program or upon follow-up, Paxton noted a trend for more frequent repayments to be associated with more rapid approach to abstinence. He concluded that effectiveness of stop-smoking programs, whatever specific interventions might be used, would be enhanced by requiring larger deposits and extending repayments over longer periods of time. In effect, this would tend to extend the subjects' experience (learning) with non-smoking so that it was a more stable condition before therapy contact ceased. So far these smoking therapy endeavors, with many variations, have achieved very limited success. A major problem is that a large portion of individuals who have achieved nicotine abstinence at the end of treatment relapse and return to smoking within a year or less; the relapse rate is discouragingly high. Psychologists continue to refine the theory of addictive behavior (Hunt & Matarazzo, 1973) and continue to investigate new methods of treatment and to design treatment programs that will enhance the client's motivation with an optimal complex of psychological reinforcement (Pomerleau, 1979).

The contribution of a social psychologist to this public health problem is represented in the innovative study of Schachter (1982). Surveying everyone in a limited population, he investigated the smoking and weight-loss (dieting) experiences in two groups: (1) an urban, ethnically diverse sample of academicians, and (2) a small-town "blue collar" and entrepreneurial sample. Collecting smoking and weight histories by direct, structured interview, he ascertained that nearly two-thirds of persons who had attempted to quit smoking had been successfully abstinent for an average of seven years. This is a considerably higher success rate than reported for subjects of specific treatment programs. This finding suggests that detailed search for differences between individuals who self-cure and those who fail with professional help may considerably advance the understanding of nicotine addiction and, more importantly, may yield important insight into the psychological forces that undergird successful cessation.

Obesity ▪ The problem of obesity is similar to that of smoking in several respects: (1) it is a characteristic of a large segment of our population, (2) it plays a causal role in increasing the risk of cardiovascular and other diseases and can be a life-threatening condition, (3) the obese individual typically experiences very great difficulty in permanently altering the behaviors responsible for his or her pathological overweight. Psychologists approach this problem primarily, as the problem of smoking, by applying the principles of learning and behavior modification. And, as is true for treatment programs for smokers, the results of such programs are modest as measured in terms of the number of patients who sustain a long-term significant weight loss (Jeffrey, Wing, & Stunkard, 1978; Kincey, 1981; Loro, Levenkorn, & Fisher, 1979; Stunkard and Penick, 1979).

In a typical application of behavioral modification techniques with overweight subjects, groups are formed that meet weekly over a period of several months. Participants are weighed in before each meeting; this provides regular feedback on their status and a basis for group reward for progress. The meeting agenda provides didactic instruction on diet (calorie counting), control (or avoidance) of stimuli for eating behavior, slowing the rate of eating at meal time, etc. Such a program may also use a pre-treatment deposit with refund contingent upon goal achievement. In one such program (Jeffrey et al., 1978), subjects achieved an average weight loss of 11 pounds. The loss was generally maintained by individuals but without further loss over a follow-up period of 12–18 months. There were wide individual differences among subjects in their weight stability or fluctuations (increases and decreases) over the follow-up period.

Kincey (1981) found no correlation between personality variables and weight loss in the early stages of a treatment program. However, as the program continued, there was increasing correlation between amount of weight loss and the individual's "locus of control" status, with subjects who were more internally oriented achieving greater loss.

Stunkard and Penick's (1979) review of 30 controlled studies led to the conclusion that behaviorally oriented programs for persons who are moderately overweight produce greater weight losses than traditional "medical" therapy (diet prescription). As with smoking therapy programs, a persistent challenge is to devise methods that will increase the likelihood that individuals will at least maintain their weight losses after treatment even if they do not achieve further reductions. The loss of group support appears to be an important element in the phenomenon of post-therapy regression or relapse. Again, Schachter's (1982) finding of a nearly two-thirds rate of successful weight losses in "non-clinical" samples suggests the need for a searching study of how self-cures achieve their goals. The application of psychological principles and methods to the problems of smoking and obesity represent two of the more extensive research endeavors of psychologists, especially as expressed in the number of individual (clients) involved.

Alcoholism • Alcoholism is another major health problem for our population. While it is not listed in statistical summaries as a major cause of death, it is undoubtedly a major contributor to death by accident, especially via automobile accidents, and accidents of all types are the fourth most frequent source of fatalities. Public concern with alcoholism and the development of medical and social programs of treatment antedate the development of health psychology, and psychologists have played a less prominent role in alcoholism research than is true for the problems of smoking and obesity. "Alcoholism research is in a much more primitive state than is the case in the other self-destructive disorders. Part of the problem may be the lack of separation between research and treatment programs, which often results in a reluctance to withhold treatment from control subjects or to randomly assign subjects to different treatments. Evaluation is complicated further because, unlike treatments developed for smoking and obesity, alcoholism treatments almost always have combined modalities. Most treatments include counseling, in both individual and group contexts, and the use of drugs as adjunctive therapy" (Henderson, Hall, & Lipton, 1979, p. 158).

Again, in this area, the application of behavior modification techniques has been a primary effort. The work of Sobell and Sobell (1978) stimulated considerable controversy because their early findings refuted the widely accepted principle that complete abstinence was the only valid therapeutic goal in the treatment of hard-core alcoholics. They carried out a treatment program with 20 male alcoholics with a goal of retraining these problem drinkers to become "controlled" or social drinkers. Treatment consisted of 17 individualized sessions involved aversive conditioning with electric shock in the bar setting. drinking behavior were videotaped for later playback to the subjects. Later sessions involved aversive condtiioning with electric shock in the bar setting. Shocks were systematically applied when subjects ordered straight liquor rather than a mixed drink, when they gulped drinks rather than sipping, and when their drink orders exceeded a frequency limit. The experimental sessions included discussion of substitute behaviors for coping with stress or frustration. Final sessions presented videotapes of the subject's drunken and "controlled" behavior respectively. For comparison, a sample of 20 equally hard-core drinkers were processed through a traditional treatment program that included group therapy, chemotherapy, and the Alcoholic's Anonymous program, and had complete abstinence as a goal. The Sobells reported their findings from a two-year follow-up of the "controlled drinking" and "abstinent" subjects. They concluded that the "controlled" subjects had a significantly better history than the "abstinent" subjects, as measured by the percentage of days when each subject was "functioning well" and the number of days each was incarcerated either in a jail or hospital. Given the extensive role of social drinking in our culture, these findings gave hope that problem drinkers could be retrained to become social drinkers with a greater success rate than was generally true for the more difficult goal of total abstinence.

The results of a ten-year follow-up of the 20 "controlled drinking" subjects, with an exhaustive study of hard data on their post-treatment histories, bring grave doubt to this hope (Pendery, Maltzman, & West, 1982). These investigators concluded that only 16 of the 20 subjects in the experimental treatment program were in fact hard-core alcoholics. Of these 16, it was determined that 13 had been rehospitalized for alcoholism within an average of four to five months following their discharge from the treatment facility. Only one of the 20 subjects was found to have consistently controlled his drinking over the ten-year post-treatment period; subjects who had been unable to control their drinking in the short-term post-discharge period were still drinking excessively and with serious consequences or had become totally abstinent. In these findings we see further illustration that the long-term success of intensive treatment programs for chronic behavior problems may require regular post-treatment contact for "refresher courses."

Chronic pain ▪ There are patients whose physical ailments are accompanied by chronic pain. Such pain not only leads to a progressive restriction of activity but may also be accompanied by addiction to anodynes (pain killers). The combination of restricted activity plus drug dependence has serious implications for the patient, for his or her family, and for society, which loses the patient's productivity. Psychologists have played a notable role in the treatment of such patients by developing management programs based on the principles of behavior modification (Fordyce, 1976; Sternbach, 1974).

The essence of such programs entails an explicit commitment of the patient to participate in a therapy program (usually as an inpatient), and an explicit, formal contract that spells out the details of the program, including the specific, agreed-upon goals and the steps that are to be involved in achieving those goals. The general goal is to bring about a progressive decrease in the patient's pain behaviors (e.g., staying in bed, demanding medication) and a progressive increase in non-pain behaviors (e.g., engaging in social behavior, performing exercises to increase mobility). These desired changes in behavior are not only agreed to by the patient but are communicated to the treatment staff. The staff consistently withholds rewards (attention and response) to the patient's pain behaviors and consistently reinforces (rewards) the patient's non-pain behavior (by being attentive, responsive, and encouraging). During this behavior modification program, the patient who has been extensively self-medicating with pain killers is treated with a gradual reduction in amounts and frequency of such medication. Most importantly, graphic records of specific behaviors are maintained on an hourly and daily basis and are shared with the patient, who also may have some responsibility for recording his or her activity. These graphic records are an important, regular "feedback" to the patient who is motivated and rewarded by the evidence of progress toward goals.

Outcomes of such behaviorally oriented pain management programs have generally seen a significant degree of improvement in a majority of patients, with increased mobility and activation, decreased pain-oriented behavior such as complaining, and independence from medication. Follow-up studies indicate a fair rate of maintenance of these gains; however, as noted with the problems of smoking, drinking, and eating disorders, there are a significant number of patients who demonstrate a partial relapse and a return to some of their former restricting behaviors.

Other research issues ▪ The research activity reported briefly above relates to specific methodology applied to specific and common health problems. Health psychologists are also active in applying a variety of psychotherapeutic interventions to a range of illness behaviors. Prominent among these have been studies of the incidence of significant emotional problems in patients who consult general physicians and studies of the impact on the utilization of medical services when psychological referral and consultation is readily available (Cummings and Follette, 1975; Goldberg, Krantz, and Locke, 1970). With growing concern for the enormous increase in the cost of our medical care delivery, costs that reflect the development of valuable but highly expensive technology (e.g., computerized axial tomography, CAT) and the particular increase in the costs of hospitalization, psychologists can play a valuable role in identifying the "non-organic" patient whose very real and distressing symptoms can be alleviated by psychological intervention (Olbrisch, 1977).

The development of effective treatment for health/illness problems is undermined when patients are neglectful or refuse to observe medical recommendations. The problem of the noncooperative patient has long been recognized; in recent years there have been increasing efforts to investigate the causes of noncompliance and to develop programs and procedures to improve the rate and level of patient compliance with prescribed regimens. Psychologists, with a variety of specialty backgrounds, have been prominent among researchers in this area (Epstein & Masek, 1978). It has been estimated that from 20 percent to 80 percent of patients with serious medical problems do not consistently observe the medical regimen prescribed for their condition. Compliance is a function of the patient's perception of the seriousness of the condition and the relative ease or difficulty of carrying out the prescribed care. Compliance is a particular problem in those conditions such as hypertension and mild diabetes when the patient is relatively symptom-free. The availability of self-monitoring procedures and proper instruction of the patient in their use can play a significant role in compliance. But consistent self-monitoring requires the patient to acquire specific behavior patterns (habits) and here the psychology of instruction and learning are a focal element. Covert methods of checking on compliance (by serological tests, for example) can identify the noncompliant patient who can then be directed to special programs of psychological counseling.

Finally, note should be made of one of the more recent avenues of research into psychological dimensions of the causal matrix for physical illness. This is represented by studies of the relationship between environmental factors (and the perception of those factors) and the incidence of illness (Moos, 1976). These studies have examined both variables descriptive of the physical environment and those characterizing the social environment. A particular example of such research is study of the relationship between crowding (i.e., number of individuals housed in the same living unit) and the frequency of illness in those individuals. Moos (1979) has presented an excellent overview of what he calls "socioecological" factors, to encompass place and person variables, and concludes, "It is necessary to develop health care professionals who understand environments, the kinds of reactions people have to them, and the environmental dimensions and mediating mechanisms involved" (p. 545).

Clinician

The health psychologist as a clinican brings his or her expertise to specific problems in a clinical setting. This expertise has two components: (1) thorough knowledge of basic principles of psychology and of the research studies exemplified in the preceding section, and (2) progressive experience as a direct service provider or as a consultant. Health psychologists may be experts in the management of behavioral complications of a specific disorder, e.g., spinal cord injury (Hohmann, 1975), hemophilia (Varni, 1980), cancer (Kellerman, 1980; Kellerman et al., 1976), asthma (Renne and Creer, 1976). Or, health psychologists may be generalists who are "on call" to a range of medical specialties. Which of these roles pertains will depend to a large extent on the setting in which they work and on their specific assignments (see next section).

Either as specialist or generalist, most health care psychologists engage in some clinical work involving direct patient contact. In this, over and above specific technical expertise (e.g., with biofeedback procedures), they bring into play broad clinical skills that are involved in establishing rapport with patients, observing the patient's psychological status (e.g., assessing degree of anxiety or depression), and eliciting the patient's interest and cooperation with procedures.

Apart from direct clinical services, most health psychologists find a primary role as consultants to physicians, nurses, and other allied health professionals. In this role they bring the insights of psychology and the principles of behavioral management to assisting the health care team in a coordinated approach to the patient's illness and the patient's response to his or her symptoms. In both inpatient and outpatient settings, the psychologist may be requested to conduct a diagnostic study to determine the nature and extent of any emotional, cognitive, or psychiatric problem that may underlie the patient's complaints, contribute to the symptom picture, or complicate response to treatment. In a hospital setting, the psychologist is likely to be in active and continuing consultation with the nursing staff, assisting the nurses to an understanding of a patient's behavior (e.g., excessive demands or excessive dependence) and to the development of a program of patient management. In an outpatient clinic, the psychologist may receive referrals from the medical staff who wish to have the psychologist undertake direct treatment of psychological problems that have been uncovered in the course of medical treatment.

Whether as clinician or consultant, the health care psychologist almost without exception works in an interdisciplinary setting. In such settings, communication skills are of the utmost importance. The psychologist must appreciate the priorities of other professionals. He or she must acquire an under-standing of the technical terminology of medicine while becoming skilled in putting the technical concepts of psychology into "layman's" language.

Evaluator

As psychologists through their research studies have developed specific meth-ods of treatment for major health problems and programs of health education, there has been a need to evaluate the effectiveness of such methods and pro-grams. Evaluation research is both crucial and difficult. There are ethical issues concerning "control" patients (those who are untreated). There are problems with variables other than treatment procedures that may affect outcome (such as the illness being acute or chronic). Additionally, the "representativeness" of the patient group is important to consider. When the question of cost-effective-ness is added, the problem of meaningful evaluation is still further compli-cated. The goals of an intervention program and of the professionals responsible for it, the goals of the program recipients, and the goals of the administrators may differ significantly.

While many disciplines contribute to the technology of evaluation, psy-chologists have made notable advances in increasing the sophistication of research methodology. "Psychologists have methodological skills that are of great value in developing ways of assessing the effectiveness of various pro-grams, including those in health. The research design and statistical skills of psychologists are highly developed, and their measurement skills may be unique, unmatched by researchers trained in any other discipline. Conse-quently, psychologists are in a good position to contribute to the measurement of health outcomes. It is no mere happenstance that such efforts as the Sick-ness Impact Profile, the Index of Well-Being, and the measures of consumer sat-isfaction with health care by Ware and others have seen substantial involve-ment by psychologists" (Sechrest & Cohen, 1979, p. 393). The method of Goal Attainment Scaling (GAS) (Kiresuk & Sherman, 1968) is an excellent example of bringing relevance and objectivity to what are frequently overly global and subjective indices of program accomplishment. Developed originally to provide measurement of outcome for a community mental health program, the GAS method has had increasing application to a variety of other health programs.

■ WORK SETTINGS

The work setting of the health psychologist is determined by (or a determiner of) his or her primary role. Those whose major activity is the teaching of health professionals are found on the faculties of medical, dental, and nursing schools. Psychologists with primary research appointments may be found in university affiliated hospitals, or in special hospitals (such as the National Jewish Hospital and Research Center in Denver). Within medical school–university hospital complexes, the research and clinical activity of the psychologist is a function of his or her particular departmental appointment. While such centers still have a majority of psychologists appointed in departments of psychiatry or divisions of behavioral science, there is a trend for psychologists to be attached to specific clinical departments, as noted in the section on Teaching above. Research and clinical activity is particularly visible among psychologists attached to departments of pediatrics, neurology, neurosurgery, and physical medicine and rehabilitation. In recent time, psychologists have been active as researchers and clinicians in oncology (cancer) services.

Health psychologists who function primarily as clinicians are found in general medical outpatient clinics and in general hospitals. In marked difference to the older, established specialty of clinical psychology, health psychologists (defined as those teaching, researching, or giving service *outside* of the mental health area) are very rarely engaged in full-time independent private practice. From its essential nature as an interdisciplinary field of psychology, it follows that health psychology is identified with medical care facilities. The development of Health Maintenance Organizations (HMO's), which has been fostered by federal legislation, provides a special opportunity for psychologists. The HMO, as a prepaid insurance plan, emphasizes health maintenance and preventive health care. Outpatient care and reducing the need for hospitalization gives special impetus to the identification and treatment of the psychological needs of the client; this affords a special role for the health psychologist (Schofield, 1976; Wright, 1976).

■ FUTURE PROSPECTS

Training

In light of the very recent origins of the field of health psychology, there does not exist presently any uniform and widespread system for preparing psychologists to enter this new field. "Since, in the past, there have been no formal training programs in health psychology, all of those who currently function in the field have come from one of the existing specializations. Now, however, it is important to consider the kind of training that is appropriate for those who will be the next generation of health psychologists. As we view the field, it is broad and complex and many different kinds of psychologists will be necessary to meet its various needs. If every core field of psychology is relevant to health psychology, then we need training that will adopt the theories and methods of these core fields to the requirements of work in the health system" (Adler, Cohen, & Stone, 1979).

A viable profession requires some minimal degree of cohesive structure and a basis for functional identity of its members. For the established professions this is provided by standardization of training programs (e.g., the traditional four-year program for the M.D.) that are subsequently validated through a process of licensing or certification. Standardization (i.e., a uniform doctoral curriculum) of training for the health psychologist is both improbable and undesirable, given the recognition that the domain of health/illness behavior requires the research and intervention expertise of psychologists with a variety of area specializations.

However, whether the student's interest lies primarily in research or in clinical service work, and regardless of the core field of pre-doctoral study, it will be necessary that he or she have the direct, supervised experience of not less than a year of full-time internship in a general medical setting (Schofield, 1976). There is no substitute for first-hand experience with the complexity of the health care system and the challenges provided by a wide variety of illnesses, each imposing different stresses on patients and each requiring a comprehensive plan of management that recognizes the socioenvironmental and psychological as well as the physical requirements of the patient.

Opportunities

Of all of the recent advances in the areas of medicine, illness, and health, there is probably none that has greater significance than the discovery that those illnesses which are among the most frequent causes of death and disability in our population (heart disease, cerebrovascular disease, chronic pulmonary disease, cirrhosis of the liver, atherosclerosis) have as a significant causal factor certain patterns of behavior. It is increasingly clear that the behavior of individuals—the choices they make (e.g., as to diet and exercise) and the acts they engage in or refrain from (e.g., smoking and drinking)— plays an important role as contributors to their resistance or susceptibility to other causal variables in the complex of factors that lead to health or to illness. With respect to these major illnesses, individuals are no longer perceived as passive victims of the chance mixture of heredity and exposure that ends with illness or disability. To the extent that individuals' positions on the health-illness axis are a product of their specific behaviors, they have the possibility of being responsible.

As experts in the many specialties of the science of *behavior*, psychologists can contribute both indirectly and directly to the total of those efforts that are directed at reducing the incidence of illness and improving the overall level of our nation's health. Of great importance is the contribution of health psychologists in pursuing basic research and applied research—basic research to clarify, define, and measure the psychological variables most pertinent to health/illness behavior, and applied research to evaluate programs that incorporate psychological assessment and methods in altering health/illness behavior.

The direct contributions of health psychology are found in the clinic, the hospital, and the rehabilitation center where the clinician as service provider or consultant brings into play psychological forces so that the patient becomes increasingly responsible, increasingly in control, reducing his or her sympto-matology, or coping more effectively with unavoidable aspects of his or her ill-ness or disability. It follows that there is a special opportunity for psychologists to join with other health professionals in mounting programs of research and of intervention with a goal of helping our population to achieve better health and greater freedom from illness.

Thus far, the research contributions of psychology in the health area have been exciting and promising. Each area of research (such as the relation of per-sonality to susceptibility to coronary disease, or the relation of recent life events to illness) requires the continuance of data collection in order to provide a reliable basis for generalization. Refinement of methodology and improve-ment of instruments (illustrated in both of the preceding research areas) is a continuing challenge to psychology.

At a time when economic-political policy leads to shrinkage of funds avail-able generally for behavioral science research, it is encouraging to note a steady growth in the extent of funding for social and behavioral science studies in those medical research programs funded by the federal government (Weiss, 1982). In 1980, funding of social and behavioral science research in the National Institutes of Health exceeded $100 million dollars.

It appears likely that the concept of the Health Maintenance Organization will prove to be a stable part of our health care system. With the focus of HMO's on cost-effectiveness, reduced demand for expensive medical treat-ment, and the screening for psychosocial factors in service recipients, there will be a continuing and possibly growing opportunity for psychologists to be directly involved in the provision of health-related services (Schofield, 1976). A promising development is the interest of large industries in developing health care, educational programs for their employees and in monitoring the impact of such programs on the level of employee health, the frequency of hospitaliza-tion, and absenteeism. Psychologists with varied backgrounds are finding opportunities in such programs.

Health psychology as a branch of applied psychology and as an interest area for many "basic science" psychologists is an evolution of the 1980s. While still in the very early stages of development, there are enough signs of solid achieve-ment and significant research funding to suggest that by the year 2000 every general medical facility—hospital, clinic, or specialized care center—will have at least one health psychologist on its staff.

■ SUGGESTED READINGS

Gatchel, R. J., & Baum, A. (1983). *An introduction to health psychology.* Reading, MA: Addison-Wesley.

This book covers major psychological facts, concepts, and techniques as they apply to health and illness. It is a thorough survey of various aspects of health psychology, including patient behavior in medical settings, pain management, and psychophysiological disorders. This book is suitable for advanced undergraduate or beginning level graduate students.

Hamburg, D. A., Elliott, G. R., & Parron, D. L. (Eds.). (1982). *Health behavior: Frontiers of research in the biobehavioral sciences.* Washington, D.C.: National Academy Press.

This professional-level review of current research clarifies psychosocial determinants of illness and health. The emphasis within this book is biomedical.

Jospe, M., Nieberding, J., & Cohen, B. D. (1980). *Psychological factors in health care: A practitioners' manual.* Lexington, MA: Lexington Books, D. C. Heath.

This manual is a good overview of the application of psychology to specific medical problems. Related to practice in medical settings, it is suitable for advanced undergraduate or beginning graduate students.

Stone, G. C., Cohen, F., & Adler, N. E. (Eds.). (1979). *Health psychology.* San Francisco: Jossey-Bass.

This handbook is a comprehensive overview of the relevance of psychological principles and psychological research to the American system of health care, including both prevention and treatment of illness. It is a basic reference source for researchers, clinicians, and policy makers and provides a good perspective on the emerging field of health psychology.

UNIT II

PSYCHOLOGY APPLIED IN EDUCATIONAL SETTINGS

Psychology has had a long history of application within educational settings. This tradition has occurred for two primary reasons. First, since the science of psychology often focuses on investigating the processes by which people learn, psychologists have many answers to questions of educational effectiveness. Second, since educational institutions are where we spend a large proportion of our lives, psychology's applications with regard to learning, mental health, and normal development can be used to benefit many people.

This unit contains three chapters that discuss the various roles of psychology within educational settings. The chapter on school psychology presents applications of psychology that focus on mental health, academic adjustment, and personal adjustment. The chapter on instructional psychology emphasizes the applications of psychology in the improvement of the learning process. The chapter on the teaching of psychology approaches the role of psychology within educational settings from a different perspective, namely as subject matter. When "psychology" is taught in schools, what content is taught? And how does the content vary as a function of the setting in which the teaching occurs?

As you read these chapters, you will notice that the setting of these three specialties—namely, schools—has influenced their development. Schools are an institution of society designed to provide learning experiences to students. As such, schools are responsive to many different groups of people. Schools must provide instruction in subject matter that is required by state law or the institution's guidelines. Schools also are settings in which teachers attempt to convey broader values and standards to students. As such, schools must be accountable to parents and to the community in which the school is located. In each of these specialties, this multifaceted accountability has led to the specialty developing interventions that meet a broad variety of needs and requirements. This is the special challenge of working within school and educational settings.

Given the importance that society places upon education, and the recent emphasis upon increasing educational quality, the work of psychology in educational settings is likely to broaden in the future. Thus, these chapters not only discuss current applications, but also point toward the future of psychology within educational settings.

VIRGINIA C. BENNETT

SCHOOL PSYCHOLOGY

■ INTRODUCTION

Definition

School psychology is a psychological specialty defined as the application of knowledge and skills to the prevention or solution of problems children face in learning what society deems essential for success. Such goals are often couched in language such as "takes his or her place in society," "develops his or her full potential," or "becomes a contributing member of society." While these are vague goals that are worded abstractly, they can be translated into needs of children that society has entrusted to schools. A concept that is basic to the practice of school psychology is that American schools are designed as societal institutions. In these institutions, children learn the academic skills needed for successful coping with life in the United States.

The major responsibility for the social acculturation of children has historically been attributed to the schools, and schools have been entrusted with instructing children to learn such values as appreciation for rules, independence of thought, and responsibility (Cohen, 1975; Shimahara, 1975).

Today's schools are involved not only in the teaching of reading, writing, and mathematics, and the ramifications of these basic skills (history, literature, economics), but also in physical education, affective education, family education, driver education, music and art education, home economics, and a host of other offerings. However, the school's primary charge remains to provide all children with a set of specific, purposeful, and formally directed processes designed toward mastering certain types of knowledge and cognitive skills (Popenoe, 1971). A school psychologist, therefore, may be defined as the practitioner of psychology who uses professional knowledge and skills to help schools achieve learning and socioculture adaptation goals for children.

There is another way of defining a school psychologist. School psychologists must be certified, as are teachers, administrators, and others employed by public school districts, by State Departments of Education. Each State Department of Education has its own requirements (Sewall & Brown, 1976). These requirements vary from state to state, just as do requirements for teacher certification. Nonetheless, a school psychologist could be defined as a professional who holds a school psychology certificate from a state department of education.

How does school psychology differ then from other psychological specialties? Applied psychology is basically the use of psychology as a science to provide psychological services to people. As you have seen and will see in this text, applied specialties frequently overlap in the kinds of techniques used and in the settings in which practice takes place. While school psychology has much in common with clinical psychology, counseling psychology, and industrial/ organizational psychology, the concern of school psychologists is children, adolescents, and college students in their "world of work" (Erikson, 1960), the school setting.

Those of us who have practiced school psychology for many years like to think of ourselves as the original community psychologists, in that we have long focused upon how chidren interact with schooling—a community enterprise. We have concentrated on the public schools in the recognition that children spend 12 to 13 years in elementary and high schools, five days a week, five to six hours a day. As there is compulsory education for all children from age 6 to 16, school psychologists view the schools as the most appropriate setting in which to attempt to prevent and ameliorate children's problems. The community for school psychologists is primarily the schools, although when one deals with children, other community agencies, as well as parents, become part of the school psychologist's domain.

Sometimes the difference between school psychologists and educational psychologists can become confusing. While in a few states, school psychologists are eligible to practice privately as "educational psychologists," in general, educational psychologists do not deliver services directly to children and youth, but are engaged in research on instruction and learning. These distinctions are admittedly somewhat arbitrary, as is inevitable considering the base of core psychology that underlies all good psychological practice. School psychologists must have mastered many "clinical" skills, must know the research findings from educational psychology, must be knowledgeable about community agencies and institutions that serve children and youth in addition to the schools, must be able to assist guidance counselors in vocational and occupational counseling, must be able to integrate the concerns of a social system with concerns for the individual functioning within that system, and must understand not only how children grow and develop normally and abnormally but also about how adults function in order to deal effectively with parents, teachers, and others important in the lives of children.

■ HISTORICAL DEVELOPMENT

As school psychology is based upon psychology as a science, its roots are those of psychology in general. The contributions of the earliest philosophers are well documented elsewhere (Murphy, 1968) as well as the early scientific approaches to psychology by such greats as Darwin, Fechner, Galton, Pearson, and Wundt. Less well known, perhaps, is that Francis Galton (a cousin of Charles Darwin) extended his interest in possible inherited characteristics to encompass that rich source of available children, the schools. In the late 1800s Galton induced a number of schools to keep systematic records of how pupils performed on tests he devised on keenness of vision and hearing, reaction time, and discrimination (Anastasi, 1957). Galton's measurement of children's behavior is considered by some writers to be the first example of school psychological services (White & Harris, 1961).

As is true of the development of any specialty area, school psychology arose from a perceived societal need. As society changed from simple agrarian families and artisans in colonial America to a society of rapid industrialization and tremendous immigration, societal values and needs changed concomitantly. In 1753, the message to American parents and educators was "The first duties of Children are . . . mechanical; an obedient Child makes a Bow, comes and goes, speaks, or is silent, just as he is bid . . ." (Kessen, 1979, p. 815). By the nineteenth century, however, a concern for the growth and development of children began to be expressed.

Interest in psychology as applied to schooling erupted in the late nineteenth century. Witmer established the first "psychological clinic" at the University of Pennsylvania, primarily to serve children with learning problems and as a training site for psychologists to investigate ". . . the phenomena of mental development of school children . . . (and) . . . the training of students for a new profession—that of the psychological expert, who should find his career in connection with the school system . . ." (Brotemarkle, 1931, p. 346).

Other events important to the establishment of school psychology followed. In 1888, the Chicago Board of Education established a Department of Child Study (Munson, 1947). In 1894, John Dewey founded his Laboratory School; in his presidential address to the American Psychological Association in 1899, he pointed out that "The school is an especially favorable place in which to study the availability of psychology for social practice . . ." (Hilgard, 1978, p. 76).

The development of mental measurement

One of the major contributions to all psychology, but particularly for school psychology, was the development of the "quantitative method." Considering that Francis Galton's measurements of physical traits fell along a normal distribution curve, it was postulated that other equally human but less observable characteristics might also be normally distributed. The development of measurement of "mental ability" was given credence as well as impetus from the discovery that there were possible ways to measure and to quantify human characteristics.

Concern for the measurement of children's "mental abilities" was an outgrowth of the social and cultural revolutions that were taking place, primarily in the United States, England, and France. In the late nineteenth century, as part of the atmosphere created by its philosophers and exemplified by its Revolution, France became a leader in humanitarian and educational efforts; by 1894 the British had formed the Child Study Association while the French had the Societé Libre pour l'Étude de L'Enfant (White & Harris, 1961). An American psychologist, James McKeen Cattell (who like many pioneering American psychologists had studied in Europe), is credited with the first use of the term "mental test" in an article written in 1890 (Cattell, 1890).

As early as 1895, Alfred Binet, a psychologist, and Théodore Simon, a psychiatrist, criticized the testing movement's emphasis on psychological functions (sensory discrimination and reaction time) typical of the German psychologists (Kraepelin, Oehrn, Ebbinghaus) (Anastasi, 1957). In France, Binet and Simon pointed out that functions of memory, imagination, attention, comprehension, and aesthetic appreciation were better indicators of mental ability, even if more difficult to measure, than the measurement of physical traits and simple sensory-motor processes.

Most important for school psychology was the appointment of a commission of the Ministry of Public Instruction in Paris to investigate the learning potential of children who were having difficulty with school tasks. Binet and Simon collaborated to carry out the commission's charge (Binet & Simon, 1905). They questioned teachers about the kinds of learning difficulties children had, as well as asking about the intellectual tasks most children were able to master at given ages. Binet and Simon sifted, collated, and compared what teachers said. They found, for example, that most children can carry out three simple, sequential requests at age four and one-half. Most seven-year-olds are able to copy a diamond-shaped line drawing with fair approximation. Binet and Simon developed 30 such problems and arranged them in ascending order of difficulty. Their work was not only careful but thoughtful; many of those original 30 items have survived extensive statistical analyses that support the claim that they represent the extent to which individual children have mastered basic, developmental tasks.

The Binet-Simon scale, the acknowledged patriarch of all tests of "intelligence," promised help for educators interested in school children's ability to cope with academic tasks, a notion far beyond the scale's early use to distinguish children who could learn the three R's from those who, apparently, could not. Because the ascending order of item difficulty permitted an estimate of "mental age," a teacher could make a judgment of whether Jill could learn as well as most other ten-year-olds when Jill's responses to Binet and Simon's tasks were like those of most five-year-olds.

The development of classes for "slow learners," the recognition that delinquents tended to do poorly in school, the American dedication to the notion of compulsory education to promulgate universal literacy, the strides in the recognition of individual differences, all contributed to the rapid adoption of Binet and Simon's work in the United States. Henry H. Goddard, a psychologist at The Training School in Vineland, N.J. (a pioneer school in research into the psychology of mental retardation as well as in humane provision for and the teaching of mentally retarded children) published an article (1910) translating, describing, and proscribing "The Binet-Simon Measuring Scale for Intelligence."

On the west coast, Lewis Terman of Stanford University was also adapting the work of Binet and Simon for use in American schools. The Stanford-Binet, as Terman named his version, introduced the *ratio* between mental age and chronological age, the intelligence quotient (IQ). Most simply, our hypothetical ten-year-old Jill who completed Binet's tasks like a five-year-old has a mental age of five; the ratio of five to ten is one-half; multiply by 100 (for convenience) and Jill's IQ is 50. The ten-year-old who performs like most ten-year-olds has a ratio of 10 over 10, times 100, leading to an IQ of 100, which is presumed to be "average."

Following Terman's work, many other tests were developed to measure children's general learning aptitudes, especially for school achievement. The rapid development of the testing movement was boosted further by the need of the military in World War I to evaluate the general intellectual level of its recruits. Intelligence tests that could be administered to groups were developed, leading to widespread "testing programs" in the public schools. In contrast to the Stanford-Binet, administered individually by a skilled examiner, whole classes could be administered group IQ tests by teachers. The testing boom was in full swing by the 1930s; the "IQ" became a household word (Anastasi, 1957).

During the first quarter of the twentieth century, a few schools employed persons sometimes called "psychologists," sometimes "psychological examiners," to administer to individual children and to interpret the Stanford-Binet. Assignment of children into special classes for the retarded required that someone be responsible for deciding which children should be so placed, and the

Binet test served to sort out those children who learned little and/or very slowly. Exactly when these test administrators and interpreters were given the title *school psychologist* is not clear, and there are conflicting claims for "firsts," but it is reported that Dr. Arnold Gesell was appointed in 1915 to the Connecticut State Board of Education ". . . to make mental examinations of backward and defective children in rural, village, and urban schools, and to devise methods for their better care in the public schools" (Connecticut Special Education Association, 1936, p. v). By the early 1920s, T. Ernest Newland (1981) was testing juvenile delinquents, and in 1927 he was testing children for a preschool program. In 1923, an article appeared titled "The School Psychologist" (Hutt, 1923). By the 1930s the title and function were appearing regularly in the literature (Cornell, 1936; Mullen, 1981; Watson, 1931) although services were extremely scattered geographically, and found mostly in larger cities. By the 1940s the specialty was considered sufficiently identified to warrant an entire issue of the *Journal of Consulting Psychology* (1942, 6) on the subject of school psychology.

The development of concern for mental health

Although psychologists working in the schools were originally primarily mental testers (Symonds, 1942), there was early recognition that factors other than those measured by an IQ test contribute to a child's school success or failure. As early as 1911, Wallin was concerned with the mental health of school children, and schools in Pennsylvania, Missouri, Illinois, and Ohio were establishing psychological services to deal with "the whole child" rather than on the basis of a child's IQ score alone (Mullen, 1981; Newland, 1981; Wallin, 1942).

Freud's writings were becoming known in the United States; he was developing new and startling theories to explain the origins of emotional reactions and how people develop different personality patterns (Hall, 1962). Freud's disciple-turned-dissenter, Alfred Adler, lectured widely in the United States, and his ideas were found to be relevant by educators. The psychoanalytic viewpoint in general emphasized the importance of events and relationships in early childhood in the development of emotional adjustment; psychologists began to be concerned about the psychological health of children in schools as well as about measureable intellectual capacities.

The writings of Clifford Beers (1908) generated interest in mental hygiene, or the prevention of mental illness. Child guidance clinics appeared in increasing numbers. Universities were beginning to offer coursework in psychoanalytic theories and the newly developing techniques to assess personality functioning in psychoanalytic terms. By the end of World War II, courses in mental hygiene were becoming mandatory in teacher training institutions, along with the study of child growth and development. Teachers and parents became concerned about pupils' emotional health. States that already supported classes for the mentally retarded began to offer partial state funding to support the creation of classes for emotionally disturbed children.

Social awareness of the need to prevent as well as solve the problems of children put pressure on legislators to mandate educational practices that involved psychology. Parents of children with problems formed pressure groups to urge legislators to pass laws mandating a variety of "special" education services. Some states began to require the services of a psychologist to perform, in addition to the testing services, mental health services, such as providing counseling services to children and parents and offering psychological consultation to teachers. For a psychologist to be employed by a school district to work with a school population, certification by a state Board of Education to perform such services became required. This Education certificate universally bore the title "school psychologist," even though there were few psychologists trained specifically to work in the schools before the late 1950s. Clinically trained psychologists who had interest in working with school children, guidance counselors, and teachers who had had training in testing became the first certified school psychologists. One commonality among them (and one that still exists) was that they administered individual intelligence tests.

By the late 1950s, the job market was excellent for school psychologists, while the training needed for the positions was ill-defined and not readily available. The first graduate from a doctoral program in school psychology was in 1958, the second in 1959 (University of Illinois and Rutgers University, respectively). As jobs proliferated, so did programs for training school psychologists. By 1980, training programs reported 642 graduates at the specialist (non-doctoral) level and 176 graduates at the doctoral level, representing the greatest percentage of increase since 1970 among *all* the psychological specialties.

■ THE PUBLIC SCHOOLS AS PSYCHOLOGICAL WORK SETTINGS

Schools are a very important part of life for American children and youth. Schools are the social institution given the responsibility for the care, nurture, social development, *and* education of children, second only to parents in influencing children's development. Because of compulsory education in the United States, most of us have experienced public schools as learners. We all know schools very well from the student's side of the desk, and to be a school psychologist, it is good that we do. If we remember some of our problems, it helps us understand how children can be troubled about inner feelings and outer events that, while seemingly inconsequential to adults, are very scary to kids.

Over and above understanding the special climates of classrooms is understanding school administration. How are Boards of Education, to whom school administrators are responsible (and who hire and fire them), elected or appointed? What kind of tax structure supports local schools (a combination of local, state, and federal, but they vary), and what do changes in economy and changes in the politics of administrations mean for schools? Who decides what is to be taught, and by whom? Most of these questions cannot be answered here, nor are they always satisfactorily answered in the tons of literature available on education; the point being made is that schools, as social systems, are very complex and very political. As a work setting for psychologists, however, the answers are very important. To function in a school district as a psychologist is very different from functioning in a mental hospital, in a clinic, even in a business organization. It is because of the idiosyncrasies of schools that school psychology has developed as an identifiable professional specialty within psychology.

■ TARGET PROBLEMS

While school psychologists work with individual students, they also work with teachers, parents, and school administrators. This part of the chapter will discuss typical problems faced by school psychologists as they work with their variety of clients. In a later part of the chapter, we will discuss the ways in which school psychologists attempt to solve these problems.

The problems of individual children

Probably no parent or teacher would disagree with the statement "All children have problems—it's just a matter of degree." If you think about your own growing-up, you'll probably agree, too. Most of us struggle and bumble through childhood and adolescence, learning to cope without professional help. It would be ideal if all of us could have had an "outsider" who was understanding and helpful with whom to share our anxieties and concerns, and sometimes we found a teacher, a guidance counselor, a physical education teacher/coach, or a school nurse to be a person who offered wise counsel. There are normal developmental problems of growing up. However, many children believe at the time that these scary feelings, fantasies, or confusions are unique and they fear admitting their feelings even to parents or a best friend.

Sometimes these normal problems of growing up do get a youngster to the school psychologist. However, school districts range from providing one psychologist to 1500 school children (in the best serviced districts) to one psychologist to 20,000 school children. It is immediately apparent that unless youngsters present themselves as needing psychological help (unlikely), or someone else (parent, teacher) asks for help, these "normal" problems seldom reach the school psychologist.

It is estimated that approximately 10 to 15 percent of children exhibit behavior that causes either parents or school personnel to refer the youngster to the school psychologist. These problems run the gamut; it is arbitrary to try to categorize them precisely. For purposes of identification in schools, they are usually spoken of as *behavioral problems* (the kid won't sit still, always talks out, is always truant), as *academic problems* (won't do homework, can't read at grade level), as *social problems* (has no friends, is always teased, is too quiet and withdrawn, provokes others, or has the wrong friends), or as *emotional problems* (is always lashing out verbally or fighting with others, has tantrums, steals, may be on drugs, is anorexic, obese, is abused, neglected). Usually a child is "identified" as a problem child for some combination of these behavioral, social, emotional, and academic problems. There are, too, those who have very specific problems that are physical in origin—those who are deaf, blind, cerebral palsied, hydrocephalic, Down's syndrome, and a host of other possibilities.

The cause of a problem may be of prime importance for children themselves and their parents, but the "why" the child has a problem, for schools, is not as important as "what do we do?"

The problems of teachers

Schools are certainly densely populated institutions, but teachers within them are the loneliest workers in the world (Sarason, 1971; Sarason, Davidson, & Blatt, 1962). By law, classrooms must never be left without the presence of an authorized adult; teachers spend most of their day with children. Many teachers really love children, but interaction with children is not a substitute for peer interaction. Some teachers have no "break" at all, and supervise lunchroom and playground duty as well as the regular classroom activities. If teachers do lunch together in a faculty lunch room, the time is brief and conversation hurried. At faculty meetings, most teachers say very little (if anything), as the principal does most of the talking.

There are rewards for teaching, and nothing is more satisfying for the dedicated teacher than the realization that a child has grasped a new concept, has experienced the joy of learning. But there are also many, many frustrations: teacher motivation is discouraged, their behavior becomes routinized. Sometimes it seems that if just one or two particularly difficult or disruptive children could be removed from the class, the job of teaching the others would become more rewarding and easier; or if the teacher did not have to spend so much time going over and over material for a few that the majority have already mastered (and become bored with), all kinds of fascinating and challenging activities could take place in the classroom.

Should the teacher, then, seek help with these problems? And from whom? Some seek help from the school psychologist. Many do not. In the first place, some teachers view seeking outside (of the classroom) help tantamount to admitting failure as a teacher. Next, with the kinds of psychologist/student ratios quoted earlier, only the most desperate of events is likely to result in action (on the part of the psychologist) in the near future. There is almost always a backlog of "referrals" on the school psychologist's desk. In the third place, there is never a magic answer, even from the most competent of psychologists. As mentioned earlier, many teachers wish and hope that a psychologist can "work with" a troubled and troublesome child and "cure" the child, so the child will become a positively active, learning, well-behaved member of the class. A variety of techniques can assist, but rarely, if ever, can a problem be "cured" by the psychologist alone. In other words, the teacher has to do something as well as the psychologist.

There is even a fourth problem for the teacher. The child may indeed exhibit a problem so severe that the teacher believes the child is eligible for removal from the regular class and assignment to special education. As this child is the most problematic, how much easier the teaching job will become if the teacher no longer has to have the responsibility of coping! The teacher usually genuinely sees this kind of situation as "If Jill were in a special education class—which is where she ought to be—then I'd be free to teach the others." Sometimes, perhaps too frequently, children are removed from regular classrooms and placed in special education classes for the entire school day. Others may be so difficult and problematic that they cannot function even in a special education classroom, and therefore attend special schools. Some even, unfortunately, must be institutionalized. However, most children can learn within the regular classroom, and even those with problems can frequently learn in a combination of special education class (usually now known as a "resource room") or some "remediation" (small group or individual tutoring in math, reading) with regular classroom placement. Federal law (PL 94-142) requires "the least restrictive environment" and urges "mainstreaming" for children classified as having educational handicaps.

The teacher, therefore, may view removal from the classroom as the best solution to the problem, but is told instead that the child will remain in the regular class. Despite suggestions, techniques, and other assistance with the difficult child, teachers become discouraged and again frustrated.

The problems of parents

Parents, even those who seem most indifferent to their children, want their children to learn the academic skills. Parents vary widely in their beliefs about the best methods of teaching those skills, and they certainly vary in how they communicate this belief to their children, but they recognize the societal value of education and the relationship between school achievement and societal "success."

Well-meaning parents have alternately been blamed by philosophers, psychologists, and educators for being too strict, or too permissive, and in general directly responsible for whatever is perceived to be the wrongs committed by their children. The discovery of the DNA factor and implications that there is a genetic component to whether a child is "easy" or "difficult" to rear has alleviated, to some extent, parents' guilt feelings about their behavior being totally responsible for how their children develop (Thomas, Birik, Chess, Hertzig, & Korn, 1963). Parents unfortunate enough to have a child who is severely intellectually or physically handicapped are burdened by the extra care involved in bringing up such a child, and, in addition, are frequently traumatized psychologically by their feelings of genetic responsibility. In the experience of this writer, one of the most common questions posed by a parent of a child experiencing behavior/academic problems is "What did I do wrong?" However, another frequent comment is "He's just like his father (mother)!"

Some parents seem to care too much. Other parents relinquish all efforts at control. Still other parents nag and torment their children or abuse them physically. Some parents are psychologically torn by their own problems of separation and divorce. Other single and working parents worry about their children being unsupervised between school dismissal and parent quitting time (latchkey children). Many parents are torn by feelings of helplessness and confusion about how to deal with their children.

The problems of other school personnel

When we think of schools we always think of teachers first, and surely they are the key professionals who deal most intimately with children. Teachers are the most numerous of school personnel, but they are only one part of a hierarchy of school personnel, all of whom play an important part in the growth and development of children.

Boards of Education are the ultimate school authorities. In small communities, Boards of Education are usually elected directly by the voters, a process which, along with direct voting for the school budget, gives the individual voter a relatively unique sense of direct control over school policy. Boards prepare the budget, hire and fire the personnel, and shape school curriculum by cutting out "frills" and determining pupil/teacher ratio. Boards also determine policies such as minimum age for entrance into kindergartens. There are restraints in that budgets may be voted down by the community, but the board members usually represent powerful constituencies among the community groups. Some smaller communities band together to form Boards of Education whose members represent differing but nearby communities, and who oversee a regional school that serves several communities. Some states operate on regional levels; others (usually in the older, smaller northeastern states), on the "grass roots" basis.

Cities generally have Boards of Education appointed by the city governing group; in large cities, the operations of the school are extremely complex and voters have less direct control. However, powerful interest groups such as well-organized parent or community groups can exercise considerable and effective pressure upon school operations (as in the city of New York, for example).

School administrators are hired by the Board of Education; these school officials have enormous power, but power that can be withdrawn, sometimes very suddenly: unlike teachers, school superintendents do not have tenure in their position. It is the school superintendent who proposes policies and budgets and submits them to the board; a "good" superintendent is one who can convince a board of the efficacy of his or her plans and policies. Between the superintendent and the teachers are the school principals, the deputies for the superintendent's policies within their particular school building. Larger districts may have a variety of assistant superintendents.

Schools, as you remember, are populated by a great number of persons other than the classroom teachers and the administrators. There are school nurses, librarians, social workers. There are also "staff" who frequently are important members of the school community: the teacher's aides, the secretaries, the custodians, the school bus drivers, the cafeteria personnel. All of these people have an impact upon how and under what kind of circumstances education is offered to children and youth.

School-wide problems

Understanding the climate and culture of the schools (for the school psychologist) includes knowing what White (1978) refers to as "the real agenda of the schools" (p. 292). Community expectation for its children varies widely, and these variations are reflected in schools. In some urban communities, problems such as racial tensions have received so much publicity that we are all aware of them. Urban school problems frequently include those of children and parents whose language is other than English, disproportionate numbers of minority group children in classes labeled for the mentally retarded, high "drop-out" rates, and high truancy.

As White (1978) points out, the best simple predictor for future occupations (and educational level) of school children is the occupational level of their parents. A community that expects most of its children to complete a college education has different expectations for its schools than a community that does not. Rural communities have different educational values than either urban or suburban. The population growth obviously affects schools; the "baby boom" of the 1940s and 1950s resulted in crowded classrooms, building programs, and teacher shortage. The recent decline in population growth has resulted in decline in school population, with some empty classrooms and a surfeit of available teachers. All of these factors have a direct effect upon school policies and procedures.

■ PROBLEM SOLUTIONS

Working with an individual child

Individual problems are usually identified first by the teacher, although sometimes by a parent. The teacher's question is usually framed along these lines: "Is Johnny having trouble learning because he doesn't apply himself? Or, is it possible that Johnny can't learn at the same rate as the others, and am I expecting too much of him?" There are usually concomitants to the basic problem of not learning—"He doesn't seem to be able to work independently; if I'm busy with the reading group, he wanders around the room, distracts other children, gets into trouble."

Most schools have a procedure for referral of a child to the school psychologist; the teacher fills out a "referral form" that briefly describes the teacher's view of the problem and why help is sought from the school psychologist. Referrals are usually cleared through (or screened by) the building principal before sending them to the school psychologist, or to a group of professionals usually known as the "child study team" (frequently consisting of the school psychologist, a school social worker, and a learning disability teacher consultant). Ideally, but not always, the teacher has voiced his or her concern to the parent(s) in a regular parent-teacher conference. At this point, the school psychologist is likely to talk with the teacher to encourage elaboration of the brief "reason for referral." This encounter can be as informal as a few minutes in the hall, in the cafeteria, or during a teacher's free period. The psychologist will probably ask the teacher's permission to observe Johnny in the classroom setting.

It should be noted immediately that these practices vary among schools and among school psychologists. However, ideally, any attempt at a determination of the nature of a child's problem and what can be done to alleviate that problem should include consideration of the *setting* in which the problem is observed to exist, i.e., the classroom (Bardon & Bennett, 1974; Sarason, 1971). It is possible, for example, that Johnny's "problem" is easily remediated by the teacher's following some suggestions about curriculum materials, seating arrangements, or some rewards to enhance Johnny's motivation. The classroom visit, however, may cause the psychologist to believe that further data are needed about Johnny's potential for learning. This conclusion usually leads to the psychologist suggesting additional testing.

For an assessment session to be scheduled by the psychologist with Johnny, parental consent must be obtained (PL 94-142). Parents have the right to refuse a psychological evaluation; some do. Usually, however, parents are as eager as the teacher to discover more about Johnny's problems. If they refuse, it is sometimes because they "don't want anything on Johnny's record," or "there's nothing wrong with Johnny . . . it's the fault of the teacher (school, other children)." In the instance of parental refusal, the school psychologist (or school social worker), the principal, or any combination thereof, attempt to convince the parents that the proposed evaluation is for Johnny's benefit, not detriment. Conferences with reluctant, angry, or hostile parents are frequently instances of the psychologist's need for understanding, empathy, and consummate interpersonal skills as well as knowledge about family structures, parents, and parenting. The parent conference is also the source of needed data about Johnny, such as what stresses he may be experiencing at home or in the neighborhood that have an effect upon how he functions in school. Only parents can communicate to the school how they view Johnny and what their expectations are, and a good psychologist is frequently the best-trained school professional to enhance that communication and to engender trust.

There are other data to be collected, e.g., precisely what is Johnny's academic record? Most schools routinely administer group achievement tests, usually sometime in the spring of each academic year. Group achievement tests yield scores (machine provided) in terms of percentile ranks or grade level. The norms provided are usually nationally based, although many school districts have determined (or should have) their own local norms. Percentile ranks need to be explained: a percentile rank of 50% does not mean Johnny got a 50 on a test based on 100; it means that Johnny did as well as 50% of the children who took the test as part of the norming group. There are school districts whose total school population scores at an average percentile rank of 60% or 70%, demonstrating the need for local norms.

Grade-level performance means that machine scoring provides the information that Johnny is, for example, reading at grade level 1.7, performing math functions expected at grade level 2.4, and the like. Without going into all the details of standard deviations on these scores, suffice it to say that these grade-level assignments are suggestive rather than definitive. If, however, Johnny's group testing scores are the above, and Johnny is in the fourth grade, the inference is clear. Johnny is not functioning academically at grade level (or perhaps he had a temperature of 103° the testing day, or perhaps he was upset, tired, and simply marked his answer sheet at random—these are the problems of group testing).

But if Johnny is indeed in the fourth grade, there are other data, such as previous years' testing scores. Are they consistent? And, importantly, how does the teacher view Johnny's academic performance? What kinds of grades has Johnny been receiving all along? Has he ever been retained a grade ("left back")? What has Johnny's attendance record been? What about his health record? Are his vision and hearing of sufficient acuity? All of these data are recorded in Johnny's cumulative record folder maintained in school offices.

Next the psychologist interviews Johnny. Here the psychologist must be reassuring and help Johnny recognize that the procedures to which he is being subjected are to help him. It should be noted, however, that most children enjoy the individual attention and interest of a warm, empathic, noncritical adult. The trick for the school psychologist is, of course, to fit that description in the eyes of the youngster—whether age 2 or age 18. It should be apparent by now that professional skills and knowledge are necessary attributes of a school psychologist, but equally important are interpersonal skills, the ability to be nonjudgmental, to understand and speak the jargon of the age group, as well as to know the school itself, the climate of the youngster's classroom, even the personality of the teacher.

Professional judgment determines the choice of instruments selected for the individual assessment. Considering the reason for Johnny's referral, certainly an instrument designed to give information about his cognitive functioning is in order. As Johnny is in the fourth grade, he is probably, if he has not previously repeated a grade, nine years old, and the instrument most likely to be selected is the Wechsler Intelligence Scale for Children–Revised (1974). The WISC-R, as it is known, yields an IQ number. Despite many criticisms of the Wechsler tests, the instrument does provide information about how Johnny performs certain cognitive tasks that are, in general, quite accurately predictive of how he can and will be able to perform academic tasks (Buros, 1978; Sattler, 1982). As the various tasks are presented by the psychologist, reading is not a prerequisite for task completion as it frequently is on group tests. Language acquisition and knowledge are needed for the verbal subtests, but there is also a "performance" scale that is sufficiently nonverbal that portions can be used with children who do not speak English (there is also a version in Spanish).

All tests of so-called "intelligence" are inferential. They are based on a sampling of behavior found to be predictive of other behaviors that are related to cognitive functioning. Of course they reflect a child's environment. The children of articulate, highly educated parents who talk a lot to their children, read to them, expose them to a variety of experiences and explain those experiences are likely to get better scores on the verbal portions of the WISC-R than are the children of parents who do none of those "enriching" things. The point is, however, that the IQ score itself is not as important a piece of information as how Johnny goes about solving the various problems, how successful he is, and in what areas of cognitive functioning he shows relative strengths and/or weaknesses. The WISC-R is a sample of behavior. Unlike group testing, an individual test permits a psychologist to encourage Johnny to try to solve the problem rather than simply give up. The psychologist needs to differentiate between the child's "I don't know" that means that the child really doesn't know from the "I don't know" that means the child isn't sure and doesn't want to give a wrong answer. The skill of the psychologist is applied to finding out what Johnny does know and can do as well as how he handles tasks that are difficult or even impossible for him.

In general, the school psychologist's major concern is what Johnny can and can't do academically, but frequently there is the additional question of "Why can he or can't he." To separate personality functioning from intellectual functioning is to make an arbitrary distinction, for the two are not separable. For Johnny, however, it is helpful to try to understand (considering the reason for referral) why he loses interest in his work, feels impelled to wander around the room, and distracts other children. The reasons may be perfectly apparent to the psychologist after talking with the teacher, the parents, observing in class, and talking to Johnny himself, but in some instances a psychologist needs to know more about the conflicts, fantasies, and unrecognized and unverbalized problems a child may be experiencing.

Following the Freudian notion that the unconscious constantly struggles for expression in seemingly innocuous ways, "projective techniques" are a series of devices that seek to reveal unconscious motivation. For example, a child may be asked to draw a picture of a person. The picture the child produces reveals self-concept, ideal self, sex role identification, and developmental maturity (Bennet, 1964, 1966; Buck, 1948; Harris, 1963; Machover, 1949). Children may also be asked to tell stories about pictures of situations and people (Morgan & Murray, 1935), another way of eliciting how they see other adults, other children, and themselves. Of course the most famous of projective techniques is the series of inkblots known as the Rorschach Technique (Rorschach, 1949). A relatively amorphous inkblot looks like different things to different people, depending upon how a person views his or her world.

The end product of a psychoeducational assessment battery conducted with an individual child by a school psychologist is information that will be helpful to teachers and to parents in planning educational placement and techniques. Secondarily, the information should be helpful to parents and teachers in child behavior management and in child rearing practices.

The identification and classification of children with educational handicaps

Public Law 94:142 ▪ This law, passed in 1974, has had significant impact on the practice of psychology in the public schools (Bennett & Bardon, 1975). Public law 94:142 mandates free and appropriate education to *all* children, regardless of physical or psychological handicapping condition, and charges schools to ensure such education for handicapped children. The teeth in the law is that federal funding is provided to assist in the expense of providing such education, and that *all* federal funding, even for regular education, will be withheld if special education is not provided.

In order to provide appropriate education for handicapped children, the children must be identified as in need of special educational plans and techniques. A totally blind or severely physically handicapped child is fairly easy to identify; other educationally handicapping conditions such as mild mental retardation, perceptual-motor deficits, partial deafness, and emotional problems are not necessarily self-evident. In some instances, it is a physician who must attest that a child has an educational handicap, but usually the major responsibility falls upon the school psychologist, who, along with other special services personnel, must classify a handicapped child into a category and work out an individual educational program (IEP) for that child. Another facet of PL 94:142 is that the handicapped child's education must take place in the *least-restrictive environment*. In order from least to most restrictive placements are (1) regular class *(mainstreaming)*, (2) regular class with part of the school day spent with a remedial teacher, (3) regular class with part of the day in a resource room (special teacher, special materials, perhaps a small group), (4) special class placement (classroom within the public school with a small group of children and a teacher certified in special education), (5) placement out of the public school (in a nearby day school devoted to children with special problems), and (6) residential placement in an institution devoted to children with special problems.

The above paragraph is a condensed description of a very elaborate process that consumes, today, the greatest portion of the school psychologist's time. As mentioned, parents must be consulted and must consent to every step of the process. Decisions about appropriate placement and educational techniques are crucial to a child's growth and development. The effect on a child of being labeled (e.g., as mentally retarded, as emotionally maladjusted) is much argued about, but really unknown.

Bias in classification and placement ▪ Within psychology, possible bias in the assessment of intellectual functioning continues to evoke concern and dissent. Is an IQ score on a Stanford-Binet or one of the Wechsler Intelligence Scales really indicative of the intellectual ability of a child whose cultural milieu is different from that of the dominant white, middle class? This brief chapter cannot detail or even adequately discuss the material published defending or criticizing the use of intelligence tests by psychologists. However, the school psychologist needs to know this literature thoroughly, as well as be aware of the nature and outcome of the litigation that has proliferated on the basis of possible bias in testing, especially when that testing results in some kind of "label" (as, for example, mentally retarded). The psychologist also needs to be aware of the alternatives or supplements to the well-known individual tests (Mercer & Lewis, 1978).

One point, perhaps, can be made: An IQ number derived from one of the individual intelligence tests is relatively unimportant in and of itself in a school situation. What is important (and much of this information can be obtained from the classic intelligence tests) is the level of language development, the level of conceptual development, the child's understanding of numerical functions, the child's perceptual-motor development, the amount of short-term and long-term memory, the ability to make inferences, the ability to use the known to solve a new problem, and the ability to learn from every-day happenings in one's environment.

Assuredly a child like Diana, the plaintiff in the classic court case on bias in testing (*Diana* v. *State Board of Education*), who spoke Spanish but not English should not be classified as mentally retarded on the basis of a test administered in English. Nor should a special class for the mentally retarded, in a mixed-race school, consist of primarily black children (*Larry P.* v. *Riles*). On the other hand, psychologists need the best tools available to help sort out children who need special educational techniques and to find the kinds of techniques appropriate for that particular child. As PL 94:142 proclaims, all children are entitled to a free and appropriate education, regardless of educational handicap.

If it is discoverable that the lack of knowledge of middle-class white English is the primary educational handicap, then appropriate measures, whether providing for bi-lingual education or teaching English as a second language, can be proscribed.

Intervention procedures

The practice of school psychology incorporates a wide variety of professional activities. Some of us have conceived this practice as occurring on three levels: psychology applied to the problems of (1) the individual, (2) groups, and (3) systems (Bardon & Bennett, 1974; Comtois & Clark, 1976; Peterson, 1976). Psychological procedures designed to effect change or modification of the behavior of individual children, their parents, teachers, entire classrooms, or even curriculum practices and school system-wide programs are usually called *intervention* procedures. Intervention can take place not only on the three levels mentioned above but also on three levels of directness. *Direct intervention* occurs with the person who is experiencing the problem. *Indirect intervention* occurs by offering consultation or counseling with people who work with or live with the person experiencing the problem. *Primary prevention* occurs when the intervention is designed to prevent problems rather than to remediate them.

Many school psychologists have adopted the knowledge and techniques of behavioral approaches to intervention because of their demonstrated efficacy (Wilson & Franks, 1982), their emphasis on short term rather than long term "therapy", and their adaptability for use with teachers and parents (O'Leary & O'Leary, 1972). These classroom procedures have taken the form of systematic praise of children for desired behavior, rewards of "tokens" (to be turned in for a desired reward), programmed instruction, and establishment of clear rules and directions. Other methods in schools have been soft reprimands, "time-out" periods, relaxation, gradual presentation of fearful stimuli, and desensitization (O'Leary & O'Leary, 1972).

More recently, school psychologists have shifted away from an emphasis on decreasing disruptive behaviors, partially because of the dubious effectiveness of these approaches on actual learning (Franks, 1982), to a concern with educational tasks involving thinking skills (Craighead, 1982). These approaches involve programs designed to teach children skills necessary for success in education, such as problem solving (Gesten, Rores De Apocada, Rains, Weisberg, & Cowen, 1979), decision making (Meichenbaum, 1977), and self-discipline. The cognitive behavior modification approach, as it is known, is built on theories of cognitive development, information processing, and learning (Morris & Cohen, 1982).

Individual intervention ▪ Assessment of individual children and devising educational plans for them is easily categorized as psychological intervention on an individual level. Sometimes the school psychologist will schedule regular counseling sessions with a child who has social or emotional adjustment problems. Helpful as individual counseling (the word "therapy" is generally not used in public schools) may be, the aforementioned ratios of pupil to psychologist and the psychologist's workload make it unrealistic for the psychologist to devote large segments of time to a necessarily small number of students. The counseling offered by the psychologist is more likely to take the form of "crisis counseling" or very short-term sessions with an individual youngster. If long-term therapy is needed, school psychologists usually refer the child and parents to an agency that specializes in therapy (Conti, 1971).

Group intervention ▪ In addition to the practical advantage of seeing several children simultaneously rather than one at a time, there are other advantages to counseling groups of children. Many psychological problems are essentially those of interpersonal relationships, and groups permit an opportunity for children to learn successful interaction skills within a small, protected (by the psychologist) milieu. Some groups are formed on the basis of a shared problem—children of parents going through separation and divorce, for example (Drake, 1981). Other groups are formed for the purpose of modifying aggressive behavior or helping withdrawn children become more assertive (Rotheram, Armstrong, & Booream, 1982).

Classroom management ▪ A common problem for teachers, and an area in which school psychologists can be helpful, is classroom management. Although individual children are frequently perceived as responsible for a disruptive class, the procedures used in classroom management are designed to modify the behavior of individuals within a group situation. Thus, classroom management uses peer pressure and the teacher's authority as part of the intervention procedure (Bardon & Bennett, 1976). Token economies (turning in earned chips for rewards) are offered the entire class, not just targeted children (Andronico & Guerney, 1967). The psychologist observing the classroom can lead to changes that improve both the individual's situation as well as all of the childrens' work. Examples are getting an isolated child to participate with others by successively approximating the desired behavior in small steps, forming within-class project teams, and enlisting the aid of other children to form "buddy systems." It is difficult for the harried teacher to be objective. A trained observer, the psychologist, can offer (carefully, tactfully, insightfully) suggestions to the teacher concerning effective management of the whole classroom, including the "problem child."

Teacher consultation ▪ Frequently, a group for teachers will be formed so that teachers can share solutions among themselves for problems such as how to handle sex education, what to do about substance abuse, how to handle parent conferences, and how to deal with problems common to certain age groups. A neglected but cogent facet of school problems is that teaching behaviors are as likely to be the products of pupils' actions as their causes (Copeland, 1980). Successful teacher consultation requires great psychological knowledge and skill on the part of the psychologist; as mentioned earlier in this chapter, teachers are often lonely and overworked, and all are vulnerable to criticism by their principals and superintendents, by parents, and by the community.

Parent consultation ▪ As mentioned, the law (PL 94:142) requires that parents participate in all the procedures and steps that are part of special education. Fortunately, 85 to 90 percent of children in schools do not require special educational procedures, but these "normal" children have normal developmental problems, and their "normal" parents can experience problems with their children. School psychologists can offer considerable help to parents individually, and to groups of parents who share similar problems. These problems can range from "My child is gifted, what should I (and the school) be doing?" to "Can we, as parents, prevent future substance abuse?" to the problems shared by parents whose children have substantial learning deficits or disabilities.

The legal requirement for continuous parental involvement in the schooling of their children has helped school psychologists to become much more involved with parents. Parents formerly considered "unreachable" are now available. Many of the barriers perceived by parents to be put up by schools to prevent their interaction have been removed. Concomitant to, or perhaps partially because of, the need for psychologists to include the family as well as the school in consideration of the problems of a child, family therapy has recently emerged as an intervention technique of choice. The nature of the American family has changed drastically in recent years (Bronfenbrenner, 1979) and there now exists an identifiable set of theoretical structures underlying intervention techniques with families (Guerin, 1976; Gurman & Kniskern, 1981; Haley, 1976; Loven, 1978; Minuchin & Fishman, 1981). Just as it is impossible for a school psychologist to consider a child's problems without considering the context of the classroom and the school, it is impossible to deal adequately with children's problems without considering the context of their families.

Referral to other agencies ▪ As pointed out earlier in this chapter, some children unfortunately have handicapping conditions so serious they cannot function within the public school system, even within "special classes." Profoundly handicapping conditions are usually, fortunately, also known as "low incidence" handicapping conditions. Day schools, to which children can be transported by bus, are provided in some communities for these children. Residential schools are provided for children who cannot be maintained either in a day class or at home. These schools vary in their sources of support; while some have tuition fees, special residential treatment centers usually reserve places for children of parents who cannot pay the full amount. The school psychologist's role in the placement of these children is very important, and the school psychologist must be knowledgeable about these resources in order to make appropriate referrals.

Intervention at the systems level

Another development with implications for the practice of school psychology is the recognition that school systems need consultation and technical assistance in planning, developing, and evaluating school service delivery systems (Bardon & Bennett, 1974; Maher, 1981; Reilly, 1973). A school is a service delivery system that must respond to the needs of various clients (administrators, teachers, parents, and communities as well as children).

A child may be having "a problem" in learning academic skills; the child's problem is also the teacher's problem and the parents' problem. In seeing individual children, teachers, and sets of parents, the school psychologist may discover that there really exists a system-wide problem of primary grade children's acquisition of reading recognition and comprehension skills. In order to effect change at the level of the individual, struggling child, a whole organizational change is needed (Gallesich, 1973; Schmuck & Miles, 1971). School systems, however, do not change easily but tend to continue to offer the same procedures and the same programs (Sarason, 1971).

An entire set of skills is needed for the school psychologist to be able to define the problem for the system, define the system structure, plan programs, and then—most importantly—evaluate the effectiveness of those programs. Only in this way can real changes be made in how children are taught and how they learn in schools. Psychologists trained at a very high level of knowledge and skills are perhaps uniquely qualified to fill the role of a "change agent" or "change facilitator" (Bardon & Bennett, 1974).

■ TRAINING PROGRAMS IN SCHOOL PSYCHOLOGY

The growth of training programs in school psychology exceeds that of any other psychological specialty. Although titles and content may vary slightly, there are, in general, three levels of training available, and all are at the graduate level.

Psychometricians

As the title implies, these training programs graduate, usually with a master's degree, technicians who have had course work and supervised experience in the administration and scoring of the classic psychological tests (the Binet and the Wechsler tests) and the development of written, discursive reports based on their findings. As a master's degree usually encompasses about thirty graduate credit hours, it is apparent that these programs can teach little beyond testing for cognitive functioning. There is, however, a place for these personnel in many school districts under the supervision of a qualified professional school psychologist. In some states, graduates of these programs are eligible for a state department of education certification, permitting their employment by schools as long as supervision is provided.

Psychoeducational specialists

In some states, the department of education issues a certificate in this name, but in many states this level of education and training is certified with the title *school psychologist.* In most states, these programs require a minimum of 60 graduate credits, and some colleges/universities award a Professional Diploma (P.D.) or a degree as Educational Specialist (Ed.S.) to indicate these graduates have completed work beyond a master's degree, yet do not hold a doctoral degree. Since the American Psychological Association does not recognize the use of the title "psychologist" without the doctoral degree, the title "school psychologist," if used by a nondoctoral program or person, is disputed.

Doctoral programs

The increase in training programs for school psychologists is true also for doctoral programs. Doctoral programs vary in the specific doctoral degree offered. Some offer the doctorate in education (Ed.D.), particularly likely if the program is housed in a school of education in a department of educational psychology. Some schools of education offer a Ph.D. in education. Other programs offer a Ph.D. in school psychology, more likely to occur in universities in which the training program is housed in a department of psychology. The most recent addition to doctoral degrees in all of professional psychology, but including school psychology, is the doctorate in psychology (Psy.D.). The rationale for this degree is that the Ph.D. has traditionally been the degree that reflects the academic/researcher/scientist; the Psy.D. accurately reflects the practitioner just as do the degrees in medicine, veterinary medicine, dentistry, law, and education (M.D., D.V.M., D.D.S., J.D., and Ed.D.).

A recurring concern in the profession of psychology is the amount of education and training needed for the delivery of services to the public. The American Psychological Association reaffirmed in 1982 its position that the doctoral degree represents the appropriate amount of training and education in order to represent oneself as a *psychologist* and to engage in the delivery of psychological services without supervision (APA, 1982). Yet there are many professionals with master's degrees who graduate from training programs in psychology and call themselves psychologists. In school psychology, as mentioned earlier, state departments of education issue certificates to persons who vary in the amount of training they have had, from thirty graduate credits to two years of graduate study (60 graduate credits) plus an internship. With the growing market for psychologists in the schools, the number of nondoctoral persons certified by departments of education as school psychologists is greater than those practicing holding a doctoral degree (Trachtman, 1981). There is no disagreement about the need for practitioners, whether in school, clinical, counseling, or industrial/organizational psychology, whose graduate training is less than doctoral. Disagreement arises over the title (psychologist) and the entry level (amount of education and training to practice as a psychologist) (Fagan, 1982). This disagreement with the APA is heard most vociferously among school psychologists, and the attempts at resolution have so far been fairly well confined to school psychology.

Certified school psychologists who do not hold the doctorate degree have frequently complained that the APA has not been an adequate professional parent. As psychologists who are elected to positions in the Division of School Psychology in APA have tended to be university faculty rather than practitioners, many school psychologists working in school settings believed their problems of everyday practice were not being addressed by the APA. In 1968, the Ohio School Psychologists' Association hosted a planning conference that resulted, in 1969, in the formation of the National Association of School Psychologists (NASP) (Farling & Agner, 1979). NASP, recognizing non-doctoral certified school psychologists as psychologists, in less than two decades has become an organization of approximately 7000 members (National Association of School Psychologists, 1982) that concerns itself exclusively with school psychology.

The APA point of view, as represented by Division 16 school psychologists, is that there is a qualitative gap between the specialist degree and the doctorate, and that this difference is represented by nondoctoral training programs that are psychoeducational versus doctoral programs in psychology (Bennett, 1980). Well-trained and needed as the nondoctoral practitioners are, they are essentially technicians as opposed to being professional psychologists. The difference is not merely a requirement to complete a dissertation, but an entire sequence of psychological training and experience of which the process of participation in applied research is very important. The doctoral level school psychologist is considered a planner and innovator as well as a highly skilled school clinician; the evaluation of the effectiveness of one's techniques and skills requires more than being an intelligent consumer of research.

The job market

Anyone considering graduate work in school psychology should be aware that the possibilities of employment after graduation (as in almost any other profession) depend upon many societal factors: the state of the economy, the particular point of view and policy of the majority in Congress, the President and Cabinets. The whole issue of governmental support for services is, at this writing, heatedly debated. Funding for education, whether for pre-school culturally disadvantaged children (Headstart) or for government subsidy of college student loans, is uncertain. Similar debates are occurring in state legislatures. Because funds for psychological services in the schools are provided by a combination of federal, state, and local funds, the number of positions available in schools will largely depend upon decisions made by legislators.

On the other hand, legislators at the state and federal level have created positions for school psychologists by enacting certain laws that were designed to protect the interests of school children. The Education for All Handicapped Children Act (PL 94:142) at current writing will operate much as originally written, despite proposals for sweeping changes in 1982 (Dwyer, 1982). This law, as mentioned earlier, provides for psychological services to identify and to determine what is "free and appropriate education" for handicapped children.

Some states had enacted similar legislation prior to the federal legislation's enactment. In such states, school psychologists are already numerous, and with declining funding at the state and local levels, the job market is not likely to increase. In other states, however, the federal law has created a need for school psychologists that previously did not exist, and so there are openings for school psychologists. There are also positions available for faculty to teach in school psychology programs, although these positions too are dependent upon the state of the economy and the extent to which a college/university has access to state and federal funding for its program offerings.

A number of school psychologists function in settings other than public schools. Almost any institution, residential treatment center, or day school for handicapped persons that provides educational services for children employs the services of psychologists, especially school psychologists. Many mental health clinics that provide services for children employ school psychologists to offer consultation to school districts in their "catchment" areas.

■ THE FUTURE OF THE SPECIALTY

This section must indeed be speculation. Psychologists may be capable (to the layperson) of sometimes startling insights about human behavior, but they are not readers of crystal balls or tea leaves, nor, for that matter, can they always accurately predict human behavior. Similarly, predictions about the future in school psychology are dependent upon so many social and economic factors as well as the state of the art and the science that the answer to "Will school psychology continue to be a rewarding profession for socially conscious, responsible, and able young people?" is "It all depends."

The fact that school psychology has its roots in both psychology and education is inescapable; this marriage, uneasy as it may be, is also desirable. School psychologists work in schools with the problems of schools; they are employed by schools and to be eligible for such employment must be certified by state departments of education. At current writing, no endorsement or document of any kind by psychology as a profession is required for such employment. Yet school psychologists bring the expertise of psychology to educational settings.

While conflict and disagreement over issues are not going to be resolved in the immediate future, the two groups as represented by NASP and APA have in common their sincere dedication to helping children in schools, and neither wants completely to alienate the other. In fact, many school psychologists are members of both organizations. Psychologists have recognized the importance and value of working in the schools from Witmer and John Dewey's time through the present. There is no question that major contributions to both psychology and education will continue to be made by school psychologists.

■ SUGGESTED READINGS

Bardon, J. I., & Bennett, V. C. (1974). *School psychology.* Englewood Cliffs, NJ: Prentice Hall.

An easy-to-read "primer" on school psychology, this paperback covers the basic details of school psychology. Although prepared as one of a series to introduce the psychology student to a variety of professional specialties in psychology, this book is the most frequently used text for beginning graduate students in school psychology training programs.

Journal of School Psychology. This publication is a journal devoted to articles of interest to school psychologists or students in school psychology. Topics include philosophy, research findings, and position papers.

School Psychology Review. This journal consists of reports of research, position papers, and discussion of issues relevant to the practice of school psychology. The review frequently publishes special issues that are collections of papers on a single topic; recent examples are "program planning and evaluation in special education programs" and "school based family interventions."

Three Publications from The National Association of School Psychologists

Selecting a School Psychology Training Program ($2.00): This guide to applicants for graduate training in school psychology spells out differences between doctoral and nondoctoral programs and discusses different emphases among program offerings.

Directory of School Psychology Training Programs ($2.00): As its name implies, this paperback lists every school psychology training program in the United States that the authors were able to identify. The programs are listed by state, and there is considerable detail about their accreditation status, number of students enrolled, degrees awarded, program requirements, financial assistance available, and so on.

Handbook on Certification/Licensure in the United States and Canada ($7.00): This publication lists each state's requirements to become certified (by a state department of education) and thereby eligible for employment as a school psychologist. Requirements for licensure for private practice as a psychologist are also listed.

All three are available from NASP Publications, 10 Overland Drive, Stratford, Connecticut 06497.

SUSAN M. MARKLE

INSTRUCTIONAL PSYCHOLOGY

■ INTRODUCTION

Anyone who has studied much psychology will have to admit that theories of learning constitute a major portion of the scientific discipline. Laboratory studies of learning are a large part of the research emphasis of the discipline. Studies of learning in natural environments are shared with other disciplines, such as ethology and biology. And, of course, there are numerous studies of learning in the environment of the school system. Deliberate instruction can be found in other species, as, for example, the lioness teaching her cubs how to hunt, but people are the only species with institutions—the schools—devoted to creating learning in the young and with professionals—teachers—who devote their lives to the training of youngsters not related to themselves. One would expect that psychology would have a great deal to say about how schools should operate.

Educational psychology as an application of scientific psychology has a long history. The famous psychologist-philosopher William James wrote his wise and charming *Talks to Teachers* in 1899; books from psychologists John Dewey and Edward Thorndike appeared not long thereafter. While most teachers must take a course in educational psychology, not all have found what they learned to be very useful in their day-to-day attempts to cope with the classroom. William James put it succinctly: "Psychology is a science and teaching is an art; and sciences never generate arts directly out of themselves. An intermediary inventive mind must make the application, by using its originality" (James, 1899).

155

In his book *The Sciences of the Artificial* (1969), Herbert Simon made the point that natural science is concerned with what things are and how they work, while the "engineer is concerned with how things ought to be—ought to be, that is, in order to attain goals and to function." The educational system as it exists is, in Simon's terms, an artifact designed to achieve human purposes, and the laws of nature—about how people learn—constitute only one piece of information needed to improve the system so that it achieves its purposes most effectively.

Many psychologists, among them Robert Glaser (1976), have postulated the need for a science of design devoted to solving instructional problems. *Instructional psychology* is thus a recent development, a "linking science" devoted to discovering the principles involved in academic learning and applying these principles to the design of instructional materials, procedures, and environments to attain goals.

The application of science and technology to improving the human condition is a strong part of our culture, although not one that is universally welcomed. The educational system has felt the impact of technology in some of its functions, but surprisingly little in its main function of teaching. Unless you attend one of the more fortunate school systems, modern communication devices such as video equipment and computers probably have more impact on your home environment than on your school day. Education is said to be a "labor-intensive" system, using people without technological assistance to help them do their jobs more efficiently and effectively. Most teachers are more like the country doctors of a generation ago, with a small black bag in hand going from one patient to the next, than like the modern medical practitioner with all the resources of the hospital laboratory and computerized information systems to call upon.

A strong movement for technology as a solution to the low productivity of the school system arose in the 1960s. To most people, technology means machinery. Notice, however, what is implied in this definition given by the President's Commission on Instructional Technology in its Report to Congress (1970):

> Instructional technology is a systematic way of designing, carrying out, and evaluating the total process of learning and teaching in terms of specific objectives, based on research in human learning and communication, and employing a combination of human and nonhuman resources to bring about more effective instruction.

Simon's point about engineering as a design science involving goals is very much a part of the definition: a systematic way of achieving objectives more effectively. Research in human learning of complex materials is what instructional science is about, while design of effective materials and methods (includ-

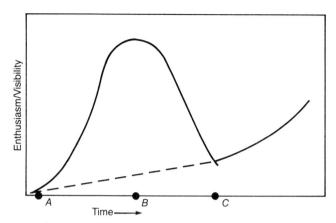

FIGURE 7.1   The development curve for new technologies (after Mager, 1966). At point *A*, a useful application of scientific knowledge is suggested. At point *B*, maximum enthusiasm is evident from supporters who promise too much. Disillusionment drops the curve to point *C*, where workable applications are becoming available based on research and development underway since point A.

ing what teachers do) is the activity of instructional designers. Both scientist and designer are a part of instructional psychology.

■ HISTORICAL DEVELOPMENT

The historical development of instructional technology looks more like the boom and bust of our economic cycles than like the orderly development of a systematic discipline. Robert Mager, when president of the National Society for Programmed Instruction*, drew a "development curve" for technological fads, of which programmed instruction had been one. Figure 7.1, slightly revised, shows the action: an initial burst of activity with glowing promises for the future followed by disillusionment and decreasing publicity. As Mager (1966) put it: "It is discovered that the first applications of the technology leave something to be desired, and those whose vision is short conclude that these limited applications demonstrate the failure of the technology." Throughout the initial burst of enthusiasm, shown in the steeply rising curve, a small and less noisy group works steadily on the new idea, developing the full implications of the new technology which will, in time, take its place as one of the elements in the whole fabric. This curve that Mager drew for programmed instruction applies equally to the sudden bursts of enthusiasm generated by many new developments taken by some educators to be *the* panacea; such bursts have appeared for new curricula and then for "back-to-basics," for inquiry training and discovery learning, for television, for behavioral objectives, for Keller plans, for comput-

---

*The Society changed its name in 1972 to "National Society for Performance and Instruction."

ers, and a host of other developments. At the time this is being written, the bandwagon surging toward its peak is the microcomputer "revolution," another technology that will find its place in the system when sufficient hard work has been done on how and when to use such machines.

Instructional technology as hardware

Only a few machines have entered the school system as tools deliberately designed to satisfy some need identified by research. Machines such as film projectors and video equipment were developed for quite different purposes, as, of course, were computers. Instructional designers can ask how such machinery can be used to foster school goals but such machines constitute a solution in search of a problem rather than a solution developed because a problem had first been identified.

Edward L. Thorndike wrote some of the earliest texts on educational psychology and is still referenced as the ancestor of Skinner's reinforcement theory. Thorndike's Law of Effect, that responses are "stamped in" by positive consequences, is still very much with us as developed and elaborated by Skinner and his associates. The gist of the law is that, when students exert effort to solve a problem or answer questions, feedback about what they have done right should be given as soon as possible. The feedback should emphasize the successful response rather than simply correcting what they have done wrong. If you think about what often happens to you in school (and is still to happen in college), you will realize how far we have to go to implement this turn-of-the-century bit of wisdom. It is not rare for a student to get a paper back from a teacher a week or so later, with ample red ink on the errors and only a grade to show how adequate it is. If the grade is A, you know you did something right, but the specific feedback usually emphasizes what you did wrong.

Designing an instructional environment that provides frequent positive feedback to the learner is one of the principles "based on research in human learning" that an instructional engineer would seek to implement to bring about "more effective instruction" (as noted in the Instructional Technology Report cited above). Skinner (1958) estimated that teachers ought to be delivering such feedback to 10,000 to 15,000 responses per pupil per year! Obviously this is beyond the capacity of a single human teacher confronted with a large group of busy students, so a nonhuman resource is suggested. Immediately, an engineer would envision a machine to solve the technological problem of delivering feedback to each student in a class at the moment that the student comes up with a correct response.

One of the earliest "teaching machines" was designed for just such a purpose. Sidney Pressey, an educational psychologist, introduced a device at the 1924 convention of the American Psychological Association which gives *and* scores a test, and will also teach informational and drill material efficiently. In its testing mode, the machine would present a multiple-choice question and keep a tally of correct choices, yielding a test score when the student completed the test. It could even be set to deliver a piece of candy to a student who was doing well, assuming that being correct was not a strong enough reward and that candy was. In its "teaching" mode, the machine could present multiple-choice questions as before, but would refuse to move on to the next question until the student had answered the presented one correctly. This simple little device was a mechanical solution to the problem educational psychologists posed for teachers when they told teachers to provide positive feedback as often as possible and as immediately as possible and then sent teachers out into an environment in which following the advice was humanly impossible!

In 1958, Skinner introduced the next generation of teaching machines designed to provide resources for the embattled teacher. Following the initial burst of enthusiasm in the late 1950s, as shown in Figure 7.1 above, for the second generation of capital equipment, teaching machines again became hard-to-find tools in the school system. Skinner's machines constituted an advance on two fronts. First, much emphasized by Skinner, they allowed students to compose answers rather than select them in the multiple-choice format. Second, unlike Pressey's presentation mode, which had no instruction but only the test, Skinner's involved instructional input as well. At least a small amount of information could be given to students before they were confronted with a question. After composing an answer to the question, students moved a lever that exposed the model correct answer. If they had answered correctly, the correct answer constituted positive feedback of the sort called for by Thorn-dike's Law of Effect and Skinner's own reinforcement theory. If not, there was a problem. A student who was wrong and who had seen the correct answer could not think through the problem again. This "second chance" had been built into Pressey's early multiple-choice format but sacrificed in Skinner's in order to allow the students to compose answers. We are now watching the third generation of capital equipment knocking at the schoolhouse door—the computer. With computers as teaching machines, the problem is solved. Computers can be programed to evaluate all sorts of input from students, allowing an infinite number of chances to get it right.

Another technology, that of video, is coming on to the educational scene. Rather than knocking at the schoolroom door, it threatens to remove the door entirely! Courses for college credit can now be taken in many communities by watching broadcast presentations at home and by sending homework assignments into the college by mail. The most famous application of broadcast technology is Sesame Street, beamed to the homes of preschoolers at least once a day. With almost every home having a television set, broadcasting is one of the least expensive media for distributing an instructional program. Now that more affluent homes are acquiring videocassette recorders and videodisc machines, viewers are able to check out instructional video programs as they would a book from their library, or even purchase video instruction for self-improvement. Many libraries have equipment for less-than-affluent viewers to use. The videocassette technology gives people new options not available to school attendees: not only can we do our lessons whenever it fits into our schedules but also we can repeat a lesson or portion of a lesson as often as desired, advantages that have always been available with books but not with classroom activities. The advent of personal computers promises to give the same options for computer-based lessons.

Television is a one-directional medium. It talks to you but it cannot listen to you. It can ask questions, but like Skinner's teaching machines, it cannot evaluate your answer. But tie your videocassette machine or your videodisc machine to your computer, and you have the technological panacea! Every student can sit in front of the greatest instructors who have at their command all the devices of motion visuals and animation. No longer merely passive viewers, students can respond to significant questions asked by the program, with the computer evaluating their answers and individually tailoring the next step. Such is the promise that engineers have created for us.

Is the world of education ready for such marvels? All that is needed to make such systems work is *software*, or as it is sometimes called, "courseware," the programs of instruction that will put the equipment to its full use. Therein lies the challenge for instructional psychologists.

Instructional technology as software

Beginning at the turn of the century, psychologists have researched how instruction should be handled in schools. However, much of this research, continuing throughout the 1930s and 1940s, took place in the laboratory and did not affect school procedures.

A surge of applications involving psychologists took place during World War II, with many of them working on training problems in military training establishments. There the outcomes of the research had better luck affecting training procedures than was true in the educational world. Other chapters in this book will pick up the activity in military and industrial psychology.

During the 1950s and 1960s, two main areas of research occurred. One of these was the sudden burst of activity creating software (programmed instruction) for Skinner's second-generation teaching machines and the "programmed" textbooks that were modeled after the machines. The second trend, heavily financed by the Office of Education and the National Science Foundation, was launched under the threat to our national pride presented by the Soviet Union's launching of Sputnik. Prodded by test results showing an increasing illiteracy in science and math in our schools, psychologists joined teams of teachers and media specialists to develop major curriculum packages to foster scientific and mathematical literacy. Among these were materials to teach mathematics, science, physics, chemistry, and biology. No longer content to tell teachers and textbook publishers how instruction should be designed, psychologists were now actively creating materials and methods for use in the schools.

In the same era, social policy also dictated a concentration of effort aimed at increasing the chances of underprivileged children to escape poverty and failure in school by participating in preschool Headstart projects. Again, psychologists were involved. All of this activity found us working as part of curriculum development committees, bringing to the teams special skills as task analysts and empirical researchers, attempting to answer questions such as: "What should be taught?" "How should it be taught?," and, when some designs had been created, "Is what has been designed working?"

■ INSTRUCTIONAL PSYCHOLOGY AS A PROFESSION

Quite a few persons who would call themselves "instructional psychologists" hold academic posts at colleges and universities, teaching courses and doing research as other professors do, while others are in the field doing instructional development, generally indistinguishable from the profession of instructional technologist. There are several pathways to becoming an instructional technologist, not all of them involving degrees in psychology. Some advanced degrees in education aim at such a specialty; some professional curricula in media (such as television, film, or computers) may include an instructional development component, and some degrees in disciplines other than psychology might specialize in instruction in that discipline. Programs aimed specifically at training people to be instructional technologists/designers/developers (all three designations can be found in the titles of such programs) exist at several universities.

Unlike some of the other specialties described in this book, there is no one professional society to which such persons uniformly belong. They can be found in the American Psychological Association, in the American Educational Research Association, in the Association for Educational Communications and Technology, in the National Society for Performance and Instruction, and in the American Society of Training Directors. Articles relevant to the profession can be found in journals of each of these societies and elsewhere. No one group has been able to establish sufficient credibility to create a credentialing system of the sort in several other applied specialties whose practitioners are based primarily in the American Psychological Association. If you were to inspect the course catalogues of the training curricula mentioned above, you would find considerable overlap but certainly not complete agreement.

Instructional psychologists may specialize in their work according to level of instruction, anywhere from preschool to college and beyond. They may be found in industrial and military training establishments, major retail stores, banks, or the Air Force Training Command. The past two decades have seen the establishment of a network of educational development centers sponsored by the National Institutes of Education where research-and-development activities attacked major problems of curriculum materials and other unmet needs in the public school system. The Children's Television Workshop employs many instructional psychologists. Some colleges and universities have a center or office dedicated to improving instruction on that specific campus, assisting their faculty to employ new media, design better evaluation methods, and revitalize their teaching. New universities dedicated to off-campus teaching and consortia of community colleges employ instructional technologists to help design broadcast and correspondence lesson materials.

In industrial training, instructional technologists can be found in many roles. A few major industrial giants, such as the American Telephone and Telegraph Company, have groups doing basic research on instruction as well as teams developing better training for jobs in the Bell telephone system. Some instructional technologists have their own corporations, serving as consultants for industry and designing programmed texts, video lessons, and computer lessons for the general market.

Instructional psychology, then, is a relatively new and somewhat diverse specialty. While the history can be traced back to the turn of the century, the feeling of a separate identity is very recent. However, instructional psychology is a specialty that investigates who is learning what under what conditions, primarily in applied settings. Although it could be difficult to distinguish instructional psychology from its psychological parent, educational psychology, one potential distinguishing characteristic is that it is applied.

■ THE SYSTEMATIC INSTRUCTIONAL DEVELOPMENT PROCESS

The ideal held by instructional designers is rarely followed exactly in the real world. Both time and costs prevent most projects from attaining such perfection. Ideally, one first determines the goals to be achieved by the system, analyzes these into clear and specific objectives, carefully determines what the students already know, and then proceeds to develop an instructional treatment that should fill the gap between what students can already do and what one wishes them to be able to do after instruction. As is true with any other engineering effort, every portion of the instructional treatment should be tried out with students and revised until it works well. This process is so rational that it seems that everyone ought to follow such steps, but in practice few projects can approach such an ideal. While the process can be divided into stages in several ways, we will divide it into four major stages.

Task analysis

The first step in designing instruction is to define carefully the knowledge and skills that a learner should exhibit when successfully taught. Attempts to define "the educated citizen" are beyond what most instructional psychologists feel called upon to do, except in their roles as educated citizens or as members of school boards. The skills chosen for analysis are at a more manageable level, from areas such as verbal sophistication (reading and writing skills), mathematical competencies, scientific knowledge and attitudes, vocational skills, and so forth. In recent years a major area of concentration at all levels of education has been on thinking or problem-solving skills, competencies that seem to be absolutely crucial for being "good at" any of the usual subjects that are taught in schools and colleges (Markle, 1981; Pellegrino & Glaser, 1980).

Notice that task analysis has nothing to do with deciding what to talk about (Gagne, 1974). Task analysis is an analysis of what learners ought to be able to do. The analyst might be looking at and cataloguing all the different activities (tasks) that a person does while doing a job, for instance diagnosing and repairing a television set, filling a prescription in a pharmacy, filling a tooth, driving an automobile or tank, flying an airplane, making a hamburger, and so forth. Or the analyst might be looking at what the well-trained person does when solving word problems in arithmetic, proving a geometry theorem, or constructing an essay in history. The concentration is on the skilled behavior—the outward physical responses people do to operate things or the inner information-processing activities that go on before the analyst can see "answers" or steps in solving problems.

A case study (Short, 1973) may clarify how task analysis contributes to training. The job for which people were being trained was a craft in the telephone company involving 40 different job assignments. Previous trainees had been given a course stressing the electronic fundamentals underlying the long-distance system. However, even the best trainees (defined by test scores in this course) learned how to build and repair such systems on the job. Rather than improve the course so that more trainees would get higher scores in it, the job analysts went out into the field and observed skilled craftsmen at work. These observations, gathered in five-minute segments, were analyzed and classified so that the job analysts could detail what the conditions were under which some activity began, what the worker actually did, and what outcome indicated successful task completion. From these data, the job analysts could then determine what to teach the trainees.

This project took two years, cost $200,000, and required considerable skills and problem solving from the analysts. But the project, when completed, reduced the time required for training from nine weeks to nine days, which saves the company over two million dollars per year in wages paid to workers. The difference between the old course and the new one, developed after the project, was not a difference in training methods but rather a difference in training objectives. This change in objectives was based on the task analysis.

A similar anecdote indicates the applicability of job analysis to school-related tasks. Landa (1976), a Russian instructional psychologist, reported an interaction with a teacher who was concerned about a bright student who knew the geometry theorems, but could not use them to solve problems. When

Landa wondered why the student couldn't figure it out, the teacher responded that the student couldn't figure it out because he couldn't figure it out. Unfortunately, the actual thinking operations that occur when a skilled person solves a problem are, first of all, probably discovered by trial and error. Second, these thinking operations because of their familiarity are probably almost unconscious. Third, these thinking operations are rarely taught to students even in courses that involve problem solving as the major task. The Russian geometry student was in the same position as were the telephone craftsmen described above when asked to construct telephone circuits after a course in electronic theory. While analysis of what teachers and textbooks say is an appropriate way of describing what can be known, task analysis describes what students ought to be able to do (Tieman & Markle, 1978).

As you might expect, our knowledge of what goes on when people wrestle with intellectual problems is far from complete. In her recent review of instructional psychology, Resnick (1981) noted: "A richly detailed picture of the ways in which people perform many of the tasks central to education is beginning to emerge. . . . The task remains to consider how useful all of this might be to those concerned with the practical problems of education." Similar points can be found in other papers by cognitive psychologists working on school-related learning (e.g., Calfee, 1981).

What is the outcome of task analysis? Task analysis enables an instructional developer to arrive at a set of objectives describing what the competent person is able to do. It seems intuitively obvious that a teacher, textbook author, or designer of a lesson cannot make rational decisions about what to teach unless the outcome is clear, but school systems have a long history of "covering" the subject matter in courses without being very clear about what students are supposed to accomplish. Robert Mager, whose early book *Preparing Instructional Objectives* (1962) is widely read, later developed a marvelously descriptive term for the way most schools and colleges express their objectives. He called them "Fuzzies." Example "fuzzies" are "be a good citizen," "have pride in work," and "appreciate" any art form such as music, painting, or dance. While these are worthy goals, they require analysis so that we may translate them into specific objectives. These specific objectives will then allow an instructor to know when students have achieved them and how such achievement is to be evaluated.

Criterion measures

Even though making judgments may not be simple, task analysis makes the procedures for judging whether learners have obtained objectives clear. A technology for developing the tests with which you are most familiar, aptitude and norm-referenced achievement tests, has existed for a long time. Criterion tests are not so well understood. If we want to find out if a learner can change spark-plugs (a specific objective), the procedure for measuring this competence is fairly obvious. It is not at all obvious how to measure competence in important educational skills such as problem solving in physics or historical knowledge or essay writing (Gagné & Beard, 1978).

The problem for designers of criterion tests is simple to state but enormously complex to solve. We need to be able to specify the *universe* (all) of the situations that the learner should be able to handle. A criterion score is supposed to tell how much of this universe a learner has mastered. Take the sparkplug example and ask: How many different machines will your learner be able to handle? Only one automobile? All makes of American cars five years old or less? All cars, American and foreign, of any age? Tractors too? And so forth. The technology on which most of the tests used in schools is based does not face this problem of specifying the total universe. What scores on these tests tell you is how much you know compared to others in some group (the "norm" your score is referenced to). Thus, if you know that you read at the 11th grade level, you know that your score is like the average student in the 11th grade. The score does not tell you what portion of reading skills are yet to be mastered. Thus, if we have determined that the average student completing driver education can change sparkplugs on two makes of cars, we can say you are above average if you can handle three different makes. But how much more is there to learn to become a champion sparkplug changer? That is what a criterion test score attempts to make clear (Hively, 1974).

Developing procedures to achieve goals

Once goals are carefully defined and ways of measuring them developed, the first issue faced in many training departments is whether instruction is the appropriate solution. If people are not doing what they should be doing, do they need training? Engineering psychologists and industrial psychologists consider other possibilities. If a pilot cannot handle all the information provided in a new cockpit layout, perhaps the layout could be simplified. If there is too much to remember and people are making mistakes, perhaps a manual could be provided. Training is only one solution to a problem.

Often a task analyst will find that the basic problem on the job is not lack of knowledge but rather lack of feedback on how well the worker is performing. A famous case was reported in *Business Week* (December 18, 1971). Workers at Emery Air Freight had to decide for each package the company was shipping whether to put the package in a container with lots of others or whether to ship it separately, which cost a lot more. The workers thought they were making the right decision most of the time, but an analyst found they were right less than half the time. A feedback system was designed with workers scoring themselves and with their supervisors providing praise for improvement and good performance. In a short period of time, performance was almost perfect. It seems apparent that these workers knew what to do, but did not seem to do it well when no feedback or rewards existed. Sending these workers back to school for more training would have been a waste of money and time and would not have solved the problem.

Many professionals working in industrial training departments think of themselves as "performance problem solvers" rather than purely instructional developers because so many of the problems they are called upon to solve resemble the Emery Air Freight case. Mager and Pipe (1970) suggested a simple question to ask to resolve this question: Could the worker do it if his or her life depended on it? If the answer is yes, then training is not the solution. Performance problem solvers in industry and behavior modification specialists in school systems are engineers in a certain sense. They attempt to redesign the social system or the learning situation in such a way that feedback and positive consequences occur when appropriate behavior occurs. However, our society tends to work otherwise. For example, with regard to driving behavior, our current system waits until you, the driver, do something wrong and then delivers punishment in the form of police summons, arrests, tickets, and fines. However, this system is a human design and could be changed. Think about how you would make a positive consequence system for driving behavior.

Job aids are another technique performance problem solvers have developed to avoid instruction. One of the reasons people cannot perform adequately is that necessary information is not stored in their memories. While analyzing a task, we can raise the question of whether it needs to be stored in memory or is there an easier way of designing the task so that memory would not be required. All of us are used to reference materials such as dictionaries, almanacs, and encyclopedias for facts we have forgotten or never knew. Similarly, manuals remind an operator how to use some infrequently used function of complex machines. Also, computers make tremendous stores of information available to workers.

Because most jobs require a certain level of efficiency, the skill in designing job aids is that of arranging for the most-needed information to be "at your fingertips." A simple example is the reference you will find on many secretaries' desks containing the "100 most often misspelled words." A big dictionary would be inefficient for these simple facts although just as effective.

A recent research topic for instructional psychologists is the area of "document design." Laws have recently been passed insisting that documents designed to be used by consumers ought to be usable by consumers. A familiar example of the need for this law is the inability of the average person to understand the manual that accompanies income tax forms. It is not clear what decisions the tax preparer has to make nor the order in which steps should be taken; in the task analysis mentioned above, these are the conditions (if such and such is the case) and the action (then do so and so). Explaining in normal prose a complicated series of decisions in which the next step to be taken depends on the answer to the question at the previous step takes a master prose writer. Many designers prefer an algorithm expressed as a flowchart to make the thinking process clear to a user. Algorithms do force us to be brief and clear and to get things in order (Lewis & Horabin, 1977).

As a simple illustration, the first few decisions an umpire has to take into account when the pitcher throws the ball in baseball are shown as an algorithm in Figure 7.2. If you know baseball, you will be able to see that the umpire has still more decisions to make at each of the lowest points before calling the event a strike, ball, out, or foul. For instance, coming down the leftmost track (Was the ball hit? No; Was the pitch good? No), umpires must still decide whether the batter swung at it—yes or no. A writer who had to write a training manual for umpires would most likely try to tell readers what "strikes" and "fouls" and "balls" are. Such prose tends to weave in and out of these simple decisions in ways that readers simply cannot follow. Getting lost in such prose has happened to all of us, including the best readers. Translating prose into algorithms in complex subject matters such as medical diagnosis and income tax regulations is one of the most challenging tasks instructional designers face.

A decision chart such as the mini-flowchart in Figure 7.2 can be used as a reference once the learner has mastered the key concepts in it or simply as a way to make the structure of the task more obvious while the learner commits the procedures to memory. It should be apparent that a person with no experience in baseball could not use the algorithm in Figure 7.2. Key concepts such as "good pitch" would have to be learned first. Obviously a real umpire must commit these decisions to memory. Any umpire who had to pull such a crib sheet out in the middle of a game would be booed off the field!

Many teachers feel they have "taught" when they have told students what they know. Likewise many students feel they have "learned" when they can recite what the teacher has said. Suppose you had memorized this:

> *strike:* a pitched ball which is (a) struck at but missed; (b) fairly delivered but not struck at; (c) hit foul but not caught (unless there are already two strikes); . . .
> (Webster's *New World Dictionary*).

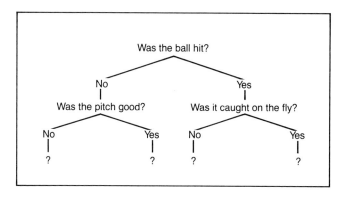

FIGURE 7.2   The first two stages of deciding how to call an event in baseball—the umpire's algorithm.

Buried in that definition is the very complex sequence of decisions underlying the algorithm in Figure 7.2. The logic is difficult to unlock as is true of most stated rules and definitions. In (c), for instance, there are four decisions: the ball was hit AND the ball was not caught AND the ball's track was foul AND there are fewer than two strikes already counted. Not written out for you in so many words is the implication in the definition that a strike is (a) or (b) or (c). The significance of programmed instruction derives from the fact that instructional phenomena are analyzed carefully and described algorithmically (Landa, 1976).

Few instructional programs now in use in schools and colleges represent the level of sophistication Landa was talking about. There is a great deal of analytical and developmental research to be done. Notice also how different this kind of programming is from that of the scholar or teacher who sits down to write as clearly as possible what is known in a discipline. It is the student's thought processes, the sequence of decisions made in solving problems, that the designer must search for and build into the instruction. (See Pellegrino and Glaser, 1980, for an example.)

To build instruction that will enable students to solve problems, the designer must determine all the skills and knowledge each student must have to succeed and then determine a logical order in which to develop both at once. Resnik, Wang, and Kaplan (1973) published a detailed analysis of early arithmetic skills that showed the progression from simple skills to complex skills and the order in which they had to be taught. Some of the relations between skills and knowledge to be mastered first and the ones to come later are pretty obvious. For instance, if a child is to count a set of objects (the objective), being able to recite the numbers in order is obviously a prerequisite bit of knowledge. But some children who can recite the numbers correctly still cannot count in an orderly fashion. What, Resnick asked, was the missing skill? As she defined it, it was being able to "synchronize touching an object and saying a word." Children who had not mastered this skill could not count in an orderly fashion even though they could recite the numbers. Likewise, of course, children who had the synchronization skill but did not know the numbers could not count either. Both skills are necessary in order to meet the counting objective. The knowledge (reciting the numbers) was a standard part of early arithmetic lessons, while the skill (synchronizing) was not.

Examples of this kind of analytical insight occur in many papers by instructional psychologists attempting to figure out why some students are not learning. The discovery of missing skills that are not being taught challenges an old principle in the educational system that we must wait until the learner is "ready" for some lesson. Too many learners do not seem to get ready for some of the more complicated objectives. Rather than wait, or permit learners to fail, why not discover the missing prerequisite skills and teach them directly?

Anyone who develops instruction must come to grips with sequencing—some sort of logical order has to be used. Research studies of the sort done by

Resnick and her colleagues go beyond sequencing on the basis of what "feels" right or seems logical. The process requires close observation of learner breakdowns, analysis of potential missing components, development of instruction to teach such components, and finally demonstration that the solution works, i.e., that further breakdowns do not occur. This type of research in instructional psychology goes beyond the describing of natural science and into the prescribing of engineered solutions to achieve goals (Glaser, 1976).

Tryout and revision

In discussing his generation of teaching machines, Skinner (1958) noted: "Whether good programming is to remain an art or to become a scientific technology, it is reassuring to know that there is a final authority—the student. An unexpected advantage of machine instruction has proved to be the feedback to the *programmer.*" Shortly thereafter, Gilbert (1960) put it more bluntly: "Think of the process as an exploratory experiment in which you do not know what the effective variables are. . . . Take your first crude effort to the student. Remember, he is going to teach you. This student cannot fail. If he doesn't get where you want him to go, you have failed. Try something else." Two decades later, a great deal is known about good programming; additionally, instructional design is far beyond a first crude effort. However, the empirical process of taking the draft to the learner is still a necessary one (Markle, 1978).

Those who have discussed the tryout and revision process (Markle, 1967) are operating with a set of intertwined assumptions expressed in the definition of instructional technology given in the early part of this chapter. First, you have a clear goal (not a "fuzzy") in mind, which you have defined with enough specificity to be able to measure its attainment. Second, you hold yourself accountable for reaching that goal—it is not the student who will fail. If an engineer designs a bridge that collapses, we don't blame the bridge! Third, you are dealing with a lawful process, human learning, about which we may not know everything but at least we know enough to get us started on the design process.

The first phase of testing an instructional design involves close observation of individual students, if at all practical. Its purpose is to gather as much detailed data as humanly possible on exactly what is going on in each student's head at each stage of instruction. Whether sitting in front of a computer, or watching a prototype of a videotape, or reading written materials, students are doing most of the interesting activities covertly—in their heads. That is where the "ideas" for possible answers occur, where decisions that a phrase or paragraph has to be read (or listened to) again are made, and other decisions of interest to programmers trying to guide thought processes. Designers work with individual students to find out what is going on during the instructional episode. Young children have trouble verbalizing what the problems are, but from older students much helpful information and solid suggestions for improvement arise. Of course, these students must understand their job as helping make the materials better rather than as a measure of their own "intelligence." Even at a distance from the designers, students can be extremely helpful, as Nathensen and Henderson (1980) found in testing materials to be used at Britain's Open University. The Open University mails out course texts and broadcasts lectures and demonstrations over television and radio, making it difficult for programmers to get the feedback about student problems that teachers usually get in the classroom. Although trying out materials under these conditions is difficult, Nathensen and Henderson found that students were willing to write out lengthy critiques of the materials, willing to admit where they had problems, and often able to give very fine suggestions on how to improve the instruction. The two investigators were able to show that revisions of the instruction based on this feedback from the first small group of students did indeed measurably improve the workability of the college course in terms of how well the next group of students did with the materials.

Tryout is an empirical process. When data indicate problems with the instruction, the designer tries "something else," whatever it is, but this new approach also needs to be tried out with students to be sure that it is indeed an improvement. In theory, instruction should be tested, revised, retested, and revised again, with the cycle repeating itself until the outcome—what students learn and their attitude toward the instruction—is satisfactory. In the early 1960s, the Air Force Training Command had a policy that their programmers would keep at the process of tryout and revision until 90 percent of the learners achieved a score of 90 percent or better on the criterion performance test. Such rigid standards are usually unworkable, as this one proved to be. In some cases, such as pilot training, competence needs to be at the 100 percent level before the trainee is allowed to fly a multi-million dollar plane. In other cases, some of the less costly errors can be tolerated while the new worker gains a higher level of skill on the job.

An interesting sidelight on tryout procedures is provided by psychologists testing out Sesame Street ideas. Because a youngster who is not watching the show carefully will not learn much from it, the early drafts of lessons are tested first for their ability to hold attention. Children watch these drafts in playrooms where there is plenty to do if they get bored. If a child turns away, the designer tries again.

Early tryouts are designed to provide the kinds of information needed to revise the instruction until it works under very controlled conditions. A second stage of testing usually follows. This two-stage process should remind you of the sort of product testing cycles followed by many industrial concerns researching new technology, new drugs, and so forth. A new drug will be tried out on animals and/or human volunteers before it is tried out in the field on "real" patients, a second stage that precedes its release to all doctors. In the second stage, an instructional evaluator is concerned with collecting data to show what the instruction package accomplishes in ordinary use in the classroom. Product testing of this sort is still relatively rare in education, although instances of it occur in developing instruction in industrial, military, and medical training. Some massive evaluation studies have been done of major curricula such as Sesame Street and various Headstart projects, as well as other curricula mentioned in this chapter. Evaluation research is a major professional activity of many instructional psychologists.

■ INSTRUCTIONAL MANAGEMENT SYSTEMS

Instructional psychologists have been involved in redesigning general procedures in school systems as well as doing research on intellectual skills and designing instructional materials to achieve goals. In most educational systems at present, time is the primary unit of measurement: you spend so many hours in your English course, you spend so many years in elementary school, you need so many hours of credits to graduate or to get into college. What each student learns in this predetermined amount of time is permitted to vary, at least up to a point. It should be obvious how drastic the change has to be from the way the educational system is now designed if we change the primary unit of measurement to achievement of specific objectives. Individual progress plans, in which each student works as long as necessary to reach a criterion of success, have been tried again and again since the turn of the century in one or another forward-looking school system. They have yet to become the "conventional system."

The problems that a true achievement-oriented system creates are enormous. One problem is finding enough instructional materials that work well enough. Each student is going to be at a different point in the sequence of lessons, and teachers cannot pick up the pieces the way they do now when everyone is having a problem at the same moment. Another problem is keeping the less-motivated student hard at work; when a test can be postponed until each student feels ready, some will coast. A further problem, much in the headlines in the past few years, is what to do about students who fail to come up to the achievement standard, those students who would have been passed on to the next grade or allowed to graduate with poor records. More resources are needed to help such students achieve the higher standards.

Instructional systems in schools

Several recently developed instructional systems appear to be working well in school systems that have adopted them. Glaser and his colleagues at the University of Pittsburgh, Klausmeier and his colleagues at the University of Wisconsin, and several other such teams have shepherded large numbers of psychologists, graduate assistants, and others in developing individualized instruction for a whole elementary school system from first to eighth grade. In each case, these scholars have been involved in redesign from the ground up.

The materials the students use are redesigned; testing systems must be developed; what teachers do in their job is redesigned; the way classrooms are arranged is redesigned (30 students facing a teacher at immovable desks has to go!); the kinds of teacher aides and the work they do are redesigned. As clearly stated in the definition of instructional technology, human resources are as much a fundamental part of the redesign of the total system as are those other resources, the new machines and new methods. But what they do is quite different.

From experience, it seems clear that a single teacher working in a single course, or even a few working together, are going to face insurmountable problems introducing individualized instruction in one small part of a time-based system. Classes are too heterogeneous for one set of materials or one approach to work with all students. Different students work at different rates in different courses. To guarantee success for all, the whole system has to change.

Instructional systems at the college level

Attempts have been made at the college level to introduce a mastery approach, following the suggestions of Fred Keller, a well-known behavioral psychologist. Keller had a chance to design a whole college system when he was a consultant for a newly founded university in Brazil. His system, sometimes called the Keller Plan and sometimes the "Personalized System of Instruction," involves: (1) students working at their own pace, coming for tests when ready; (2) mastery of each unit of instruction before starting the next; (3) the use of text and study questions as the main source of instruction, with lectures only for motivational purposes and only occasionally; and (4) the use of student (peer) proctors to manage the tests and test scoring and to give tutorial help and personal interaction for every student in the typically large introductory course. Keller suggested that automation (the machinery in instructional technology) was a luxury and concentrated most of his thinking on arranging the human resources so that all students would experience a lot of success and considerable "personal-social interaction" with other human beings while mastering a course. Social interaction is a worthy goal and, when so stated, the system can be designed to be sure that it is reached along with student mastery of the cognitive content of a course.

Research studies on the effectiveness of the Keller Plan (Keller, 1966) appeared in many journals devoted to studies of teaching in physics, chemistry, and other disciplines. Most of these studies compared the achievement of classes taught by the Keller method with other classes taught by conventional methods. While the research generally supported Keller's proposals, widespread adoption of this method has not yet occurred.

Future research directions

With the relatively recent explosion of communication technology, the horizon is full of promises to revise the school system, along with the promised revision in the way we shop, bank, and perform many other daily duties. The most fundamental assumption that students will go to the place where instruction is available is being challenged. As transportation costs go up and communication costs go down, it seems obvious that the instruction could go to the students more cheaply. Correspondence courses have existed for many decades, with lonely persons struggling to maintain the motivation to complete each lesson and send in their test results. At the preschool level, Sesame Street is an example of what could be done to reach a large number of students without the expense of building new classrooms and hiring new teachers. But parents expect to have their three-year-old underfoot. It is not so obvious that the average family would consider it a useful change in their routines to have all their children at home getting their lessons through television and computers! These are issues we have yet to face. With adults, particularly adults already working full time, sending well-prepared lessons through the mails, over the broadcast media, and to homes via videotapes and audiotapes makes sense and, if well thought out, can be a considerable success.

There is a drastic change of purpose occurring in education at the present. You can easily find signs of conflict in news stories all over the country. Students have sued schools because they have graduated without basic reading skills. Students are being held back because they have not achieved a set level of competence. It seems that a new educational purpose is emerging: namely, to cause each student to reach at least a minimum level of mastery of skills needed to cope with modern society. Traditional methods and materials, designed to achieve the purpose of transmitting information content from scholar to student, do not work well for this new purpose. When a total educational system needs redesign, the promise of instructional technology holds forth a systematic approach to making education more efficient and more effective. Instructional psychologists are devoting long hours to the enormous problem of trying to make specific the exact nature of thinking and performance that constitute the outcomes of good instruction. Such research, however, is rarely published as a journal article or a research report. Instead, the result is a new instructional system or a change in practice in a real world teaching situation.

■ CONCLUSION

Instructional psychology is a broad area with individuals performing varied tasks. As an application of psychology, it is relatively new although its roots go back to some of our well-known predecessors. Some instructional scientists prefer the academic life, searching for clear answers to questions raised by the need to teach specific content and skills and passing these answers on to the instructional developers. The scientists need all the research skills that any other academic psychologists needs. The instructional developers usually work in teams with subject matter experts, teachers, and, in the evaluation phase, with students. Expertise in the analytical models and especially in writing are terribly important if the resulting products are to be valid and at the same time interesting. Instruction is certainly one of the more challenging areas to which psychologists can bring their expertise.

■ SUGGESTED READINGS

Davis, R. H., Alexander, L. T., & Yelon, S. L. (1974). *Learning system design.* New York: McGraw-Hill.

> This well-written text emphasizes practical applications for people intending to be instructional developers. It draws from the authors' experience with developing adult learning systems, and would be of interest to anyone going step-by-step through the process of instructional development.

Gagné, R. M. (1970). *The conditions of learning* (2nd ed.). New York: Holt, Rinehart & Winston.

> Historically, this is one of the most influential books in the field, describing a theoretical approach to types of learning, from the most simple to the most complex cognitive outcomes. The guiding generalization is that there are different kinds of learning which require different approaches to instruction. While this text requires some background in psychology, it would be interesting to an upper level undergraduate student.

Mager, R. F. (1975). *Preparing instructional objectives* (2nd ed.). Belmont, CA: Fearon Publishers.

> Probably the most widely read in the field, this text is a humorous and effective example of branching programming. It teaches what a usable objective should look like while subtly informing the reader via an underlying philosophy that you can't teach if you don't know what you are trying to accomplish, that students can't learn if they don't know what to expect, and that the whole educational experience is better for everyone if teachers and students work toward explicit goals.

Skinner, B. F. (1968). *The technology of teaching.* New York: Appleton-Century-Crofts.

> This book is a collection of Skinner's published papers on the potential of teaching machines including a theoretical background from which his ideas for education developed. Since most of these articles were addressed to educators and scholars in other disciplines, this book would be understandable and interesting to the average undergraduate student.

Tiemann, P. W., & Markle, S. M. (1983). *Analyzing instructional content* (2nd ed.). Champaign, IL: Stipes.

> This is an active-response workbook designed for teachers and others who need to develop skills in analyzing their subject matters in order to develop good objectives, lesson plans, and evaluation schemes. It would be suitable for an advanced undergraduate or graduate student.

DOUGLAS K. CANDLAND

THE TEACHING OF PSYCHOLOGY

■ INTRODUCTION

Psychology is taught in a variety of settings, ranging from the newspaper or magazine article to postdoctoral training in universities and medical schools. Psychology is taught by persons with varied preparations: Those teaching courses called psychology may have taken an undergraduate program with a major in education (as is often true of secondary and two-year college teachers), or they may have studied psychology exclusively and have never taken a course in education (as is likely to be true of college and university teachers of psychology). Psychology may be taught in the public schools; in a college or university; in a medical, law, nursing, architecture, or business school; or in a program designed especially to train and educate those who apply psychology in any of the many ways described in other chapters of this book.

Although the teaching of psychology, as an applied specialty within psychology, may seem to differ from other applied specialties described in this text, there are certainly many similarities. The teaching of psychology is often undertaken in contexts in which its applications are stressed. In teaching psychology to nurses, for example, the uses of psychology in working with people who are ill may be emphasized. In law, the teaching of psychology with an applied emphasis may focus on the applications of psychology within the courtroom (for example, in jury selection). Psychologists as a group have had a strong interest in the teaching of psychology. One of the pioneer divisions in the American Psychological Association (Division 2) is composed of those psychologists who have interests in the teaching of psychology. The teaching of psychology now occurs in broader contexts, often those with an applied emphasis.

175

The purpose of this chapter is to describe four places in which psychology is taught (the high school, the two-year college, the college or university, the professional school), to consider the duties typical of teaching in each setting, to describe the educational requisites for being considered for a position in each setting, and to discuss what can be guessed about the future. In order to provide firsthand information on teaching in each of the settings, the chapter includes a description of "typical" activities written by a teacher active in each of these settings. The chapter then considers ways in which psychology is now being taught and suggests ways in which the teacher of psychology may influence the goals and achievements of education.

Goldman (1983), among many others, has noted that there have been two approaches to the teaching of psychology. In the first, psychology is taught as a scientific discipline with emphasis on how psychology acquires its information. In the second approach, the teaching of psychology is intended to help the student in matters of practical concern such as information on sexual practices, individual and group relationships, child-rearing, and citizenship.

Variations of these different views of education are commonplace and not limited to psychology. Those who design and administer the curricula disagree as to what should be taught to whom. Should one teach physics, or one of its practical uses, plumbing? Chemistry, or a practical use, following recipes? The reading of literature, or the writing of it? Speaking a foreign language, or reading its literature? Is it more important to appreciate the problems of evaluating psychological data or to attempt to apply psychological principles to our lives?

One's answer depends on one's view of the purpose of education, a topic regrettably beyond the point of this chapter, but if a comment is permitted it is this: The purpose of teaching is not to gain control over the mind of another, to force the mind to this conclusion or that, but the reverse—to present ideas previously unthought by the student; to suggest ways of thinking, whether or not they are contrary to established thought; and to encourage the mind to explore its own reasons, emotions, and memories. If these goals be those of the teacher, the student may be helped to see applications, to judge options, the better to make choices, but never to be indoctrinated. The subject matter of psychology is ideal for the training of the mind, for it offers hypotheses of obvious interest—those regarding our own behavior—and methods of acquiring, measuring, testing, and evaluating data.

■ THE TEACHER'S ENVIRONMENT

We now review the chief situations in which teachers of psychology perform in order to understand better the nature of the work required of the successful teacher. Recognize that these descriptions are but generalities: There is no single person who performs each of these tasks to the degree described. The purpose is to describe, by emphasizing the teachers' work, aspects of the profession that may not be evident to the non-teacher.

The secondary school teacher

The teaching of psychology remains adjunct to the main purposes of secondary schools. The major curricula in secondary schools—college preparatory, technical, and commercial—are not perceived as requiring specialized teaching in psychology. In secondary schools in which psychology is taught, the subject is almost always offered as an optional course, emphasis is placed on the application of psychology to personal life, the scientific aspects are not thought to be so important as teaching self-understanding and social skills, and some teachers are unlikely to have had college training in psychology equivalent to that of a college graduate who was a major in psychology.

Principles of psychology are often taught in other course work in the secondary, and sometimes the primary, school curriculum. For example, psychological discoveries concerning how the mind interprets perceptions such as illusions; the different functions of the two hemispheres of the brain; discoveries regarding how people and animals learn, forget, and organize what they have learned; and the physiological aspects of human emotional experience are topics that are taught frequently in the secondary school, perhaps as biology, perhaps as social science.

Training of the secondary school teacher • In the United States, the certification of secondary school teachers is a process decided by the state legislatures. In some states, decisions as to certification are made by departments of education within certain colleges and universities while in others the decision is made by a body appointed by the state legislature to interpret state laws regarding education. In general, the elementary school teacher has taken instruction from a department of education amounting to approximately 30 to 40 percent of the total college course work, not including a lengthy period during the senior year when the student undertakes classroom teaching under the supervision of a certified teacher and the college's department of education. The remainder of the course work includes the electives in English, science, the humanities, and social sciences generally required by American colleges for a degree.

The person preparing for secondary school teaching will take fewer courses within the department of education and a larger number within the field in which the student wishes to teach; e.g., English, history, science. In many states, graduates are certified to teach in broadly defined fields, such as social science. For this person to receive certification to teach social science, the person will have studied, for example, some aspects of economics, sociology, history, philosophy, psychology, geography, political science, or government. It is most likely that the student will have taken a number of these courses at the introductory level only and unlikely that any subject will have been studied in depth. This is so because the certification is for social science in general and not for a particular social science.

In most states, the field of psychology is not certified as a separate discipline (as are English, science, and physical education, for example) thereby requiring those whose primary interest is in teaching psychology to prepare themselves for certification in another field. Although psychologists have pleaded for a separate certification in psychology for those who wish to teach this field as a specialty, only a few states have approved the request. Nonetheless, the quality of the teaching of psychology in the high schools can be excellent, although much depends upon the attitude of the school administration toward the qualities they seek in teachers and in the views of the community, students, and school administrators as to whether psychology should be taught as a science or as a means of aiding social relations.

What the secondary school teacher does ▪ It is unlikely that the secondary school teacher is able to teach psychology exclusively. Usually only one course is offered, an introductory course, and facilities are rarely available in secondary schools for the introduction of laboratory work or demonstrations involving equipment. The teacher most often teaches psychology along with, perhaps, government, history, philosophy, English, or physical education.

The discipline of psychology has natural connections to a number of fields of inquiry. Some examples would be biology to physiological psychology and sensation and perception, economics and management to social psychology, mathematics and computers to psychological statistics, and social sciences and personality theories to social psychology. If one is able to consider the principles, practice, and findings of psychology as a core, with relationships to other disciplines serving as an exchange of ideas and discoveries beneficial to psychology and the other fields, psychology may be seen as having a place in the curriculum that is at once unique in subject matter and comprehensive in spirit.

In order to describe the task of the teacher, Ms. Len McCord, who teaches high school in Des Moines, Iowa, has provided us with some thoughts about her work as well as some sample hours from her day (Box 8.1).

In recent years, the number of school-age children has been fewer than in the previous decades, leading to there being fewer positions available in secondary school teaching. Some analysts argue that it is foolish to base one's career choice on present circumstances: Because fewer teachers are now being trained implies that there will be a shortage in the future. It would appear that the teaching of the social sciences is being taken more seriously by educational authorities presently than has been true in the past. Should this trend continue, the person who is well trained and capable of teaching more than a single subject matter is likely to be chosen when school systems face the twin demands of greater student interest in the social sciences and the lack of teachers trained

---

B O X 8.1   ON BEING A HIGH SCHOOL PSYCHOLOGY TEACHER

LEN McCORD

A FEW CONSIDERATIONS ON BECOMING A HIGH SCHOOL TEACHER OF PSYCHOLOGY

While a decision to enter this field is laudable, the prospective teacher must keep in mind that the trend of marked increases in enrollment by high school seniors and juniors in psychology courses over the last decade is circumvented by the growing surplus of secondary school teachers in general and by the fact that some states require only one course in psychology as preparation for teaching it or none at all. Full-time teachers of psychology are few. In some areas, the counselor counsels half the day then teaches half-time psychology or sociology. In other areas, the course is contained within the social studies department.

For all intents and purposes the instructor is the course. Most schools don't have required course outlines that identify the major concepts you are expected to cover. Will the class be college preparatory, average track, or a dumping ground for students of low motivation? Usually the new teacher must adapt to the existing students, then slowly upgrade the course, a task that is harder than it may seem.

Beyond considering grade or IQ level, the new teacher must make a basic decision about the nature of the material itself. Will the course be science oriented? Will it be an applied self-knowledge course? Will it be an eclectic overview of the discipline or will it focus on the major teachings of one model? Will the teacher incorporate a science laboratory format occasionally into the classroom-lecture model? How much career education will be presented (required in some states)? Will the teacher develop student experimental work and compete in local science fairs? Will the teacher attempt psychodramas and other role-playing skits in class? Will students and teacher, alike, produce filmstrips and slides for class demonstrations?

Teachers have been criticized for the type of grading systems they have adopted in the past. This area can be of considerable concern, unless the new teacher protects himself/herself from charges of favoritism or subjectivity. The best possible solution is the setting of criteria for each assignment. The more subjectivity in your grading, the more open to criticism from administrators, parents, and students. The assigning of total point values is one method a teacher can use to protect themselves. Students consistently think their grades are higher than they really are.

For all practical purposes, two people sit in the same classroom seat. One is a human being that deserves your respect and concern, a person you relate to as another person. The other personality is someone for whom you must keep a number score in your grade book, someone that is a series of numbers that represents a percentage of possible points. You don't give this person points; they earn their score through a variety of quizzes, projects, and discussion. The grade book belongs to the students, not the teacher. Always have easy access for the students so they know where they stand on total points. There should be no surprises at the nine weeks or semester grading. This practice lessens student anxiety and graphically shows those students who don't keep up with assignments what a disastrous effect it is having on their grade. The grade book is open to all students.

Discipline is probably one of the most important potential pitfalls for beginning teachers and unfortunately very rarely covered in education courses. Make yourself aware from

BOX 8.1 *(Continued)*

the beginning of all school rules contained in the discipline handbook. As a new teacher you will be tested by every student. Most, even the "good" kids, get a charge out of hassling new teachers in discipline settings, primarily because they have been rewarded for it in the past. As a symbol of authority, the sight of you in a confused or ignorant state is quite pleasurable. Once you get a reputation for being a pushover you will be taken advantage of by everyone. This doesn't mean you need to adopt a fascist policy. What this means is that you need to know what the rules are and make a decision ahead of time on how you will handle common situations as they arise. When in doubt send students to the vice principal in charge of discipline. This lets everyone know you mean business, particularly on fuzzy points you would rather not handle yourself. Discuss difficult situations with department members.

Whatever grading, theoretical model, or discipline procedures are chosen, guard the reputation of your course well. Sometimes the public views a psychology course and its instructor as a little kinky from the beginning. Don't give fuel to irresponsible rumors of tortured animals, hordes of sobbing students (the material was so intense), or "perverted" sex surveys (some communities feel any survey about attitudes on physical contact to be perverted).

Circumvent some of these problems by keeping your principal informed on class projects and the subject matter covered. He or she has to defend you if trouble arises.

SELECTED HOURS FROM AN ORDINARY DAY

Every day is a new challenge to the high school teacher. The schedule of classes can give basic structure to the time management problems faced by all teachers. Organization is very important. Without it, you cannot possibly keep up with your work unless you enjoy correcting tests at 3:00 A.M. Time budgeting becomes an all-important duty to the teacher.

Teachers are expected to report to the building by 7:45 A.M. The day ends at 3:30 and teachers can leave between 3:45 and 4:00 depending on duties.

Before school ▪ (1) Arrive ten minutes early; it's your turn to fill the department coffee pot. (2) Write agenda for the day on board.

First period ▪ 8:00–8:55, Hall Supervision. (1) Make several rounds of the building looking for any unauthorized individuals in building. (2) All students without passes or adults without office visitor pass are to be taken to the vice principal. (3) If possible find filmstrip projector not returned to audiovisual room for today's use (signed up a week ago, first choice is yours). (4) Pick up attendance cards from all doors at 8:30 during second round of building. (5) Escort tardy students to office. (6) Check bathrooms on each wing, first and second stories. (7) Break up morning cigarette group in girl's bathroom. (8) Take offenders to office and fill out discipline report. (9) Pick up filmstrip for today in library.

Second period ▪ 9:00–9:55. (1) Take attendance and lunch count. (2) Record number of students. Admit girl absent yesterday. (3) Hand-deliver attendance card to office because of student theft of cards in your hall. (4) Lecture for 30 minutes on operant conditioning and include class demonstration. (5) Pass out filmstrip worksheet to fill out while teacher runs machine. (6) Show 15-minute filmstrip of B. F. Skinner to reinforce lecture. (7) Ten-minute oral quiz over classical conditioning includes 5-minute correction time. (8) Collect filmstrip worksheet and place in grade book for correction during planning period.

Fifth period ▪ 12:30–1:15. (1) Find out you forgot afternoon classes were shortened to 45 minutes due to unexpected pep assembly. (2) Make decision to attempt to cover lecture, demonstrations, and quiz in 45 minutes and correct quizzes yourself over weekend. (3) Band members will leave 10 minutes before everyone else and miss quiz. They will come in your planning period to make it up or before and after school.

Seventh period ▪ 2:35–3:25. Back to a 55-minute class. (1) 30-minute lecture and demonstration on operant conditioning. (2) Bulb blows out on machine—in desperation send student to library for another bulb. No more bulbs; quota for month exhausted. (3) Decision made to give 7th hour students answers to filmstrip questions because material will be on Tuesday's test.

After school ▪ 10 minutes until faculty meeting. (1) Erase old lecture outline, put Monday's lecture outline on board as fast as possible. (2) Student from last year drops in to say how much he enjoys college and your psychology course really helped in preparation. (3) Apologize for having to leave for faculty meeting.

Faculty meeting ▪ 3:40–4:45. (1) Discussion of community group attempting to ban four books from the library. One is a supplemental book for psychology, *"I Never Promised You A Rose Garden."* Four are English required readers, *Good Earth, Slaughterhouse Five, Lord of Flies,* and *Working.* (2) Various school items discussed. (3) Smoke bomb scandal in senior hall, at least three bombs per day. All teachers requested to stand in hall beside classrooms between periods. (4) Found out school board announced reduction in force. High school must lose two teachers, smallest number in district. (5) Association member reports attempt by administration to reduce salary increases.

---

with depth in these subject matters. It would appear that the certification laws, laws intended to protect the student from incompetent teachers, have also worked to restrict the number of teachers qualified to teach the several social sciences in the depth that competent teaching requires.

The two-year college teacher

In 1980, two-thirds of first-year college students were enrolled in two-year colleges (Hill, 1980). This statistic points both to the recent growth of the two-year or community college and to a general change in the pattern of college attendance by American students.

A psychology course in two-year colleges is likely to be more diverse in attainment and goals than a secondary school class. The reason is that psychology is taught in the secondary school usually to college-preparatory students while in the two-year college, psychology courses are open to all students. These students are identified by Friedlander (1979) as having at least five distinct characteristics that influence their goals and expectations. Some are students who began college elsewhere; some are interested in general education and have no specific educational or vocational goals; some have definite occupational plans, plans that may or may not be suitable given their talents; some are not prepared for college work either in motivation or background; and some students are taking courses for "cultural, recreational, or community interests." As Hill (1980) points out, this diversity leads to far greater problems in setting curricula than is the case in either the secondary school or the four-year college or university. Curriculum plans developed for colleges and universities are not applicable to the ability or goals of the student in the two-year college.

Two-year colleges normally offer four courses in psychology, including a general course that is offered by almost all two-year colleges. Those courses most often offered, in addition to the introductory course, are child and developmental psychology, personal adjustment, social psychology, and abnormal psychology. The teaching of the scientific-oriented subject matter of psychology appears to be common, if not universal, although such subject matter tends to be the standard fare of the four-year college. The texts used are those that would be found in four-year college introductory courses, suggesting that the perception of the two-year college student as doing the underclass work typical of the four-year college is maintained in the choice of text, but not always in the emphasis on material placed by the instructor.

A characteristic of the two-year college is the transient nature of the student body. Students are likely to visit the campus or facility for their classes only, while in the four-year college/university, students often live on the campus and campus life melds into classroom life. Even in the secondary school, one finds that students are likely to have in common a geographical base. The emphasis of the two-year college on the classroom, the offering of courses at times convenient to working students, and the lack of expectation that the teacher is to undertake research or scholarly activities points to the notion that the teacher of psychology in the two-year college is not in a position to converse or exchange information with colleagues and not likely to see students outside the class. The logistics of the two-year college works against a network of communication developing among either teachers or students.

Training of the two-year college teacher ▪ In 1973 (Nazzaro, 1974), the American Psychological Association prepared, by questionnaire, information on the characteristics of two-year college teachers of psychology. It is noteworthy that the first problem encountered by the association was how to make contact with those who teach psychology in these institutions. This difficulty makes evident the problem that such teachers are not organized through any professional society devoted to the study of psychology.

The survey found that teaching occupied 62% of the respondents' time; counseling students, 25%; and administration, 12%. The large amount of time devoted to counseling dovetails with the *ad hoc* committee on the two-year college's statement that the community college teacher is "called upon by administrators, fellow teachers, and students for service he or she is presumed to be expert in—for example, curriculum development and evaluation, counseling, human relations, community relations, and student learning" (1974, p. 2). Neither secondary school teachers nor college/university teachers would be expected to perform these services so extensively. The data also suggest that teachers in the two-year colleges are more frequently trained in counseling, testing, and personnel work than in the scientific aspects of psychology.

James Bell of Howard Community College, Columbia, Maryland has provided the description in Box 8.2 of his activities and responsibilities.

B O X 8.2   A PARTIAL DIARY OF YESTERDAY

JAMES BELL

8:30 A.M. ▪ I arrived at Howard Community College, which is located in Howard County, Maryland. The college is 12 years old, has five buildings, and over 3300 credit students. Only a small percent of the students attend full time. The average age is around 28, with about 60% of the students being women. All of the day classes are offered on campus, while in the evening several locations off campus are also used. I am the only full-time psychology teacher, which has resulted in very short department meetings.

8:45 A.M. ▪ I walked over to the Word Processing Center, which is our typist pool, and got a revision of a handout on positive reinforcement that I had been working on. Later in the afternoon or evening I will continue working on it. I also picked up 20 copies of a new handout for Social Psychology that the Print Shop had run off for me. I stopped by the Audiovisual Equipment room to leave my film requests for the rest of the semester. Projectors and films are brought to our classrooms just before class.

9:20 A.M. ▪ I arrived at class early to set up the projector and handle individual questions. General Psychology has 62 students; ⅓ between 18 and 21, ⅓ from 22 to 30, and ⅓ over age 30. About 25% are taking General Psychology as their first college course while 10% have completed over 90 credits.

9:30 A.M. ▪ General Psychology was designed with ideas from research, ideas on teaching, ideas from other faculty, students' performance, and students' opinions. These ideas were fit into a framework of systematic instruction that stresses specific written objectives careful design of instruction, analysis of information about student learning, and change based on the idea that if courses don't improve they deteriorate. Along with the very organized approach that comes from systematic instruction, the ideas from the viewpoint of humanistic education also provide a framework for the course. Mastery learning is used along with a heavy emphasis on written assignments rather than tests. Specific objectives for each assignment were given out the first day of the class for the full course.

BOX 8.2 *(Continued)*

I have been working on getting one attention-grabber per week to start class. Today, I used a "Candid Camera" sequence showing conformity on an elevator. After the brief film, I asked for identification of the psychological concept demonstrated and a listing of factors that might increase conformity. I collected the homework, which was based on a booklet on psychological research methods called *Getting the Facts*, which I had written for the class.

1:00 P.M. ▪ Two students who are working more rapidly than other students in Advanced General Psychology came by to take the tests before class at 1:30 P.M. Advanced General Psychology is a course that uses mastery learning, self-pacing, and independent study. Two students came in because they were behind and I had called them and asked them to come in early. I talked with one of them about her goals in the course and the need to set up a study schedule to catch up. The second student had been sick for two weeks and I reviewed with her what she needed to do to catch up.

A student who is taking Abnormal Psychology through self-directed learning was seen for 15 minutes. Self-directed learning involves the student and I developing a set of unique objectives for that student, deciding how to accomplish those objectives, and getting agreement on how to evaluate the learning. This student has a MA in music, has been a teacher for ten years, and now wants to go to graduate school in psychology. The Abnormal Psychology class that I planned did not meet her needs, so she chose self-directed learning. She turned in her weekly time log, one written assignment, and talked with me about the film she had viewed entitled Reinforcement Therapy. Before she left, I returned her previous work and we talked about her plans for the week.

2:30 P.M. ▪ The Retention Committee met. The Director of Counseling chaired the committee of four staff. I had done a review of the literature for the committee on the various ideas and research on retention. The committee's task was to recommend specifically what our college should do and when. We agreed that retention is most influenced by what happens in the classroom. One of the major questions we posed to ourselves was "How can we get more time to faculty for improving their teaching?" We also agreed that calling students who miss class during the first three weeks was effective although some faculty and administrators wondered if we weren't going too far. "Shouldn't the students accept responsibility for attending class?"

4:30 P.M. ▪ I met with my supervisor, the division chairperson for the Humanities/Social Sciences. This session is to review my progress on my objectives. At the start of the school year, I worked out with my supervisor what I wanted to accomplish during the year and what the institution wished me to do. I am expected to teach five 3-credit courses each semester, have office hours, advise about 30 students, handle administrative routines, spend 120 hours on projects to improve my teaching beyond normal class preparation (this year I am revising the book of readings that I put together for General Psychology and rewriting the study guides that are a part of the book), serve on several college committees, participate in the community by lending my expertise (this year I am working on a committee looking at the mental health resources for the aged), and spend at least 60 hours in keeping up in my field and keeping up on ideas on improving teaching.

Merit projects are above the just-mentioned categories. I am working on a retention project and am finding that calling students throughout the semester when they miss twice in a row usually does get them back. Once a student misses more than four times he or she rarely finishes my course. A second merit project is the designing and conducting of workshops for high school psychology teachers. My third merit project involves three library projects. One project is to develop a list of interesting topics and related readings pulled from 25 child psychology books of readings. I will be putting the 25 books on reserve and will have a master list of the most interesting articles grouped according to topic. Our library subscribes to only three psychology journals so that the books of readings fill in at a very low cost. The second library project is the development of a Psychology File. Articles from journals, newspapers, and magazines are filed by topic. The Psychology File will have about 1,000 sources that will be more useful to our students than technical journals. The third library project is the pulling together of the films, articles, and books on the topic of behavior modification that cut across several of our psychology courses. Students who wish just an introduction will find several useful sources as will students doing research papers.

I requested that the objective involving an articulation meeting with the University of Maryland be dropped since no meeting was scheduled this year for the first time in about six years. I also added an objective dealing with working with faculty on their teaching. Our senior faculty are being asked to share their expertise with other faculty.

PERSONAL OPINION

If I were hiring a person to teach psychology, I would communicate the following ideas to persons I would be interviewing.

1. I am looking for teachers who are enthusiastic about helping students learn. This focus on student learning calls for a reorientation of what a teacher is. Helping students learn requires teachers who have many more skills than simply that of conveying information. In general, information is easily available through all types of written materials, through a wide variety of audiovisual aids, and computers. Written lectures, videotaped lectures, and audiotaped lectures can fill in for what can't be purchased.

2. I am looking for teachers who are dedicated to placing primary focus on teaching and student learning. Fifteen hours in the classroom each week along with five office hours indicates our commitment to teaching and helping students learn. In addition, each faculty member is expected to plan and use 120 hours each year to improve their teaching beyond normal course preparation.

3. I am looking for teachers who have a broad knowledge about psychology. Two-year college teachers cannot teach on their graduate school education. The beginning courses taught at community colleges demand much more breadth than is acquired in graduate school. Consequently, I am looking for teachers who are learners and want to continue to learn about psychology.

4. I am looking for teachers who are open to continued growth about teaching and student learning. Too few teachers continue to grow as teachers. Once a comfortable approach has been found, many teachers continue in that framework without searching out new ideas and approaches or rethinking old ideas and approaches that were previously rejected. Getting feedback from students on how they are learning and their feelings about the learning process is extremely important. I am looking for teachers who value the criticism and views of both students and other faculty. When a criti-

BOX 8.2 *(Continued)*

cism is made, the approach should be "In what ways can I use this criticism to make this a better course?" Unless we systematically collect and analyze feedback, we will miss many helpful ideas.

5. I am looking for teachers who know how to work with other staff members. Our faculty work with part-time faculty in their disciplines, with the library staff in previewing and purchasing audiovisual materials, with Word Processing to type our handouts and tests, with the Print Shop to get copies of course materials run off, with the computer center for feedback information, with agencies in the community for field placements, with guest speakers who bring the "real world" into the classroom, with the Test Center for placement and repeated testing, with the Counseling Center for help with students whose problems go beyond our counseling skills, and with other faculty and administrators in overall curriculum planning and the running of the college. I am looking for teachers, who will be teaching into the 21st century, who will need flexibility to adapt to the changing circumstances of higher education.

Educational requirements ▪ The usual degree for the two-year college teacher is a master's degree in psychology. Of the sample examined by Nazzaro, 56% held degrees in psychology, 24% in education, and 20% in other fields. Of those holding degrees in psychology, 41% held the MA; and 12%, the Ph.D. It would appear that a variety of educational backgrounds is to be found among two-year college teachers of psychology and that there is no single pathway to such positions, a finding that gives additional credence to the view that such teachers are diverse in interests, training, and the ways they view the subject matter of psychology.

The future ▪ If there is an identifiable sector of education in which one can expect growth in the teaching of psychology, it would appear to be in the two-year college. It is regrettable that less has been done to assist such instructors than is true of teachers in the secondary schools or in colleges/universities. The absence of professional affiliation by teachers and the logistics of teaching in the two-year college make it difficult for networks of communication to develop among teachers, students, and professional organizations interested in psychology. Most teachers in these institutions hold the master's degree. This degree does not usually qualify one for membership in the American Psychological Association, although Division 2 of the Association, the division concerned with the teaching of psychology, has made special efforts to send the journal, *Teaching of Psychology*, to non-APA members. The future must promote ways in which two-year college teachers can be recognized by a professional organization, and there are encouraging signs that the American Psychological Association is noticing this problem.

For many persons interested in the teaching of psychology, the two-year college is less able to supply collegial relations with teachers interested in the field and presents a curriculum that is undecided whether to teach psychology as an empirical science as is characteristic of the four-year college level or to recognize the wishes of students to attend directly to their vocational needs.

It would appear that many of the problems to be found in the teaching of psychology at the secondary level that involve administrative demands are also to be found in the two-year college. Most often the two-year college is supported by local taxes and is thereby subject to some of the same strictures upon the public schools. The immediate future may include a demand for teachers of psychology in the two-year college; these teachers may well be those with graduate training in psychology. James Bell has commented on other abilities to be found among successful teachers in the two-year colleges in his description of his work day (Box 8-2). If so, the two-year college may become an institution in which personal development is possible and where the imaginative teacher can be successful and appreciated.

The college/university teacher

In American education, the distinction between a college and a university is muddled, if not lost. In this section the term college refers to an institution that grants the baccalaureate degree as its chief purpose. The university, while offering such degrees, offers graduate degrees (MA, MS, Ph.D.) and often includes professional schools in law, medicine, and business. The chief difference in function between the college teacher and the university teacher is that the former teaches undergraduate students exclusively, while the latter will teach both undergraduate and graduate students and supervise graduate students. It is sometimes thought that the requirements for successful teaching differ within these institutions in that teaching is held to be more important than research in the college setting, while the reverse is said to be true in the university setting. Although this generality may apply to many situations, the exceptions are so numerous as to render the generality of limited value.

Training of the college/university teacher ▪ Unlike the secondary or two-year college teacher, the college/university teacher is unlikely to have had any background in course work in education. Most teachers hold the Ph.D. degree. Recipients will have graduated from a four-year college and undertaken four or more years of graduate study involving psychology course work, research, and training in fields allied to psychology (biology, mathematics and computing, sociology). The Ph.D. degree also requires a dissertation. Generally, the dissertation contains a set of publishable research findings. Usually, an oral examination is given the candidate by the graduate faculty as the final step in acquiring the degree.

Certain other degrees are occasionally held by teachers. The Ed.D. (Doctor of Education) places greater emphasis on course work, applied experience, and less on research and training in scholarly fields. The Psy.D. (Psychology Doctor) is given by a few universities as a degree in applied psychology. This degree is intended for those whose interests in research are limited, but whose career goals are aimed toward applied concerns or clinical practice. The MA, MS, or MEd is awarded for a variety of educational achievements. At times the degree represents one or two years of course work; sometimes a dissertation is involved; sometimes research is required; and at times a reading knowlege of languages is required.

Whatever the holder of the Ph.D. may have learned about teaching is likely to have come from observing teachers and serving as a graduate assistant while studying for the degree. Few graduate programs for Ph.D. candidates include course work in the teaching of psychology, for it is assumed by graduate programs that knowledge of subject matter and research techniques is far more important than formal training in how to teach. In some schools, especially universities, professional advancement is judged by contributions to research and scholarship with there being no similar high expectations for successful teaching. In other institutions, contributions to research are important to advancement, but such contributions do not replace successful teaching. Many college/university teachers will have undertaken postdoctoral training at a major research institution in their research specialty. During their teaching careers, leaves of absence are often used to assist the teacher to remain active in research and scholarship.

What the college/university teacher does ▪ Most teachers are hired because of their potential ability to teach or do research in a particular area of psychology (social, developmental, physiological, comparative), for departments believe it important to offer course work in basic areas of psychology. The teacher may be responsible for from two to four classes each quarter or semester (meeting from three to five times a week). In general, the more time required for classroom instruction, the less the requirement that the teacher do research of publishable quality. In addition to the responsibility for classes, the teacher will spend time in research; supervising independent study of students; attending meetings concerned with the educational program, such as the setting of the curriculum; meeting with students regarding course work or, at times, academic or social difficulties; pursuing research and scholarship; and reading literature in psychology.

Perhaps the most compelling task of the teacher is the preparation of lectures. Most teachers will give from 6 to 15 lectures a week with the audience varying from 6 to 1000 students. Lectures in psychology require setting out what is currently known about a topic, and therefore the material must be revised consistently. It is unlikely that the teacher who gives the same lecture yearly will survive the system of evaluation that determines retention, promotion, or the granting of tenure. When the institution is not in session, the teacher is apt to be involved in research, scholarship, or taking additional workshops or course work intended to keep the teacher informed of current developments. Successful teaching in psychology requires a lifetime's commitment to studentship. Those who prefer employment with set hours, who find working at night and on weekends to be onerous, or who are uninterested in developing their knowledge and skills over a lifetime will be unsuccessful and disappointed in the selection of college/university teaching as a career.

Robert Sommer of the Department of Psychology at the University of California at Davis has prepared a description of his work as a teacher of psychology at the college/university level (Box 8.3).

B O X 8.3   DIARY OF A COLLEGE/UNIVERSITY TEACHER

ROBERT SOMMER

Most of my students are not psychology majors. They enroll in psychology courses to learn more about themselves and other people. I try to give them that, and also exposure to ways of asking answerable questions about human behavior. My classes are large; most contain 100 students or more. Lecturing to a large group is a skill acquired over time. The first time I stood in front of a large group of strangers to talk for 50 minutes, my heart pounded and my perspiration glands worked overtime. This apprehension went away after the first few lectures and has not returned. I was also bothered that students wrote down everything I said. I did not believe that my words were so important. After a while, I became so accustomed to this undivided attention that it puzzled me when I would toss out equally good lines at home or at parties and no one took notes. It took a while to overcome this attitude also.

I do not feel that I must fill every moment of the hour. Some of the responsibility of making the class a success belongs to the students. Silences should be friendly, supportive, and thought-provoking, not leaden or oppressive. Silence should be a time to think, focus, pull things together, and not to squirm, feel embarrassed, and look at the clock. There is no point in looking at the room clock anyway, since it's always wrong. One of the first requirements for a college teacher is an accurate watch. If the students can trust the instructor to adhere to the class schedule, they won't need to set their calculator alarms, shuffle papers, and pack their belongings halfway through the hour.

The rhythms of college teaching are predictable. Years are divided up into quarters, quarters into mid-terms, and mid-terms into lecture slots. I can predict with relative certainty where I will be six months from now on Tuesday at 10:00 A.M. and what I will be talking about. Since most of my students are non-majors who may not take any other psychology courses, I will have only three months to reach them. Our time together is brief and important for me, and I want it to be important for them. They are the reason why I am in the classroom, partial justification of all those lectures I attended myself, and all the reading

BOX 8.3 *(Continued)*

that I still do. Much of my self-image is built around teaching. It defines my role in society. Yet I will never see most of my students after the course ends. Yesterday on the PBS news program "All Things Considered" one of the broadcasters identified herself as Lisa D. She was a student of mine 10 years ago. So was her husband and brother-in-law. I've not seen any of them since they left here. I hope I gave them something. They come, they move on, and we stay; that is what college teaching is all about. Faculty provide the stability and the direction of the university. Students provide the enthusiasm, the energy, and idealism. Every year I get one year older, but the students remain the same age.

Teaching in a university is more than giving lectures. It is staying current in the field, serving as academic advisor and personal counselor, composing and scoring exams, writing letters of recommendation, and endless committees. I sometimes feel that the campus is a vast paper mill and cringe for all the forests that have been decimated for us to write papers and send memos. I receive daily reports from assorted administrators with impressive titles like the Assistant to the Associate Vice Chancellor. I used to toss them into the circular file but now I put them in a recycling bin. I try to keep in mind that I'm really a college instructor and not only a paper recycler.

I hold scheduled office hours two or three times a week and my door is open the rest of the time. Most students wait until examination time to drop in. Students occasionally bring me their personal problems. This is unavoidable for a psychology instructor. Sometimes a student will miss an examination because a parent is ill, an important relationship has ended, or a roommate has a serious problem. Such incidents are inevitable in any American university. Sometimes I refer the students to the counseling service. Occasionally I have escorted a student undergoing a personal crisis over to the Health Center. I have also counseled students myself, even though I have no formal training as a counselor. I have also had students in wheelchairs, who were blind, who had reading disabilities, or problems with the English language. I deal with each case individually and try to provide special assistance and separate examinations where possible. Working with individuals with special needs makes my job more than that of a teaching machine.

I do my serious thinking and writing at home where there are fewer distractions than at the office. I rise early in the morning, let the cats in and feed them, make a pot of coffee, and write. By the time I go over to school at 9:00 A.M., my writing day is finished. I learned to work this way when my children were very young and early morning was the only time when there were no demands on my time. I do most of my course preparation at home also. I have my own system but I am sure that it would not fit everyone. I store lecture notes in individual file folders according to topic. For my class in Abnormal Psychology, I have one folder for alcoholism, another for depression, another for mental retardation, etc. Each folder contains a basic lecture outline as well as corollary materials. It is these additional materials that keep the lectures current. In the alcoholism folder, there is an autobiographical article by a woman alcoholic from *Ms.* magazine, clippings about prominent individuals with admitted alcohol problems, posters and pamphlets used in alcohol education programs, some materials from Alcoholics Anonymous, and accounts of alcohol treatment in other nations. I weave the material into the general lecture outline. Use of the folders allows me to insert new material and remove outdated material easily. This system minimizes preparation time in courses taught previously. The night before a given lecture, I look through the folder and decide what to include and in what order. Preparing a lecture on a new topic requires more time. Then I will sit down at the kitchen table with several texts, articles, and reference books and "steal" whatever is relevant to the topic. Teaching requires not so much original research but the synthesis of existing information and the identification of ambiguity, contradictions, and unanswered questions.

Examinations and grading are the most irksome aspects of teaching. They are part of the credentialing process, in which I as a teacher certify that the student has learned a specific body of information. Whether they have "really learned the information" or have just learned enough to pass the examination is an unanswerable question. As an experienced teacher, I have an exam file that extends back many years. I place all the old tests on reserve in the library, along with the answer sheets. This lets students know what to expect on the examinations.

The type of teaching that I enjoy most involves group projects. Here the students and I work together to accomplish something. We share a common objective and learn together. Typically there is a product at the end of our quest in the form of a written report. Some of these reports have later been published. Given the choice, I would much rather work with groups of students on specific projects than teach survey courses. Yet I realize that both have their place in an academic curriculum.

Meetings and committees are necessary parts of university life. Most meetings are boring. No one who cannot sit still in meetings should become a college instructor. A university is run by its faculty and this means committees, committees, and still more committees. There is a committee for everything on this campus, and even a Committee on Committees. I cannot describe how dull most of these sessions are. I do most of my serious doodling at committee meetings. Yet I would be abdicating my responsibilities as a teacher if I did not take part in these discussions of curriculum and related matters. This year I served on the committee to appoint a visiting lecturer to the College of Letters and Sciences, chaired a committee to conduct a five-year review of the Design Department, was a member of the Physical Planning Advisory Committee, and served on departmental committees on Undergraduate Instruction and Equipment Purchases. I have not calculated the amount of time I spent attending these meetings, and reading and writing reports connected with them.

I look forward to the end of classes each year, but also to the start of classes in the fall. This ambivalence reflects the duality of university life, in which duties are split between teaching and research. I have made deliberate efforts to see that my teaching enriches my research and vice versa. I do not want the parts of my academic life to remain separate any more than I want the parts of my personal life to remain separate. If I were to do research without teaching, teach without doing research, or do either without writing about them, I would feel less than complete. Putting something down on paper requires a discipline that compels an author to confront and correct inconsistencies, ambiguities, and omissions. Writing this essay has helped me to understand better my own teaching style. The excitement in research, teaching, and writing is connected with the constant sense of discovery and renewal. This fall I will teach a course that I have taught 25 times. Yet the students will be different and the materials will be different. This will be a meeting of particular students, professor, and content that has never occurred before and will never be duplicated. I carry the responsibility for seeing that our brief one-time encounter is mutually productive.

Educational requirements ▪ The typical degree requirement for employment in teaching at the college/university level is the Ph.D., although persons with the Ed.D., or one of several master's degrees, will be found on faculties. Continuing education in the way of workshops, leaves, and sabbaticals—times during which the teacher develops or learns new areas of scholarship—are usually requisite.

The college teacher is evaluated at set intervals, usually by the department but at times by the college administration or professors in other fields or, at times, by psychologists at other institutions. Promotion is offered from instructor, assistant professor, associate professor, to professor, based on success as a teacher and research and scholarship. Tenure, if it is given, is usually awarded between the sixth and eighth years. If tenure is not given within this span, the teacher is usually not rehired. Advancement within the college/university is through a funnel: Many more persons are hired than will be promoted or offered tenure.

When we consider the number of Ph.D.'s given in psychology during the last fifty years in relation to the number of college/university positions available, we find a classic representation of supply-and-demand market conditions. In the 1930s, the number of such degrees was flat, for the number corresponded with the relatively few new teaching positions becoming available. In the 1940s, persons of the appropriate age and sex were involved, during the first half of the decade, in war, but so were the students who would normally have provided the demand for the teachers. The 1940s and 1950s were periods of slow growth, both in an increase in the number of Ph.D.s and the number of students needing them. The number of persons gaining the degree roughly matched the need for such persons. Beginning in the 1960s, psychology, and teaching, experienced a boom: Babies born after the war when families were reunited were beginning college in large numbers, but few teachers had been prepared to greet them. The result was a fine job market for those who held the requisite degree or training and a sudden interest by the federal government in the training of Ph.D. psychologists. The situation of undersupply and overdemand continued through the early 1970s when the wartime-produced baby-boom ended, leaving universities with heavy investments in Ph.D. programs, but with those acquiring the degree beginning to experience difficulty in finding academic positions. By the end of the decade and into the 1980s, the supply of Ph.D.s was excessive compared to demand by colleges and universities. An immediate result was that persons with the degree began to combine jobs, by teaching courses at various institutions or combining clinical practice with teaching.

Two comments appear to be in order. First, the well-publicized lack of academic positions for scholars needs to be considered historically. The supply-and-demand characteristic has been out of order before and will be again. It takes many years to train a scholar, and the absence of positions now should not deter the student intent upon a career in scholarship from beginning the requisite preparation. A student, now a sophomore in college, will be in the work force, approximately, until the year 2030. The only thing that can be predicted about the kind and nature of jobs or skills that will be needed during this period is my second point. It seems senseless to choose a career based solely on today's market conditions. What one feels constructive and productive doing would appear to be a far more important consideration, since someone who feels productive at their work is more likely to do well at it and therefore to be wanted and needed.

Teaching psychology in other settings

Teachers of psychology are to be found in educational institutions in addition to those described. These include medical schools, nursing schools, business schools, schools of social work, and in other institutions dedicated to educating practitioners whose training requires some background in psychology. Often these departments are part of universities that include a four-year college. Teaching in these settings is often dedicated to a specialized purpose, such as teaching practitioners how to apply their skills in particular situations. For example, law and architecture students receive training in sensation and perception. Medical students receive some training in psychological and biological statistics and in physiological psychology. Nurses receive some training in theories of personality, development, and learning. Business students learn some aspects of social psychology, personnel management, and industrial and organizational psychology.

There appears to be no evident route or training for these appointments. There are no courses specific to teaching psychology to architects, lawyers, nurses, physicians, or business persons. Appointment to such a teaching position usually arises from the individual's special training in research and is dependent on the training and research received during graduate and postdoctoral years.

Kathryn Anthony of California State Polytechnic University, Pomona, has provided a description of her activities and duties as a psychologist who teaches design to architecture students (Box 8.4).

The future ▪ There are no bases on which to predict whether the number of such unusual positions will increase or decline. It would appear that some aspects of psychology are being taught more often in applied settings, but it also appears that such teaching is being done increasingly by those trained in fields only distantly related to psychology.

One evident exception is persons trained in both medicine and psychology. Some medical schools cooperate with universities to make possible the achieving of both the MD and Ph.D. Such a melding of education provides opportunities in both practice and research. For a number of reasons, such programs seem not to have achieved their primary goal. The number of persons completing both degree programs appears to be very small.

B O X   8.4   DIARY OF A PSYCHOLOGY TEACHER
                     WHO TEACHES ARCHITECTS

KATHRYN ANTHONY

Teaching psychology to architects is a fascinating, but not an easy, task. It requires creativity, imagination, resourcefulness, and a bit of patience. It can be extremely rewarding, however, to introduce students to a new way of thinking about design.

I have taught both undergraduate and graduate architecture students, as well as professional architects, landscape architects, interior designers, and city planners. My courses are called Environmental Psychology, Behavioral Factors in Architecture, and Social and Cultural Factors in Architectural and Urban Design. Along with other specialists in structures, environmental controls, and interior architecture, I have also team-taught a design lecture series.

The emphasis of my courses has been on applied, rather than pure, research. In my lecture series to undergraduate design classes, I have been called upon to serve as a "behavioral consultant." The coordinator for the course assigns a design project, such as a small urban museum, in which case my role would be to teach about social and psychological issues in museum design. Some of the other design projects have included a small restaurant and nightclub, a new School of Environmental Design, a city hall, and a high-rise "mixed-use" building containing shops, restaurants, offices, and apartment units.

My creativity is called upon in that virtually no one has written specifically about behavioral issues in these building types. Consequently, I must often extract information and present findings from comparable research settings, or else I simply raise questions about issues I believe are important. For example, what different types of users frequent a museum? What kinds of special environmental needs might these groups have?

My next task is to teach architects the tools with which to answer these questions and test some of their assumptions about design. Among the exercises I have given are learn-

A second exception may occur in the development of curricula in schools of business. It appears that many such institutions are revising their ways of teaching. It is possible that these revisions could lead to the addition of positions for persons whose central training is in psychology.

■ CONTRIBUTION OF PSYCHOLOGY TO EDUCATION: WHAT IS TAUGHT

The previous sections are marked by both generality and diversity. In order to discuss the salient characteristics of the teaching of psychology, generalities have been stated, yet in order to show the many ways in which psychology is taught, diversity has been evident. Reasons for both the generality and diversity

ing how to observe and interview users of the built environment. These are two techniques commonly used in psychological research, but rarely in architectural teaching and practice. I often ask students to observe how people behave in a given setting such as a park, a hotel lobby, or a school lounge, and to record what they are doing and where. Does a certain spot seem to encourage or discourage people from talking to one another? Is there any one location in the setting void of activity? Then I may ask them to interview users by asking them such questions as "What do you like most about this building?" "What do you like least?" "What changes, if any, could be made to improve this building?"

I also ask students to study the physical traces in the environment, to try to understand clues to previous behavior in places. Are there any worn spots on the grass? Any graffiti on the walls? Any pieces of litter on the sidewalk? What can these pieces of information tell us about how people use the environment?

After completing these exercises, I often ask students to redesign a setting in light of what they have learned about people's behavior in and attitudes about the place. We sometimes compare drawings of a project before and after research.

One of the lessons I have learned from teaching psychology to designers is that I must be willing to teach a new vocabulary. Words like "cognition" and "perception" are new to architecture students, and it is important that they understand their meaning. Many have never heard of Carl Jung, whose notions of the "archetype" have provided some basis for research in environmental symbolism.

Similarly, I have had to learn to communicate in the language of designers, too. Designers generally communicate visually, through drawings, sketches, plans, and slides, while psychologists communicate verbally, through writing. As a result I have tried to incorporate slides into almost all my lectures. I also have attempted to become relatively fluent in architectural lingo by familiarizing myself with well-known architects and their work.

My biggest challenge in teaching psychology to architects has been to try to think like a designer. My academic training has taught me to examine research questions that are of theoretical interest. In my current position, however, I must also put myself in the architects' shoes and center my teaching around architecturally relevant issues.

can be found in the origins of psychology itself. We began the chapter by asking: Who teaches psychology to whom? Let us now consider what is taught, for in so doing we shall come to see why the teaching of psychology can involve different topics and be done for different purposes.

The sources of the psychology we teach can be found chiefly in the last century in European intellectual thought. There were four traditions of thinking that contributed to psychology. The first tradition is from physiology, for it examines human behavior in terms of what is sensed and perceived. This tradition today is seen in the interest of psychology in physiology, the sensory systems, neurology, and the workings of the brain. A second tradition is from philosophy, where the manner in which the mind makes associations, forgets and remembers, and interprets experiences is emphasized. This tradition is now seen in cognitive psychology. The third tradition is that of medicine, where treating illnesses of unknown physical cause occurred. This tradition is to be found today in the interest in psychology in abnormal psychology, social psychology, testing, and other applied psychological areas. The last tradition emphasizes the learning or acquiring of behaviors and is active today in the study of learning, developmental psychology, and personality theory.

The first three of these traditions came from Germany, Britain, and France/Germany respectively. The fourth has its sources in Russian and American psychology. All of these traditions have their identifiable origins from approximately 1850 to 1890. In the United States in the 1880s, we find evidence of courses in psychology being taught in secondary schools (although under the rubric of philosophy or mental health) and in the colleges/universities. Here we find the source of the diversity in contemporary teaching of psychology represented by two views. From the medical tradition we are able to see the contemporary interest in the teaching of psychology as a social, humanitarian, and practical subject matter. From the other traditions, we can see the origins of the psychologist's concern with understanding behavior through the methods of empirical science.

What determines which kind of psychology is taught to whom? Sometimes the student is the indirect judge. Whether courses in psychology are offered in the secondary school appears to be in part a matter of whether there is student interest, since such courses are usually electives. It is understandable that secondary school students would be interested more in the aspects of psychology that appear to have a direct and meaningful effect on social relations, self-understanding, and humanitarian goals. The teaching of psychology as a science-oriented discipline almost requires that the students be familiar with basic science, especially anatomy, physiology, and chemistry. Because the secondary school student is not likely to have had training in all of these subject matters, the teaching of psychology in the secondary school concentrates on what students understand and want to learn: namely, the medical/abnormal/social relations aspects of psychology.

Much the same situation is to be found in the two-year college, although it may be that the diverse interests of this population of students makes it all the more challenging to teach aspects of psychology that are both informative and useful to the students. The two-year college student is not likely to have a more sound background in the basic sciences than is the secondary school student and is apt to be as interested or more interested in self-improvement.

Colleges and universities most often insist that basic training in psychology emphasize the experimental nature of the discipline. In understanding the research and theories concerning behavior, both human and animal, the students are able to appreciate the science of psychology and make informed applications to other contexts.

■ RESEARCH CONCERNS

In this section we focus on theory and research relevant to the teaching of psychology. In so doing, we discover that two opposite rationales have guided such research. The first is that techniques themselves can be investigated in order to determine which are most effective or efficient. The second is that research should attend first to how the mind learns, retains, and functions. We have met the seeming antagonism between discovery and the application of discovery often in this chapter and it is repeated when we consider research on the teaching process itself. As we have learned, the availability of two rationales does not mean that either is quieted: Research continues following either rationale, sometimes both. Inquiry is the more robust and healthy for such disagreements on principle.

There appears to be an enormous time-lapse between discoveries regarding how the human mind learns and the using of such information by teachers. The lecture, almost certainly the most widely used teaching method throughout the world, arose in medieval times when only the teacher had a text: Students copied as the professor read and commented. Socrates is said to have favored the method in which teacher questioned student, and took each reply to phrase a new question. Note Socrates' assumption that the mind already possesses knowledge and that it is the teacher's task to help the holder to release such information. Aristotle favored observation and the categorization of empirical events. His methods resemble the laboratory or empirical approach to education in which the student is trained to ask questions of the world, to collect data, and to interpret the findings into broader, theoretical statements.

The views expressed in the Socratic and Aristotelian methods remain with us: Shall the teacher assist the learner by bringing out what is already in the mind or shall the teacher instruct by providing hypotheses, data, and interpretive conclusions? If the former, the task of the teacher is to come to understand the workings of the mind, the better to develop its powers among the student. If the latter, the task of the teacher is to instruct the student in methodology.

One strategy is to emphasize research that attempts to discover how we learn. This tradition is descended from the study of learning, of how behavior is acquired and retained. One can determine empirically whether it is more efficient to memorize a sonata or Krebs cycle by first learning the parts and afterward joining them into the learning of the whole passage or cycle, or whether it is more efficient to learn the passage or cycle in its entirety. The data show clearly that the answer as to which method is best depends on such factors as the nature and length of the material. To apply the empirical answer to a question of educational significance, we may ask whether the traditional means of teaching spelling or multiplication tables are sensible techniques in terms of what is known about how the human mind learns and retains information.

The answer, a negative one, is but an example of the fact that the psychologist's discoveries of how the mind functions appear to have little effect on techniques used in teaching. Teachers are among the last to alter or adapt techniques of teaching to suit our increased understanding of how human beings learn. Why should this be so? One reason is that the process of teaching has built into it the psychological equivalent of the physical process, "drag." At the secondary level, as Len McCord makes evident in her statement (Box 8.1), community, parents, administrators, and students alike prefer traditional modes of teaching, whether or not the methods are effective or efficient, to what appear to be untried and untested methods. At the college/university level, the lecture is the centerpiece of education, at least from the teacher's viewpoint, and there is evidence that students prefer it and are unsettled by other procedures.

We have available an example of the introduction of a technique based both on empirical findings regarding how the mind works and on how to engage students in learning. The principles of operant conditioning stress the importance of reinforcing small acts and proceeding to new acts or concepts only when the previous bit has been learned. In the 1960s, a number of subject matters were so arranged to follow principles uncovered by operant conditioning under the name "programmed instruction." A sample program is shown in Table 8.1 where the development of a concept begins with the notion of a hungry animal receiving food and ends with an analysis of how an air traffic controller functions psychologically.

Programmed instruction tests were developed for a number of topics, including playing bridge and electronics. Academic subjects included programmed instruction texts for subjects as diverse as psychology, spelling, and arithmetic. Some colleges use an adaptation of the programmed instruction system to teach elementary or introductory psychology and a variety of appraisals suggests that students learn the content of psychology as well or more rapidly through this technique as by the standard lecture format. Why, then, has the use of programmed instruction not become the standard way of teaching? Why have psychologists themselves appeared to be resistant to use the techniques? An uncharitable answer is that the teacher has an interest in not being replaced by programmed devices, but the true answer is that we do not know. It is evident from this example, however, that among the research questions that need attention and clarification is how teachers may be shown discoveries regarding the ways in which the mind works and be encouraged to use techniques of teaching that correspond with contemporary understanding of how information is acquired and retained.

A second area of psychology in which basic research has influenced teaching is the physiological approach. Teaching, from elementary school to university, assumes that students have vision, hearing, and the ability to write and remember that are within what is considered a normal range. In recent decades, psychologists concerned with sensory and brain functions have assisted in

TABLE 8.1   **Items from the psychology program (Holland and Skinner). These items illustrate the gradual development of a new concept.**

Item	Correct answer	Percentage of students giving the answer
1. Performing animals are sometimes trained with "rewards." The behavior of a hungry animal can be "rewarded" with _____.	Food	96
2. A technical term for "reward" is reinforcement. To "reward" an organism with food is to _____ it with food.	Reinforce	100
3. *Technically* speaking, a thirsty organism can be _____ with water.	Reinforced	100
50. A school teacher is likely, whenever possible, to dismiss a class when students are rowdy because he/she has been _____ by elimination of the stimuli arising from a rowdy class.	Reinforced	92
51. The teacher who dismisses a class when it is rowdy causes the frequency of future rowdy behavior to (1)_____, since dismissal from class is probably a(n) (2)_____ for rowdy children.	(1) Increase (2) Reinforcement	86
54. If an airplane spotter never sees the kind of plane he or she is to spot, his frequency of scanning the sky (1)_____. In other words, his "looking" behavior is (2)_____.	(1) Decreases (2) Extinguished (or: Not Reinforced)	94

pointing out a number of aspects of the brain that suggest that variations in how one perceives and learns are far greater than has been supposed by the teaching profession. Following the model imposed by medicine, many of these variations have been given names, such as dyslexia and hyperactivity.

The last two decades included remarkable discoveries concerning the function of the sensory systems and the brain in learning, many of which, such as the role of the hemispheres, remain too untested to produce definitive conclusions. It is essential that these findings be communicated to the teacher for this reason: Children with learning abilities different from the assumed norm are apt to be judged unintelligent or uncooperative in the early years of elementary school. Unless what we have learned about brain functions and learning is applied at this time in the educational regimen, these children will never reach the level of intellectual attainment described in this chapter. An adequate secondary education, much less an adequate college/university education, will not become available to them.

A third way in which psychological research has affected education is the growth of tests as measures of abilities and traits. The purpose of any test is to discriminate, and it is the act of discrimination itself that encourages proper and serious questions about the reliability and validity of tests. Few who use tests are familiar with the mathematical methods used in constructing and therefore in forming conclusions from tests. Teachers are offered course work in "Tests and Measurements," but often these courses emphasize the giving and scoring of tests and ignore the mathematics of testing. The result is that the interpreter of tests does not have the knowledge required to answer questions regarding the reliability and validity of tests sensibly.

The effects of tests on our lives are enormous. In part, they determine students' track in school, which college students attend, and admittance to particular professions. On the one hand, tests may be used to assist educators to provide the most useful and fulfilling education to the greatest number of students. On the other hand, tests may be used thoughtlessly to limit the education of those who for reasons psychological, physiological, or economic do less well on tests than other students. The research findings regarding how tests are designed and used need publication, and teachers need the education requisite to permit them to use, evaluate, and explain adequately the use of tests to discriminate the capacities of students. Testing is no longer merely a researchers' tool: It has become an industry that affects the lives of those who have no means to judge its fairness. The research findings regarding how tests are designed and used need publication, and teachers need to understand, evaluate, and explain adequately the use of tests.

When we consider the research contributions to education of the traditions described in the previous section, we see that each tradition continues to explore areas of research that should have a direct influence on the processes of teaching. The success in translating research findings to alterations in teaching techniques is limited. Given the choice of arguing for more such research or the dissemination of what is now known, one would almost certainly choose to emphasize the latter. How is this to be done? A simple answer is to imitate the ways other professions have elected to meet similar problems; these being introduction at specific intervals to new knowledge, providing an environment where such learning is expected and rewarded, providing professional groups that address the subject matter and techniques used by teachers, and assisting researchers to prepare their findings in ways that can be understood by the diverse audience that represent the teaching profession.

If there is a common theme among the diaries of the four teachers who wrote for this chapter of their activities, it is that one's training to be a teacher never ends: To commit one's professional life to teaching is to commit oneself to always being a student.

■ THE AMERICAN TEACHER'S DILEMMA

The American system of education is sometimes viewed as an industry that provides skills, through education and training, that are perceived as beneficial to society. An alternative, and older model, is that the purpose of higher education is to care for what has been learned, to pass such knowledge to each new generation, and to provide research and scholarship into new kinds of knowledge. We may see signs of the use of the business model in the ways in which colleges/universities are organized with a chairman of the board of trustees, president, chancellor, deans, and departments, the departments being represented by a person designed as the head. This organization mimics that found in larger businesses. As is true of business, institutions and teachers are sometimes evaluated by their "output"; namely, how many students take courses, how many are graduated, and how many are employed. Decisions regarding the retention, promotion, dismissal, or granting of tenure to faculty are sometimes based on "output" such as papers or books published.

However simple it may be to evaluate teaching in terms of the number of students who register for a class, the number who receive degrees in certain fields, the numbers given by students on forms that intend to evaluate faculty teaching abilities, or the number of articles published, no set of numbers can ever be more meaningful than the precision of the question that is asked. If we wish to ask how many students register for a class, the number 12 may be a correct and informative answer. If we want to know whether a teacher has taught subject matter clearly, a standard test may be given the students. Even these scores, however, would not tell anyone how well the teacher has succeeded in teaching the student to inquire, to use skepticism wisely, to find solutions to problems, to evaluate data, and to organize one's knowledge into a coherent if questioning philosophy of life and knowledge. What the teacher does of most importance to students may be never directly measurable.

Consider the following questions, thinking of them as test questions:

1. Define standard deviation,
2. A sample has an n of 30, a mean of 45, a standard deviation of 6.0, and a range from 5.0 to 89.0. If I score 86, how many persons' scores are below mine?
3. Define the relationships among n, the mean, standard deviation, range, and percentile.

The asking of each question makes quite different assumptions about how knowledge is retained and used. To answer 1, memorization of a definition is required; to answer 2, the ability to calculate and understand relations among two such definitions is required; to answer 3, the ability to understand the relationships between five definitions is required, but not the skill to manipulate specific numbers. The nature of these questions demonstrates different views on the part of the question-maker or teacher as to what it is that students are expected to learn. Is the goal of the teacher to teach definition, a particular skill, or the ability to manipulate concepts?

Those who believe the purpose of teaching to be the sharing of definition would believe that, for example, a multiple-choice test determines how well the teacher has communicated. Those who believe that the purpose of teaching is to assure the acquisition of specific skills would ask for a calculation, as is required in question 2; those who favor the manipulation of concepts as the purpose of the teacher would argue that there is no assured way of assessing the teacher's success, for such success often cannot be measured for many years, as one sees how students use their knowledge and lead their lives.

Simply said, this nation does not agree on the purposes of education and we cannot expect to find agreement on the qualities of the successful teacher. Our lack of agreement regarding the qualities of successful teaching may be considered a blessing: Probably no single kind of teacher or teaching is appropriate for everyone who wishes to learn. As is true of both evolution and democracy, the variation may well be the strength of the system. Unlike the educational systems of most other countries, the United States accepts, if tacitly, the notion that all students should be provided with education equal, if not beyond, their proven abilities. Whatever obstinate problems this tactic may create for our teachers, it may be argued that this policy is superior to any that refuses to teach students who fail to show promise while very young, who cannot finance their education, or whose disabilities in one area may mask their achievements in another.

Acknowledgements

I wish to thank several persons who assisted in the writing of this chapter: Frederic J. Medway, Jeri J. Goldman, John K. Bare, Susan M. Markle, Tom Bond, Samuel Cameron, Richard Kasschau, Fay-Tyler Norton, Anne M. Rogers, Randall C. Kyes, Kay R. Ocker, and the four persons who contributed descriptions of their teaching activities. This work was encouraged by a grant from the Ethel Ward Fund administered by Bucknell University.

■ SUGGESTED READINGS

Bare, J. K. (1974). *Psychology: Where to begin*. Washington, DC: American Psychological Association.

This pamphlet is an outstanding guide to the teaching of psychology. It provides useful information on both content and process of psychology teaching.

Hill, A. (1980). *Science education in two-year colleges: Psychology.* Los Angeles: Center for the Study of Community Colleges and ERIC Clearing House for Junior Colleges.

The growth of the teaching of psychology in two-year institutions is reviewed in this publication. It also provides valuable information on the methods of teaching psychology in community colleges.

Johnson, M., & Wertheimer, M. (Eds.). (1979). *Psychology teacher's resource book: First course (3rd ed.).* Washington, D.C.: American Psychological Association.

This valuable work is intended to assist the high school psychology teacher in locating instructional materials. It also provides considerable information on the teaching of psychology in secondary schools. It would be of interest to the advanced undergraduate student although of more benefit to the professional.

Rolison, M. A., & Medway, F. J. (1982). A review of the teaching of psychology in high school. *Professional Psychology, 13,* 453–561.

This paper reviews the teaching of psychology in high schools. The authors consider methods of teaching psychology that are both content-oriented and process-oriented. Also included is an analysis of teaching methods used in secondary schools, a discussion of the involvement of the American Psychological Association in secondary school teaching, and a discussion of research on the effects of teaching psychology in secondary schools.

Walker, E., & McKeachie, W. (1967). *Some thoughts about teaching the beginning course in psychology.* Belmont, CA: Brooks/Cole.

This book is an important statement on necessary curriculum in psychology, especially the introductory course. It would be interesting and appropriate for an advanced undergraduate student to read.

| UNIT III | PSYCHOLOGY APPLIED IN BUSINESS SETTINGS |

While the traditional view of psychology's applications may emphasize mental health promotion, another widely held view of the applied role of psychology emphasizes problems connected with employment. Psychologists have historically been interested in helping individuals find employment that is a good match to the individuals' interests and abilities and in assisting individuals, once on the job, to achieve better performance. The chapters in this unit—industrial and organizational psychology, engineering psychology, and consumer psychology—share the setting of the business world.

You will notice a similar emphasis among these three chapters on the uses of psychological research. The specialties in this unit share a concern with the effective application of research findings. Therefore, within each of these specialties, research findings are a prime determinant of the types of applications that are undertaken. In addition, research on the effectiveness of the applications then becomes part of the specialty's knowledge base. While we may think of the term "scientist–practitioner" within the context of clinical and counseling psychology, this term also describes the activities of psychologists who identify with one of the three specialties in this unit.

These chapters are similar in the tone of enthusiasm they portray concerning their specialty. Perhaps

more than other specialties, the setting of these specialties—the business world—and its emphasis on
accountability and visible results has led to the stimulation of these three specialties toward interesting ideas
with ready application.

C H A P T E R ■ 9

LAURENCE SIEGEL

INDUSTRIAL AND
ORGANIZATIONAL PSYCHOLOGY

■ INTRODUCTION

Like the other applied specialties, industrial and organizational (I/O) psychology proceeds from a scientific perspective. I/O psychology is the science of behavior applied to persons in industrial and other organizations. Its objective is to enhance organizational effectiveness.

What, for example, can be done to alleviate the national shortage of registered nurses? Or to counteract "burnout" experienced by air traffic controllers? Or to ensure that police officers will use their weapons judiciously? Solving such real problems in the real world requires that the issues be defined, alternative solutions be evaluated, and the optimal solution implemented. The answers at each step come from research.

With respect to problem definition, we must investigate whether the shortage of nurses is pervasive, or whether it is experienced only in certain work settings (like general hospitals). Is the shortage the result of having too few trained nurses, or does it rather reflect a decision by many trained nurses against employment in their specialty?

Once the answers to such questions are known, remedial measures can be proposed and evaluated for effectiveness. Empirical issues are raised here again. Does the suggested solution accomplish its objective? And, if there are alternative solutions, which is more appropriate both from the standpoint of dealing with the problem and cost effectiveness?

I/O psychology rests on a body of basic research and theory about behavior in general and behavior in organizational contexts in particular. The relationships between the basic and applied aspects are reciprocal. Thus, I/O psychology both draws from and contributes to the broad base of knowledge about human behavior.

Some indication of the scope of professional activities encompassed by this field is provided by the following job description reprinted, with slight modifications, from the *Dictionary of Occupational Titles* (1977):

PSYCHOLOGIST, INDUSTRIAL-ORGANIZATIONAL

Develops and applies psychological techniques to personnel administration, management, and marketing problems. Observes details of work and interviews workers and supervisors to establish physical, mental, educational, and other job requirements. Develops interview techniques, rating scales, and psychological tests to assess skills, abilities, aptitudes, and interests as aids in selection, placement, and promotion. Organizes training programs, applying principles of learning and individual differences, and evaluates and measures effectiveness of training methods by statistical analysis of production rate, reduction of accidents, absenteeism, and turnover. Counsels workers to improve job and personal adjustments. Conducts research studies of organizational structure, communications systems, group interactions, and motivational systems, and recommends changes to improve efficiency and effectiveness of individuals, organizational units, and organization. Investigates problems related to physical environment of work . . . and recommends changes to increase efficiency and decrease accident rate. Conducts surveys and research studies to ascertain nature of effective supervision and leadership and to analyze factors affecting morale and motivation. . . .

This job description continues with references to the I/O psychologist's possible involvement in the types of studies central to the two following chapters of this book: Engineering Psychology, and Consumer Psychology. Hence, this chapter is the first of three which are closely related.

As you examine the above job description, you will note its frequent reference, one way or another, to the assessment and enhancement of employee, supervisory, and managerial performance. *Performance* serves as the organizing concept for this chapter. Two of the major sections discuss issues in defining, measuring, and predicting job performance. (These matters are ordinarily considered to be the province of Personnel Psychology.) A third section considers various factors related to facilitating or improving the quality of job performance.

■ HISTORICAL DEVELOPMENT

You may wonder why this field is referred to as Industrial/Organizational psychology instead of by some simpler designation like industrial psychology, or business psychology, or organizational psychology. Actually, the I/O designation is a fairly recent name change (dating to 1973) for a division of the American Psychological Association that formerly had been designated the Division of Industrial Psychology. The newer designation is meant to imply that the field has broadened throughout its history.

Before World War I

We can identify at least three major threads in the early differentiation of an industrial/organizational specialty from the broad science of psychology: (1) Studies of individual differences and their measurement, leading to a technology of psychological testing and eventually culminating in personnel psychology; (2) attempts to enhance job performance by manipulating the physical working environment, leading to an interest in task standardization and simplification, and eventually culminating in engineering psychology; (3) the human relations movement in psychology growing out of the Hawthorne Studies and creating the background for activities in organizational psychology.

Psychological testing ▪ Between the time the first laboratory for psychological studies was established under Wundt's directorship in 1879 and the beginning of World War I, the emerging science of psychology was largely directed towards studying individual differences. Variations in abilities and performance were identified and techniques for measuring these variations were noted as early as 1883 by Sir Francis Galton in his book, *Inquiries Into Human Faculty and Its Development*.

Just seven years later, James McKeen Cattell fathered the mental testing movement by coining the phrase "mental test" and initiating investigations of the relationships between such nonphysical characteristics as attentiveness and task performance. And by the turn of the century, Alfred Binet, a French psychologist, had demonstrated the correspondence between scores on his intelligence test and independently made teacher appraisals of learning ability. Binet's test, and test-building technology generally, were rapidly imported into the United States, elaborated, and applied to nonscholastic as well as school settings.

World War I provided an additional impetus for the further development of psychological testing. The army needed to screen inductees rapidly for optimal assignments. Thus psychologists devised tests to facilitate matching inductees to the particular assignments for which they had the prerequisite skills and abilities. Related psychological activities included task performance evaluations and training procedures. Together, these activities—personnel selection, placement, training, and performance evaluation—comprise the essence of the personnel component of I/O psychology.

Task standardization and simplification ▪ In contrast to the emphasis on selection and placement, which sought to match people with jobs, a second parallel approach emphasized job simplification. Initially, this approach developed largely outside of psychology and was known as industrial engineering. The introduction of the assembly line led to a search for ways to enhance the efficiency of its human operators. Two approaches were (a) setting output criteria for a fair day's work (Taylor, 1911), and (b) task simplification (Gilbreth, 1911). The former emphasized standardization of worker activities and, most particularly, the speed with which each was performed. The latter emphasized utilization of efficient movements in doing the job.

Although not part of these particular efforts, psychologists had a very sound tradition of experimental research, particularly on sensation and perception. The growing interest in fitting jobs to workers led some of the early experimental psychologists to study the impact of adverse work environments (noise, heat, and so on) upon job performance, fatigue, and boredom.

Human relations movement ▪ Inadvertently, this interest in work environment lead to the third major thread in I/O psychology's history. Studies conducted in the Hawthorne plant of the Western Electric Company, beginning in 1927, were in the tradition of experimental psychology. The initial intent was to investigate the effect of different illumination levels upon job performance.

What began as a one-year study of a relatively simple issue became progressively more involved as the investigation progressed. The expected negative consequences of decreasing illumination did not always materialize because of what has come to be known as the "Hawthorne effect." This term refers to the confounding effects upon human motivation and performance of being singled out for special attention and study. Recognizing the complex influences upon job-related behavior, the investigators gradually turned their attention to studying the effects of such distinctly human factors as employee attitudes, informal interpersonal relationships at work, employee perceptions about supervision, and structure of the work group. By the time the studies were ended in 1939 (Roethlisberger & Dickson), the horizons of industrial psychology, as this field was then designated, were considerably broadened.

Chronology ▪ Hugo Münsterberg is usually credited as the father of industrial psychology because of publication, in 1913, of *Psychology and Industrial Efficiency*. Although he was the first writer to designate a psychological specialty involving applications to work—he termed it "economic psychology"—the distinction of writing the first book in the field probably belongs to Walter D. Scott. In 1903, Scott wrote *The Theory of Advertising*, followed during the years prior to Münsterberg's publication by several other books on what must be regarded as industrial psychology.

You can gain some additional feeling for the three historical roots— personnel testing, task standardization and simplification, and human relations—by thinking about them in the context of the post-war era. The flush of victory and the armistice were shortly followed by the Depression. The associated scarcity of jobs implied opportunities to use psychological testing technology for selecting personnel from an overabundant labor supply. But the general atmosphere was one of shattered economic self-confidence. Doing a good day's work no longer ensured continued employment. Management exercised its "right" to establish ground rules for working hours, pay, and production quotas in the interest of improved efficiency; employees who were dissatisfied were easily replaced.

Labor organizations developed to give their constituents a power base from which to negotiate with management from strength rather than weakness. And, given the flavor of the associated labor-management strife, the times were right for ameliorative efforts like those brought into focus by the human relations movement.

World War II and after

Military manpower needs in World War II once again required an enormous personnel effort to which psychologists responded. The techniques of personnel psychology leapt rapidly ahead. The human relations movement also gathered force in the civilian sector because of the urgent national need to involve virtually all nonmilitary personnel in the war effort. Long shifts, short vacations, and nontraditional employment (for example, women engaged in heavy manufacturing) were the rule. Both employers and employees were concerned with maintaining productivity through high morale and good supervision, and welcomed contributions from the human relations movement.

The earlier studies of task standardization and simplification were now given a new direction. Inexperienced manufacturing employees and untrained military recruits were suddenly required to operate complicated equipment. One solution was to redesign equipment to capitalize upon the human operators' unique strengths and minimize the negative impact of their weaknesses. Operators and their equipment were conceptualized as interactive parts of a single functional system. In consequence, industrial psychology now had an additional subspecialty, engineering psychology.

By 1973 it had become evident to the members of the Division of Industrial Psychology of the American Psychological Association that the designation for their division was unduly restrictive. Partly because of increased maturity of the field itself, and partly because of broad social and economic influences (like passage of the Civil Rights Act of 1964, automation, computerization, hard core unemployment, and so on) industrial psychologists were increasingly making important contributions to such non-industrial organizational settings as government, education, and health care. This increased breadth of activity is responsible for the change of that division's designation to the Division of Industrial and Organizational Psychology.

Another important change became evident with the publication in 1976 of Dunnette's *Handbook of Industrial and Organizational Psychology*. The earlier Fryer and Henry *Handbook*, which summarized the state of the field as of 1950, emphasized "cookbook" solutions to those problems likely to be encountered by the practitioner. In contrast, Dunnette's *Handbook* clearly demonstrates that practical applications are now grounded in a solid base of behavioral theory. Theory and practice are interdependent and mutually reinforcing, each furthering the development of the other.

■ TRAINING AND WORK SETTINGS

Training in I/O psychology has much in common with that in any other psychological specialty. All psychological training emphasizes a concern for understanding, predicting, and changing behavior. The main distinguishing feature of I/O training is that it emphasizes the application of psychological principles to behavior in work or other organizational settings. Towards that end, most doctoral students in I/O psychology are provided with supervised on-the-job experience as part of their training.

I/O psychologists typically are employed in three primary settings: colleges/universities, industrial organizations, and consulting firms (including private practice). The distribution among these settings of the American Psychological Association Division 14 (Industrial and Organizational Psychology) membership has been reported as 35 percent, 36 percent, and 18 percent, respectively (Madden, 1980). The remaining 11 percent reported being engaged in various administrative, governmental, military, and other miscellaneous assignments.

The activities of an I/O psychologist on a psychology faculty are rather traditional. In addition to providing course instruction, the faculty member is ordinarily engaged in a program of scholarly research contributing to the theoretical base for the discipline, and may be conducting one or more applied research projects for organizations that have contracted for such service.

Full-time employment by an industrial organization provides I/O psychologists with opportunities to apply their research skills to a broad range of psychological issues. One way or another, of course, management anticipates that its I/O staff members will help to reduce costs, improve employee job satisfaction, and produce a better product or deliver a better service.

Thus, the staff psychologist may at various times undertake projects to initiate or improve personnel selection and placement programs, programs for evaluating employee performance relative to assigning merit increases and making promotions, training and development programs for employees at all levels (including supervisors and managers), wage and salary schedules, and so on. Additionally, the staff psychologist might engage in research to analyze human factors in plant accidents with a view toward reducing accident frequency, evaluate sources of employee dissatisfaction with a view toward possible amelioration and reduction of voluntary turnover, conduct a management talent search of incumbent nonmanagerial employees in order to structure appropriate staff development programs for them, and identify the skills prerequisite to operating a new piece of plant equipment so that proper job applicants can be recruited.

The projects above are merely illustrative. The I/O psychologist employed by an industrial organization is, in a sense, a general practitioner to whom management is likely to turn for answers or research-based solutions to a wide array of concerns or questions about human behavior in the workplace.

The I/O psychologist in a consulting practice engages in much the same types of activities, except that these typically are accomplished under contract on a project-by-project basis. Unlike the staff psychologist, the consultant's responsibilities to the organization typically end upon completion of the contract. Such completion might be marked by submission of a set of recommendations to management. Alternatively, in instances when the objective is to assist the organization in implementing a new program, the contract could provide for installing the new program and training in-house personnel to implement it on a day-to-day basis.

At the beginning of this chapter, "performance" was indicated as this chapter's organizing theme. We begin our overview of research and practice in I/O psychology by considering selected issues in psychological measurement as these relate specifically to measuring performance.

■ ISSUES IN PSYCHOLOGICAL MEASUREMENT

Hiring a new employee is an exercise in predicting future performance. The employer screens applicants with a view toward hiring only those who have the best potential for performing the job. Therefore, the decision rests upon some indication available before employment that the particular applicant will, if hired, prove to be a satisfactory employee.

You are familiar with several predictors of likely future job performance. For example, the applicant's scholastic record and previous work history might provide evidence that he or she has the required skills or, at least, is capable of learning them easily. Alternatively, the prospective employer may require applicants actually to demonstrate their skill at, say, welding, by giving them a welding test. Of course, many jobs (like operating some new piece of equipment, selling, or supervising) require a fairly broad array of knowledge, skills, and abilities not readily evaluated by any one particular predictor. For these, the prospective employer might seek predictive evidence from several sources, including tests, each tapping one or more of the components of the job-related skill or knowledge. Finally, there is the predictor that probably first came to your mind when you began this paragraph: the employment interview.

Whatever the approach to preemployment selection, it is clear that the accuracy of the resulting decisions rests upon three things:

1. The use of a particular predictor must be justifiable. Each predictor must either measure (a) some critical aspect of the task that this applicant will be expected to do as an employee, or (b) some characteristic known to be related to successful task performance. There is no point, for example, to requiring bank tellers to know how to program a computer. Even though they may have occasion to use computer terminals, the actual programming is not part of a teller's job.

2. There must be a clear demonstration that the predictor "works" as intended. It must be shown that the applicants identified by predictors as most promising do, in fact, prove to be the more satisfactory employees.

3. Each predictor must satisfy certain psychometric (psychological measurement) requirements. These include the requirements of consistency and accuracy. We cannot expect to make accurate predictions from measures that are themselves fallible.

Much of our subsequent discussion will elaborate these statements, but in a context that is broader than that provided by a concern solely for preemployment testing. From this broader perspective, all devices contributing to personnel decisions are, in a sense, psychological "tests," and therefore must satisfy psychometric requirements. This means, of course, that employment interviews and application blanks must be regarded as "tests." But it also means that such practices as periodic evaluation of employee performance to determine salary increases or promotability are likewise held accountable as psychometric instruments.

Psychometric bias and error

All measurement, both psychological and physical, contains a certain amount of error. This is true because all measuring instruments are subject to potential sources of inaccuracy. The instrument may measure in units that are too gross to permit the needed discriminations. Or it may have some inherent defect (like an electronic short circuit in a voltmeter) causing it to yield inconsistent, and therefore untrustworthy, readings even under successively identical circumstances.

Thus, it is important to recognize that a score provided by any psychometric measure is only an estimate of that person's hypothetical "true" score. The more accurate the instrument, the smaller is the discrepancy between the earned and hypothetically true scores. It follows that such accuracy is fundamental to an instrument's usefulness, both for measuring present performance and predicting subsequent performance.

The deviation between obtained and true scores may occur in either direction. That is, the obtained score may either overestimate or underestimate the true situation. If we designate the hypothetical true score as T and the actual earned score as X, the relationship between these scores can be expressed:

$$X = T + B + E,$$

where B = bias and E = error.

This formulation (Brogden & Taylor, 1950) clarifies that there are two major factors that degrade the accuracy of obtained test scores. One of these is bias (B); the other is a group of error (E) factors. One of the primary concerns in personnel psychology is to increase the accuracy of psychometric measures used for making personnel decisions. This is accomplished by reducing the unwanted influence of bias and error factors.

Subjectivity is probably the most obvious potential source of bias in measurement. Any time judgment enters into a score, the personal characteristics, preferences, idiosyncracies, and predilections of the grader are made part of the measuring instrument. The evaluator may be deliberately or unwittingly biased in favor of or against a particular employee or group. Either way, the resulting judgment of performance misrepresents the true situation. There is considerable potential for this source of bias to degrade evaluations made, for example, from personal interviews or supervisory ratings.

Even objectively scored (that is, where judgment is not required) instruments are potentially open to bias from another source: contamination. A measure is contaminated whenever some factor that should actually be irrelevant exerts an influence on the obtained score. Thus, a multiple-choice test taken by the person sitting next to you would be contaminated (for better or worse) if that person copied some of your answers. More to the point, gross sales taken as a measure of a salesperson's performance may be contaminated by such aspects as the season, the potential of the sales territory, the level of advertising support, and so on. Although these are matters beyond the salesperson's control they may systematically affect the amount of gross sales, thereby biasing this measure.

Even if our psychometric measure could provide a perfectly unbiased estimate of a person's hypothetical true score, this estimate would still be subject to measurement errors from three major sources: chance, transitory personal factors, and sampling distortion. All three can be illustrated by considering their influence on the score you obtain on a course examination. The instructor takes this exam score as an indication of how much of the content you truly know. But your actual earned score may signify a greater or lesser level of knowledge than you possess depending upon how well you guess on certain items (chance), whether you slept well or are fatigued at the time you take the test (a transitory personal factor), and whether the test questions fairly cover all of the content you were expected to learn (sampling).

Reliability and validity

Correlation (r) is a statistic computed to express the magnitude and direction of the relationship between two or more variables. It may already have occurred to you that one way to determine whether bias and error are operating is to correlate two independently made estimates of the true score. If scoring the psychometric device requires subjective judgment, we might correlate the scores generated by two different readers. If it is an objective measure, we could administer parallel forms (that is, two sets of questions designed to cover the same content) on different occasions. In either procedure, discrepancies between the scores earned on the two administrations would result in a low correlation, thereby providing evidence that the instrument is subject to bias, or error, or both.

This application of r provides an indication of an instrument's *reliability*. One way to think about reliability is that a reliable instrument yields stable or consistent scores. The correlation coefficient required as evidence of satisfactory reliability using the parallel-forms design described above ordinarily is quite high: about 0.90.

Correlation is also central to exploring possible relationships between pre-employment variables (applicant test scores, age, sex, and so on) and postemployment measures of actual job success. Here the investigator begins by hypothesizing the existence of a relationship between applicants' characteristics and applicants' subsequent effectiveness as employees (Guion, 1976). The two sets of data are collected and correlated in order to determine whether the hypothesized relationship is confirmed. The correlation obtained from such a study is termed a predictive *validity* coefficient. A satisfactory validity coefficient signifies that the preemployment measure is a sufficiently powerful predictor of subsequent performance to permit its use in preemployment selection.

These two concepts—reliability and validity—are central to all measurement and prediction efforts. Validity studies entail correlations between scores on a potential predictor with some independently measured criterion—usually, job performance. Reliability refers to the correlation between two separately made estimates of the true score yielded by an instrument. Is it possible for a measure to be reliable and yet be invalid? Absolutely. In spite of evidence that a test of physical dexterity measures reliably, for example, that test would be quite invalid for predicting a faculty member's instructional effectiveness.

■ AN OVERVIEW OF SELECTION

Figure 9.1 provides a context for the remainder of our discussion of performance evaluation and prediction. It summarizes the elements and chronology of research to establish employee selection programs.

Most research in I/O psychology begins with a job analysis. This analysis summarizes information about employee duties, responsibilities, and the surroundings (both physical and social) in which the work is performed. In addition to its importance to employee selection, such information has clear relevance to research in such areas as training, leadership and supervision, improving working conditions, and job satisfaction.

As the initial step in developing a selection program, *job analysis* provides information from which the I/O psychologist makes two sets of inferences. First, the job analysis is a basis for hypothesizing the likely prerequisites to satisfactory job performance. These prerequisites may include certain skills and knowledge, abilities, educational background, prior experience, and so on. Once such prerequisites are hypothesized, they in turn suggest promising trial predictors: that is, psychometric devices appropriate to their assessment. Second, by providing a comprehensive description of employee responsibilities, the job analysis serves as a basis for inferring potential indices of employee performance.

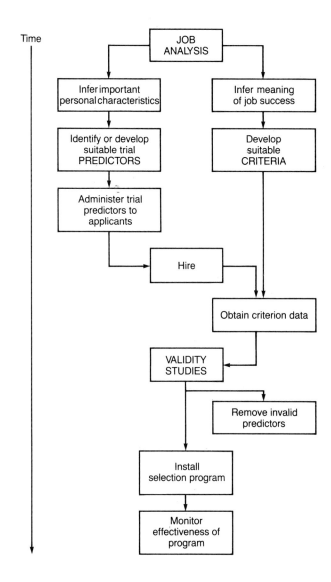

FIGURE 9.1 Employment selection: Investigating predictive validity. (From *Personnel and Organizational Psychology* (p. 112) by L. Siegel and I. M. Lane, 1982, Homewood, IL: Richard D. Irwin, Inc.)

These inferences, in turn, provide the basis for developing measures of the quality of job performance (criteria).

Thus, job analysis suggests hypotheses about relationships between certain applicant characteristics (measured by the predictors) and his or her subsequent effectiveness as an employee (as measured by the criteria). The next step is to determine whether these relationships actually exist.

Although there are alternatives, the particular research model shown in Figure 9.1 requires that we administer the trial predictors to applicants, hire them irrespective of predictor scores (since we do not yet know whether the preemployment measures actually predict the criterion), and subsequently obtain criterion data. Only then are we in a position to conduct validity studies by correlating the predictor scores obtained from this sample of applicants with criterion measures subscquently available for these same persons as employees. Using these validity studies, invalid predictors can be identified and discarded. We will examine these steps now in somewhat greater detail.

■ DEFINING AND MEASURING PERFORMANCE

We begin with the right side of Figure 9.1, that is, the development and implementation of performance measures (criteria).

Multidimensionality of criteria

Criteria reflect differences between persons or groups. In the context of employee selection, the groups of interest are satisfactory and unsatisfactory employees. The job analysis will ordinarily suggest several performance distinctions between them.

What, for example, distinguishes the more- from the less-effective faculty members? The ultimate objective in selecting new faculty members is ordinarily expressed in terms of identifying those persons who will excel as teachers, scholar/researchers, and university representatives to the community. Clearly, no single criterion measure can reflect all three of these broadly stated performance expectations. In common with most jobs, that of faculty member is comprised of several duties. Further, the several aspects of expected performance are often relatively uncorrelated: better scholar/researchers are not necessarily better representatives to the community. Jobs are multidimensional.

Yet the realities of selection require a unidimensional decision: hire or reject. And once hired, there are other similarly unidimensional decisions: do or do not promote, or award tenure, or increase salary, and so on. The practical issue is self evident: How can various criterion measures, each reflecting performance on different and often uncorrelated aspects of job performance, be used to help make such unidimensional decisions?

There are several alternatives; either the several criteria can be combined into a single composite index, or each separate criterion can be separately predicted. The former is defensible only when the several criterion measures have been demonstrated to sample different aspects of a single performance dimension (Dunnette, 1963). Attempts to predict a composite of relatively uncorrelated criteria tend to limit the predictive power of the selection program (Wallace, 1965).

Criterion measures

In turning to specific kinds of criteria, it is useful to distinguish between objectively and subjectively derived measures. Objective measures are ones for which the data are matters of record; they are relatively judgment-free. Job tenure (length of employment), salary, and sales volume are illustrations. In contrast, the data for subjectively derived criteria are totally judgmental: they rest upon someone's (usually the supervisor's) evaluation of employee performance. Their use is required whenever more objective evidence is unavailable. This is usually the case, for example, when evaluating the performance of employees in service- rather than product-oriented jobs.

Even though a measure of work output might seem to you to be the best possible criterion, productivity counts are rarely used. Two conditions must prevail in order for a production measure to provide a useful criterion: (1) A relatively large number of employees must perform essentially the same task in the same circumstances; (2) the task must be sufficiently short-cycle and free of external constraints that the output reflects only worker productivity (uncontaminated by such things as availability of raw materials). These circumstances tend to apply to only the most routine jobs. For most jobs, there are differences in the nature of the task even for persons doing what may appear to be the same kind of work.

Among other job behaviors sometimes used as criteria are employee promotion rate, tenure (and its opposite, turnover), accidents, tardiness, and absenteeism. It is usually incorrect to take such measures as indirect indications either of employee productivity or job satisfaction. All can be influenced by circumstances of the job environment, many of which are beyond management's control and some of which are beyond the employee's control. Therefore, if they are to be used as criteria at all, their use must be justified on the basis of their own merit rather than because of their presumed relationship to other criteria.

We have already noted that there are many jobs for which objectively based data are either not available or are unsuitable for criterion purposes. The alternative is to rely upon judgments. Other things being equal, judgments tend to be less reliable and less valid than are objectively obtained measures. This is so because of their greater susceptibility to evaluator biases and errors. One of the major challenges in designing rating forms and training raters in their use is to minimize the influence of these unwanted contaminants.

There are several potential sources of error inherent in subjective measurement. A first type of error is *distributional*. Some evaluators are disposed to be either overly lenient or overly severe. A second source of error, the *halo* effect, is the carry-over of impressions. The source of these impressions may be internal to the instrument (i.e., carryover between items) or external to the instrument. So, for example, if a rating form contains 10 separate scales, the supervisor may respond carefully to only the first few. The remaining scales are marked on the basis of these initial impressions. Third, subjective appraisals are susceptible to *sequential* effects. When judging several persons in a row, the evaluator may become progressively more or less stringent.

An illustrative rating procedure

Most of the research on rating procedures has been directed toward improving their reliability and validity by reducing their susceptibility to error and bias. Rather than attempt to summarize the range of available procedures, we will discuss just one: behaviorally anchored rating scales (BARS). This particular procedure has been selected for emphasis because it is a relatively recent elaboration of a rating format with which you are probably familiar, and it illustrates a type of scaling research.

You may not know graphic rating scales by their proper name but you have undoubtedly encountered them. These scales typically consist of a label, like dependability, a brief description of the trait, and a line or series of boxes on which you mark your judgment. Although graphic scales are widely used, they are susceptible to all of the sources of error described earlier. This susceptibility stems largely from their ambiguity: both the trait (such as dependability) and the scale points (such as above average, extremely dependable, and so on) mean very different things to different raters. An example of a graphic rating scale is as follows:

Conscientious

| |_____|_____|_____| |

Not at all   Moderately   Very much so

The BARS approach was developed specifically to address this problem. Instead of using potentially ambiguous rating anchors, positions on the BARS continuum are illustrated by examples of actual behaviors (Smith & Kendall, 1963). A BARS developed to evaluate grocery checkers is shown in Figure 9.2. This particular scale, designed to measure "knowledge and judgment," is one of seven developed to measure performance in various aspects of that particular job (Fogli, Hulin, & Blood, 1971).

How were the behavioral anchors identified and scaled? The procedure entailed three steps:

1. Instances of effective and ineffective behavior by grocery checkers were isolated through interviews with the staff of a large grocery chain.
2. The investigators reviewed these critical behaviors and identified provisional organizing categories to encompass them. Thereafter, some staff members were asked independently to allocate each behavior to one of these provisional categories. Those behavioral descriptions allocated by a majority of

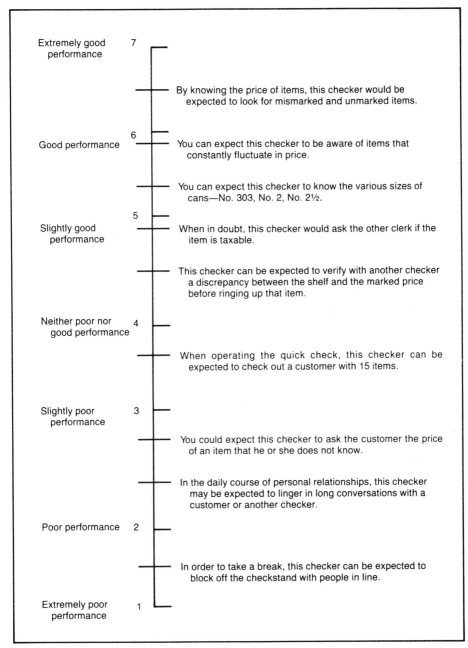

FIGURE 9.2   A behaviorally anchored rating scale: Knowledge and judgment. (From "Development of first-level behavorial job criteria" by L. Fogli, C. L. Hulin, and M. R. Blood, 1971, *Journal of Applied Psychology, 55,* p. 6. Copyright 1971 by The American Psychological Association. Reprinted by permission).

these judges to the "knowledge and judgment" category were further analyzed as described below.

3. Another larger staff sample was asked independently to consider each behavioral statement. Their task was to rate on a 7-point scale the level of knowledge and judgment evidenced by checkers displaying each particular behavior. These ratings were used to generate two types of information about each behavioral description. First, if some judges rated a behavioral description as good performance and other judges rated the same description as poor performance, it would mean that the description meant different things to the different raters. Therefore, that description was eliminated because it was ambiguous. Second, for unambiguous descriptions, the average rating could be used as that behavior's appropriate location on the rating continuum.

The resulting BARS (shown in Figure 9.2) provides concrete illustrations of the meaning of various points on the rating continuum. As the investigators intended, the consequent reduction in ambiguity was responsible for improving the reliability of this format, as evidenced by high interrater agreement, over that obtained from graphic rating scales. However, the costs of developing BARS probably restricts their use to relatively large organizations (Landy & Farr, 1980).

■ PREDICTING PERFORMANCE

We next consider the remaining aspects of Figure 9.1, beginning with a discussion of predictors.

Predictors

There are three basic sources of preemployment data: personal history, interviews, and psychological tests. All three are properly regarded as psychometric devices. Job analyses typically point to some combination of the three as likely predictors of subsequent job performance. However, job predictors may or may not be confirmed by validity research. For example, employers are sometimes inclined to impose a minimum educational requirement because it "makes sense." Or, employers may routinely reject female applicants because "they lack the endurance to do the job." It is important to emphasize that any information used for personnel decisions, including selection, in the absence of demonstrated validity is potentially discriminatory.

Personal history ▪ Job analyses often identify such aspects as previous work experience and educational background as likely predictors. Most often, such information is obtained on an application form. In rare instances a single application item may eliminate candidates from further consideration. (The job may require, for example, that you be licensed to drive a truck.) More typically, the application blank contains several items, each with some degree of demonstrated relationship to expected job success.

Some application blanks are scored much like more conventional psychological tests. A scoring key is developed by analyzing the item responses of known groups of persons. We might wish, for example, to use a blank to predict job tenure. Preliminary research would be conducted to identify questions to which known groups of short- and long-tenure employees have responded differently. Assuming these differences meet certain requirements of statistical significance, those replies associated with long tenure could be assigned positive weights.

Personal history is sometimes evaluated also by a Biographical Information Blank (BIB). Like the application blank, the BIB asks for autobiographical information. However, BIB questions tend to range more widely over topics like health, hobbies, and family history.

Interviews ▪ When used to assist with selection, the interview has one unique feature: its interpersonal character. Its potential value rests upon evidence that certain characteristics (for example, diction) are better evaluated by an interview than by other means, and that these characteristics are important to the quality of job performance. In spite of the almost universal use of employment interviews, evidence concerning their validity is relatively sparse and largely negative (Mayfield, 1964). Furthermore, interviewer agreement (reliability) tends in most studies to be below acceptable levels.

One reviewer of a large body of research on the selection interview concludes that (1) its scope should be limited to evaluating just two areas—interpersonal behavior and job motivation; (2) the process should be standardized by asking all persons essentially the same sequence of questions under similar circumstances; (3) interviewers must be trained to be unbiased evaluators (Schmitt, 1976).

Psychological tests ▪ We cannot here catalog and describe the tremendous variety of available psychological tests. If you are interested in knowing more about this matter, you might wish to consult a basic text on testing (e.g., Anastasi, 1982).

A consideration of the characteristics of carefully conceived tests used by I/O psychologists is more to the point of the present discussion. Although we have alluded to some of them previously, they are enumerated below for clarity.

1. An almost infinite number of test questions could be constructed on any topic. However, practical considerations limit test length. Therefore, the particular questions chosen for inclusion in a test must adequately represent the universe of all test questions that could have been written.

2. Test administration is *standardized*; that is, all conditions are uniform. Otherwise, it would be impossible to make meaningful comparisons between test-takers.

3. Test scores order persons along some kind of relevant scale. If the test is to be used as a predictor, the passing or critical score must be established by research such as that discussed in this chapter.

4. There must be clear evidence of test reliability and of validity.

5. Finally, the predictor must be equally *fair* for everyone. The test scores must predict criterion performance without having a systematic adverse impact for any applicant subgroup.

Validity

In its broadest definition, validity signifies two concepts. A valid test (1) accurately reflects the characteristic it purports to measure and (2) permits reasonably accurate predictions of some criterion. The essential distinction between these concepts is that the former, designated descriptive validity, emphasizes a property of the test itself. The other, criterion-related validity, emphasizes the usefulness of the test in providing information about those other characteristics with which the test score correlates (Messick, 1980).

Descriptive validity ▪ A test is merely a device for making systematic observations and measurements. The accuracy of the resulting description of the test-taker is at issue when we speak of descriptive validity. Such accuracy can be judged in two ways.

The first is *content validity*. The underlying issue here is that of the appropriateness of the particular set of test questions to the desired content coverage. This is largely a matter of judgment. The full range of content must be representatively sampled by the questions comprising the test.

Construct validity is a second descriptive issue. Test scores are often taken as evidence about some underlying construct which itself cannot be seen or otherwise sensed. Motivation, sociability, intelligence, and similar traits are constructs that have been developed to explain patterns of behavior. The construct validity question is "Does this presumed measure of motivation really measure motivation? Does this so-called intelligence test really measure intelligence?"

Ultimately, the evidence for construct validity must come from testing behavior that is hypothesized as associated with the construct. If intelligence is a reasonable construct, it ought to be associated with such skills as learning speed. Therefore, if the purported intelligence test really has construct validity, the resulting scores should correlate positively with the rapidity of learning. If not, there is something wrong either with the construct (because it led to an incorrect hypothesis) or with the new test.

Both content and construct validity are prerequisite to the potential predictive usefulness of a test. But we must look to criterion-related validity for evidence that the test actually contributes to criterion prediction.

Criterion-related validity ▪ We have already presented (Figure 9.1) one approach to investigating test–criterion relationships, that is, *predictive validity*. This research design requires time to elapse between acquiring the potential predictor and criterion scores. The evidence being sought is that predictor scores earned by applicants correlate with that same group's job performance as employees. In order to conduct this study, all of the applicants must be hired irrespective of predictor score. (The predictor cannot be used for actual selection until after its validity has been established.) As you can imagine, implementing this design presents some problems, particularly in organizations that have relatively few applicants and job openings.

As an alternative, it is often desirable to investigate the prediction question by correlating pairs of scores from a sample of incumbent employees. Here, no time elapses between administration of the "predictor" and availability of the criterion measure. This approach is termed *concurrent validity*. The zero-time interval in concurrent validity studies has potentially important ramifications. Employees' "predictor" scores may differ from what they would have been were they applicants. As applicants, they would not have had actual job experience; therefore, their test scores might be lower. Also, their test-taking motivation, were they applicants seeking employment, might have been higher.

In spite of the conceptual differences between predictive and concurrent validity, there is growing evidence that, for certain predictors, the two may yield comparable results (Barrett, Philips, & Alexander, 1981; Jensen, 1980).

Fairness in selection ▪ Title VII of the *Civil Rights Act of 1964* specifically prohibits hiring (or promoting, or setting salaries) on the basis of tests that selectively penalize protected groups of persons. In a landmark legal decision (*Griggs v. Duke Power Company*, 1971) the U.S. Supreme Court held that the employer bears the burden of proving that employment selection measures are job related. Further, the administrative interpretation of this act (Equal Employment Opportunity Coordinating Council, 1978) clarifies the meaning of tests to include all personnel screening measures including interviews, application blanks, tests of physical strength or coordination, and so on.

Fairness and validity are related but separate concepts. The required proof that tests are job related implies a demonstration of criterion-related validity. Fairness implies the absence of adverse impact upon a protected group of persons.

To appreciate both the distinctions and relationships between validity and fairness requires that you realize that test scores have no intrinsic value. Their only value comes from the accuracy of predictions that may be made from them. Thus, whether or not a selection test is fair depends upon its effects. Assuming two applicants who would prove to be equally satisfactory employees if given the opportunity, a test causing one to be hired and the other to be rejected is unfair to the rejected applicant (Guion, 1966).

Note that the fairness issue does not revolve about test scores. Merely because women on the average may score lower than men on a test of strength does not signify that the test is therefore biased. We must ask about the relative rates of prediction errors from the test. It is only biased if it leads us erroneously to reject a greater proportion of the minority or protected group than of the majority group (Dunnette, 1974).

Thus, the essence of civil rights legislation is its emphasis upon the conservation of human talent without regard to such aspects as race or sex. This is, of course, also the objective of psychological testing (Dunnette & Borman, 1979). Employment testing, carefully conceived and implemented, is the best tool available to society for matching organizations' needs to employ talented persons with individual's needs to use their talents effectively.

■ FACILITATING PERFORMANCE

We turn next to some of the activities of I/O psychologists emphasizing performance facilitation to the mutual benefit of the employee and the organization. Five major topics are treated in this section: training, motivation, job satisfaction, leadership and supervision, and organizational theory.

Training

Training is any deliberate organizational effort to help employees adapt to their jobs. Thus, training programs may emphasize learning knowledge, skill, or attitudes; be directed toward newly hired employees or more senior ones; or focus on the present job assignment or contemplated future assignments. A useful classification of training strategies is divided into three groups: simulation methods, on-the-job training, and information presentation techniques (Campbell, Dunnette, Lawler, & Weick, 1970).

The first thing most of us think of in connection with simulation is something like pilot training. Such mechanical simulations are clearly useful when training under operational circumstances is potentially hazardous to the trainee or others, and the complexities of doing the real task or operating the real equipment preclude isolating separate task components for intensive practice.

However, tasks other than those requiring equipment operation can also be effectively simulated for training purposes. Simulations are frequently used to help trainees improve their interpersonal (supervision, sales, interviewing) and decision-making skills. Thus, supervisory trainees can prepare for likely eventualities on the job by role playing them in the classroom, and managerial trainees can learn to improve their ability to establish priorities by an *in-basket* exercise wherein they sort and respond to various memoranda, phone messages, letters, and computer print-outs placed in their hypothetical in-basket.

It is assumed that skills learned during simulation will transfer to real task performance. No such assumption is required to justify the most widely used training strategy: on-the-job training (Utgaard & Dawis, 1970). This can range from a systematic apprenticeship program, to less structured job training under the supervision of an experienced employee. Aside from bypassing the transfer issue, this strategy usually is cheaper than others, and facilitates employee adjustment to the actual job environment while encouraging the development of job-related skills.

A third strategy, information presentation (by lecture, discussion, films, programmed instruction, computer-assisted instruction, and so on), often supplements other strategies by providing trainees with the required background knowledge.

Effectiveness of training ▪ New training programs are sometimes instituted in the context of other simultaneously occuring changes (Goldstein, 1980)—like a new selection program or profit sharing plan. When several organizational changes occur simultaneously, it is very difficult to isolate the effects of any one of them from the effects of the others. Thus from a research standpoint, it is sometimes difficult to sort out the beneficial effects of training from those of other organizational programs initiated at about the same time.

Even granting the fact that training is itself useful, no strategy can be regarded as the most effective under all circumstances. Both trainee characteristics and training objectives influence the choice of an optimum strategy. Furthermore, some strategies (like simulation) tend to be considerably more expensive than others. Hence, it may be necessary to compromise by implementing a slightly less effective but considerably less expensive training procedure.

Enhancing motivation

Perhaps the one question most frequently asked by managers is "How can I motivate my employees to do better work and be more conscientious?" Managers ask this question even when they know about the importance of dispensing rewards contingent upon satisfactory job performance. That, after all, is the rationale for merit pay increases, promotions, and so on.

The question implies an awareness that rewards are not uniformly effective. Different factors motivate different people. And the power of a particular motivator differs even for the same person under different circumstances or in various phases of his or her life. Thus, in addition to providing contingent rewards, management must provide employees with appropriate ones.

The motivational issue is sufficiently complex that it has been addressed by two sets of complementary theories: need theories and process theories. As applicable to the industrial/organizational context, the former focus on the nature of employees' job-related needs; the latter guide managerial action to satisfy those particular needs.

Need theories ▪ In formulating his theory of human needs, Maslow (1954, 1965, 1970) postulated that the normal human condition is continually striving to satisfy needs. Maslow arranged these needs in a hierarchy. This arrangement implies that, once satisfied, a particular need is immediately replaced by another.

Maslow's hierarchy consists of five levels, with needs at any one level taking precedence over needs at all higher levels. The lowest level on the hierarchy is physiological. These needs are those relating to survival, such as food and water. The second level is safety needs. These are needs relating to protection from physical danger and threat as well as to the need for psychological safety (security). Needs for friendship, belonging, and love are social needs, the third level of the hierarchy. The fourth level is esteem needs. First, we need to feel competent in order to experience feelings of self-respect. Second, we need our reputation, with its satisfaction of our needs for recognition, appreciation, and status. Since it is likely that most employees experience reasonable degrees of satisfaction of the needs at the first three levels, this fourth level of the hierarchy is presumed to be of great significance in organizations. The last level is needs relating to self-actualization. Maslow includes here needs relating to a sense of self-fulfillment, to creativity, and to realizing one's potential.

Research evidence has contradicted certain predictions from Maslow's needs hierarchy theory. In particular, it has been found that certain needs may continue to operate as important motivators even though they have been satisfied (Lawler & Suttle, 1972). However, such disconfirming evidence has given rise to a modification of the needs hierarchy theory. The reformulation (Alderfer, 1969, 1972) postulates three sets of needs: existence needs, for material substances and goods; relatedness needs, for interpersonal relationships and communications; and growth needs, for developing one's abilities to the fullest.

The similarities between Maslow's theory and the reformulation are self-evident. The important difference between the theories is that the reformulation introduces the possibility of "frustration-regression." This concept means that when higher-level needs are not satisfied, employees may regress in search of additional gratification of lower-level needs. This part of the Existence-Relatedness-Growth (ERG) theory is intuitively appealing. It implies that motivation can be maintained at a reasonable level even for relatively unchallenging jobs. Although the evidence on this theory is still being accumulated, the available data are largely supportive (Wanous & Zwany, 1977).

Process theories ▪ Assuming that management knows about an employee's needs, how can it respond to them in ways that will encourage desirable work behavior and discourage undesirable behavior? How does the motivational process operate? We have selected two theoretical approaches to illustrate present-day thinking about this matter: reinforcement theory and expectancy theory.

Reinforcement theory is based upon much of Skinner's (1953, 1969) research on operant conditioning. The theory has two sets of principles: one related to acquisition of desired behaviors and the other related to elimination of undesirable behaviors. The key concept for both sets of principles is reinforcement of behavior. The reinforcer may be positive (a reward) or negative (removal of an aversive condition). Either way, reinforcement of desired behavior leads to its acquisition or continuation; the absence of reinforcement leads to the discontinuation (extinction) of undesirable behavior.

In spite of supporting evidence, reinforcement theory alone is regarded by many as too limited to provide a truly comprehensive basis for managerial strategies. Human beings reason and have a rich variety of feelings—both of which are largely ignored by reinforcement theories, but are central to expectancy theories (e.g., Porter & Lawler, 1968; Vroom, 1964).These theories emphasize that employees decide on a course of action to follow and on the amount of effort to expend in pursuing it. Those decisions result from their expectations: that is, their analyses of the anticipated consequences of alternative courses of action. Expectancy formulations address the various factors influencing these expectations and their links to decision-making.

From a practical standpoint, the strength of expectancy theories is in their power to explain and predict the likely motivational consequences of such organizational efforts as improving the match between employee job assignments and abilities, redesigning the physical and social work environment, and modifying training programs (Campbell & Pritchard, 1976).

Job satisfaction

Job satisfaction has been one of the major theoretical and practical concerns of I/O psychologists since the Hawthorne studies were conducted. This general research area, perhaps better than most others, illustrates some of the difficulties in attempting to attribute causal directions to established relationships.

Job satisfaction and performance ▪ Common sense suggests that productivity will be higher when employees experience job satisfaction. As discussed below, this commonsense view is incorrect! Although job satisfaction is an important issue in the context of our broad concern for facilitating performance, its importance does not lie in a causal link between these feelings and productivity. By way of clarification, we will consider the relationship between job satisfaction and performance indicators of productivity and turnover.

Repeated investigations of the relationship between job satisfaction and productivity confirm that this relationship is very weak (Organ, 1977). In reviewing a large number of studies of the issue, Vroom (1964) reported that the median obtained correlation was only .14. Why is this relationship not stronger? A first explanation is evident from your own experiences in various courses. You know first hand that you do well in some courses in spite of negative feelings about the particular instructor and course, and poorly in others in spite of positive feelings. Your personal feelings are not the sole, or even the most important, determinants of your willingness to do the work required in the course. Similarly, job satisfaction is neither the sole nor most important determinant of job performance (Schwab & Cummings, 1970). Employees who are quite dissatisfied may yet perform satisfactorily in order not to be fired. And the level of job performance of even highly satisfied employees can be limited by such factors as their ability and level of skill, or pressures from coworkers to reduce productivity.

Second, the causal linkage between productivity and satisfaction operates both ways. Indeed, in certain circumstances, performance may be a much more powerful determinant of satisfaction than vice versa. Thus, we can anticipate satisfaction resulting from performance when (a) the employee perceives performance at work as a way of gratifying personally important needs (as discussed in the previous section on motivation), and (b) when that performance does not entail undue personal cost (in fatigue, marital problems, and so on) (Locke, 1976).

Evidence from a number of studies confirms that satisfied employees are less likely than unsatisfied ones to quit their jobs (Brayfield & Crockett, 1955; Herzberg, Mausner, Peterson, & Capwell, 1957; Vroom, 1964). Again, the causal linkages are complex and indirect. Job dissatisfaction may well encourage an employee to think of quitting. But whether or not this leads to action probably depends upon other factors—such as the employee's age and tenure, and the condition of the economy—which, in turn, influence the probability of finding an acceptable alternative job (Mobley, Horne, & Hollingworth, 1978).

Determinants of job satisfaction ▪ What aspects of the job environment encourage feelings of satisfaction? We have already cited productivity as one such potential factor. We now examine two others: features intrinsic to the job and pay.

Of the many ways in which jobs may differ intrinsically from each other, several aspects have been isolated as particularly relevant to feelings of job satisfaction (Hackman & Oldham, 1975). First, the variety of skills in the job seems to be important. The greater the variety of skills required by the employee, the less boring the job and the greater the satisfaction. Second, *task identity* appears to be related to job satisfaction. Task identity can be provided by arranging jobs to require the completion of a meaningful piece of work (such as an entire car engine) rather than a subunit of an entire piece (such as the construction of fan belts). Third, the perceived social significance of the task (task significance) is related to job satisfaction. A fourth aspect potentially relevant to job satisfaction is permitting the employee freedom, independence, and discretion in determining work procedure. Last, structuring tasks so that the employee can receive feedback on the quality of his or her performance seems to increase job satisfaction.

The power of intrinsic dimensions, such as those cited above, to determine job satisfaction is dependent upon the degree to which the employee believes that his or her worth is reflected in his or her job performance (Wanous, 1974). It appears that, for persons with a high work ethic, intrinsic factors are more related to job satisfaction. However, for persons with a low work ethic, extrinsic factors (such as pay) seem to be more powerful influences upon job satisfaction.

For many years I/O psychologists erroneously minimized the importance of pay as a factor contributing to job satisfaction (Nash & Carroll, 1975). The early view was that pay is relatively unimportant in relation to job satisfaction. Therefore, these investigators treated pay as if it were a uniform and uncomplicated variable, looking only at the absolute amount of pay as a possible determinant of job satisfaction or dissatisfaction. A different picture emerges, however, when employee perceptions concerning the adequacy of their pay relative to personal needs and worth is considered. Irrespective of the absolute amount of pay, persons who regard themselves as being underpaid express dissatisfaction and reduce their productivity (Pritchard, Dunnette, & Jorgenson, 1972).

Leadership and supervision

From an organizational perspective, all of us are members of various groups, and groups need leaders (supervisors, section leaders, foremen, managers) in order to accomplish their assignments effectively. On this topic, we can merely hint at the findings of an enormous body of research and theory by addressing just two questions:

1. What characterizes the behavior of leaders?
2. What distinguishes effective from ineffective leadership behavior?

Leadership behavior ▪ The early systematic research was less concerned with studying the behavior of leaders than it was with searching for personal characteristics (or traits) inevitably linked to leadership. This approach assumed that "great men" or "natural leaders" are genetically endowed with certain characteristics predisposing their effectiveness in widely ranging situations. By and large, this search proved fruitless. Effective leaders have been tall and short, intellectually bright and not so bright, socially outgoing and reclusive. Since no pattern of traits was found consistently to be associated with leadership, the research took another direction: Do leaders exhibit consistent patterns of behavior?

Search for such patterns began about thirty years ago at The Ohio State University, and has proven to be a fertile direction for investigation. Research led initially to the important discovery that leader behavior can be characterized in terms of two primary dimensions: consideration and initiating structure (Fleishman, 1953, 1973). *Consideration* is the degree to which the supervisor indicates respect for subordinates' ideas, needs, and feelings. *Initiating structure* refers to those supervisory actions that mobilize subordinates to deal effectively with the tasks.

A similar conclusion was reached by Fiedler (1967) using quite a different research approach. Whereas Fleishman's Ohio State studies identified dimensions of leader behavior by analyzing descriptions of leaders at work, Fiedler asked leaders to describe the kind of person with whom they found it especially difficult to work. The conclusion (Fiedler, 1978) is that at one extreme there are leaders who are more concerned with interpersonal relations than with task activities; those at the other extreme have the converse concerns.

The similarity between these two conclusions is self-evident. The difference is subtle. Fiedler's approach produced a continuum of dominant leader concerns ranging at the extremes from high interpersonal/low task to high task/low interpersonal. Fleishman's approach emphasized the leader's behavior rather than disposition, and concluded that behavior is characterized by two relatively independent dimensions: consideration and initiating structure. Thus, a leader who acts considerately, for example, might or might not also behave in ways designed to initiate structure.

Effective leadership ▪ It is clear that leadership entails concerns for tasks and subordinates. Which of these concerns is more important? Or, does a leader need to be concerned about both in order to be effective?

As you might expect, the supervisor's level of consideration is an important factor in subordinates' job satisfaction and consistent work attendance (Fleishman, 1973; Fleishman, Harris, & Burtt, 1955). Although job satisfaction and consistent attendance are undoubtedly worthwhile objectives, considerate leader behavior is not always regarded as desirable. For example, consideration scores correlated negatively with the rated effectiveness of combat air-crew commanders (Halpin & Winer, 1957), presumably because high-consideration leaders were less able to make the required life-and-death decisions.

Thus, there is not a simple answer to whether effective leadership requires supervisors to be considerate (or be concerned with interpersonal relations), to initiate structure (or be concerned with task activities), or both. It depends upon the particular subordinates and circumstances. Leadership is situational. The various situational theories of effective leadership tend to build either upon Fleishman's consideration and initiation of structure as independent dimensions of how the leader acts, or upon Fiedler's continuum of leader orientations.

Both theoretical approaches have stimulated considerable research and scientific debate, quite beyond the scope of this discussion. The debate focuses less on whether one or the other theoretical approach is "right" than it does on stretching our comprehension of the kinds of situations in which particular supervisory styles are effective or ineffective. As our understanding of this issue has continued to improve, I/O psychologists have made stronger contributions in three practical areas. First, I/O psychologists have designed improved procedures and specified better criteria for selecting prospective supervisors and managers. Second, psychologists have drawn upon research on leadership effectiveness for improving supervisory training and management development programs. Third, organizational structures have been evaluated for their potential impact on both leaders and employees. This latter topic is one with which we will end our discussion of performance facilitation.

Organizational theory

Our consideration of performance facilitation has followed a progression from individual-centered to group-centered concerns. We first examined training, motivation, and job satisfaction as factors in individual performance. Next, we discussed certain aspects of leadership and supervision as these influence performance by persons comprising a discrete work group. Now we turn to the influence of the total organizational structure whereby the activities of the separate functional groups are integrated.

As noted earlier, the Hawthorne studies of the 1930s must be credited with stimulating an awareness of the importance to organizational effectiveness of concern for human relations. Nevertheless, the full impact of this awareness was not realized until some thirty years later. Prior to the 1960s, organizations were structured primarily to facilitate the performance of highly fragmented tasks.

This is not especially surprising. The assembly line, with its attendant limitations upon the responsibilities and activities of individual employees, was characteristic of manufacturing industries. The era of craftsmen and cottage industries, with total responsibility from raw materials to finished product, had come and gone. Their productivity was too low, the quality was too variable to meet market demands, and the cost of the resulting product was too high for the mass market.

Task fragmentation encouraged the development of classical organizational structures characterized by clear-cut divisions of work responsibilities, delegation of authority, a hierarchical chain of command, and delimited supervisory control. Some of the assumptions implicit in this structure were described as *Theory X* assumptions by McGregor (1960, pp. 33–35):

1. "The average human being has an inherent dislike of work and will avoid it if he can."

2. "Because of this human characteristic of dislike of work, most people must be coerced, controlled, directed, threatened with punishment to get them to put forth adequate effort toward achievement of organizational objectives."

3. "The average human being prefers to be directed, wishes to avoid responsibility, has relatively little ambition, wants security above all."

Theory X assumptions were certainly not held by all organizations or managers, nor were these assumptions endorsed wholeheartedly. Nevertheless, Theory X assumptions did describe, for the most part, bureaucratic structures prior to the 1960s.

This organizational structure was criticized by McGregor (1960). He argued that any organizational structure must facilitate the integration of individual and organizational objectives, rather than encouraging conflict between them. McGregor, therefore, developed a different approach to management that emphasized the desirability of increasing individuals' autonomy and self-direction. These contrasting managerial assumptions became titled *Theory Y.*

1. "The expenditure of physical and mental effort in work is as natural as play or rest."

2. "External control and the threat of punishment are not the only means for bringing about effort toward organizational objectives. Man will exercise self-direction and self-control in the service of objectives to which he is committed."

3. "Commitment to objectives is a function of the rewards associated with their achievement."

4. "The average human being learns, under proper conditions, not only to accept but to seek responsibility."

5. "The capacity to exercise a relatively high degree of imagination, ingenuity, and creativity in the solution of organizational problems is widely, not narrowly distributed in the population."

6. "Under conditions of modern industrial life, the intellectual potentialities of the average human being are only partially utilized." (McGregor, 1960, pp. 47–48).

The time was right for American management to pay particular attention to McGregor's theory. There was mounting evidence that the United States was no longer the world's industrial giant that we once were. While our plants continued to make use of relatively antiquated equipment following World War II, Japan and West Germany, in particular, replaced much of theirs. The replacements were considerably more efficient because of improved automation technology. And the efficiency of their manufacturing operations was further enhanced by the kinds of organizational designs required by the newer equipment. Machines handled more of the hazardous, odious, monotonous, tasks; people were engaged more in such duties as anticipating, trouble-shooting, and planning. Therefore, McGregor's Theory Y became influential in the redesign of organizational structures.

Current organizational theories emphasize the implementation of optimal interpersonal arrangements and employee responsibilities. The best possible use of human talent and capabilities is the objective of many organizational theories (Likert, 1961). However, there is not a single best structure for all organizations. Theory X and Theory Y structures are both appropriate for particular organizations, just as optimal leadership styles are contingent upon several interacting circumstances.

Two interactive dimensions of organizational structure have been described as particularly pertinent to the effectiveness of organizational structures: differentiation and integration (Lawrence & Lorsch, 1969). *Differentiation* refers to the range of the differences in orientation and objectives of the various managers within an organization. These differences result from the individual manager's personality and from the nature of the particular task handled by his or her unit. As has been noted earlier, some managers are oriented more toward consideration while others are oriented more toward task accomplishment. Additionally, some are disposed toward more formal structures than others. Secondly, *integration* refers to the range of demands within the organization for collaboration and cooperation. Whereas some units (for example, sales and marketing) may dovetail their activities very closely, other units (such as personnel and engineering) may be less interdependent.

It appears that the most effective organizations succeed in attaining a high level of integration, even among units that had not formerly been accustomed to working together. While it had been theorized that the dimensions of integration and differentiation are antagonistic, newer structures are being created in organizational environments to facilitate integration in spite of required differentiation. Thus, specific persons or groups may be given new kinds of job responsibilities: that of helping integrate activities of relatively large organizational segments. *Project teams* and *quality circles* illustrate this type of responsibility (see Box 9.1). Both structures effect higher levels of integration by giving individual employees increased responsibility for making and implementing decisions.

BOX 9.1   SERVICES PROVIDED BY I/O CONSULTANTS

BEN B. MORGAN, JR. AND SCOTT I. TANNENBAUM

As illustrated by the examples given at the beginning of this chapter, organizations are continually faced with a variety of "people problems." As they attempt to solve such problems, organizations sometimes rely on the expertise of industrial and organizational (I/O) consult-

BOX 9.1 *(Continued)*

ants. These consultants usually are trained as I/O psychologists, but they may also be experts in business, management, human resource planning, human-factors engineering, operations research, or organizational development. In many cases, they are employees of the organization that experiences the problem. These "internal consultants" may be required to help solve almost any type of personnel or organizational problem. On the other hand, a consultant may be a member of the faculty of a college or university or of a private consulting firm that provides services to a variety of different organizations. These "external consultants" usually provide more specialized services. That is, they may be hired specifically because of their experience in dealing with a particular kind of problem.

One of the major services provided by I/O consultants is the *identification* and *diagnosis* of problems. When a company realizes that it is not meeting its objectives—as evidenced by low morale, high turnover, low productivity, conflict, etc.—it may engage a consultant to help determine the precise cause, location, type, and severity of its problem(s). In making this assessment, the consultant may conduct interviews, surveys, observations of workers, and a variety of statistical analyses. Based upon the obtained information, he or she will make recommendations concerning possible solutions to the problem. This service is extremely important because without a clear understanding of the nature and cause of organizational problems, improvement is unlikely.

After problems have been diagnosed, I/O consultants are often asked to assist in the *development* and *implementation* of programs (interventions) to alleviate or avoid the problems. Depending on the nature of the problem being addressed, these activities will focus upon (a) the individual worker—testing job applicants, developing training programs, providing counseling, etc.; (b) specific work groups—conducting team development programs, resolving intergroup conflicts, etc.; (c) the tasks performed by certain workers—redesigning jobs to make them more interesting or challenging, improving the fit between the employee and equipment, etc.; or (d) an entire personnel or organizational system—developing a selection, training, performance evaluation, or compensation system, or even redesigning the structure of the entire organization. When engaged in these activities the consultant is sometimes called a "change agent." As such, he or she must be sensitive to the needs of the employees, and must work closely with them in order to ensure their acceptance of the interventions.

Consultants also assist companies in *evaluating* the effectiveness of programs or organizational changes. Specifically, they may be asked to determine whether an intervention is operating as designed (e.g., are employees performing better after they have completed training?), to assess a program's cost effectiveness (e.g., do the benefits of a stress management program outweigh its costs?), and/or to compare potential alternative programs (e.g., is a testing program more likely to select successful employees than interviews?). This evaluation process may involve observing and interviewing employees, reviewing company records, examining the products of the program under evaluation, and developing and administering surveys. Based on data collected in these ways, the consultant will make recommendations for maintaining, revising, or discontinuing programs.

The variety of services provided by I/O consultants is illustrated by the following example: An external consultant was contacted by the manager of a midsized company that manufactures industrial parts. This manager had become alarmed by increasing waste, turnover, and product rejection rates within his plant. In order to identify and diagnose the cause(s) of these problems, an initial round of interviews was held with the plant managers, supervisors, and employees. It was determined that the employees felt as though they were unappreciated, that their needs and desires were not being considered by management, and that they had little control of, or input to, the operation of the plant. As a partial solution to this problem, the consultant recommended the institution of procedures to increase the participation of employees in the problem-solving and decision-making within the plant.

With the agreement and support of the plant manager, the consultant met with union and management officials in order to discuss the nature and necessity of employee participation programs. As a result of these discussions, the group agreed to establish a steering committee to examine the company's problems and to search for ways to increase employee participation in the solution of these problems. Volunteers from both labor and management were appointed to this committee.

With the assistance of the consultant, the steering committee decided to develop and implement a series of "quality circles," i.e., groups of about a dozen employees that were led by a zone-supervisor in the study of specific problems. The committee agreed to test the effectiveness of quality circles in one area of the plant and to determine how well they were accepted by employees before establishing them throughout the plant. In order to help reduce resistance to this participation program, information was communicated to all employees, and volunteers were solicited from the designated test area of the plant in order to form the initial quality circles. In addition, the consultant developed a program to train quality circle leaders to solicit input and to foster a supportive environment. He also developed a series of exercises that would help the leaders facilitate group interaction, participation, and teamwork.

After the developmental work was completed, these groups held a series of meetings designed to help identify problems, propose solutions, and evaluate the feasability of potential solutions. As a result of these circle meetings, several recommendations were made to upper management. While not all the recommendations were instituted, two of them were. The first was a revision of the work layout that could help reduce waste; the second was a method for improving communications within the plant.

Reactions to the quality circles were favorable and the steering committee (with the approval of upper management) decided to extend them gradually to other sections in the plant. Leaders of successful groups were asked to help train new group leaders. Evaluation of the quality circles is continuing, and they are being modified where necessary. However, it appears that waste is being reduced, quality is being improved, and the employees are pleased with their participation in plant improvements.

As indicated above, "people problems" abound in organizations, and the need to provide solutions to these problems is an important concern of most companies. The way in which employees are treated, and the way in which employees respond to the organization, is often the difference between success and failure for a company. Until this ceases to be true, I/O consultants will be called upon to assist in developing solutions that will allow the organization to operate more smoothly, productively, safely, and with higher levels of job satisfaction.

■ CONCLUSION

We have scratched the surface of scientific and practical concerns of I/O psychology. If there is a single pervasive goal of all activities in this field, it is that of facilitating the creation of work environments that are physically and psychologically safe and healthy. With special regard to the latter, I/O psychologists strive in all directions that encourage persons to make the most effective use of their present abilities, to develop new ones, and to do work that is intellectually and emotionally satisfying. Reviewing the aspects of I/O psychology presented in this chapter, I/O psychologists are most likely to be found creating and assessing new methods of measuring and predicting performance, and involving themselves to facilitate and improve the performance of trainees, workers, and leaders.

■ SUGGESTED READINGS

Dunnette, M.D. (Ed.) (1976). *Handbook of industrial and organizational psychology.* Chicago: Rand McNally.

> This comprehensive handbook is a basic reference source for graduate students and professionals in industrial-organizational psychology. It surveys methodology, theory, and practice in the field.

Landy, F. J., & Farr, J. F. (1980). Performance rating. *Psychological Bulletin, 87,* 72–107.

> This is a professional-level review of studies of performance ratings and the sources of their susceptibility to error. The authors integrate the literature by deriving a model that suggests the process of making performance judgments in applied settings.

Landy, F. J., & Trumbo, D. A. (1980). *Psychology of work behavior.* Homewood, IL: The Dorsey Press.

> This excellent survey of personnel and organizational psychology is written primarily for undergraduate students who have some familiarity with basic statistics and with the content of an introductory psychology course.

Schmitt, N. (1976). Social and situational determinants of interview decisions: Implications for the employment interview. *Personnel Psychology, 29,* 79–101.

> This article reviews research on interviews and their contributions to decision-making. It cites studies indicating the interview's unique contribution to employment selection, and presents a model concerned with the determinants of interview outcomes. Several practical suggestions are offered for the personnel interviewer.

Siegel, L., & Lane, I. M. (1982). *Personnel and organizational psychology.* Homewood, IL: Richard D. Irwin, Inc.

> A text written for a first undergraduate course in industrial-organizational psychology, the authors do not assume that the reader has taken previous coursework in psychology.

WILLIAM C. HOWELL

ENGINEERING PSYCHOLOGY

■ INTRODUCTION

Person–machine system design: The concept

Suppose you were asked to assemble a team of experts to design something—say a new kind of wrench, or a space shuttle, or a fifty story office building. What kinds of specialists would you choose? If you are like most of us, you would probably start with engineers or architects, the traditional design professions. Next you might add an expert user—in this case, perhaps, an auto mechanic, astronaut, or realtor—to contribute practical insights. Depending on your background and creativity, you might also include marketing specialists, lawyers, and a host of other professions. But the chances are that you would never think to recruit a psychologist.

You would not be alone in this oversight. Design teams have traditionally been more concerned with the cost, efficiency, reliability, and attractiveness of their creations than with the characteristics of the people who must use them. And it is in the latter domain, the scientific description of human capabilities and tendencies, that psychology has something to offer. There is an important

Over the past two years, I have had the opportunity to review prepublication manuscripts of several published or forthcoming books on this topic: (1) McCormick, E. J. and Sanders, M. S. (1982). *Human Factors in Engineering Design.* New York: McGraw-Hill; (2) Kantowitz, B.H., and Sorkin, R.D. (1983). *Human Factors.* New York: Wiley; and (3) Wickens, C. (under review) *Engineering Psychology and Human Performance.* Columbus, Ohio: Merrill. While I have attempted to reference all specific material drawn from these sources, I am sure that they influenced my thinking in many places and ways that cannot be so neatly pinned down. Therefore, I would like here to recognize the considerable contribution they have made to this chapter. W. C. H.

contrast in design philosophies involved here. The traditional approach might be called "machine-oriented" in that its aim is to construct something that works properly irrespective of the user. In fact, according to this philosophy, the less a design relies on people the better, since everyone knows that "to err is human." If a machine has met the predetermined design criteria and people have trouble using it, well, the human is obviously at fault.

The more enlightened approach holds that people and machines are partners, not antagonists. Together they constitute *systems* for accomplishing things—usually work. Each has a legitimate role to play, and it is the designer's job to strive for an efficient, reliable, and safe combination of human and nonhuman components. If a particular design results in a lot of errors or accidents, one does not bemoan the stupidity of the human operator; one tries to isolate those design features that contribute to the problem. Perhaps the only solution is more automation, which in essence designs the human out of the system. But in many, if not most, instances, a careful analysis will suggest a less radical solution: an improved information display, communication link, control device, or even training program. This more "user-oriented" view is generally referred to as the *person–machine system* philosophy. It calls, naturally, for an understanding of the strengths, operating limits, and tendencies of all components, including the human ones.

A useful way of depicting the person–machine philosophy is to trace the flow of information and/or energy through the various components of an abstracted system as shown in Figure 10.1. We assume that the object of the system is to achieve or maintain some desired state, such as keeping your car on the road and within the speed limit. The relevant information comes to you, the human component, in either literal or "processed" form via machine elements known as *displays* (e.g., the scene through your windshield and the speedometer, respectively). You use various *sense systems* to pick up this information and transform it into impulses that undergo a series of transformations as they traverse your *nervous system* (including your brain) and eventually deliver instructions for corrective action to an appropriate set of *muscles*. At this point the transition is made from person to machine, and from information to energy transfer as the muscles execute the action via *controls* (e.g., the steering wheel, accelerator, and brake). Thereupon a sequence of machine processes ensues similar to that for the person, and the car's position and speed change. You pick up the new state of affairs as before, decide whether it meets the criteria that you have stored in your memory, and the entire cycle is repeated. Finally, the whole process takes place within an *environment* that can greatly affect how well some or all of the components function: flooding might interfere with machine operation; fog or nerve gas with person operation; and so on.

This is, of course, a greatly simplified picture of what happens in most systems, but it is sufficient to illustrate the logic and the main principles involved in the person–machine design philosophy. First, it emphasizes the importance of

FIGURE 10.1   Illustration of the primary route of information flow through the person–machine system. *Source:* Chapanis, A. "Engineering Psychology," in Marvin D. Dunnette (Ed.) *Handbook of Industrial and Organizational Psychology.* Chicago: Rand McNally, 1976. (By permission of the editor.)

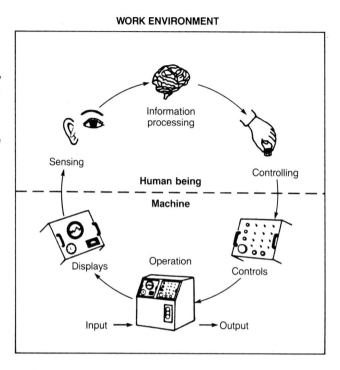

understanding both human and nonhuman components with an eye toward integrating them into an effective combination. A breakdown anywhere in the flow can cause problems. Second, it suggests that there are usually many alternative ways to allocate functions to achieve a given result (a principle sometimes referred to as *equipotentiality*). For example, your car might be equipped with "cruise control," a device that takes the functions of monitoring speed, computing corrections, and executing control action away from the human subsystem and puts them into a machine subsystem. Or, you might have a broken speedometer, which would make you responsible for computing speed in your head—a function, it turns out, for which you are not particularly well suited (Chubb, 1963). Much of the problem of system design reduces to questions of what functions should be assigned to which components.

Third, Figure 10.1 emphasizes some particularly vulnerable points in the system, notably those where person meets machine (known in the trade as *person–machine interfaces*). Misreading or ignoring human factors at these critical junctures has led to some costly and tragic design flaws as we shall see in the next section. And finally, the illustration implies that it makes more sense to consider human factors in the initial design of a system than after the cry of "human error" has gone up. Unfortunately, even though designers today are showing a greater interest in human factors than they have in the past, the typical application is still an after-the-fact correction. Far too seldom is the total system considered in the initial planning stage.

Some graphic illustrations

This chapter describes and illustrates a branch of psychology that is concerned explicitly with the human factors aspect of system design. It is called *engineering psychology*. In a moment we shall explore this discipline more fully, particularly with respect to how it developed and how it relates to several others. First, however, it might be well to establish that such a discipline is, indeed, necessary for the design of modern systems, and that the need is likely to grow rather than diminish as systems become more complex. So far we have made the case only in rather abstract terms. Let us look now at a few concrete examples to contrast what can happen when human factors are and are not properly recognized.

The Three-Mile Island accident ▪ One of the most serious peacetime nuclear accidents occurred at Three Mile Island in Pennsylvania on March 28, 1979. Accounts in the popular media pointed to a whole succession of "human errors" leading up to and exacerbating the disaster: failure to detect critical information, misinterpretation of what was detected, poor decisions based on that misinterpretation, more misinterpretation, and so on. Closer analysis, however, revealed an appalling lack of attention to human factors principles in the design of the plant and its operator tasks. Displays were poorly arranged and hard to read; key information was obscured or missing; tasks were designed in ways that are known to cause people problems in time of stress (Kemeny, 1979). While no one can say for sure that good human factors design would have prevented the accident, it is obviously a real possibility. Consequently, the Nuclear Regulatory Commission has begun a major project to work toward improvement in this aspect of existing and future plants (Hopkins, 1981).

Power presses ▪ Since the earliest days of modern industrialization, one of the most widely used pieces of manufacturing equipment has been the manually controlled power press—a device that brings tremendous force to bear on a point of contact to stamp, cut, or shape metal parts. It also has proved to be among the most dangerous, for it is equally adept at stamping out human parts such as fingers, hands, and arms. Since the danger is "open and obvious," however, it was many years before adequate safeguards were developed; and even today, guarding is not mandated as a condition of sale for presses in the United States (although it is in most European countries). The problem, of course, has always been failure to appreciate fully the human factors aspects of power press operation. Most of these tasks are repetitive and dull, features that are known to induce inattention and carelessness in human operators (Howell, Johnston, & Goldstein, 1966; Sussman & Morris, 1971). Most also put a premium on quantity of output, a feature that encourages operators to take short-cuts and risks—as in using one's fingers to clear material when it jams or binds on one of the plates. The only effective solution to this problem, short of complete automation, is a design principle that removes from the human subsystem the option of performing the clearing and activating tasks concurrently. This principle, *fail-safe design*, lies at one end of a continuum of approaches to safeguarding that is anchored on the other with simple warnings. The underlying difference, of course, is the extent to which responsibility for safety is vested in human consciousness as opposed to a machine element. Where a particular system belongs on this continuum requires careful consideration of human cognitive processes and the relative costs involved—not only of the design but of its predictable consequences. Warnings are cheap, but they will not prevent power-press accidents. Fail-safe devices, on the other hand, will prevent such accidents but are costly. While one could justify the cost to prevent serious bodily injury, one would have greater difficulty doing so as a deterrent to, for example, illegal parking.

Photoreconnaissance ▪ One of the major sources of information used by the defense establishment in both tactical and strategic operations is aerial photography. Pictures are taken from aircraft and space satellites using very sophisticated photographic techniques in an effort to monitor what is going on within some defined territory. For these records to be useful, however, they must ultimately be interpreted by a human, there being no adequate substitute for human visual perception in viewing complex scenes.

Several human factors principles have been used to improve the quality of these interpretations. One involves modifying the distribution of lightness–darkness over the scene in accordance with known properties of the visual system so as to "sharpen up" the image (Brainard & Ornstein, 1965). Another takes advantage of a perceptual illusion known as the "phi phenomenon" in which spatially separated lights activated in sequence appear to move. This works through time-lapse photography: The same scene is photographed at different times, and the resulting images are projected in rapid alternation or succession on a screen. Features that have changed between exposures (e.g., troop movements) will show up vividly as "phi" movement against a background of everything that has remained fairly constant. Still a third human factors principle recognizes that photointerpretation consists not only of perception but also of judgment of what is perceived (Brainard, Sadacca, Lopez, & Ornstein, 1966). As we shall see later, it is possible to estimate—and even manipulate—an individual's decision criterion (i.e., how much evidence is needed before a "target" is reported). Knowing this, we can "calibrate" the photointerpretor within limits to whatever level of assurance is deemed best for the system.

A household color-coding problem ▪ Recently I replaced a defective fan motor in my home air conditioning unit with the factory-authorized replacement part. The warehouseman assured me that the hook-up was identical to that for the original motor. Upon unpacking it, however, I discovered a slight difference in the color of the wires (the usual mode of designating the various leads): The green, white, black, and yellow of the original motor were replaced with green, *brown*, black, and yellow in the new one. "No problem," I thought; "since all the others are the same, brown must simply have been substituted for white." After an hour or so of pain and suffering under a 100-degree Houston sun, the new motor was mounted, wired up, and running. For about 15 minutes! Another hour of pain and suffering and a very irate amateur serviceman was on his way back to the warehouse with one "defective" new motor and some very dark thoughts concerning the offending company. Of course, the motor checked out just fine. Puzzled, the warehouseman dug through a pile of old manuals and eventually found the wiring diagram. White had been changed to yellow, and yellow to brown several years ago! Thus my hook-up caused the motor to run backwards (which I failed to notice in my excitement over the fact that it ran at all), it overheated, and that eventually activated the automatic cutoff, which is designed in to protect the motor from burning itself out.

This incident, though trivial in the greater scheme of things, is by no means an isolated illustration of poor design in everyday household products. Manufacturers have neglected human factors in this area as much—if not more so—than in the design of power plants and military systems. Only recently, with the growing incidence of product liability suits, has much thought been given to the user, and that is mainly with respect to safety. One does not have to look far to find many examples of products that are unnecessarily difficult to use, easy to misuse, or impossible to maintain. Returning to our illustration, one can only wonder what considerations went into the change in color coding (a sale on brown wire, perhaps?). Certainly anticipation of problems created for the potential user was not among them. On the other hand, anticipating a common threat to the welfare of the machine component, the designers saw fit to build in an overload switch. Here we see a classic case of the traditional "machine-oriented" philosophy. By contrast, good human factors design would have dictated against *any* coding change. Were one absolutely necessary for economic or other reasons, every effort would have been made to minimize the confusion (e.g., preserve as much as possible of the original code—green, black, and yellow—and indicate "brown replaces white" in a conspicuous place on the brown wire or motor). At the very least, an explanation of the code could have been affixed to each unit so that the installer would not have had to depend on an informed and cooperative distributor or an easily lost instruction sheet for the necessary information.

Four examples cannot, of course, do justice to the full scope of design problems to which engineering psychology either has made or could make an important contribution. They do, however, illustrate four major areas of application: military, energy, industrial, and everyday household systems. They also give some idea of the diverse forms that such a contribution can take, and the kind of benefits to be expected. Inputs range from little more than "common sense" (which, nonetheless, traditional designers seem rather prone to overlook) to specialized information on how people perceive things, make decisions, or react under stress. Potential benefits range from reducing inconvenience to improving performance, from saving time or money to saving limbs or lives, from making our everyday existence a little more pleasant to reducing the chances of a nuclear holocaust.

Some confusing labels

The main purpose in what you have read so far was to give you a "feel" for the field of engineering psychology and a justification for its existence. There are also some subtle distinctions—not all of which, I might add, are universally accepted—in the field (Alluisi & Morgan, 1976; Howell & Goldstein, 1970). *Engineering psychology* is a specialty of psychology which, as we shall see, had its origin in the basic science of psychology. While it is an applied specialty, concerning itself with using what we know about people, it retains a strong research orientation as well. *Human factors engineering* is the broader, more interdisciplinary field of which engineering psychology is an important part (Huchingson, 1981; Meister & Rabideau, 1965). Other specialties represented in human factors engineering include several branches of engineering (especially electrical and industrial), biomechanics, physiology, medicine, and anthropology. Many writers view the orientation of this larger field to be more "applied" and pragmatic than that of engineering psychology. To confuse matters even further, there is a third term for this general activity that is preferred everywhere in the world except the United States: *ergonomics* (McCormick & Sanders, 1982).

Since the present book is about psychology, we shall devote our primary attention and the remainder of this chapter to those aspects of human factors that clearly belong within the domain of engineering psychology. We shall explore its history in psychology, the principal places where it is applied in today's world of work, and the principal kinds of human functions with which it is presently most concerned.

■ HISTORICAL DEVELOPMENT

The early years: World War II

Engineering psychology was an outgrowth of World War II. During the war, systems development progressed on a crash basis (Taylor, 1957). Scientists and engineers of various kinds were recruited in large numbers and organized into project-oriented teams. In some cases, their task was to correct a design problem discovered through system failure, such as rifles that tended to "jam" under battle conditions. In other cases, their task involved creation of an entirely new concept, such as the atomic bomb. This multidisciplinary team approach was something new. Since it also proved quite effective, it became a model for peacetime systems development.

Many of the problems to which task forces were assigned turned out to have what we would now recognize as human factors implications: aiming weapons under low illumination, landing aircraft under poor visual conditions, receiving radio messages under severe distortion or noise (Meister & Rabideau, 1965; Taylor, 1957). It was discovered that research psychologists had been studying human sensing and perceiving capabilities for years, and as a result, had access to information that could be applied directly in the solution of such problems. Thus, psychologists began showing up on trouble-shooting teams and, as word of their contribution spread, their input was occasionally solicited in the conceptual stages of design as well. As the problems addressed became more complicated, the answers very often did not lie in existing psychological literature. It became necessary to undertake new human performance research in order to answer these questions, and topics thus were added to the mainstream of psychology that, in peacetime, might never have arisen. A good example was multichannel listening. The question was, how well can people follow voice communication that is superimposed on other conversations sharing the same channel? And what can be done to improve performance under these conditions? The resulting research produced not only practical answers to this question, but a whole new theory of human attention (Broadbent, 1958).

The kind of psychologists recruited for this role in system design and research were primarily experimentalists—scientists whose peacetime activities focused on the discovery of general principles of normal adult thought and action (Fitts, 1963). Other branches of the field, notably those specializing in clinical and industrial applications, also contributed mightily to the war effort, but in more traditional psychological activities—testing, selection, placement, counseling, training, etc. Engineering psychology thus grew out of the wartime discovery by psychological science and engineering practice that the two fields could interact to the profit of both.

The post-war era: 1940s to 1960s

After the war, engineering psychology continued and became formalized. The *Society of Engineering Psychologists* was founded and incorporated into the American Psychological Association (as Division 21) in 1957. That same year the *Human Factors Society* held its constitutional convention (Knowles, 1982). The *Ergonomics Society*, founded earlier in Great Britain, preceded both. Graduate programs and research institutes devoted exclusively to the field of engineering psychology were established at several major universities by the early 1950s (notably Ohio State, Michigan, Illinois, Johns Hopkins, and Tufts in the United States; the Applied Research Unit at Cambridge in England). Of course, even in peacetime, the field had a very strong military orientation, since much of the funding for research and training came directly or indirectly from agencies in the Department of Defense. In fact, every branch of the military operated one or more of its own laboratories, and these organizations worked very closely with their nonmilitary counterparts on both "basic" and "applied" issues in system design. Much of the seminal work on human information processing, decision-making, attention, and motor skill processes came directly out of Army, Navy,

Air Force, and Marine laboratories, or the civilian laboratories with which they were linked. So, too, did research on human tolerance for and ability to perform under unusual or stressful conditions (high and low "G" forces, heat and cold, high and low information input rates) as well as many other practical military and space-age issues.

The modern era: 1960s to 1980s

The fact that it was born and raised in a military setting, and spent its earliest years under the exigencies of war, did not predestine engineering psychology to a military career. One should always remember that its genetic heritage was not in application but in pure science—*experimental* psychology. Probably for this reason, it retained an abiding interest in fundamental principles of human performance, and therefore has had little difficulty adapting itself to other kinds of design problems. With the advent of the "space age" in the mid 1960s, it became deeply involved in the design of space vehicles and the tasks to be performed by astronauts (Chapanis, 1963). With the advent of the "computer age" in the 1970s, it turned its attention to improving person–computer interfaces, languages, and computer-assisted instruction (Parsons, 1981; Williges, 1982). Throughout, it has maintained an active role in the improvement of highway and automotive safety (Forbes, 1972; McFarland, 1963), industrial accident prevention (Cohen, Smith, & Anger, 1979), air-traffic control system design (Wiener, 1980), and the host of other civilian problems to which we referred earlier.

Changing systems, changing roles

There is one other thread that should be noted in tracing the field's history from the 1940s to the present. In its earliest days, the systems with which it was concerned were largely human-controlled. That is, though aided tremendously by machine components, people flew the aircraft, aimed and fired the guns, drove the tanks, and navigated the ships. Today, as everyone knows, automated or largely automated control is central to many of these activities. Humans are slipping much more into the role of monitor, planner, programmer; advanced systems draw more upon their intellectual and cognitive skills than upon their perceptual-motor skills (although the latter functions have by no means disappeared). What this has meant for engineering psychology is that its focus has shifted a bit in accordance with the new system demands (Bennett, Degan, & Spiegel, 1963). Studies of mental work-load measurement, divided attention, judgment, and decision-making have replaced those of display legibility, control "feel," and manual "tracking functions" in domination of the research literature.

Perhaps this trend can be best illustrated with reference to the changing demands of one particular kind of military activity: battlefield command, control, and communication (often referred to as C³I functions and systems). As summarized recently by Wohl (1981), the mobility of forces and the capability of

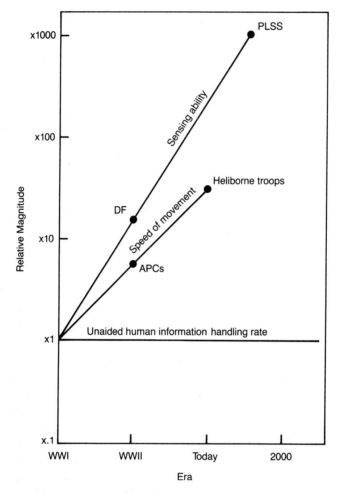

FIGURE 10.2   Battle-field information rate trends from the era of World War II to the end of the century. DF and PLSS refer to "direction finder" and "precision location and srike system" respectively; APCs are "armored personnel carriers." Adapted, with permission, from IEEE TRANSACTIONS ON SYSTEMS, MAN, AND CYBERNETICS, Vol SMC-11, No. 9, page 619, September 1981. Copyright © 1981 IEEE.

information-gathering (sensing) equipment have increased dramatically since WWI (see Figure 10.2). This means that to be effective, the commander must act upon more information in less time than ever before in the heat of battle. Strategies must often be changed in midcourse; revised plans must be coordinated quickly; any action can have immediate and profound consequences. The human capacity to process information, however, is the same as it always has been, i.e., limited. Therefore, it remains for the system designer to figure out how to augment the human capability. But in order to know what kinds of "aids" would help the most, the designer must understand the specifics of peoples' processing limitations. Otherwise, an "aid" might do little more than add further to the user's burden. Thus, whereas forty years ago, the main concern may have been providing the wing commander with more maneuverable aircraft or a better "picture" of enemy targets, today it is providing more intelligent use of both weapon systems and information.

As it exists today, then, engineering psychology studies human-performance capabilities and tendencies for the purpose of improving system design. It deals with both general questions about the way people function and specific design issues that arise in conjunction with specific systems. While the range of applications is large and growing, encompassing a host of military and civilian design problems, our technology has a lot to do with which human performance functions are of greatest interest at any particular time (Bennett, Degan, & Spiegel, 1963). Today, those functions involving human cognition (thought processes) and response capability under assorted stresses seem to occupy center stage.

■ WORK SETTINGS

It should be fairly apparent, in view of our preceding discussion, where one is likely to find engineering psychologists. They are employed full time by large academic, government, industrial, and independent research laboratories, often as part of identifiable engineering psychology or human factors groups. Many more serve as individual human factors experts on design or trouble-shooting teams in industrial, government, city planning, architecture, medical, legal, and other settings. Some of these are regular employees of the organizations; some are associated with consulting firms or work as independent consultants. Table 10.1 summarizes and illustrates these employment patterns.

T A B L E 10.1   **Approximate Distribution of Human Factors Society Members by Type of Employment in U.S.**

Employment category	Percentage of those classifiable (Total N = 1600)*
Federal government	13%
a. military	(9)
b. nonmilitary	(4)
State and local government	1
Medical	2
Industrial	41
Consulting	23
a. independent, smaller firms	(20)
b. larger fims	(3)
Academic	18
Nonacademic research institutes	2

*Since total membership is nearly 3000, our tabulation is obviously far from complete. Excluded were foreign members and individuals whose employment was not apparent from directory listings. Still, the above distribution gives a rough indication of employment patterns.

Source: 1982 *Human Factors Directory*

Perhaps the best way to explain what a typical engineering psychologist (if there is such a thing) might be found doing in these various contexts is again through examples. Let us take a quick tour of a few hypothetical work settings. Our focus here will not be so much on the subject matter or method used, but rather on the setting itself.

Government setting

Our guide is Captain Susan Falcone, working in an office complex assigned to the engineering psychology branch of an air force research and development (R&D) laboratory. She is surrounded by other human factors specialists and support personnel, both military and civilian. At present she is working on four projects, all related to the general problem of reducing the "down time" on a particular type of aircraft. An earlier design modification introduced to resolve this problem seems to be failing: it involved in-flight test and replacement of electronic components. The difficulty with the in-flight repair approach is that the technicians are replacing a lot of modules that are later shown to be good at a total cost that is becoming prohibitive. Fully 40 percent of their rejections turn out to be false alarms!

One of Capt. Falcone's current projects is a laboratory study designed to determine whether the high false-alarm rate is attributable to perceptual or decision aspects of the task. She has a research assistant conducting this study in an adjacent building, where a mock-up of the in-flight test equipment has been constructed. There, it will be possible to record hundreds of responses by technicians under a carefully controlled set of test conditions. When it is finished, the study will be written up as a technical report and, if it yields findings of more general applicability, may be submitted to a professional journal (e.g., *Human Factors*) for publication.

Her other three projects involve, respectively, a review and analysis of all reported in-flight failures of the components (a field study), experiments on human decision making being conducted at Forest State University under the direction of Dr. Ron Tower (Dr. Falcone serves as the air force technical monitor on this contract), and preparation of a "request for quotation" (RFQ) on a new contract for component development that will soon go out for competitive bids. In the field study and RFQ projects, she serves with engineers and systems analysts as part of a project team. As technical monitor, she performs an individual liaison function between the sponsoring Air Force laboratory and Dr. Tower's group.

In addition to her four ongoing responsibilities, Capt. Falcone is often asked to provide temporary help with other projects. In this capacity she serves as a resident human factors consultant, advising or assisting design teams on specific problems. As we are about to leave, for example, she is on her way to help resolve a dispute over where a new display should be placed in a proposed cockpit layout.

This illustration is fairly representative of the engineering psychologist's function in both military and nonmilitary government organizations (such as NASA, the Department of Transportation, and the Federal Aviation Administration). The mix of laboratory research, field studies, monitoring, specifications writing, and internal consulting might vary, but some combination of these activities usually defines the job.

Academic setting

Dr. Tower's laboratory is located in the basement of the Psychology wing of the new Social Science Building at Forest State. It consists of a large central area in which research planning, data analysis, data and equipment storage, and a variety of other research-support activities are carried on; several "cubicles" that serve as graduate student offices; and a half-dozen completely enclosed rooms that house the actual experimentation. The latter range in size from small booths, which are designed for testing individual "subjects," to a large conference-type room which, at present, is outfitted to resemble a military command post. Several contain small laboratory computers on which various experimental tasks are programmed. Two of these are currently being used to run the decision experiments for Capt. Falcone's Air Force project.

As we tour the facilities, Dr. Tower explains how he and other engineering psychologists function in the academic world. We learn that he spends about 75 percent of his time during the nine-month academic year on the teaching and "service" activities that occupy all professors. Another 15 percent is taken up by professional duties, such as editing manuscripts, and doing committee work. The remaining 10 percent, plus the summer months, he devotes primarily to research—reading the literature, writing proposals and reports, designing and managing experiments, and supervising a small research staff (currently three graduate assistants, a part-time clerk-typist, and a full-time technician). He also spends an average of several days a month as a paid consultant, advising design teams on specific human factors problems and, occasionally, even rendering expert testimony in legal actions. One such case in which he is currently involved hinges upon the question of whether, from a human factors standpoint, the warnings on a can of drain cleaner are sufficient to protect the reasonably prudent user from serious harm.

Noting the variety of experimental set-ups around the lab, we wonder how all these projects are funded and organized. That, Dr. Tower admits, is his number one headache! His whole research operation, it turns out, is largely entrepreneurial. To keep it going, he must compete against other researchers in other institutions for the limited number of grants and contracts awarded each year by various funding agencies (e.g., the Air Force, the Department of Transportation, the National Science Foundation, large aerospace firms). Since most awards are for one- or two-year projects, and few are large enough to underwrite his entire laboratory, he spends a great deal of his research time developing grant proposals as well as initiating and concluding activities for those contracts he has been able to win.

While Dr. Tower's situation is fairly typical, he hastens to add that there are many variations on this general theme. Some professors, particularly in smaller institutions, carry on a single line of research in their primary interest area with whatever support they can muster (usually modest "outside" funding plus considerable help from the university itself). Others, particularly at large state universities, combine their efforts, often across disciplines, to form large-scale research institutes.

Our visit at an end, we thank Dr. Tower for his time, and ask whether he could recommend any further sites to round out our education in the working environment of the engineering psychologist. His only suggestion is private industry. It happens that a former Forest student, Dr. Tom Cash, is now employed at the Product Development Laboratories of Communication Services, Inc.; Dr. Tower suggests that we contact him.

Industrial setting

Dr. Cash begins his description of the engineering psychologist role at Product Development Laboratories by referring to a flip chart mounted on a tripod behind his desk. He has obviously given this briefing before. Running quickly through the organization chart on the first page, he explains that there are three human factors groups in all: one in the Advanced Concepts Division, a basic research group funded largely out of patent revenues; another under Military Products, a division devoted exclusively to Department of Defense Contracts; and the third under Consumer Products, an internally funded division concerned with research and development on existing product lines. In addition, there are a few engineering psychologists assigned to special projects in operations, such as a nationwide changeover to a new system for handling customer repair orders that is currently in progress.

The people in Advanced Concepts are free to pursue virtually any research idea that they consider relevant to any facet of the company's operations. Those at Military Products are also mainly engaged in research; however, like Dr. Tower, they spend a lot of time on proposal writing and other contract matters. Unlike him, they are limited by corporate policy to pursuing projects that are consistent with the company's overall mission. This, however, is considerably more flexibility than is enjoyed by Consumer Products. There, projects are simply assigned to individuals or teams in priority according to what management perceives as the greatest practical urgency.

Basically, then, the engineering psychologists at Product Development Laboratories may function in any of a number of roles, from basic researcher to applied problem solver, to middle-level manager. The main difference between the industrial and military setting seems to be the extent to which, in the former, corporate policies and objectives (notably profitability) operate to direct his or her activities.

Other settings and methods

If someone wanted a first-hand look at engineering psychologists in their work habitat, a tour of the sort just described would present a fairly accurate picture. However, the hypothetical itinerary was far from complete. Had time permitted, we might have visited a few full-time consultants, a nonprofit research institute, a large medical center, and some of the other locations noted earlier. Each would have added something to our evolving job description, but once we got past the specific problem context, most of what we saw would have seemed quite familiar.

Before moving on to a consideration of some of the main problem areas, it might be well to mention one final aspect of the work setting: methodology. Obviously, engineering psychologists who spend some or all of their time in the laboratory (as was the case for all three of our hypothetical hosts) rely on experimentation to answer design questions. One might find them using very simple, abstract tasks (such as a device to measure human reaction times to lights or tones) or very elaborate, realistic ones (such as an automobile driving simulator). In either case the object would be to discover how human response varies as conditions of interest are changed in a systematic, controlled fashion. Does display X or display Y produce better overall performance? How does speed and accuracy drop off as progressively larger amounts of irrelevant information are fed into the display, or doses of alcohol are fed into the body?

By contrast, those who work mainly in field locations are more likely to use analytic methods. Their aim is primarily to describe the system for purposes of understanding it, evaluating it, or improving it. Analysis, of course, can take many forms, and the descriptive data have many potential uses. For example, we might find our analyst measuring physical features (sound and light levels, display formatting, anthropometric characteristics of operators), task features (amount and kind of information to be processed, speed and accuracy norms, communication linkages), and even subjective features (user complaints, questionnaire responses). These data might be used to construct a physical or computer simulation which, in turn, might be used in training system operators, modeling (and evaluating) alternative design options, or conducting experimental research. Or the analyst might simply wish to search the descriptive data for logical design flaws.

Some engineering psychologists are involved relatively little in either experimentation or analysis, serving instead as human factors experts on design teams. For them, the principal methodology may be little more than reviewing plans and referring to data in human factors handbooks (e.g., Parsons, 1972; Shackel, 1974; Van Cott & Kinkade, 1972; Woodson, 1981) and the scientific literature. However, in this capacity, they may find it necessary to make frequent use of statistical and computer techniques.

■ FOCAL AREAS FOR RESEARCH AND APPLICATION

In the preceding pages we have touched upon a variety of human factors issues in the course of exploring what engineering psychology and those who practice it are all about. Now it is time to consider such issues a bit more systematically and in a little greater depth. Naturally, it is impossible to do justice to any of these topics in the few pages available. Therefore we shall look only at problem areas that seem to be of particular current interest, and even then, without much attention to the vast literature that has accumulated on each.

A convenient way to organize this material is in terms of the general flow of information through the system (see Figure 10.1) with particular emphasis on the human functions involved. While we know that it is a gross oversimplification, classification in terms of *input, central processing, output*, and *work environment* issues has proven useful. Thus we shall examine a few of the problems involved in detecting and interpreting signals (the display–person interface), in "mentally" processing or transforming the information (human information processing functions), in choosing and executing responses (the person–control interface), and in functioning under various stresses and strains imposed by the task setting.

Problems in detecting and interpreting signals

It almost goes without saying that humans can be of little use to the system unless they are able to pick up key information about the system's mission: its current status, the desired state, feedback from corrective action, or some combination thereof. Although accurate and timely reception of signals conveying such information is not a sufficient condition for system performance, it is certainly a necessary one. Therefore, good human factors design requires that we know what characteristics of signals affect human receiving proficiency as well as how the two are functionally related. Of course, the better we understand the basic ways in which human sensing and perceiving systems work, the easier time we have identifying potentially important signal or display properties.

There exists at this point a great deal of pertinent information on both the fundamental properties of sensory and perceptual systems and desirable features for signals and displays to have. We know, however, that the best designs cannot be determined completely without considering how the person must use the information: Task and display variables often have an interactive effect on system performance.

A good example of this interaction may be seen in a study of five different coding (display) schemes used in combination with five different system tasks. Subjects were required to count, identify, verify, locate, or compare items on a map-like display when presented as numerals, letters, geometric shapes, configurations, or colors. As shown in Figure 10.3, people generally performed well with numeral designations and not so well with configural ones. But within dif-

FIGURE 10.3   Relative performance on five different tasks as a function of the type of code used to convey the information. Points are connected only to facilitate task comparisons—the shape of the "functions" has no meaning. From *Human Factors Engineering and Design* by E. J. McCormick and M. S. Sanders. Copyright © 1982 McGraw-Hill Book Company. Used with permission of McGraw-Hill Book Company.

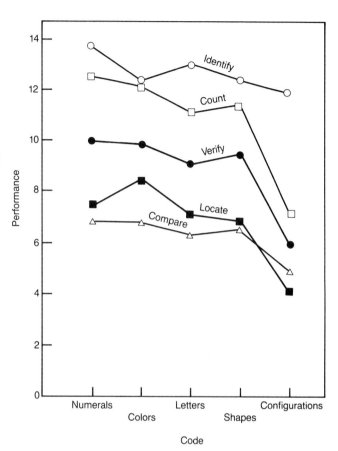

ferent tasks, the best code was not always the same: color was best for location but relatively poor for identification; shape was good for verifying and counting, but not so good for either locating or identifying. It is because such interactions are common that it is desirable to test any proposed set of display options in either the actual system or a simulation of it before finally implementing them.

Despite all we know about presenting information to people, many practical issues still remain. We shall consider just two of these: the low-frequency input problem and symbolic representation of everyday information.

Low-frequency input ▪ Technological advances have made it increasingly rare for human operators to deal with anything but highly processed input signals. In fact, in many cases their principal function is to monitor largely automated processes for the occasional malfunction or the unanticipated occurrence that cannot be incorporated into the program. Sometimes, the to-be-reported events are well defined and easily identifiable; in other cases, their characteristics are not known precisely in advance, so that identification involves an element of judgment. Very often the consequences of missed signals, misinterpreted (or falsely reported) signals, or delays in reporting signals are most severe. Consider, for example, the Three Mile Island situation, the anesthesiologist monitoring the vital signs of a patient, the air traffic controller watching for potential midair collisions, or the missile warning officer surveying his CRT for evidence of nuclear attack. It is, in fact, precisely because of the critical nature of mistakes that we do not care to relinquish complete control over certain situations to machines.

The problem is that people are generally not very good at maintaining their proficiency over prolonged periods of watch-keeping. As illustrated in Figure 10.4, it has been shown repeatedly in a wide variety of studies that a substantial "vigilance decrement" occurs after as little as an hour on the job. Recognizing

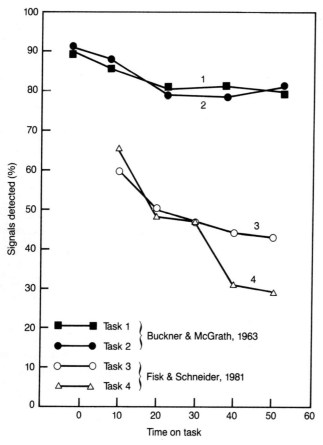

FIGURE 10.4 Decrements in monitoring performance reported in two different studies using four different tasks. (Adapted from sources cited and included in the list of references.)

this problem, researchers have explored the phenomenon from many different angles hoping, on the one hand, to gain a better understanding of the human processes responsible for it, and on the other, to formulate human factors recommendations to help overcome this threat to system performance.

Progress has been made on both fronts. One approach that has proven particularly useful in analysis of the problem derives from a general theory of signal detection (TSD or Theory of Signal Detectability). The basic premise of TSD is that devices for distinguishing between the occurrence of signals (which always appear in conjunction with some level of background "noise") and nonsignals (i.e., the "noise" alone) operate by transforming the evidence available at any given time into a likelihood estimate (i.e., the "odds" that the observation at hand came from a distribution of evidence generated by "noise" alone vs. one generated by "signal + noise").

As you can see from the hypothetical case in Figure 10.5, as the observed evidence (point on the x-axis) shifts from left to right, the odds (indicated by the relative position of that point on the two curves) move from strongly favoring the N *alone* to strongly favoring the S + N interpretation. If our signal detection device isn't allowed to respond with "odds," but must tell us whether or not it thinks a signal is present, it must pick some point on the x-axis (i.e., some odds level) above which it will say "signal" and below which it will say "noise." This is called a decision *criterion* or β. All other things being equal, an ideal device would choose the point where the curves cross (dashed line) as its β, since this criterion will be as accurate when it says "signal" as when it says "noise." In the case shown (arrow), however, the point chosen is conservative, suggesting that the device considers false alarms more serious than missed signals. Naturally, anything that brings the S + N and N distributions closer together will increase

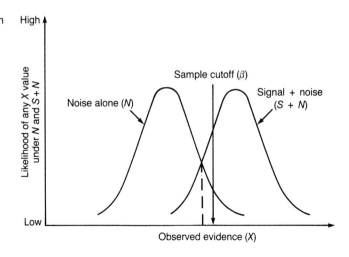

FIGURE 10.5   Illustration of the conceptual elements of the Theory of Signal Detectability (TSD) using hypothetical S and S + N distributions, and a rather conservative decision cutoff (i.e., one that, for the assumed distributions, requires nearly a 3:1 likelihood favoring the presence of a signal).

the overlap and therefore move the odds for whatever β is chosen closer to even, making the decision tougher. Spreading them apart will have the opposite effect. Separation, then, increases discriminability, and is indexed by a measure called d', which should be independent of β.

When people are serving as monitors, they are behaving as signal detection devices. Using a TSD analysis, it is possible to estimate what condition they are using as their internal decision criterion (β), and how well they are able to distinguish the two distributions $(d'$ or pure discriminability). The advantage of this sort of analysis is that it allows one to pinpoint where in the human receiving process any variable has its principal effect, and that, in turn, suggests what might be done about it. If, for example, a vigilance decrement represented a progressive relaxation in β, one would take steps to maintain the operator's decision standards (possibly through training). If, instead, ability to distinguish signal and nonsignal conditions (d') deteriorated over the watch, the solution might be to increase the signal's distinctiveness. As it turns out, both kinds of effects can occur under certain task conditions (Broadbent & Gregory, 1965), and both potential remedies have been used together with a number of others (Buckner & McGrath, 1963).

The TSD model is not, of course, the only way to look at monitoring performance. One team of researchers, for example, has suggested recently that vigilance declines only if the task requires expenditure of "mental effort." Some monitoring tasks, it seems, can be performed almost "automatically," and on these, people hold up very well (Fisk & Schneider, 1981). Nevertheless, the TSD approach has proven both theoretically and practically useful in a host of human performance contexts—monitoring is just one of them.

Symbolic coding ▪ You have undoubtedly noticed over the past few years a dramatic increase in the number of public signs that are coded as symbols rather than words. Perhaps you thought it was just another indication of what some see as our growing illiteracy crisis! Actually, the trend is in part due to the increase in international trade and travel, and in part the result of solid human factors evidence (Mackett-Stout & Dewar, 1981). It turns out that symbols have been found superior to printed messages in a number of different studies using a number of different performance indexes (Cahill, 1975; Dewar & Ells, 1974; Walker, Nicolay, & Stearns, 1965).

Why, then, does this pose a problem? There are at least two reasons, both illustrative of more general coding issues. One has to do with the origin and standardization of symbols, the other, with the way they are evaluated (Howell & Fuchs, 1968). For the most part, the specific symbols we see are not the result of any systematic, scientific, or even standardized development process. In fact, one can find a number of different representations of the same concept in different locales, and as more items are added to the lexicon, the confusion can only increase. Eventually, whatever advantage they may have had may be overwhelmed by sheer lack of a sound development strategy. A similar situation has occurred, incidentally, in the case of stop lights. The most common forms of colorblindness involve confusion of reds with greens. Recognizing this, one can make traffic lights suitable for both normal and color-weak drivers by adding a lot of blue to either the red or green light, and yellow to the other. And many local governments have, in fact, done just that. The only problem is, some have elected to add the blue to the green signal, others, to the red! Therefore, as the color-weak driver goes from town to town, the additional cue does absolutely no good. The message is, of course, that the time to evaluate symbols for any widespread use is before they are adopted; and once adopted, the use should be standardized.

This leads to the second issue: method of evaluation. The engineering psychologist would typically measure the quality of a symbol set by having subjects use them in actual task performance. The question is, what task? A host of different ones have been used—preference ratings, comprehension tests, reaction-time measures, legibility tests, etc.—under various display conditions, and the results have been far from uniform. Recently, several investigators have attempted to develop more defensible and general approaches to evaluation. Mackett-Stout and Dewar (1981), for example, have devised and tested an "efficiency index" comprised of four subtasks: legibility distance, comprehension, preference, and glance legibility. Geiselman, Landee, and Christen (1982) have developed another "index," a measure of perceptual discriminability, for use in expanding an existing symbols set. Despite these positive steps, however, the question of how to generate and choose the best symbols is still far from answered.

Problems in central processing

The aspect of human performance that has received more attention than any other over the past few decades is the set of cognitive or "mental" operations that people use to transform input signals into a form appropriate for the task at hand. How do they encode the information they have received? Store it for later use? Retrieve it when needed? Combine it with other information? Filter out competing or irrelevant signals? What are their capacity limits in these functions, and what happens when capacities are exceeded?

Much of the research on these processes has been carried out at a very basic level. That is to say, tasks and experimental conditions have been designed principally to isolate cognitive *structures*—the elementary mental operations that people apply fairly consistently to a rather narrow range of problems. Posner and McLeod (1982) distinguish the structural approach from studies of cognitive *traits* (the individual's typical mode of dealing with all kinds of problems), *states* (mode of dealing with them at some particular time), and *strategies* (typical mode of dealing with a narrow range of problems). Since the cognitive tasks posed by real-world systems rarely involve simple structures, and successful performance undoubtedly depends upon trait, state, and strategy considerations as well, it is often difficult to translate cognitive-process principles into human factors recommendations. For this reason, we shall not venture into the vast body of literature on cognitive structures—the interested reader should consult works by Bourne, Dominowski, and Loftus (1979), Wicklegren (1979), Lachman, Lachman, and Butterfield (1979), or Nickerson (1980) for this material.

Again, we shall direct our attention to a few selected problems that are of current practical interest and seem to be generating applicable research.

S–R compatibility ▪ It has been recognized for some years that people can transform inputs into outputs better under some display–control arrangements than under others. They will do a more accurate job of controlling a vehicle, for example, if the control movement is in the direction they want the vehicle to go rather than where they would like the target to be. Physical correspondence, in other words, is obviously an important relationship, especially when physical control is involved.

However, once one gets beyond the realm of simple spatial and movement relationships, the situation becomes much less clear. Should the up or down position of a switch turn things on (the norm on this, incidentally, is different in the U.S. and in England)? What about the arrangement of keyboards? How should inputs be coded for the "cerebral" kinds of tasks that we have said are coming to dominate the human role in system affairs? It turns out that even in these situations, the mapping of the stimulus set onto the response set usually matters. Sometimes there is a logical principle involved; sometimes the only apparent explanation is convention (i.e., population stereotypes that have evolved, as in the case of the light switches). Sometimes, as in the case of the standard typewriter keyboard, the logical principle, and the convention work in opposition. We know that a more efficient arrangement is possible; however, the present stereotype is so firmly entrenched that to adopt the more efficient version would create total chaos in the clerical workforce!

Because the "best" coding relationship is not immediately obvious in many cases, it falls to the engineering psychologist to measure the relative effectiveness of alternative schemes. The result of this measurement, and the concept it measures, is usually called *S–R compatibility*. While ways to do this are limited only by the ingenuity of the experimenter, a very common approach is one that conceptualizes the human as a communication channel. Communication engineers have a convenient way of specifying quantity of information (the *bit*), which is based on the number and probability of all the messages that could be sent over a channel: the more likely a particular message is, the less information (fewer bits) it can convey even if transmitted perfectly (see, for example, Fitts & Posner, 1967, or Howell & Goldstein, 1971, for further description). Using this measure, one can evaluate a channel by comparing the information going in with that coming out in terms of either absolute amount (bits transmitted) or, more often, rate of transmission (bits/sec). Now, the basic idea of S–R compatibility is that the "human channel" is more efficient under some coding arrangements than others; consequently, those arrangements that produce the highest bit rates are taken as the most compatible (e.g., Howell & Fuchs, 1968).

Processing capacity and mental work load ▪ Measures such as transmission rate, reaction time, and correct response rate can be used to tell us things about human processing capabilities as well as the efficiency of coding arrangements. In fact, much of our understanding of cognitive structures comes from studies in which a subject's speed and/or accuracy in responding to inputs is measured as a function of systematic variations in task conditions. The logic behind this approach is that any information processing activity involves a series of mental operations, each of which takes time and adds a potential for error. Greater delays and more errors imply more processing steps. If the experimenter is clever in choosing task conditions, the functions attributable to specific steps (structures), such as encoding, central processing, response selection, and response execution, can be isolated (Briggs & Swanson, 1970; Posner & McLeod, 1982). One implication of this logic is that a highly compatible S–R pair requires fewer steps than an incompatible pair.

It turns out, however, that the processing picture is much more complicated than this because, for one thing, not all "steps" happen in serial order: some work in parallel (e.g., Taylor, 1976). Another complication is that people seem to have a limited amount of total processing capability (*capacity*), and how they allocate it is somewhat under their control (Lane, 1982). Thus, for example, investing a lot of attentive effort in a difficult encoding operation (say, trying to decipher a garbled message) might make you forget a phone number you were about to dial or fail to see an important warning on your CRT. And finally, there is growing evidence that not all kinds of processing operations draw on a common store (Kantowitz, 1982); some, in fact, may be so "cheap" in capacity demand that they are virtually automatic (e.g., driving car under nonstressful conditions; Shiffrin & Schneider, 1977).

What all this means is that it is virtually impossible to specify the human capacity for handling information in any absolute sense. But the capacity question is among the most important practical issues in human factors today. Despite the fact that, as we saw earlier, people are not as directly involved in system control as they once were, they are far from inactive. Very often, mental effort has been substituted for physical effort. Even though overt action may be called for less frequently, and, when taken, may just involve pushing a few buttons, the mental activity leading up to that act may be intense, and the potential consequences, catastrophic (Sheridan, 1980).

So, we have a problem. Many tasks to which people are being assigned require them to process more and more information under greater and greater pressure, but we have no handy means of predicting when their capacity is about to be overtaxed, nor have we a convenient way to express the total work load under which they are operating. Both of these aspects of the problem, however, are being actively pursued by engineering psychologists today.

Attempts to quantify mental work load have produced a number of physiological, subjective, and performance measures (Beatty, 1982; Moray, 1982). Unfortunately, they do not agree very well as they should if they were all measuring the same construct. Moreover, little is known about the specific mental processes that underlie them. Still, some have proven of considerable practical value for particular task settings. The scales shown in Figure 10.6, for example, are used to describe the subjective "flyability" of aircraft. Measures obtained using these scales agree very nicely with objective measures of system characteristics that are known to influence control difficulty. Also, the obtained ratings correspond closely to actual performance measures.

Progress is also being made in the measurement of human capacity for dealing with particular kinds of tasks. The way this is generally done is by having subjects perform multiple tasks singly and in combination, and measuring their performance under single- and multiple-task conditions using some typical index such as reaction time or processing rate. The extent to which proficiency on each single task drops off as others are added (or to which combined performance falls short of what one would get by combining the component single-task scores) is taken as an index of the capacity limitation. In this way one can compute a "Performance Operating Characteristic" (POC) that describes the extent to which pairs of tasks draw upon the same mental resource.

In one such study, for example, Wickens and his associates (1981) plotted POC functions for all combinations of four common tasks: tracking, classification, line judgment, and auditory running memory. These tasks were chosen because they typify activities that are believed to use somewhat distinct stores of mental capacity. As shown in Figure 10.7, the results generally supported their expectations. That is, the pairs that are supposed to be most distinct (hence to produce the least dual-task decrement) plotted in the upper-right portion of each graph (i.e., in the direction of 0 decrement on both tasks). Those involving similar activities (e.g., LL, LC, CC, TT) were generally below the midpoint. Pairing two classification tasks (CC) turned out to have a large and equal effect on both; pairing line-judgment with classification (LC), however, hurt classification proficiency much more than it did line judgment.

Judgment and decision making ▪ In citing death and taxes as the only sure things in life, Mark Twain may have been guilty of overstating the case, but not by much. There are few situations we face that are totally predictable, very few tasks we perform that require absolutely no judgment of future prospects, contingencies, or relationships. Take, for example, the simple case of loosening a "frozen" bolt. An inexperienced mechanic, if strong enough, will increase the applied torque until the bolt either comes free or breaks off. An experienced one

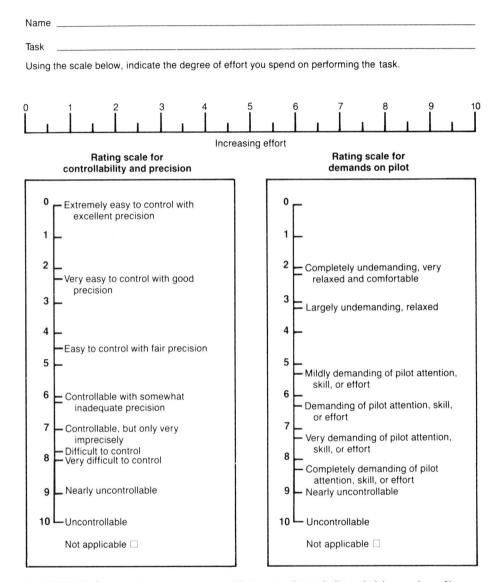

Name _____

Task _____

Using the scale below, indicate the degree of effort you spend on performing the task.

0   1   2   3   4   5   6   7   8   9   10

Increasing effort

Rating scale for controllability and precision

0 — Extremely easy to control with excellent precision

1

2
  — Very easy to control with good precision

3

4
  — Easy to control with fair precision

5

6 — Controllable with somewhat inadequate precision

7 — Controllable, but only very imprecisely
  — Difficult to control
8 — Very difficult to control

9 — Nearly uncontrollable

10 — Uncontrollable

Not applicable ☐

Rating scale for demands on pilot

0

1

2 — Completely undemanding, very relaxed and comfortable

3 — Largely undemanding, relaxed

4

5 — Mildly demanding of pilot attention, skill, or effort

6 — Demanding of pilot attention, skill, or effort

7 — Very demanding of pilot attention, skill, or effort

8 — Completely demanding of pilot attention, skill, or effort

9 — Nearly uncontrollable

10 — Uncontrollable

Not applicable ☐

FIGURE 10.6   A set of questionnaire items filled out by pilots to indicate their impressions of how demanding a particular aircraft is to fly. (From *Human Factors,* 1982, *24*, 25–41. Copyright © 1982 by the Human Factors Society, Inc., and reproduced by permission.)

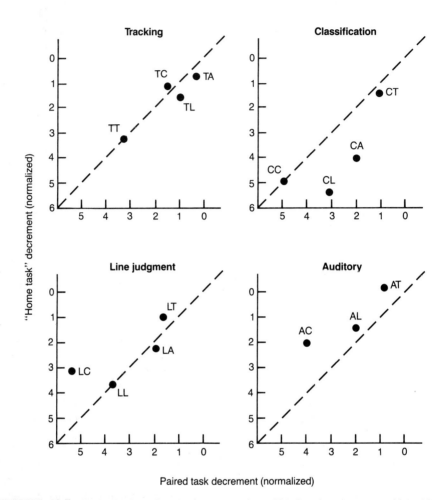

FIGURE 10.7 Reduction in performance on one task resulting from its concurrent pairing with another. Each point represents a pair; nine pairings of four different tasks are shown (some twice). No decrement in either task would be plotted at 0-0; the dashed lines represent all points of equal decrement in both members of a pair. Pairing a task with itself (TT, LL, CC) necessarily results in a point on that line. (From *Human Factors*, 1981, *23*, 221–229. Copyright © 1981 by the Human Factors Society, Inc., and reproduced by permission.)

will stop short of the break point, recognizing, from a combination of stored information and sensory input, that the chances of a successful outcome are dropping off fast while those of a disasterous outcome are becoming prohibitive.

In the long run, of course, system performance reflects the quality of a host of such judgments and decisions. Broken bolts add up to wasted time and money; misinterpreted intelligence data adds up to situations such as the Bay of Pigs and the embassy takeover in Iran (and could bring us World War III). It is therefore important to understand how people process the information that they use in making decisions under conditions of uncertainty, to determine how good the resulting decisions are, and to explore ways to make them better.

Until a few decades ago, the only scientists interested in such matters were the economists, for whom people were seen as rational decision-making entities who, though perhaps imperfectly, operate to maximize their marginal expected profit or utility. Since the laws of probability define rationality in risky situations, the economic view assumed that such rules also serve as a model for human judgment. Most psychologists probably knew better, but it took another economist (Herbert Simon, who, incidentally, is also a psychologist and won a Nobel Prize for his effort) to point out that people just do not approach risky decisions in so reasoned a fashion (Simon, 1957). Often they settle for the first acceptable option that comes along rather than trying to maximize profit, utility, or anything else. Thus, "rationality," in the classical sense, is a poor starting point for an account of human decision behavior.

Somewhat surprisingly, when psychology finally got into the act, it was the classical economic view—not Simon's—that dominated its first decade of decision research (roughly, the 1960s). The assumption was that, yes, people do act rationally, seek to maximize utility, and intuitively apply the right rules. The only problem is, they are limited in what they can do mentally (see previous topic), and also have certain biases. Therefore, the proper approach to understanding and predicting human decision behavior is (a) to rescale "objective" quantities, such as probabilities and dollars, into "subjective" ones, such as uncertainty and utility values, and (b) to determine how far (and in what way) people go wrong in their efforts to apply the optimization rules (Slovic, Fischhoff, & Lichtenstein, 1977).

Not all the work during the 1950s and 1960s, however, was in the economic tradition. Several investigators, notably Hammond and Naylor (see Slovic & Lichtenstein, 1971, for review), took a more descriptive direction. Like Simon, they were not inclined to view human decision behavior as an approximation to any rational model; rather, they used statistical methods (linear regression analysis) to infer what "policy" people were, in fact, applying. This work, too, has resulted in practical applications. For example, through a procedure known as "bootstrapping," a decision maker's policy is "captured" (or described statistically), a model of it is created, and the model is used in making subsequent choices (Slovic, 1982). The advantage of this approach is that it allows the human's value system to be applied in decision-making more consistently than is humanly possible.

Early in the 1970s Simon's original argument was rediscovered and given additional impetus through a series of studies by Tversky and Kahneman (see Kahneman, Slovic, & Tversky, 1982). What they showed was, in essence, that behavior often does not even approximate normatively optional rules. Rather, people seem to rely on handy rules of thumb or "heuristics" that, while not the best they could do, probably have served them reasonably well in the past, or so it seems to them. After all, they rarely get the kind of feedback that would indicate the existence of a better way (Einhorn, 1980).

The Tversky and Kahneman work has led to a whole decade of descriptive research—attempts to identify the kinds of biases heuristic processing yields and to understand some of the causal factors. From a practical standpoint, attempts have also been made to find ways to reduce the biases (Fischhoff, 1982).

All of the major lines of decision research, then, have increased our understanding and led to suggestions for improving the performance of decision systems. At the present time, however, concern seems to be growing over the fact that specific task conditions may have a lot to do with how the decision maker approaches various problems (Einhorn & Hogarth, 1981). The project for the 1980s, therefore, seems to be one of teasing out and organizing these (often subtle) task influences (Einhorn & Hogarth, 1981; Payne, 1982).

Problems in executing responses

Despite the trend toward automated and semiautomated control, there will probably always be system tasks that require skilled movements of one sort or another. Thus, while it is no longer the central issue that it once was, how people execute skilled movements still concerns engineering psychologists. Today, they share that interest with researchers from other fields (notably physical education).

Research in this area has generally taken one of two forms: attempting to describe, analyze, or model the movement pattern produced by the human controller in relation to a time-varying input signal and attempting to analyze the processes involved in discrete movements. The former has tended to favor use of so-called "tracking" tasks in which the controller attempts to follow as closely as possible a programmed course by moving a wheel, joystick, or some other control device. The target and response signals are usually displayed either separately (*pursuit* tracking) or as to-be-corrected error (*compensatory* tracking) on a CRT display, much in the fashion of modern video games; performance is measured in terms of various error indexes (e.g., time-on-target, average error, "lead" or "lag" error, and so on; see Briggs, 1966). Discrete movement research, on the other hand, has tended to use fairly simple tasks such as "aiming," in which the subject moves a stylus from a "home" position to a "target" position as quickly as possible on command. Success in hitting the target and travel time (measured from leaving the home position to contacting the target) are common measures of performance.

The great appeal of the laboratory tracking task lay in its close resemblance to real-world vehicular control. In fact, it allowed researchers to incorporate any sort of machine dynamics they wished in order to study human proficiency or the relative merit of different design features under realistic control conditions.

A host of studies were carried out on everything from display features to control "feel" to the dynamic properties of the task itself.

While this work was undoubtedly useful in many aspects of system design (and still is), it never produced the insight into human control processes that many had hoped it would. Today, the tracking task is still widely used in research on other issues, such as stress effects; as a way of studying basic motor processes, however, it has been largely replaced by simpler tasks. Just the opposite trend has characterized research on discrete movement. Let us turn now to two examples of the many issues that are being studied within this general framework (see Kantowitz & Sorkin, 1983; Schmidt, Zelazmik, Hawkins, Frank & Quinn, 1979; and Welford, 1976, for more complete accounts).

Open-loop vs. closed-loop processes ▪ It has generally been assumed that any skilled movement results from two kinds of processes: a preplanned "program" that, once initiated, follows its course without further adjustment (as in a ballistic missile or a thrown football); and a controlled aspect in which status information is monitored and in-course adjustments are made. The former is referred to as an *open-loop* process; the latter, as a *closed-loop* process. The issue involved is essentially how much of a role the two kinds of processes play in various types of skills.

Today, the predominant view favors the "motor program" emphasis, the idea being that the key to most skills lies in building up and refining prototypic sets of instructions that are delivered to muscle groups as required by the task. Evidence for this position includes studies in which the nerves that convey the main feedback by which closed-loop control could be exercised are effectively anesthetized. Despite "breaking the loop," the skill survives (Kelso, 1977). It is difficult, however, to eliminate all feedback information, so even such an apparently conclusive test can be questioned. One of the central issues yet to be resolved is the minimum time required to process feedback. If, as some suggest, it is very short, the possibility of closed-loop control in even rapidly paced skills (such as typing or playing the piano) becomes more tenable. Probably the most plausible view is that response patterns are selected in accordance with a motor program, but that errors in execution can be detected (and minor corrections made) without changing the whole pattern (Schmidt, 1976).

Parameters of difficulty in simple movement execution ▪ Moving a stylus (or anything else) from point A to point B is obviously harder the greater the distance involved, the smaller the target area, and the shorter the time available. Knowing how these and other properties of the task (such as the mass of the thing moved) interact to affect performance is useful both for its task design implications and for what it says about basic motor processes. For example, if we know these functions, we can avoid certain conditions in which human error will exceed tolerable limits; or at least we can specify how much accuracy we will have to sacrifice to gain a desired increment in speed. And, by analyzing the function, we can infer what sorts of control processes govern the levels of precision (or error) and speed achieved.

Experiments employing a number of variations on this theme have produced several important generalizations. The earliest, named after the man who pioneered such work, is known as *Fitts' law*. What this says is that difficulty (ID) increases in direct proportion to the distance moved (*A*) and inversely proportional to the target width (*W*). Specifically,

$$ID = \log_2 (2A/W).$$

This equation, coupled with certain other assumptions, allows one to predict how fast or accurately a particular response can be executed. For example, movement time (MT) in a tapping task is given by,

$$MT = a + b \log_2 (2A/W).$$

As illustrated in Figure 10.8, these predictions have accounted well for results obtained in a number of studies over the years.

More recent work, however, has shown that Fitts' law is more a first approximation than a final answer—even though it is a very good first approximation. Kantowitz and his coworkers, for instance, demonstrated that an equation that takes into account the acceleration and deceleration component of movement does an even better job of fitting Fitts' data than Fitts' law does (see Kantowitz & Sorkin, 1983). Then Schmidt and his associates (1979) found that single-aiming tasks, rapid-timing tasks (where one must move a fixed distance in a certain time), and reciprocal-movement tasks (where one moves back and forth between two targets at a fixed rate) all require somewhat different equations.

The mere fact that one can find different equations to fit sets of data such as these is not, of course, very illuminating. What is of interest is that they all represent somewhat different theories of the underlying motor processes. Fitts thought of movement in terms of the linear *information* model discussed earlier. Kantowitz recognized important *nonlinearities* in movement (acceleration and deceleration). Schmidt saw the amount of *force* applied as the main determinant of spatial error, the total amount of *time* involved as the main determinant of temporal error. Unfortunately, space does not permit us to examine these distinctions in greater depth.

Problems in the work context

Human performance in a system is not just a matter of task characteristics and basic information processing functions. Simple input–output relationships never tell the complete story. For one thing, people learn; thus the most carefully defined functions can change with experience. The student in a driver's education class not only is less proficient than a seasoned taxi driver, he or she probably

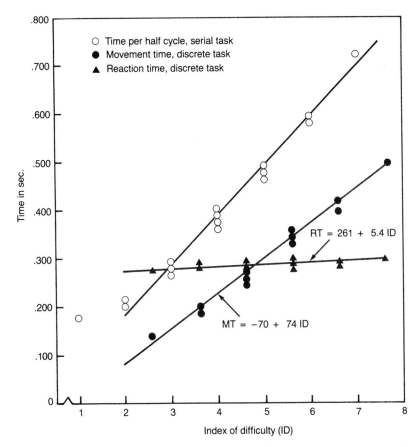

FIGURE 10.8 Reaction and movement times for several different types of tasks as a function of the *difficulty index* (see text). (From P. M. Fitts and J. R. Peterson, "Information capacity of discrete motor responses," *Journal of Experimental Psychology*, 1964, *67*, 103–112. Copyright © 1964 by the American Psychological Association. Reprinted/adapted by permission of the author.)

uses an entirely different set of control functions. For another thing, individuals differ a great deal in ability and personality—enduring traits that can greatly affect performance. And finally, a person's proficiency may vary as a function of his or her physiological or mental *state*. Alcohol affects one's ability to control an automobile (as well as other functions), biorhythms may affect one's ability to put forth sustained effort (Alluisi & Morgan, 1982), and the feeling of intense pressure or great physical discomfort can reduce one's ability to work effectively. Engineering psychology has paid some attention to learning issues (chiefly as they relate to training procedures) and almost none to individual traits. But it has concerned itself a great deal with states, particularly as they are induced by the environment or context within which human operators find themselves. Therefore, we shall end our excursion into the problem areas of the field with a brief look at this amorphous set of issues.

Stress ▪ A common way in which environmental influences are organized conceptually is through the notion of *stress*. A *stressor* is anything that affects a person's general state of arousal. Temperature conditions can do it; work load (mental or physical) can do it, noise can do it; an obnoxious officemate can do it—a lot of things singly and in combination. *Stress*, then, is the biological and psychological reaction of the organism to stressors. This sounds rather circular, and indeed it is an extremely difficult concept to pin down. Its main justification rests on the evidence that a variety of different conditions seem to bring about a very similar nonspecific response pattern (Selye, 1976).

The effects of stress are also many and varied. So far as task performance is concerned, the relationship is generally regarded as having an inverted U shape: too much or too little stress hurts performance. One way this seems to happen is by limiting our capacity to attend to things, as we saw earlier. Whether this same function describes the equally important matter of the person's subjective feelings has not been clearly established, although some argue that without the perception there can be no stress (Hogan & Hogan, 1982). Instances are commonplace, however, in which an operator will express discomfort but continue to perform at a high level (we shall examine one of these in a moment). Finally, as Chapter 5 detailed, one must consider the long-term consequences: people can suffer severe mental and physical problems from prolonged stress (it is even listed as one of the major contributing factors in heart disease).

The practical problem from a system design standpoint, of course, is that of measuring stress effects for particular stressors and for their various combinations. Without some such index, plus a general idea of what constitutes tolerable (or even desirable) and intolerable ranges of stress, we are hard pressed to set design standards. This is why the "mental work load" issue is prominent today—and, as we saw, no single measure of that has yet emerged. One of the reasons this task is so difficult is that people differ tremendously in stress tolerance; moreover, conditions at work are but one set of life's stressors. Thus the best level for me and my life situation may be a poor one for you. Another is the fact that there are so many potential stressors and the interactions among them are not simple. Adding two of them to a situation may be worse than either alone, the same, or even better in some cases (Poulton, 1966).

Thermal conditions ▪ One set of potential stressors about which volumes of research literature have appeared is that defining the operator's thermal environment (hot, cold, humidity, air velocity, clothing insulation, etc.). Unlike mental work load, both physical and physiological measurements are well developed here: what the body does under various conditions is described in quantitative terms and is fairly well understood. Also fairly well established are a number of task performance functions. The surprising thing revealed by these data is how resistent performance is to seemingly miserable conditions. One must work at least three hours at temperatures above 86°F before performance declines at all (see Kantowitz & Sorkin, 1983), and it takes almost 100°F for 43 minutes to disturb performance on mental tasks (Wing, 1965).

What is not so firmly established is how people react subjectively to these conditions. Not that the topic has suffered from neglect; thermal comfort has received much the same treatment at the hands of the heating, refrigeration and air-conditioning (ASHRAE) research community as has physiological response. Precise functions have been developed relating the distribution of comfort measure to all combinations of physical parameters (Fanger, 1972). And from these "comfort equations" have come standards that are in general use throughout the worlds of engineering and design.

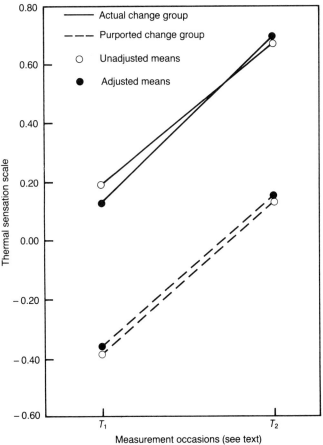

FIGURE 10.9   Mean "thermal sensation votes" obtained under the original (T_1) and shifted (T_2) conditions for groups subjected to actual and "psychological" temperature changes. (Adjustment was in terms of several variables used as covariates.)

The only problem is, these neat, orderly functions misrepresent reality. In fact, they illustrate quite nicely the cardinal sin in design for which engineering psychology and human factors engineering were sent to save the world: the neglect of psychological variables. In the case of the "comfort equations," the only predictors are physical—despite the fact that the measure being predicted is entirely subjective. Even the scale that defines "comfort" is mislabeled: it is actually a measure of perceived warmth or coldness. There is growing evidence, however, that how warm someone feels (and thus how much the thermal environment is stressful) depends on psychological as well as physical conditions.

We and others have found that what temperature one thinks it is, what one believes (erroneously, in most cases) is one's preferred temperature, and similar factors all affect the person's judgment (Howell & Kennedy, 1979; Howell & Stramler, 1981; Rohles, 1971). In one study, for example, we compared the comfort-scale responses of two large classes of students: one in which temperature was shifted by 5°F without their knowing it; the other in which they were told it had been shifted, but it wasn't. The results (see Figure 10.9) showed exactly the same perceived change in comfort regardless of whether the manipulation was physical or psychological.

■ CONCLUSION

As you can see even from this very cursory exposure, engineering psychology has its work cut out for it in the years ahead. The problems it is now addressing—mental work load, stress, decision-making, etc.—are not soon to be resolved. Many more that we did not even glimpse—human–computer interface (see Williges, 1982), air traffic safety (see Wiener, 1980), and others—present at least as many difficulties. Still, considering its short history, the field's progress to date seems encouraging. If I have done my job even half as well as I should, you may join me in the conviction that at least it is headed in the right direction.

■ SUGGESTED READINGS

Chapanis, A. (1976). Engineering psychology. In M. D. Dunnette (Ed.), *Handbook of industrial and organizational psychology* (pp. 697–744). Chicago: Rand McNally.

This brief overview of engineering psychology is suitable for any reader and is a good introduction to the field. Particular attention is given to the interface between engineering and industrial-organizational psychology.

Howell, W. C., & Goldstein, I. L. (1971). *Engineering psychology: Current perspectives in research.* New York: Appleton-Century.

This collection of readings—classic papers and illustrations of then-current research—is suitable for a graduate or professional audience.

Kantowitz, B. H., & Sorkin, R. D. (1983). *Human factors*. New York: Wiley.

A first edition text that is more extensive in coverage than the McCormick and Sanders text and concentrates more on research and theory. While this text is more suitable for engineering or psychology students, some of the chapters could be read and appreciated by the layperson.

McCormick, E. J., & Sanders, M. S. (1982). *Human factors in engineering design*. New York: McGraw-Hill.

This undergraduate–graduate text of about 600 pages attempts to present an overview of the entire human-factors domain. It has gone through many editions, and specifies applications more clearly than psychological research and theory.

Welford, A. T. (1976). *Skilled performance: Perceptual and motor skills*. Glenview, IL: Scott, Foresman.

This brief overview of theory and research on one facet of the engineering psychology domain is a readable but somewhat dated account of the skills area. It is suitable for a general audience with some background in psychology.

RICHARD J. LUTZ

CONSUMER PSYCHOLOGY

■ INTRODUCTION

Consumer psychology is that portion of the broader discipline of psychology that is devoted to the study of consumer behavior. What exactly is consumer behavior and why should we worry about studying it? Consumer behavior is a pervasive, almost omnipresent set of human behaviors that can range from the highly complex and involved (e.g., the purchase of a home) to the nearly automatic. For example, if you are highlighting or taking notes on this chapter, you are "consuming" a marker or pen or pencil, some paper, and this book. You are probably also "consuming" a desk and a chair, as well as a lamp, a lightbulb, and some electricity. You are "consuming" the clothing you are wearing and the snack you occasionally pop into your mouth. The list could go on, but the point is that consumer behavior is something in which we all engage virtually continuously.

Every day each of us is exposed to literally hundreds of advertising messages from television, radio, newspapers, magazines, billboards, the sides of busses, etc. Response to advertising (including ignoring it) is consumer behavior. Going to the supermarket and purchasing a shopping cart full of items is an obvious form of consumer behavior, but a less obvious form, perhaps, is the decision-making that led to those items being chosen. Why those 50 items and not some others of the roughly 10,000 different items in the typical supermarket? Answers to these and countless other questions regarding consumer behavior are the goal of researchers in the field of consumer psychology.

Consumer psychology defined

Consumer psychology is the study of the psychological processes involved in the performance of that set of behaviors generally identified as consumer behavior.

Two aspects of this definition need amplification. First, like any other scientific discipline, consumer psychology focuses on a particular domain of phenomena to be studied. In this case, the domain is *consumer behavior*, which includes such activities as the acquisition of product-related information, the actual purchase of products, and the use (i.e., consumption) of products.

By far the dominant thrust in consumer behavior research has been with respect to physical products produced by business organizations seeking profits. However, significant research efforts have also been directed at consumer behavior related to services and to a variety of "nonprofit" behaviors such as blood and organ donorship, voting, and charitable donations. These latter topics, while important, are clearly at the fringe of the domain of consumer behavior and are also studied intensely by social psychologists and political scientists, among others. For the purposes of simplicity of exposition and to concentrate attention on the "core" of the consumer behavior domain, the term "product" will be used throughout this chapter. In the last section of the chapter, the extension of consumer behavior research into nonbusiness arenas will be given explicit treatment.

A second key aspect of the above definition of consumer psychology is its focus on the study of the psychological processes involved in consumer behavior. The domain of consumer behavior can be approached from a number of perspectives, e.g., sociological, economic, anthropological, etc. Hence, consumer psychology represents that approach to the study of consumer behavior that attempts to explain consumer behaviors by focusing on intraindividual processes.

Although only the domains of consumer behavior and psychology are necessary to define consumer psychology, a third domain—marketing—also is of importance in capturing the essence of consumer psychology. As noted earlier, consumer psychology has dealt primarily with consumers' behavior with respect to products sold for a profit by businesses. Marketing is the function within a business organization whose role it is to ensure that the firm is producing the right products for its intended customers and selling those products effectively. In fact, it was within the field of marketing that concern about consumer behavior first arose. Since marketing is so often misunderstood, a brief digression to outline some basic concepts is in order before proceeding further.

Marketing: A brief introduction

Marketing entails the study of economic exchange relationships in society, historically from the perspective of the firm wishing to exchange its products for consumers' dollars. Although marketing is most often seen by consumers as consisting of advertising and personal selling activity, in reality marketing encompasses a much broader range of activities. An important marketing term is the *marketing mix*, which refers to the four interrelated decision areas of product, price, promotion, and place (often identified as the 4 Ps).

Any firm engaged in a marketing effort must make decisions with respect to each element in the marketing mix. *Product* decisions entail such aspects as the level of product quality, the types of ingredients or features to offer, the depth and breadth of the product line (e.g., different product forms and sizes), branding, and packaging. *Price* decisions must take into account not only the cost of producing the product, but also its perceived value to the consumer. *Promotion* decisions are very complex, involving the amount and type of mass media advertising, which particular media to use, the brand image to be conveyed, the size and organization of the sales force, the type and frequency of sales promotion (e.g., coupons, samples), and the publicity campaign. *Place* decisions refer to the distribution of the product and include such considerations as intense versus exclusive availability and the interaction of brand image and retail outlet image. Decisions regarding the many subelements of the marketing mix are coordinated and integrated, so that the resultant marketing program represents a consistent and unified effort with respect to the market it is attempting to reach.

In marketing parlance, a *market* is any group of current and potential customers to whom the firm can choose to direct its marketing effort. The guiding philosophy of many of the largest companies in the U.S. and abroad is the marketing concept, which asserts that customer orientation is the key to success. A *customer orientation* means that the firm actively seeks information on consumer wants and needs, and only then designs products and marketing programs in an attempt to satisfy these wants and needs. This is why companies spend so much money on marketing research studies; it is because they believe that knowing as much about the consumer as possible is the starting point for successful, responsible marketing.

Marketing is a discipline concerned primarily (at least historically) with assisting business organizations in their attempts to be more effective marketers. As such, marketing is a heavily normative discipline; that is, a great deal of emphasis is placed on research that address "How to" questions, e.g., "How should a firm set its advertising budget?" "How should a new product be introduced?" Marketers have long realized that the answers to these and myriad other questions lie with the consumer. Hence, within the normatively focused marketing discipline exists the more descriptively oriented subfield of consumer behavior. Instead of "How to" questions, consumer behavior research is most often characterized by "what and why" questions, e.g., "What is the nature of consumers' responses to advertising and why?" "How do consumers come to try new products and why?"

In attempting to answer these latter types of questions regarding consumer behavior, marketing researchers have, over the years, turned to other more basic disciplines (especially psychology) for potential explanations. Reflecting this pattern, there is a high degree of overlap between marketing and consumer psychology as well as between marketing and consumer behavior in general. The bulk of the research on consumer behavior, and especially that portion of it that can be labeled consumer psychology, has been conducted by researchers in the field of marketing. Marketing, with its necessary focus on the consumer, not only initiated consumer behavior research, but has also dominated all other disciplines in its active pursuit of consumer behavior research. As will be seen in a subsequent section of this chapter, much of this research is heavily psychological in content and conduct and hence qualifies as consumer psychology. The student interested in pursuing a career in consumer psychology should be aware that such a career will almost certainly be within the general sphere of marketing.

■ HISTORICAL DEVELOPMENT*

The 1950s

Beginning at roughly the turn of the century, psychologists occasionally turned their attention to topics that fall within the domain of consumer psychology. However, with the possible exception of the psychology of advertising, this work was quite scattered and did not constitute a unified or identifiable domain of psychological research activity. Until the late 1950s, practicing consumer psychologists, who tended to be almost exclusively in nonacademic positions in industry, had no separate identity within the American Psychological Association. Instead, they were typically housed in other related divisions of APA, such as Measurement, Personality and Social, and Industrial. In 1959, Division 23 (Consumer Psychology) was formed, and for the first time consumer psychologists had a home of their own within APA.

Concomitant with the emergence of consumer psychology within APA was the development of the study of consumer behavior within the fields of economics and marketing. In the early 1950s, economist George Katona and his colleagues at the University of Michigan Survey Research Center introduced the concept of *psychological economics*. Whereas economists previously had focused on consumers' ability to purchase products based on consumer income vis-a-vis the prices of products, psychological economics includes as a key determinant of purchase behavior consumers' willingness to buy. Questions of what causes a consumer to be willing to buy a product quickly give rise to the need for psychological theories and methods.

Meanwhile, in the marketing arena, the early 1950s marked the introduction and rapid acceptance of the marketing concept, which, as discussed earlier in this chapter, incorporates customer satisfaction as the central means to the end of attaining various marketing goals. Thus, during the 1950s, marketing

---

*Much of the historical material in this section was abstracted from an outstanding APA Division 23 Presidential Address delivered by Ivan Ross at the 1981 APA Convention in Los Angeles. For the full citation, see Ross (1981).

researchers began to study consumer behavior in a serious manner, since it was seen as the key to successful marketing. The work of Katona and his associates was very influential, as was the clinically based thinking of people such as Ernest Dichter. The latter's work was labeled "motivation research" and purported to offer insights into the deeper underlying psychological processes that motivated consumer purchase behavior. Borrowing liberally the tools of the clinical psychologist, the motivation researchers "explained" consumers' reactions to products. For example, motivation researchers asserted that the act of baking a cake was, for many women, symbolically (and subconsciously) related to the act of giving birth. On this basis, manufacturers decided to call for an egg to be added to boxed cake mix, even though the product would have worked perfectly well without the egg being added. More generally, early resistance to convenience foods like instant coffee was diagnosed as relating to housewives' subconscious guilt that using such products was "cheating" their families. Resistance was then overcome by advertising campaigns depicting the user of convenience items having even more "quality time" to spend with her spouse and children.

Motivation researchers were most important in the 1950s although many are still at work in industry today. However, motivation research never attained academic respectability due to its ad hoc "explanations" and lack of verifiability. Yet, the notion of products somehow reflecting consumers' personalities was a pervasive one in the 1950s, and many researchers turned to an array of personality inventories (e.g., the MMPI) in an attempt to build quantitative models relating personality to product use. Literally hundreds of such studies have been reported over the past thirty years, investigating the predictive power of personality traits for a wide variety of consumer behaviors (e.g., orange juice brand loyalty, preference for one-ply versus two-ply toilet tissue). In his classic review of this literature, Kassarjian (1971) pointed out the weak results of this approach. Very little personality research is currently being conducted in the realm of consumer psychology.

The 1960s

The 1960s witnessed rapid growth in consumer psychology. Spurred by the growth of business schools across the country, many psychologists found marketing departments attractive settings in which to pursue their research interests. Courses entitled "Consumer Behavior" began showing up in major schools' marketing curricula, and these courses were taught initially out of social psychology textbooks, coupled with reprints from various psychology journals. Consumer behavior research at this time was in the tradition of social psychology, emphasizing such theories and concepts as cognitive dissonance, reference group influence, and models of persuasion. However, as we shall see in a later section of this chapter, research and consumer psychology has closely paralleled trends in psychological research in general. Specifically, research in consumer psychology was initiated with a strong social psychology orientation in the early 1960s, and shifted in the late 1960s and throughout the 1970s to an emphasis on cognitive psychology. Recently, the field has begun to embrace the hybrid approach labeled cognitive social psychology (or social cognition).

By the mid-to-late 1960s, the first consumer behavior texts were written for use in the consumer behavior courses. *Consumer Behavior* (Engel, Kollatt, & Blackwell, 1968) was the first full-length text and focused on the individual consumer as a problem solver who attempted to satisfy wants and needs through the purchase and consumption of products. Additionally, the consumer was also seen as acting within a set of cultural and social constraints, particularly the family. Even though the text was written by marketing professors, the dominant conceptual thrust is clearly psychological.

Most of the psychological research cited in current consumer behavior texts was neither conducted by researchers trained in psychology nor reported in psychology journals. The majority of the research has been conducted by marketing-trained researchers and reported in marketing journals, although many psychologists, primarily those working with the marketing domain, have contributed heavily to the marketing literature on consumer behavior.

Throughout the 1960s, Division 23 of APA served as a focal point for sophisticated psychological research on consumer behavior. Research papers were presented at the annual convention of APA and were published in the proceedings of that convention. However, many marketing researchers participated in the conventions but relatively few became members of APA. Since most consumer behavior researchers were not psychologists by training, they maintained their professional attachment to marketing.

The 1970s

By 1969, consumer behavior was experiencing "growing pains" within the marketing discipline. There was so much attention given to consumer behavior that professional marketing associations and marketing journals were unable to devote sufficient space to consumer behavior activities and research. Also, new theories were proposed in the late 1960s that generated additional interest in consumer research. For example, a theory of buyer behavior was proposed by Howard and Sheth (1969) that was an attempt to integrate different streams of consumer behavior research in a comprehensive model. Therefore, in 1969, marketing researchers joined with consumer researchers in other fields to form the multidisciplinary Association for Consumer Research (ACR). This association seeks to foster research aimed at explaining consumer behavior, regardless of the particular research orientation taken. In its relatively brief existence, ACR has clearly become a focal organization for consumer research.

The decade of the 1970s saw tremendous growth in the amount and sophistication of consumer behavior research. The field retreated from the so-called comprehensive models of consumer behavior by the mid-1970s, primarily because of the analytical intractibility of these complex networks. Instead, middle-range theories appeared. Paralleling developments in cognitive psychology, consumer behavior research turned to attribution theory and information-processing models. As the decade ended, attention was focused on models of memory, schema theory, and other similar explanations. However, a counterpoint to these explanations, all of which assume a highly motivated consumer decision-maker, is low-involvement theory, which proposes that consumer behavior is largely uninvolving. The upshot of this lack of involvement is much simpler decision processes than most researchers had previously assumed. At the outset of the 1980s, low-involvement theory was one of the field's "hottest" research topics.

At this point in its evolution, consumer psychology research is quite sophisticated and at its best rivals the quality of research in other areas of psychology. Increasing numbers of new Ph.D.s in psychology are pursuing their careers in the marketing (both academic and nonacademic) domain, and more and more psychologists who are affiliated with a university psychology department are joining ACR and participating actively in its conferences. Consumer behavior research has "come of age" and offers a vital and stimulating research arena for the applied psychologist. In the next section we turn to a consideration of the types of work settings in which one might find a consumer psychologist.

■ WORK SETTINGS

Consumer psychologists enjoy a wide range of career opportunities that can be loosely grouped into three main categories: *academic, industrial,* and *governmental.* The vignettes in Box 11.1 provide a brief glimpse into the professional lives of three hypothetical consumer psychologists, one from each of the three categories. The positions depicted differ dramatically in terms of their day-to-day routine and their ultimate goals, but they share the basic psychological orientation to the solution of the research questions with which they are presented.

Academic

An academic position is the only one of the categories for which a Ph.D. is required. By and large, academic positions are limited to marketing departments in business schools. There are few if any psychology faculty in this country whose primary emphasis is consumer psychology. A psychology professor may do research on consumer psychology, but almost always as a secondary research stream. As a marketing professor, the consumer psychologist can generally expect to teach not only courses in consumer behavior but also courses in other aspects of marketing, such as marketing principles, market research, and advertising. In addition to teaching responsibilities, the faculty member is expected to maintain a program of research, the majority of which would be published in marketing journals. Scholarly research productivity is the primary standard of

---

B O X   11.1   WORK-RELATED ACTIVITIES IN CONSUMER
                    PSYCHOLOGY

At a major Midwestern university, Professor Terry Houston is preparing lecture notes for his
undergraduate Consumer Behavior course. The topic of this particular lecture is the role of
memory processes in consumer decision-making, and Professor Houston is particularly
excited about covering that topic in class. His research, which has recently been published
in the *Journal of Consumer Research,* deals with the effects of visual imagery in advertising
as a facilitator of consumers' recall of product information, so this week's lecture material
will be closely related to Professor Houston's research interests. He has located several television and magazine advertisements which aptly illustrate the key theoretical concepts,
and he is looking forward to a lot of class discussion and interaction on the topic.
    In New York City, one of Professor Houston's friends from their doctoral student days,
Dr. Michele Locander of the ad agency BBS & M, is completing a statistical analysis of the
potential market for cable television (CATV) service in the U.S. A key factor in her analysis is
the identification of market segments that contain consumers receptive to innovative products like CATV. To accomplish this, she has used the results of a nationwide survey of over
1500 households, each of which provided responses to a host of demographic and psychographic questions. Her desk is piled high with computer printouts as she punches in
one final analysis on her computer. Time is short, for next week she is to present her findings to the board of directors of the cable company that the agency represents.
    Meanwhile in Washington, D.C., at the Consumer Safety Assurance Bureau, Dr. Wil-
liam Childers, another colleague of Professor Houston and Dr. Locander, is designing an
experiment to test the relative effectiveness of various alternative warning labels on appli-
ances. Dr. Childers holds the position of staff Research Director at the CPSC, and he is
responsible for advising the commissioners regarding the likely impact on consumers of
certain actions under consideration by the commission. Dr. Childers specialized in cognitive psychology, and he uses the theories and methods of that subfield to design maximally
effective public policy recommendations.

---

evaluation for marketing faculty, just as it is for psychology faculty, with teaching ability an important but secondary criterion.

Industrial

The consumer psychologist in an industrial setting may or may not hold a Ph.D.
but generally has completed at least an M.A. degree. The variety of research positions available is literally as great as the range of companies in the U.S. economy,
but the positions tend to be concentrated in the following types of organizations:
consumer products manufacturers (e.g., Procter and Gamble, General Mills),
advertising agencies, market research firms, and independent consulting firms.

Consumer products manufacturers were among the first companies to adopt the marketing concept described earlier in this chapter. Large companies have literally dozens of research professionals whose responsibility it is to develop in-depth knowledge of the firm's customers. Unlike academic researchers, consumer psychologists in industry focus on using psychological theory rather than developing it. For example, a consumer psychologist with a clinical background may conduct "focus group" discussions with small groups of consumers in order to uncover ideas for new products. A psychologist with expertise in psychophysical judgment may be called upon to determine how a new hand lotion can be formulated to be "luxurious and creamy" without being perceived as "greasy." A cognitive psychologist may be involved in designing product packaging so that it attracts maximum attention on the supermarket shelf. An expert on persuasive communications may work in conjunction with the company's ad agency to design tests of television commercial effectiveness. In general, the consumer psychologist is likely to be involved in most aspects of the firm's marketing activity, from spotting new product opportunities, through product and communication strategy design, to assessing marketing effectiveness.

The consumer psychologist working in an advertising agency will typically be involved in all aspects of the communications program for the client company. Current and potential customers are profiled psychographically to discover potential advertising appeals; e.g., is the target market group likely to respond favorably to a humorous commercial? Many agencies conduct extensive pretesting of alternative advertising executions before purchasing expensive media space. Pretesting can take many forms, from unstructured focus group discussions to laboratory and field experiments. In some cases, the ad agency actually serves as the market research department for a smaller client, in which case the agency researcher may be involved in the kinds of research described in the preceding paragraph (e.g., product and package design).

Market research firms come in all shapes and sizes and are often hired by consumer products companies to conduct a range of marketing-related studies. The consumer psychologist in a market research firm may moderate focus groups, design market surveys and experiments, or conduct sophisticated data analysis. Unlike their counterparts in manufacturing firms and ad agencies, consumer psychologists in market research firms are likely to be simultaneously working on projects for a number of client organizations. Hence, this type of position requires an ability to grasp quickly the nature of the client's business and particular marketing problem. In larger firms the consumer psychologist may have the luxury of specializing in a particular type of study (e.g., focus group interviews or advertising experiments), while in smaller firms the consumer psychologist may be forced to wear several hats, not only conducting a variety of studies but also participating in the initial client contact (i.e., assisting in selling the firm's services).

The consumer psychologist as an independent consultant may perform all the same functions as the full-line market research firm. Often, however, the consultant has a particular expertise and chooses to specialize in a certain type of research study. The typical route to becoming an independent consultant is to work for an ad agency or market research firm for a period of time and later spin off to form a consulting organization, relying on contacts with previous client firms to provide the foundation for the fledgling consulting firm. Consulting firms may consist of one person or a partnership of two or three individuals, but at least one of the individuals involved must have a strong entrepreneurial orientation and a good head for business. More so than any of the other occupations discussed previously, independent consulting requires the consumer psychologist to be a jack of all trades, not only conducting research but also raising capital to start the business, promoting the business, selling the research services, and arranging for appropriate bookkeeping and billing functions.

Governmental

Opportunities for consumer psychologists are somewhat limited in the governmental and closely related nonprofit sectors. Governmental agencies that are responsible for public safety or information sometimes maintain a small staff of researchers to assist them in designing public policy, but this task is often accomplished by contracting with outside consultants. Similarly, some of the larger nonprofit organizations (e.g., charities, environmental groups, consumerist "watchdog" organizations) employ consumer psychologists to assist them in their marketing efforts. The kinds of research activities engaged in by consumer psychologists in these organizations are very similar to those in the industrial sector; the focus is on understanding how consumers will react to certain programs and/or information campaigns instead of products or advertisements.

This brief introduction to the world of the working consumer psychologist has revealed a wide range of career opportunities. The consumer psychologist may develop theory or use theory to solve marketing problems; he or she may work in a large or a small organization, the goals of which range from generating new knowledge, to aiding society, to profits through consumer satisfaction. The consumer psychologist may be a generalist or a specialist, a business entrepeneur or an academic researcher. The common thread uniting all these individuals is the study of consumers' psychological processes.

■ THEORIES AND RESEARCH IN CONSUMER PSYCHOLOGY

In this final major section of the chapter, we will turn our attention to some of the dominant research themes in consumer psychology. Earlier in the chapter a thumbnail historical overview of past research trends was presented; this section will focus on the current state of the art in consumer research. As alluded to earlier, research in consumer psychology has closely paralleled research in social psychology, cognitive psychology, and, more recently, cognitive social psychology. Evidence of contributions from all three of these fields will be seen below.

Characteristic of research in consumer psychology is a bit more attention to the applicability, or the external validity, of the research findings than is often apparent in the other subfields of psychology upon which it draws. Obviously, consumer research conducted in the industrial and governmental sectors is highly action-oriented, but most of it is also proprietary and hence does not appear in research journals. Therefore, this section will reflect primarily the research themes of academic researchers whose work appears in journals and textbooks. However, it is a safe assumption that the same topics are important in the other sectors as well, due to the close interaction of academic and industrial researchers at conferences and sometimes in a consulting capacity.

The research domains that we will be examining are organized into four broad categories: individual differences, attitude and attitude change, communications effects, and decision process models. These general categories are neither mutually exclusive nor collectively exhaustive, but they do reflect the most important topic areas within consumer psychology.

Individual differences

Perhaps the topic with the greatest longevity in the consumer psychology literature is that of individual differences. One of the dominant ideas in modern marketing thought is the concept of *market segmentation*, wherein the firm seeks relatively homogeneous subgroups, or *segments*, within the widely heterogeneous mass market. The segmentation concept holds that a firm can serve its market more effectively by, first, recognizing that consumers are different in important ways, and second, developing products and marketing programs tailored more specifically to different segments. Virtually every major consumer goods marketer practices market segmentation to some degree.

The desire of marketers to identify segments of consumers has led to a vast number of studies aimed at discovering useful *segmentation bases*, i.e., individual difference variables. Initially, consumer researchers turned to straightforward and readily available demographic and socioeconomic status (SES) descriptors such as age, sex, income, religion, family size, etc. Over time, however, a range of psychologically based variables filtered into the segmentation literature, most notably personality trait measures assessed by instruments such as the Minnesota Multiphasic Personality Inventory (MMPI) and the Edwards Personal Preference Schedule (EPPS). As discussed in an earlier section of this chapter, these general personality inventories did not prove to be very successful when applied to the study of consumer behavior. As shown in Table 11.1, the categories of demographics (and SES) and personality fall into the broader classification of general characteristics, which refer to descriptors of consumers that are constant (for any given consumer) across product classes; e.g., a person's age,

T A B L E 11.1 **A Typology of Individual Difference Variables Used in Segmentation Research**

	General characteristics	Product-specific variables
Overt characteristics	Demographics Socioeconomic status	Past usage rate Repeat purchase patterns
Covert Constructs	Personality Self-concept Life-style	Brand loyalty Benefits sought Usage situation

occupation, and degree of introversion are the same regardless of the product being marketed to that consumer. In most cases, as noted by Frank, Massy, and Wind (1972) in their review of the segmentation literature, general characteristics, whether overt or covert, have not proven to be effective segmentation bases.

One very important exception to the above conclusion regarding the utility of general characteristics in segmentation research is the approach based on consumer *life-style* analysis. Also labeled *psychographic segmentation*, life-style analysis was pioneered in the early 1960s by William Wells and others for the purpose of developing a "richer" portrayal of consumers than that provided by simple demographics and SES variables. Life-style is a rather loosely defined multidimensional concept that refers to how the individual consumer thinks, feels, and acts in relation to his or her surrounding environment, particularly as related to the consumption of goods and services. Measurement of consumer life-styles is accomplished through the use of large questionnaires containing batteries of questions tapping individuals' *activities, interests,* and *opinions* (known as AIOs), as well as a range of product usage questions and media behavior.

Figure 11.1 is an example of commonly used AIOs; a typical AIO questionnaire may contain 200 to 300 such items which, taken together, can paint a vivid picture of the consumers of a particular product of concern. For example, Figure 11.2 shows a partial life-style analysis of two segments of the commercial air travel market: people who fly predominantly for business purposes versus those who most often fly for personal reasons. A casual scanning of the pattern of results shows business flyers to be more confident, more dedicated to their careers, more adventurous and more pro-business. An airline and/or its advertising agency could apply these findings to the development of suitable advertising themes in approaching these two distinct segments of the air travel market.

Life-style analysis has been an extremely popular research topic among both academic and business researchers. In his award-winning review paper, Wells (1975) cited nearly 150 articles dealing with life-style and closely related approaches, and the bulk of that research had been conducted since 1970. The

FIGURE 11.1   Sample AIO items.

Activities

How many times in the past 12 months have you . . .

	None	1–4 Times	5–16 Times	17–24 Times	25–51 Times	52 + Times
Ridden a bicycle	_____	_____	_____	_____	_____	_____
Gone boating	_____	_____	_____	_____	_____	_____
Played cards	_____	_____	_____	_____	_____	_____
Done volunteer work	_____	_____	_____	_____	_____	_____

Interests and Opinions

Please indicate the extent to which you agree or disagree with each statement below. Use the following response scale to record a number next to each statement:

Definitely disagree	1	2	3	4	5	6	Definitely agree

_____ I am a homebody

_____ I like to watch disaster movies

_____ I am influential in my neighborhood

_____ I work very hard most of the time

_____ There should be a gun in every home

_____ I would like to spend a year in London or Paris

FIGURE 11.2   Life-style analysis of business flyers vs. personal flyers.

	BF*	PF*
I have more self-confidence than my friends.	89%	82%
I like to be considered a leader.	88	78
Job security is more important than money.	59	69
It's hard to get a good job these days.	56	65
I work under a great deal of pressure.	76	64
I work very hard most of the time.	89	78
My greatest achievements are ahead of me.	77	65
I often skip lunch or have a light snack.	11	18
I have the same thing for breakfast daily.	41	48
I'd feel lost alone in a foreign country.	32	40
I'd like to own and fly my own plane.	57	49
I'd do better than average in a fist fight.	54	45
My days follow a definite routine.	51	59
Ralph Nader does a lot to protect the American consumer.	58	69
The energy shortage is a hoax.	40	49
Our family has moved more than most of our neighbors.	33	24
I am interested in politics.	68	61

*Percent agreeing with each statement

volume of life-style research diminished somewhat during the latter half of the 1970s, but it remains one of the dominant segmentation approaches and an important consumer individual difference variable. It should be noted, however, that life-style segmentation is not without its critics. Questions have been raised regarding its rather weak conceptual foundations, the reliability and validity of measurement, and the general predictive power of AIOs (Wells, 1975). Thus, despite its widespread use and intuitive appeal, life-style is nevertheless subject to many of the frailties of general characteristics as predictors of consumer behavior.

Most segmentation researchers place greater reliance on the kinds of product-specific individual differences shown on the right-hand side of Table 11.1. Product-specific variables measure aspects of consumer behavior that are relevant only to the product class of interest. For example, in Table 11.1, past usage rate characterizes the consumer as a "heavy," "moderate," or "light" user of the product category. A pervasive phenomenon in marketing is the so-called "heavy half" effect, which refers to the observation that, in virtually every product category, a relatively small percentage of the total customers account for a disproportionately large share of the total purchases of the product. For example, one study (Twedt, 1964) reported that 17% of U.S. households purchased 88% of all beer sold; 33% of households purchased 83% of the paper towels sold; and 49% of households accounted for 74% of toilet paper sales! Obviously, a firm interested in promoting its brand(s) in any particular product class would prefer to attract heavy rather than light users.

From the perspective of the consumer psychologist, the shortcoming of the usage rate approach to segmentation is its lack of attention to the reasons why a consumer or household purchases heavily. This criticism is also applicable to another form of individual difference variable, repeat purchase patterns, which represents a household's tendency to concentrate its purchases on one or sometimes two brands within a product class. This tendency is often labeled *brand loyalty*, though Jacoby and Kyner (1973) argued persuasively that true brand loyalty reflects a form of psychological commitment to the brand, over and above the repeated purchase of that brand. Although there is by no means consensus on this issue, it seems more appropriate to incorporate some sort of attitudinal construct in the conceptualization of brand loyalty, such that a brand-loyal consumer genuinely prefers the brand over others in the product class. In contrast, repeat purchase may take place without attitudinal commitment, due to reasons of ready availability of the brand, lower price, or simply "mindless" repetitive buying (see, for example, Langer, 1978). A truly brand-loyal consumer is thought to be more responsive to the brand's marketing efforts and, conversely, resistant to the efforts of competitors, making brand loyalty a potentially important individual-difference variable. Conceptualization and measurement of brand loyalty (especially as opposed to simple repeat purchase) remain intriguing issues for consumer psychologists (Jacoby & Chestnut, 1978).

Two final individual difference research topics drawing much attention currently are *benefit segmentation* and segmentation based on *usage situations*. Reflecting the movement of the field away from personality research, both of these approaches to segmentation rely on more transient product-related characteristics rather than enduring individual traits. As such, these two topics bridge over into other areas of consumer psychology research. Benefit segmentation will be treated in the next section, attitudes and attitude change, while the usage situations concept will be dealt with in the final section of this chapter.

Attitudes and attitude change

As was mentioned earlier in this chapter, the study of consumer attitudes has been the dominant consumer behavior research topic over the past decade. Similar to its role in social psychological research, the attitude construct is viewed as a precursor to overt behavior; as such, consumer attitudes toward brands, product classes, and firms are of interest in the prediction and explanation of consumer behavior.

By far the dominant theoretical approach to the study of consumer attitudes derives from the work of Fishbein (1963, 1967), in what has come to be known in consumer psychology as the *multiattribute model of attitude*. Fishbein's theory of attitude formation and change can be succinctly represented by

$$A_O = \sum_{i=1}^{n} b_i e_i, \tag{11.1}$$

where

A_O is the individual's attitude (i.e., affective feelings of favorability/unfavorability) toward any object (e.g., a brand or a firm);

b_i is the *strength* of the individual's *belief* (expressed as a subjective probability) that the attitude object is characterized by attribute i (e.g., the likelihood that Listerine mouthwash tastes "mediciney");

e_i is the individual's *evaluative aspect* attached to attribute i (i.e., how good or bad "mediciney taste" is to the individual); and i is the number of salient attributes of the attitude object.

Fishbein's formulation conforms to a general expectancy-times-value perspective on the underlying force behind behavior; beliefs about brand attributes can be seen as expectations about how the brand will perform, and the value to the individual of that attribute is assessed by the evaluative aspect. Together, the beliefs and evaluations form the basis for the attitude in question. Figure 11.3 shows some examples of the types of scales used to measure the b_i and e_i components in Fishbein's model; attitude is typically measured via the semantic differential procedure.

It is important to note that the beliefs and their evaluative aspects are seen as the determinants of attitude. It is this property of Fishbein's theory that makes it

---

Belief strength (b_i)

Charmin toilet tissue is strong

very likely   +3 : ____: ____: ____: ____: ____: -3 :   very unlikely

Charmin toilet tissue is soft

very likely   +3 : ____: ____: ____: ____: ____: -3 :   very unlikely

Evaluative Aspect (e_i)

With respect to toilet tissue, strength Is

very good   +3 : ____: ____: ____: ____: ____: -3 :   very bad

With respect to toilet tissue, softness is

very good   +3 : ____: ____: ____: ____: ____: -3 :   very bad

---

FIGURE 11.3   Examples of multiattribute attitude model measures.

so attractive to consumer researchers. Essentially, if the rcsearcher measures the salient attributes that determine attitude, he or she not only can predict the level of a consumer's attitude, but also can diagnose the reasons why the consumer holds that attitude. This diagnostic property of the multiattribute model is important in offering suggestions with respect to strategies for attitude change, a topic that will be treated in more detail shortly.

Fishbein's theory and other closely related variants of the multiattribute attitude model have received much empirical support in the consumer psychology literature. Wilkie and Pessemier (1973) and Lutz and Bettman (1977) reviewed this literature and concluded that the model accurately predicts consumer behavior. Among the research issues that have not been fully resolved with respect to this model are how to determine if the proper set of salient attributes has been identified (Kanwar, Olson, & Sims, 1981), whether the attributes combine additively or via an averaging process (Bettman, Capon, & Lutz, 1975; Troutman & Shanteau, 1976), and the efficacy of the model for explaining attitude change (Mitchell & Olson, 1981).

Identification of the true underlying attribute determinants of attitude, as required by the Fishbein model, has been a persistent problem. Researchers have used several different methods (see Collins & Loftus, 1975, and Kelley, 1955). Sometimes determining the attributes is undertaken in a focus-group setting (see Box 11.2). Whichever method is chosen, taking an open-ended approach to defining the attribute determinants is a problem in conducting research on the model because weak results can be explained with an argument that certain important attributes must have been omitted from measurement because they were not brought up.

As mentioned briefly earlier, the postulated diagnostic value of the multiattribute attitude model has, to a large degree, accounted for its prominent role in the consumer research literature. Whether or not the model is a powerful one for suggesting attititude change strategies remains an open issue in the sense that little empirical work has been undertaken to test the validity of the model's predictions in a dynamic setting. An example will help to clarify the issue.

Figure 11.4 portrays the responses of a hypothetical consumer to a multiattribute questionnaire regarding alternative radio stations. The responses reflect the types of measurement scales shown in Fig. 11.3. Note that the consumer has one set of e_i measures but three sets of b_i measures (one set for each radio station). Using the computational formula (Eq. 11.1), the consumer's attitude toward each station can be computed, as shown at the bottom of Fig. 11.4. Based on the model's predictions, WIPP would be the consumer's preferred station, with WHET and WYLD trailing.

B O X 11.2   THE FOCUS GROUP: A CONSUMER RESEARCH
                   STAPLE

The focus-group discussion is the most widely used primary research methodology in commercial consumer research. It is also used frequently in academic research settings for certain purposes, such as the elicitation of salient product attributes.

Essentially, a focus group is a group of 6 to 10 consumers who have been pre-screened and invited to participate in a market research study. The focus group is generally conducted in a market research firm's specially designed facility. The room looks much like a large living room, with comfortable sofas and chairs and attractive decor. Almost always, one wall contains a large one-way glass mirror with an observation room behind it to permit clients to view the focus group firsthand. The rooms are always equipped with audio (and sometimes video) taping equipment to record the discussion for later transcription and/or analysis.

Focus groups are conducted by a professional moderator (often a clinical psychologist) who is adept at creating an atmosphere conducive to a free-flowing discussion. The ideal focus group is quite open ended, with a short list of general questions being provided initially to launch the discussion. The real value of the focus group is thought to lie in the responses to follow-up questions, or *probes,* posed by the moderator in response to comments made by the participants.

Focus groups are used in a wide variety of research activities, such as preliminary advertising or new product concept testing and brand image studies. The role of the focus group is exploratory, with the goal of generating hypotheses for further testing through more statistically based research procedures. Due to its small and necessarily nonrepresentative sample of consumers, the focus group should never be used to draw important conclusions; unfortunately, many firms misuse focus groups by placing too much reliance on their findings.

For more information on focus groups, see Calder (1977).

Attribute	e_i	Station b_i		
		WIPP	WHET	WYLD
Plays lots of music	+3	+2	+1	-2
Plays lots of commercials	-2	+2	+2	-2
Gives news updates	+1	+1	+2	-1
Has interesting DJs	+2	+2	0	+1
Overall Attitude		+7	+1	-1

FIGURE 11.4   A hypothetical consumer's responses to a radio station questionnaire.

Using the diagnostic power of the model, the management of WHET could undertake an attitude change program in order to improve the station's market position. In particular, they might hire new, interesting, exciting DJs and raise their b_i on that dimension from 0 to +3, which when multiplied by the e_i of +2, would add +6 to the consumer's attitude toward WHET. This approach has been characterized as a *belief change* strategy and has been supported empirically in a number of investigations (Lutz, 1975; Mazis & Adkinson, 1976; Mitchell & Olson, 1981).

Alternatively, the management of WHET might adopt a *value change* strategy by attempting to alter the consumer's e_i for news updates from +1 to +3. This change, if accomplished, would have the effect of adding +4 to the consumer's attitude toward WHET (an e_i change of +2 multiplied by the b_i of +2). Evidence in support of the power of the value change approach is scant (Lutz, 1975), and it appears that value change is more difficult to achieve than is belief change. This apparent difficulty is due, in part, to the presumed greater centrality of e_i components as compared with b_i components. However, more research is needed to clarify this issue.

The basic multiattribute attitude model has been extended (Fishbein, 1980; Fishbein & Ajzen, 1975) to incorporate social normative influences on behavior as well as attitudinal influences. The *theory of reasoned action*, as it has been labeled, has generated a large amount of consumer research over the past 10 years (Kassarjian, 1982; Ryan & Bonfield, 1975). The theory consists of the series of relationships depicted in Fig. 11.5. As shown, Attitude toward the Behavior (A_B) is seen as being a function of underlying beliefs (b_i) and evaluations (e_i), just as in the original multiattribute attitude model. Here, however, the attitude of interest is with respect to a particular behavior (e.g., *purchasing* Brand X) rather than simply an object. This behavioral focus is required due to the theory of reasoned action's specific focus on addressing the time-worn research issue of the relationship between attitude and behavior. As shown in Fig. 11.5, A_B is seen as an immediate precursor of Behavioral intention (BI), which in turn determines actual Overt behavior (OB).

Supplementing the consumer's attitude toward performing a behavior is a normative component. Subjective norm (SN) is the individual's perception of what important referents, taken as a whole, expect him or her to do in the situation—should the behavior be performed or not? Determining SN are two underlying components, Normative beliefs (b_j) and Motivation to comply (m_j), which refer to what the individual believes specific referent others expect him or her to do and the degree to which the individual desires to comply with each of those other referent's expectations. For example, in considering the purchase of a new brand of toothpaste, the consumer may hold normative beliefs (b_j) with respect to spouse, children, and the family dentist. Tempering those b_j would be the associated motivation to comply with each (m_j). Thus, a recommendation by the dentist to try a new decay-fighting toothpaste may outweigh or offset the spouse's and children's expectations that the new brand not be substituted for

FIGURE 11.5   Diagrammatic representation of the theory of reasoned action.

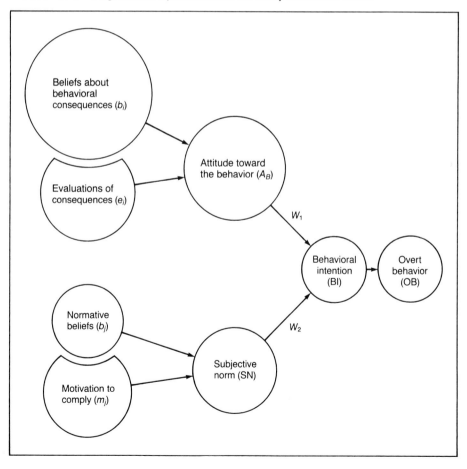

the one used in the past. Subjective norm (SN) reflects the amalgamation of the various b_j and m_j components just as A_B summarizes the joint influence of b_i and e_i components.

In Figure 11.5, W_1 and W_2 refer to the relative weights of A_B and SN in determining BI. These weights are typically estimated through the use of multiple regression. When W_1 is greater than W_2, the behavior in question is said to be under *attitudinal control*; when W_2 exceeds W_1, the behavior is under *normative control*. Determination of whether A_B or SN is governing behavior is important to the consumer psychologist conducting applied research because it provides clues as to how best to cause behavioral change. Unless the behavior is under attitudinal control, the attitude change strategies discussed earlier will be futile in affecting subsequent behavior. Instead, a change strategy based on peer group pressure (e.g., through word-of-mouth communication) or expert endorsement is dictated. To date, the theory of reasoned action has proven to be moderately succcssful in directing behavior change programs (e.g., Ryan & Bonfield, 1980), and thus serves as a potentially useful extension of the basic multiattribute attitude model.

Examples of applied research domains in which multiattribute models have proven useful include advertising and promotional strategy, benefit segmentation, product positioning, and new product design and concept testing. As was discussed above in conjunction with the hypothetical data in Fig. 11.4, multiattribute models form the basis for promotional strategy formulation. Attribute beliefs and evaluations are measured and diagnosed for appropriate change avenues. Advertising campaigns are then developed to implement the multiattribute-based strategies, and studies of advertising effectiveness incorporate the same attribute dimensions (Boyd, Ray, & Strong, 1982; Lutz, 1979).

Benefit segmentation, which was pioneered by Haley (1968), has proven to be the most powerful approach to market segmentation over the past decade (Wind, 1978). Essentially, benefit segmentation clusters individual consumers into homogeneous segments based upon the evaluations (e_i components) they attach to salient product attributes. For example, the hypothetical consumer in Fig. 11.4 valued the amount of music played by radio stations most highly and was "turned off" by lots of commercials. A second hypothetical consumer might have a completely different e_i vector, say $+1, 0, +3$, and $+1$. This consumer values news very highly and is completely indifferent to the number of commercials. Benefit segmentation fits into the Covert/Product-specific cell of Table 11.1 (in the Individual differences section), and is, in most cases, the single best approach (though a costly one) to segmenting a market.

Product positioning refers to the perceptual "niche" a brand occupies in the mind of the consumer. How consumers view the attributes of competing brands is tapped by the b_i measures in the multiattribute model. Because of various selective processes involved in consumer perception, consumers' subjective perceptions of brands often disagree with objective reality. For instance, Cohen and

Houston (1972) found that two groups of consumers loyal to different brands of toothpaste (one Crest, the other Colgate) rated their brand significantly higher on all five attribute dimensions included in a questionnaire, while a control group, loyal to neither brand, perceived virtually no differences between the two. While this type of finding has been interpreted by some as a *halo effect* (Beckwith & Lehmann, 1975), it serves to point out that brands occupy different positions in the minds of different consumers.

Product positioning research is characterized by a technique known as *perceptual mapping*, wherein competing brands' positions are depicted spatially for analytic and diagnostic purposes. Figure 11.6 portrays the positions of the three radio stations from Fig. 11.4 on the music and DJ dimensions, using the b_i measures from Fig. 11.4. Numerous approaches to building perceptual maps have been devised, but all are based on multiattribute logic (Green & Wind, 1973).

A final area receiving a great deal of multiattribute research is new product design and concept testing. Potential new products are described on a number of attribute dimensions, and a sample of consumers is asked to rate the attractiveness of each product. Using a statistical procedure known as *conjoint analysis*, researchers are then able to determine which levels of the various product attributes are maximally valued by consumers and hence design the best possi-

FIGURE 11.6   Example of a perceptual map.

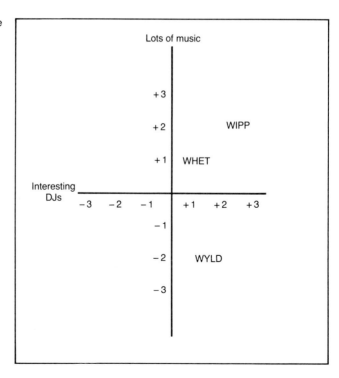

ble new product. Shocker and Srinivasan (1979) have provided an excellent review of these multiattribute-based concept testing procedures.

In summary, research on attitudes and attitude change in consumer psychology has been dominated by the multiattribute attitude model. The model has much empirical support in a variety of contexts, although there has been relatively little attitude change research reported. Attitude research is used heavily in a wide array of applied research settings, and it is safe to say that the multiattribute model is the single research area in which consumer psychology has made its greatest contributions.

Communications effects

Closely related to attitude change research has been the somewhat more general topic of communications effects. Of primary interest to consumer psychologists is the nature and magnitude of consumer response to advertising communications (e.g., Maxis & Adkinson, 1976), although some studies have investigated consumer reactions to personal selling efforts (e.g., Busch & Wilson, 1976).

The dominant theoretical approach to the study of communications effects has been quite consistent with classical communication theory in its reliance on a series of interrelated responses as indicative of the effectiveness of a persuasive message. In a classic paper, Lavidge and Steiner (1961) posited the *hierarchy of effects* model of advertising effectiveness shown in Fig. 11.7. As indicated in the figure, the six response stages are seen as being sequentially (and causally)

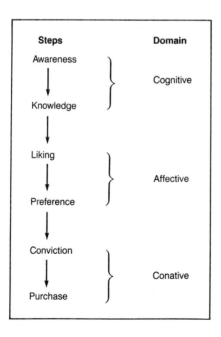

FIGURE 11.7   The Lavidge and Steiner hierarchy of effects model of advertising effectiveness.

related, with each successive response stage dependent on the immediately preceding one. Also, as shown, successive pairs of the response hierarchy correspond to the three domains of the well-known tripartite conception of attitude. That is, the general flow of communications effects is seen as initiating with cognitive impact, then affective reactions, and, finally, conative change. Fishbein and Ajzen (1975) incorporated this basic idea into their model as well. This rather pervasive view of the communications process has dominated consumer research in both academic and applied settings. Recently, however, many consumer psychologists have begun to question the validity of the standard hierarchy of effects and have offered an alternative explanation based upon "low-involvement" learning.

The initial statement of the low-involvement hypothesis was made by Krugman (1965), but it was not until the mid 1970s that the notion was widely embraced and began to generate empirical research. Krugman's position was that consumer response to advertising communications was simply not as personally involving as response to political speeches or other forms of persuasive messages typically studied by psychologists. Further, he argued, the classic hierarchy of effects assumed a highly involved message recipient and was therefore not appropriate for explaining the responses of low-involved recipients. Krugman's revised hierarchy, called the *low-involvement hierarchy*, initiated with cognitive change, followed by behavioral change, and culminated with attitudinal (or affective) change.

Ray (1973) extended Krugman's thinking in proposing his "three hierarchies" model of communications effects shown in Fig. 11.8. Both the high- and low-involvement hierarchies begin with cognition. At that juncture, however, the low- and high-involvement processes part ways. Highly involved consumers form brand attitudes on the basis of their beliefs about the brand (b_j in multiattribute model notation), while low-involvement consumers move directly to purchasing the brand on a trial basis. Thus, low-involvement consumers use initial trial purchase as a *basis* for forming brand attitudes whereas high-involvement consumers purchase (or decline to purchase) as a *result* of their

FIGURE 11.8   Ray's three hierarchies model of communications effects.

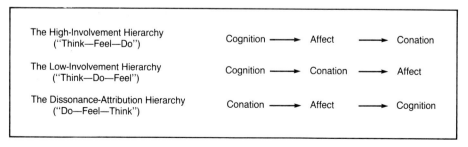

brand attitudes. The reversal in the ordering of the affective and conative response stages has far-reaching implications for consumer communications. Under high-involvement conditions, marketers emphasize the quality of persuasive argumentation in advertising and personal selling appeals. For the low-involvement situation, which appears to characterize most consumer package goods, marketers strive to create and maintain high brand awareness, stimulate trial purchase through special sales promotion activities (e.g., coupons), and rely on the quality of the product to generate customer satisfaction and repeat purchase.

The third hierarchy depicted in Fig. 11.8, the *dissonance–attribution hierarchy*, is one that was abstracted by Ray (1973) from the considerable literatures in dissonance theory and attribution theory. Under both theories, covert reactions such as cognition and affect are seen as resulting from the individual's analysis of his or her own behavior. This form of introspection, while (apparently) prevalent in many social psychological contexts, has not proven to be very powerful in the consumer psychological domain. In retrospect, it seems clear that the dissonance–attribution flow of effects requires reasonably high involvement on the part of the individual; hence, the low-involvement nature of much consumer behavior mitigates against the power of this hierarchy. As Ray (1982) reports, much empirical support has been generated for the low-involvement hierarchy, some for the high-involvement, and very little for the dissonance–attribution hierarchy. A continuing emphasis of 1980s consumer communications research is further explication of consumer response in low-involvement situations.

Another major research thrust in the area of consumer communications is the *cognitive-response* approach pioneered in social psychology by Greenwald (1968). Under the cognitive-response approach, message recipients are viewed not as passive receivers but rather as active participants in the communications process. In particular, recipients are thought to argue for or against points made in the message, disparage the source of the message, or express confusion or curiosity, among other possible responses. Importantly, these cognitive responses are viewed as intervening psychological processes that determine ultimate message response (e.g., attitude or behavior change). For instance, Wright (1973), in the initial test of cognitive–response theory in consumer psychology, found that a set of four cognitive-response mediators—counterarguing, support arguing, source derogation, and curiosity—were significantly related to attitudes and intentions following exposure to radio and print ads. In contrast, recall of message content was totally unrelated to attitudes and intentions. This convincing demonstration of the importance of the consumer's active role in communications response has given risen to a great deal of cognitive–response research over the past decade. For an outstanding review of this literature, see Wright (1980).

Cognitive–response data are generated by asking consumers open-ended questions following exposure to a persuasive message. Box 11.3 shows a typical cognitive–response question as well as some examples of the kinds of responses

B O X 11.3   TYPICAL COGNITIVE RESPONSE QUESTION AND
                  SAMPLE RESPONSES TO AN ADVERTISEMENT

QUESTION

"As you saw the commercial, what were some of the thoughts that went through your mind? Please write down everything that you thought of, regardless of whether it pertained to the commercial, the product advertised, or any other thought that went through your mind."

SAMPLE RESPONSES

"Alaska could be a good place to test automobile parts."
"I don't like Muhammed Ali."
"Motorcraft parts must be tough to stand that test in Alaska."
"Ali doesn't know anything about cars."
"Driving in Wisconsin winters. Going over ruts and potholes. Overall durability of my car."
"I like Ford products. Motorcraft shock absorbers are probably good."
"The commercial stressed tough."
"Motorcraft is durable. It has been tested."
"Not him again! He should stick to boxing."
"I like Ali."
"Commercial is believable."
"Only 3 shocks failed."

*Note: These responses taken from actual consumer responses to a television commercial in which Muhammed Ali endorsed Motorcraft parts by presenting the results of a test in which Motorcraft shock absorbers were "tested tough in Alaska."

consumers make. Commercial market research firms and advertising agencies have used this form of questioning for years but typically did not analyze the resultant data in any systematic fashion. The open-ended nature of the question permits consumers to provide any and all reactions to the ad, which is valuable in and of itself. However, the cognitive–response model, by providing the previously absent analytical framework, adds even more power. Hence, advertising researchers have readily embraced cognitive–response theory as a useful approach to communications research (e.g., Wolpert, 1982).

At its simplest level, cognitive–response theory is no more than a theoretical basis for *content analysis* of open-ended responses to communications. That is, a categorization scheme is developed that helps to uncover the nature of intervening processes. Some research attention has been directed to the development of response categories that are more appropriate for consumer communication stimuli. In general, social psychological research on cognitive response has utilized high-involvement messages such as speeches or editorials. In contrast, consumer communications researchers are more interested in relatively short, uninvolving messages like TV commercials and magazine ads. Evidence has begun to accumulate that suggests that a different set of response categories is needed in consumer communications research (Belch, 1981; Lutz & MacKenzie, 1982). In particular, large numbers of responses seem to be directed at evaluating the quality of the ad *per se* (labeled Ad Execution responses). This response category is quite important, especially in low involvement situations, and represents an important extension of the theory to accommodate the consumer psychology domain.

Decision–process models

The final major research area to be discussed in this chapter is the general body of research that characterizes consumer behavior in terms of decision–process models. The focus of this research is on the consumer as a decision maker or problem solver. Numerous decision process models have been proposed by various authors (e.g., Bettman, 1979; Howard & Sheth, 1969), but the most succinct example is probably the model first proposed by Engel, Kollat, and Blackwell in 1968, the core of which is depicted in Fig. 11.9.

As shown in the figure, consumer purchase decisions are seen as initiating with the consumer recognizing some sort of problem (e.g., "I am about to run out of toothpaste."). At this juncture, the consumer engages in both internal search (i.e., a memory scan) and external search for brands and relevant choice criteria. The set of brands that the consumer considers as possible problem solutions is sometimes referred to as the *evoked set* (Howard & Sheth, 1969), and the set of decision criteria correspond to the *salient attribute* dimensions central to the multiattribute attitude model. In fact, the Alternative evaluation stage in Fig.

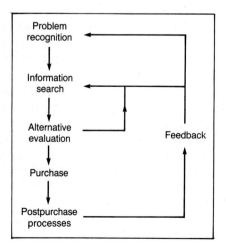

FIGURE 11.9   A generalized consumer decision process model.

11.9 has been characterized by some authors as being essentially a process of forming attitudes toward the various brands in the evoked set. As shown in the figure, the evaluation of these brands often requires further information search. As will be seen shortly, the bulk of consumer decision process research has focused on the Information search and Alternative evaluation stages.

Based on the evaluation of alternatives, actual purchase occurs, followed by postpurchase behaviors and outcomes. Here, researchers often examine the processes involved in consumer satisfaction/dissatisfaction (e.g., Oliver, 1980). The process of consumption is seen as providing feedback to the consumer, perhaps causing new problems to be recognized ("I can't use this new toothpaste until I buy a toothbrush.") or serving as a form of information search, i.e., the "trial" purchase behavior discussed under the low-involvement model of communications effectiveness.

Because of the focus of attention on the second and third stages of the general decision process model shown in Fig. 11.9, much of the research conducted in this domain has been labeled *consumer-information processing* research. That is, the consumer seeks information about goods and services and then processes that information through a variety of mechanisms to arrive at a purchase decision. This perspective of the consumer as an information processor has been the dominant over-arching paradigm in consumer psychology over the past decade. The three research areas discussed previously here all fit under a general information-processing umbrella to some degree. In addition, other heavily researched topics are clearly inspired by an information processing view of consumer behavior.

The initial consumer information processing research involved the construction of *decision nets* based on consumer *protocols* (i.e., self-reports of thought processes) generated during shopping trips (e.g., Bettman, 1970). Decision nets provided pictorial descriptions of decision sequences, but were cumbersome analytically and not powerful in an explanatory sense.

Consumer-information processing research next moved into a phase wherein mathematical modeling of decisions was the main focus. Under this approach, the central formula of the multiattribute attitude model was characterized as a *linear additive* model or, alternatively, as a linear compensatory model. Thus, the model's mathematical characteristics are such that a "strong" attribute could "compensate" for a "weak" attribute because all attributes are summed. In contrast, other views of consumer information processing are *noncompensatory*, or configural, in that a particularly weak or strong attribute can totally govern the outcome of the decision process. Examples of these alternative mathematical formulations are lexicographic, conjunctive, disjunctive, and additive difference models (Bettman, 1979). In recent years, interest in mathematical models of consumer-information processing has waned, primarily due to the fact that they generally do not predict significantly better than the simple linear additive model. Furthermore, consumer psychologists have become dis-

TABLE 11.2   **An Information Display Board**

Attributes	Brands				
	A	**B**	**C**	**D**	**E**
1	A1	B1	C1	D1	E1
2	A2	B2	C2	D2	E2
3	A3	B3	C3	D3	E3
4	A4	B4	C4	D4	E4

enchanted with the ability of these models to capture adequately true decision processes and have turned instead to other more process-related methodologies.

An important approach to the study of consumer-information search and processing has been centered on the *information display board* (IDB) first used by Jacoby and his associates (Jacoby, Speller, & Kohn, 1974a,b). A typical IDB arrays brand-attribute information in a matrix format, as shown in Table 11.2. Brands are ordered along one axis and relevant choice criteria along the other. Cell entries contain specific pieces of information about the level of each brand on each attribute. The specific cell information is initially covered, and consumers are asked to uncover the items of information necessary to make their purchase decision. Researchers track the total amount of information accessed and the order in which it is accessed for the purposes of uncovering the underlying processing which is taking place. Thus, the IDB provides data similar to that which is obtained through the use of eye movement monitoring equipment (Bettman, 1979).

To date, the most significant general finding that has been forthcoming from the IDB research is that consumers tend to select information along an attribute dimension (known as *attribute processing*) across brands, given that the brand attribute information is readily available in the IDB context. In reality, however, brand information is rarely available in matrix form, forcing consumers who are unwilling to juggle, say, ten cereal boxes at a time, to resort to *brand processing*, i.e., accessing relevant information one brand at a time. Brand processing hampers brand comparisons and is thus of interest to public policy makers interested in fostering better consumer decision making. In one clever study, Russo, Krieser, and Miyashita (1975) posted unit price information in a matrix format in supermarkets and found that, over time, the average price paid for certain grocery items dropped, even though the unit price information had been available previously in the standard form on shelf facings. Russo and his colleagues interpreted this effect as representing the greater ease of processing afforded by the matrix presentation.

The most recent trend in consumer information processing research has been the incorporation of memory constructs into the study of consumer choice. Critics of the IDB methodology described above pointed out that the IDB measured only external search for information and ignored potential internal memory scanning being conducted by consumers in the process of making purchase decisions. Hence, consumer researchers have become concerned with prior product knowledge as it has an impact on choice. The topics of memory encoding, distortion, decay, and retrieval are becoming increasingly popular in the consumer psychology literature (e.g., Bettman, 1979). And, paralleling the trend in cognitive psychology, consumer psychology has moved from the *levels of processing* view of memory (Craik & Lockhart, 1972) to the more currently fashionable *schema theory* view (e.g., Abelson, 1976). At the present time, consumer product class knowledge and how it is organized in memory is a hotbed of research activity.

Consumer-information processing research is relevant to several more applied research questions. For instance, the nature of information search and processing is of interest to both marketers and public policy makers. If information that is most easily processed is that which tends to be used in decision making, then there are substantial implications for packaging (e.g., nutritional labeling) and advertising decisions.

In another vein, several studies have demonstrated that consumer information processing varies, sometimes rather dramatically, with the surrounding situational context (e.g., Wright & Weitz, 1977). This situational effect is important, for example, in market segmentation research. For many products, the anticipated situation in which the product is to be consumed (e.g., at home alone vs. at a party with others) is the single most powerful basis for segmentation (Young, Ott, & Feigen, 1978). Fuller understanding of the processes is of obvious importance to marketers of these kinds of products.

Finally, memory research has begun to reshape consumer psychologists' views of advertising effectiveness investigations. While past research has relied on consumers' recall of information, current thinking suggests that analyzing consumers' recognition of information may be more appropriate (Bettman, 1979). This shift in theorization may have a dramatic impact on the nature of advertising pretesting methods.

■ CONCLUSION

Consumer psychology is a fascinating domain in which the professional psychologist can pursue his or her career. There is room for both the pragmatic, action-oriented individual who enjoys applied research and the more theoretically oriented person who enjoys pushing back the frontiers of knowledge. Consumer behavior is a pervasive set of phenomena, ranging from the important and complex to the trivial and repetitive. As such, the milieu of consumer behavior provides an excellent crucible for the study of human behavior.

■ SUGGESTED READINGS

Assael, H. (1980). *Consumer behavior and marketing action.* Boston: Kent.

This best-selling consumer behavior text serves as an excellent introduction to the field and is acclaimed for its real-world examples. This book is a good source for learning about how consumer psychology is used in making marketing decisions.

Bettman, J. R. (1979). *An information processing theory of consumer choice.* Reading, MA: Addison-Wesley.

This scholarly monograph outlines a general theory of consumer behavior, working primarily from the perspective of cognitive psychology. This book is a good introduction to consumer research for the advanced student.

Engel, J., & Blackwell, R. D. (1982). *Consumer behavior* (4th ed.). Hinsdale, IL: Dryden.

This recent edition of the classic consumer behavior text represents an encyclopedia of current research distilled for the novice. This text is noted for its completeness of coverage and its organization around the decision–process model of consumer behavior.

Kassarjian, H. H. (1982). Consumer psychology. *Annual Review of Psychology, 33,* 619–649.

The most recent of the Annual Review chapters on Consumer Psychology, this chapter is authored by a researcher generally regarded as one of the founding fathers of the consumer behavior discipline. This chapter would be primarily of use to the advanced researcher.

Journal of Consumer Research (1974–1985).

This journal is the leading scholarly journal in the field of consumer research. It contains many excellent articles examining consumer behavior from a psychological perspective.

UNIT IV

PSYCHOLOGY APPLIED IN THE PUBLIC DOMAIN

A recent and exciting area of application for psychology is in those areas that might be considered "public domain." Thus, each of the chapters in this unit describes a psychological specialty whose practitioners work for the betterment of society as a whole. While most psychologists have been involved in activities that meet this goal in general, the chapters in this unit detail activities whose direct outcome is improvement of our society and the world in which we live.

The first chapter in this unit, environmental psychology, discusses what psychologists have learned concerning our environment's influence on us and the impact of our actions on our environment. Thus, noisy environments or stressful environments may cause certain responses among us. We, in turn, can reciprocally influence our environment, as when we redesign neighborhoods to promote social behaviors.

Another aspect of society that affects all of us is the criminal justice and legal system. Psychology has broadened its influence within this system. Traditionally, psychologists have interacted with the criminal justice system primarily through expert testimony on issues of insanity and competence to stand trial. Lately, psychologists have begun to investigate the nature of jury selection, the effect of other aspects of the courtroom setting on the eventual verdict, and the outcome of certain verdicts upon the defendants. Law psychology is a rapidly growing specialty with many new avenues of application.

The final chapter in this unit is on psychologists' role in the formulation and investigation of public policy. Perhaps more than any of the other chapters in this text, the setting of "public policy" poses a formidable challenge to the science of psychology and an equally challenging setting for employment.

RALPH B. TAYLOR

ENVIRONMENTAL PSYCHOLOGY

■ INTRODUCTION

In the short story "Rammer" (Niven, 1974), an aging cancer-ridden architect is put into a frozen sleep. As he drifts off, he wonders about the future. He is awakened, two hundred years later, to find an omnipotent state, and a city where buildings, all of the same cubistic design, were close packed. He is tested and trained by the state to be a space pilot, an opportunity he exploits to fly to a far-away planet. Unlike this hero, we are not likely to have the chance to escape to other worlds. And, our future is not two hundred years away. There are many forces currently sculpting the face of the future—governments, corporations, and historical figures. But, at the same time, the future is made up of behaviors of individuals.

It is difficult to feel that we determine the future. We feel a sense of helplessness, to which we attempt to adapt. We learn how to cope with noise, bad air, gasoline lines, and high utility costs. But adaptation may not be desirable; we may learn to live in cities with endless concrete and become primed to accept further degrading of the quality of our world. Thus, if we think of ourselves in relation to our environment, there are important themes: Through our behaviors, we improve or degrade the environment. Second, we try to cope with stressors in environments where we live, work, and have recreation. Part of this coping may be instrumental in our attempts to improve things. Part of this coping may also be palliative; that is, we just accept things as they are.

The author was partially supported by grant CJ-IX-80-0077 from the National Institute of Justice during the preparation of this chapter. Opinions are solely those of the author.

It is these themes that are the main concern of environmental psychology. To illustrate these themes and to illustrate environmental psychology, this chapter will use the device of the case study. That is, several studies, or series of studies, will be examined. Each is closely linked with a particular theoretical perspective of central interest to environmental psychology. These case studies include two investigations that rely on a stress perspective—first, a study of chronic stress among residents around the Three Mile Island Nuclear Power Plant, and the other, a study of the effects of airport noise on school children. We shall examine concepts of human territoriality in an urban residential environment. We also will use crowding concepts to analyze the stressful consequences of over-crowding in prisons. Last, we shall examine efforts to promote anti-littering behavior. We will conclude by examining problems likely to be with us in the year 2000 and beyond.

Environmental psychology has many other areas to offer that cannot be examined in this chapter, including hospital redesign (Holohan & Saegert, 1973; Winkel, 1981), rerouting traffic (Appleyard, 1981), and queuing systems at crowded bus stops in national parks (Wicker & Kirmeyer, 1976). The interested reader is encouraged to investigate these additional cases.

■ THE BACKGROUND OF ENVIRONMENTAL PSYCHOLOGY

The environmental psychological orientation

Many people are environmental psychologists but call themselves something different, such as environmental design researcher, ecological psychologist, human ecologist, or social ecologist. Regardless of the label, there are several common characteristics among environmental psychologists. First, they are interested in solving, or at the very least understanding, real-world problems. Theories they use may, in fact, have been developed specifically to address these real-world problems. Second, they include one or more aspects of the physical environment either as a predictor (something that helps cause the problem), or as an outcome (something that may be a problem now but could be altered through change). Third, they are interested in a particular level of analysis, namely, related to individuals and small or medium-sized predominantly face-to-face groups (Stokols, 1977). If the person is concerned with smaller-scale systems within a person (such as visual tracking), then he or she is probably an experimental psychologist and not an environmental psychologist. If the person would rather discuss larger groups of people (such as social classes), then he or she is probably a social psychologist or a sociologist. Environmental psychologists study whole people or groups as entities in and of themselves. Fourth, they believe in the inherent integrity of person-setting units (Barker, 1968; Proshansky, 1976). Environmental psychologists believe that a person's behavior only makes sense in the particular context in which it occurs. Last, environmental psychologists have a strong preference for performing field studies or field experiments rather than laboratory experiments.

Environmental psychologists believe that the laboratory setting imposes some disadvantages on research: an artificial setting, "subject pool" subjects, and a narrow focus. While there are advantages to laboratory setting research—the ability of the experimenter to clearly control the population being studied and the effect of variables not of interest—environmental psychologists believe that the disadvantages of the laboratory setting outweigh its advantages. And conversely, although field settings impose limits on experimentation, environmental psychologists believe field settings have the strong advantage of allowing naturally occurring behaviors and attitudes to be examined in a real environment.

An additional aspect relevant to many environmental psychologists is that they work in interdisciplinary or multidisciplinary contexts. They are likely to incorporate ideas and methods from other areas of psychology as well as from related disciplines such as architecture, geography, anthropology, and so on. This broad view is necessary because many of the problems addressed by environmental psychology, such as energy conservation, noise, and wilderness use, have no disciplinary bounds. Working on such teams can be difficult, because an initial learning period is required where each member learns about the other's definitions and approaches; but the final results are ultimately more powerful than could have been obtained otherwise.

Figure 12.1 sums up the broad conceptual outlines of environmental psychology. Links between attitudinal, affective, and behavioral consequences and the physical environment, as mediated or carried or influenced by intervening social, cultural, and psychological processes, are the variables of interest. Behaviors and intervening processes at the individual or small-group level may be examined. Note that according to this approach, *direct* effects of the physical environment on human behavior are not possible. Such a fallacy has been labeled "architectural determinism" (Broady, 1972). Physical variables do not determine what we do, although they may make certain events more or less likely. For example, consider the well-known finding by Festinger, Schachter, and Back (1950) that in a student housing project people were much more likely to pick people living close at hand, only one or two doors away, as friends. The

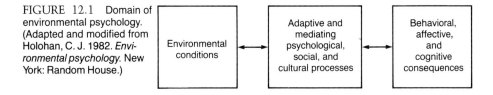

FIGURE 12.1   Domain of environmental psychology. (Adapted and modified from Holohan, C. J. 1982. *Environmental psychology.* New York: Random House.)

Environmental conditions ←→ Adaptive and mediating psychological, social, and cultural processes ←→ Behavioral, affective, and cognitive consequences

authors did not suggest that the proximity "determined" friendship. Rather, they suggested that proximity resulted in two people "bumping into" each other more often and, since they were very similar on several characteristics (education, interest, class, war experience), these unplanned or passive contacts were reinforcing, so the two people would be likely to follow them up, eventually, with some "planned" contacts, like getting together for an evening. Thus, although the physical environment is clearly of interest to environmental psychologists, they must also be very careful and clear about the roles it can play in influencing behavior.

■ HISTORICAL DEVELOPMENT

There is disagreement on when environmental psychology became a distinct discipline. Some say 1970, when a book, a volume of edited readings, appeared with that title (Proshansky, Ittelson, & Rivlin, 1970). Others (Ittelson, Proshansky, Rivlin, & Winkel, 1974) push the date back to the late 1950s when psychologists began investigating links between design and behavior on psychiatric wards. A case can also be made for identifying the beginning in the early 1940s when Barker, Dembo, and Lewin (1943) published their paper on the behavioral effects of interposing a physical barrier between children and their toys. These small beginnings led to a surge in the 1970s, when environmental psychology became increasingly important.

There were several reasons for this sudden blooming of environmental psychology. Relevance was an issue, and people wanted a field of psychology that could more clearly speak to the problems around them. The ecological movement, in conjunction with Apollo pictures of a delicate globe floating in empty space, brought into popular awareness the fragility and potentially perilous condition of our ecosystem. The civil disorders of the 1960s suggested to people that maybe something was really wrong in our big cities, and many wondered how much of the problem was the physical environment. There was a resurgence of interest in nature, "getting back to nature," and even "living off the land," singly or in a collective group.

Since the early 1970s, the field and the researchers working in it have evolved substantially. Craik (1977) has suggested that, early on, environmental psychology was simply a set of issues to which psychologists in other areas could apply their conceptual and methodological expertise. Social psychological researchers, for example, were applying their theories and methods to environmental problems. One such instance is Worchel and Teddlie's (1976) study of crowding. They hypothesized that if one person was physically close to another, he or she would become aroused, and would then seek an explanation for that arousal. If an environmental explanation was possible, the arousal would be attributed to that cause. (An "environmental" explanation might be exciting pictures on the wall, or telling the person that inaudible subsonic noise was being pumped into the room.) Lacking an external explanation, however, the person would attribute the arousal to crowding, and thus say that he or she felt crowded. Although Worchel and Teddlie's experimental setup was elegant in many respects, and although they did obtain the predicted pattern of results, the experiment represents a process of stripping down the problem being examined. In this experiment, the experience of crowding was reduced to what subjects thought about some explanations they were given. This experience of crowding is certainly quite different from what people in an inner-city classroom or an over-crowded prison experience. The traditional approaches used in the early work may have precluded a complete appreciation of the environmental issues.

Subsequently, however, and to the credit of the field, there has been less and less fitting of environmental issues to the methodologies of other areas of psychology. Workers in the environmental area have placed increasing emphasis on the use of appropriate methods such as behavioral observation, assessment of physical environments, postoccupancy evaluation, and, where possible, of multiple methods. The field has also had considerable success in developing its own theories, many times accomplishing this by completing a unique fusion of several concepts from other areas of psychology, or from outside the discipline (Taylor, 1983).

Environmental psychologists are finding acceptance in interdisciplinary research centers, and in related departments such as housing, interior design, architecture schools, social work programs, planning programs, and so on. Many have gone on to public sector or service-oriented positions with federal or state agencies.

■ RESEARCH CASE STUDIES

Because the field of environmental psychology is so diverse, we will present six case studies to demonstrate the variety within the discipline.

The first two cases to be discussed, Three Mile Island and schools near airports, draw on a *stress* perspective, which in environmental and health psychology has been applied to many topics. The third and fourth case studies are concerned, respectively, with neighborhood redesign to prevent crime and use of small urban open spaces; both draw on a *territorial* perspective. The fifth case study is concerned with prisons and draws on a *crowding* perspective. The last case study is concerned with the promotion of anti-littering behaviors and uses *learning principles*. Thus, although these six case studies do not cover all of the areas in which environmental psychologists work, they do include some of the major theories that have been investigated.

Three Mile Island

As many vividly recall, the nuclear station at Three Mile Island (TMI), near Harrisburg, Penn., experienced a malfunction in the No. 2 reactor on March 28, 1979. Subsequently, it was determined that it would be necessary to vent a large volume of radioactive Kr-85 gas, which had built up during and after the accident, from one of the containment buildings. The actual venting took place a little over a year after the accident, and its impact on surrounding residents was monitored by Andy Baum and his colleagues. Although the explicit focus of the study was on reactions to the venting, it really serves in a larger sense as a documentation of the chronic stress associated with proximity to a crippled, and still potentially dangerous, nuclear power plant.

Some relevant theoretical background ▪ Baum and his colleagues (Baum, Gatchel, Fleming, & Lake, 1982) placed their TMI research squarely in the tradition of research that has focused on human stress. In their review article on environmental stress, Baum, Singer, and Baum (1981) suggested that the components involved in determining the stress response can be broken down into three sets: (1) the source of stress and its physical characteristics; (2) how the stressor is appraised or interpreted by the affected person, which usually concerns the extent to which the person perceives the stressor as threatening or dangerous, and (3) the characteristics of the person or audience. The stress response, which is determined by these elements, is complex. It may include a physiological component, a performance component, an affect (mood) component, and a social behavior dimension. Also, these different levels of stress response may not all be present all the time. A certain stressor may affect physiological functioning in one way but have a different influence on, for example, cognitive performance.

Responses to a stressor are complex for two additional and important reasons. First, stress *aftereffects* may be much more sizable than effects while the stressor is present. For example, Glass and Singer (1972) found that people adapted physiologically quite rapidly to loud, intermittent noise. The adaptation was reflected by a measure of electrodermal activity—galvanic skin response (GSR)—returning to normal levels soon after the onset of the noise. But, when the noise was over and subjects were taken to a different room, they showed stress aftereffects in terms of poorer performance on various cognitive tasks and/ or less persistence on these tasks. The strength of the stress aftereffects was related to the nature of the noise stressor, i.e., how irregular it was and whether subjects thought they had control over the noise.

This pattern of response to stress makes sense because it has survival value. When things are difficult, we cope effectively by turning quickly to avoid a stopped car on the freeway or by pulling a child out of the path of an oncoming vehicle. It is only after the danger is past that our heart rate increases, we sweat profusely, and our hands shake. Thus, to determine stress effects accurately, it is important to identify how people respond both during and after the occurrence of the stressor.

A second difficult feature of stress responses is that they are often shaped by repeated exposure to a stressor. Generally, two patterns are discussed. The first is one of simple *adaptation*, where people learn to cope more effectively to repeated presentations of the stressor or to the continuation of the stressor. A second pattern is *accumulation* over time, where stress effects build up over time, resulting in severe long-term impacts if a stressor is repeatedly presented. Prolonged exposure may deplete physiological resources, thus inhibiting people's capability to respond and cope with future stressors. Severe emotional consequences, such as free-floating anxiety, may also develop. In instances where a stressor continues over time and the person is continually being forced to cope and adjust, he or she may be said to be suffering from chronic stress.

Hypotheses ▪ Baum et al. hypothesized that residents around TMI would suffer acute stress in anticipation of and during the venting of the Kr-85 gas, but that this stress would be lower after the venting had been successfully completed. They also hypothesized that residents around TMI would suffer chronic stress, due to living in proximity to a damaged and still potentially dangerous nuclear reactor. Thus, TMI residents would show more stress symptoms than comparable residents from different communities who were not living near a damaged nuclear facility.

Design of study ▪ Respondents living within 5 miles of TMI, on the opposite side of the Susquehanna River, were interviewed four times: 3 to 5 days before the venting began, after the venting had been in progress for several days, 3 to 5 days *after* the announced conclusion of the venting, and six weeks after the announced conclusion of the venting. (The last assessment occurred about 18 months after the accident.)

In the town of Frederick, Md., a sample of residents was also tested at the same points in time. These residents lived 80 miles from TMI and more than 20 miles from the nearest power plant (of any type). Frederick was selected as the primary control group, against which TMI respondents would be compared, based on socioeconomic and demographic similarities between the two communities.

For the final assessment session, two additional control groups were added: residents living within five miles of the undamaged Oyster Creek, N.J. nuclear power plant, and residents from Dickerson, Md., who lived within five miles of a traditional coal-fired power plant.

Procedure ▪ Interviewers contacted potential respondents at their homes and solicited their participation. The testing sessions were scheduled if the resident was willing to participate. At each session, a battery of protocols was completed to measure levels of emotional disturbance and depression; attitudes toward TMI; and several dimensions of cognitive performance, including a proofreading task and an embedded-figures task. Respondents were also asked to provide urine samples, which were later measured for levels of epinephrine and norepinephrine (substances that represent some of the catecholamines secreted in the body and reflect levels of adrenal medulla activity, and hence stress).

Results ▪ TMI residents, as compared to residents in the Frederick control group, demonstrated several differences. The TMI residents perceived a higher level of threat and hazard from TMI, and these significantly higher levels persisted throughout the study, remaining higher even six weeks after venting had ended. The TMI residents also reported more somatic symptoms and mood effects (e.g., depression), some of which declined slightly after venting was completed but some of which (e.g., anxiety) remained high. Poorer performance on the proofreading task was shown by TMI residents; this difference remained constant throughout the four testing sessions. Last, the TMI residents showed higher norepinephrine levels during the first two testing sessions; by the last testing session, these levels were only somewhat higher.

The availability of data from the three different control groups at the last testing session allowed the experimenters to determine if the stress was caused by living close to a power plant, a nuclear power plant, or a crippled power plant. Results indicated that the primary source of distress was the latter. TMI residents, as compared to all three control groups, perceived higher levels of threat from the nearby plant, showed higher rates of somatic complaints, performed more poorly on the cognitive tasks, and had higher epinephrine levels in their urine. Bear in mind that the data from the last testing session were collected almost a year and a half after the original accident. These results suggest that, on several parameters, TMI residents were suffering from a chronic stress syndrome that was not totally alleviated by the venting procedure. Results suggest that the cumulative effects of this chronic stress may have been substantial.

Practical consequences and implications ▪ The results of this study have had an impact in the legal arena. When the company that owns TMI petitioned to start up the undamaged reactor there, the court ruled that this could not be carried out because of the adverse impact it was likely to have on residents' already high fear and perceived threat levels. In essence, the court ruled that mental stress was an environmental impact that the utility must propose to ameliorate, not exacerbate (Marshall, 1982a). Subsequent legal rulings, much to the relief of utilities, have put this ruling in the very narrow context of the TMI incident itself, thus not mandating that it apply to other utilities who want to start their nuclear plants.

One final point about TMI. One reason the plant may be such a potent stressor for the residents close by, for such a long period of time, may be due, as Baum has suggested, to the topography: Residents can see the cooling stacks at TMI from their property. This vista may have served as a persistent symbol of the danger they confronted.

Leaving on a jet plane: Schools in the flight path of Los Angeles Airport

Airports, unfortunately, do not exist in a vacuum. Somebody must live and work and go to school near them, and it is not desirable to place them at a great distance from centers of human activity and commerce because this makes them inaccessible and uneconomical. It is also unfortunate that airplanes make intense noise when taking off and landing. Studies in the U.S. and in other countries have established that, although levels of airport noise may not be high enough to cause physical damage, they can cause other health problems such as heart trouble and elevated blood pressure levels (see Cohen & Weinstein, 1981, for a review of such studies). There are also studies that correlate noisy school environments with poor performance. This research, however, has not yet revealed the underlying process that causes this result.

Some relevant theoretical background ▪ There may be several mechanisms through which noise leads to poor performance on cognitive tasks, such as reading tests, and achievement. One explanation relies largely on an attentional model: It argues that when confronted with noise, we allocate some portion of our finite capacity for attention to that source (Kahneman, 1973). This means that we have less attention to allocate elsewhere, resulting in selective inattention to those other areas.

An alternative and more stress-oriented explanation would be a "learned helplessness" one (Seligman, 1975). According to this explanation, when we initially encounter aversive environmental events, we try to cope in some fashion (leave, turn on air conditioner, etc.), but if our efforts are unsuccessful, and the aversive event continues over a period of time, then eventually we "give up" trying to cope and exhibit a learned-helplessness syndrome. This is a psychological state that includes such motivational and emotional disturbances as apathy and depression.

Laboratory work on noise (Glass & Singer, 1972) provides some evidence of how the psychological state of "giving up" may develop. In experiments, some subjects were exposed to controllable noise whereas other subjects were exposed to uncontrollable noise. The only difference was that in the controllable condition, subjects were shown a button, and the experimenter told them that if the noise became intolerable, all they had to do was push that button and everything would stop. None of the subjects actually pushed the button. After the exposure to the noise was over, subjects were given a frustration task (how many times they would attempt to trace an anagram, which was untraceable, without lifting their pencils). Subjects in the uncontrollable condition gave up sooner and made fewer attempts to solve the anagram. Thus, at least in a lab setting, it looked as if uncontrollable noise could lead to helplessness. The question then became, for Cohen and his colleagues, does it happen this way in the real world too?

Study design ▪ The study (Cohen, Evans, Krantz, & Stokols, 1980; Cohen, Krantz, Evans, & Stokols, 1981; Cohen, Krantz, Evans, Stokols, & Kelly, 1981) took place in the four noisiest elementary schools in the Los Angeles (LA) Airport air corridor and in three control "quiet" schools, matched with the noisy schools on background characteristics. In the noisy schools there was, on average, one overflight every 2½ minutes, and sound levels in those schools reached as high as 95 decibels. Furthermore, in the noisy schools there were some "quiet" class-rooms, where sound reducing material had been installed some years earlier. After the first testing session, several more classrooms received a noise abate-ment re-design. The researchers came back a year later for a second testing ses-sion. Thus, they could carry out cross-sectional analyses (comparing several different settings at one point in time), and longitudinal analyses, comparing how children did after they had been transferred to the noise-abated classrooms for a year. They could also examine the effects of noise over time by comparing children who had been at the noisy schools for varying lengths of time.

The researchers obtained physiological measures—systolic and diastolic blood pressure—on all participants. They also had the participants complete a variety of cognitive tasks—proofreading, puzzle solving, and so on—in a sound-proof trailer brought up to the school on testing days. Some of these tasks were performed under distracting conditions, with noise in the background. The researchers also collected records of academic performance from the schools.

Hypotheses ▪ The basic expectation was that children in noisy as compared to quiet schools would have poorer health (higher blood pressure), poorer academic scores, poorer performance on cognitive tasks, and be more distractible. It was expected that these negative effects would intensify with increased exposure to the noisy schools, reflecting an accumulation of stress effects over time and not successful adaptation.

Results ▪ The main results of the cross-sectional analysis, that compared stu-dents from noisy and quiet schools at one point in time, found that the children from the noisy schools had higher systolic and diastolic blood pressure than their quiet-school counterparts and that the differences were largest for those children who had been fewer years at the noisy school. (These analyses, and all others, controlled for other differences between the noisy and quiet schools, such as race and social status of parents.) These results suggest that there may have been some degree of physiological adaptation to the noisier school environment as a result of increased exposure.

On cognitive tasks, there was evidence for lower levels of performance and for the expected learned-helplessness syndrome. Children from noisy schools were more likely to fail to solve a puzzle task within the allotted time, and were more likely to give up on the task before the allotted time had passed. Another finding that supports a helplessness explanation came from the task where the children did simple proofreading while being distracted by a taped voice in the background. Children who had been at the noisy schools for a longer period of time, more than four years, were much more distractible than children who had been at the noisy schools for less than two years. This finding suggests that when children first come to a noisy school, they try to cope by tuning out extra-neous noise; however, after a period of time and persistence of the stressor, chil-dren give up on this kind of coping and no longer tune out extraneous noises.

When the researchers came back a year later, they found that many of the patterns of differences discussed above still remained. Noisy-school children were still more distractible the longer they had been there. Thus, it appears that the helplessness syndrome persisted. And, noisy-school children still performed more poorly, and had a longer time to completion, on the cognitive puzzle task. Differences in blood pressure were not observed a year later because the children from the noisy schools who had high blood pressure had moved out of the noisy neighborhoods! Noisy-school students with the highest blood pressure scores at the initial testing were the most likely group to have moved out of the noise-impacted area within two years of initial testing. (Again, these findings control for race and class.)

The authors suggest that there are several possible explanations for these results. The one they tended to favor was that parents of children with elevated blood pressure were sensitive to the noise-induced stress their children were under, and consequently moved away. (Other analyses also support this interpretation.) If this interpretation is correct, this study has revealed a striking and unanticipated consequence of noise-induced stress. These results also illustrate the difficulty with field studies in that natural attrition (subjects dropping out of research) tends to occur and is a potential source for error in interpretation of results.

Comparisons of children who had been in noise-abated classrooms for a year, where objective noise levels were lower, with children who had remained in noisy classrooms for a year revealed some improvements due to the abatement procedures. First, they helped reduce the helplessness syndrome: Children from noise-abated classrooms did slightly better than their noisy-classroom counterparts on the puzzle-solving task. Second, math scores for third grade children in abated classrooms were somewhat higher than scores from their noisy-classroom counterparts. Thus, although the noise-abated classrooms were much quieter, objectively, than the nonabated classrooms, the abatement procedures were less successful than had been anticipated.

Practical consequences and implications ▪ The noise-abated classrooms discussed in this study had come about as a result of a legal decision in a case involving the local community vs. the LA Airport. The community had won, and it received money to modify the classrooms. The data from this study suggest, however, that such an intervention may not have been enough. The abatement procedure resulted in only marginal improvements and did not even effect a wide range of stress-related measures. This suggests that the intervention was too weak. It is likely that in addition to less noise in the classroom, less noise in the community is needed as well. "Thus, decreasing overall community noise levels by creating buffer zones between airports and other sources of high intensity noise and the surrounding communities would be one way of providing more adequate protection for community residents" (Cohen, Krantz, Evans, Stokols, & Kelly, 1981, p. 345). In sum, community noise seems to induce stress responses in children, who in turn do not appear to adapt over time to the stressor. A wide-ranging and comprehensive intervention appears to be necessary to reduce the stress.

The next two case studies are of a different nature than the previous two in that they focus on places, not on individuals. Also, these case studies are *demonstration projects*, where the bulk of resources is committed to changing something and resources left over for evaluation are fewer. Furthermore, because of planning, implementation, and community involvement, such demonstration efforts tend to take place over a period of time. This time factor may make evaluation difficult, because it is hard to determine if changes in attitudes and behaviors that are observed are due to the actual intervention or to larger scale changes in the surrounding area. For example, a neighborhood may implement physical changes and find that, afterwards, crime has decreased. However, crime in the entire city may have decreased as well during that same time period. This problem of "what causes what" crops up in any longitudinal investigation.

There are two ways that the researcher can increase his or her ability to unravel causal effects. One approach is to compare what happens in the demonstration sites with what happens in similar "control" areas that did not receive the intervention. An even better method is to assign areas randomly to either receive the intervention or to receive no intervention (Fairweather & Tornatzky, 1977). The random assignment assures that differences between the control and treatment areas are due to the intervention. This approach, although it can and has been achieved in many instances, is difficult to implement.

Crime running rampant: Turning the streets back to the people

Some relevant theoretical background ▪ The suggestion that there may be links between the physical design of streets, neighborhoods, and projects, and crime in those locales was first made by Jane Jacobs (1961) over 20 years ago. Subsequently, Oscar Newman (1972) systematized these suggestions into what he called "defensible space theory." The basic idea was that certain design features of the public housing environment (surveillance by locating windows overlooking playgrounds and walkways, clear boundaries between public and semiprivate spaces through the use of barriers or low walls) could be implemented, which would "unleash" the latent territorial instincts of residents who would then take a more active role in policing their own area and thus reduce crime and other antisocial behavior.

Although subsequent research has established that design features are associated with crime rates, Newman's original statement of the process underlying this linkage has been discarded (Taylor, Gottfredson, & Brower, 1980). People do not have latent territorial "instincts" that are "unleashed" by certain design features. Rather, it appears to be the case that if certain social preconditions are met, and if the crime problem is not overwhelming, physical features, such as real and symbolic barriers or surveillance opportunities, and local social ties can support residents' territorial functioning (Merry, 1981; Newman & Franck, 1982; Taylor, Gottfredson, & Brower, 1980).

In the present case, the researchers sought to apply defensible space "spin offs" at the neighborhood level: What they planned was to reduce unwanted vehicular and pedestrian traffic in the neighborhood by changing traffic patterns in the neighborhood and by making entrances to the neighborhood more distinctive. Previous work by Appleyard (1981) showed that heavy traffic volume on a street caused the residents to feel less territorial about their street, and to spend less time sitting outside socializing with their neighbors. Heavy pedestrian traffic can also have the same kind of impact (Baum, Davis & Aiello, 1978). Thus, reducing traffic levels should "turn the streets back to the residents" and make the streets less anonymous. It was then expected that residents would be more on the lookout, that potential criminals would be aware of this change, and thus that crime and related fear would decrease (Fowler & Mangione, 1981; Fowler, McCalla, & Mangione, 1979).

Study design ▪ The study took place in the Asylum Hill neighborhood of Hartford, Conn. The most important part of the design of the study was that the changes were phased in sequentially over a period of years. This aspect of the study allowed researchers to assess changes in the measures of interest also over a period of years.

The first step was to promote and support local community organizations that were concerned about crime. This step took place beginning in late 1974 and early 1975. These organizations also took part in later shaping and approving the physical changes in the neighborhood. Policing changes, which involved assigning the same police officers to the same area over time (geographic stability of assignment), took place in 1975 and 1976. Police officers also developed closer ties with community organizations and local business people. The physical design changes were completed in late 1976. The final design changes involved, first, the creation of four cul-de-sacs that inhibited through traffic. Second, seven gateways, with planters and special entrances, better defined the neighborhood as a distinct area. Third, one major artery was changed to allow one-way traffic only. Initially, more changes (street closings) had been planned, but opposition by local businesses led to their being dropped. In addition, since the changes were of unknown effectiveness, it was agreed that they would be viewed as temporary and could be removed at a later date if they were not working.

For evaluators' purposes, residents were surveyed periodically throughout the study period, one year after the changes were complete, and three years after the changes were complete. Also, as a "control" group, residents from the rest of the city were interviewed at the same times. Data on crime, for the neighborhood and the entire city, were collected from the local police department. Also, observers recorded levels of street activity at various times.

Hypotheses ▪ The hypotheses were fairly straightforward: After the implementation of these changes, residents would report greater use of streets, easier distinction between who does and who does not belong in the neighborhood, less fear, fewer problems, and fewer instances of being victimized. Also, it was expected that crime rates for the study area would decrease.

Results ▪ Crime did not start to show a drop until after the physical changes were in place, suggesting that the earlier changes in policing and community organizing had not been sufficient (although perhaps they were necessary) to deter crime. By a year after the physical changes were in place, burglary showed a statistically significant drop; that is, it wasn't as high as it should have been based on crime rate trends elsewhere in the city. Robberies and purse snatches showed a (nonstatistically significant) drop as well. But, at the same time, robbery/purse snatch offenses had been shifted away from the residential streets, and a larger portion of them were happening on the main streets than before. This suggests that some of the streets had been made safer than they were before.

One year after implementation, residents reported attitudinal and behavioral changes which, in part, help explain the crime changes. First, residents reported a higher level of neighborhood activities (e.g., walking in the neighborhood). Also, levels of informal social control (e.g., ease of recognizing strangers) improved. Finally, objective measures indicated the traffic in the neighborhood had decreased. Unfortunately, by three years after the completion of the changes, burglary levels had risen to what would have been expected based on preprogram levels. But, in contrast with this change, residents' general perceptions of the neighborhood that had not improved by one year after implementation had improved by three years after implementation.

In sum then, the physical changes did have dampening impacts on crime that were fairly immediate, but these positive effects appeared to decay or "wash out" as time passed. Most residents' specific perceptions showed immediate improvement and tended to stay high, despite the wearing off of the actual deterrent effect.

Practical consequences and implications ▪ Physical design changes can make a difference in the crime problems experienced by a community, but that deterrent effect appears only when those physical elements are backed up by active social elements, such as community groups with an active crime prevention program or involved local police officers. These various elements are needed in combination so that they can supplement each other.

The study also shows that such a large-scale intervention is feasible and actually can be carried out. While such an effort requires considerable coordination among the different sectors that are affected—residents, community groups, local businesses, politicians, and police—it can be done.

Finally, this program suggests that, if changes (such as the development of community groups) are initiated, such programs need maintenance efforts or "refreshment" attempts over time. The social processes that "back up" the physical changes need support if they are to persist (Taylor & Shumaker, 1982).

Naturally, a question arises as to the cost-effectiveness of the intervention. The policing and organization charges did not require any additional resources. The physical changes did require about $150,000 (1977 dollars). Was it worth it? To answer this question means putting a "dollar amount" on each crime that was prevented. That is, each burglary or purse snatch prevented was a savings of X dollars for the community and its residents. But how much is it worth to have a crime prevented? We know that with burglary, for example, the experience can be very traumatic for the victim (Waller & Okihiro, 1978). He or she may experience trauma for months or years afterwards—being afraid to come into the house alone, jumping at every little noise, and chronically worrying that it will happen again. If a woman is a victim of a purse snatching and doesn't then go out much at night, sees friends less, uses local stores less, then how many dollars in "cost" is that? If a program reduces people's fear levels and makes them feel better about the neighborhood, and perhaps think more seriously about staying there or investing, how much is that worth?

In short, although we can estimate some of the savings produced by the program, such as police resources conserved, other benefits are almost impossible to calculate. Thus, those who would say that such a program is too costly are, implicitly, putting a very low value on the crimes, fears, and traumas that may be prevented through such a program.

Folsom Prison blues: Overcrowding and its impact

In this country, there are a large number of people who are in prison, at the federal and state level, and in jails, at the local level. In 1981 there were 369,009 persons incarcerated in state and federal institutions. Perhaps even more distressing than the absolute number of people locked up, though, is the rate at which incarceration is increasing. Last year, nationwide, 12% more people were incarcerated than the year before. This is the largest jump in prison populations recorded since the statistics became available in 1925 (*Justice Assistance News*, June/July, 1982).

Needless to say, such changes cause immense headaches for prison administrators and local officials. There is *very* strong pressure, in many states, to build more prisons. But, prison construction is a delicate issue for local communities because, although residents want secure lockups to ensure public safety, no one wants a prison in his or her backyard. And, prisons already in existence are jammed to the ceiling. In many states, cells originally designed for one person now hold two or sometimes three persons. Such developments have not been met gladly by the prisoners. In fact, in over 32 states, prisoners are involved in litigation with the authorities concerning their rights. One of the central elements in almost all of these suits is "prison overcrowding" which, the prisoners maintain, constitutes "cruel and unusual punishment." In some states, courts have issued rulings to reduce double celling, and thus crowding.

Some prison administrators have developed their own ad hoc solutions. In some states, prisoners are occupying temporary quarters, sometimes in mobile homes adjacent to the prison. In Texas, one jurisdiction closed its prison and refused to allow any more prisoners to enter the facility. One local sheriff there threatened that, if they did that, he would bring his prisoner to the main gate of the prison, handcuff him there, and then leave. In another state where the system was trying desperately to come into compliance with court-ordered reductions in double celling, the prison administration threatened to let the courts, if they weren't happy with the progress, take over and run the system. These desperate measures bespeak the severity of this problem at the national level.

Theoretical background ▪ The most favored perspective to explain the impact of prison overcrowding is a simple arousal and stress model. The basic notion is that high levels of prison density lead to physiological arousal within the person as he or she attempts to cope with the stressor. Over time, the arousal continues but the person's resources become depleted, thus side effects of the stress, such as increased blood pressure, psychiatric symptoms, and so on, occur. (Cox, Paulus, McCain, & Schkade, 1979; D'Atri, 1975; D'Atri & Ostfield, 1975). High density within a prison is a particularly potent stressor for several reasons: it continues over a long period of time, it is involuntary and unescapable, and the persons one is proximate to are very dangerous people.

In other environments, the impact of crowding has been found to be much more conditional; that is, negative effects do or do not occur depending upon what else is happening. For example, in the case of the residential environment, density effects depend upon whether or not a person feels in control of his or her life, whether the person has a place to go and be alone if he or she wishes, whether he or she has friends on the street, and so on (Verbrugge & Taylor, 1980). And, in addition to being negative, density can also have positive effects, for example, having someone close by to run an errand. But, in the prison environment, density is a more powerful and more unambiguously negative stressor than in other settings.

Method ▪ In the study discussed here (McCain, Cox, & Paulus, 1980; see also Paulus, Cox, McCain, & Chandler, 1975, and Paulus, McCain, & Cox, 1978), the researchers traveled to several different prisons that offered various types of living arrangements. At each site, they had volunteer prisoners fill out questionnaires about mood, health, and social behavior. They also took blood pressure readings. From archival files they were able to determine when the prisoner arrived, how long he had been there, what type of living arrangement he was currently in, how often he had complained of illness, and so on. The analysis then involved correlating the density and type of living arrangement with these various outcomes.

Hypotheses ▪ The main hypotheses were that increased density would be associated with negative mood, feeling crowded, and higher blood pressure.

Results ▪ The results were similar across the different institutions, attesting to the generalizability and reliability of the findings.

Repeatedly, higher-density living arrangements were associated with more problems (i.e., double cells were worse than single cells, dormitories were worse than doubles). Higher density was associated with greater feelings of being crowded, more negative evaluations of the living units, higher illness complaints, and, in some cases, higher rates of disciplinary infractions and higher blood pressure.

One clear and policy-relevant finding was that the placement of low walls in dormitories—turning dormitories into cubicles—resulted in much less crowding stress. On almost all measures, inmates living in cubicles most closely resembled inmates living in singles, and were unlike inmates living in open dormitories. Thus, by dividing up the public space in a dorm and giving each person a bit of his own territory, crowding stress was significantly reduced. Analyses on the relative contributions of group size (social density) and spatial density showed that both were strongly and independently associated with perceived crowding, but that, of the two, social density was more strongly tied to illness complaints.

The authors' archival analyses showed that when more people were locked up in a prison, without increases in facilities, a host of negative consequences such as higher disciplinary infraction rates, suicide rates, and death rates of older prisoners occurred.

Practical implications ▪ High density is a significant stressor for prisoners. One might argue, though, that we should not be worried about this because prisoners have broken the law and thus deserve some high-stress settings. There are at least two reasons, however, why we should be concerned about prison crowding effects even if we think the prisoners deserve it. First, these stressed prisoners are more likely to commit a crime again when released. Farrington and Nuttal (1980) found that releasees from institutions that were overcapacity, i.e., held more prisoners than they were intended to, were more likely to recidivate after release. Thus, the consequences of prison overcrowding include costs to society. (Note that this finding is in keeping with the earlier discussion of stress after-effects.) Second, people have to run prisons. Guards and administrators must somehow manage a large volume of violent and dangerous people in a small area, and it looks as if those dangerous people become more violent, and in a worse mood, as density goes up. Thus, high density and the resulting pattern of crowding stress makes the jobs of guards and other administrators in prisons more stressful and difficult.

Finally, the most important result of the study is that reductions in perceived crowding can be achieved effectively and cheaply by turning dorms into cubicles, separated by low-rise partitions. This rather modest architectural intervention appears to have a substantial psychological impact. Without major renovations and without dramatic costs, it appears possible to modify spaces so that they cause less crowding stress to prisoners.

Be a litter bit helpful: Prompting anti-litter behavior

There is a wide range of behaviors that people perform that serve to degrade the environment: littering; wasting gas and electricity in the home by using air conditioning and heating when it is not necessary; pouring toxic wastes into rivers and sewers; throwing away and not recycling cans, bottles, paper, and motor oil; buying and driving gas guzzling cars instead of gas misers; and driving over 55 mph. The list could go on and on. And, even though it is true that governments and companies and utilities are doing much to pollute and otherwise spoil the environment, people by themselves do a great deal also. Thus, by changing our behaviors, we can contribute to preserving the environment instead of degrading it.

Theoretical background ▪ We are encouraged in many different ways to preserve the environment. Woodsy the Owl tells us to "Give a hoot, don't pollute!" Every month, our local utility company sends flyers telling us how we can save energy (even though their very rate structure encourages us to use energy). Soda cans tell us "Please dispose of properly." Signs along some highways threaten us with $100 dollar fines for littering. Our nation's leaders have appealed to us to drive 55 mph and to save energy in the home. Thus, it seems that we are bombarded from every side with messages that encourage us to behave in a pro-environmental manner.

But, it should be obvious to most of us that none of these tactics are working well. For example, many do not observe the 55 mph speed limit. One study (Holmes & Solomon, 1980) found that average speeds on the highway dropped closer to 55 mph for a couple of days after a plea for this cause, but returned to normal by a week later. We are surrounded by messages and prompts that are unsuccessful.

Why don't these messages work? There are a number of reasons. First, these prompts are often very general (e.g., "Don't pollute!") and don't tell us what specific behaviors we should be doing in which places. Second, the prompts are often not in physical or temporal proximity to the site where the pro-environmental behavior should occur. For example, you see a sign along the highway warning of a penalty for littering, but there is almost never a trash can placed next to the sign. Or your utility sends you a flyer about how to conserve, but when you go to flick the switch on your air conditioner or heater, that message, in terms of your thoughts, is likely to be a "million miles away." In addition, it is not clear that if we did follow these prompts, there would be any rewards or we would avoid any punishment. When was the last time you saw a state trooper pull somebody over for littering? Or, even more unlikely, when was the last time you saw someone rewarded for not littering? Of course there are long-term effects that build up over time in our neighborhood or city or the world, but these are not consequences that anyone really "sees"; in fact, it is conceptually difficult for most of us to see such linkages.

Platt (1973) has stated this problem in learning terms. Our (environmentally destructive) behavior has immediate short-term positive consequences, but long-term negative consequences. Graphically:

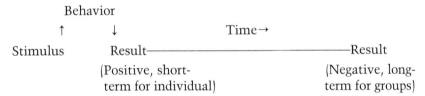

(adapted from Edney, 1980). Littering gives us relief from the burden of carrying trash (a short-term, positive consequence), but the long-term negative consequence is a littered environment. The same perspective can be applied to other environmentally destructive behaviors (of individuals or companies), such as burying toxic waste in inadequate repositories.

It is not surprising, given the failure of attempts to encourage pro-environmental behaviors through the use of general prompts, that people have turned to different methods. One school of researchers has focused on the application of learning principles to the problem of pro-environmental behaviors. There are essentially two types of strategies that can be used with this approach: *antecedent strategies* and *consequent strategies*. Antecedent strategies attempt to modify the social or physical environment or context surrounding the desired behavior in order to make it more likely that the person will demonstrate the pro-environmental behavior. Consequent strategies focus on something positive happening to the person once the desired behavior is performed. Such a positive outcome would, it is hoped, make the person more likely to perform the desired behavior again at a later time. Of course, it is always possible to combine the two types of strategies. For example, a trash can might be very brightly colored and in the shape of a bird with a big beak (antecedent), and the can might say "thank you" when litter is deposited in it (consequent) (See Fig. 12.2).

Method ▪ Research conducted by Geller and his colleagues will be discussed to illustrate several approaches (see Geller, 1982; Geller, Winett, & Everett, 1982 for

FIGURE 12.2   Talking cardinal trash can.

a review). One study used trash can design, another explored the effectiveness of anti-litter prompts, and a third examined the impact of offering a reward for litter bags in use in cars.

In the trash can experiment, the degree to which a normal 50 gallon drum versus a bird-shaped brightly colored trash can inspired people to pick up litter lying around was investigated. Experimenters spread some trash around a trash can, and then retired to an unobtrusive distance to record how many people walked by and how many picked up litter. The normal vs. fancy can appeared in the same location, thus the comparison of interest was across the different days.

In the anti-litter–prompts study, researchers handed out flyers advertising the specials of the week at a supermarket. At the bottom of the flyer appeared one of several messages. The prompt could read "Please dispose of this handbill properly. Please do not litter." Or, the prompt could be more specific, such as "Please help us recycle. Please dispose for recycling in green trash can at rear of store." Handbills with different messages were handed out on different days. When the store closed, the research assistants would collect all the handbills and determine the proportion that had been disposed of properly. (This was a time-consuming process. Sometimes handbills would be stuck underneath bananas in the produce section or behind the peas on a shelf!) Again, the relevant comparison is across days.

In the study that used a consequent strategy—a reward for litter bags in use— a stand was placed at a Wendy's fast-food drive-in where drivers gave their orders into the microphone. The stand had litter bags that could be taken and a sign that informed drivers that if they had one in use when they drove up to the window, they would get a free drink. The comparison is the proportion of cars driving through Wendy's that had litter bags in use on days when the reward contingency was in application versus those in use on days when the reward contingency was not in application.

Hypothesis ▪ It was hypothesized that these various interventions would, in each case, increase the proportion of people engaging in pro-environmental behaviors.

Results ▪ In the trash can study, the fancy trash can inspired a higher proportion of passers-by to pick up the litter that was around it. With the standard trash can, almost nobody picked up the litter, even though in some instances they might walk right through the garbage.

In the supermarket study, on days when handbills were distributed with specific prompts, e.g., "Please help us recycle. Please dispose for recycling in green trash can at rear of store," there was a higher rate of proper disposal of handbills (25 percent instead of 3 percent).

In the Wendy's study, the contingency worked. On days when the free drink was offered, a higher proportion of the cars that drove through had litterbags in use in their cars (30 percent vs. 5 percent).

Practical implications ▪ Each of these experiments was really an intervention, an attempt to change the level of pro-environmental behavior by changing the surrounding environment. And these interventions worked. Although they never got everybody to show the desired behavior, they often succeeded with a fair-sized minority. Obviously these techniques are not perfect and there is room for improvement. Nonetheless, the important point is that fairly minor changes (e.g., trash can design) can result in sizable changes in behavior. These findings suggest that numerous small-scale changes made in our environment might result in considerably improved levels of pro-environmental behaviors.

Closing comments on case studies

The previous presentation has covered a few examples of what environmental psychologists do. The sampling of types of issues, since limited, is not very representative. For a fuller understanding of the field as a whole, the interested reader should consult recent reviews of the area (e.g., Stokols, 1977, 1978). However, an important thread that has run through each of the studies is the assessment of interventions or changes and the implications of the assessment. The TMI venting, using noise-abated classrooms, redesigning neighborhoods in Hartford, constructing cubicles in prison dormitories, and using cans and messages to prompt anti-littering all constitute environmental changes. Sometimes these changes worked, sometimes they didn't, and sometimes they had only a minor effect. Out of the evaluation of each of these interventions came a fuller understanding of the processes involved in the environment-behavior linkages. Often, when programs had a mild effect, we achieved a greater understanding afterward of contextual factors such as social climate, setting demands, and so on. Thus, a wider focus appears needed for the researcher or evaluator. Such a broad focus is often more accurate and more effective in the long run as a perspective to guide solution planning.

■ THE FUTURE

President Carter commissioned a study in 1977, involving numerous federal agencies, to assess the "probable changes in the world's population, natural resources, and environment, through the end of the century." The results, published in *the Global 2000 Report to the President* (Barney, 1982), are extremely sobering.

> Our conclusions . . . indicate the potential for global problems of alarming proportions by the year 2000. Environmental, resource, and population stressors are intensifying and will increasingly determine the quality of human life on our planet. At the same time the Earth's carrying capacity—the ability of biological systems to provide resources for human needs—is eroding.

Africa is turning to desert because people burn trees and grass as cooking fuel. Rivers, like the Colorado, will soon be so diverted into irrigation that the "river" will be a "trickle." Underground water supplies, like the huge aquifer in the southwest U.S., which took thousands of years to form, are dropping by several feet per year. By the year 2000, world population will be almost 6½ billion, and some 40 percent of the remaining forest cover in less-developed countries will be gone. Deterioration of soil for crops will continue at a progressive rate through the end of the century. In considering these projections, it is important to bear in mind that these estimates may be very conservative. That is, there is a good chance that things could be worse than expected.

Environmental psychologists have a role to play in meeting the challenges of the future. This contribution will not, however, be realized by psychologists working alone, but rather by their working in collaboration with governments, relief organizations, demographers, farmers, family planners, and so on. It means that environmental psychologists will have to develop a sensitivity to the social, cultural, and economic backgrounds in various parts of their country and the world that play a part in these problems.

There are two ways in which environmental psychologists can be of assistance. First, they can identify significant stressors operating on various populations and propose how to reduce exposure to stressors and/or promote more effective coping styles. Second, they may help design, implement, and evaluate programs and contingencies for individuals, communities, or companies that increase the probability of pro-environmental behaviors. In short, they can assist in the formulation of public policy to promote conservation and pro-environmental behaviors.

■ SUGGESTED READINGS

Baum, A., Fleming, R., & Davidson, L. M. (1983). Natural disaster and technological catastrophe. *Environment and Behavior, 15,* 333–354.

This conceptual paper discusses the characteristics of natural hazards and technological catastrophes, and explores their differences. The authors suggest, for example, that impacts of the latter are often invisible and endure over a longer period of time. These differences have important implications for understanding the nature of the human response to such situations. The article is suitable for both undergraduate and graduate students.

Evans, G. W. (Ed.). (1982). *Environmental stress.* New York: Cambridge University Press.

This edited volume includes several broad-ranging and thorough chapters on particular aspects of stress and the physical environment. There are chapters on settings such as neighborhoods, schools, offices, and hospitals. The text is highly recommended for upper level undergraduate and graduate students.

Fisher, J.D., Bell, P.A., & Baum, A. (1984). *Environmental psychology* (2nd ed.). New York: Holt, Rinehart & Winston.

This introductory text reviews recent research in several areas of environmental psychology. It is broad ranging and accessible. Topics such as stress, design, and environment and social behavior are well covered. It is an excellent introduction to the area for undergraduates.

Geller, E. S., Winett, R. A., & Everett, P. B. (1982). *Preserving the environment*. New York: Pergamon Press.

This text covers the "forgotten" side of environmental psychology: how behavior influences the environment. The text includes very thorough reviews of research in areas of litter control, recycling, energy conservation, transportation energy conservation, and water conservation. The authors also discuss how behavioral change can be related to changes at the policy level.

Wicker, A.W. (1979). *An introduction to ecological psychology.* Monterey, CA: Brooks/Cole.

Ecological psychology is the best developed and tested theory in the entire area of environmental psychology. This book provides an excellent, readable, and personal account of the theory and the research it has spawned over the years. This beginning undergraduate text is a must for those interested in issues of organizational functioning.

BRUCE D. SALES AND
THOMAS L. HAFEMEISTER

LAW AND PSYCHOLOGY

Since the 1970s, we have witnessed a virtual explosion of interest in the law–psychology interface. Many books and journals cover the developments in it, people are being trained to work within it, psychologists with training in traditional areas (e.g., clinical, counseling) are becoming more involved with it, and national societies (American Psychology-Law Society and the American Association of Correctional Psychologists) were organized because of it or include specialists from this field within it (Law and Society Association). Yet what is law-psychology? Is it a research or a practice area? Is it limited to clinicians or can people from other areas of psychology contribute to and participate within it? The next section addresses these questions.

■ INTRODUCTION

In integrating psychology with the law, we are typically focusing on psychology as a science studying the law; as a profession providing input into the legal process; or on how the law affects the science and profession of psychology. In all cases, what the law is becomes critical. Thus, it is helpful to start off by first focusing on the law and employing the concept of LAW. By this term we are referring to all laws, legal systems, and legal processes.

Laws refer to all federal, state, and local laws whether they come from a constitution (i.e., constitutional law), a statute passed by a legislature (i.e.,

Parts of this manuscript are drawn from other writings by the first author, particularly Sales (1983a,b), Sales and Elwork (1980), and Elwork, Sales, and Suggs (1981).

statutory law), a court decision (i.e., case law, also known as common law), an administrative agency ruling that was promulgated by the agency pursuant to a constitutional delegation of authority from the legislature or Congress, or a local/municipal ordinance. All of the above are law. They do have different force and effects when one type is pitted against another, but they are all law.

Legal systems refer to those systems (for example, a state agency) that are created and operated pursuant to a law. This category includes all federal agencies such as the U.S. Department of Health and Human Services, the Energy Department, the National Institute of Mental Health, and the National Science Foundation, and all agencies of state government such as a Department of Mental Health, a State Education Department, a Department of Welfare, law enforcement, and the court system.

Finally, *legal processes* refers to the way people are processed through or participate in a legal system pursuant to the law. Some may find it easier not to have this category since its scope and function can be included within the definition of the preceding two categories. We list it separately since it forces us to focus on the way professionals and clients are actually being treated and handled rather than focusing on the black letter of the law (i.e., the actual wording of a law) or the structure, organization, and operation of a system.

We have now identified the LAW, but where is the psychology? Turning to Fig. 13.1, you will note that under the LAW is the phrase "Behavioral Assumptions." It is here that the two fields relate. Almost all of the LAW is based upon assumptions about how people act and how their actions can be controlled. Although lawyers are equipped to draft the legal language, they have not been trained to identify these behavioral assumptions or study their validity (Special Commission on the Social Sciences of the National Science Board, 1969). Psychologists, on the other hand, are uniquely qualified for this task. They can empirically identify invalid assumptions and inappropriate LAW that results. Where the behavioral assumptions are valid, psychologists can aid the policy process by monitoring and evaluating whether the LAW is meeting its intended behavioral goals, as well as detecting if there are unintended consequences. Finally, they can provide behavioral expertise that is often required for the LAW to operate. Hence their potential contribution to the creation, implementation, and revision of public and legal policy is unquestionable.

Behavioral assumptions

Let us consider an example of these behavioral assumptions within each of the three components of the LAW. As to an actual law, consider the case law that generally holds that juveniles arrested for a crime must be told their rights— i.e., given a Miranda warning. Legal policy underlying this law is admirable; namely, that juveniles, like adults, have very serious interests at stake when they become involved in the criminal/juvenile justice systems, and thus should

FIGURE 13.1 A model for integrating law and psychology.

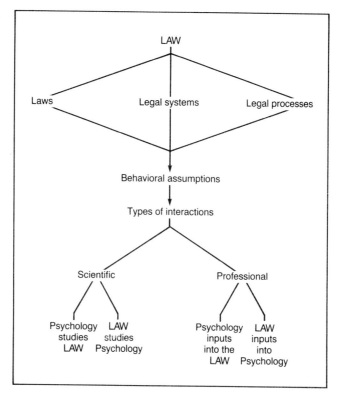

be told their rights before they inadvertently, or out of ignorance of the law, waive them. As Grisso (1981) has argued, this law makes a number of behavioral assumptions that need to be clearly articulated and whose validity needs to be assessed. Among the basic ones are that once read these rights, juveniles will understand them, will remember them, and will be able to logically and rationally apply them to the situation at hand. In fact, his research clearly and forcefully demonstrates the partial invalidity of each assumption and strongly suggests the need for carefully rethinking and possibly restructuring the way in which the policy goal is implemented. Grisso's work on this topic represents a fine example of the importance of rigorous psychological analysis and research for the law.

For an example of behavioral assumptions underlying the creation and operation of a legal system, consider the courts. They are structured such that a litigant often has a right to a jury trial so as to ensure fairness and impartiality. There are numerous behavioral assumptions here. For example, it is assumed that the jury selection techniques used during the voir dire (jury selection process prior to a trial) will result in a jury that is neutral at the start of the trial. In fact, many experienced trial lawyers take great pride in their ability to select juries they believe are prejudiced toward their side of the case (e.g., Adkins, 1968–1969; Darrow, 1936; Goldstein, 1938; Rothblatt, 1966).

However, what research there is on the voir dire as a means of eliminating incompetent and biased jurors suggests that it is not an effective legal procedure. For instance, Broeder (1965) concluded that the "voir dire was grossly ineffective in weeding out 'unfavorable' jurors and in eliciting the data which would have shown particular jurors as very likely to prove 'unfavorable' " (p. 505). More recently Zeisel and Diamond (1978) stated:

> Our experiment suggests that, on the whole, the voir dire as conducted in these trials did not provide sufficient information for attorneys to identify prejudiced jurors. The average performance score of the prosecution was near the zero point. . . indicating an inability to distinguish potential bias; defense counsel performed only slightly better. (p. 528)

If most lawyers, and arguably judges, are incompetent at weeding out biased and prejudiced jurors, the behavioral assumption about the trial beginning with an impartial jury is invalid.

But even if the impaneled jury is neutral and fair minded at the start of the trial, and hence the first assumption is valid, there are other assumptions that exist and need to be questioned. For example, the jurors' task is to listen to the evidence, remember it accurately, and reach their verdict by weighing the evidence in light of the law that the judge will read to them at the end of the trial. There are several assumptions here. First, it is assumed that jurors will be able to understand and remember the evidence that was presented in the case. That might seem like a simple task until we realize that some cases require the presentation of extremely complex information, such as complex economic fact and theory in an antitrust case. Will the average juror with only a high school education be able to understand this evidence? In addition, some cases require six or more months just to present all of the evidence. Is it humanly possible to remember every material fact that was presented in that type of case? Common sense would say no. Second, it is assumed that jurors will be able to understand the law that is read to them by the judge to guide their deliberations. Psycholegal research has regretfully shown that this assumption is invalid. Jurors often do not understand the law as read and thus are creating their own decision rules to reach a verdict—rules that are based upon the jurors' own sense of justice, or more accurately, their own whim, sympathy, and prejudice (Elwork, Sales, & Alfini, 1977, 1982). Third, and finally, it is assumed that jurors will reach their verdict based only upon the evidence that was presented at the trial. But numerous studies have shown that jurors use other factors in reaching a verdict (see generally, Sales, 1981). Therefore, as with our prior example of a law, we see how legal systems are also created and operated based upon a series of underlying behavioral assumptions that are assumed to be valid but may not withstand close scrutiny.

For an example of the behavioral assumptions underlying the legal process, consider an individual who is alleged to be mentally ill and dangerous and, because of these allegations, is the subject of an involuntary civil commitment petition. Civil commitment is a legal action to have a person who is mentally ill *and* a danger to self or others, or gravely disabled, involuntarily committed for treatment. In virtually all states today, the law provides this individual with substantial due process rights from the time the petition is filed until the individual is released. The rights include such things as the right to counsel and the right to present and cross-examine witnesses. Among the behavioral assumptions underlying this law that specifically relate to the processing of the individual are that the person will understand his or her rights and will have the opportunity to fully and appropriately exercise them. Yet, from our previous example, we know that the legal system does not always operate as intended. How might that affect the processing of this individual through the mental health system pursuant to mental health law? In fact, research has demonstrated that subjects of civil commitment petitions do not always have the opportunity to rigorously exercise their rights. Studies have shown that these individuals, if indigent, often will not have the opportunity to see their attorney for more than a few minutes before the case begins and that these attorneys may not attempt to defend their client vigorously during the trial (Poythress, Jr., 1978; Wexler, 1981). If committed, a major assumption is that the person will receive appropriate therapy.* But numerous cases have demonstrated that commitment to a large institution can result in nothing more than custodial care without therapy (see, for example, *O'Connor v. Donaldson*, 1975). Thus, the legal process is also based upon behavioral assumptions whose validity must be empirically assessed if we are to improve the operation of the LAW.

Scientific interactions

Given that behavioral assumptions underlie the LAW and that the scientific study of behavior is within the domain of psychology, psychologists should be interacting with the LAW. But in what ways? Mirroring the dualism that exists among the membership of the American Psychological Association, there are two types of interaction, scientific and professional.

---

*Because the standard for commitment has changed in the last decade from mental illness and the need for hospitalization to mental illness and dangerousness, the police power of the state has been added to the *parens patriae* power as a justification for commitment. Under the later theory, treatment is clearly warranted. Under the former, however, protection of society, and hence custodial care, would be a justifiable basis for commitment. Although the U.S. Supreme Court has not spoken on this issue, it seems reasonable to suggest that if the *parens patriae* power is invoked as even a partial rationale for the state action, then treatment should be made available (see Wexler, 1981, for further discussion of this issue).

As Fig. 13.1 shows, the scientific interaction has two components. The first is where psychology as a science can be used to study the LAW, or more precisely, study the validity of the behavioral assumptions underlying the LAW. Almost every area of psychology, if not every one, will ultimately be demonstrated to have relevant contributions to make to this process. For example, the recent explosion in scientific research on the LAW has involved cognitive psychology including perceptual studies (e.g., Wells, 1980), memorial studies (e.g., Loftus, 1979), and language studies (e.g., Elwork, Sales, & Alfini, 1982), social psychology (e.g., Carroll & Perlman, 1978; Diamond, 1979; Greenberg & Ruback, 1982; Konečni & Ebbesen, 1982; Saks & Hastie, 1978; Sales, 1981), developmental psychology (e.g., Grisso, 1981; Melton, Koocher, & Saks, 1983), personality psychology (e.g., Bray & Noble, 1978), clinical psychology (e.g., Brodsky & Smitherman, 1983; Monahan, 1981; Monahan & Steadman, 1983; Roesch & Golding, 1980; Shah, 1978, 1981), counseling psychology (Feldman & Wilson, 1981), and we could go on.

Typically this scientific research and writing follows the model laid out in the following steps:

1. Identify the LAW (legal issue),
2. Identify the behavioral assumption(s) underlying it,
3. Review the existing research relevant to the validity of (2),
4. Conduct new research directly relevant to (2),
5. Assess the likelihood that each assumption (2) is valid,
6. Determine the appropriateness of (1) given conclusions of (5),
7. Make needed recommendations for revision of (1).

The researcher first identifies the legal issue (LAW) that is to be the focus of the study. Then the behavioral assumption or assumptions underlying this issue are identified. For each assumption, the researcher must then review the existing literature for studies that have directly tested the validity of the assumption in the particular legal context under question. Where there are no studies or where the results of this prior research are inconclusive, other research that indirectly relates is reviewed. These other studies may have manipulated relevant independent and/or dependent variables but in a nonlegal context. Their results often can provide a reasonable basis for generating an hypothesis or hypotheses about the validity of the assumption. Based upon the findings of the literature review, and the goals of the manuscript being written, the researcher either designs and carries out new research directly on the issue, suggests a design for future research on the issue without actually carrying it out and proceeds to the next step, or proceeds directly to the next step. In this step the findings of previous research and the results of any new research that is conducted are compared to each behavioral assumption that was identified in step (2). Whatever conclusions that can be drawn about the validity of these assumptions are then made. Where conclusions are drawn they are then compared to the legal issue and its goals as enunciated in step (1). Finally, based upon this comparison, recommendations are made for revision of the LAW either to bring it into conformity with the behavioral reality or to suggest that if the LAW is maintained then the public should be given an honest appraisal of what it is, and is not, accomplishing behaviorally.

There are variants on this model. For example, for some psychologists, the critical issue is not the LAW but rather a psychological theory that they wish to study. In this case, the law becomes another testing ground for the theory. If, however, their research is designed to maximize external validity (see generally, Diamond, 1979) then the model is still appropriate, with it adding to the traditional psychological approach of theory formulation, hypothesis generation, research, comparison of the results to the theory, refinement and validation of the theory.* For other psychologists, the goal is the study of a behavioral phenomenon. As with theory testing, if the research design has high external validity, the psycholegal model remains appropriate with small differences we need not elaborate here.

The other type of scientific interaction is where the LAW, and in particular legal theory and legal procedure, is used to study some aspect of psychology. Of all of the scientific and professional interactions between law and psychology, this is the least well developed. Examples, however, of this approach are using legal theory to generate hypotheses about group behavior, or studying the effects of using the adversarial model of truth seeking (a hallmark of the American judicial system) as an alternative to the scientific model for discovering facts and truth in psychology (Levine, 1974).

Professional interactions

Now let us consider the professional interactions. As professionals, psychologists have regularly provided input into the LAW. The most common instance is where the psychologist as an expert is asked to testify in court. For example, consider the clinical or counseling psychologist who is employed by the court or one of the parties to evaluate and testify about a defendant who, in a murder trial, alleges that he was insane at the time of the crime. Professional psychologists have also testified in a wide variety of other criminal (e.g., sexual sociopathy, incompetency to stand trial, sentencing) and civil (e.g., child custody, workmen's compensation, vocational disability, involuntary civil commitment) proceedings. Most often these are situations where a psychologist

---

*This approach is not meant to imply that research using the model presented in the previous list is atheoretical. Although the LAW is the first step, and the study of it is the ultimate goal, theory is typically used in step (4) to generate researchable hypotheses, and the findings are then also used as a test of the theory. In addition, findings on how the law actually operates may be used to build a theory of behavior in legal contexts (e.g., Konečni & Ebbesen, 1981); theory building would be added on as a step (8) in the model.

whose primary identification is as a professional, as opposed to a scientist, is interacting with the LAW. But it is not the primary identification of the psychologist outside of the legal arena that is important. Psychologists who are scientists also wind up acting as experts in court cases and in that capacity are also professional psychologists.

The relationship between psychologists acting in their professional capacity and in the science of psychology does not end with scientists testifying in court. In fact, the "Ethical principles of psychologists" (APA, 1981), the *Standards for providers of psychological services* (APA, 1977b), and the "Specialty guidelines for the delivery of services" (APA Committee on Professional Standards, 1981) require psychologists to be familiar with the scientific research that is relevant to the issues about which they are testifying. Thus, the professional interaction of psychology and the LAW is dependent upon the scientific interaction of psychologists studying the LAW.

As professionals, psychologists also provide input into the LAW in a variety of other ways. For instance, the traditional role of teacher and researcher at a university or college will indirectly contribute to the LAW if the psychologist is working in a law–psychology training program, a criminal justice training program, a traditional psychology training program offering some law–psychology training, a law school, etc. There also are several nontraditional settings available, however. For example, the psychologist can be hired by a police department or a police academy to teach such topics as effective methods of riot or crowd control, interviewing eyewitnesses, handling family disputes, or anticipating the actions of a criminal. Similarly, the psychologist can be used in training correctional officers, legal agency administrators, judges, lawyers, etc., since each of these personnel have a need for information from the social and behavioral sciences.

Another role that the psychologist can play is that of evaluator–consultant. This is a role that requires psychologists to use their expertise to evaluate some aspect of laws, legal systems, and legal processes and/or use this expertise to advise people within the legal system on how to proceed with some problem. For example, a specialist in social psychology can be called upon to evaluate the effectiveness of punishment as a deterrent to crime or to evaluate the effectiveness of a prison system in rehabilitating criminals. A specialist in clinical psychology may be asked to evaluate whether a defendant is competent to stand trial or was insane when the crime was committed. In more of a consulting role, a counseling psychologist could be called upon to advise the court or a parole board as to what should be done with a prisoner or, in a custody case, what familial environment would be most advantageous for a child. Social and personality psychologists can be called upon to consult with lawyers in choosing a jury and/or in presenting a convincing case.

To some extent, this role of evaluator–consultant is related to that of the applied researcher who uses research skills to study applied problems in the LAW. For example, what is the impact of allowing cameras into the courtroom (see generally, Miller & Fontes, 1979)? Can we develop valid techniques for evaluating the performance of judges (see generally, Ryan, Ashman, Sales, & Shane-DuBow, 1980)? In this role, the researchers may work full time for a professional research organization, a local organization that has a research section, a state or federal government, or a university.

A psychologist also can take the role of a clinical practitioner within the legal system. This includes the practice of clinical and counseling psychology in terms of providing assessment, therapy, and counseling to populations who are in direct contact with laws and legal systems (e.g., prison populations, law enforcement officers, persons undergoing divorce). What makes such work different from other practice is the fact that the legal environment must be taken into account in preparing a successful therapy/counseling plan.

Finally, the psychologist may act as a policy analyst for state or federal government. In this role, the professional is concerned with ensuring that lawmakers and administrative agency personnel are making and implementing decisions with a firm understanding of the teachings of behavioral and social science on the topic under consideration. Typically, the individual is not conducting new research but rather is reviewing and interpreting existing research to aid policy makers and policy implementers in reaching their decisions.

The other side of the professional interaction is comprised of the law having input into psychology, that is, regulating and, more generally, affecting psychology. This interaction has not received much attention in the legal or psychological literature, when compared to the amount of writing that has taken place on psychology as a science studying the LAW, or as a profession providing expert services to the LAW (Sales, 1983a,b; Schwitzgebel & Schwitzgebel, 1980).

One obvious reason for the lack of attention is that psychologists are typically not equipped to find and analyze the law. As with the acquisition of any skill, this deficiency can be overcome. Another possible reason is that the law's impact is just not that important to the science and profession of psychology. This argument was made by Foreman and Shackar (1981) who responded negatively to recent writings of psychologists that suggested the need for legislative lobbying to achieve laws favorable to psychologists and psychology. (Chapter 15 presents more details on this kind of lobbying.) Foreman and Shackar were arguing that the impact of the law did not substantially affect the practice of psychology, a difficult point to agree with since in today's complex society it is almost impossible to avoid a consideration of the law's impact on psychological practice—whether it is scientific or professional. And, since this law often involves the creation and operation of legal systems and legal processes, all parts of the LAW are at least implicitly, and often explicitly, relevant to it and justify the study of the LAW's input into psychology.

In fact, there are at least four main goals for psychologists studying this part of the interface. First, the major professional standards controlling our behavior dictate that all psychologists (scientists and professionals) stay informed about not only current organizational standards but also current legal developments (for example, see Principle 3 of the "Ethical principles of psychologists" [APA, 1981]). Compliance with this mandate is important since standards regulating psychology enjoy the sanctioning power of the government and can be used as the basis for private lawsuits. Thus, we do not have the option of ignoring them. In addition, laws can often confer very important benefits but usually only if we are aware of these laws and invoke them properly.

Second, only by identifying these laws will we have the opportunity to determine how they affect the conduct of our science and the delivery of our services. In studying their impact, it is helpful to categorize them in four broad topics. First are those that regulate scientific practice. For example, for years social science researchers have promised subjects that their responses would be held in strictest confidence. These promises were mandated by professional ethics, federal statutes, and institutional research review boards. It has become increasingly clear, however, that it may not be possible to keep these promises of confidentiality, since there are several conditions under which a researcher may be legally compelled to disclose this information to another party. Some of these laws are contained in the courts' subpoena power (Comment, 1977; Knerr & Carroll, 1978). Reseachers may find themselves confronted with a subpoena in those situations in which their data may provide necessary evidence in a legal action. Another pervasive threat to researcher confidentiality may be the federal Freedom of Information Act (Morris, Sales, & Berman, 1981) and similar laws that exist in some states; these not only threaten researchers' confidential relationships with their subjects but also their property interests* in the data. Examples of other laws in this category include laws regulating animal experimentation (Sales & Overcast, 1984) and laws regulating the development and use of psychological tests (Bersoff, 1981; Lerner, 1981).

The second topic includes those laws that regulate the delivery of our professional services. Examples include licensure and certification laws that regulate the title and practice of psychology (Stigall, 1983) and laws that affect the professional's role in providing services (e.g., Morse, 1983; Sales, Powell, Van Duizend, & Associates, 1982). In order for the psychologist to successfully provide services, the legal context for these services must be understood. For example, when the psychologist is asked to evaluate an individual to determine if he or she is competent to stand trial, the psychologist is not being asked to determine whether the person is mentally ill. Rather, the law sets its own definition of competency for which the professional must assess. The application of an incorrect standard for assessment can lead the judge to disregard the psychologist's testimony and can create serious consequences for the client.

---

*A property interest "means a right to have the advantage of accruing from anything . . . the exclusive right of possessing, enjoying, and disposing of a thing" (Black, 1968, p. 1382).

The third topic includes those laws that regulate the organization and administration of our professional business enterprises. A prime example of direct concern to health service providers is the law affecting whether health insurers will have to pay psychologists for their independent provision of a service to the client/purchaser of the insurance. Prior to state laws (known as freedom of choice laws) mandating that these insurers pay psychologists directly, many insurers kept their coverage narrow, reimbursing only psychiatrists or psychologists who were supervised by psychiatrists. Clearly a knowledge of this law and its requirements, and a critical review of its structure, is essential to professional psychologists who provide health services (Dorken, 1983).

The final topic includes those laws that regulate the way clients of professional services enter into the service system and are processed through that system, and the rights they receive while in it. It is important that the professional understand how the law controls the behavior of the client that is related to the professional's services (e.g, Wexler, 1981). For example, a civil commitment statute will specify what behaviors must be present before the individual will be subject to commitment, what procedures must be followed for commitment to take place, where the person will go once committed, and what rights the person has during each stage of the process. For the health service provider in psychology, such knowledge is critical since that professional may wish to initiate such proceedings on behalf of a client or may be asked to assess, testify about, or treat such an individual.

The first two goals for identifying and understanding the law will naturally lead us to the third, which is identifying and assessing the validity of the behavioral assumptions underlying this law. To exemplify this goal, consider confidentiality and privileged communications laws (DeKraai & Sales, 1982, in press). *Confidentiality* is a broad concept originating in professional ethics codes but today covered by many types of statutes and case law. Generally, a confidential communication is information that is known by or communicated between two or more persons, the knowledge of which is limited by law or ethics to those persons or other designated individuals. A subarea of confidentiality law is termed *privileged communications* law. This law developed because confidentiality law was not applicable when the psychologist appeared in court and did not provide the psychologist with the right to refuse to reveal information when called as a witness in a legal proceeding. In most states, legislatures have attempted to remedy this situation by enacting privileged communication statutes that protect the client's confidential communications when the psychologist is called to the witness stand.

Underlying this law is a series of behavioral assumptions (Shuman & Weiner, 1982) that need to be identified and tested if we are ever to know if this law is even needed, and if needed, to what extent, and if it is structured appropriately. The assumptions are as follows. First, without confidentiality, potential clients will not seek out psychotherapy for fear that their confidences and the fact that they sought therapy will be disclosed to third parties. Second, if not totally deterring, a lack of confidentiality will delay potential clients from seeking help. Third, clients already in therapy will be reluctant to divulge essential information, making therapy ineffectual or only partially effective. Fourth, the absence of confidentiality will result in premature termination of therapy either when the therapist informs the client of this absence or when the therapist actually reveals the confidence. Unfortunately, what research there is on these points is contradictory on the validity of these assumptions (e.g., Meyer & Smith, 1977; Meyer & Willage, 1980; Shuman & Weiner, 1982; Woods & McNamara, 1980). And because of methodological limitations of these studies, the findings that are available are of questionable accuracy or generalizability (Dekraai & Sales, 1982, in press). But clearly the ability to study the validity of the assumptions underlying the law of psychology will present an important opportunity for the two types of psychology–law interactions, scientific and professional, to build upon each other, both in regard to confidentiality and privileged communications laws in particular, and in regard to the law of psychology in general.

This leads us into the fourth reason for seeking this information—to enhance our ability to make recommendations for policy changes in this law. Once we have identified the laws that affect psychology and the services that we perform, and have identified and studied the validity of the behavioral assumptions underlying this law, then we are in a unique position to make recommendations on how the law should be restructured to increase its appropriateness for governing psychologists and the clients of psychological services.

Now that you understand the model presented in Fig. 13.1, there is still one lingering conceptual issue that needs to be addressed: what is the relationship between law-psychology, psycholegal research, and forensic psychology? Unfortunately not all people use these terms distinctly or correctly. Law-psychology is the most inclusive descriptor. It covers both scientific and professional interactions. Psycholegal research refers to the more limited set of activities of psychologists and/or lawyers studying the validity of the behavioral assumptions underlying the law. This work typically derives from the left-hand node under scientific interactions and the right-hand node under professional interactions in Fig. 13.1. "Forensic" is defined to include only court-related activities (Black, 1968). Since it typically refers to psychologists working as experts in the court, its activities fall under the left-hand node under professional interactions in Fig. 13.1

At this point, you are probably wondering why the confusion between terms has arisen at all. The reason is that to be a competent court expert, the forensic practitioner must stay abreast of the psycholegal research relevant to the topic of the testimony. Thus, these practitioners' interests cross the various nodes. Yet to be interested in learning about the findings of psycholegal research does not make you a psycholegal researcher. Hence, forensics is distinct from psycholegal research, with both being sub-areas of law-psychology.

Approaches for obtaining training

Realizing the opportunities and needs for psychological researchers and professionals, there are at least five training approaches that an individual interested in law-psychology could pursue.

The first, the disciplinary-unstructured program, is one in which the trainee has to learn each discipline independently of the other. Since there is no structured relationship between the psychology department and the law college, the psychology student must independently seek out one or more law courses to take, and obtain the instructor's permission. However, the contents of the courses are rarely directed to the student's needs since the course was designed for law students. Finally, the student must solve problems such as transferring credits between colleges, being graded on a separate scale from the law students, and enrolling in a different college.

The second approach, the disciplinary-structured model, encourages students to cross disciplinary lines by taking courses in the other discipline for credit within their major department and/or by offering specially developed courses and seminars in the psychology department that are jointly taught by a psychologist and a lawyer or by one skilled in both fields. These courses may be used for undergraduate, graduate, and postgraduate training, and they encourage student participation by defining the subject manner in a way that is relevant to both psychology and law students. Many universities currently offer such coursework on various topics within law-psychology (Grisso, Sales, & Bayless, 1982).

The third approach, the integrated-interdisciplinary model, is intended to produce people with degrees in both psychology and law. This approach takes the trainee through the two programs as well as a core set of courses and research experiences aimed at bridging the two fields. It requires cooperation between a law college and a psychology department and most likely the hiring of a J.D./Ph.D. to develop courses that will truly integrate the two fields. The benefits of such a program are that it will train scholars with an overview of the entire interface and the ability to identify, understand, and reason in the languages and thought processes of the two disciplines. Four universities currently offer this formal training: University of Arizona; Hahneman University Department of Mental Health Sciences combined with Villanova College of Law; Johns Hopkins University Department of Psychology combined with University of Maryland College of Law; and the University of Nebraska-Lincoln. Stanford University is also developing training in this direction. It should be noted, however, that the double degree is not necessary to ensure quality psychological research and practice within particular areas of law (e.g, see Poythress, 1979 for a discussion of a model for forensic training).

The fourth approach, the multidisciplinary model, is based on the assumption that problems, especially those of society, need a multidisciplinary approach to reach the proper solutions. The argument for such a program is that since many of the disciplines in the behavioral/social sciences have distinctive expertise to contribute, a team of scientists/practitioners representing various disciplines will be better able to solve them. Thus, for example, the faculty for such a program could include people from psychology, law, sociology, political science, etc. The Department of Social Ecology at the University of California, Irvine, exemplifies this model.

As already noted, in order to contribute to the law-psychology interface, not everyone need seek a formal program of study in law-psychology prior to obtaining their degree. In fact, the history of this field is such that most psychologists probably obtained their expertise in it after they completed their Ph.D. or Psy.D., or at least after they completed all coursework prior to completing the dissertation. This approach is not necessarily inappropriate. There are viable postdoctoral options for a psychologist given the high level of training and skill the individual has already attained in psychology. For example, some psychologists may need only a brief excursion into a branch of law in order to gain the minimal insight and skills necessary to direct a specific program of psycholegal research, teaching, or service. Other approaches to getting such brief and specialized training include reading the literature, attending special workshops and paper sessions at universities and annual meetings of relevant national organizations, and working in a formal postdoctoral training program under the direct and continuing supervision of a specialist in the field. Finally, clinical and counseling psychologists may receive their forensic training as part of their internship since many APA approved internship programs provide such experiences (Levine, Wilson, & Sales, 1980). Obviously, the critical issue is not what type of training psychologists receive but rather that the training has provided sufficient knowledge to truly understand and appreciate the legal problems on which, and the legal context in which, the students intend to work.

Given that you now have an overview of law-psychology, the rest of this chapter will review representative psycholegal research on two topics in order to give you a better appreciation of the type of issues that this field addresses and why increasing numbers of psychologists are being attracted to it.

■ THE TRIAL PROCESS

The adversary system

One of the more distinctive features of the American legal system is its use of an adversarial approach to resolve disputes between opposing private parties (plaintiff vs. defendant) in a civil suit, and between the state and an accused individual (prosecutor vs. defendant) in a criminal case. It is based on the belief that the fairest possible outcome will be assured if both sides in a legal controversy have their own attorneys who are obligated to represent their clients, and only their clients, to the best of their ability. A lawyer will present those evidentiary facts that place his or her client in the most favorable light possible. It is up to the opposing attorney to bring out those facts that detract from the picture portrayed. Thus, neither side will present a complete representation of the events that transpired. Although the attorneys cannot lie, they will be highly selective in what they look for in preparing their case and what they present in court. The truth is envisioned as lying somewhere in between these two opposing positions, with the judge and jury being the impartial determiners of where that point is. The underlying assumption is that, by having the opposing attorneys pulling in opposite directions, the breadth of the materials and concepts discovered will be maximized, allowing the decision-making process of the court to be based upon the greatest amount of information possible.

In contrast, in most of the other countries of the world, an inquisitorial type of legal system is utilized. An attorney is assigned by the court to obtain information from the disputants. Sworn to find the truth, these attorneys remain free of personal commitment to either side in the controversy. Their responsibility is to find out what actually occurred and report this to the court, which will then apply the law to the facts uncovered. The basic premise of this approach is that by minimizing bias and interest, an accurate representation of what actually transpired is more likely to be discovered.

A series of research studies have attempted to compare the effectiveness of these contrasting legal systems, with perhaps the most widely noted being performed by Thibaut and Walker (1975). They conducted a series of experiments to compare a number of decision-making procedures that approximated and reflected the key components of the adversarial and inquisitorial legal systems. The studies were designed to determine the ability of these procedures to produce justice, which they defined as the ability to (1) cancel out the initial bias of the decision maker; (2) cancel out biases resulting from the order of presentation of evidence during the trial; and (3) compensate for sampling error in the discovered facts. Volunteer law students were given either client-centered instructions or court-centered instructions, with observations made of how a simulated case was built and argued. Thibaut and Walker found that justice as they defined it was most successfully accomplished by those individuals given the adversarial instruction. Unlike court-centered (inquisitorial) attorneys who were content to end the information search once they had achieved stable, confident (though not necessarily accurate) beliefs about the case, client-centered (adversarial) attorneys searched for more facts when initially the facts were skewed against their client. Furthermore, Thibaut and Walker concluded that the type of system makes a major difference in the psychological atmosphere it creates in the courtroom. Participants were more likely to perceive the procedure as fair and satisfying, with parties found guilty less dissatisfied with the verdict when it resulted from an adversarial process where control of the case presentation is placed in the hands of the disputants.

The jury

Another distinctive feature of the American judicial system is the use of the jury trial in which members of the community are utilized to determine the facts of a case. Much research has been conducted concerning jurors' competency, impartiality, and efficiency in reaching decisions. In general, these studies utilized mock juries so that different courtroom procedures and influences on juries could be isolated, manipulated, and studied without disturbing the sanctity of an ongoing trial. Some concern has been expressed over the methodology of such studies as well as their applicability and generalizability to real-world cases. For a broader review of these methodological issues, see Kerr & Bray (1982), Saks & Hastie (1978), and Sales (1981).

Bench vs. jury trial ▪ One of the initial decisions the participants in a trial must make is whether to opt for a bench trial (where the judge makes the decisions on what actually occurred, the facts of a case, as well as the law to be applied, with a jury not involved at all) or for a jury trial (where the judge will decide the applicable law in a case while the jury will decide the facts of the case and how the law will be applied to those facts). The crucial question for the litigants is whether the judge and the jury are likely to differ in the verdicts they arrive at, and which is likely to be more favorable to their position.

Kalven and Zeisel (1966) conducted one of the first and most frequently cited studies on the question. They mailed questionnaires to trial judges across the country asking them to report how juries decided the cases they had tried, and how they would have decided the issues had they alone been responsible for making such decisions. Responses were provided on 3576 criminal cases. It was found that judge and jury agreed 78% of the time. In 19% of the cases the juries were more lenient than the judges, and in 3% the judges would have been more lenient than the juries. Thus, 16% of the time the defendant fared better with a jury than with a bench trial.

In addition, Kalven and Zeisel had the judges attempt to identify the bases of their disagreements with the jurys' verdicts. In general the judges felt that, when the evidence was close, juries utilized a higher threshold of doubt, as well as being more willing to rely on their sentiments and personal values as a basis for a decision. Among the specifics the judges delineated were that juries (1) were less apt to stick to the letter of the law when extentuating circumstances were present (e.g., they were more likely to feel that a defendant had been "punished" enough, either from time spent in jail awaiting trial or from life itself); (2) were more lenient when they felt that it would be unjust to place all of the blame on the defendant (e.g., when the blame should be shared by accomplices or by the victim; when an unpopular law or a law violated by everyone was involved; or when they felt that the punishment was too severe in light of the trivial nature of the wrong, the victim had been more than adequately compensated, or the victim was one toward whom the jury felt little compassion or was biased); (3) were likely to be more strict when they felt there was little chance for reparation (e.g., in narcotics cases or sex crimes against children) or the defendant exhibited certain unfavorable characteristics (e.g., undignified occupations, divorced several times, acted arrogantly); and (4) were affected by the impact and attractiveness of the lawyers. In short, Kalven and Zeisel described a wide array of factors that were believed by judges to be affecting the verdicts reached by juries. Although they did not present empirical evidence showing that such factors actually did influence juries, or in what particular circumstances these factors were most likely to be decisive, their descriptive survey provided the impetus and direction for a large number of ensuing jury studies.

Extra-evidential influences ▪ A predominant research concern in the psychology of the trial has been to document the existence of various extra-evidential influences on juries, influences that the judges in the Kalven and Zeisel (1966) study saw playing a large role in the determinations reached by juries. Typically, juries are to limit their considerations to that information that is admitted into evidence by the presiding judge in the course of the trial. Because jury deliberations are secret, it has been difficult to determine exactly what it is on which juries base their determinations. Nevertheless, studies have identified a number of extra-evidential influences that are most likely improperly considered.

Concerned about the fairness of the criminal trial, studies have manipulated the psychological attractiveness of the defendant by varying the defendant's background characteristics (e.g., whether or not the defendant is a family person, holds a good job, has a prior arrest record) to see what effect this has on jury decision making. Even though all individuals are considered equal before the law, as Kalven and Zeisel suggested some individuals may be more or less equal, with these background characteristics improperly used to determine the likelihood that the individual committed the acts alleged, or the blameworthiness of those acts.

In a review of such studies conducted by Elwork, Sales, and Suggs (1981), it was found that jurors will be less certain of a guilty verdict when the defendant is psychologically attractive, will find high socioeconomic status defendants less blameworthy, and will suggest higher prison sentences for psychologically unattractive defendants. The relationship between psychological attractiveness and judgment is not always direct, however. For example, it was found that when a psychologically attractive defendant had little external justification for the acts committed, that individual would be dealt with more severely.

There have also been attempts to show that jurors are likely to be influenced by the physical characteristics of a defendant. For example, females are more likely to be found not guilty by reason of insanity than are males, black males are generally more likely to be found guilty than white males, and physically attractive defendants were evaluated with less certainty of guilt than less attractive defendants. The latter has been shown, however, to involve a complex relationship, with physical attractiveness serving as a handicap and resulting in more severe sanctions when the crime was facilitated by the physical attractiveness (e.g., embezzlement). Furthermore, even though white males were less likely to be found guilty than black males, white males received harsher penalties when they were found guilty (see generally, Elwork, et al., 1981).

Researchers have also manipulated certain characteristics of the victim to determine what effect these have on juror judgments. Stephan and Tully (1977) reported that jurors are more likely to find in favor of a physically attractive civil plaintiff (the avowed victim in the suit), and award them significantly more money damages, than for a physically unattractive plaintiff. Howitt (1977) found confirmation for the hypothesis that a defendant will be dealt with more severely when the victim is seen as helpless; in his study, greater prison sentences were assigned to the defendant when a rape victim was described as being of subnormal intelligence. However, Boor (1976) did not find this hypothesis confirmed when the victim was merely poor.

Even though in most jurisdictions the jury is to be concerned only with the question of guilt or innocence, and not with the possible penalties that may ensue from a finding of guilt, research has shown that jurors do concern themselves with those penalties. For example, Vidmar (1972) found in one simulation study that when subjects were given a choice of first-degree murder or not guilty, 54 percent of those subjects chose not guilty. Yet for the same fact situation, when the defendant was charged with manslaughter, an offense carrying a lesser sentence, 92 percent of the subjects opted for a guilty verdict.

Deliberation processes of the jury ▪ Another line of research has focused on the intercommunicative dynamics of the jury after they retire to deliberate on a verdict. The interaction between the individual jurors as modified by certain structural variables imposed on jury deliberations are postulated to have an effect on the determination that the jury ultimately reaches.

The initial task facing the jury after they retire is the selection of a foreman who is nominally charged with directing the jury's deliberations and ultimately reporting the result obtained to the court. As a result of the role, the foreman may have a greater impact on the final verdict than other jurors. In light of this, several investigators have attempted to ascertain those factors likely to lead to the selection of a particular juror as foreman. Strodtbeck, James, and Hawkins (1957) in a study with mock jurors found that only one-fifth as many women were made foremen as would be expected by chance. They also concluded that the person who spoke first in the group after the jury retired was more likely to be selected foreman, as well as those individuals whose occupation was higher in socioeconomic status. Strodtbeck and Hook (1961) subsequently found that the location of the juror around the jury table affected the likelihood of a juror's being selected foreman. Those jurors occupying the end positions of a rectangular table tended to be selected nearly three times more than would be expected by chance.

Strodtbeck, et al. (1957) also attempted to determine how much the foreman influences the jury verdict. They found that the foreman accounted for about 25 percent of the verbalizations during deliberations after a mock trial. Whether this predominant participation was intended and served to persuade other jurors or merely regulated and coordinated the deliberations remained ambiguous, however. Part of the answer to this question may be found eventually in research based on a distinction pursued by Bevan, Albert, Loiseaux, Mayfield, and Wright (1958). They found that autocratic as opposed to democratic foremen tend to suppress discussion and lead jurors to quicker decisions, suggesting the assumption of a more deliberately persuasive role.

Two approaches are generally used in studies to determine the nature of the deliberation that ensues after the jury has retired to reach a verdict. The first line of research assesses the characteristics of those jurors who dominate the conversation within the jury. The assumption is that these "high participators" will be the most influential in shaping the verdict ultimately given by the jury. Researchers have found that males participate more than females (although this dominance appears to be lessening in recent years); individuals with an occupation higher in socioeconomic status and those with higher levels of education tend to speak more than their respective counterparts; and individuals occupying the end and middle positions are more involved than those sitting at the other positions of a rectangular table (Saks & Hastie, 1978).

A second line of research has studied the formation of subgroups and factions during deliberations, considering this a key variable in explaining the verdicts reached by juries. The amount of participation of an individual juror has been found to vary with the size of the faction a person is a member of. Hawkins (1962) reported that the average individual interaction rates in a mock jury dropped from about 23 percent when the faction contained a single juror to 7 percent when it had from 7 to 11 members. He concluded that the larger the faction, the less time each member spoke, but the greater the total length of time the faction used as a group, suggesting that small factions are being browbeaten as the majority faction increases in size.

The question of juror participation acquired increased and significant general interest when the United States Supreme Court relied on the behavioral assumption that the presence and amount of consideration given to divergent points of view would not be diminished by utilizing a six-member rather than a twelve-member jury. Although the Court in *Colgrove v. Battin* (1973) cited four empirical studies showing that there was no difference between the verdicts of six- and twelve-member juries, some researchers have disagreed with the Supreme Court's decision and questioned the validity of the studies cited (Diamond, 1974; Zeisel & Diamond, 1974). Saks (1977) concluded that as an individual, a member of a minority faction gets to talk more in a small jury (as does everyone else), but as a faction minorities do the same or better when they are in large juries in terms of the proportional share of the conversation they account for. Zeisel (1971) suggested that a dissident juror was more likely to hold out if joined by a fellow dissident, and that it was the absolute, not the proportional size of the faction that was crucial. Elwork, et al. (1981), in their review of the research conducted on the differences between six- and twelve-member juries, concluded

> Although researchers have been unable to find statistically significant differences in the verdicts between six- and twelve-member juries, they have found significant differences in the quality of the deliberations; that is, twelve-member juries are more likely to engage in the type of robust discussion that should take place when an individual's liberty or civil liability is at stake. . . . twelve-member juries are less likely to force people with minority opinions to give in to the majority opinion, less likely to be influenced by a single aggressive juror, more likely to be composed of members with a variety of backgrounds, less likely to have reached a clear-cut predeliberation consensus, and more likely to deliberate longer (p. 32).

The U.S. Supreme Court did not remain oblivious to this research. In *Ballew v. Georgia* (1978) the Court specifically cited and discussed numerous empirical studies on jury size. Based on this work, the Court ruled that five jurors for a criminal trial was too few, setting the constitutional minimum at six for such cases.

Another spate of social science research was generated by a related line of Supreme Court cases that ruled jury verdicts need not be unanimous. In *Apocada v. Oregon* (1972) and *Johnson v. Louisiana* (1972), the Court, in a fashion similar to that in *Colgrove*, concluded that nonunanimous verdicts will make no difference in the way jurors reach their decisions. Subsequent research was unable to demonstrate empirically that there was a higher probability of conviction when a nonunanimous decision rule was utilized, but did show that hung juries were more likely to occur (Kerr, Atkin, Stasser, Meek, Holt, & Davis, 1976; Nemeth, 1977; Saks, 1977). Researchers again found, however, that the decision rule affected the quality of the deliberations. Nemeth (1977) reported that juries required to reach a unanimous decision underwent more opinion changes and conflicts during their deliberations, but were more confident in their verdicts as opposed to juries working under a majority requirement, who sometimes cut off discussion as soon as the required majority was reached, disregarding the views of the minority. Saks (1977) also found that juries under a unanimity requirement deliberate longer.

Davis, Bray, and Holt (1977), in reviewing the work done on jury size, make a point that seems equally applicable to those studies that dealt with the unanimity requirement. They argue that the effect of jury size, in and of itself, is very small, and that very large samples of data would be required to pick up a verdict difference. A similar argument could be raised in explaining the non-significant results that have been obtained when the verdicts reached by juries operating under a unanimity requirement have been compared to those working with a nonunanimous decision rule. When only a few juries are observed and studied, the effect of a unanimity requirement tends to be obscured by other factors. Possibly if a large enough sample of juries was utilized, both the jury size and the decision rule might be found to have a significant impact. However, the prohibitive costs of such studies, the increased administrative efficiency the courts enjoy as a result of smaller juries and the shorter nonunanimous jury trials, and the apparent fact that only a few defendants would benefit from a unanimity requirement or a larger jury has thus far discouraged the initiation of the massive in-depth studies required. The question remains, nevertheless, whether the judicial system should continue to give any person the possibility of less than full justice under the law when the issue has not been decisively settled. If that one person in a hundred, or even a thousand, was you, how would you feel? In addition, the perception of justice may be just as important. When the question has not been decisively settled one way or the other, those convicted by, as well as the jurors participating in, a small jury or a nonunanimous jury vote may find it difficult to accept the validity of the judgment passed.

Juror selection ▪ Within the course of a jury trial, the lawyers for both sides are given three opportunities to challenge the composition of the jury that will hear the trial. These three types of challenges are (1) a challenge of the array; (2) a challenge for cause; and (3) a peremptory challenge. In a sense, this is the one segment of the trial where the previously described work on jury research can have an immediate impact on the outcome of any particular trial. The assumption is that by understanding the ways in which a jury functions, one will be able to predict the outcome of a trial, and that jury selection provides the opportunity to manipulate the key variables in that functioning.

The initial step in assembling a jury is to draw a pool of prospective jurors from the community (the *venire*). Even though an extended series of rulings by the United States Supreme Court has declared that venires are to be representative of the community from which they are drawn, researchers have found them to be widely unrepresentative (Holbrook, 1956; Mills, 1962; Vanderzell, 1966). In addition to their survey and sampling skills, which have been utilized in individual cases challenging the array assembled (Kairys, Schulman, and Harring, 1975), social scientists have also investigated which of the methods utilized to select a venire (e.g., use of voter registration lists vs. a "key man" system) is more likely to result in sampling biases and an unrepresentative venire.

After the venire has been assembled, the next step is to select a jury out of this group of prospective jurors, the *voir dire* process. Actually the process is not one of active selection, but of rejecting those prospective jurors who are deemed unsuitable, leaving the remaining jurors to comprise the actual jury. The purpose of the voir dire is to ensure that the jury will be composed of individuals competent and impartial enough to render a fair verdict. During the voir dire the judge and/or the lawyers ask the prospective jurors for personal information (e.g., occupation, marital status) and question them on a variety of issues that relate to the case. Certain bases for disqualifying a juror are specified by statute (e.g., does not speak English, is blatantly prejudiced toward one side). The attorney may make a motion alleging that the prospective juror falls within the bounds of this statutory disqualification, and if the judge agrees, that person is "excused." This is known as a challenge for cause, and little empirical research has been conducted on the use of such challenges or on what should be the appropriate statutory grounds for disqualification (generally they are rarely exercised with the statutory grounds listed being quite limited).

Also as part of the voir dire, each lawyer, through the exercise of peremptory challenges, is allowed to remove a limited number of jurors without giving any reason for those removals. The assumption is that if both attorneys eliminate those jurors most likely to be biased against them, the result will be a jury composed of people that lean to neither side, but instead let the evidence rather than their attitudes and personality dictate their decision (Saks & Hastie, 1978). Since the number of peremptory challenges allotted each side is limited, lawyers try to use them strategically. As a result, attorneys are increasingly calling upon social scientists to aid them in maximizing the effectiveness of their choices, with social scientists correspondingly increasing their research into those strategies and those factors likely to produce a favorable, or at least unbiased, jury. The two major goals of such research are to suggest more effective ways of eliciting honest answers from jurors (through changes in how and by whom the voir dire is conducted) and generating and utilizing additional information about jurors (e.g., personality traits, demographic characteristics, nonverbal cues) in conjunction with their direct answers to questions posed to them during the voir dire to compile an accurate portrait of the biases and predispositions of the prospective jurors.

Evaluators of the voir dire have concluded that it is generally not very effective in producing relevant information on which to base challenges (Broeder, 1965; Zeisel & Diamond, 1978). Two aspects of the voir dire questioning have been identified as placing social constraints on the elicited answers, tending to minimize and distort the information provided by those answers (Suggs & Sales, 1981). The first concerns the manner in which the voir dire is conducted. For example, three types of questioning techniques are used: (1) questions addressed to the entire venire at the same time; (2) questions directed toward individual jurors in the presence of the rest of the venire; and (3) questions directed toward individual jurors out of the presence of other jurors. Suggs and Sales suggest that only the third type of questioning will be optimally effective in eliciting honest answers because the first two approaches will result in pressures to conform to norms provided by the panel and a corresponding reluctance to disclose true feelings and/or discredit oneself in front of the other prospective jurors.

A second aspect of the voir dire that is likely to constrain the information provided by the prospective jurors concerns who conducts the voir dire. In many jurisdictions it is left to the judge's discretion whether the judge, the lawyers, or both will conduct the voir dire. Suggs and Sales (1981) assert that questioning by the judge will be less than optimally effective in eliciting honest and relevant answers because the judge will be less familiar with the pertinent issues than the attorneys who have already prepared their cases; will be less likely to probe deeply into relevant areas, partially because of this lack of familiarity; and as a result of the judge's neutral role, will be less likely to ask pointed and penetrating questions in an aggressive manner designed to generate self-disclosure. Although the above assertions are based on well-established social psychological knowledge, little empirical research has been conducted to test them in the context of trials.

In order to supplement the explicit content of the answers provided by the prospective jurors during the voir dire, three basic types of information have been suggested. The first assesses relevant personality traits of the prospective juror. The assumption here is that a juror's personality will affect the way in which the juror interprets the evidence and renders a judgment. Researchers have examined a wide variety of personality variables, but one construct repeatedly focused on is that of the authoritarian juror. For example, researchers have investigated the possibility that jurors with authoritarian personalities tend to be more harsh on criminal defendants than jurors with less authoritarian tendencies because they see more malice in others and see punishment as the most effective deterrent of crime. Studies have shown that high authoritarians were more consistently punitive (Centers, Shomer, & Rodrigues, 1970; Crosson, 1968; Snortum & Ashear, 1972). However, under some conditions authoritarian jurors were shown to be less likely to convict a defendant. Hamilton (1976) found that high-authoritarian jurors were less likely to convict a defendant when the defendant was "just following orders." Thus, the degree to which jurors are authoritarian may make a difference in the verdict, but the direction of the difference may depend on the facts of the case. An additional limitation of the applicability of such research is the practical problem of trying to determine the personality of potential jurors during voir dire. Rarely will a judge let a lawyer administer the written or oral personality tests that are the usual bases for identifying those individuals with a particular personality trait (such questions being generally regarded as outside the scope of the particular issues involved in the case at hand and thus likely to obscure and confuse the matters to be decided).

The second information base utilized to supplement the voir dire involves the jurors' demographic characteristics. The assumption here is that these characteristics will be predictive of an individual juror's level of participation during the deliberations, the criteria they will use in deciding on a verdict, and their final verdicts. Among the characteristics that have been investigated are age (Sealy & Cornish, 1973); sex (James, 1959; Snortum & Ashear, 1972; Snyder, 1971; Strodtbeck & Mann, 1956); occupation (Nemeth & Sosis, 1973; Reed, 1965; Simon, 1967; Strodtbeck, James, & Hawkins, 1957); education (James, 1959; Nemeth & Sosis, 1973; Reed, 1965; Simon, 1967); religious affiliation (Becker, Hildum, & Bateman, 1965); and socioeconomic status. The difficulty with this research is that the relationship between demographic characteristics and verdict are found typically in the context of one particular type of trial with one particular type of fact situation. Thus, the findings may not generalize to different cases. In addition, individuals do not always act as the other members of a particular demographic subgroup do. And finally, to which demographic subgroup does an individual most identify with: age; age and race; age and race and occupation status, etc.?

Nonverbal cues provide the third source of information that has been investigated as a possible supplement to the information provided by the voir dire. The assumption is that when a prospective juror lies during voir dire questioning, or when the juror dislikes the lawyer posing the questions or the client whom the lawyer represents, the juror will feel at least slightly more anxious than normal. This anxiety in turn will be manifested in the juror's paralinguistic behaviors (e.g., speech pauses and latencies, speech disturbances, pitch and tone of voice) and/or kinesic behaviors (e.g., facial expressions, body position, and hand movements). Although little research has been done showing the reliability and validity of such cues in a courtroom situation, a great deal of literature does exist tying specific paralinguistic and kinesic behaviors with the experience of anxiety (Davis, 1975; Eisenberg & Smith, 1971; Ekman & Friesen, 1975; Strongman, 1973; Weitz, 1974).

Three major systematic techniques utilizing social science expertise have evolved to take the general behavioral information generated by these information bases and apply it to the voir dire process of specific criminal and civil trials. The *community survey* approach relies on a survey of the community from which the jury panel will be drawn, a technique with which many social scientists are likely to be particularly well acquainted. Generally it will include questions designed to provide information regarding the respondent's attitude toward the facts of the case, the litigants, the attorneys, and matters that may be related to issues in the case, as well as certain background characteristics of the respondent. By correlating these background characteristics with the attitude measures, a number of key variables are generated that will be used to predict the attitudes of prospective jurors based upon the background characteristics of the jurors, which the jurors provide in the course of the voir dire. The assumption is that the prospective juror will share the attitudes of those members of the community with whom he or she shares key characteristics. The survey is designed specifically for the case in which it will be used and utilized only in that immediate area since the correlations may vary with the locale and the issues. Based on this survey, the level of favorability likely for each prospective juror is provided, and a strategy for the exercise of peremptory challenges is formulated.

While the community survey approach bases its predictions on the general trends it finds within the community as a whole, *information networks* focus on the jury panel members themselves. While direct contact with members of the jury panel is not allowed, it is permissible to talk with individuals who might have personal information or knowledge about these potential jurors (Hans & Vidmar, 1982). Although this approach is really quite old in that lawyers have utilized it for years, such an approach is particularly ripe for those social scientists with skills in interviewing and a basic understanding of the flow of information within a community, as well as for understanding and manipulating those aspects of the approach which will maximize the breadth, depth, and reliability of the information generated.

Unlike the community survey and the information network approaches, the *unobtrusive nonverbal technique* does not rely on information generated outside the courtroom for its predictions. As previously noted, prospective jurors manifest paralinguistic and/or kinesic behaviors during the voir dire, which a social scientist trained in the study of nonverbal cues can observe and interpret. By observing the prospective jurors' responses to the opposing attorneys and judge, a rating can be generated that will indicate which side the prospective juror is more favorable toward, with a rough estimate provided of the degree of partiality (Suggs & Sales, 1978).

Scientific jury selection, taken as a whole, has generated a great deal of controversy both as to its effectiveness and predictive power (see, e.g., Hans & Vidmar, 1982; Saks & Hastie, 1978), as well as to its ethics (see, e.g., Berman & Sales, 1977). For a comprehensive review of this topic, see Hafemeister, Sales, and Suggs (in press).

The judge

Even though the judge is equal to, if not more important than, the jury in the trial process, relatively little experimental effort has been devoted to this central figure. This may be the result of a reluctance on the part of judges to participate in studies in general or it may be connected with the difficulty of simulating the unique role of judges as well as their idiosyncratic behaviors. Nevertheless, some research in this area has been initiated.

Judicial backgrounds ▪ Ryan, Ashman, Sales, and Shane-DuBow (1980) have provided the most comprehensive and up-to-date survey of the American trial judge. They report that the prior occupation of a judge is likely to be particularly important, not only in terms of who is selected to occupy a judicial seat, but also in terms of influencing the judge's perceptions of the job. The majority

(54 percent) come directly from private legal practice, with 24 percent rising from a lower court judgeship, 10 percent from the district attorney's office, and 9 percent coming directly from other public positions (e.g., state legislature, city council, state or local administrative agencies). In addition, they found 55 percent of trial judges identify themselves as Democrats, 36 percent as Republicans, and 9 percent reported no affiliation. However, this imbalance was largely the result of a great predominance of judges who are Democrats in the South (82 percent). On the average, trial judges were selected at the age of 46. In 1977 their average age was 53 years, with only 7 percent being under 40 and 3 percent over 70. Overwhelmingly, American's trial judges are white (96 percent) and male (98 percent). One in ten judges reports a grandparent who was a lawyer, judge, or elected public official, and one in five reports a parent who held one of these positions.

Other studies have attempted to relate judicial backgrounds to behavior. Nagel (1962), for example, studied the influence of background on state and federal supreme court judicial decisions. He found that political party affiliation (Republican), bar association membership, high income, Protestant religious affiliation, lower scores on a test of liberal political attitudes, and experience as a prosecuting attorney were all correlated with a prosecutorial bias. However, Goldman (1975) found that the effect of background variables varied with the issue area involved, while Ulmer (1973) suggested that more specific and a wider range of such variables need to be taken into consideration in explaining judicial behavior. For a review of these and related studies on judicial backgrounds, see Champagne and Nagel (1982).

Judicial personalities ▪ Another attempt to explain judicial behavior focuses on the personalities of judges. Smith and Blumberg (1967) used participant observation to develop a typology of trial judges. The six personality types they identified were (1) intellectual scholar, (2) routineer hack, (3) political adventurer-careerist, (4) judicial-pensioner, (5) hatchet man, and (6) tyrant-showboat-benevolent despot. These six were distinguished, among other things, by the amount of the court's workload each handled, their political backgrounds, their career aspirations, their out-of-court connections, their images, and their style of work. Although this study is widely referenced, it should be noted that these six personality types were based on observations of nine judges who sat on one city court. Other than this one study, however, there has been almost no research on the effects that various personality variables have on judicial decision making.

Judicial socialization ▪ Regardless of their backgrounds, personalities, and prior experiences, once an individual is selected as a judge, an on-the-job socialization process begins. Both formal instruction and informal learning is involved in this transition. Ryan, et al. (1980) have attempted to document this process.

They point out that formal programs of orientation have only minimal impact, with the greatest amount of influence being provided by interactions with more experienced judges and courtroom personnel, prior occupational experience, and interchanges with the attorneys who appear before them. Alpert, Atkins, and Ziller (1979) found three stages in the process of socialization. Their first stage was "initiation/resolution," involving the first five years on the bench and characterized by a process of learning about the job and finding ways of resolving problems of initial adjustment. Their second stage was "establishment," lasting for the next ten years approximately, during which a decision would be made whether to make a career out of the judicial position. The final stage was "commitment," a period characterized by increasing certainty, loyalty, and fraternity on the job. However, Ryan, et al. (1980) take exception to the validity of this categorization scheme. They contend that it is the demands of the work environment (e.g., the structure of the court, the attorneys and courtroom personnel who surround them, and the limitations of their own age) that shapes the work patterns of judges, with few differences appearing in the organization and mix of work between veteran and less-experienced judges.

Judicial attitudes and behavior ▪ Partially as a result of this socialization process, a distinctive judicial role is commonly believed to evolve. At least in the eyes of the general public, judges are expected to be unbiased, neutral, steady, patient, of superior wisdom, and above the fray that transpires before them in the courtroom. These "judicial attitudes" in turn are expected to be translated into "judicial behaviors," which are expressed in a consistency by individual judges both within the course of a trial and from trial to trial, and in a consistency of "judicial behaviors" among the various judges. Social science investigators have attempted to determine both whether these expectations are actually fulfilled and the factors that influence the actual attitudes possessed and behaviors expressed by those who hold judicial positions.

Attitudes being very difficult to define and measure, as might be expected, most research has focused on judicial behaviors with an attempt to deduce from such behavior the attitudes that influenced those behaviors. One of the most frequently studied judicial behaviors involves the sentencing of defendants who have committed similar crimes. Several researchers have found statistically significant differences in sentences given to defendants of different races or socioeconomic status (Bullock, 1961; Howard, 1975; Nagel, 1967; Thornberry, 1973). As Saks and Hastie (1978) note, "It is something of an embarrassment to observe the great range of sentences that different judges assign to apparently indistinguishable crimes" (p. 41).

More recent studies have confirmed the earlier findings that the average length of prior sentences given convicted criminals varies widely. In addition, they explore the bases for this sentencing disparity. Diamond (1981) found support for the hypothesis that some of this disparity arises because judges differ in their handling of the mix of the facts available in a sentencing decision, emphasizing different factors. She identified both within-judge and between-judge inconsistency. In addition, she was able to paint a picture of the type of offender over whom judges generally disagreed: in Chicago this offender had stable personal relationships and no other charges pending, while in New York, the other focus of her study, the offender was well-educated and tended to be older. Ebbesen and Konečni (1981) determined that offender variables, such as race, sex, religion, age, education, and marital background, were unrelated to the final sentence, as were factors relating to specific features of the criminal activity and the offender's justification for the crime. The four factors that they found to account for almost all of the systematic variation in the sentence were (1) the type of crime; (2) the extent of the offender's prior record; (3) the status of the offender between arrest and conviction (i.e., released on own recognizance, free on bail, held in jail, originally in jail and then released on bail); and (4) the probation officer's sentence recommendation.

Another judicial behavior that has been scrutinized involves judges' bail-setting policies. In another study by Ebbesen and Konečni (1975), an attempt was made to isolate those factors that have a significant impact on the final bail decision. In their model, they identified the district attorney's recommendation, as well as the extent of the defendant's local ties and prior record as being influential, while the defense attorney's recommendation carried no weight. However, when this model was applied in an actual courtroom setting, they found the district attorney's recommendation had the greatest influence on the level bail was set at, with an additional factor, the severity of the crime, having an indirect effect, inasmuch as it altered both attorneys' recommendations.

A third judicial behavior that has been studied involves the plea bargaining stage of the criminal trial and the pretrial negotiations on the civil side. Ryan, et al. (1980) note that the level of judicial involvement in these settlement efforts varies widely, even though almost all courts rely heavily on negotiated dispositions to relieve the strain on their crowded dockets. In some courts the attorneys reach agreements in which the judge concurs. In other courts, judges themselves are active participants in the construction of an agreement. Ryan, et al. identify the following factors as influencing the role or style that a judge adopts in the negotiation setting, which in turn effects the ultimate product: the structure of the court itself; the skills, stability, and adversariness of attorneys; and the judges' perceptions of their own skills and of the caseload pressures facing them. These factors assume different weights depending on whether a civil or criminal trial is involved, but in both contexts, the judges' perception of their own skills at negotiating was found to be the most important factor.

The reliance on and utilization of precedent is a fourth judicial behavior that has been investigated. Under the principle of *stare decisis*, the law is conceived as a cumulative and progressing body of wisdom, with judicial decisions being based on the determinations reached in preceding cases. However, Becker (1966), in a study involving Hawaiian judges, found large amounts of variation in precedent orientation among judges. His results showed that the great majority of judges ranked personal factors as extremely important in making decisions. Yet, if the judges also showed a strong precedent orientation, they tended to decide hypothetical cases against their personal values and in line with precedent.

A fifth judicial behavior studied involves the interaction between the judge and the trial participants in the courtroom. Blumberg (1967) argued that the trial is a social network composed primarily of the judge and the trial attorneys. Cooperative behavior among these participants is emphasized since such cooperation maximizes case productivity for all parties. As a result, the parties learn to rely on one another.

Voting patterns involve a sixth judicial behavior that has been researched, although this technique has primarily been used to study judges at the appellate level. The voting patterns of a particular court are identified and compared among the various judges sitting on that court. A frequent approach is to rank judges along a liberal-conservative dimension and examine the ideological differences between them (Pritchett, 1948; Schubert, 1965, 1974). Certain judges might be found to favor individuals, while others tend to vote in favor of the government. Since a judge's degree of liberalism is determined relative to that of other judges, it is most easily adapted to multi-judge courts, which unlike a series of single-judge trial court justices, have all heard the same case and are thus easier to compare. However, Champagne and Nagel (1982) suggest that such underlying, influential judicial attitudes could be studied at the trial court level by distributing to those judges a liberalism questionnaire similar to the one devised by Nagel (1969) which was found to predict liberal voting behavior. Nagel found that judges who expressed liberal attitudes on the questionnaire were much more pro-defendant in criminal cases, much more pro-government in business regulation cases, somewhat in favor of the plaintiff in motor vehicle accident cases, and slightly in favor of the employee in employee injury cases. The danger of such research is, of course, that the connection betwen judicial attitudes and voting behavior always remains tenuous and subject to numerous intervening variables.

■ DEFENDANTS FOUND NOT GUILTY BY REASON OF INSANITY

Another focus of psycholegal research has been on mental health policy. Because the use of the insanity defense in criminal trials receives such intensive coverage from the media, we have chosen research on this particular topic as our second example of representative research in law-psychology.

The insanity defense is concerned with a defendant's mental condition at the time of the alleged offense, rather than with the defendant's mental condition at the time of the trial (the latter is referred to as competency to stand trial). Until quite recently there were strong disincentives to raising such a defense; namely, those found not guilty by reason of insanity (NGRI) often faced automatic and indefinite commitment in a secure mental institution. As a result, the defense tended to be raised only by those defendants facing charges carrying the most severe punishments. However, some states are now using civil commitment if the person is found NGRI. These laws require review and/ or recommitment hearings on a regular basis. In addition, in the past 30 years there has been a great upheaval in the standards by which the courts determine whether a defendant should be held responsible for his or her criminal acts. Throw into this maelstrom the heat of public scrutiny generated by a few well-publicized cases where the NGRI defense has been raised, the often critical and controversial role played by the mental health professional's testimony as to the defendant's legal sanity in such cases, and the pressures on legislators and judges from the public as well as the legal and psychological professions to revamp the NGRI system, and it becomes obvious why this issue is one of genuine importance for psycholegal research. Unfortunately, there have been few studies on the issues surrounding the NGRI plea, with Pasewark (1981) and Steadman and Braff (1983) providing the most recent and comprehensive reviews in the area.

Perceptions and use of the NGRI plea

One major series of studies has been conducted to discover how frequently various groups think the NGRI plea is entered and how often they think it has been entered successfully (Pasewark & Pantle, 1979; Pasewark & Seidenzahl, 1979; Pasewark, Seidenzahl, & Pantle, 1981). Estimates on these two items were gathered from Wyoming college students, state legislators, community and state hospital mental health personnel, and the residents of two Wyoming communities. Each group grossly overestimated both the frequency and success of the plea. In Wyoming during the two-year time period considered in the early 1970s, only 102, less than one-half of one percent of the 22,102 defendants charged with a felony, entered an insanity plea, with only one defendant being successful in the use of the plea (a success rate of 1%). The students estimated that an NGRI plea was entered in 37 percent of all cases, the legislators said 21 percent, the residents of the two communities guessed 43 percent, the state hospital professional staff did the best at 13 percent, while the state hospital aides did the worst at 57 percent. As for the success rate of those entering the plea, the students conjectured a 44 percent success rate, the legislators 40 percent, the community residents 38 percent, and the community mental health center professionals 19 percent. The authors suggest that the widespread publicity given by the media to such cases may be responsible for these findings. In addition, these surveys showed that many of the respondents were unfamiliar with the mechanics of the NGRI plea, and with the exception of the legislative group, the majority expressed disagreement with the underlying philosophy of the NGRI plea and favored its elimination.

As for the actual use and success of the NGRI plea there is little comprehensive data. Most reports are limited to brief intervals taken during different time periods, in different jurisdictions. Yet, what data there are conform to the Wyoming report noted above and suggest that the number of cases in which the defense has been raised, let alone successfully pursued, is quite small (Criss & Racine, 1980; Steadman, Keitner, Braff, & Arvanites, 1983).

Generally little interest has been shown by the states in maintaining any systematic record of the use of NGRI pleas, a most unfortunate omission in view of the continuing public and professional controversy over the use of the plea and recurring legislative and judicial attempts to tinker with, if not abolish, this defense in criminal trials. Nevertheless, it appears that the number of NGRI acquittals represents a very small portion of those individuals entering the criminal justice and mental health systems (Phillips & Pasewark, 1980).

Characteristics of persons found NGRI

In those studies that have examined NGRI acquittees, a fairly consistent portrait has emerged of these individuals (Cooke & Sikorski, 1974; Criss & Racine, 1980; Morrow & Peterson, 1966; Pasewark, Pantle & Steadman, 1979b; Phillips & Pasewark, 1980; Petrila, 1982; Rogers & Bloom, 1982; Singer, 1978). Generally they are in their mid-thirties; Caucasian; male; without a high school diploma; unskilled, semi-skilled, or unemployed; and unmarried. Although showing greater variation, roughly 40 percent have undergone prior hospitalization for mental illness and over half were diagnosed as psychotic at the time of the crime.

The two most controversial categories with the greatest fluctuation in data are the criminal histories of NGRI acquittees and the criminal charges of which they have been acquitted. Such information is critical in that it is the basis for three common stereotypes that have been influential in directing policy decisions in the field. The NGRI acquittee has been characterized as (1) a "mad killer" who attacks victims randomly and repeatedly; (2) a "crafty con" manipulating the system by faking insanity, who, after a short period of relatively soft hospitalization, will obtain release and return to a life of crime; or (3) a "desperate defendant" against whom the evidence is so heavily weighted that an insanity plea is the only legal option remaining.

Generally the data does not appear to support any of these projections, although it is not consistent or comprehensive enough to refute them totally either. If the first portrait, the Dr. Jekyll/Mr. Hyde who has run amok, accurately portrayed NGRI acquittees, one would expect most of them to be charged with murder, or at least serious personal assaults upon a number of victims.

However, there appears to be a wide fluctuation in the charges that faced the NGRI acquittee, suggesting the insanity plea is used differently in different states at different times. Oregon and Missouri report only about one in ten NGRI acquittals are of murder or manslaughter charges; New Jersey and Connecticut one in four; and Michigan and New York one in two. A similar breakdown occurs when the target of the crime is considered: In Oregon and Missouri only about one-half of the crimes for which the NGRIs have been acquitted were for what could be considered crimes against the person, that is, directly aimed at another person as the victim. In New Jersey and Connecticut, slightly over three out of four involved such crimes, while in Michigan and New York they rose to nearly nine out of ten. However, the New York study, which supplies the most support for the "mad killer" hypothesis, also specifically notes that (1) many of the crimes are of a less serious nature; (2) nine out of ten of the crimes involved either no victim or a single one; and (3) in two out of three cases the victim was known to the defendant prior to the criminal act (Pasewark, Pantle, & Steadman, 1979b). Furthermore, a later study in Michigan, the other state with the most support for this view, noted that the number of NGRI acquittals of murder represented only 1.7 percent of those arrested on that charge (Criss & Racine, 1980).

As for the second portrait of the NGRI acquittee, that of the "crafty con," again fluctuations in the data make it difficult to make firm statements for or against the image. Reports of the percentage of NGRI acquittees with a history of prior criminal convictions, which might suggest an experience with and capability for manipulating the criminal system, range from a low of 18 percent in New Jersey to a high of 66 percent in Missouri (although a later Missouri study reported 39 percent, a figure more in line with other states). However, the high percentage of NGRI acquittees with a prior mental condition history, the large number of them given the most severe diagnosis of psychosis in their evaluation, and as will be discussed shortly, their generally high rate of rehospitalization following their release on the current charge and a criminal recidivism rate lower than or equal to that of comparable felons, all suggest that at least a sizeable proportion of the group are not faking their symptons in order to manipulate the system. Rather, the NGRI plea is serving as a device to resume psychological and psychiatric treatment for many of them that predates and/or postdates the criminal offense (Petrila, 1982).

In regard to the third caricature of the NGRI acquittee as the "desperate defendant," certainly the mere fact that the evidence shows the defendant committed the criminal act does not indicate the mental state of that defendant at the time of the crime. Neither is it indicative that the insanity plea is a mere guise to protect the criminal who has been caught "red-handed." Although the low educational level might be utilized to buttress an argument why the defendant failed to conceal the crime better, such openness also might be construed to suggest an individual who truly was not in command of his or her faculties. Thus far there has not been a study conducted that compares NGRI acquittees to convicted felons matched according to the criminal charges brought against them to determine if the evidence against the former was more certain than against the latter. Nor would such a comparison necessarily prove valid, since the NGRI acquittee may expend his or her trial resources attempting to establish a showing of insanity rather than contesting the factual evidence arrayed against him or her, as would be expected for the convicted felon.

Nevertheless, many of the same points can be made against the image of the NGRI acquittee as a "desperate defendant" as against the view that such individuals are a "crafty con." The prevalent psychiatric history, the severe diagnoses, their high rate of rehospitalization, and unremarkable recidivism rate all suggest an individual who is indeed severely mentally disordered.

Based upon the above kinds of information, Pasewark, Pantle, and Steadman (1979a,b) suggest other subcategories: (1) those for whom the criminal act was directly associated with a mental disorder (such a grouping would include those with previous and subsequent psychiatric histories, but little prior and later criminal activity); (2) those who represent the larger criminal population and, like any other occupational group, contain a certain number of mentally ill individuals (such individuals would tend to have both earlier and later psychiatric histories as well as earlier and later criminal records); and (3) those for whom the classification of mental illness is a misnomer but for whom society makes special allowances, including police officers, mothers who kill their children, and the defendant for whom there is a great deal of empathy. This third group, we suggest, would not be expected to have either a prior criminal or psychiatric history, nor would they be expected to have a high recidivism or rehospitalization tendency.

The assumption of much of this work is that by identifying the characteristics of those persons found NGRI, we have thereby determined the characteristics of those individuals for whom an insanity plea is more likely to be successful. Yet such an approach is limited since we need to compare these characteristics to those defendants for whom the plea has failed. Such studies have generally been frustrated by the size and logistics problems of the investigation required, as well as local and state roadblocks to the gathering of such information (e.g., laws concerning public access to court verdicts).

Steadman and his colleagues (Steadman & Braff, 1983; Steadman, Keitner, Braff, & Arvanites, 1983) overcame these difficulties by limiting the scope of their study and focusing their efforts on the court records of a single county. In that way they could identify all defendants for whom the insanity defense was raised and thereby compare the characteristics of those for whom NGRI pleas were successful and those for whom they had failed. At the same time they limited the generalizability of their findings and exposed themselves to the distorting influence of peculiar and isolated local events. They found that in Erie County, New York, between 1970 and 1980 there had been 205 individuals for whom insanity pleas were entered, of which 65 percent were convicted, 25 percent found NGRI, and 10 percent dismissed, acquitted, pending, withdrawn, or the defendant had died prior to disposition. For the convicted and NGRI groups the average age was the same (29), while they were similar in sex (88 percent vs. 92 percent males for NGRIs and convicteds respectively), race (69 percent vs. 62 percent white), marital status (88 percent vs. 77 percent currently unmarried), employment status (72 percent vs. 73 percent unemployed or unskilled), and prior state psychiatric hospitalization (67 percent vs. 74 percent had none). Among those with prior state mental hospital admissions, the NGRIs averaged a slightly higher and statistically significant number of prior admissions (3.3 vs. 2.0), although for shorter periods (756 vs. 1245 days, not statistically significant). The majority of both groups had prior arrest histories (57 percent NGRIs, 70 percent convicteds), with the NGRIs averaging fewer arrests (3.5 vs. 4.7, not statistically significant).

An examination was also made of the offense with which these two groups were charged. Both groups were charged most frequently with violent or potentially violent crimes, though the NGRIs were more often charged with such offenses (80 percent vs. 69 percent). However, the most frequent offense, murder/manslaughter, involved NGRIs less often (35 percent vs. 41 percent). Victims were involved in a majority of the offenses for both groups (80 percent NGRI, 70 percent convicted), with the only divergence, though not statistically significant, being the involvement of a female victim (56 percent NGRI, 37 percent convicted). Otherwise the results were largely the same with the victim being predominantly white (67 percent vs. 70 percent) and of a similar age (33 vs. 34). NGRIs did tend to use a knife or gun in the offense more often (61 percent vs. 44 percent).

Finally, an analysis was made of the symptomatology reported for the two groups. Statistically significant differences were present in 4 of the 14 psychiatric impairments reported. NGRIs were diagnosed by forensic staff as more psychotic (28 percent vs. 5 percent), depressed (53 percent vs. 36 percent), and agitated (24 percent vs. 12 percent) than the convicted group, though less inclined to alcohol and drug indulgence (0 percent vs. 12 percent). However, it is difficult to determine whether the label determined the treatment, or the treatment determined the label.

What was most strongly associated with a successful versus unsuccessful pleading was the finding of the pretrial forensic examination. Even though such findings are rebuttable evidence and not binding on the court, when this evaluation declared a defendant insane, 83 percent of the time the case was dismissed or the defendant was determined to be NGRI. When the evaluation found the defendant sane, in only 2 percent of the cases was the defendant found NGRI. In turn, the major factor related to a clinical finding of insanity was a diagnosis of psychosis (where this was the diagnosis, 82 percent of the defendants were found legally insane as compared with only 28 percent of all other diagnoses). In fact, when control for this diagnosis was introduced, neither age nor number of prior mental hospitalizations remained significant. It was the diagnosis of psychosis that was the decisive factor.

In a sense Steadman's findings are reassuring in that it appears that once an NGRI plea has been entered, the legal system that is trying the defendant appears to be confining itself to those factors that are relevant to a determination of insanity. That is to say, under the law the only relevant consideration should be the defendant's mental condition at the time of the crime, not such extraneous factors as the defendant's sex, race, or prior criminal status. Although clinical studies are not encouraging as to the ability of forensic evaluators to provide accurate diagnoses or to reach back to the time of the alleged crime in forming such diagnoses, Steadman's work nevertheless indicates the appropriate issue is being considered. What is less comforting is the apparent preemption of the courts' decision-making process by mental health professionals. Although they may be the most qualified and best-equipped individuals to make determinations of mental disorder, as we shall see below, the legal test of insanity requires far more complex judgments that should require the judge or jury to take a far more active role in the ultimate decision (e.g., Morse, 1983).

Detention and subsequent release of persons found NGRI

Steadman and Braff (1983) in their studies of New York acquittees also investigated the length of hospitalization after acquittal for those individuals found NGRI and the factors related to their subsequent release. They found that 40 percent of the 278 persons found NGRI between 1965 and 1976 were still hospitalized in 1978, with an average length of stay of three and a half years. Of the 47 percent of the NGRIs released without supervision following post-acquittal hospitalization (henceforth released), their average length of stay had been 406 days. A follow-up study of those hospitalized between 1976 and 1978 indicated that the average length of stay of those released was going to considerably exceed that of the 1965–1976 group.

They also found a clear trend for more severe crimes to be associated with longer detentions. The 55 persons acquitted of murders who were released averaged 500 days of hospitalization, the 25 acquitted of assaults and released averaged 398 days, while the 6 acquitted of burglary who were released averaged 288 days. As the authors note, the appropriateness of these variations cannot be assessed in that it is not possible to ascertain which defendants were "sicker" and thus needed longer terms of treatment.

Pasewark, Pantle, and Steadman (1982), in their study of the length of detention incurred by NGRIs and a comparison group of felons convicted of the same offense in New York, found that initially the two groups had almost the same length of detention between 1965 and 1971 (1021 days for male NGRIs versus 995 days for male convicteds; 638 days for female NGRIs versus 789 days for female convicteds, with neither difference being statistically significant). However, in 1971 the responsibility for NGRIs was shifted from the Department of Correctional Services to the State Department of Mental Hygiene. Between 1971 and 1973 the NGRI men accumulated an average of 533 hospital days as opposed to the felons' 837 prison days (a significant difference), although there were no significant differences for women; the NGRI women averaged 435 hospital days, while the female felons averaged 565 days. Thus there was a major decrease in the detention time of both the NGRI and felon groups, but the NGRIs dropped considerably more (48 percent vs. 16 percent for the men, 32 percent vs. 28 percent for the women).

Steadman and Braff (1983) comment that findings such as these should not necessarily be interpreted as showing that NGRI acquittals are an easy way out since (1) hospitalization is supposed to be based on both therapeutic and protective rationales, with release to be tied to the remission of the insanity symptoms and certification that the individual is no longer dangerous; and (2) few defendants serve time for their arrest charges because of plea bargains.

Post-release recidivism rate and rehospitalization

Morrow and Peterson (1966) found that during a three-year period in Missouri, 37 percent of NGRI acquittees were rearrested for the commission of a felony (generally for economic offenses and generally a repetition of the prior arrest category). Considering the recidivism rate for released felons in Missouri during this period (35%), they concluded that the recidivism rate for NGRIs was not alarming.

Pasewark, Pantle, and Steadman (1979b) reported that of the 278 persons acquitted between 1965 and 1976 in New York, 107 were released, with 21 (20%) of them subsequently rearrested during this time period. All 21 were males, as none of the 19 women in this group were rearrested through 1976. The 21 men rearrested totaled 68 arrests, with arrests for property crimes comprising the largest category (35%), followed by crimes against persons (25%), drug charges (18%), other felonies (3%), and misdemeanors (19%). Generally these subsequent crimes were less serious than the ones for which the individuals were initially acquitted. Based on these findings, they suggest that there is a small core of repeat offenders who are the source of the inaccurate stereotype of NGRIs as repetitive offenders who quickly return to crime after having found an "easy out."

Steadman, et al. (1983), believing that the proper comparison group should be persons released from state mental hospitals and not from prisons, compared the Pasewark, et al. (1979b) results to the arrest rates of patients recently released from New York state mental facilities (Steadman, Cocozza, & Melick, 1978). He found in the latter group that 9 percent recidivated during their first 19 months after release, suggesting that the NGRI recidivism rate could be considered troubling.

Two studies have examined the subsequent mental hospitalization of NGRI acquittees. Pasewark, et al. (1979b) found that 22 percent were subsequently rehospitalized, with these 23 dischargees rehospitalized a total of 47 times (of the 88 discharged men, 16 [18%] were rehospitalized a total of 34 times; of the 19 discharged women, 7 [37%] were rehospitalized a total of 13 times). Pasewark, Pantle, and Steadman (1982), in their comparisons of NGRIs and convicted defendants who unsuccessfully used an NGRI plea, found 18 percent of the NGRI acquittees were rehospitalized, while only 6 percent of the matched convicted felons entered mental hospitals subsequent to their prison release. The six rehospitalized acquittees totaled 19 readmissions (16 civil, 3 criminal), while the two released felons incurred one hospitalization each (both civil). It seems clear from this data that at least a sizeable proportion of the NGRI population are not mere manipulators of the system but actually do display symptomatology that is serious enough to bring these individuals back under the auspices of the mental health system on a repeated basis without the intervention being initiated by the criminal courts.

Impact of laws governing NGRI pleas

One of the continuing controversies surrounding the NGRI plea concerns the language of the insanity test. The controversy has two parts: (1) what should the language be, and (2) often overlooked, what is the impact of that language on the trier of fact. The former may appear to require largely a philosophical answer, varying with individual views on whether and/or to what degree a criminal defendant should be absolved of responsibility for acts influenced by insanity. However, the issue quickly takes on an empirical cast when answers are sought to questions such as (1) what does insanity look like; (2) are there degrees of insanity, and if so, what do they look like; (3) what does the threshold between legal sanity and legal insanity look like; (4) what factors lead us to conclude one person is sane while another person is insane; (5) is it possible for a person to fake insanity, and if so, what does that look like; and (6) for people who have been found legally insane, what will the results be of treating them in various ways?

Unfortunately, space limitations preclude our reviewing the empirical work performed on the existence, manifestations, and treatment of insanity. Instead we will focus on the equally important but largely ignored second part of the NGRI controversy: the impact of the legal language governing the NGRI process. Such language dictates how and when the judge or jury is to determine that a defendant who has entered an insanity plea should receive an NGRI acquittal. Four legal tests, separately or in conjunction, have been frequently used in the American judicial system to answer these questions. These tests are described in Box 13.1. The oldest, which is still used in some form in 21 states today, is the M'Naghten "right from wrong" test. A second standard is the "irresistible impulse" test, still appearing in some form in four states today. The third approach, the Durham rule, was first used in 1954. Originally intended to broaden the scope of the insanity investigation, it was concluded to be unworkable, and is not presently being used in any American jurisdiction.

B O X 13.1   STANDARDS FOR INSANITY

The *M'Naghten standard* as originally formulated read,

> to establish a defense on the ground of insanity, it must be clearly proved that, at the time of the committing of the act, the party accused was labouring under such a defect of reason, from disease of the mind, as not to know the nature and quality of the act he was doing; or if he did know it that he did not know he was doing what was wrong (*M'Naghtens Case,* 1843, p. 722).

This standard was criticized for being too narrow in that it ignored findings by mental health professionals that while the mentally ill might be able to distinguish right from wrong, they might still be unable to control their wrongful actions (Hagan, 1982).

Originally devised as an alternative and corrective for the M'Naghten rule, the *irresistible impulse* test excused those who knew the act was wrong but were unable to stop themselves from carrying it out. However, this approach has been criticized in turn because of mental health professionals' great difficulty in differentiating an irresistible impulse from an impulse not resisted.

The *Durham rule* asked if the criminal act was "the product of a mental disease or defect." Designed to allow for the inclusion of more material concerning the alleged insanity of the defendant, it proved too general and an insufficient guide to juries and judges. In addition, the testimony of psychiatric experts was felt to usurp the decision-making function of the judges and juries under this rule, as experts inevitably, despite the courts' attempts to prevent it, provided answers to questions that were beyond their expertise, and which juries and judges found impossible to ignore in reaching their decisions (Hagan, 1982).

Intended to be broader and open to a greater spectrum of evidence concerning the alleged insanity, yet narrower in scope than the Durham rule, the *ALI test* states,

> A person is not responsible for criminal conduct if at the time of such conduct as a result of mental disease or defect he lacks substantial capacity either to appreciate the criminality (wrongfulness) of his conduct or to conform his conduct to the requirements of the law (American Law Institute, 1962).

This approach has been applauded for incorporating the modern view that the mind is a complex entity whose function may be impaired in various ways (Hagan, 1982). The ALI formulation is said to differ from the M'Naghten rule in three respects: (1) by using the term "appreciate," it introduces an affective, emotional understanding as opposed to M'Naghten's reliance solely on the cognitive understanding of the defendant; (2) it does not require total lack of appreciation by the defendant of the nature of his/her conduct, only that the defendant "lacks substantial capacity" to do so; and (3) it includes a volitional element, making the defendant's inability to control his/her actions an independent criterion for insanity (The Insanity Defense, 1983).

The most recent formulation, devised by the American Law Institute and known as the ALI test, has been adopted by the federal courts and is used in some form by 26 states (The Insanity Defense, 1983).

Despite the extensive efforts represented by the creation and application of these four standards and their variations, many people today remain unhappy with insanity pleas and acquittals. There is concern that defendants who are not actually insane are being absolved of responsibility for their acts, that all of the tests are too lenient and include defendants who are sufficiently sane that they should be held responsible even though they may show some aspects of mental illness, and that too many dangerous individuals are able to use this route as a shortcut to enable them to return to the streets where they continue their aberrant behavior. As a result, three additional proposals have recently been raised to alter insanity defense laws. First is a proposal to substitute or add the alternative of a "guilty but mentally ill" (GBMI) verdict in place of or in addition to the traditional finding of NGRI; under this approach, a defendant found GBMI receives the same sentence as a defendant found sane but some of this sentence may be served in a mental health treatment facility rather than a prison. A second proposal is to shift the burden of proof on the insanity issue from the state to the defendant. This proposal would place the burden on the defendant to generate the relevant evidence for insanity. The third proposal is to eliminate the insanity defense altogether.

Although the four traditional tests and the three recent proposals have generated extensive discussions in the journals of the legal and mental health professions, and in the popular press, very little empirical work has been done to determine how the different laws will affect the processing of mentally disordered offenders. Among the few attempts was a study by Criss and Racine (1980). In early September of 1974 a court ruling held Michigan's automatic commitment of NGRI acquittees to be unconstitutional and required a separate hearing following the criminal proceeding on the individual's current mental status before that individual could be committed for treatment. In response to this decision and with the intent of preventing defendants without a current committable mental illness from receiving an NGRI acquittal and thus immediate release back into the community, the Michigan legislature in 1975 created an alternative GBMI verdict. The authors, drawing on the earlier work of Cooke and Sikorski (1975), who studied NGRI patients in Michigan from 1967–1972, attempt to determine the effect of these legislative and judicial changes by comparing the earlier data to the information they amassed on NGRI acquittees from September 1, 1974 to August 31, 1979.

Criss and Racine found that slightly over half (56%) of the NGRI population under the new procedure was found at the subsequent civil commitment hearing to not meet the criteria for involuntary hospitalization. Furthermore, those who were committed incurred a significantly shorter length of hospitalization than had previously been the case, seemingly supporting the view of those legislators who feared an early return to the community of defendants found NGRI. However, the authors argue that these changes are the result of more effective mental health intervention throughout NGRI proceedings, implying that the NGRI system is working as intended and is, in fact, improving. Unfortunately, they do not provide data on the recidivism and/or rehospitalization rate of these NGRI acquittees, which would further substantiate their claim, nor do they provide comparable information on GBMIs.

The Pasewark, Pantle, and Steadman (1979b) study discussed earlier also noted the impact of a statutory change on NGRI proceedings. There the NGRI adjudications themselves remained essentially the same; what was altered was the subsequent fate of NGRI acquittees. Prior to 1971, NGRI acquittees were placed under the jurisdiction of the New York Department of Corrections and were committed to a mental hospital for the criminally insane. On September 1, 1971, that jurisdiction was transferred to the State Commissioner of Mental Hygiene for involuntary hospitalization in a civil mental hospital. For the five complete years prior to the change, an average of seven persons were found insane each year. For the four complete years following the change, an average of 44 persons were found insane each year.

Pasewark, et al. (1979b) concluded that the statutory language governing insanity pleas is probably not the decisive factor in determining whether an individual receives an NGRI acquittal. Rather, they suggest that largely unidentified factors other than the literal language of these rules of law control NGRI determinations. They assert that each of the legal rules is highly restrictive. And only when the law is successfully "bent" by the concerned parties (i.e., defense attorneys, judges, prosecutors, and mental health professionals) is a defendant found insane. Such manipulation, they argue, opens up the possibility that decisions on NGRI pleas are inappropriately based on factors such as residence, race, sex, and/or the empathy of the judge or jury.

This view concerning the irrelevance of the particular test utilized gains support, albeit for slightly different reasons, from a study by Elwork, Sales, and Alfini (1982). They demonstrated that most jury instructions, including those that contain the standard for judging insanity, are simply incomprehensible to the juries that hear these trials. Their study described and tested a method whereby jury instructions may be rewritten so that they are maximally understandable. With an edited version of an actual trial utilizing the M'Naghten rule, they found that mock jurors averaged 51 percent right on a questionnaire designed to test their comprehension of the original jury instructions. Even for an extremely basic question such as "Define what (the defendant) meant when he stated that he was not guilty by reason of insanity," which could be answered correctly with a simple "he did not know the difference between right and wrong," "he had a mental illness which made him not know what he was doing," or "he did not know that what he was doing was wrong," jurors given the typical M'Naghten instructions answered this question incorrectly

44 percent of the time. Thus, it was clear that jurors were arbitrarily selecting their own standards by which to judge insanity in such cases, exposing the decisions in such trials to the whims of caprice and prejudice.

Despite these findings, there are studies that have detected differences resulting when one legal standard for insanity is used in place of another. One of the first and perhaps most well-known efforts in this direction was taken by Simon (1967). As part of her study of the American jury system, she presented to her mock juries one of two recordings of condensed and recreated versions of two actual trials where an NGRI plea was raised as a defense. One trial involved a housebreaking charge, without any elements of violence toward another person, while the second involved the more heinous offense of incest. After listening to their assigned trials, a third of the juries were given jury instructions that contained the M'Naghten rule to guide their deliberations, another third received the Durham rule, while the final third received no instructions at all. These mock juries were then left alone to reach a verdict with their deliberations recorded as had been previously agreed upon.

In the housebreaking trial, it was found that those jurors who received no instructions gave the highest proportion of NGRI verdicts, followed by Durham, with the M'Naghten jurors giving the fewest NGRI acquittals. The difference between the M'Naghten jurors and the uninstructed jurors was significant, that between M'Naghten and Durham jurors was not. In the incest trial, the verdicts of jurors receiving no instructions and Durham instructions were very similar, with the M'Naghten jurors significantly less likely to vote for an NGRI acquittal than the Durham jurors (a 12 percent difference).

Based on these findings, Simon concluded there is support for those who opposed the Durham rule because they feared it would increase the number of NGRI acquittals. However, she noted that a 12 percent increase is not necessarily an alarming increase (although when jury verdicts rather than juror verdicts were considered, the difference jumped to 19 percent). In addition, she pointed out that the Durham rule seemed to be producing results closer to the jurors' natural sense of equity as reflected in how they voted when not given any instructions. Furthermore, she found that at least half of the uninstructed and Durham juries took the defendant's ability to distinguish right from wrong, the hallmark of the M'Naghten instructions, into consideration during their deliberations. This seems to support the assertion that the Durham rule added to the scope of the discussions generated by the M'Naghten standard, which contained only one aspect of what juries consider appropriate in reaching conclusions on the question of a defendant's insanity. Simon also found evidence that refuted the charge that the Durham rule would result in jurors abdicating their decision-making responsibility, blindly following the conclusions of the mental health professionals. She found that the Durham juries deliberated significantly longer than did the M'Naghten juries, suggesting greater juror involvement and responsibility, while the lack of a significant difference in the proportion of hung juries was taken to suggest it was no more difficult for them to reach consensus.

One other study provides indirect evidence that the particular legal standard chosen has little influence on the outcome of NGRI trials. Arens and Susman (1966) studied trial transcripts of NGRI cases in Washington D.C. between 1960 and 1962. Based on their content analysis they concluded that the change from a M'Naghten standard to the Durham rule in that jurisdiction made no appreciable difference in the wording of the judges' instructions to the jury on the insanity plea in such cases. Instead there was a tendency to retain the language of the M'Naghten instructions. Arens and Susman suggest this intransigency is due to the trial judges' dislike of the insanity defense in general, and their disapproval of the Durham rule in particular.

Finally, two things in reviewing this literature should be kept in mind. First, not all NGRI pleas are decided by a jury. Thus the proportion of NGRI cases in a jurisdiction that are decided by a judge and the percentage by a jury may effect the importance of the phrasing of the jury instruction and their incomprehensibility to jurors. Second, in light of the findings discussed earlier by Steadman, Keitner, Braff, and Arvanites (1983) that the controlling factor in NGRI adjudications is whether the pretrial forensic examiner found the NGRI defendant insane, how either the jury or the judge interprets the insanity standard may be irrelevant, with the impact it has on the forensic examiner being decisive.

Clearly, there are serious needs for research in this area. What research there is has been conducted in a few areas of the country for limited periods of time and often focusing on limited questions. Yet what results are available suggests that such work will be essential if we are to frame rational state and federal policies for mentally disordered offenders. For example, is the plea used often enough to warrant specialized courts to deal with the matter? And should NGRI acquittees who are subsequently committed for treatment be held to higher standards for release than civil committees because they may pose a greater danger to society? Empirical research will provide the factual foundation to help answer these and other policy questions.

■ CONCLUSION

The above noted research findings have implications for more than creating public policy. They also can be used for guiding the implementation of existing policies and the practice of professionals. A clear example is the accumulated research on jury selection. As Fig. 13.1 demonstrates, the tie between the scientific and professional interactions are strong, with both relating to the creation and implementation of policy. The opportunities for the study of legal topics and issues are considerable. It is this diversity combined with relevance that may account for the phenomenal growth in interest in law-psychology.

■ SUGGESTED READINGS

Bartol, C.R. (1983). *Psychology and American law.* Belmont, California: Wadsworth.

Dunn, J., & Farrington, D. P. (Eds.). *Current research in forensic psychiatry and psychology.* New York: John Wiley.

Current research in forensic psychiatry and psychology is a book series devoted to collecting scholarly writings that deal with forensic psychology and psychiatry topics. Each volume is edited by the series editors. It provides a valuable source of information on the developments within this field.

Ellison, K. W., & Buckhout, R. (1981). *Psychology and criminal justice.* New York: Harper & Row.

Horowitz, I. A., & Willging, T. E. (1984). *The psychology of law: Integrations and applications.* Boston: Little, Brown.

These books are introductory texts that survey significant parts of the psychology-law interface. Reviewing theory, research and practice, they collectively cover the following topics: the jury and trial process, lawyering, police behavior, processing offenders through the criminal justice system, the use of psychological assessment services by the law, and the relationship between the mental health and the criminal justice processes.

Law and human behavior. New York: Plenum.

Law and human behavior is a quarterly journal that has been produced since 1977. It is generally considered the leading single forum for law-psychology research and scholarship.

Sales, B.D. (Ed.). *Perspectives in law and psychology.* New York: Plenum.

Perspectives in law and psychology is a series of books devoted to the law and psychology interface that are authored by experts in the field. Currently, the books cover such topics as the criminal justice system, the trial process, juveniles' waiver of rights, mental health law, mentally disordered offenders, and research scales in crime and delinquency. As an on-going series, it, like the journal *Law and human behavior*, provides a valuable source of psychology-law scholarship.

CHARLES A. KIESLER
PSYCHOLOGY AND PUBLIC POLICY

■ INTRODUCTION

Most of the applied specialties described in this book are directly related to specific public policies. Some of them, such as community psychology, school psychology, and instructional psychology, are specialties that rest on literally decades of research and analysis relevant to particular public policies. Others, such as psychology and health, environmental psychology, and psychology and the law, represent more recent but rapidly developing interests and technologies. In this chapter, we hope to develop a more formal approach to applying psychology to public policy.

Of course, public policy is not really an applied specialty of psychology. That is, it is not a substantive sub-field of psychology that only psychologists can concentrate on. Nonetheless, psychologists, along with a great many others, scientists and non-scientists alike, have something to bring to the study of public policy and its analysis, formation, and change. That special flavor is what this chapter is about.

Public policy is a term used generally to describe all the choices that the public makes or could make. It involves the study of alternative choices and the trade-offs that are necessary for each. Almost any public choice for policy demands some sense of trade-offs, a comparison of costs and benefits. Suppose we are considering whether to build a dam as a conservation watershed in the Ozarks. Typical initial reasons for building a dam might be to control floods and reduce the consequent human damage and to eliminate the erosion of the topsoil that floods produce. Secondary considerations might be production of electrical power and control of the watershed for irrigation. Irrigation and control of flooding lead to increased farm production, a positive economic benefit. The construction process itself would also directly stimulate the local economy through product purchases and employment.

Those are benefits. What are the negative implications—the trade-offs? One obvious trade-off involves the cost of the dam. However, there are other sets of negative features of building such a dam, including the loss of the land, both public and private, that would be flooded by the lake created by the dam. People would have their property seized and have to move. Some of the alternatives would involve whether to build the dam at all or, if so, what size dam to build, including the amount of water to be held (which determines the amount of land to be given up for the watershed). In the policy process one either directly compares these positive and negative implications in a formal cost-benefit ratio or indirectly compares them via the trade-offs that occur in the political process.

Policy science is a field that studies such public problems or choice alternatives. The usual approach is to represent the various choice alternatives mathematically in the form of *models*. We will touch on some of the types of models later in this chapter. The mathematics underlying policy analysis will not, however, be the primary focus of the chapter. A student wishing to gain some further knowledge in this important area is recommended to read one of the good introductory books, such as that by Stokey and Zeckhauser (1978). Our approach here will not be to present the detailed mathematical structures of policy science per se, but rather to focus on what psychology and psychologists can bring to the study of public policy.

Certainly, this is not a new topic for the students who have read this book. Several of the previous chapters have focused on the relationship of psychology to particular kinds of public policies. Chapter 5 on psychology and health has a good deal to say about national public health policy in the United States. Chapters 11 on consumer psychology, 12 on environmental psychology, and 13 on psychology and the law all discuss the potential contributions of psychologists to the understanding and study of particular sorts of public policies. This chapter can be considered a supplement to those, discussing at a more general level the contributions of psychology and psychologists to public policy.

■ WHAT PSYCHOLOGISTS OFFER TO PUBLIC POLICY

In our discussion of public policy we want to emphasize both the analysis of policy and the making of policy. Policy makers would include the U.S. Congress, state legislatures, governors, mayors, heads of federal and state agencies, and the like. These are people who both make decisions regarding new public policies and resist changing the old public policies. Policy analysis is a research oriented and analytic enterprise designed to lay out public policy alternatives for the future and to analyze the often unintended consequences of current public policies. What do psychologists bring to these two types of roles?

Some things that psychologists could offer would not make them unique. That is, psychologists are obviously very bright. For example, the graduate record examination scores of entering graduate students in psychology are among the highest in the sciences. Psychologists are also very well trained in scientific method, particularly in the experimental method. Every psychologist has a good deal of practical experience in research prior to obtaining the Ph.D. Psychology is also one of the most self-consciously scientific of all sciences (Feyerabend, 1970). That is, we are very self-conscious about clarifying hidden assumptions underlying research and making our theories as explicit as possible. Perhaps this makes psychologists unique. I would like to think so. But whether they are or not, certainly other sciences and the humanities could justifiably make similar claims. That is, their graduates are obviously bright, self-critical, and well trained in scientific or analytic methods.

What distinguishes psychologists from the other fields is that the substance of our field is the understanding of human behavior. It is expertise in human behavior that, in my opinion, makes psychologists needed in policy analysis and policy making. Not all public policies need some great understanding of human behavior to be considered. Nonetheless there are many that do, such as health, mental health, and welfare, but also less obvious policies such as defense or housing. Our further discussion in this chapter will emphasize that part of public policies in which advanced understanding of human behavior would be advantageous.

What are the primary roles for psychologists in public policy?

Administration ▪ If psychologists have something unique to offer in the study and implementation of public policy, what are the contexts or ways in which it could be done? In other words, what are the roles psychologists could play? There are several. One role is *administration* of policy. There is a huge number of such administrative and leadership roles in the cities, states, and federal government that someone with an experts' knowledge in human behavior could usefully fill. For example, Chapters 6, 7, and 8 detail the involvement of psychologists in education and instruction. There are a large number of psychologists in high-level positions in the National Institute of Education, the U.S. Office of Education, and state educational planning units. Over the years, psychologists have also been very involved in university administration and, at various times, have occupied the presidencies of such universities as Yale, Chicago, Columbia, Kansas, and the University of California at Berkeley and San Diego.

Mental health administration is another area where psychologists could have much to offer. Psychologists have been deputy directors of both the National Institute of Mental Health and the National Institute of Child Health and Human Development, and a large number of psychologists serve on the staff of those institutes. Psychologists have been involved with state mental health program administration, and a number of state mental health program directors have been or are psychologists. Probably hundreds of psychologists have been directors of community mental health centers across the country.

Psychologists have also been involved more generally in the administration of science policy. A psychologist was formerly the Director of the National Science Foundation, for example. Another is currently in the Office of Science and Technology Policy, the administrative arm of the President's science advisor. A number of psychologists serve in the Office of Management and Budget and recently one was in charge of the budgets for all health and mental health in the federal budget. There is also a growing section of the Office of Management and Budget dealing with evaluation research, disproportionately staffed by psychologists. The Congressional Budget Office also employs a number of psychologists. In the welfare arena, there are a number of research psychologists employed by the Social Security Administration.

Across these diverse fields of education, health, mental health, welfare, and science policy, literally hundreds of psychologists are involved in policy-making administrative roles. I have been involved with both sides of this issue: helping federal and state agencies understand what psychologists could offer in particular administrative roles (and helping to find good psychologists to occupy these roles) and talking to psychologists about the public's need for psychologists in administrative positions. It is my own feeling that public policy needs to be informed about our knowledge of human behavior; it is in the public interest that scientific knowledge about human behavior be used in the analysis and implementation of public policy. Such knowledge can most easily be used in the formation and analysis of existing public policies if at least some psychologists are involved in administering public policy at the national, state, and local levels. Administrative roles for psychologists in these various public arenas will continue to grow and at a fairly rapid rate.

Translation ▪ The word "translation" is meant literally: to translate the findings of psychology in the behavioral sciences into a language easily understood by the educated lay public, including policy makers. This is a very important role. Historians of science tell us that the public's understanding of scientific findings typically is about 20 years out of date. That is, one would expect that typical public knowledge about physics would be based on what was discovered or ascertained in the early to mid-1960s. At minimum, psychology has a similar problem. However, there is a sort of hidden baggage to psychology that makes public understanding of our science much more difficult to accomplish. What the public typically understands about psychological science is not just what we discovered 20 years ago. Rather, the public presentation of psychology is often seriously misleading. A good deal of what one absorbs from magazines, newspapers, or television neither represents the best nor even the most reliable findings of psychological science.

The reader of this volume will already have had some contact with the science of psychology, perhaps an introductory course. Compare what you learned there with what you see and hear in the public media. Much of the latter is trivial, sometimes inaccurate, and sensation-seeking. However, the fads are eye catching and newsworthy, and seem to interfere with the public's acceptance and utilization of psychological research. Lively, but solidly based science writing is a national need, particularly in the social and behavioral sciences. As Bevan (1976) has said, a neglected role ". . .is that of the skillful integrator and interpreter of science. In the arts and humanities, this is a highly esteemed role, as evidenced by the respect shown great musical performers, great literary critics, great legal scholars, and authors of leading text books in history, economics, political science and the law" (p. 490).

This field is more open than you might think. When I was executive officer of the American Psychological Association (1975–1979), I found that the annual meeting of the American Psychological Association was considered by others to be a big media event. Over 1200 journalists and TV people would register at the convention and a great deal of time and effort was spent in assisting them in developing contact with good scientific presentations. Partly from curiosity, I employed a clipping service from which I received copies of articles published in magazines and newspapers around the country that were based on any scientific paper presented at the convention. It became very clear to me that there were probably no more than a half dozen excellent translators of psychological science in the country. When looking for excellence, I looked for articles I thought accurately represented the science of psychology and I also looked for articles that the field of journalism admired. One way you can tell if an article is admired is that it will appear either on the wire services or will be picked up in various papers around the country (often without the original journalist's knowledge). If you look at the overlap of these two groups—consisting of those people who did an excellent job of representing the scientific findings and the science behind it, and in addition wrote in a manner that gained respect from their journalistic colleagues—the number became very small. There are over 50,000 psychologists in the country today, and about half of them regard themselves as having a primary commitment to research. If only six or eight people are doing an excellent job in covering the research produced by 25,000 scientists, a lot is going uncovered, or alternatively, a good deal of it is not being accurately presented in the public press, radio, and television. Of course, one doesn't have to be a scientist to be a good science writer, but certainly the opportunities are there in the behavioral sciences.

Consultation ▪ *Consulting roles* are another method of translating scientific findings into action. A lot of psychologists actively consult with corporations and various levels of government. Sometimes the role consists of being involved in the decision-making process so that expertise in human behavior can be effectively used. Indeed, I know of one person who was offered a job in the state department, in which she could do essentially whatever research she liked, as long as she was available as a consultant on particular state department decisions. The intent was to have social psychological knowledge available for the variety of decisions and information-gathering actions that the state department had to initiate. Such resource people are used by a variety of agencies. Apparently the Secret Service is currently moving to employ behavioral science findings more actively. They are very interested in knowledge relating to terrorism and hostage-taking, and in gaining a better sense of how a deranged potential assassin might think about possible public opportunities. In a sense, all of these resident consultant roles are roles that involve the translation of behavioral science findings into the policy-making or decision-making process; undoubtedly, these roles will increase in the future.

Research ▪ We want to discuss research roles more completely later and wish now only to note that research is a primary role for psychologists in public policy. Thus, four important roles that psychologists could play in public policy are the administration of policy (including policy making), the translation of behavioral science findings relevant to public policy, expert consultation regarding alternative policies, and direct research into policy issues and policy alternatives.

Current approaches to the study of public policy

Policy science ▪ *Policy science* represents an interdisciplinary effort to understand and study public policy. We emphasize interdisciplinary, because it is not the purview of any particular discipline. However, if one had to mention the disciplines that were most influential within the policy sciences, they would have to be economics and computer science (or more specifically operations research). The issues are very complex and it is difficult to say only a little about them as a part of this chapter. However, one can point to some threads that go through a good part of policy sciences.

One theme is the computer simulation of current policies or alternative policies. This is a method of trying to simplify a very complex setting in a systematic way. For example, suppose one would try to understand the effect of the amount of money available in the market on long-term interest rates for loans. In studying the various correlations of these two events over time and noting other events that were going on at the same time, one could make a theoretical statement of what the relationship appeared to be. The computer simulation is one step further along in the scientific process. One tries to describe in computer language the basic assumptions and logical steps that the theory is attempting to specify. By putting this hypothetical theoretical process on the computer, one can develop a very fine-grained analysis of the process over time. Partly, computer simulation forces the policy scientists to specify his or her theory in great detail. Alternatively, once one has the computer simulation— the model—and the data on the machine, one can then look at what the effects of alternative policies might be.

Computer simulation is partly an approach to an intellectual problem and partly a method that one can use in other approaches. For example, cost-benefit analysis is a typical approach to studying public policy alternatives. One attempts to state in financial terms what the various costs of a potential policy are and what the full financial benefits of the policy would be. One tries to construct alternative cost-benefit ratios for alternative policies. Since public policies are typically extremely complex, the computer is a valuable aid in constructing these analyses.

There is also a considerable body of research relating to what is called preference analysis (or attribute analysis). This approach to problems attempts to determine systematically what the public's preferences for particular policy alternatives are, or more typically, what policy makers' preferences are for particular policy alternatives.

While this presentation of policy science has been brief enough to run the risk of being misleading, there are important issues worth noting in psychology's relationship to policy science. First, policy science has been developing for some time without the involvement of psychologists. This lack of involvement has led to a corresponding lack of integration of psychological findings with the technical field of policy science. Second, since policy science is an interdisciplinary field, there are opportunities in it for psychologists to contribute their knowledge of human behavior.

Evaluation research ▪ *Evaluation research* is a field oriented toward assessing the effectiveness of social programs or social actions. Obviously related to the policy sciences, it leans less on economics and mathematical decision theory. It emphasizes less the comparison of public policy alternative choices and more the evaluation of current practices.

Two main approaches to evaluation are process and outcome research. Process research tries to evaluate the implementation of a program or the way it is conducted. For example, two of the reasons underlying the formation of the Community Mental Health Center (CMHC) system were to aid deinstitutionalized patients from state hospitals and to provide outpatient care that is affordable to the ordinary citizen. Evaluation research might be directed to answering whether these two goals have been successfully implemented. One might simply count the proportion of deinstitutionalized patients who make contact with a CMHC. For the second goal one might look at the distribution of clients as a function of family income (do poorer citizens *use* the CMHCs?). This process research would, in fact, yield mixed results. Until recently, CMHCs made little contact with deinstitutionalized patients; however, the clients CMHCs do treat are disproportionately from the less-wealthy citizen categories (see Kiesler, 1980a,b).

Outcome research, on the other hand, emphasizes the effectiveness or cost-effectiveness of the program. Here, we would ask about the impact of services rendered in CMHCs. Do the clients show improvement? Are the problems they bring to the therapeutic setting ameliorated? Again the data are mixed. A recent report by the National Institute of Mental Health showed that CMHCs handled 29 percent of the nation's outpatient episodes at 4 percent of the total mental health cost. So the relative costs of the services delivered seems very reasonable, but what about their impact on patients? Surprisingly, little research has been carried out regarding the effectiveness of the treatment received (partly because the poorer patients have few treatment alternatives for comparisons).

Unlike the policy sciences, psychologists have been very involved in evaluation research. One is more likely to see typical methods and statistics used in evaluation research taught in graduate departments of psychology than those of policy science.

Evaluation research is very broad in terms of the social programs it has been or could be involved in. A brief glimpse of the field can be conveyed by some of the chapter titles in volumes 1 & 2 of the *Evaluation Studies Review Annual* (Glass, 1976; Guttentag, 1977): the economic costs and returns to educational television; a public school voucher demonstration; recent trends in school integration; trends in alcohol consumption and associated illnesses; the economic returns to increased educational spending; the effectiveness of drinking-and-driving legislation in Sweden and Norway; the impact of four possible areas of federal intervention in higher education; work release and recidivism; and the impact of employment and training programs.

Evaluation research as a field continues to grow and psychologists are increasingly involved in it. One can see by the diversity of the topics above that the possible uses and applications of evaluation research are virtually limitless.

Given that psychologists have not been as involved as they might be in formal public policy research, what would motivate a psychologist to become involved, and what would psychology have to offer to the study of public policy?

■ WHAT PSYCHOLOGISTS OFFER TO THE STUDY OF PUBLIC POLICY

The synthesis of information

If it is true that psychologists have not been much involved in the study of public policy, then it must also be true that what psychologists know must not have been very involved either. One thing that they can offer perhaps is a better knowledge base in the consideration of alternative public policies. For example, community action programs were devised to get the public more interested in a variety of public programs and to become more motivated both to support them and volunteer to help them. It is probably true that some of the underlying philosophy in the development of those programs was conservative.* The philosophy says that too much government is bad government, that citizens should undertake more public action and not wait for the federal government to do it or to pay for it, and that we should revert to an older time when neighbors helped each other. Community Action Programs were to some extent a reflection of this philosophy—to take the pressure off federally financed programs and to put more of the responsibility for such programs on the voluntary efforts of ordinary citizens. If I as a social psychologist had been sitting in on the original discussions of these programs as a public policy alternative, I think I might have had something to contribute. My role would have been to point out that it is true that people who volunteer to perform some action become more committed to it; in the process they develop positive attitudes about it and thereby enhance the possibility that they will be involved in such programs in the future. Such research has been very typical in social psychology and goes back to the early work of Kurt Lewin in the 1930s. Consequently I would have been able to assure policy makers that indeed the basic premises that they were assuming to be true had been verified in research. On the other hand I could have pointed out certain risks. In all of that research, which is related to decision making, public commitment, and involvement with group goals, what the research subject is deciding to act upon is subtly manipulated in the group context. Thus, in that research, what the person decided to do was not an issue; the research concerned the outcomes of such decisions, rather than which decision a person might reach. However, community action programs tended to be social welfare programs. Because of that, the citizens who were likely to be involved in them were also ones who were relatively unlikely to endorse the conservative philosophy of the administration. Thus, I would have said that it is very likely that what they chose to do will be at variance with the administration, and therefore people will become committed to, have positive attitudes about, and be more likely to act in the future in ways quite contrary to what the administration was trying to accomplish.

Indeed, this imagined scenario is more or less what happened. The administration was very startled to find citizen groups coming out of the community action programs that were not only disagreeing with the federal government but suing them to accomplish their goals. What the administration had done, in essence, was to crystallize its own opposition.

---

*Actually, community action programs have been, at one time or another, supported by both liberals and conservatives in the Congress and White House. The example stresses the conservatives' distress with the outcomes of the programs.

None of this should be taken to imply that either side is correct. This particular scenario happens to be very value laden, and values are always implicitly with us in public policy discussions, as we shall talk more about below. The point I wanted to stress in this example is that inadequate knowledge about the behavioral science base led to a public policy decision that was doomed from the beginning (doomed, at least, from the perspective of the policy maker). A more informed sense of psychological science would have been helpful.

Dynamic versus static preferences

In the study of preferences in public policy, typically one looks at what other people want to have happen. Those other people can be policy makers, influential people, law makers, or the ordinary citizen. Consequently when looking at the preferences for particular public policies, we are looking at *static preferences*—preferences that are more or less unchanging. These preferences reflect whatever biases or knowledge the people have who are being surveyed. That knowledge may be inaccurate or years out of date. Let me give you an example. I have recently carried out a research program investigating various aspects of mental hospitalization (Kiesler, 1982a,b). In my review of the literature on this, I conclude that there are various techniques for treating seriously disturbed people outside of a mental hospital more effectively and less expensively than in a mental hospital. This would suggest a change in public policy toward the development and funding of alternative modes of care. Further, one would look at this research closely to attempt to determine which particular modes of care seem most promising and which particular alternative programs might be best developed to use them.

Now, suppose that we do a preference analysis of the policy opinions of law makers and citizens. They might be asked general questions in the area of mental health, but they are probably not aware of up-to-date knowledge on treating seriously disturbed people outside of a mental hospital. They would probably not be enthusiastic about the funding of alternative care mechanisms and programs and would likely be much more strongly in favor of continued and perhaps even increased funding for mental hospitals. When we assess anybody's opinion about alternative public policies, ranging from lay citizens to the President of the United States, we are assessing an imperfect knowledge base. In a sense, the assumptions people have formed implicitly in expressing the opinion never become explicit. Psychology, as well as other behavioral sciences, can help to make more of the cutting edge of science findings available when discussing public policy alternatives. Thus, *dynamic preferences* should also be assessed; they are those preferences that are open to change or have the potential for change. These human sciences can speak to the point about the capacity of human beings for particular sorts of change and to speak to well-developed research findings that show one method or type of program would be more effective than another.

The study of policy strategies

Often in policy formation, the policy makers or decision makers can agree on a goal, without being aware of public actions that might accomplish the goal. For example, during World War II the federal government was concerned with the potential effects of propaganda on our soldiers and citizens. There was a wide-scale campaign conducted during the war in an attempt to make the soldiers and the citizens more resistant to foreign propaganda. The general technique to do this was to expose particular methods of propaganda, such as "the big lie" technique. The campaign conducted by our government was quite extensive. Unfortunately, research subsequently carried out indicated that this general approach to increasing the resistance of the citizens to propaganda simply did not work. Thus, in a very real sense, the goal was never reached because the policy strategy adopted was totally ineffective. Had we done some policy research instead to find out what sorts of techniques are effective in increasing one's resistance to propaganda, the policy strategy implemented would have been much more effective.

Psychology can help policy makers to discover which public actions would be effective in reaching publicly agreed-upon goals. As another example, I was once involved as an undergraduate in a research team related to the building of the Mackinac bridge to connect southern with northern Michigan. The basic problem presented to the research team was to discover better ways to affect traffic flow on the bridge when it was completed. What the policy people wanted was to vary the number of lanes going in each direction as a function of how heavy the traffic was. They wanted to have lights put on the bridge that would clearly indicate to people not to go in certain lanes but to proceed in others. The important aspect of this was to have directional signals that people would not respond to by stopping or even slowing down very much. For example, an old calculation used in the theory of traffic flow was that if cars are proceeding at a normal space apart and a given car slows ten miles per hour (from 55 mph to 45 mph, say), each car behind it will be slowing even more to accommodate conservatively to the decrease in speed. Given this extra accommodation, the seventh car in line will actually stop. This behavior would increase the likelihood of accidents on the bridge; the use of directional lights on the bridge was to avoid such events.

We started by designing a very large number of potential signals of varying shapes and colors.* We then took all of these signals into the laboratory and pretested large groups of people asking them to respond to the signals, telling us how they would interpret them if they saw them on a road. From this analysis it was clear to us that red X's and green →'s seemed to produce the clearest desired responses. That is, the green arrow obviously indicated that one could proceed in that lane. Indeed, the response to the green arrow was even better

---

*All of this research I carried out under the direction of Terrence Allen of Michigan State University.

than the ordinary green traffic signal (circle), which some people thought might change, and hence, would slow down or proceed cautiously. The more important signal was the red X, because a response of stopping or slowing quickly was very dangerous. However, our laboratory data indicated that people uniformly interpreted the red X not as a signal either for caution or stopping, but rather that the lane should not be driven on at all. A larger proportion of people said they would change lanes seeing that signal than for any other signal that we had devised. Consequently we suggested those signals to the state of Michigan; prototypes were built and installed on the bridge.

Prior to the actual formal opening of the bridge, we did field studies on the bridge itself, opening the bridge for certain periods of time, putting some barriers on particular lanes, and testing drivers' response to the signals. By doing this in advance of the public openings and only for short periods of time, traffic was very light and our tests could be carried out safely. We measured the time and the distance it took any particular car to respond to the signal. In addition we were very interested if anybody would stop after seeing the red X (none ever did). From these pragmatic field studies, we were able to ascertain that the results indicated by the laboratory research were valid for the field as well, and that the signals were indeed very safe. People responded as hoped for. This is a good example of pragmatic research in which the psychologist involved (and we were all psychologists) accepted the goals of the policy makers and merely did the research for the most effective means of reaching the goals. It is also a good example that such research can be very cost-effective. You can find numerous similar examples in this textbook.

The effects of social conditions

The basic question of this area is which parts of human behavior can be changed by external incentives and which parts are directly a function of the conditions in which the individual finds himself or herself. Research in social psychology has indicated that we tend to attribute the causes of a person's behavior to attributes of the person rather than to conditions in which the person finds himself or herself. This is a tendency that Congressman William Ryan once called "blaming the victim" in a well-known book. In this view, the poor are poor because they are lazy and not because environmental conditions inhibit their ability to respond. When one adopts this view, then one would not be in favor of public policies that would, say, offer incentives for job training, or provide better tax breaks such as a negative income tax for the poor. Why? In the former case, the poor presumably would not respond favorably to job training opportunities, because of the very reasons they are poor. In the latter case, there is no sense in this view in giving them more money since they wouldn't spend it in socially desirable ways. Indeed, congressmen throughout the decades have voted against many programs for the poor on the basis that the cause of poverty is in the individual, not in the social conditions surrounding poverty.

There was a large social experiment of a potential policy called the negative income tax during the Nixon years (Haveman & Watts, 1976). It is a good example of an effective public policy gone awry through political action. The basic notion was to feed money directly back to the poor by giving them an income tax refund that exceeded the amount that they had paid in. More specifically, in the New Jersey experiment, 1357 families participated, of which 622 formed the control group. There were several experimental variations, but in general families were guaranteed a certain income during a four-year period. They received payments averaging about $100.00 every four weeks. The plan was graduated such that the more a family earned working, the less it received from the plan (but on a percentage basis rather than a one-to-one ratio). The ratio varied from 30 percent to 70 percent across experimental conditions. Political controversy swirled around whether this money would be put to good use by the poor. Some of the arguments used in Congress and in the Executive Branch were much like those outlined above. The arguments against the negative income tax were that the poor would not use the money to improve their lives and the lives of their children, but would "blow it" on non-essentials. Further, people argued that it provided a disincentive for working, since the payment the poor received would be reduced somewhat for additional money earned.

The New Jersey negative income tax experiment was conducted over a four-year period. The data are reasonably clear: the recipients of the extra money used it for food, for clothes, and for other household items. In short, they definitely did not "blow it." People also did not reduce the number of hours per week that they worked. If anything, there was a slight tendency to increase hours worked. In spite of the data of the social experiment being very clear, there was still great resistance in the Congress to implementing the negative income tax. Indeed, the policy never was implemented.

Research can be a valuable aid in determining the most effective way to implement a policy. However, it does not guarantee that the policy will be implemented. This is a part of a research area called knowledge use and knowledge utilization. Many psychologists and other behavioral scientists are involved in this area in which people attempt to discover what the underlying processes are that lead certain scientific information to be used in policy formation and other information not to be used.

A change of values maintaining current policies

Often particular public policies are supported by the values or the opinions of the citizens in ways that inhibit the change of ineffective or outmoded policies. The negative income tax described above is one good example in which a potentially effective new policy was undercut by an invalid public opinion about potential outcomes of the policy. Inaccurate or misleading assumptions about causes and effects of human behavior can be seen intertwined in various other current national policies. Mental hospitalization is one. Various data suggest there are more effective and less expensive techniques of treating people outside of hospitals (Kiesler, 1982b), as well as new techniques for getting people out even when they have been there a very long time (e.g., Paul & Lentz, 1977). Essentially no new public policy initiatives have been designed to capitalize on these data. The notion of mental hospitalization is ingrained in our society and the public seems to support, at least implicitly, its continuation. Why? One possible reason is that the population also regards the mentally ill as dangerous and unpredictable and the mental hospital is one place to get them out of our sight and to be reassured that they do not constitute a personal danger to us. Therefore, changes in public policy will be very difficult. The resistance of the public and policy makers to enlightened and well documented alternative policy strategies is a topic worthy of considerable investigation in itself (Kiesler, 1981).

Implicit assumptions regarding human behavior and current policy

In most of our public policies that affect human beings, we make some implicit assumptions about human behavior. Some of these assumptions have been discussed before. Think of the laws and policies that we have that make some assumptions about why people do well or badly in school, why they are poor, why some teenagers become pregnant and not others, why people become mentally ill, and the like. In most cases the assumptions made should be the topic of research because research might lead us to have more effective and enlightened public policy. In the Congress and in various state legislatures, for example, there has been extensive debate regarding teenage pregnancy—an increasingly important national problem. Related to this public policy debate are the discussions we hold about teaching human sexuality or contraception in high school. One side of this public debate implicitly assumes (sometimes explicitly) that discussion about human sexuality or contraception increases one's desire or propensity to have a sexual relationship. That side does not want to have such courses because it would only make the problem worse in their view. But such implicit assumptions are often empirical questions, and can be researched as such. This set of problems is an interesting psychological one, because often we find that the empirical questions that are implicitly raised in the discussion will not decide the issue one way or another. The implicit assumptions that people are making are only reflecting more central values that are extremely resistant to change. Thus, clear evidence that courses on human sexuality and contraception decrease teenage pregnancy probably will not change the tenor of the discussion of whether to have such courses.

We have described some ways in which psychologists can make significant contributions to public policy. As mentioned, this is less a specialty in psychology than it is an interdisciplinary problem-focused effort to which psychologists can contribute. However, the contribution that they might make is an extremely important one and well worth considering for the budding student of psychology. If one were to be a psychologist with an interest in public policy, what kinds of background, training, and intellectual tools would one need to make a significant contribution?

■ PREPARATION FOR WORK IN PUBLIC POLICY

We assume here that the student considering this alternative is intending to go to graduate school in psychology with the usual training and background that implies. That includes four or five years of graduate study in psychology, along with extensive laboratory or other research experience, and a heavy course in statistical methods and research design. However, one would need more than this in order to make a reasonable contribution to the study of public policy.

Public policy is an interdisciplinary field. Consequently one needs to know something about the other fields that contribute to it—in particular, this means some study in economics, sociology, epidemiology, and political science. Some of this work would be taken at the undergraduate level where one becomes at least accustomed to the terminology and methods of the various fields. In addition, some other course work could be taken as one proceeds along in graduate school. Many graduate programs in psychology require minors outside of psychology and this requirement can effectively be met by an organized program of interdisciplinary training and coursework.

Some further training in statistics and methodology would be needed outside that typically taught in psychology. In particular, calculus and differential equations are important as well as some other higher mathematics. Computer simulation would be helpful (at my university the study of computer simulation is a requirement for graduate study in psychology). Some background in the general approach of the policy sciences to policy research would be important. This would include various kinds of modeling techniques, such as decision analysis, preference analysis, and the like.

Some practical experience is important as well in the study of public policy, particularly some first-hand experience in a setting stressing policy formation and change. There are several post-doctoral programs related to public policy, for example, a year of experience in a pragmatic setting in Washington. Taking a position in some part of the administrative policy hierarchy in Washington or a state capital or even a large city could be a helpful practical experience.

From the perspective of a student reading this book, this may sound like an onerous and lengthy preparation for a career. It is certainly not a simple one. However, the career implied here would certainly be an interesting and exciting one. This set of research problems is among the more important that we have as a country. There are not now very many departments of psychology in the country that offer general training in policy research, other than that specifically related to such specialties as engineering psychology, community psychology, or organizational psychology. Consequently any student electing to embark on such a career would probably have to take more initiative than for other careers in psychology.

However, the decision to specialize in this area does not have to be an abrupt one at all. I have described above a few courses that you should be taking at an undergraduate level. A few more at the graduate level in other fields would allow you to get some sense of how well this specialty matched up with your strengths and interests. In short there are some very low cost ways to test the strength of your interest without making a formal commitment to a specific career, other than general psychology. Further, some of these courses that I have suggested can be important sets of knowledge for other applied specialties described in this volume. Indeed, the best advice to a student is to test out a very broad intellectual net before deciding on any particular specialty.

■ SUGGESTED READINGS

Bevan, W. (1979). The sound of the wind that's blowing. *American Psychologist, 31,* 481–491.

This article is a readable discussion of science policy questions for psychology. It would be interesting and appropriate to an advanced undergraduate student.

Kiesler, C. A. (1980). Mental health policy as a field of inquiry for psychology. *American Psychologist, 35,* 1066–1080.

This article reviews issues in mental health policy and discusses research questions addressing these issues. The field of mental health policy as a potential field of study for psychologists is emphasized.

Kiesler, C. A. (1980). Psychology and public policy. In L. Bickman (Ed.), *Applied Social Psychology Annual* (Vol. 1). Beverly Hills, CA: Sage.

This non-technical discussion of the relationship of psychology to public policy would be informative and stimulating to interested undergraduate or graduate students.

U N I T   V   **APPLIED PSYCHOLOGY: TRANSITION TO THE FUTURE**

The previous chapters in this text have described the work of many different specialties in psychology. The chapter in this unit takes a different focus on applied psychology, namely issues related to the practice of psychology. No matter what specialty a psychologist identifies with, he or she practices (completes research, obtains funding, conducts psychotherapy, develops and implements industrial interventions, provides career counseling, and so on) in a larger context, namely the role of psychology within the United States. This context contains several developments that are important to any psychologist. An example of such a development would be the necessity for psychologists to obtain licensure to practice psychology.

The chapter in this unit discusses many issues related to this broader theme, the practice of psychology in the United States. It overviews the current and future job market for psychologists. It discusses many issues of applied psychology that are being addressed by professional organizations, and it directly considers an issue that has been indirectly touched upon in many chapters, namely the methods by which we can assure the quality of psychological services which are delivered in various settings. This chapter will provide a different focus to many of the specialties that have been previously presented by considering the work of those specialties within a larger context.

RICHARD KILBURG

MARK R. GINSBERG

MARY JANSEN

ELIZABETH MEID

SHARON SHUEMAN

CURRENT ISSUES AND FUTURE TRENDS IN APPLIED PSYCHOLOGY

■ OVERVIEW

One chooses a career in a particular profession, trade, or field for several major reasons. Most importantly, the context of the work performed should be interesting and give the individual a sense of self-worth, personal identity, and achievement. If this characteristic is present, most people are able to make a long-term, personal commitment to a particular career. Next, the financial rewards of the work should be sufficient so as to allow one to be self-supporting and to develop a capacity for long-term economic stability. Finally, the profession, trade, or field should offer sufficient opportunities so that a variety of flexible and creative career paths is possible.

The previous chapters of this book have described many of the major sub-areas of applied psychology, provided a general description of what psychologists do in those areas, and given some insight into the problems and prospects in each area. The purposes of this chapter are somewhat different. In it, we will attempt to provide a general review of many of the trends and issues that confront the whole profession of psychology, with an emphasis upon psychology in health care, education, and industry. We will focus on competitive and regulatory problems, reviewing developments at the federal and state level as well as initiatives from within the profession itself.

Where the jobs are: The major markets for psychological services

The November, 1981 issue of the *American Psychologist* was devoted entirely to a comprehensive presentation of the human resources data currently available about psychologists. For our purposes, several important themes were discussed in this volume.

Table 15.1 presents the data from Stapp and Fulcher (1981) on the employment status of doctoral-level American Psychological Association members by

TABLE 15.1 Employment Status of Doctoral-Level APA Members by Sex, Race/Ethnicity, and Specialty Area

Sex, race/ethnicity, and specialty area	Employed full-time		Employed part-time		Unemployed, seeking		Unemployed, not seeking		Retired		Not specified		Total weighted respondents (100%)	(Unweighted N)
	N	(%)	N	(%)	N	(%)	N	(%)	N	(%)	N	(%)	N	
Total doctoral-level respondents	21,432	(86.9)	1,745	(7.1)	259	(1.0)	205	(0.8)	855	(3.5)	157	(0.6)	24,653	(5,076)
Sex														
Men	16,759	(91.0)	686	(3.7)	135	(0.7)	94	(0.5)	631	(3.4)	118	(0.6)	18,424	(3,127)
Women	4,673	(75.0)	1,059	(17.0)	123	(2.0)	111	(1.8)	224	(3.6)	39	(0.6)	6,229	(1,949)
Race/ethnicity														
White	20,492	(86.8)	1,711	(7.2)	249	(1.1)	200	(0.8)	837	(3.5)	126	(0.5)	23,614	(4,551)
Black	259	(93.7)	6	(2.2)	0	(0.0)	5	(1.7)	7	(2.5)	0	(0.0)	276	(186)
Hispanic	167	(90.5)	17	(9.0)	1	(0.5)	0	(0.0)	0	(0.0)	0	(0.0)	185	(92)
Asian	250	(96.9)	5	(2.0)	2	(0.8)	0	(0.0)	1	(0.4)	0	(0.0)	258	(167)
American Indian	45	(97.8)	1	(2.2)	0	(0.0)	0	(0.0)	0	(0.0)	0	(0.0)	46	(21)
Not specified	219	(80.0)	6	(2.0)	7	(2.6)	0	(0.0)	11	(4.0)	31	(11.5)	274	(59)
Specialty area														
Clinical	9,444	(85.5)	1,141	(10.3)	107	(1.0)	71	(0.6)	220	(2.0)	65	(0.6)	11,048	(2,300)
Cognitive	159	(88.2)	8	(4.4)	3	(1.4)	0	(0.0)	4	(2.1)	7	(3.9)	181	(32)
Community	313	(87.1)	11	(3.0)	14	(3.8)	9	(2.5)	13	(3.6)	0	(0.0)	360	(74)
Comparative	77	(95.8)	3	(4.2)	0	(0.0)	0	(0.0)	0	(0.0)	0	(0.0)	80	(14)

Counseling	2,377 (85.8)	168 (6.1)	51 (1.8)	19 (0.7)	133 (4.8)	22 (0.8)	2,770 (595)
Developmental	854 (87.1)	63 (6.5)	12 (1.2)	9 (0.9)	36 (3.6)	7 (0.7)	981 (237)
Educational	1,187 (89.2)	19 (1.4)	5 (0.4)	14 (1.0)	101 (7.6)	6 (0.4)	1,331 (282)
Engineering	188 (94.2)	0 (0.0)	0 (0.0)	3 (1.3)	9 (4.5)	0 (0.0)	199 (29)
Experimental	1,274 (91.4)	38 (2.7)	16 (1.1)	7 (0.5)	55 (4.0)	4 (0.3)	1,395 (249)
General	216 (81.7)	16 (5.9)	0 (0.0)	7 (2.7)	26 (9.8)	0 (0.0)	264 (47)
Industrial/organizational	1,200 (88.4)	36 (2.7)	7 (0.5)	7 (0.5)	88 (6.4)	19 (1.4)	1,358 (236)
Personality	347 (81.8)	21 (5.0)	7 (1.6)	17 (4.1)	32 (7.4)	0 (0.0)	425 (81)
Physiological	283 (92.4)	12 (3.8)	0 (0.0)	4 (1.2)	0 (0.0)	8 (2.6)	306 (63)
Psycholinguistics	57 (92.5)	5 (7.5)	0 (0.0)	0 (0.0)	0 (0.0)	0 (0.0)	62 (13)
Psychometrics	152 (90.7)	6 (3.5)	2 (1.2)	0 (0.0)	8 (4.6)	0 (0.0)	167 (40)
Psychopharmacology	73 (100.0)	0 (0.0)	0 (0.0)	0 (0.0)	0 (0.0)	0 (0.0)	73 (11)
Quantitative	173 (98.6)	0 (0.0)	0 (0.0)	3 (1.4)	0 (0.0)	0 (0.0)	176 (33)
School	975 (89.8)	60 (5.5)	7 (0.6)	12 (1.1)	33 (3.0)	0 (0.0)	1,086 (259)
Social	1,052 (91.4)	41 (3.6)	10 (0.9)	17 (1.4)	31 (2.7)	0 (0.0)	1,151 (288)
Systems/history/methods	72 (88.9)	0 (0.0)	0 (0.0)	0 (0.0)	9 (11.1)	0 (0.0)	81 (13)
Other, in psychology	502 (82.1)	59 (9.6)	19 (3.1)	5 (0.7)	20 (3.3)	7 (1.1)	612 (128)
Other, not in psychology	387 (84.9)	28 (6.0)	0 (0.0)	3 (0.6)	31 (6.8)	8 (1.8)	456 (90)
Not specified	70 (74.0)	11 (11.7)	0 (0.0)	0 (0.0)	9 (9.5)	5 (4.8)	95 (22)

Note: Row percentages are given. The application of fractional weights and rounding may result in total percentages and N's that differ slightly from the sums of subgroup percentages and N's. In each case, N's have been rounded to the nearest whole respondent.

Source: This table is from "The employment of APA members" by Stapp, J., and Fulcher, R., 1981, *American Psychologist, 36,* p. 1281. Copyright © 1981 by the American Psychological Association. Reprinted by permission.

sex, race/ethnicity, and specialty area. First, as can be seen, less than 2 percent of the sample reported themselves as being unemployed; 86.9 percent reported being employed full-time, 7.1 percent part-time, and 3.5 percent retired. One can therefore safely conclude that psychologists readily find employment in a wide variety of settings. Second, the same table presents a breakdown of employment by self-reported specialty area. The largest number of psychologists were employed in the areas of clinical, counseling, experimental, industrial/organizational, educational, social, and school psychology. Employment in these fields accounted for approximately 80 percent of the total sample size. When grouped in a slightly different fashion, we can state that the major areas in which psychologists find jobs are education, (including higher, secondary, and elementary settings), health care, and industry. These areas, or markets, provide the vast majority of job opportunities for psychologists. A final point, made by Stapp, Fulcher, Nelson, Pallak, & Wicheriski (1981), is that, despite early predictions of a Ph.D. glut, recent graduates have been able to find meaningful employment in a variety of settings not previously thought suitable for employment of psychologists. Such flexibility and adaptability have become a hallmark of psychologists. This has been summarized neatly by Meredith Crawford, a venerable military psychologist, who has said "Psychologists do their best work when they stick their noses into other people's business." The capacity to use psychological knowledge, skills, and abilities in nearly any conceivable setting is truly the essense of applied psychology. The articles in the special issues of *American Psychologist* edited by VandenBos, Stapp, and Pallak (1981) speak eloquently to these themes.

In a subsequent analysis of some of this information plus additional data, Jansen and Fulcher (1982) provided an overview/estimate of the total dollar value of salaries in the three major markets of psychological services: health care, academic/education, and industry/government. Table 15.2 presents the full-time salaries of doctoral-level members of the APA as of 1979 (the most recent information available) in each of these major markets. As you can see, the sum of the salaries is greatest in the academic area, followed by health and then industry/government, although the mean salary figures are in the reverse order. These figures account for the salaries of approximately 31,000 APA members, or 60 percent of the total membership. The total figure approaches one billion dollars in income for 60 percent of APA members in 1979. Since APA's membership represents a significant percentage of all psychologists in the United States, but by no means all, when the effects of inflation are added to the figures in Table 15.2, we can safely say that currently, psychology in this country is a two-to-four-*billion* dollar business. Projecting from these figures, approximately 40 percent of the business volume is done in academic settings, 40 percent in health care settings, and 20 percent in industrial/governmental and other settings.

TABLE 15.2 Full-Time Salary of Doctoral-Level APA Members as of 1979

Employment setting		Years since doctorate					
		0 – 4	5 – 8	10 – 14	15 – 19	20 or more	All
Academic	$\bar{x}$	$ 19,100	$ 21,490	$ 24,720	$ 28,410	$ 32,350	$ 24,990
	S.D.	5,620	6,400	5,610	6,900	9,620	8,470
	SUM	49,125,000	88,995,000	75,472,000	57,441,000	103,352,000	374,384,000
	N	2,572	4,140	3,054	2,022	3,195	14,982
Health	$\bar{x}$	24,580	30,380	33,890	37,060	40,230	31,980
	S.D.	10,430	13,630	14,490	17,240	17,360	15,120
	SUM	59,027,000	129,454,000	70,913,000	37,960,000	75,324,000	372,678,000
	N	2,402	4,261	2,093	1,024	1,872	11,652
Industry, Government, and Other	$\bar{x}$	25,760	29,770	35,410	39,740	45,620	35,220
	S.D.	8,390	9,560	11,030	15,920	15,060	14,170
	SUM	19,214,000	33,333,000	24,954,000	20,318,000	46,908,000	144,728,000
	N	746	1,120	705	511	1,028	4,110
							Totals*
All Settings	$\bar{x}$	22,270	26,440	29,280	32,530	37,010	29,010
	S.D.	8,800	11,430	11,370	13,110	14,370	12,840
	SUM	127,366,000	251,782,000	171,339,000	115,719,000	225,585,000	891,789,000
	N	5,720	9,521	5,851	3,557	6,095	30,744

Note: The N's in this table represent population estimates derived from the application of fractional weights to the number of survey respondents. The use of fractional weights results in total N's that differ slightly from the sums of subgroup N's.

*This represents the cumulative totals for all years and all settings, i.e., for all full-time doctoral-level employed APA members in 1979. Therefore $29,010 is the mean salary, 12,840 is the S.D., $891,789,000 is the total salary of all full-time doctoral-level employed APA members in 1979 based on an N of 30,744.

Source: This table is from Jansen, M., & Fulcher, R. Salaries of doctoral level psychologists. Agenda of the Board of Professional Affairs of the American Psychological Association meeting, February 19–21, 1982.

397

These data provide a rough estimate of the economic size and scope of the psychological profession, some idea as to where the majority of psychologists are employed, and what size salaries they are making. Clearly, it is a sprawling and complex enterprise with many challenges and a wide variety of opportunities. In the remainder of this section of this chapter, we would like to touch upon the major trends in each of these three segments of the psychology market.

Trends in education

Traditionally, education has represented the largest market for psychological services. For purposes of discussion, we include higher education (junior colleges, four-year colleges, and graduate universities), secondary, and elementary schools in this category. For decades, psychology has participated in the enormous growth of this country's educational system. Psychologists with doctoral degrees were, for the most part, completely absorbed by colleges and universities. Those individuals who sought employment off campus did so usually out of personal preference. Because there were more positions than people to fill them, in some institutions persons with master's degrees in psychology were hired because of the lack of people with doctoral degrees. Because of the shortages, most practitioners in secondary and elementary schools possessed a master's degree in psychology, and some not even that degree.

Recently, this traditional picture has been altered radically. College and university departments have become largely a market to replace retiring senior faculty members, and there are many applicants for each vacancy. A few enterprising departments have developed new program areas, and some universities with access to private resources are still expanding. However, in general, colleges and universities face a shortage of resources, a middle-aged and largely tenured faculty, equal opportunity employment pressures to correct past discriminatory practices, and declining enrollments of students. Psychology is still one of the most popular undergraduate majors and graduate programs continue to operate well, but the general picture is quite mixed, with considerable economic pressure existing in a large number of programs. Federal and state support for education has been declining, as the burden of regulations regarding employment, use of human and animal subjects in research, and requirements for paper documentation of administrative details have simultaneously increased. Briefly then, the employment picture for psychology in higher education continues to be fairly positive, but there are challenging problems to be faced.

In elementary and secondary education, the largest number of employed practitioners still possess the master's degree. The squeeze on financial resources as well as the problems produced by declining enrollments also are present here. However, due largely to the impact of the federal "Education for All Handicapped Children Act," or Public Law 14-142, which requires multidisciplinary evaluations of children, the number of jobs for psychological practitioners has increased dramatically during the past decade. Simultaneously, a large number of other behaviorally based professions have emerged to provide part of the services psychologists are trained to do. For example, social workers and counselors evaluate and treat children with behavioral problems. Also, special educators and other specialists in reading, mathematics, and so on provide evaluation and remediation services. Increasingly, legal and administrative requirements have led to the development of formal systems of accountability. New laws have been created to guarantee students and parents access to student records. And, legal restrictions on the use of psychological tests have created a problem when courts have ordered what tests should and should not be administered. It seems that in educational settings, the future will continue to hold much of the same level of complexity. Psychology will need to define its services clearly, compete for jobs, and use skills and abilities derived from its knowledge base on behalf of clients.

Trends in health care

The largest expansion in markets for psychological services has come in the health care industry. Since World War II, over 25,000 clinical and counseling psychologists have been trained. The vast majority of these professionals are practicing in health-related settings, where they live and work in an industry that was built largely by and for physicians. While the average American has profited enormously by the health care system, there has also been a price to pay for this structural domination.

To describe the organization and operation of the health care sector of the economy is beyond the scope of this or any other single chapter. Suffice it to say that there is a large body of state and federal law and regulation that provides the framework for health care in this country. These laws and regulations establish institutions in which care is delivered (hospitals, nursing homes, community mental health centers, hospices, etc.), the types of care that can be rendered (usually anything a physician says is appropriate, but a large number of treatments are listed in laws and regulations), who can deliver such services (via licensing and certification laws), and how these services are to be paid for (usually by health insurance and other reimbursement programs provided for by law). At the center of this structure stands the physician who is legally empowered to make decisions in this system and who, through this legal and administrative power, and the institutions it has created, directs the health industry.

For many decades, psychology has struggled to develop its own place as an independent health care profession that can stand beside medicine in the provision of psychological services. It has come a long way in this struggle. As will be detailed later, psychology has had good success in establishing its own legal, regulatory, and financial foundations. In doing so, psychology has had to overcome the opposition of organized medicine, especially psychiatry. More recently, a variety of other behaviorally based helping professions (i.e., counselors, social workers) have worked to modify psychology's legal foundation so as to be included in organized medicine themselves. Increasingly, medicine, psychology, and other health professions are in competition within and through insurance companies, health maintenance organizations, and state and federal governments to determine the future shape of health care in this country.

On the regulatory scene, one fact now towers over everything: the high cost of health care. During the past 20 years, health care has grown to the point that it accounts for almost 10 percent of the United States' gross national product, a figure approaching 300 billion dollars. Nearly every policy maker in the country is now asking how we can continue to pay for these services. A wide variety of proposals are being debated that focus on two major approaches. The first emphasizes increasing competition in the industry as a way of regulating its growth. Various methods of "deregulation" have been proposed that would increase and/or modify the types of organizations and service delivery patterns which would receive payments. In this way, it is hoped that the enormous increases in costs can be contained. The second approach has the same goal, cost containment, but takes a more traditional legal and regulatory route. These proposals would provide ceilings or "caps" on payment schemes and would try to control more directly which organizations and providers would be paid. A related phenomenon is called cost shifting. Providers of services, institutions and professionals alike, state that the costs of providing services to an individual are the same regardless of whether the individual, an insurance company, or a government pays the bill. If anyone reduces or stops paying for part or all of these costs, then either the service will not be delivered or the portion of the costs that was unpaid will be shifted, via various administrative and accounting procedures, to someone or some organization who will pay. Otherwise, the institution or professional goes out of business. Thus, proposals to "cap" payments for services are quite controversial because they usually lead to a great deal of cost shifting. As the nation's population ages and the demand for health services continues to increase, these debates will become sharper and more urgent. However, at the present time no clear direction has been set for this industry.

In the midst of these forces, psychology has continued to assert itself as an independent profession that must be able to receive reimbursement directly, without the intervention of any other profession. As the health industry develops larger and larger organizations that control more resources in the same fashion as other industries, psychology increasingly will need to create a structure of its own in which to practice. Although many individuals have called for this to be done, few concrete steps have been taken to initiate such a development. This is perhaps understandable given the energy that has been focused on basic organizational tasks. As these larger health care corporations begin to dominate more and more of the health market, efforts to build an independent psychology organization that can compete directly and equitably will become more necessary. The overall picture of employment of psychologists in health care is quite optimistic despite the problems that have been discussed.

Trends in industry

Psychologists who work in industry face a dramatically different set of conditions than those in education or health care. Psychology has long been recognized as the dominant behavioral science in industry. Its research and practice bases have contributed significantly to the growth and development of many firms. No other profession has arisen to compete directly with psychology although managers, personnel professionals, and a variety of management consultants have worked their way into major shares in the market. This has all happened with no noticeable decrement in the demand for psychological services. It is one of the areas of psychology where there continues to be an increasing number of jobs. One factor that is having an impact involves a divergence in the types of practice in which psychologists engage. On the one hand, the demand has remained high for traditionally trained scientists who work on testing, assessment, human factors, and a variety of other industrial applications. On the other hand, a growing number of psychologists have been working on decision making, group dynamics, and other human-relations problems. A small but growing segment in this area also overlaps with health care as psychologists provide stress management, employee assistance, and other types of human services in various organizations.

On the regulatory side, the greatest challenge has come from the impact of the civil rights movement on industrial hiring practices. The passage of the Fair Employment Practices Act and the adoption of the Guidelines for Testing in Employment by the Equal Employment Opportunities Commission have brought many changes into industrial practices. For psychology, it has meant new challenges to demonstrate the reliability and validity of their assessment and testing procedures. Such procedures, which are designed to discriminate cheaply and effectively between individuals who are likely to be better performers on the job than others, now must demonstrate that the discrimination is related to how people perform on the job rather than on various demographic characteristics such as ethnicity, sex, or age. This has forced psychologists to go to court in increasing numbers to defend the "job-relatedness" of their assessment procedures.

In general, the market for psychological services in industry remains strong. Traditional areas continue to present job opportunities. In addition, many new markets for applied psychological science are beginning to appear. This is particularly true in such areas as cognition and computerization, robotization of factories and equipment, human decision making, human resource development, and helping organizations to change. It is likely that industry will provide some of the greatest challenges for psychology in the future.

In light of the foregoing, and necessarily brief, review of the chief issues in the major markets for psychological services, we would now like to concentrate more specifically on two prominent areas of significance. In the following sections, we will cover in somewhat more detail current legal and advocacy issues in psychology, and the efforts to ensure the quality of services that psychologists provide.

■ LEGAL AND ADVOCACY ISSUES IN APPLIED PSYCHOLOGY

State and federal legislative and regulatory processes, together with the judicial system, combine to set important policy and legal directions for applied psychology. Increasingly, matters affecting the practice of psychology are decided by officials in state and federal government. For example, the states' right to regulate occupations and professions empowers state governments to adopt statutes and rules licensing the professions, including psychology. In addition, many of the laws governing the health care industry, including reimbursement for health care services, payment for social programs, funds for education, and rules concerning a range of other services provided by psychologists are established by state and federal governments. Clearly, then, a review of pertinent state and federal policies will help the reader to an understanding of many current advocacy and legal issues in applied psychology.

Licensure

Historically, occupational regulation, including laws regulating the professions, has been entrusted to the states. This important states' right has meant that state legislatures have the authority to enact legislation, state executive branches have the mandate to implement legislation and regulations, and state judiciaries have been required to review legislation and regulations that establish procedures for occupational controls. Regulation of a profession by the state is critically important, as it provides a legal definition of and identity for the profession. Such a definition is the foundation upon which rests the future growth and development of an occupation or profession.

In most states, the process of regulation begins with legislative advocacy directed toward the enactment of licensing or certification legislation. Once legislation has been enacted, the governor of the state is mandated to appoint citizens, usually psychologists and consumer representatives, to a State Board of Examiners in Psychology. This board is charged with the actual implementation of the statute and is a component of the state's executive branch of government. It is not linked formally to private groups or organizations such as state professional associations.

An important task of the board is to issue regulations that are required to define operationally the language of the statute. The board screens candidates for licensure or certification to be certain that they meet education, credentialing, and experience requirements, and reviews the ethical conduct of persons regulated by the board. The board also arranges for and conducts examinations of candidates for licensure or certification. Applicants for licensure or certification in every state are required to pass, at a level defined either by law or by the state board, a national examination in psychology known as the "Examination for the Professional Practice of Psychology" (EPPP). At present, this examination, prepared and administered bi-annually by a test development corporation under contract to the American Association of State Psychology Boards, is comprised of 200 multiple-choice questions. In addition, some states require applicants to pass a written examination specially prepared by the state and/or an oral examination administered by the board or its designees.

During the last 35 years, American psychologists have worked to establish and maintain licensure statutes that describe the types of services and activities that psychologists typically perform. Beginning in Connecticut in 1946, states began to adopt regulatory statutes for psychology. By 1977, all of the states and the District of Columbia had enacted statutes to regulate psychology. In the United States, the statutes that exist today are of two general types: licensure statutes and certification statutes. *Licensure statutes*, the preferred and most common form of statutory regulation, exist in 44 jurisdictions. A licensure statute regulates both the title, in this case psychologist, and the practice of psychology. Licensure statutes restrict the use of the noun "psychologist" to those persons so licensed and also enable the licensee to practice that which the statute authorizes as the activities of psychologists. The practice of psychology is also defined in licensure statutes. Licensure laws, in theory, restrict the practice of psychology, as defined in the law, to licensed psychologists or persons specifically exempted from the law. All other persons are prohibited from the practice of psychology unless they are supervised by a licensed psychologist. On the other hand, *certification statutes* regulate only the title, as in the case of psychology certification statutes, the title "psychologist." Unlike licensure statutes, certification statutes do not regulate actual practice. Therefore, uncertified persons are prohibited only from using the title "psychologist" even though they may actually perform some of the same activities as certified psychologists. At present, seven states have certification laws.

In general, the licensure laws regulating the practice of psychology are generic. That is, they define the scope of practice as wide-ranging, rather than defining the practice of psychology in narrow or specialty oriented terms. For example, most laws license "psychologists," not clinical psychologists, school psychologists, experimental psychologists, etc. However, the section of most laws concerning ethical conduct mandates that psychologists only practice within their areas of training, experience, and expertise. There are a few laws that regulate only the specialty area in psychology known as health care. These licensure laws, currently in place in Hawaii, Michigan, and South Dakota, require that only psychologists engaged in the delivery of health care services—generally clinical, counseling, and school psychological services—be licensed. All other persons trained as psychologists are unregulated by the state. In addition, a subset of states has enacted licensure laws that provide for a generic license in psychology, with licensees then specifying and documenting their own specialty areas, which become adjunct certifications. For example, in Tennessee one is licensed as a psychologist and then given a specialty title in the area of expertise chosen from a list of eleven substantive areas in psychology.

A final issue concerning licensure is the educational and experiential requirements necessary for licensure or certification. As part of a model licensure statute, the American Psychological Association adopted a policy in 1967 which recommends that

> Legislation regulating the practice of psychology should be restricted to one level, requiring the doctoral degree from an accredited university or college in a program that is primarily psychological, and no less than 2 years of supervised experience, one of which is subsequent to the granting of the doctoral degree. This level should be designated by the title of "psychologist." Psychology should depend on the profession itself for higher level certification or licensure (of which American Board of Professional Psychology is an example).
>
> However, in some states it has been necessary to certify or license at more than one level. When this occurs, the legislation should reflect the following recommendations:
>
> If a state desires legislation below the psychologist level, this level should be designated by a title which includes the adjective "psychological" followed by a noun such as "examiner," "assistant," "technician," etc. It should require a defined program of at least 1 year of graduate training in an accredited university or college, plus experience leading to qualifications in the practice of certain defined psychological functions, under the supervision of a psychologist. In addition, the law should contain a provision prohibiting independent practice by such individuals (American Psychologist, 1967, p. 1099).

At present, 34 states license providers only at the doctoral level. The other states have enacted some form of regulation for doctoral-level providers as well as for persons at less than the doctoral level.

The entire matter of licensure traditionally has been, and continues to be, quite controversial with much of the debate centering on the basic question of the necessity for the laws. In this particular debate, some psychologists believe that licensing laws protect only the profession, while other psychologists believe that licensing laws are needed to protect the public. Additionally, groups outside of psychology (including physicians, social workers, mental health counselors, marriage and family counselors, etc.) have strong views about the regulation of psychology and the related right-to-practice issues. These controversies have been most dramatic during "sunset" review periods in different states.

Sunset review, first developed as a concept in the mid-1970s in Colorado, refers to the periodic review of state statutes, policies, and programs by state legislatures. Sunset has focused directly on occupational regulation, an often-criticized component of state government. Without re-enactment of the regulatory statute within a finite time, a statute under sunset review "dies" and is terminated. Working with state legislatures on regulation of psychological practice has resulted in an increase in the legislative advocacy activities of psychologists.

The regulation of psychology by the state forms the foundation for a wide range of other laws and rules which affect applied psychology. Some of these other substantive areas will be reviewed below.

Recognition and reimbursement

One of the most critical issues confronting psychologists working in health care settings is the matter of recognition and reimbursement. Recognition and reimbursement refers to the concept that psychology, or any other profession, is recognized by a state or federal government as a profession whose members, if properly trained and credentialed, are eligible for reimbursement for services provided to persons where this reimbursement is included as an insurance or other program benefit. For example, in the specific case of psychology, such recognition and reimbursement laws mandate that psychologists are reimbursed for their services in the same manner that physicians and other providers are reimbursed when mental health services are covered in insurance policies. Generally, recognition and reimbursement laws are referred to as "freedom-of-choice" laws. The matters of recognition, reimbursement, and freedom of choice relate most directly to payment to a psychologist by someone other than the client, usually through insurance. This other party is referred to as a third party and such insurance coverage is identified as "third-party reimbursement." Examples of third-party reimbursement include Medicare, Medicaid, and individual and group insurance plans. At present, freedom-of-choice legislation has been adopted by 37 states and the District of Columbia. These laws advance the notion of economic parity between physician and non-physician providers of health care.

A landmark court decision related to freedom-of-choice and third-party reimbursement for licensed professional psychologists occurred in 1981 in the *Virginia Academy of Clinical Psychologists v. Blue Shield of Virginia* case. In this legal battle, the United States Appellate Court for the Fourth District reversed a federal district court decision by stating that in Virginia, a state with a freedom-of-choice statute, the services of licensed psychologists must be reimbursed by individual insurance plans and that physician supervision and billing is not required for reimbursement. This decision helps to prevent attempts by insurance companies to refuse to reimburse psychologists in Virginia and other states that have freedom-of-choice laws. The U.S. Supreme

Court refused to review this Appellate Court decision, thus leaving it stand as a legal precedent. In a follow-up case to the "Virginia Blues" case, *Blue Shield of Virginia v. McCready* (1982), a consumer in Virginia charged that she was entitled to treble damages under Section IV of the Clayton Antitrust Act because she was denied reimbursement for the services of a licensed clinical psychologist. This denial substantially increased her net or out-of-pocket cost for psychological services. The Supreme Court recently decided that McCready is entitled to sue for damages under antitrust law, thus reaffirming that freedom of choice is a legally binding concept.

Medicare and Medicaid

Two important federally initiated third-party reimbursement programs are Medicare and Medicaid. Both Medicare and Medicaid were established by Congress in 1965 as components of the Social Security Act (1972). Medicare provides health care services for the disabled and the aged. It is funded and regulated by the federal government. Unlike Medicare, Medicaid is principally a state regulated program despite the fact that the enabling legislation and the majority of the funding comes from the federal government. Medicaid was designed to provide for health care services to the aged, blind, disabled, and/or medically needy and to families with dependent children. Many states have passed state laws or regulations that provide reimbursement for mental health services provided by psychologists under Medicaid.

Psychologists currently are not included in the Medicare amendments to the federal Social Security Act as independent providers of mental health services. Although organized psychology has worked for more than 10 years to modify this situation, the profession has been unsuccessful in accomplishing legislative changes. Medicare constitutes a critical piece of federal legislation because it often is cited as the basis upon which other legislation is drafted, and indeed, even arguments in some court cases have been based on it.

Health maintenance organizations

The Health Maintenance Act of 1973 is another federal statute that affects psychologists nationwide. This act establishes health maintenance organizations (HMOs), a major and relatively new structure for the delivery of health care services. In 1970, there were 29 HMOs in operation in the United States, but by 1980, more than 280 had been successfully organized. HMOs provide health care services to a subscriber group on a prepaid basis. In most HMOs, this basis means that subscribers pay the HMO a set amount of money each month, which entitles them to use the available services of the HMO. The subscriber's fee does not change regardless of the amount of services received, so the HMO does not make more money for delivering more services. As this statute is written, physicians control the administration of HMOs. Psychologists therefore are employed by physicians rather than working as independent providers within the structure of the HMO. This situation is problematic, as psychologists are licensed for the independent practice of psychology but are often unable to function in HMOs to the full extent permitted by their licenses.

The hospital practice of psychology

Many of the state and federal programs that have been discussed in this chapter are examples of governmental policies that extend the notion of equality or parity between physician and non-physician providers of mental health services. Another example of a parity issue involves the matter of the hospital practice of psychology. Whereas psychology has made great strides in recognition in almost every setting, the issue of parity in the hospital setting has proven problematic. Although the reasons are complex, generally they involve the tradition of physicians administering hospitals, the equation of health care with medical care, and the accreditation criteria of the Joint Commission on the Accreditation of Hospitals (JCAH, 1980). The current JCAH accreditation criteria do not permit psychologists to be part of medical staffs in hospital settings or to become voting members of the hospital governance structure unless permitted by a state law. This means that in most hospitals, psychologists cannot practice independently the way they are permitted by state licensure laws. A range of alternative strategies, including both legislation and litigation, has been considered to facilitate free entry and access to independent provider status by psychologists in hospitals. This is a very important area of concern to psychologists, as many hospitals recently have expanded their programs to include both inpatient and outpatient mental health services and other health care services, such as biofeedback, which traditionally have been within the domain of psychology. It is likely that the hospital practice of psychology will be a major issue for applied psychologists during this decade (Zaro, Batchelor, Ginsberg, & Pallak, 1982).

Clients' rights

Although licensed professional psychologists are ethically bound to ensure the confidentiality of client information, except in cases where the patient presents a serious threat to him- or herself or to someone else (APA, 1981), psychologists, in some states, are not legally protected by privileged communication statutes (Dekraai & Sales, 1982). Furthermore, at the present time only physicians, clergymen, and lawyers are protected by the United States Department of Justice guidelines requiring a search warrant for sensitive or confidential information. This same privilege has not been extended to psychologists and other mental health professionals despite protests from major provider groups including the American Psychological Association, the American Psychoanalytic Association, and the American Psychiatric Association. Each of these provider groups has recognized that mental health providers, including non-physician providers of mental health services, should be entitled to protection from unnecessary searches and that clients' rights related to confidentiality must be protected.

In addition to being guaranteed the right to confidentiality, clients of professional psychologists have the right to treatment in the least restrictive environment. This right is now guaranteed by a recent decision of the U.S. Supreme Court, which decided in 1981 that clients must be afforded treatment in an environment that is the least restrictive and enables them to function optimally within their capabilities (*Pennhurst State School and Hospital v. Halderman*, 1981). Recently an elaboration on this same theme was tested in *Youngberg v. Romeo* (1982), in which the Supreme Court affirmed a mentally retarded individual's right to safe conditions of confinement, freedom from undue bodily restraint, and training or habilitation.

Another important issue within the domain of clients' rights is that of an institutionalized patient's right to refuse antipsychotic medication or any other form of treatment. This issue was recently reviewed by the U.S. Supreme Court in the case of *Mills, et al. v. Rogers, et al.* (1982). In this case, a client, institutionalized in a state hospital, refused to take antipsychotic medication prescribed by a physician. The state held that it had the right and power to force medication on the patient. The patient argued that since such medications could be dangerous and harmful and, since there were other treatments available that were less dangerous, patients should have the right to choose less harmful treatments. The U.S. Supreme Court ruled that the state Supreme Court must re-review this case in light of recently established state legislation that protects the right of patients to choose appropriate treatment. These and other clients' rights issues will continue to provide challenges for psychologists in the future.

Entry level for independent practice

Professional psychologists have also been confronted with an issue that relates to health care and educational settings. This issue involved the provision of services by master's-level as opposed to doctoral-level providers.

As Chapter 7 noted, the area of school psychology has been involved in a long-standing controversy concerning this issue. The doctoral degree has been the APA standard for entry level to professional practice since 1955. However, in most states, school psychologists trained at the master's level are certified by state departments of education as school psychologists, but are not licensed as psychologists by state licensing boards. In order to address the issues involved, representatives of the APA and the National Association of School Psychologists (NASP) have been working for several years to develop mutually acceptable solutions. As of this writing, the two organizations are about to undertake a pilot joint accreditation program and are working on the entry-level standards issues.

Education of the handicapped

The Education for All Handicapped Children Act, P.L. 94-142, was designed to guarantee an appropriate education for all children regardless of the nature or severity of their handicap. This act, which is similar to federal civil rights legislation, stipulates that a "separate but equal" education is neither necessarily appropriate nor acceptable for a handicapped child.

Unfortunately, there has been resistance to implementing this legislation. Parents, by and large, have supported the legislation although some were concerned that their handicapped children would not receive specialized attention. Teachers and other school personnel were hesitant to incorporate handicapped children into regular classrooms because of potential management problems. Also, the federal government has attempted to dismantle the Department of Education, to cut funds for services under P.L. 94-142, and to modify the law and its regulations.

A major test of the issues involved with the delivery of psychological services in special education has been occurring in *Forrest v. Ambach*, a 1981 case which was brought in New York State court by a school psychologist. This psychologist (Forrest) was fired from her job for refusing to follow the directions of her principal. The administrator changed the content and recommendations of psychological reports, refused to allow Ms. Forrest to discuss service alternatives with parents, and dictated the direction that psychological services should take. When the psychologist both challenged and disobeyed these orders because they violated her professional ethics and standards, she was fired. In an appeal in this case, the court upheld the principle that psychologists be permitted to function in accordance with professional standards, but ruled that the psychologist's firing was justified on other administrative/personnel grounds. This decision is being appealed. This case represents a test of the independent status of psychology as it is practiced in the schools.

With regard to the issues surrounding testing and evaluation of children for placement in special education classes, particularly classes for mentally retarded children, two landmark federal cases were decided in the late 1970s. In *Larry P. v. Riles* (1979) and *PASE v. Hannon* (1980), the question of the constitutionality of using group intelligence tests to place minority children in classes for the educable mentally retarded was tested in court. In the *Larry P. v. Riles* case, the federal district court in California ruled that standardized intelligence tests could not be used as the sole basis to identify or place children in classes. This case currently is on appeal before the federal appellate court. In *PASE v. Hannon*, a contradictory decision was rendered by the federal district court in Illinois, which held that traditional standardized tests used for determining educational placement for children do not discriminate against minority children. This case is also on appeal at this time. In each case, the court relied on professional psychologists to testify concerning test construction, reliability, validity, and cultural bias. Since the decisions are contradictory, it is impossible to tell at this point which way the courts will decide on this issue. However, the future delivery of psychological services in schools is dependent on the ultimate results of these court tests.

Professional psychologists working in educational settings are responsible for assessing and evaluating the potential of this country's youth, be they handicapped or nonhandicapped. That responsibility is one that state and federal legislatures, via legislation like 94-142, and the courts, via cases like *Larry P. v. Riles* and *PASE v. Hannon*, will help to decide. Professional school psychologists are playing an important role in helping to shape those decisions that affect children, their families, and the entire educational system.

Testing issues in industry

Professional psychologists also work in a variety of settings related to business and government. In these settings also the use of tests to evaluate an employee's performance or to assist with employee selection has been challenged in the courts. The first major challenge to employment tests came in *Griggs v. Duke Power Company* (1971). In this case, black employees challenged the use of general ability tests to hire and advance employees. In 1971, the Supreme Court decided that employers had a responsibility to show that "any given requirement . . . had a manifest relationship to the employment in question" (p. 432). This decision was based on the Equal Employment Opportunity Commission (EEOC, 1966) "Guidelines on Employment Testing." These guidelines note that tests used in industry must "fairly measure the knowledge or skills required by the particular job" and further state that the instruments used must be "predictive of or significantly correlated with important elements of work behavior which are relevant to the job for which candidates are being evaluated" (29 C.S.R. 1607). This court decision and the EEOC Guidelines have thus established that tests should be able to demonstrate their "job-relatedness" if they are to be used to aid in hiring and promotional decisions.

A subsequent case, *Albermarle Paper Company v. Moody* (1975), tested the question of whether or not distinct criteria had been achieved by which employers could judge the job-relatedness of any test. In this case, the company hired an industrial psychologist to validate the company's use of an ability test. All potential employees were then required to take the validated test. The psychologist's validation procedures were challenged in court and the court found that the particular skills needed to perform the job in question had not been analyzed by the validation study. Again, the EEOC Guidelines were invoked as the judge ruled that the ability test should not be used. The court further stated its desire to increase the Guidelines' effectiveness by emphasizing that the Guidelines reference the Standards for Educational and Psychological Tests (APA, 1966, 1974) of the American Psychological Association.

In the case of *Washington v. Davis* (1976), the U.S. Supreme Court reviewed a claim of employment discrimination that was brought under the Equal Protection Clause of the Constitution. The Court held that the rigorous standard, which had been established in *Griggs* and *Albermarle*, was inappropriate and could not be applied under the Equal Protection Clause of the Constitution. In that light, the Court stated that there was no need to validate a test by showing a positive relationship between the test and job performance. The decision that was rendered in *Washington v. Davis* evoked a great deal of criticism from civil rights groups. The decision also evoked concern on the part of psychologists because of what was seen as a fundamental error in conceptualizing test validation. Disagreeing with the Supreme Court, many psychologists concerned with industrial testing issues noted that construct validity must be established if fair employee selection procedures are to be carried out and discrimination avoided. In these situations, construct validity is "demonstrated by data showing that the selection procedure measures the degree to which candidates have identifiable characteristics which have been determined to be important for successful job performance" (EEOC, 1978).

Psychologists have played an integral role in helping the courts define appropriate uses of tests and in helping courts determine what are the most fair and effective means of assessing particular job situations and characteristics needed to perform those jobs. Assisting the courts in their attempt to guarantee equal opportunities for all is a major policy endeavor that psychologists likely will continue to be involved in and responsible for in the near future.

Organizing for advocacy

Professional psychologists have only recently become aware of the need for systematic advocacy, or speaking out, on behalf of the profession. While traditionally many psychologists have not worried about issues such as recognition and reimbursement, inclusion in proposals for national health insurance, court decisions on the use of tests, and other such issues, legislation and the courts have begun to enact laws, statutes, and decisions which in fact influence the practice of the profession of psychology.

Applied professional psychologists now realize that, as they struggle to protect their legislated right to practice independently, they also address the very core of their identification as professionals. The fact that professional psychologists are working to enhance and empower psychology does not eliminate the real problems that face the profession. The empowerment brought about by forms of legal recognition of psychology as well as the knowledge that psychology is being threatened on a variety of fronts have helped bring psychologists together in organized advocacy efforts. Professional psychologists now realize that if they are to survive the battles that are occurring both legislatively and in the courts, individual psychologists must stand collectively and speak with a unified voice. To this end, psychologists have engaged in a variety of advocacy activities. The major foci of these activities are to encourage legislative action at state and federal levels and to present expert testimony before legislative and administrative bodies on issues that relate to health and human services in general and to psychology in particular.

The Association for the Advancement of Psychology and the American Psychological Association have been involved actively in a wide variety of federal legislative and regulatory issues. Simultaneously, at the state level, psychologists are working toward effective political advocacy through their state psychological associations. Each state and the District of Columbia has a state psychological association affiliated with the American Psychological Association. Generally, the state associations are organized to represent the interests of the community of psychologists at the state level.

The advocacy activities of the state associations have included the development of legislative committees and political influencing strategies. Generally, the legislative committee attempts to implement the legislative policies of the state association. Strategies typically used include meeting with legislators and decision makers to discuss issues of concern to psychology, the use of lobbyists to represent further the interests of psychology, and the generation of "grass roots" financial and political support by psychologists and others to enhance the legislative and policy advocacy activities of the state association.

Issues of concern to psychologists active in state level affairs include matters of professional importance, such as licensure and freedom of choice, and matters of social concern, such as custody decisions in divorce proceedings and gun control. An important component of psychology's advocacy efforts at the state level has been public information. The "publics" that psychologists attempt to inform include: (1) the broad community of psychology; (2) the legislature; and (3) the general public. In addition, leaders of the APA and the state psychological associations frequently consider the merits of psychology entering as a friend of the court (amicus curiae) in relevant cases being litigated in the judicial system.

As psychology has grown, its need to advocate and to defend its principles and values also has increased. Fortunately for the future of the field, the capacity of psychology to undertake these types of activities has steadily improved at all levels of policy development. As we move through the rest of this decade, psychology will continue to be challenged in these various areas. How psychology performs will determine the shape of the field as well as the shape of many critical government policies which will guide our country's actions. This is the most complex and important issue that psychology must face.

■ ASSURING THE QUALITY OF PSYCHOLOGICAL SERVICES

During the last decade, there has been an increased demand to assure the quality of psychological practice. The growth of consumerism and increased public awareness due to public education have resulted in more sophisticated consumers who ask that products and services perform as they are "advertised." Also, new resources that are available to be expended for human services in both the public and private sectors have diminished significantly in recent years, while costs for these services have risen. Consequently, the emphasis has been on ensuring that available funds are spent for services of value. The term *quality assurance* has come to embrace a range of techniques, concepts, and approaches to address the problem of assuring quality of psychological practice.

For its part, the psychological profession has embraced accountability as the mark of a mature profession. The argument has been made that the more a profession seeks acceptance for its products and services from the community at large, the greater that profession's obligation to ensure that its conduct and practices are "guaranteed," as it were, to embody the highest professional standards. As the national organization for professional psychologists, the American Psychological Association has embodied its commitment to accountability in documents such as the *Standards for Providers of Psychological Services* (APA, 1977b), *Specialty Guidelines for the Delivery of Services by Clinical, Counseling, School, Industrial/Organizational Psychologists* (APA, 1981), and the *Ethical Principles of Psychologists* (APA, 1981). In addition, increased competition among the mental health professions has contributed to the desirability of and push for demonstrating the quality of psychological services. This has led to the development of "peer review" mechanisms in psychology, which also contribute significantly to the overall quality assurance effort. These approaches to accountability will be described in more detail below.

Quality assurance in psychological practice involves a process of monitoring and evaluating professional service activities in order to ensure that the products of the professional psychologist attain pre-established levels of acceptability. Quality assurance procedures include the monitoring and assessment of both process and outcome. Simply put, process is the means (e.g., training) and outcome is the end (e.g., the effectiveness of services delivered) in the functioning of a professional psychologist.

There are two primary mechanisms commonly utilized by organized psychology to ensure the quality of services. They are the establishment of standards for the professional conduct of members of the profession and the monitoring of the process of professional education and training. The former is manifested in published documents such as the above mentioned *Standards, Guidelines,* and *Principles;* the latter, in the process for accreditation of psychology programs and internships as conducted by the American Psychological Association and as outlined in the APA *Accreditation Handbook* (APA, 1980).

A third type of mechanism that has been the subject of much attention and controversy in the last few years is *peer review*. Peer review systems were developed to address the questions concerning the outcomes of psychological services. Peer review is a formal procedure in which the judgments concerning quality of care are made by one's professional colleagues. Peer review has been more common in medicine, and only recently has it developed as a quality assurance mechanism endorsed within organized psychology through the APA.

Other quality assurance mechanisms within professional psychology involve licensure to practice as a psychologist, membership in professional associations, continuing education requirements, and specialized credentialing through the efforts of such organizations as the Council for the National Register of Health Service Providers in Psychology and the American Board of Professional Psychology. These methods of quality assurance are focused on process, credentials, and experience rather than outcome.

The "Standards" approach to quality assurance

Standards ▪ In 1974, the American Psychological Association adopted the first national standards for providers of psychological services. As stated in the introduction to the 1977 revision of these Standards (APA, 1977), their intent was to "improve the quality, effectiveness, and accessibility of psychological services to all who require them (p. 1)." They were promulgated as a uniform set of standards for practice and were intended to be useful to providers, users, and third-party purchasers of services.

The Standards reflect minimally acceptable levels of quality and performance on the part of "psychological service units" and individual providers in all settings. Standards apply to (1) providers, (2) programs, (3) accountability, and (4) environment.

The Standards pertaining to *providers* attempt to define desired qualifications, areas of professional functioning, relationships with other professionals, and professional roles within the organizational structure. For example:

> 1.1 Each psychological service unit offering psychological services shall have available at least one professional psychologist and as many more professional psychologists as are necessary to assure the quality of services offered (p. 4).

Standards pertaining to *programs* define services, staffing, organization, and functioning relevant to the delivery of psychological services. For example:

> 2.1.1 The composition and programs of a psychological service unit shall be responsive to the needs of the persons or settings served (p. 6).

Standards for *accountability* relate to the responsibility of the psychologist or service unit to ensure the effectiveness and appropriateness of their services. For example:

> 3.1 Psychologists' professional activity shall be primarily guided by the principle of promoting human welfare (p. 9).

The standard dealing with the *environment* directs:

> 4.1 Providers of psychological services shall promote the development in the service setting of a physical, organizational, and social environment that facilitates optimal human functioning (p. 11).

Specialty Guidelines ▪ The Standards for Providers are generic, having been developed to apply to all psychologists delivering psychological services. In 1980, the American Psychological Association promulgated Specialty Guidelines for the Delivery of Services. There are four sets of Guidelines, each one applying to services delivered by one of the four recognized *(de facto)* specialties: clinical, counseling, industrial/organizational, and school psychology. They are modeled upon and parallel to the generic standards but have been modified to meet the unique needs of the four specialties. For example, Standard 1.1 (above) corresponds to the following Guidelines for the delivery of clinical psychological services:

> 1.1 Each clinical psychological service unit offering psychological services has available at least one professional clinical psychologist and as many more professional clinical psychologists as are necessary to assure the adequacy and quality of services offered (p. 643).

Together, the Standards for Providers and the Specialty Guidelines state the official policy of the APA with respect to services delivered by each of the four specialty groups. The two policy documents are intended to contribute to a higher quality of psychological services by defining a structure and a process for delivery of these services. There is no formal enforcement mechanism associated with either document. That is, if a psychologist is "guilty" of nonadherence to one or more Standards or Guidelines, that psychologist does not necessarily face disciplinary action by the APA or any other body. He or she might face referral to a state or national ethics committee, a state Professional Standards Review Committee, or a state licensing board for psychology. Such a procedure could be invoked if the psychologist's behavior is blatantly in conflict with Standards and Guidelines. Enforcement or disciplinary action, however, would be contingent upon the particular behavior being in violation of the state licensing/certification law or the ethical code of the state or national association.

Ethical Principles ▪ Since 1953, APA members have been required to abide by a code of professional ethics (APA, 1981). Members of state psychological associations are similarly bound by this code, since all affiliated state associations use the APA's code as their own. The existing Ethical Principles of Psychologists (formerly called Ethical Standards of Psychologists) were promulgated by the Association in 1981. The Ethical Principles are a set of normative "prescriptions" and designate behaviors which are seen as intrinsically desirable or are valued by the psychological profession. For example, Principle 2, "Competence," states:

> The maintenance of high standards of competence is a responsibility shared by all psychologists in the interest of the public and the profession as a whole. Psychologists recognize the boundaries of their competence and the limitations of their techniques. They only provide services and only use techniques for which they are

qualified by training and experience. In those areas in which recognized standards do not yet exist, psychologists take whatever precautions are necessary to protect the welfare of their clients. They maintain knowledge of current scientific and professional information related to the services they render (p. 634).

Each principle is exemplified by additional, more explicit statements. For example, subprinciple *a* of Principle 2 states:

Psychologists accurately represent their competence, education, training, and experience. They claim as evidence of educational qualifications only those degrees obtained from institutions acceptable under the Bylaws and Rules of Council of the American Psychological Association (p. 634).

The Ethical Principles have an associated enforcement mechanism. If a psychologist member of APA is judged by the Association's Ethics Committee to have been in violation of an Ethical Principle, that psychologist is subject to one of a series of disciplinary actions, ranging from a simple reprimand to expulsion from the Association. Additional actions could include referral to a state licensing or certification board for a review of the individual's fitness to practice in that state, or to a state association ethics committee.

If a psychologist is not a member of a national or state psychological association, he or she would not be subject to the disciplinary action described above. Many states, however, have written into their licensing or certification laws that a psychologist must abide by the APA Ethical Principles. Consequently, a licensed psychologist who is in violation of an Ethical Principle is also in violation of the law and could be disciplined or prosecuted as a result of action by the licensing board or the state attorney general.

As mentioned above, the focus of the "standards" approaches to quality assurance is on process. That is, the profession makes statements about what are minimally acceptable and desired behaviors for professionals calling themselves psychologists. These statements are widely disseminated to the profession and the public and subsequently are incorporated in the graduate training programs. The behaviors specified in the Standards, Guidelines, and Principles are valued highly by the profession. An explicit assumption is that psychologists who behave in this way deliver acceptable quality services.

The second primary mechanism used by organized psychology to ensure the quality of services also focuses on process—monitoring the process of education and training for the profession.

Assuring the quality of education and training

Quality assurance efforts in the education and training of psychologists are directed toward ensuring that programs designated as "accredited" meet certain criteria that are judged to influence positively the performance of their graduates. This section will discuss briefly the history and nature of the accreditation process and will outline how the accreditation criteria have been developed.

Accreditation is concerned with assessment of the nature and quality of education and training of psychologist practitioners. In response to inquiries from the Veterans Administration, the Public Health Service, and the Army Surgeon General concerning the quality of doctoral programs in psychology, the APA initiated efforts to assess and accredit these training programs. The APA developed criteria for the accreditation of clinical psychology doctoral programs in 1947 and undertook accreditation of these programs the following year. In 1950, the Association began applying the accreditation procedure to counseling psychology doctoral programs and in the late 1960s acted similarly with regard to school psychology programs. In 1956, the Association began the accreditation of predoctoral internship programs. Currently, the APA accredits 205 psychology training programs (clinical, counseling, school, and professional) and 275 internship programs.

The process of the assessment of a doctoral program focuses on seven areas: institutional settings, cultural and individual differences, training models and curricula, faculty, students, facilities, and practicum and internship training. The criteria are generic (or general), even though they are specified as criteria for evaluation of programs in specialty areas. For example, one criterion [III.D.] specifies skills required for competent professional functioning but does not differentiate among the skills required of clinical, counseling, or school psychologists. Criteria are revised periodically (the last revision was 1979) under the direction of the APA's Council of Representatives. Recommendations for revisions originate with a task force made up of representatives from the relevant specialty areas of psychology, various APA governance groups, and other special interest groups within psychology.

The accreditation procedures attempt to ensure quality by focusing on the education process. An implicit assumption of this quality assurance effort is that a training program that satisfies specified criteria for quality, defined primarily by professional values and judgment, will produce professional psychologists whose services meet high standards of quality. There has, however, been no empirically tested validation of the criteria to determine whether this assumption is warranted. Training programs submit detailed information describing the way they meet the criteria. This information is augmented by the reports of three psychologists who conduct a site visit of the training program to observe first-hand if the criteria are being met. Programs meeting the criteria are then granted "accredited" status by APA, and they are permitted to advertise themselves as an APA-accredited program.

The third major quality assurance mechanism to be discussed—peer review—focuses on the quality of services actually rendered by the psychologist practitioner.

Peer review

As it is applied to mental health services delivered by psychologists, peer review is a quality assurance mechanism focused on outcome. Peer review involves obtaining professional judgments of the services provided by one psychologist by other health service providers in psychology, i.e., the psychologist's peers. Peer review also occurs in other areas within psychology, such as the academic sector's peer review of grant proposals, journal articles, and the use of human subjects. The APA's peer review systems generally are aimed toward psychologists in private practice who are not subject to institutional systems of review such as those existing in hospitals, community mental health centers, schools, etc.

Peer review of psychological services may occur in a face-to-face manner between the provider and the peer reviewer, it may be based on documents submitted by the provider, or it may consist of some combination of the two procedures. In any case, information supplied by the provider must address questions about the treatment being provided, the basic questions that underlie the purpose of the peer review. When peer review is a mechanism to assure the quality of services being provided, these questions most often concern whether the treatment is necessary, appropriate, and effective. Peer review also may have other purposes besides quality assurance. Among these are cost containment (review of services with the purpose of eliminating those that are unnecessary, fall below a minimum level of quality, or which exceed specified limits), use review (monitoring the pattern of utilization of existing resources), "policing" (the elimination of fraudulent or incompetent providers), and education of providers. These various purposes of peer review may at times all have a link to maintaining, improving, or assuring the quality of services provided by psychologists to the public.

Peer review as a formal system of assuring the quality of psychological services has developed primarily within the past decade. Its foundations lie in more long-standing customs of training and practice such as the case conference, supervision by senior practitioners, and problem-oriented record-keeping (Stricker, Claiborn, & Bent, 1982). In 1972, federal legislation established Professional Standards Review Organizations (PSROs) to provide comprehensive, ongoing, federally supported review of medical care provided under Medicare (services to the elderly), Medicaid (services to the indigent), and Maternal and Child Health (services to indigent pregnant women and mothers) programs. The PSRO program was the first nationwide health review system operating at local and state levels with federal aid having the goal of evaluation of the medical necessity, appropriateness, and quality of health and mental health services delivered under these federal programs. The aims of the PSRO program were both cost control and quality assurance. The program has not been entirely successful, however, as it has encountered organizational problems and has not been demonstrated to be cost-effective. Psychologists have had difficulty gaining acceptance into the PSRO review system, which has focused primarily on inpatient services.

At approximately the same time that the PSRO system was evolving under federal auspices for review of inpatient medical care, the APA was developing a review system for outpatient psychological services. The APA's review system was in response to the growing acceptance of psychologists' services for reimbursement by insurance companies, the so-called "third-party payers." While the third-party payers were reimbursing the services of psychologists, they also wanted some mechanism whereby the necessity and quality of services and appropriateness of fees charged could be assessed. In 1975, culminating a seven-year developmental process, the APA issued guidelines for establishment and functioning of Professional Standards Review Committees (PSRCs) to operate in conjunction with each state psychological association to review questions about fees and about quality of service (APA, 1975). PSRCs serve both to review and to educate with regard to cases initiated by the third-party payer, the provider, or the consumer of service. Currently, PSRCs operate at varying levels of activity in all states under the auspices of the state psychological associations.

An additional seminal event in the development of the concept of peer review as a quality assurance mechanism has been the contractual peer review project developed and implemented by APA in cooperation with the Civilian Health and Medical Program of the Uniformed Services (CHAMPUS). CHAMPUS is a health benefits program for over six million dependents of active duty military and retired military personnel. This project, first funded in 1977, became operational in 1980. It has resulted in the establishment of a roster of approximately 400 APA-approved psychologist peer reviewers located in all fifty states, the District of Columbia, and Puerto Rico, and the development of written criteria for selecting cases to go to peer review based on questions about necessity and quality of outpatient psychological services. A similar peer review program has been developed by the American Psychiatric Association for CHAMPUS-reimbursed services provided by psychiatrists. Current plans are for three other professional groups (the National Association of Social Workers; the American Nurses Association; and the American Association of Marriage and Family Therapists) to have their own peer review systems under CHAMPUS.

The peer review process within the APA/CHAMPUS system presently is based entirely on documents. Over and above routine claims review common to all third-party payers, the initial stage of the peer review process is performed by trained personnel within claims processing centers around the country under contract with CHAMPUS. At pre-determined times during the course of treatment, the claims processor asks the provider to submit a Mental Health Treatment Report containing specific information about the case. The Mental Health Treatment Report requires information about the patient's problems, the goals of treatment, therapeutic strategies, and progress achieved. The claims processor applies the APA-developed criteria for evaluation of necessity and quality of treatment to this information and on that basis decides which cases to send to peer review.

Peer review in the APA/CHAMPUS system is based upon the professional judgments of three psychologist reviewers selected by the claims processor from the APA-approved roster. The reviewers receive the case documents by mail after the names of the patient and provider and any other identifying data have been removed by the claims processor to ensure confidentiality. The reviewers make judgments independently about the necessity and appropriateness of the treatment as documented. They make recommendations as to whether CHAMPUS should reimburse past services and whether future treatment as planned should be reimbursed in full or in part. The final decision about reimbursement is made by the claims processor.

The APA/CHAMPUS project is the most widely implemented system of peer review of psychological services that has occurred to date. Private insurance companies have demonstrated increasing interest in peer review, and since 1979 several have contracted with the APA for peer review services directed toward outpatient mental health treatment provided by psychologists. As with any major change in the status quo, the APA/CHAMPUS peer review project has met with considerable comment. Initial concerns focused on the threat to confidentiality implied by the requirement for information about treatment from the provider. Providers also protested that the paperwork involved with the peer review process is burdensome, and that peer review is an unwarranted intrusion into the treatment process. More recent issues concern whether the criteria of necessity and appropriateness of treatment reflect usual and customary patterns of practice nationwide.

With the proliferation of mental health disciplines whose members practice psychotherapy, and with third-party payment increasingly becoming the base on which treatment rests fiscally, the climate is right for a growing trend toward open and standardized accountability in the mental health field. For professional psychology not to meet the challenge posed by the development of peer review and other quality assurance mechanisms might well risk the arbitrary limitation or exclusion of mental health benefits or certain providers within health plans financed by third-party payers. As with any large-scale innovation, there have been problems associated with the development and implementation of peer review mechanisms. For example, peer review's critics argue that those who endorse and practice peer review are in league with the third-party payers to save the latter money. Other criticisms have focused on the awkwardness of the system, the lack of empirically based criteria, the qualifications of reviewers, the lack of sensitivity to local standards, and the whole system of paper review.

The effort to provide for increased accountability, however, has resulted in a number of benefits to the profession: an improved image from without, an increase in the perception that the consumer is receiving service of good quality for good reason, an opportunity for the individual provider to receive consultation on a case in the form of peer reviewers' feedback, and the opportunity for experienced psychologists to share their knowledge and expertise in their role as peer reviewers.

Organized psychology, as represented by the APA, has clearly had a commitment to quality assurance efforts, as demonstrated by its history. There are multiple mechanisms now operating to assure the quality of psychological services and there are others on the horizon. Future demands for quality assurance will arise from both within and without professional psychology. Fortunately, the profession has striven to keep pace with the challenge as both have developed, and there is every likelihood that it will continue to do so. In the future, these developments will continue to occupy a major portion of psychology's agenda. Providing adequate quality assurance systems while maintaining the independence and integrity of psychological practice involves the whole field in a major challenge.

■ SUMMARY

At this point, you may be asking yourself what these current issues and future trends have to do with you as a student. Where the jobs are for graduates, the legal and regulatory foundations of the profession, current challenges, and quality assurance mechanisms may seem like arcane and mysterious subjects for the student who is struggling to master the basic concepts in learning theory, cognition, or abnormal psychology. We can only state that the material we have reviewed constitutes a brief summary of the issues that dominate our professional lives. As those psychologists working on professional issues within the APA, it seemed logical for us to present a coherent statement on the central issues from our national perspective. The only major themes we did not discuss are the trend toward specialization and the continuing evolution of the body of knowledge and practice in psychology. These latter issues have been covered explicitly and implicitly in the foregoing chapters.

What should be obvious to you is that psychology is a vibrant, growing, and challenging field. It is full of opportunities and problems. It has a rich history and a heritage of scientific progress and concern for human welfare. The profession is comprised of large numbers of gifted individuals who are working toward a greatly expanded and enriched field. As psychologists open up new frontiers and solve old problems, they will beckon for others such as yourself to follow. As individuals who have heeded that call, we have found that the challenges and rewards have been well worth the sacrifice necessary to gain entry into the profession of psychology.

■ SUGGESTED READINGS

American Psychological Association Committee on Legislation. (1967). A model for state legislation affecting the practice of psychology. *American Psychologist, 22,* 1095–1103.

This publication of the American Psychological Association describes the content and rationale recommended for state laws which govern the practice of psychology. The model is a policy of the APA and is recommended for use in all states. This brief article, although written at the professional level, would be interesting for advanced students.

American Psychological Association. (1981). Ethical principles of psychologists. *American Psychologist, 36,* 633–638.

This is the latest version of the most important policy of the American Psychological Association. These ethical principles lay down the fundamental code of behavior for psychologists.

Dekraai, M. B., & Sales, B. D. (1982). Privileged communications of psychologists. *Professional Psychology, 13,* 372–388.

This article reviews all state laws covering the rights of psychologists and their clients to have their communication remain privileged information. It presents an excellent summary of the vital information, and would be interesting to the advanced student.

Stapp, J., & Fulcher, R. (1981). The employment of APA members. *American Psychologist, 36,* 1263–1314.

This article summarizes the results of a 1978 survey of a large sample of the membership of the American Psychological Association. Data are presented on employment settings, fields of specialization, salaries, and so on.

REFERENCES

Abelson, R. P. (1976). Script processing in attitude formation and decision making. In J. S. Carroll & J. W. Payne (Eds.), *Cognition and social behavior* (pp. 33–45). Hillsdale, NJ: Erlbaum.

Abrams, A. M., & Stanley, J. C. (1967). Preparation of high school psychology teachers by colleges. *American Psychologist, 22,* 166–169.

Abramson, L. Y., Seligman, M. E. P., & Teasdale, J. (1978). Learned helplessness in humans: Critique and reformulation. *Journal of Abnormal Psychology, 87,* 79–94.

Accreditation Manual for Hospitals. (1980). Chicago: Joint Commission on Accreditation of Hospitals.

Adkins, J. C. (1968–1969). An art? A science? Or luck? *Trial, 5,* 37–39.

Adler, N. E., Cohen, F., & Stone, G. C. (1979). Themes and professional prospects in health psychology. In G. C. Stone, F. Cohen, & N. E. Adler (Eds.), *Health Psychology* (pp. 573–590). San Francisco: Jossey-Bass.

Albee, G. (1959). *Mental health manpower trends.* New York: Basic Books.

Albermarle Paper Company v. Moody, 422 U. S. 405 (1975).

Alderfer, C. P. (1969). An empirical test of a new theory of human needs. *Organizational Behavior and Human Performance, 4,* 142–175.

Alderfer, C. P. (1972). *Existence, relatedness, and growth: Human needs in organizational settings.* New York: Free Press.

Alloy, L. B., & Abramson, L. Y. (1979). Judgment of contingency in depressed and nondepressed students: Sadder but wiser? *Journal of Experimental Psychology: General, 108,* 441–485.

Alloy, L. B., Abramson, L. Y., & Viscusi, D. (1981). Induced mood and the illusion of control. *Journal of Personality and Social Psychology, 41,* 1129–1140.

Alluisi, E. A., & Morgan, B. B., Jr. (1976). Engineering psychology and human performance. *Annual Review of Psychology, 27,* 305–330.

Alluisi, E. A., & Morgan, B. B., Jr. (1982). Temporal factors in human performance and productivity. In E. A. Alluisi & E. A. Fleishman (Eds.), *Human performance and productivity* (Vol. 3, pp. 165–247). Hillsdale, NJ: Erlbaum.

Alpert, L., Atkins, B. M., & Ziller, R. C. (1979). Becoming a judge: The transition from advocate to arbiter. *Judicature, 62*, 325–335.

Altmaier, E. M., & Woodward, M. (1981). Group vicarious desensitization of test anxiety. *Journal of Counseling Psychology, 28*, 467–469.

Altrocchi, J., Spielberger, C. D., & Eisdorfer, C. (1965). Mental health consultation with groups. *Community Mental Health Journal, 1*, 127–134.

American Law Institute. (1962). *Model penal code: Section 401.* Philadelphia: American Law Institute.

American Psychological Association. (1952). Recommended standards for training counseling psychologists at the doctorate level. *American Psychologist, 7*, 175–181.

American Psychological Association. (1966). *Standards for educational and psychological tests.* Washington, DC: American Psychological Association.

American Psychological Association. (1967). *Casebook on ethical standards of psychologists.* Washington, DC: American Psychological Association.

American Psychological Association. (1972, August). Minutes of the Council of Representatives Meeting. Washington, DC.

American Psychological Association. (1974). *Standards for educational and psychological tests.* Washington, DC: American Psychological Association.

American Psychological Association. (1975). *Procedures manual for professional standards review committees of state psychological associations.* Washington, DC: American Psychological Association.

American Psychological Association. (1977). *Resolution on the Master's level issue.* Report to the Council of Representatives, Jan. 28–30.

American Psychological Association. (1978). *Report of the committee of state legislation.* Washington, DC: American Psychological Association.

American Psychological Association. (1981). Ethical principles of psychologists. *American Psychologist, 36*, 633–638.

American Psychological Association. (1982). *Ethical principles in the conduct of research with human participants.* Washington, DC: American Psychological Association.

American Psychological Association, Committee on Accreditation. (1980). *Accreditation handbook.* Washington, DC: American Psychological Association.

American Psychological Association, Committee on Legislation. (1976). A model for state legislation affecting the practice of psychology. *American Psychologist, 31*, 1095–1103.

American Psychological Association, Committee on Professional Standards. (1977). *Standards for providers of psychological services.* Washington, DC: American Psychological Association.

American Psychological Association, Committee on Professional Standards. (1981). Specialty guidelines for the delivery of services. *American Psychologist, 36*, 640–681.

American Psychological Association, Committee on Training in Clinical Psychology.

(1947). Recommended graduate training program in clinical psychology. *American Psychologist, 2,* 539–558.

American Psychological Association Task Force. (1976). Contributions of psychology to health research: Patterns, problems, and potentials. *American Psychologist, 31,* 263–274.

Anastasi, A. (1957). *Psychological testing.* New York: MacMillan.

Anastasi, A. (1982). *Psychological testing* (5th ed.). New York: MacMillan.

Andronico, M. P., & Guerney, B., Jr. (1967). The potential application of filial therapy to the school situation. *Journal of School Psychology, 6,* 2–7.

Apocada v. Oregon, 406 U. S. 404 (1972).

Appleman, J. A. (1968). Selection of the jury. *Trial Lawyer's Guide, 12,* 207–239.

Appleyard, D. (1981). *Livable streets.* Berkeley: University of California Press.

Arens, R., Granfield, D. D., & Susman, J. (1965). Jurors, jury charges and insanity. *Catholic University Law Review, 14,* 1–29.

Arens, R., & Susman, J. (1966). Judges, jury charges and insanity. *Howard Law Journal, 12,* 1–34.

Bachman, S., Smith, T., & Jason, L. A. (1981). Characteristics of community psychologists in 1974 and 1978. *American Journal of Community Psychology, 9,* 283–291.

Ballew v. Georgia, 435 U. S. 223 (1978).

Bandura, A. (1977). *Social learning theory.* Englewood Cliffs, NJ: Prentice-Hall.

Banikiotes, P. G. (1977). The training of counseling psychologists. *The Counseling Psychologist, 7(2),* 23–26.

Banikiotes, P. G. (1980). Counseling psychology training: Data and perceptions. *The Counseling Psychologist, 8(4),* 73–74.

Bardon, J. L., & Bennett, V. C. (1974). *School psychology.* Englewood Cliffs, NJ: Prentice-Hall.

Bardon, J. L., & Bennett, V. C. (1976). Psychosituational classroom invervention: Rationale and description. *Journal of School Psychology, 14,* 97–104.

Bare, J. K. (1974). *Psychology: Where to begin.* Washington, DC: American Psychological Association, and Boulder, CO: ERIC Clearinghouse for Social Studies/Social Science Education.

Barker, R. (1968). *Ecological psychology.* Stanford: Stanford University Press.

Barker, R. G., Dembo, T., & Lewin, K. (1943). Frustration and regression. In R. G. Barker, J. S. Kounin, & H. F. Wright (Eds.), *Child behavior and development* (pp. 441–458). New York: McGraw-Hill.

Barnard, M. V. (1980) Behavioral approaches to nursing. *Behavior Therapist, 3,* 11–12.

Barney, G. O. (1982). *The Global 2000 Report to the President: Entering the twenty-first century.* New York: Penguin.

Barrett, G., Phillips, J., & Alexander, R. (1981). Concurrent and predictive validity designs: A critical reanalysis. *Journal of Applied Psychology, 66,* 1–6.

Barrett-Lennard, G. T. (1962). Dimensions of therapist response as causal factors in therapeutic change. *Psychological Monographs, 76,* (43, Whole No. 562).

Barrett-Lennard, G. T. (1981). The empathy cycle: Refinement of a nuclear concept. *Journal of Counseling Psychology, 28*, 91 -100.

Baum, A. (1982, August). *Chronic Stress at Three Mile Island.* Paper presented at the annual meeting of the American Psychological Association, Washington, DC.

Baum, A., Davis, G. G., & Aiello, J. R. (1978). Crowding and neighborhood mediation of urban density. *Journal of Population, 1*, 266–279.

Baum, A., Gatchel, R. J., Fleming, R., & Lake, C. R. (1982, July). *Chronic and acute stress associated with the Three Mile Island accident and decontamination: Preliminary findings of a longitudinal study.* Draft Report. USUHS, Unpublished manuscript.

Baum, A., Singer, J. E., & Baum, C. S. (1981). Stress and the environment. *Journal of Social Issues, 37*, 4–36.

Beatty, J. (1982). Task-evoked pupillary responses, processing load, and the structure of processing resources. *Psychological Bulletin, 91*, 276–292.

Beck, A. T. (1967). *Depression: Clinical, experimental, and theoretical aspects.* New York: Harper & Row.

Beck, A. T. (1976). *Cognitive therapy and the emotional disorders.* New York: International Universities Press.

Becker, T. (1966). A survey study of Hawaiian judges: The effects of judicial role variations. *American Political Science Review, 60*, 677–680.

Becker, T. L., Hildum, D. C., & Bateman, K. (1965). The influence of jurors' values on their verdicts: A court and politics experiment. *The Southwestern Social Science Quarterly, 46*, 130–140.

Beckwith, N. E., & Lehmann, D. R. (1975). The importance of halo effects in multiattribute attitude models. *Journal of Marketing Research, 12*, 265–275.

Beers, C. W. (1908). *A mind that found itself.* New York: Longmans, Green. (7th ed., 1948, Doubleday).

Belch, G. E. (1981). An examination of comparative and noncomparative television commercials: The effects of claim variation and repetition on cognitive response and message acceptance. *Journal of Marketing Research, 18*, 333–349.

Bell, J. (1982, May). Two-year colleges hold key to future. *APA Monitor,* p. 26.

Bennett, C. C., Anderson, L. S., Cooper, S., Hassol, L., Klein, D. C., & Rosenblum, G. (Eds.). (1966). *Community psychology: A report of the Boston Conference on the Education of Psychologists for Community Mental Health.* Boston: Boston University Press.

Bennett, E., Degan, J., & Spiegel, J. (1963). Human factors in a technological society. In E. Bennett, J. Degan, & J. Spiegel (Eds.), *Human factors in technology* (pp. 3–11). New York: McGraw-Hill.

Bennett, V. C. (1964). Does size of figure drawing reflect self-concept? *Journal of Consulting Psychology, 28*, 285–286.

Bennett, V. C. (1966). Combinations of figure drawing characteristics related to the drawer's self concept. *Journal of Projective Techniques and Personality Assessment, 30*, 192 - 196.

Bennett, V. C. (1980). Should non-doctoral school psychologists be licensed for private practice? *Rutgers Professional Psychology Review, 2*, 18–23.

Bennett, V. C., & Bardon, J. I. (1975). Law, professional practices and professional organizations. *Journal of School Psychology, 13*, 349–358.

Benson, H. (1980). Behavioral medicine: A perspective from within the field of medicine. *National Forum, LX*, 3–5.

Bergin, A. E. (1971). The evaluation of therapeutic outcomes. In A. E. Bergin & S. L. Garfield (Eds.), *Handbook of psychotherapy and behavior change* (pp. 217–270). New York: Wiley.

Bergin, A. E., & Lambert, M. J. (1978). The evaluation of therapeutic outcomes. In S. L. Garfield & A. E. Bergin (Eds.), *Handbook of psychotherapy and behavior change* (2nd ed., pp. 139–190). New York: Wiley.

Berman, J., & Sales, B. D. (1977). A critical evaluation of the systematic approach to jury selection. *Criminal Justice and Behavior, 4*, 219–240.

Bersoff, D. N. (1981). Testing and the law. *American Psychologist, 36*, 1047–1056.

Bettman, J. R. (1970). Information processing models of consumer behavior. *Journal of Marketing Research, 7*, 370–376.

Bettman, J. R. (1979). *An information processing theory of consumer choice.* Reading, MA: Addison-Wesley.

Bettman, J. R., Capon, N., & Lutz, R. J. (1975). Multiattribute measurement models and multiattribute attitude theory: A test of construct validity. *Journal of Consumer Research, 1*, 1–15.

Bevan, W. (1976). The sound of the wind that's blowing. *American Psychologist, 31*, 481–491.

Bevan, W., Albert, R. S., Loiseaux, P. R., Mayfield, P. N., & Wright, G. (1958). Jury behavior as a function of the prestige of the foreman and the nature of his leadership. *Journal of Public Law, 7*, 419–449.

Binet, A., & Simon, T. (1905). Methodes nouvelles pour le diagnostic du niveau intellectual des anormaux. *Anee psychologie, 11*, 191–244.

Black, H. C. (1968). *Black's law dictionary.* St. Paul, MN: West.

Blanchard, E. B., & Epstein, L. H. (1978). *A biofeedback primer.* Reading, MA: Addison-Wesley.

Blanchard, E. B., Miller, S. T., Haynes, G. G., & Wicker, R. (1979). Evaluation of biofeedback in the treatment of borderline essential hypertension. *Journal of Applied Behavior Analysis, 12*, 99–109.

Bloom, B. L. (1972). Mental health program evaluation. In S. E. Golann & C. Eisdorfer (Eds.), *Handbook of community mental health* (pp. 819–839). New York: Appleton-Century-Crofts.

Bloom, B. L. (1977). *Community mental health: A general introduction.* Monterey, CA: Brooks/Cole.

Blue Shield of Virginia v. McCready, 73 Led 2d. 149 (1982).

Blumberg, A. (1967). *Criminal justice.* New York: Quadrangle.

Bodin, H. S. (1954). *Selecting a jury.* New York: Practicing Law Institute.

Bolles, R. N. (1978). *What color is your parachute?* Berkeley, CA: Ten Speed Press.

Boor, M. (1976). Effects of victim injury, victim competence, and defendant opportunism on the decision of simulated jurors. *Journal of Social Psychology, 100*, 315–316.

Bourne, L. E., Jr., Dominowski, R. L., & Loftus, E. F. (1979). *Cognitive processes*. Englewood Cliffs, NJ: Prentice-Hall.

Boyd, H. W., Jr., Ray, M., & Strong, E. C. (1972). An attitudinal framework for advertising strategy. *Journal of Marketing, 36*, 27–33.

Bradford, L. P., & Bradford, M. I. (1979). *Retirement*. Chicago: Nelson-Hall.

Brainard, R. W., & Ornstein, G. N. (1965, April). *Image quality enhancement* (USAF Tech. Rep. No. 65-28).

Brainard, R. W., Sadacca, R., Lopez, L. J., & Ornstein, G. N. (1966, August). *Development and evaluation of a catalog technique for measuring image quality* (U. S. Army Personnel Research Office Tech. Rep. No. 1150).

Bray, R. M., & Noble, A. M. (1978). Authoritarianism and decisions of mock juries: Evidence of jury bias and group polarization. *Journal of Personality and Social Psychology, 36*, 1424–1430.

Brayfield, A. H., & Crockett, W. H. (1955). Employee attitudes and employee performance. *Psychological Bulletin, 52*, 396–424.

Briggs, G. E. (1966). Tracking behavior. In E. A. Bilodeau (Ed.), *Acquisition of skill* (pp. 411–424). New York:Academic Press.

Briggs, G. E., & Swanson, J. M. (1970). Encoding, decoding, and central functions in human information processing. *Journal of Experimental Psychology, 86*, 296–308.

Broadbent, D. E. (1958). *Perception and communication*. New York: Pergamon Press.

Broadbent, D. E., & Gregory, M. (1965). Effects of noise and signal rate upon vigilance analysed by means of decision theory. *Human Factors, 7*, 155–162.

Broady, M. (1972). Social theory in architectural design. In R. Gutman (Ed.), *People and buildings* (pp. 170–185). New York: Basic Books.

Brodsky, S., & Smitherman, O. (1983). *Handbook of scales for research in crime and delinquency*. New York: Plenum.

Broeder, D. W. (1965). The voir dire examination—An empirical study. *Southern California Law Review, 38*, 503–528.

Brogden, H. E., & Taylor, E. K. (1950). The dollar criterion—applying the cost accounting concept to criterion construction. *Personnel Psychology, 3*, 133–154.

Bronfenbrenner, V. (1979). *The ecology of human development: Experiments by nature and design*. Boston: Harvard University Press.

Brotemarkle, R. A. (Ed.). (1931). *Clinical psychology: Studies in honor of Lightner Witmer to commemorate the thirty-fifth anniversary of the founding of the first psychological clinic*. Philadelphia: University of Pennsylvania Press.

Brown, S. D. (1980). Coping skills training: An evaluation of a psycho-educational program in a community mental health setting. *Journal of Counseling Psychology, 27*, 340–345.

Buck, J. N. (1948). The H-T-P technique: A qualitative and quantitative scoring technique. *Journal of Clinical Psychology, 5*, 317–396.

Buckner, D. N., & McGrath, J. J. (Eds.). (1963). *Vigilance: A symposium*. New York: McGraw-Hill.

Bullock, H. A. (1961). Significance of the racial factor in the length of prison sentence. *Journal of Criminal Law, Criminology, and Police Science, 52*, 411–415.

Buros, O. K. (1978). *The eighth mental measurements yearbook* (Vols. I & II). Highland Park, NJ: Gryphon Press.

Busch, P., & Wilson, D. T. (1976). An experimental analysis of a salesman's expert and referent bases of power in the buyer-seller dyad. *Journal of Marketing Research, 13,* 3–11.

Cahill, M. C. (1975). Interpretability of graphic symbols as a function of context and experience factors. *Journal of Applied Psychology, 60,* 376–380.

Calder, B. J. (1977). Focus groups and the nature of qualitative data. *Journal of Marketing Research, 14,* 353–364.

Calfee, R. (1981). Cognitive psychology and educational practice. In D. C. Berliner (Ed.), *Review of research in education, 9,* 3–73. Washington, DC: American Educational Research Association.

Campbell, J. P., Dunnette, M. D., Lawler, E. E., III, & Weick, K. E., Jr. (1970). *Managerial behavior, performance, and effectiveness.* New York: McGraw-Hill.

Campbell, J. P., & Pritchard, R. D. (1976). Motivation theory in industrial and organizational psychology. In M. D. Dunnette (Ed.), *Handbook of industrial and organizational psychology* (pp. 63–130). Chicago: Rand McNally.

Caplan, G. (1964). *Principles of preventive psychiatry.* New York: Basic Books.

Carkhuff, R. R. (1969). *Helping and human relations: A primer for lay and professional helpers* (Vols. 1 & 2). New York: Holt, Rinehart & Winston.

Carkhuff, R. R. (1972). *The art of helping.* Amherst, MA: Human Resource Development Press.

Carroll, J. S., & Perlman, D. (Eds.). (1978). Attributions in the criminal justice system (Special issue). *Law and Human Behavior, 2* (4).

Carskadon, J. G. (1978). Thrillers among the journals: A technique to increase graduate students' reading of research. *Professional Psychology, 9,* 83–86.

Cattell, J. M. (1890). Mental tests and measurements. *Mind, 15,* 373–380.

Centers, R., Shomer, R., & Rodrigues, A. (1970). A field experiment in interpersonal persuasion using authoritative influence. *Journal of Personality, 38,* 392–403.

Champagne, A., & Nagel, S. (1982). The psychology of judging. In N. L. Kerr & R. M. Bray (Eds.), *The psychology of the courtroom* (pp. 257–283). New York: Academic Press.

Chapanis, A. (1963). Engineering psychology. *Annual Review of Psychology, 14,* 285–318.

Chickering, A. W. (1969). *Education and identity.* San Francisco: Jossey-Bass.

Chubb, P. (1963). *Drivers' ability to control the velocity of an automobile as a function of initial velocity and extent of change.* Unpublished master's thesis, Ohio State University, Columbus, OH.

Cleary, P. J. (1980). A checklist for life event research. *Journal of Psychosomatic Research, 24,* 199–207.

Closurdo, J. S. (1975). Behavior modification and the nursing process. *Perspectives in Psychiatric Care, 8,* 25–36.

Cohen, A., Smith, M. J., & Anger, W. K. (1979). Self-protective measures against workplace hazards. *Journal of Safety Research, 11,* 121–131.

Cohen, J. B., & Houston, M. J. (1972). Cognitive consequences of brand loyalty. *Journal of Marketing Research, 9,* 97–99.

Cohen, L. D., & Goldman, J. R. (1980). Sunset-Sunrise. *Professional Practice of Psychology, 1,* 51–56.

Cohen, S., Evans, G. W., Krantz, D. S., & Stokols, D. (1980). Psychological, motivational, and cognitive effects of aircraft noise on children: Moving from the laboratory to the field. *American Psychologist, 35,* 231–243.

Cohen, S., Krantz, D. S., Evans, G. W., & Stokols, D. (1981). Cardiovascular and behavioral effects of community noise. *American Scientist, 69,* 528–535.

Cohen, S., Krantz, D. S., Evans, G. W., Stokols, D., & Kelly, S. (1981). Aircraft noise and children: Longitudinal and cross-sectional evidence on adaptation to noise and the effectiveness of noise abatement. *Journal of Personality and Social Psychology, 40,* 331–345.

Cohen, S., & Weinstein, N. (1981). Nonauditory effects of noise on behavior and health. *Journal of Social Issues, 37,* 95–125.

Cohen, Y. A. (1975). The state system, schooling, and cognitive and motivational patterns. In N. K. Shimahara & A. Scrupski (Eds.), *Social forces and schooling: An anthropological and sociological perspective* (pp. 103–140). New York: David McKay.

Colgrove v. Battin, 413 U. S. 149 (1973).

Collins, A. M., & Loftus, E. F. (1975). A spreading-activation theory of semantic processing. *Psychological Review, 83,* 407–428.

Comment. Academic researchers and the First Amendment: Constitutional protection for confidential sources. (1977). *San Diego Law Review, 14,* 876–903.

Comtois, R. J., & Clark, W. D. (1976). A framework for a scientific practice and practitioner training. *Psychological Documents, 6,* 74. (Ms. No. 1301).

Connecticut Special Education Association. (1936). *History of special education for mentally deficient children in Connecticut.* New Haven, CT: The Association.

Conti, A. P. (1971). A follow-up study of families referred to outside agencies. *Psychology in the Schools, 8,* 338–340.

Cooke, G., & Sikorski, C. R. (1974). Factors affecting length of hospitalization in persons adjudicated not guilty by reason of insanity. *Bulletin of the American Academy of Psychiatry and the Law, 2,* 251–261.

Copeland, W. D. (1980). Teaching-learning behaviors and the demands of the classroom environment. *Elementary School Journal, 80,* 163–177.

Cornell, E. L. (1936). The school psychologist's contribution. *National Elementary Principals, 15,* 561–566.

Corrigan, J. D., Dell, D. M., Lewis, K. N., & Schmidt, L. D. (1980). Counseling as a social influence process: A review (Monograph). *Journal of Counseling Psychology, 27,* 395–441.

Corsini, R. (Ed.). (1979). *Current psychotherapies.* Itasca, IL: Peacock.

Cowen, E. L. (1970). Training clinical psychologists for community mental health functions. In I. Iscoe & C. D. Spielberger (Eds.), *Community psychology: Perspectives in training and research* (pp. 99–124). New York: Appleton-Century-Crofts.

Cox, V. C., Paulus, P. B., McCain, G., & Schkade, J. K. (1979). Field research on the effects of crowding in prisons and on offshore drilling platforms. In J.R. Aiello & A. Baum (Eds.), *Residential crowding and design* (pp. 95–106). New York: Plenum.

Craighead, W.E. (1982). A brief clinical history of cognitive behavior therapy with children. *School Psychology Review, 11*, 5–13.

Craik, F.I.M., & Lockhart, R.S. (1972). Levels of processing: A framework for memory research. *Journal of Verbal Learning and Verbal Behavior, 11*, 671–684.

Craik, K.H. (1977). Multiple scientific paradigm in environmental psychology. *International Journal of Psychology, 12*, 147–157.

Criss, M.L., & Racine, D.R. (1980). Impact of change in legal standard for those adjudicated not guilty by reason of insanity: 1975–1979. *Bulletin of the American Academy of Psychiatry and the Law, 8*, 261–271.

Crites, J.O. (1969). *Vocational psychology.* New York: McGraw-Hill.

Crites, J.O. (1978). *Theory and research handbook for the Career Maturity Inventory.* Monterey, CA: McGraw-Hill.

Crites, J.O. (1981). *Career counseling.* New York: McGraw-Hill.

Crosson, R.F. (1968). An investigation into certain personality variables among capital trial jurors summary. *Proceedings of the 76th Annual Convention of the American Psychological Association, 3*, 287–288.

Cummings, N.A., & Follette, W.T. (1975). Brief psychotherapy and medical utilization: An eight year follow-up. In H. Dorken and Associates (Eds.), *The professional psychologist today: New developments in law, health, insurance and health practice* (pp. 165–174), San Francisco: Jossey-Bass.

Daniel, E. (1970). Teaching psychology in the community and junior college. *American Psychologist, 25*, 537–543.

Darrow, C. (1936, May). Attorney for the defense. *Esquire Magazine*, 36–37, 211–213.

D'Atri, D.A. (1975). Psychophysiological responses to crowding. *Environment and Behavior, 7*, 237–252.

D'Atri, D.A., & Ostfield, A.M. (1975). Crowding: Its effects on the elevation of blood pressure in a prison setting. *Preventative Medicine, 4*, 550–566.

Davis, B.E., & Wiley, R.E. (1965). Forty-nine thoughts on jury selection. *Trial Lawyer's Guide, 9*, 351–356.

Davis, F. (1975). *Inside intuition.* New York: The New American Library.

Davis, H.G., Bray, R.M., & Holt, R.W. (1977). The empirical study of decision processes in juries: A critical review. In J.L. Tapp & F.J. Levine (Eds.), *Law, justice, and the individual in society: Psychological and legal issues* (pp. 326–361). New York: Holt, Rinehart, & Winston.

Davis, M., McKay, M., & Eshelman, E.R. (1980). *Relaxation and stress reduction handbook.* Richmond, CA: New Harbinger.

Deffenbacher, J.L., & Michaels, A.C. (1981). Anxiety management training and self control desensitization—fifteen months later. *Journal of Counseling Psychology, 28*, 459–462.

Dekraai, M.B., & Sales, B.D. (1982). Privileged communications of psychologists. *Professional Psychology, 13*, 372–388.

Dekraai, M.B., & Sales, B.D. (in press). Confidential communications of psychotherapists. *Psychotherapy: Theory, Research and Practice.*

Department of Health, Education and Welfare. (1979). *Smoking and health: A report of the Surgeon General.* (DHEW Publication No. (PHS) 79-5006). Washington, DC: U.S. Government Printing Office.

Dewar, R. E., & Ells, J. G. (1974). A comparison of three methods of evaluating traffic signs. *Transportation Research Record, 503,* 38–47.

Diamond, S. S. (1974). A jury experiment re-analyzed. *University of Michigan Journal of Law Reform, 7,* 520–532.

Diamond, S. S. (Ed.). (1979). Simulation research and the law (Special Issue). *Law and Human Behavior, 3,* 1–148.

Diamond, S. S. (1981). Exploring sources of sentence disparity. In B. D. Sales (Ed.), *The trial process* (pp. 387–411). New York: Plenum.

Diana v. State Board of Education, C-70-37-RFP (N.D. Cal.) 1973.

Dorken, H. (1983). Health insurance and third-party reimbursement. In B. D. Sales (Ed.), *Professional psychologist's handbook.* New York: Plenum.

Drake, E. A. (1981). Children of separation and divorce: A review of school programs and implications for the psychologist. *School Psychology Review, 10,* 54–61.

Drum, D. J., & Knott, J. E. (1977). *Structured groups for facilitating development.* New York: Human Sciences.

Dunnette, M. D. (1963). A note on the criterion. *Journal of Applied Psychology, 47,* 251–254.

Dunnette, M. D. (1974). Personnel selection and job replacement of the disadvantaged: Problems, issues, and suggestions. In H. L. Fromkin & J. J. Sherwood (Eds.), *Integrating the organization* (pp. 55–74). New York: Free Press.

Dunnette, M. D. (Ed.). (1976). *Handbook of industrial and organizational psychology.* Chicago: Rand McNally.

Dunnette, M. D., & Borman, W. D. (1979). Personnel selection and classification systems. *Annual Review of Psychology, 30,* 477–525.

Dworkin, B. (1982). Instrumental learning for the treatment of disease. *Health Psychology, 1,* 45–59.

Dwyer, B. J. (1982). *Update . . . education* (Vol. 3). Washington, DC: House of Representatives, U. S. Congress.

Ebbesen, E. B., & Konečni, V. J. (1975). Decision-making and information integration in the courts: The setting of bail. *Journal of Personality and Social Psychology, 32,* 805–821.

Ebbesen, E. B., & Konečni, V. J. (1981). The process of sentencing adult felons: A causal analysis of judicial decisions. In B. D. Sales (Ed.), *The trial process* (pp. 413–458). New York: Plenum.

Edney, J. J. (1980). The commons problem: Alternative perspectives. *American Psychologist, 35,* 131–150.

Education for All Handicapped Children's Act, P.L. 94-142 (1974).

Egan, G. (1982). *The skilled helper* (2nd ed.). Monterey, CA: Brooks/Cole.

Einhorn, H. J. (1980). Learning from experience and suboptimal rules in decision making. In. T. S. Wallsten (Ed.), *Cognitive processes in choice and decision behavior* (pp. 1–20). Hillsdale, NJ: Erlbaum.

Einhorn, H. J., & Hogarth, R. M. (1981). Behavioral decision theory: Processes of judgment and choice. *Annual Review of Psychology, 32,* 53–88.

Eisenberg, A.M., & Smith, R.R. (1971). *Nonverbal communication*. New York: Bobbs-Merrill.

Ekman, P., & Friesen, V.W. (1975). *Unmasking the face*. Englewood Cliffs, NJ: Prentice-Hall.

Ellis, A. (1962). *Reason and emotion in psychotherapy*. New York: L. Stuart.

Elwork, A., Sales, B.D., & Alfini, J. (1977). Juridic decisions: In ignorance of the law or in light of it? *Law and Human Behavior, 1*, 163–189.

Elwork, A., Sales, B.D., & Alfini, J. (1982). *Making jury instructions understandable*. Charlottesville, VA: Michie/Bobbs-Merrill.

Elwork, A., Sales, B.D., & Suggs, D. (1981). The trial: A research review. In B.D. Sales (Ed.), *The trial process* (pp. 1–68). New York: Plenum.

Engel, G.L. (1977). The need for a new medical model: A challenge for biomedicine. *Science, 196*, 129–136.

Engel, J.F., Kollat, D.T., & Blackwell, R.D. (1968). *Consumer behavior*. New York: Holt, Rinehart & Winston.

Engle, T.L. (1967). Teaching psychology at secondary school level: Past, present, possible future. *Journal of School Psychology, 5*, 168–176.

Epstein, L.H., & Masek, B.J. (1978). Behavioral control of medicine compliance. *Journal of Applied Behavioral Analysis, 11*, 1–9.

Equal Employment Opportunity Commission (EEOC). (1966). *Guidelines on employee selection procedures* (29 C.F.R. 1607). Washington, DC: EEOC.

Equal Employment Opportunity Coordinating Council. (1978). Uniform guidelines on employee selection procedures. *Federal Register*, 38290–38315.

Erikson, E.H. (1960). Industry versus inferiority. In M.L. Harmowitz & N.W. Harmowitz (Eds.), *Human development* (pp. 248–256). New York: Thomas Crowell.

Erikson, E.H. (1963). *Childhood and society*. New York: Norton.

Ewalt, J. (1961). *Action for mental health*. New York: Basic Books.

Eysenck, H.J. (1952). The effects of psychotherapy: An evaluation. *Journal of Consulting Psychology, 16*, 319–324.

Eysenck, H.J. (1961). The effects of psychotherapy. In H.J. Eysenck (Ed.), *Handbook of abnormal psychology* (pp. 697–725). New York: Basic Books.

Eysenck, H.J. (1966). *The effects of psychotherapy*. New York: International Science Press.

Eysenck, H.J. (1978). An exercise in mega-silliness. *American Psychologist, 33*, 517.

Fagan, T. (1982). The struggle to achieve a joint resolution on entry-level and title. *Communique, XI*, 1–8.

Fairweather, G.W., & Tornatzky, L.G. (1977). *Experimental methods for social policy research*. New York: Pergamon Press.

Fanger, P.O. (1972) *Thermal comfort*. New York: McGraw-Hill.

Farling, W.H., & Agner, J. (1979). History of the National Association of School Psychologists: The first decade. *School Psychology Digest, VIII*, 140–152.

Farrington, D.P., & Nuttall, C.P. (1980). Prison size, overcrowding, prison violence, and recidivism. *Journal of Criminal Justice, 8*, 221–231.

Feldman, S., & Wilson, K. (1981). The value of interpersonal skills in lawyering. *Law and Human Behavior, 5*, 311–324.

Felix, R. H. (1956). The role of psychology in the mental health effort. In C. R. Strother (Ed.), *Psychology and mental health* (pp. 4–20). Washington, DC: American Psychological Association.

Festinger, L., Schachter, S., & Back, K. (1950). *Social pressures in informal groups.* Stanford, CA: Stanford University Press.

Feyerabend, P. K. (1970). Against method: Outline of an anarchistic theory of knowledge. In M. Radner & S. Winokur (Eds.), *Minnesota studies in the philosophy of science* (pp. 17–130). Minneapolis, MN: University of Minnesota Press.

Fiedler, F. E. (1950). A comparison of therapeutic relationships in psychoanalytic, nondirective, and Adlerian therapy. *Journal of Consulting Psychology, 14*, 436–445.

Fiedler, F. E. (1967). *A theory of leadership effectiveness.* New York: McGraw-Hill.

Fiedler, F. E. (1978). The contingency model and the dynamics of the leadership process. In L. Berkowitz (Ed.), *Advances in experimental social psychology* (Vol. 11, pp. 59–112). New York: Academic Press.

Field, L. (1965). Voir dire examination—A neglected art. *University of Missouri at Kansas City Law Review, 33*, 171 - 178.

Fischhoff, B. (1982). Debiasing. In D. Kahneman, P. Slovic, & A. Tversky (Eds.), *Judgment under uncertainty: Heuristics and biases* (pp. 422–444). New York: Cambridge.

Fishbein, M. (1963). An investigation of the relationships between beliefs about an object and the attitude toward that object. *Human Relations, 16*, 233–239.

Fishbein, M. (1967). Attitude and the prediction of behavior. In M. Fishbein (Ed.), *Readings in attitude theory and measurement* (pp. 477–492). New York: Wiley.

Fishbein, M. (1980). A theory of reasoned action: Some applications and implications. In H. E. Howe, Jr. & M. M. Page (Eds.), *Nebraska symposium on motivation 1979: Beliefs, attitudes, and values* (pp. 65–116). Lincoln: University of Nebraska Press.

Fishbein, M., & Ajzen, I. (1975). *Beliefs, attitude, intention and behavior: An introduction to theory and research.* Reading, MA: Addison-Wesley.

Fisk, A. D., & Schneider, W. (1981). Control and automatic processing during tasks requiring sustained attention: A new approach to vigilance. *Human Factors, 23*, 737–750.

Fitts, P. M. (1963). Engineering psychology. In S. Koch (Ed.), *Psychology: A study of science* (pp. 908–933). New York: McGraw-Hill.

Fitts, P. M., & Peterson, J. R. (1964). Information capacity of discrete motor responses. *Journal of Experimental Psychology, 67*, 103–112.

Fitts, P. M., & Posner, M. I. (1967). *Human performance.* Belmont, CA: Brooks/Cole.

Fleishman, E. A. (1953). The description of supervisory behavior. *Journal of Applied Psychology, 38*, 1–6.

Fleishman, E. A. (1973). Twenty years of consideration and structure. In E. A. Fleishman & J. G. Hunt (Eds.), *Current developments in the study of leadership* (pp. 1–37). Carbondale: Southern Illinois University Press.

Fleishman, E. A., Harris, E. F., & Burtt, H. E. (1955). *Leadership and supervision in industry.* Columbus: Ohio State University, Bureau of Educational Research.

Fogli, L., Hulin, C. L., & Blood, M. R. (1971). Development of first-level behavioral job criteria. *Journal of Applied Psychology, 55*, 3–8.

Forbes, T. W. (Ed.). (1972). *Human factors in highway traffic safety research*. New York: Wiley.

Fordyce, W. E. (1976). *Behavioral methods for chronic pain and illness*. St. Louis: C. F. Mosby.

Foreman, B. D., & Schackar, S. A. (1981). Elevating the status of psychologists: A simple solution. *Professional Psychology, 12*, 291–292.

Forrest v. Ambach, 436 NYS 2d, 119 (1981).

Fowler, F. J., & Mangione, T. W. (1981). *An experimental effort to reduce crime and fear of crime in an urban residential neighborhood: Re-evaluation of the Hartford Neighborhood Crime Prevention Program*. Boston: Center for Survey Research.

Fowler, F. J., McCalla, M. E., & Mangione, T. W. (1979). *The Hartford Residential Crime Prevention Program*. Washington, DC: U. S. Government Printing Office.

Frank, R. E., Massy, W. F., & Wind, Y. (1972). *Market segmentation*. Englewood Cliffs, NJ: Prentice-Hall.

Franks, C. M. (1982). Behavior therapy: An overview. In C. M. Franks, G. T. Wilson, P. C. Kendall, & K. D. Brownell (Eds.), *Annual review of behavior therapy* (pp. 1–38). New York: Guilford.

Fretz, B. R., & Leong, F. T. (1982a). Career development status as a predictor of career intervention outcomes. *Journal of Counseling Psychology, 29*, 388–393.

Fretz, B. R., & Leong, F. T. (1982b). Vocational behavior and career development, 1981: A review. *Journal of Vocational Behavior, 21*, 123–163.

Fretz, B. R., & Mills, D. H. (1980). *Licensing and certification of psychologists and counselors*. San Francisco: Jossey-Bass.

Freud, S. (1938). The history of the psychoanalytic movement. In *The basic writings of Sigmund Freud* (pp. 931–977). New York: Modern Library, Random House.

Friar, L. R., & Beatty, J. (1976). Migraine: Management by trained control of vasoconstriction. *Journal of Consulting and Clinical Psychology, 44*, 46–53.

Friedlander, J. (1979). The science and social science curriculum in the two-year college. *Community College Review, 7*, 60–67.

Fryer, D. H., & Henry, E. R. (1950). *Handbook of applied psychology* (Vols. 1 and 2). New York: Holt, Rinehart, & Winston.

Gagne, R. M. (1974). Task analysis—its relation to content analysis. *Educational Psychologist, 2*, 11–18.

Gagne, R. M., & Beard, J. G. (1978). Assessment of learning outcomes. In R. Glaser (Ed.), *Advances in instructional psychology* (Vol. 1, pp. 261–294). Hillsdale, NJ: Erlbaum.

Gallesich, J. (1973). Organizational factors influencing consultation in the schools. *Journal of School Psychology, 11*, 57–65.

Gallesich, J. (1982). *The profession and practice of consultation*. San Francisco: Jossey-Bass.

Gallo, P. S., Jr. (1978). Meta-analysis—A mixed metaphor? *American Psychologist, 33*, 515–517.

Garfield, S. L. (1980). *Psychotherapy: An eclectic approach*. New York: Wiley.

Garfield, S. L. (1983). *Clinical psychology: The study of personality and behavior* (2nd ed.). Hawthorne, NY: Aldine.

Garfield, S. L., & Bergin, A. E. (Eds.). (1978). *Handbook of psychotherapy and behavior change* (2nd ed.). New York: Wiley.

Garfield, S. L., & Kurtz, R. M. (1973). Attitudes toward training in diagnostic testing—A survey of directors of internship training. *Journal of Consulting and Clinical Psychology, 40,* 350–355.

Garfield, S. L., & Kurtz, R. M. (1976). Clinical psychologists in the 1970s. *American Psychologist, 31,* 1–9.

Garfield, S. L., & Kurtz, R. M. (1977). A study of eclectic views. *Journal of Consulting and Clinical Psychology, 45,* 78–83.

Geiselman, R. E., Landee, B. M., & Christen, F. G. (1982). Perceptual discriminability as a basis of selecting graphic symbols. *Human Factors, 24,* 329–337.

Geller, E. S. (1982, August). *Beyond an uneasy alliance: Applied behavioral analysis and environmental psychology.* Paper presented at the meeting of the American Psychological Association, Washington, DC.

Geller, E. S., Winett, R. A., & Everett, P. B. (1982). *Preserving the environment: New strategies for behavior change.* New York: Pergamon Press.

Gelso, C. G., & Johnson, D. H. (1983). *Explorations in time-limited counseling and psychotherapy.* New York: Columbia University, Teachers College Press.

Gerbasi, K. C., Zuckerman, M., & Reis, H. T. (1977). Justice needs a new blindfold: A review of mock jury research. *Psychological Bulletin, 84,* 323–345.

Gesten, E. L., Rores De Apocada, R., Rains, M., Weisberg, R. P., & Cowen, E. L. (1979). Promoting peer related social competence in schools. In M. W. Kent & J. E. Rolf (Eds.), *The primary prevention of pathology. Vol. 3: Social competence in children* (pp. 220–247). Hanover, NH: University Press of New England.

Gilbert, T. F. (1960). On the relevance of laboratory investigation of learning to self-instructional programming. In A. A. Lumsdaine & R. Glaser (Eds.), *Teaching machines and programmed learning* (pp. 475–485). Washington, DC: National Education Association.

Gilbreth, F. B. (1911). *Brick laying system.* New York: Clark.

Glaser, R. (1976). Components of a psychology of instruction: Toward a science of design. *Review of Educational Research, 46,* 1–24.

Glass, D., & Singer, J. (1972). *Urban stress.* New York: Academic Press.

Glass, G. V. (1976). *Evaluation studies review annual, I.* Beverly Hills, CA: Sage Publications.

Goddard, H. H. (1910, January). The Binet-Simon measuring scale for intelligence. *The Training School,* 2–16.

Goldberg, I. D., Krantz, G., & Locke, B. Z. (1970). Effects of short-term outpatient psychiatric therapy benefit on utilization of medical services in a prepaid group practice medical program. *Medical Care, 8,* 419–427.

Goldman, J. J. (1983). Recent trends in secondary school psychology: The decade from Oberlin to the HBCP. *Psychological Documents, 13(1),* 2.

Goldman, S. (1975). Voting behavior on the U. S. Courts of Appeals revisited. *American Political Science Review, 69,* 334–351.

Goldstein, I. (1938). *Trial technique.* Chicago: Callaghan.

Goldstein, I. L. (1980). Training in work organizations. *Annual Review of Psychology, 31,* 229–272.

Green, P. E., & Wind, Y. (1973). *Multiattribute decisions in marketing.* New York: Academic Press.

Greenberg, M. S., & Ruback, R. B. (1982). *Social psychology and the criminal justice system.* Monterey, CA: Brooks/Cole.

Greenwald, A. (1968). Cognitive learning, cognitive response to persuasion, and attitude change. In A. Greenwald, T. Brock, & T. Ostrom (Eds.), *Psychological foundations of attitude* (pp. 147-170). New York: Academic Press.

Gregg, A. (1947). *The place of psychology in an ideal university.* Cambridge, MA: Harvard University Press.

Griggs v. Duke Power Company, 401 U. S. 424 (1971).

Grisso, T. (1981). *Juveniles' waiver of rights: Legal and psychological competence.* New York: Plenum.

Grisso, T., Sales, B. D., & Bayless, S. (1982). Law related courses and programs in graduate psychology departments. *American Psychologist, 37,* 267-278.

Gross, M. L. (1978). *The psychological society: A critical analysis of psychiatry, psychotherapy, psychoanalysis, and the psychological revolution.* New York: Random House.

Guerin, P. (Ed.). (1976). *Family therapy.* New York: Gardner Press.

Guion, R. M. (1966). Employment tests and discriminatory hiring. *Industrial Relations, 5,* 20-37.

Guion, R. M. (1976). Recruiting, selection, and placement. In M. D. Dunnette (Ed.), *Handbook of industrial and organizational psychology* (pp. 777-828). Chicago: Rand McNally.

Gurin, G., Veroff, J., & Feld, S. (1960). *Americans view their mental health.* New York: Basic Books.

Gurman, A. S., & Kniskern, D. P. (Eds.). (1981). *Handbook of family therapy.* New York: Brunner/Mazel.

Guttentag, M. (1977). *Evaluation studies review annual, II.* Beverly Hills, CA: Sage Publications.

Hackman, J. R., & Oldham, G. R. (1975). Development of the Job Diagnostic Survey. *Journal of Applied Psychology, 60,* 159 - 170.

Hafemeister, T. L., Sales, B. D., & Suggs, D. L. (in press). Behavioral expertise in jury selection. In D. Weisstub (Ed.), *International yearbook on law and mental health.* Elmsford, NY: Pergamon Press.

Hagan, C. A. (1982). The insanity defense: A review of recent statutory changes. *Journal of Legal Medicine, 3,* 617-641.

Hagan, J. (1974). Extra-legal attributes and sentencing: An assessment of a sociological viewpoint. *Law and Society Review, 8,* 357-383.

Haley, J. (1976). *Problem solving therapy.* San Francisco: Jossey-Bass.

Haley, R. I. (1968). Benefit segmentation: A decision-oriented research tool. *Journal of Marketing, 32,* 30-35.

Hall, C. S. (1962). *Primer of Freudian psychology.* New York: Mentor.

Hall, C. S., & Lindzey, G. (1978). *Theories of personality* (3rd ed.). New York: Wiley.

Hallam, R. S. (1975). The training of nurses as therapists: Outcome and implications. *Bulletin of the British Psychological Society, 28,* 331-336.

Halpin, A. W., & Winer, B. J. (1957). A factorial study of the leader behavior descriptions. In R. M. Stogdill & A. E. Coons (Eds.), *Leader behavior: Its description and measurement* (pp. 39–51). Columbus: Ohio State University Bureau of Business Research.

Hamilton, L. V. (1976). Individual differences in ascriptions of responsibility, guilt, and appropriate punishment. In G. Bermant, C. Nemeth, & N. Vidmar (Eds.), *Psychology and the law* (pp. 239–264). Lexington, MA: D. C. Heath.

Hans, V. P., & Vidmar, N. (1982). Jury selection. In N. L. Kerr & R. M. Bray (Eds.), *The psychology of the courtroom* (pp. 39–82). New York: Academic Press.

Harmon, L. W. (1982). Scientific affairs—the next decade. *The Counseling Psychologist, 10(2)*, 31–38.

Harrington, D. C., & Dempsey, J. (1969). Psychological factors in jury selection. *Tennessee Law Review, 37*, 173–184.

Harris, D. B. (1963). *Children's drawings as measures of intellectual maturity.* New York: Harcourt, Brace, & World.

Hathaway, S. R., & McKinley, J. C. (1951). *Minnesota Multiphasic Personality Inventory* (rev. ed.). New York: Psychological Corporation.

Haveman, R. H., & Watts, H. W. (1976). Social experiments as policy research: A review of negative income tax experiments. In G. V. Glass (Ed.), *Evaluation studies review annual* (pp. 425–441). Beverly Hills, CA: Sage Publications.

Hawkins, C. H. (1962). Interaction rates of jurors aligned in factions. *American Sociological Review, 27*, 689–691.

Health Maintenance Act of 1973 (P. L. 93-222).

Healy, E. S., Kales, A., Monroe, L. J., Bixler, E. D., Chamberlin, K., & Soldatos, C. R. (1981). Onset of insomnia: Role of life stress events. *Psychosomatic Medicine, 43*, 439–451.

Heath, R. (1964). *The reasonable adventurer.* Pittsburgh: University of Pittsburgh Press.

Heesacker, M., Heppner, P. P., & Rogers, M. E. (1982). Classics and emerging classics in counseling psychology. *Journal of Counseling Psychology, 29*, 400–405.

Heffernan, T., & Richards, C. S. (1981). Self-control and study behavior: Identification and evaluation of natural methods. *Journal of Counseling Psychology, 28*, 361–364.

Henderson, J. B., Hall, S. M., & Lipton, H. L. (1979). Changing self-destructive behaviors. In G. C. Stone, F. Cohen, & N. E. Adler (Eds.), *Health psychology* (pp. 141–160). San Francisco: Jossey-Bass.

Herink, R. (Ed.). (1980). *The psychotherapy handbook: The A to Z guide to more than 250 different therapies in use today.* New York: A Meridan Book, New American Library.

Herzberg, F., Mausner, B., Peterson, R. D., & Capwell, D. F. (1957). *Job attitudes: Review of research and opinion.* Pittsburgh: Pittsburgh Psychological Services.

Hilgard, E. R. (Ed.). (1978). *American psychology in historical perspective.* Washington, DC: American Psychological Association.

Hill, A. (1980). *Science education in two-year colleges: Psychology.* Los Angeles: Center for the Study of Community Colleges and ERIC Clearinghouse for Junior Colleges.

Hill, C. E. (1978). Development of a counselor verbal category system. *Journal of Counseling Psychology, 25*, 461–468.

Hively, W. (1974). Domain-referenced testing: Basic ideas. *Educational Technology, 14,* 5–10.

Hogan, R., & Hogan, J.C. (1982). Subjective correlates of stress and human performance. In E.A. Alluisi & E.A. Fleishman (Eds.), *Human performance and productivity* (Vol. 3, pp. 141–163). Hillsdale, NJ: Erlbaum.

Hohmann, G.W. (1975). Psychological aspects of treatment and rehabilitation of the spinal cord injured person. *Clinical Orthopedics and Related Research, 112,* 81.

Holbrook, J.C. (1956). *A survey of metropolitan trial courts in Los Angeles.* Los Angeles: University of Southern California Press.

Holland, J.G., & Skinner, B.F. (1961). *The analysis of behavior, a program for self instruction.* New York: McGraw-Hill.

Holland, J.L. (1965). *Manual for the Vocational Preference Inventory.* Palo Alto, CA: Consulting Psychologists Press.

Holland, J.L. (1973). *Making vocational choices: A theory of careers.* Englewood Cliffs, NJ: Prentice-Hall.

Holland, J.L. (1974). *The self-directed search.* Palo Alto, CA: Consulting Psychologists Press.

Holland, J.L., Magoon, T.M., & Spokane, A.R. (1981). Counseling psychology: Career intervention research and theory. *Annual Review of Psychology, 32,* 279–305.

Holmes, D.S., & Solomon, S. (1980, September). *The effectiveness of presidential pleas and legal limits on driving speed.* Paper presented at the meeting of the American Psychological Association, Montreal.

Holmes, T.H., & Rahe, R.H. (1967). The social readjustment rating scale. *Journal of Psychosomatic Research, 11,* 213–218.

Holohan, C.J. (1982). *Environmental psychology.* New York: Random House.

Holohan, C.J., & Saegert, S. (1973). Behavioral and attitudinal effects of large-scale variation in the physical environment of psychiatric wards. *Journal of Abnormal Psychology, 82,* 454–462.

Hopkins, C.O. (1981). HFS developing long-range plan for Nuclear Regulatory Commission. *Human Factors Bulletin, 24,* 1–3.

House, R.J. (1971). A path-goals theory of leadership effectiveness. *Administrative Science Quarterly, 16,* 321–338.

House, R.J., & Dessler, G. (1974). The path-goal theory of leadership: Some post hoc and a priori tests. In J.G. Hunt & L.L. Larson (Eds.), *Contingency approaches to leadership* (pp. 29–55). Carbondale: Southern Illinois University Press.

House, R.J., & Mitchell, T.R. (1974). Path-goal theory of leadership. *Journal of Contemporary Business, 3,* 81–97.

Howard, J.A., & Sheth, J.N. (1969). *The theory of buyer behavior.* New York: Wiley.

Howard, J.C. (1975). Racial discrimination in sentencing. *Judicature, 59,* 120–125.

Howell, W.C., & Fuchs, A.H. (1968). Population stereotype in code design. *Organizational Behavior and Human Performance, 3,* 310–339.

Howell, W.C., & Goldstein, I.L. (1970). Engineering psychology today: Some views from the ivory tower. *Organizational Behavior and Human Performance, 5,* 159–169.

Howell, W. C., & Goldstein, I. L. (1971). *Engineering psychology: Current perspectives on research.* New York: Appleton-Century-Crofts.

Howell, W. C., Johnston, W. A., & Goldstein, I. L. (1966). Complex monitoring and its relation to the classical problem of vigilance. *Organizational Behavior and Human Performance, 1,* 129–150.

Howell, W. C., & Kennedy, P. A. (1979). Field validation of the Fanger Thermal Comfort Model. *Human Factors, 21,* 229–239.

Howell, W. C., & Stramler, C. S. (1981). The contribution of psychological variables to the prediction of thermal comfort judgments in real work settings. *ASHRAE Transactions, 87,* Pt. 1.

Howitt, D. (1977). Situational and victims' characteristics in simulated penal judgments. *Psychological Reports, 40,* 55–58.

Huchingson, R. D. (1981). *New horizons for human factors in design.* New York: McGraw-Hill.

Hume, W. (1977). Biofeedback. *Annual Research Reviews: Biofeedback, 2,* 72.

Hunt, W. A., & Matarazzo, J. D. (1973). Recent developments in the experimental modification of smoking behavior. *Journal of Abnormal Psychology, 81,* 107–114.

Hutt, R. B. W. (1923). The school psychologist. *Psychological Clinic, 15,* 48–51.

Ittleson, W. H., Proshansky, H. M., Rivlin, L., & Winkel, G. (1974). *Introduction to environmental psychology.* New York: Holt, Rinehart & Winston.

Ivey, A. (1971). *Microcounseling: Innovations in interviewing training.* Springfield, IL: Thomas.

Jacobs, J. (1961). *The death and life of the American city.* New York: Vintage.

Jacoby, J., & Chestnut, R. W. (1978). *Brand loyalty: Measurement and management.* New York: Wiley.

Jacoby, J., & Kyner, D. B. (1973). Brand loyalty vs. repeat purchasing behavior. *Journal of Marketing Research, 10,* 1–9.

Jacoby, J., Speller, D. E., & Kohn, C. A. (1974a). Brand choice behavior as a function of information load. *Journal of Marketing Research, 11,* 63–69.

Jacoby, J., Speller, D. E., & Kohn, C. A. (1974b). Brand choice behavior as a function of information load: Replication and extension. *Journal of Consumer Research, 1,* 33–42.

James, R. (1959). Status and competence of jurors. *American Journal of Sociology, 64,* 563–570.

James, W. (1899). *Talks to teachers on psychology.* New York: Henry Holt.

Jansen, M., & Fulcher, R. Salaries of doctoral level psychologists. Agenda of the Board of Professional Affairs of the American Psychological Association meeting, February 19–21, 1982.

Jason, L. A., Zolik, E. S., & Matese, F. J. (1979). Prompting dog owners to pick up dog droppings. *American Journal of Community Psychology, 7,* 339–351.

Jeffrey, R. W., Wing, R. R., & Stunkard, A. J. (1978). Behavioral treatment of obesity: The state of the art, 1976. *Behavior Therapy, 9,* 189–199.

Jenkins, C. D., Rosenman, R. H., & Friedman, M. (1967). Development of an objective psychological test for determination of the coronary-prone behavior pattern in employed men. *Journal of Chronic Diseases, 20,* 371–379.

Jensen, A. R. (1980). *Bias in mental testing.* New York: Free Press.

Johnson v. Louisiana, 406 U. S. 356 (1972).

Johnson, J. H., & Sarason, I. G. (1978). Life stress, depression and anxiety: Internal-external control as a moderator variable. *Journal of Psychosomatic Research, 22,* 205–208.

Johnson, M., & Wertheimer, M. (Eds.). (1979). *Psychology teacher's resource book: First course* (3rd ed.). Washington, DC: American Psychological Association.

Joint Commission on Accreditation of Hospitals. (1980). *Accreditation manual for hospitals.* Chicago: JCAH.

Jones, M. C. (1924a). The elimination of children's fears. *Journal of Experimental Psychology, 7,* 382–390.

Jones, M. C. (1924b). A laboratory study of fear: The case of Peter. *Journal of Genetic Psychology, 31,* 308–315.

Jordaan, J. P. (1968). *The counseling psychologist.* Washington, DC: American Psychological Association.

Kagan, N. (1979). Counseling psychology, interpersonal skills and health care. In G. C. Stone, F. Cohen, & N. E. Adler (Eds.), *Health psychology* (pp. 465–485). San Francisco: Jossey-Bass.

Kagan, N., & Krathwohl, D. R. (1967). *Studies in human interaction: Interpersonal process recall stimulated by videotape.* East Lansing, MI: Educational Publications Services, College of Education, Michigan State University.

Kahneman, D. (1973). *Attention and effort.* Englewood Cliffs, NJ: Prentice-Hall.

Kahneman, D., Slovic, P., & Tversky, A. (1982). *Judgment under uncertainty: Heuristics and biases.* New York: Cambridge.

Kairys, D., Schulman, J., & Harring, S. (Eds.). (1975). *The jury system: New methods for reducing prejudice.* Philadelphia: National Lawyers Guild.

Kalven, H., Jr., & Zeisel, H. (1966). *The American jury.* Boston: Little, Brown.

Kantowitz, B. H. (1982). Interfacing human information processing and engineering psychology. In W. C. Howell & E. A. Fleishman (Eds.), *Human performance and productivity* (Vol. 2, pp. 31 - 81). Hillsdale, NJ: Erlbaum.

Kantowitz, B. H., & Sorkin, R. D. (1983). *Human factors.* New York: Wiley.

Kanwar, R., Olson, J. C., & Sims, L. S. (1981). Toward conceptualizing and measuring cognitive structures. In K. B. Monroe (Ed.), *Advances in consumer research* (Vol. 3, pp. 122–127). Ann Arbor, MI: Association for Consumer Research.

Karnosh, L. J., & Zucker, E. M. (1945). *Handbook of psychiatry.* St. Louis: C. F. Mosby.

Kassarjian, H. H. (1971). Personality and consumer behavior: A review. *Journal of Marketing Research, 8,* 409–418.

Kassarjian, H. H. (1982). Consumer psychology. *Annual Review of Psychology, 33,* 619–649.

Kasschau, R., & Wertheimer, M. (1974). *Teaching psychology in secondary schools.* Washington, DC: American Psychological Association.

Katz, D., & Kahn, R. L. (1978). *The social psychology of organizations.* New York: Wiley.

Katz, L. S. (1968-1969). The twelve man jury. *Trial, 5,* 39–40, 42.

Kaufman, H. G. (1982). *Professionals in search of work.* New York: Wiley.

Kazdin, A. E. (1978). The application of operant techniques in treatment, rehabilitation, and education. In S. L. Garfield & A. E. Bergin (Eds.), *Handbook of psychotherapy and behavior change* (2nd ed., pp. 549–589). New York: Wiley.

Keegan, L., Sinha, B. N., Merriman, J. E., & Shipley, C. (1979). Type A behavior pattern: Relationship to coronary heart disease, personality and life adjustment. *Canadian Journal of Psychiatry, 24,* 724–730.

Keller, F. S. (1966). A personal course in psychology. In R. E. Ulrich, T. Stachnik, & J. Mabry (Eds.), *Control of human behavior* (Vol. 1, pp. 91–93). Glenview, IL: Scott, Foresman.

Kellerman, J. (1980). Psychological interventions in pediatric oncology. In M. Jospe, J. Neiberding, & B. D. Cohen (Eds.), *Psychological factors in health care* (pp. 113–128). Lexington, MA: Lexington Books.

Kellerman, J., Rigler, D., Siegal, S. E., McCue, K., Pospisil, J., & Uno, R. (1976). Psychological evaluation and management of pediatric oncology patients in protected environments. *Medical and Pediatric Oncology, 2,* 353.

Kelly, E. L. (1961, Winter). Clinical Psychology—1960. Report of survey findings. *Newsletter, Division of Clinical Psychology,* 1–11.

Kelly, G. A. (1955). *The psychology of personal constructs* (Vols. 1 and 2). New York: Norton.

Kelso, J. A. S. (1977). Motor control mechanisms underlying human movement reproduction. *Journal of Experimental Psychology: Human Perception and Performance, 3,* 529–543.

Kemeny, J. G. (1979). *Report of the President's commission on the accident at Three Mile Island.* Washington, DC: U. S. Government Printing Office.

Kendall, P. C., & Hollon, S. D. (1979). *Cognitive–behavioral interventions: Theory, research and procedures.* New York: Academic Press.

Kerr, N. L., Atkin, R. S., Stasser, G., Meek, D., Holt, R. W., & Davis, J. H. (1976). Guilt beyond a reasonable doubt: Effect of concept definition and assigned decision rule on the judgments of mock jurors. *Journal of Personality and Social Psychology, 34,* 282–295.

Kerr, N. L, & Bray, R. M. (1982). *The psychology of the courtroom.* New York: Academic Press.

Kessen, W. (1979). The American child and other cultural inventions. *American Psychologist, 34,* 815–820.

Kiesler, C. A. (1979). National health insurance testimony to the House of Representatives, November 14, 1975. In C. A. Kiesler, N. A. Cummings, & G. R. VandenBos (Eds.), *Psychology and National Health Insurance: A sourcebook* (pp. 36–44). Washington, DC: American Psychological Association.

Kiesler, C. A. (1980a). Mental health policy as a field of inquiry for psychology. *American Psychologist, 35,* 1066–1080.

Kiesler, C. A. (1980b). Psychology and public policy. In L. Bickman (Ed.), *Applied social psychology annual* (Vol. 1, pp. 49–67). Beverly Hills, CA: Sage Publications.

Kiesler, C. A. (1981). Barriers to effective knowledge use in national mental health policy. *Health Policy Quarterly, 1,* 201–215.

Kiesler, C. A. (1982a). Mental hospitals and alternative care: Non-institutionalization as potential public policy for mental patients. *American Psychologist, 37,* 349–360.

Kiesler, C. A. (1982b). Public and professional myths about mental hospitalization: An empirical reassessment of policy-related beliefs. *American Psychologist, 37,* 1323–1339.

Kincey, J. (1981). Internal-external control and weight loss in the obese: Predictive and discriminant validity and some possible clinical implications. *Journal of Clinical Psychology, 37,* 100–103.

Kiresuk, T. J., & Sherman, R. E. (1968). Goal attainment scaling: A general method for evaluating comprehensive community health programs. *Community Mental Health Journal, 4,* 443–453.

Kirk, D. (1978, August). *High school psychology.* Paper presented at the meeting of the American Psychological Association, Toronto. (ERIC Document Reproduction Service No. ED 170 223.)

Knefelkamp, L. L., & Slepitza, R. A. (1976). A cognitive-developmental model of career development—An adaptation of the Perry scheme. *The Counseling Psychologist, 6(3),* 53–58.

Knefelkamp, L. L., Widick, C., & Parker, C. A. (Eds.). (1978). *New directions in student services,* No. 4: *Applying new developmental findings.* San Francisco: Jossey-Bass.

Knerr, C. R., & Carroll, J. D. (1978). Confidentiality and criminal research: The evolving body of law. *Journal of Criminal Law and Criminology, 69,* 311–321.

Knopf, I. J. (1984). *Childhood psychopathology: A developmental approach* (2nd ed.). Englewood Cliffs, NJ: Prentice-Hall.

Knowles, M. G. (Ed.). (1982). The Human Factors Society. *Human Factors: Directory and Yearbook,* 1–2.

Konečni, V. J., & Ebbesen, E. B. (1981). Theory and method in social-psychological approaches to legal issues. In B. D. Sales (Ed.), *The trial process* (pp. 481–498). New York: Plenum.

Konečni, V. J., & Ebbesen, E. B. (1982). *The criminal justice system: A social-psychological analysis.* San Francisco: W. H. Freeman.

Korman, M. (Ed.). (1976). *Levels and patterns of professional training in psychology.* Washington, DC: American Psychological Association.

Krugman, H. E. (1965). The impact of television advertising: Learning without involvement. *Public Opinion Quarterly, 29,* 349–356.

Kulik, J., Brown, D., Vestewig, R., & Wright, J. (1973). *Undergraduate education in psychology.* Washington, DC: American Psychological Association.

Lachman, R., Lachman, J. C., & Butterfield, E. C. (1979). *Psychology and information processing.* Hillsdale, NJ: Erlbaum.

LaFromboise, T. D., & Dixon, D. N. (1981). American Indian perceptions of trustworthiness in a counseling interview. *Journal of Counseling Psychology, 28,* 135–139.

Landa, L. N. (1976). *Instructional regulation and control.* Englewood Cliffs, NJ: Educational Technology Publications.

Landy, F. J., & Farr, J. L. (1980). Performance rating. *Psychological Bulletin, 87,* 72–107.

Landy, F. J., & Trumbo, D. A. (1980). *Psychology of work behavior.* Homewood, IL: Dorsey.

Lane, D. M. (1982). Limited capacity, attention allocation, and productivity. In W. C. Howell & E. A. Fleishman (Eds.), *Human performance and productivity* (Vol. 2, pp. 121–156). Hillsdale, NJ: Erlbaum.

Langer, E. (1978). Rethinking the role of thought in social interaction. In J. Harvey, W. Ickes, & R. Kidd (Eds.), *New directions in attribution research* (Vol. 2, pp. 35–58). Hillsdale, NJ: Erlbaum.

Larry P. v. Riles, 495 F. Supp. 926 (1979).

Lavidge, R. J., & Steiner, G. A. (1961). A model for predictive measurements of advertising effectiveness. *Journal of Marketing, 25,* 59–62.

Lawler, E. E., & Suttle, J. L. (1972). A causal correlational test of the need hierarchy concept. *Organizational Behavior and Human Performance, 7,* 265–287.

Lawrence, P. R., & Lorsch, J. (1969). *Organization and environment: Managing differentiation and integration.* Homewood, IL: Irwin.

Lazarus, R. S. (1966). *Psychological stress and the coping process.* New York: McGraw-Hill.

Lehrer, S. (1980). Life change and gastric cancer. *Psychosomatic Medicine, 42,* 499–502.

Lerner, B. (1981). The minimum competence testing movement: Social, scientific, and legal implications. *American Psychologist, 36,* 1057–1066.

Levine, A. (1982). *Love Canal: Science, politics, & people.* Lexington, MA: Lexington Books.

Levine, D., Wilson, K., & Sales, B. D. (1980). An exploratory assessment of APA internships with legal/forensic experience. *Professional Psychology, 11,* 64–71.

Levine, M. (1974). Scientific method and the adversarial model: Some preliminary thoughts. *American Psychologist, 29,* 661 - 677.

Levinson, D. J., Darrow, C., Klien, E., Levinson, M., & McKee, B. (1978). *The seasons of a man's life.* New York: Knopf.

Levy, R. I., & Moskowitz, J. (1982). Cardiovascular research: Decades of progress, a decade of promise. *Science, 217,* 121–129.

Lewinsohn, P. M., Mischel, W., Chaplain, W., & Barton, R. (1980). Social competence and depression: The role of illusory self-perceptions? *Journal of Abnormal Psychology, 89,* 203–212.

Lewis, B. N., & Horabin, I. S. (1977). Algorithmics 1967. *Improving Human Performance Quarterly, 6,* 55–86.

Likert, R. (1961). *New patterns of management.* New York: McGraw-Hill.

Locke, E. A. (1976). Nature and causes of job satisfaction. In M. D. Dunnette (Ed.), *Handbook of industrial and organizational psychology* (pp. 1297–1349). Chicago: Rand McNally.

Loftus, E. (1979). *Eyewitness testimony.* Cambridge: Harvard University Press.

Loro, A. D., Levenkorn, J. C., & Fisher, E. B. (1979). Critical clinical issues in the behavioral treatment of obesity. *Addictive Behaviors, 4,* 383–391.

Louttit, C. M. (1939). The nature of clinical psychology. *Psychological Bulletin, 36,* 361–389.

Lovaas, O. I., Freitag, G., Gold, V. J., & Kassorla, I. C. (1965). Experimental studies in childhood schizophrenia: Analysis of self-destructive behavior. *Journal of Experimental Child Psychology, 2,* 67–84.

Loven, M. D. (1978). Four alternative approaches to the family/school liaison role. *Psychology in the Schools, 15,* 553–559.

Luborsky, L., Singer, B., & Luborsky, L. (1975). Comparative studies of psychotherapies. *Archives of General Psychiatry, 32*, 995–1008.

Lurie, E. E. (1981). Nurse practitioners: Issues in professional socialization. *Journal of Health and Social Behavior, 22*, 31–48.

Lutz, R. J. (1975). Changing brand attitudes through modification of cognitive structure. *Journal of Consumer Research, 1*, 49–59.

Lutz, R. J. (1979). A functional theory framework for designing and pretesting advertising themes. In J. C. Maloney & B. Silverman (Eds.), *Attitude research plays for high stakes* (pp. 37–44). Chicago: American Marketing Association.

Lutz, R. J., & Bettman, J. R. (1977). Multiattribute attitude models in marketing: A bicentennial review. In A. G. Woodside, J. N. Sheth, & P. D. Bennett (Eds.), *Consumer and industrial buying behavior* (pp. 137–149). New York: North Holland.

Lutz, R. J., & MacKenzie, S. B. (1982). Construction of a diagnostic cognitive response model for use in commercial pretesting. In J. Chasin (Ed.), *Straight talk about attitude research* (pp. 145–156). Chicago: American Marketing Association.

Maas, J., & Kleiber, A. (1975). *Directory of teaching innovations in psychology.* Washington, DC: American Psychological Association.

Machover, K. (1949). *Personality projection in the drawing of the human figure.* Springfield, IL: Charles C. Thomas.

Mackett-Stout, J., & Dewar, R. (1981). Evaluation of symbolic public information signs. *Human Factors, 23*, 139–151.

Madden, J. M. (1980). Distribution of Division 14 members by state, type of work, and type of degree. *The Industrial-Organizational Psychologist, 17*, 25–27.

Mager, R. F. (1966). President's page. *Journal of the National Society for Performance and Instruction, 5*, 3.

Mager, R. F. (1975). *Preparing instructional objectives* (2nd ed.). Belmont, CA: Fearon Publishers.

Mager, R. F., & Pipe, P. (1970). *Analyzing performance problems, or "you really oughta wanna."* Belmont, CA: Fearon Publishers.

Maher, C. A. (1981). Intervention with school social systems: A behavioral-systems approach. *School Psychology Review, 4*, 499–508.

Markle, S. M. (1967). Empirical testing of programs. In P. C. Lange (Ed.), *Programmed instruction* (pp. 7–37). Chicago: University of Chicago Press.

Markle, S. M. (1978). *Designs for designers.* Champaign, IL: Stipes.

Markle, S. M. (1981). Training designers to think about thinking. *Journal of Instructional Development, 4*, 24–27.

Marshall, E. (1980). Psychotherapy works, but for whom? *Science, 207*, 506–508.

Marshall, E. (1982a). Fear as a form of pollution. *Science, 215*, 481.

Marshall, E. (1982b). NRC must weigh psychic costs. *Science, 216*, 1203–1204.

Martin, D., Abramson, L. Y., & Alloy, L. B. (1984). The illusion of control for self and others in depressed and nondepressed college students. *Journal of Personality and Social Psychology, 46*, 125–136.

Maslow, A. H. (1954). *Motivation and personality.* New York: Harper & Row.

Maslow, A. H. (1965). *Eupsychian management.* Homewood, IL: Irwin.

Maslow, A. H. (1970). *Motivation and personality* (2nd ed.). New York: Harper & Row.

Matarazzo, J. D. (1980). Behavioral health and behavioral medicine: Frontiers for a new health psychology. *American Psychologist, 35,* 807–815.

Matthews, K. A. (1982). Psychological perspectives on the Type A behavior pattern. *Psychological Bulletin, 91,* 293–323.

Matthews, K. A., & Avis, N. E. (1982). Psychologists in schools of public health: Current status, future prospects and implications for other health settings. *American Psychologist, 37,* 949–954.

May, E. P. (1977). Counseling psychologists in general medical and surgical hospitals. *The Counseling Psychologist, 7(2),* 82–85.

Mayfield, E. C. (1964). The selection interview: A reevaluation of published research. *Personnel Psychology, 17,* 239–260.

Mazis, M. B., & Adkinson, J. E. (1976). An experimental evaluation of a proposed corrective advertising remedy. *Journal of Marketing Research, 13,* 178–183.

McCain, G., Cox, V. C., & Paulus, P. B. (1980). *The effect of prison crowding on inmate behavior* (LEAA 78–N1–AX–0019). Arlington, TX: Department of Psychology, University of Texas.

McCormick, E. J., & Sanders, M. S. (1982). *Human factors in engineering and design.* New York: McGraw-Hill.

McFall, R. M. (1978). Smoking cessation research. *Journal of Consulting and Clinical Psychology, 46,* 703–712.

McFarland, R. A. (1963). The role of human engineering highway safety. In E. Bennet, J. Degan, & J. Spiegal (Eds.), *Human factors in technology* (pp. 207–229). New York: McGraw-Hill.

McGowan, J., & Schmidt, L. D. (Eds.). (1962). *Counseling: Readings in theory and practice.* New York: Holt, Rinehart, & Winston.

McGregor, D. (1960). *The human side of enterprise.* New York: McGraw-Hill.

McKeachie, W., & Milholland, J. (1961). *Undergraduate curricula in psychology.* Chicago: Scott, Foresman.

Meara, N., Pepinsky, H., Shannon, J., & Murray, W. (1981). Semantic communication and expectations for counseling across three theoretical orientations. *Journal of Counseling Psychology, 28,* 110–118.

Meichenbaum, D. H. (1977). *Cognitive behavior modification.* New York: Plenum.

Meister, D., & Rabideau, G. F. (1965). *Human factors evaluation in system development.* New York: Wiley.

Melton, G. B., Koocher, G. P., & Saks, M. J. (1983). *Children's competence to consent.* New York: Plenum.

Meltzoff, J., & Kornreich, M. (1970). *Research in psychotherapy.* New York: Atherton Press.

Mercer, J. R., & Lewis, J. L. (1978). *System of multicultural pluralistic assessment.* New York: The Psychological Corporation.

Merry, S. E. (1981). Defensible space undefended: Social factors in crime control through environmental design. *Urban Affairs Quarterly, 16,* 397–422.

Messick, S. (1980). Test validity and the ethics of assessment. *American Psychologist, 35,* 1012–1027.

Meyer, R. G., & Smith, S. (1977). A crisis in group therapy. *American Psychologist, 32,* 638–643.

Meyer, R. G., & Willage, D. E. (1980). Confidentiality and privileged communications in psychotherapy. In P. D. Lipsitt & B. D. Sales (Eds.), *New directions in psycholegal research* (pp. 237–246). New York: Van Nostrand Reinhold.

Miller, G., & Fontes, N. (1979). *Videotape on trial: A view from the jury box.* Beverly Hills, CA: Sage Publications.

Mills v. Rogers, 73 LEd 2d 16, (1982).

Mills, E. S. (1962). A statistical study of occupations of jurors in a (Maryland) United States district court. *Maryland Law Review, 22,* 205–214.

Minuchin, S., & Fishman, C. H. (1981). *Family therapy techniques.* Cambridge, MA: Harvard University Press.

Mitchell, A. A., & Olson, J. C. (1981). Are attribute beliefs the only mediator of advertising effects on brand attitude? *Journal of Marketing Research, 18,* 318–332.

M'Naghten's Case, 8 Eng. Rep. 718 (H. L. 1843).

Mobley, W. H., Horne, S. O., & Hollingworth, A. T. (1978). An evaluation of precursors of hospital employee turnover. *Journal of Applied Psychology, 63,* 408–414.

Monahan, J. (1981). *Predicting violent behavior and assessment of clinical techniques.* Beverly Hills, CA: Sage Publications.

Monahan, J., & Steadman, H. (Eds.). (1983). *Mentally disordered offenders: Perspectives from law and social science.* New York: Plenum.

Moos, R. H. (1976). *The human context: Environmental determinants of behavior.* New York: Wiley.

Moos, R. H. (1979). Social-ecological perspectives on health. In G. C. Stone, F. Cohen, & N. E. Adler (Eds.), *Health psychology* (pp. 523–548). San Francisco: Jossey-Bass.

Moray, N. (1982). Subjective mental workload. *Human Factors, 24,* 25–40.

Morgan, C. D., & Murray, H. A. (1935). A method for investigating fantasies: The Thematic Apperception Test. *Archives of Neurology and Psychiatry, 34,* 289–306.

Morris, C. W., & Cohen, R. (1982). Cognitive considerations in cognitive behavior modification. *School Psychology Review, 11,* 14–20.

Morris, R. A., Sales, B. D., & Berman, J. J. (1981). Research and the Freedom of Information Act. *American Psychologist, 36,* 819–826.

Morrow, W. R., & Peterson, D. B. (1966). Follow-up on discharged offenders—"not guilty by reason of insanity" and "criminal sexual psychopaths." *Journal of Criminal Law, Criminology, and Police Science, 57,* 31–34.

Morse, S. (1983). Mental health law: Governmental regulation of disordered persons and the role of the professional psychologist. In B. D. Sales (Ed.), *Professional psychologist's handbook* (pp. 339–422). New York: Plenum.

Mullen, I. (1981). School psychology in the U. S. A.: Reminiscences of its origin. *Journal of School Psychology, 19,* 103–119.

Munson, G. (1947). *Bureau of Child Study and the Chicago plan of adjustment service.* Chicago: Board of Education.

Münsterberg, H. (1913). *Psychology and industrial efficiency.* Boston: Houghton Mifflin.

Murphy, G. (1968). *Psychological thought from Pythagoras to Freud.* New York: Harcourt, Brace, and World.

Nagel, S. S. (1962). Judicial backgrounds and criminal cases. *Journal of Criminal Law, Criminology, and Police Science, 53*, 333–339.

Nagel, S. S. (1967). Disparities in criminal procedure. *UCLA Law Review, 14*, 1272–1305.

Nagel, S. S. (1969). *The legal process from a behavioral perspective.* Homewood, IL: Dorsey.

Napoletano, M. A. (1981). The effects of academic instruction in psychology on student nurses' attitudes toward mental illness. *Teaching of Psychology, 8*, 22–24.

Nash, A. N., & Carroll, S. J., Jr. (1975). *The management of compensation.* Monterey, CA: Brooks/Cole.

Nathan, R. G., Lubin, B., Matarazzo, J. D., & Perseley, G. W. (1979). Psychologists in schools of medicine: 1955, 1964, and 1977. *American Psychologist, 34*, 622–627.

Nathensen, M. B., & Henderson, E. S. (1980). *Using student feedback to improve learning materials.* London: Croom Helm.

National Association of School Psychologists. (1982). *1982 Membership Directory.* Washington, DC.

Nazzaro, J. R. (1974). The two-year college instructor: A profile. *American Psychologist, 29*, 554–557.

Nemeth, C. (1977). Interactions between jurors as a function of majority v. unanimity decision rules. *Journal of Applied Social Psychology, 7*, 38–56.

Nemeth, C., & Sosis, R. H. (1973). A simulated study: Characteristics of the defendant and the jurors. *Journal of Social Psychology, 90*, 221–229.

Newland, T. E. (1981). School psychology—observation and reminiscence. *Journal of School Psychology, 19*, 4–20.

Newman, O. (1972). *Defensible space.* New York: Macmillan.

Newman, O., & Franck, K. (1982). The effects of building size on personal crime and fear of crime. *Population and Environment, 5*, 203–220.

Nickerson, R. S. (1980). *Attention and performance.* Hillsdale, NJ: Erlbaum.

Niven, L. (1974). *A hole in space.* New York: Ballantine.

Norton, F. T. (1972). Two-year college instruction: Opportunities for psychology. *American Psychologist, 27*, 445–450.

O'Conner v. Donaldson, 422 U. S. 563 (1975).

Olbrisch, M. E. (1977). Psychotherapeutic interventions in physical health: Effectiveness and economic efficiency. *American Psychologist, 32*, 761–777.

O'Leary, K. D, & O'Leary, S. G. (1972). *Classroom management: The successful use of behavior modification.* New York: Pergamon Press.

Oliver, R. L. (1980). A cognitive model of the antecedents and consequences of satisfaction decisions. *Journal of Marketing Research, 17*, 460–469.

Organ, D. W. (1977). A reappraisal and reinterpretation of the satisfaction causes performance hypothesis. *Academy of Management Review, 2*, 46–53.

Orne, M. T. (1979). The efficacy of biofeedback therapy. *Annual Review of Medicine, 30*, 489–503.

Osipow, S. (1983). *Theories of career development* (3rd ed.). Englewood Cliffs, NJ: Prentice-Hall.

Osipow, S. H. (1982). Counseling psychology: Applications in the world of work. *The Counseling Psychologist, 10(2)*, 19–26.

Osterhouse, R. A. (1972). Desensitization and study skills training as treatment for two types of test anxious students. *Journal of Counseling Psychology, 19*, 301–307.

Overcast, T. D., & Sales, B. D. (1982). Elevating the status of psychologists: A simple solution is neither simple nor a solution. *Professional Psychology, 13*, 171–172.

Pallone, N. J. (1980). Counseling psychology: Toward an empirical definition. In J. M. Whiteley & B. R. Fretz (Eds.), *The present and future of counseling psychology* (pp. 39–49). Monterey, CA: Brooks/Cole.

Parloff, M. B., Waskow, I. W., & Wolfe, B. E. (1978). Research on therapist variables in relation to process and outcome. In S. L. Garfield & A. E. Bergin (Eds.), *Handbook of psychotherapy and behavior change* (2nd ed., pp. 233–282). New York: Wiley.

Parnes, H. S. (1981). *Work and retirement.* Cambridge, MA: MIT Press.

Parsons, F. (1909). *Choosing a vocation.* Boston: Houghton Mifflin.

Parsons, H. M. (1972). *Man-machine system experiments.* Baltimore: Johns Hopkins University Press.

Parsons, H. M. (1981, October). *Automation and engineering psychology: A look to the future.* Paper presented at the meeting of the Human Resources Research Organization, Washington, DC.

Pase v. Hannon, 506 F. Supp. 831 (N. D. Ill. 1980).

Pasewark, R. A. (1981). Insanity plea: A review of the research literature. *Journal of Psychiatry and Law, 9*, 357–401.

Pasewark, R. A., & Pantle, M. L. (1979). Insanity plea: Legislator's view. *American Journal of Psychiatry, 136*, 222–223.

Pasewark, R. A., Pantle, M. L., & Steadman, H. J. (1979a). Characteristics and disposition of persons found not guilty by reason of insanity in New York State, 1971–76. *American Journal of Psychiatry, 136*, 655–660.

Pasewark, R. A., Pantle, M. L., & Steadman, H. J. (1979b). The insanity plea in New York State 1965–1976. *New York State Bar Journal, 51*, 186–189, 217–225.

Pasewark, R. A., Pantle, M. L., & Steadman, H. J. (1982). Detention and rearrest rates of persons found not guilty by reason of insanity and convicted felons. *American Journal of Psychiatry, 139*, 892–897.

Pasewark, R. A., & Seidenzahl, D. (1979). Opinions concerning the insanity plea and criminality among mental patients. *Bulletin of the American Academy of Psychiatry and Law, 7*, 199–202.

Pasewark, R. A., Seidenzahl, D., & Pantle, M. L. (1981). Opinions about the insanity plea. *Journal of Forensic Psychology, 8*, 63.

Patterson, C. H. (1980). *Theories of counseling and psychotherapy* (3rd ed.). New York: Harper.

Patterson, G. R., Jones, R., Whittier, J., & Wright, M. A. (1965). A behavior modification technique for the hyperactive child. *Behaviour Research and Therapy, 2*, 217–226.

Paul, G. L., & Lentz, R. J. (1977). *Psychosocial treatment of chronic mental patients.* Cambridge, MA: Harvard University Press.

Paulus, P. B., Cox, V. C., McCain, G., & Chandler, J. (1975). Some effects of crowding in a prison environment. *Journal of Applied Social Psychology, 5*, 86–91.

Paulus, P. B., McCain, G., & Cox, V. C. (1978). Death rates, psychiatric commitments, blood pressure, and perceived crowding as a function of institutional crowding. *Environmental Psychology and Nonverbal Behavior, 3,* 107–116.

Paxton, R. (1981). Deposit contracts with smokers: Varying frequency and amount of repayments. *Behaviour Research and Therapy, 19,* 117–123.

Payne, J. (1982). Contingent decision behavior. *Psychological Bulletin, 92,* 382–402.

Pellegrino, J. W., & Glaser, R. (1980). Components of inductive reasoning. In R. E. Snow, P. A. Federico, & W. E. Montague (Eds.), *Aptitude, learning, and instruction* (Vol. 1, pp. 177–217). Hillsdale, NJ: Erlbaum.

Pendery, M. L., Maltzman, I. M., & West, L. J. (1982). Controlled drinking by alcoholics? New findings and a reevaluation of a major affirmative study. *Science, 217(4555),* 169–174.

Pennhurst State School and Hospital v. Halderman, 451 U. S. 1 (1981).

Pepitone, A. (1981). Lessons from the history of social psychology. *American Psychologist, 36,* 972–985.

Perls, F. S. (1969). *Gestalt therapy verbatim.* Moab, UT: Real People Press.

Perry, W., Jr. (1970). *Intellectual and ethical development in the college years.* New York: Holt, Rinehart & Winston.

Peterson, D. R. (1968). The Doctor of Psychology program at the University of Illinois. *American Psychologist, 23,* 511–516.

Peterson, D. R. (1976). Is psychology a profession? *American Psychologist, 31,* 572–581.

Petrila, J. (1982). The insanity defense and other mental health dispositions in Missouri. *International Journal of Law and Psychiatry, 5,* 81–101.

Phillips, B. L., & Pasewark, R. A. (1980). Insanity plea in Connecticut. *Bulletin of American Academy of Psychiatry and the Law, 8,* 335–344.

Piaget, J. (1952). *The origins of intelligence in children.* New York: International Universities Press (Norton, 1963).

Piaget, J. (1959). *The language and thought of the child.* New York: Harcourt, Brace. (Original work published 1926).

Platt, J. (1973). Social traps. *American Psychologist, 28,* 641–651.

Pomerleau, O. F. (1979). Behavioral medicine: The contribution of the experimental analysis of behavior to medical care. *American Psychologist, 34,* 654–663.

Pomerleau, O. F. (1980). Limitations of current treatment and research on smoking: A discourse on the need to understand underlying mechanisms. *Behavioral Medicine Update, 2,* 22–26.

Poole, A. D., Sanson-Fisher, R. W., & German, G. A. (1981). The rapid-smoking technique: Some physiological effects. *Behaviour Research and Therapy, 19,* 389–397.

Popenoe, D. (1971). Urban studies reconsidered: Present trends and future prospects. *Urban Education, 6,* 6–31.

Porter, L. W., & Lawler, E. E. (1968). *Managerial attitudes and performance.* Homewood, IL: Dorsey.

Posner, M. I., & McLeod, P. (1982). Information processing models—in search of elementary operations. *Annual Review of Psychology, 33,* 477–514.

Pottharst, K. E. (1970). To renew vitality and provide a challenge in training—California School of Professional Training. *Professional Psychology, 1,* 123–130.

Poulton, E. C. (1966). Engineering psychology. *Annual Review of Psychology, 17,* 177–200.

Poythress, N. G., Jr. (1978). Psychiatric expertise in civil commitment: Training attorneys to cope with expert testimony. *Law and Human Behavior, 2,* 1–24.

Poythress, N. G., Jr. (1979). A proposal for training in forensic psychology. *American Psychologist, 34,* 612–621.

Prison population grew at record rate in 1981. (1982, June/July), *Justice Assistance News, 3* (5).

Pritchard, R. D., Dunnette, M. D., & Jorgenson, D. D. (1973). Effects of perceptions of equity and inequity on worker performance and satisfaction. *Journal of Applied Psychology, 58,* 122–125.

Pritchett, C. (1948). *The Roosevelt court.* New York: Macmillan.

Proshansky, H. M. (1976). Environmental psychology and the real world. *American Psychologist, 31,* 303–310.

Proshansky, H. M., Ittelson, W., & Rivlin, L. (Eds.). (1970). *Environmental psychology.* New York: Holt, Rinehart, & Winston.

Rabkin, J. G., & Streuning, E. L. (1976). Life events, stress and illness. *Science, 194,* 1013–1020.

Rachman, S. J., & Wilson, G. T. (1980). *The effects of psychological therapy* (2nd ed.). New York: Pergamon Press.

Raimy, V. C. (Ed.). (1950). *Training in clinical psychology.* New York: Prentice-Hall.

Rapaport, D., Gill, M., & Schaefer, R. (1945). *Diagnostic psychological testing* (Vol. 1). Chicago: Year Book Publishers.

Ray, M. L. (1973). Marketing communication and the hierarchy of effects. In P. Clarke (Ed.), *New models for mass communication research* (pp. 147–176). Beverly Hills, CA: Sage Publications.

Ray, M. L. (1982). *Advertising and communications management.* Englewood Cliffs, NJ: Prentice-Hall.

Reed, J. P. (1965). Jury deliberations, voting, and verdict trends. *Southwestern Social Science Quarterly, 45,* 361–370.

Reilly, D. H. (1973). School psychology: View from the second generation. *Psychology in the Schools, 10,* 151–155.

Reitan, R. M. (1966). Diagnostic inferences of brain lesions based on psychological test results. *Canadian Psychologist, 7a,* 368–383.

Renne, C. M., & Creer, T. L. (1976). Training children with asthma to use inhalation equipment. *Journal of Applied Behavioral Analysis, 9,* 1–11.

Resnick, L. B. (1981). Instructional psychology. *Annual Review of Psychology, 32,* 659–704.

Resnick, L. B., Wang, M. C., & Kaplan, J. (1973). Task analysis in curriculum design: A hierarchically sequenced introductory mathematics curriculum. *Journal of Applied Behavior Analysis, 6,* 679–709.

Rieman, D. W. (1963). Group mental health consultation with public health nurses. In J. Rapaport (Ed.), *Consultation in social work practice* (pp. 85–98). New York: National Association of Social Workers.

Robinson, F. P. (1950). *Principles and procedures in student counseling.* New York: Harper.

Robinson, F. P. (1970). *Effective study* (4th ed.). New York: Harper.

Robinson, F. P., & Hall. P. (1941). Studies of higher level reading abilities. *Journal of Educational Psychology, 32,* 241–252.

Robinson, R., DeMarche, D. F., & Wagle, M. (1960). *Community resources in mental health.* New York: Basic Books.

Roesch, R., & Golding, S. (1980). *Competency to stand trial.* Urbana, IL: University of Illinois Press.

Roethlisberger, F. W., & Dickson, W.J. (1939). *Management and the worker.* Cambridge, MA: Harvard University Press.

Rogers, C. R. (1942). *Counseling and psychotherapy.* Boston: Houghton Mifflin.

Rogers, C. R. (1951). *Client centered therapy.* Boston: Houghton Mifflin.

Rogers, C. R. (1957). The necessary and sufficient conditions of therapeutic personality change. *Journal of Consulting Psychology, 21,* 95–103.

Rogers, C. R. (1975). Empathic: An unappreciated way of being. *The Counseling Psychologist, 5(2),* 2–10.

Rogers, J. L., & Bloom, J. D. (1982). Characteristics of persons committed to Oregon's Psychiatric Security Review Board. *Bulletin of the American Academy of Psychiatry and Law, 10,* 155–164.

Rohles, F. H., Jr. (1971). Psychological aspects of thermal comfort. *ASHRAE Journal, 13,* 86–90.

Rolison, M. A., & Medway, F. J. (1982). A review of the teaching of psychology in high schools. *Professional Psychology, 13,* 453–461.

Rorschach, H. (1949). *Psychodiagnostics.* New York: Grune & Stratton.

Rosen, G. (1976). *Don't be afraid. A program for overcoming your fears and phobias.* Englewood Cliffs, NJ: Prentice-Hall.

Rosenman, R. H. & Friedman, M. (1960). Overt behavior pattern in coronary heart disease. *Journal of the American Medical Association, 173,* 1320.

Ross, I. (1981, August). *To market, to market.* Paper presented at the meeting of the American Psychological Association, Los Angeles.

Rothblatt, H. B. (1966). Techniques for jury selection. *Criminal Law Bulletin, 2(4),* 14–29.

Rotheram, M. J., Armstrong, M., & Booream, C. (1982). Assertiveness training in fourth- and fifth-grade children. *American Journal of Community Psychology, 10,* 567–582.

Rotter, J. B. (1966). Generalized expectancies for internal versus external control of reinforcement. *Psychological Monographs, 80* (Whole No. 609).

Russo, J. E., Krieser, G., & Miyashita, S. (1975). An effective display of unit price information. *Journal of Marketing, 39,* 11–19.

Ryan, J., Ashman, A., Sales, B. D., & Shane-DuBow, S. (1980). *American trial judges: Their work styles and performance.* New York: Free Press.

Ryan, M. J., & Bonfield, E. H. (1975). The Fishbein Extended Model and consumer behavior. *Journal of Consumer Research, 2,* 118–136.

Ryan, M. J., & Bonfield, E. H. (1980). Fishbein's intentions model: A test of external and pragmatic validity. *Journal of Marketing, 44,* 82–95.

Ryan, W. (1971). *Blaming the victim.* New York: Pantheon.

Saks, M. J. (1977). *Jury verdicts.* Lexington, MA: D. C. Heath.

Saks, M. J., & Hastie, R. (1978). *Social psychology in court.* New York: Van Nostrand Reinhold.

Sales, B. D. (Ed.). (1981). *The trial process.* New York: Plenum.

Sales, B. D. (1983a). The legal regulation of psychology. In C. J. Scheirer & B. L. Hammonds (Eds.), *The master lecture series. Volume 2: Psychology and law.* Washington, DC: American Psychological Association.

Sales, B. D. (1983b). The context of professional psychology. In B. D. Sales (Ed.), *Professional psychologist's handbook* (pp. 3–15). New York: Plenum.

Sales, B. D., & Elwork, A. (1980). Issues in training forensic psychologists. In G. Cooks (Ed.), *The role of the forensic psychologist* (pp. 16–25). Springfield, IL: C. C. Thomas.

Sales, B. D., & Overcast, T. D. (1984). The legal regulation of animal experimentation. Unpublished manuscript.

Sales, B. D., Powell, D. M., Van Duizend, R. A., & Associates (1982). *Disabled persons and the law: State legislative issues.* New York: Plenum.

Sarason, S. B. (1971). *The culture of the school and the problem of change.* Boston: Allyn & Bacon.

Sarason, S. B., Davidson, K., & Blatt, B. (1962). *The preparation of teachers: An unstudied problem in education.* New York: Wiley.

Sattler, J. M. (1982). *Assessment of children's intelligence and special abilities.* Boston: Allyn & Bacon.

Sauer, R. H., & Mullens, P. M. (1976). The insanity defense: M'Naghten versus ALI. *Bulletin of American Academy of Psychiatry and the Law, 4,* 73–75.

Schachter, S. (1982). Recidivism and self-cure of smoking and obesity. *American Psychologist, 37,* 436–444.

Schinke, S. P., Blythe, B. J., & Gilchrist, L. D. (1981). Cognitive–behavioral prevention of adolescent pregnancy. *Journal of Counseling Psychology, 28,* 451–454.

Schlechty, P., & Vance, V. S. (1982, July 20). Study reported to the National Institute for Education. *New York Times,* p. C4.

Schmidt, R. A. (1976). Control processes in motor skills. *Exercise and Sport Sciences Reviews, 4,* 229–261.

Schmidt, R. A., Zelazmik, H., Hawkins, B., Frank, J. S., & Quinn, J. T., Jr. (1979). Motor-output variability: A theory for the accuracy of rapid motor acts. *Psychological Review, 86,* 415–451.

Schmitt, N. (1976). Social and situational determinants of interview decisions: Implications for the employment interview. *Personnel Psychology, 29,* 79–101.

Schmuck, R. A., & Miles, M. B. (Eds.). (1971). *Organizational development in schools.* La Jolla, CA: University Associates, Inc.

Schofield, W. (1969). The role of psychology in the delivery of health services. *American Psychologist, 24,* 565–584.

Schofield, W. (1976). The psychologist as a health professional. *Professional Psychology, 7,* 5–8.

Schofield, W. (1982). Clinical psychology in transition: The evolution of a profession. In J. R. McNamara & A. Barclay (Eds.), *Contemporary issues in professional psychology* (pp. 29–55). New York: Praeger Publishers.

Schubert, G. (1965). *The judicial mind.* Evanston, IL: Northwestern University Press.

Schubert, G. (1974). *The judicial mind revisited.* London: Oxford University Press.

Schwab, D. P., & Cummings, L. L. (1970). Theories of performance and satisfaction: A review. *Industrial Relations, 9,* 408–430.

Schwartz, G. E. (1979). The brain as a health care system. In G. C. Stone, F. Cohen, & N. E. Adler (Eds.), *Health psychology* (pp. 549–571). San Francisco: Jossey-Bass.

Schwartz, G. E., & Weiss, S. M. (1978). Behavioral medicine revisited: An amended definition. *Journal of Behavioral Medicine, 1,* 249–251.

Schwitzgebel, R. L., & Schwitzgebel, R. K. (1980). *Law and psychological practice.* New York: Wiley.

Scott, W. D. (1903). *The theory of advertising.* Boston: Small & Maynard.

Scribner, S. (1968). What is community psychology made of? American Psychological Association, Division of Community Psychology, *Newsletter, 2,* 4–6.

Sealey, A. P., & Cornish, W. R. (1973). Jurors and their verdicts. *The Modern Law Review, 36,* 496–508.

Sechrest, L., & Cohen, R. Y. (1979). Evaluating outcomes in health care. In G. C. Stone, F. Cohen, & N. E. Adler (Eds.), *Health psychology* (pp. 369–394). San Francisco: Jossey-Bass.

Seligman, M. E. P. (1975). *Helplessness: On depression, development, and death.* San Francisco: W. H. Freeman.

Selling, L. S. (1943). *Men against madness.* New York: Garden City Books.

Selye, H. (1976). *The stress of life* (Rev. ed.). New York: McGraw-Hill.

Sewall, T. J., & Brown, D. T. (1976). *The handbook of certification/licensure requirements for school psychologist.* Washington, DC: National Association of School Psychologists.

Shackel, B. (Ed.). (1974). *Applied ergonomics handbook.* Surrey, England: IPC Science and Technology Press.

Shah, S. A. (1978). Dangerousness: A paradigm for exploring some issues in law and psychology. *American Psychologist, 33,* 224–238.

Shah, S. A. (1981). Legal and mental health system interaction: Major developments and research needs. *International Journal of Law and Psychiatry, 4,* 219–270.

Shakow, D. (1938). An internship year for psychologists. *Journal of Consulting Psychology, 21,* 73–76.

Shapiro, D. (1979). Biofeedback and behavioral medicine in perspective. *Biofeedback and Self-Regulation, 4,* 371–381.

Shephard, G., Durham, R., & Foot, D. (1976). Teaching psychology to nurses: Suggestions for a new course. *Bulletin of the British Psychological Society, 29,* 45–48.

Sheridan, T. B. (1980). Mental workload—What is it? Why bother with it? *Human Factors Society Bulletin, 23,* 1–2.

Shimahara, N. K. (1975). American society, culture and socialization. In N. K. Shimahara & A. Scrupski (Eds.), *Social forces and schooling: An anthropological and sociological perspective* (pp. 49–81). New York: David McKay.

Shocker, A. D., & Srinivasan, V. (1979). Multiattribute approaches for product concept evaluation and generation: A critical review. *Journal of Marketing Research, 16,* 159–180.

Short, J. (1973). A case study of task analysis. *Improving Human Performance, 2,* 60–67.

Shriffin, R. M., & Schneider, W. (1977). Controlled and automatic human information processing: II. Perceptual learning, automatic attending, and a general theory. *Psychological Review, 84,* 127–190.

Shuman, D. W., & Weiner, M. F. (1982). The privilege study: An empirical examination of the psychotherapist-patient privilege. *North Carolina Law Review, 60,* 893–942.

Siegel, L., & Lane, I. M. (1982). *Personnel and organizational psychology.* Homewood, IL: Irwin.

Simon, H. A. (1957). *Models of man: Social and rational.* New York: Wiley.

Simon, H. A. (1969). *The sciences of the artificial.* Cambridge, MA: MIT Press.

Simon, R. J. (1967). *The jury and the defense of insanity.* Boston: Little, Brown.

Singer, A. C. (1978). Insanity acquittal in the seventies: Observations and empirical analysis of one jurisdiction. *Mental Disability Law Reporter, 2,* 406–417.

Skinner, B. F. (1953). *Science and human behavior.* New York: Macmillan.

Skinner, B. F. (1954). The science of learning and the art of teaching. *Harvard Educational Review, 24,* 86–97.

Skinner, B. F. (1958). Teaching machines. *Science, 128,* 969–977.

Skinner, B. F. (1969). *Contingencies of reinforcement.* New York: Appleton-Century-Crofts.

Skotko, V. P. (1980). Professional activities and the perceptions of needs and opportunities for community psychologists. *American Journal of Community Psychology, 8,* 709–714.

Sladen, B. J. (1982). Effects of race and socioeconomic status on the perception of process variables in counseling. *Journal of Counseling Psychology, 29,* 560–566.

Slovic, P. (1982). Toward understanding and improving decisions. In W. C. Howell & E. A. Fleishman (Eds.), *Human performance and productivity* (Vol. 2, pp. 157–183). Hillsdale, NJ: Erlbaum.

Slovic, P., Fischhoff, B., & Lichtenstein, S. (1977). Behavioral decision theory. *Annual Review of Psychology, 28,* 1–39.

Slovic, P., & Lichtenstein, S. (1971). Comparison of Bayesian and regression approaches to the study of information processing in judgment. *Organizational Behavior and Human Performance, 6,* 649–744.

Smith, A., & Blumberg, A. (1967). The problem of objectivity in judicial decision-making. *Social Forces, 46,* 96–105.

Smith, D. (1982). Trends in counseling and psychotherapy. *American Psychologist, 37,* 802–809.

Smith, E. E. (1968). Choice reaction time: An analysis of the major theoretical positions. *Psychological Bulletin, 69,* 77–110.

Smith, M. L., & Glass, G. V. (1977). Meta-analysis of psychotherapy outcome studies. *American Psychologist, 32,* 752–760.

Smith, M. L., Glass, G. V., & Miller, T. I. (1980). *The benefits of psychotherapy.* Baltimore: Johns Hopkins University Press.

Smith, P. C., & Kendall, L. M. (1963). Retranslation of expectations: An approach to the construction of unambiguous scale anchors for rating scales. *Journal of Applied Psychology, 47,* 149–155.

Snortum, J., & Ashear, V. (1972). Prejudice, punitiveness and personality. *Journal of Personality Assessment, 36,* 291–296.

Snyder, E. (1971). Sex role differential and jury decisions. *Sociology and Social Research*, 55, 442–448.

Sobell, M. B., & Sobell, L. C. (1978). *Behavioral treatment of alcohol problems*. New York: Plenum.

Social Security Amendments of 1972 (P. L. 92-603).

Special Commission on the Social Sciences of the National Science Board. (1969). *Knowledge into action: Improving the nation's use of social sciences*. Washington, DC: National Science Foundation.

Spielberger, C. D. (1967). A mental health consultation program in a small community with limited professional mental health resources. In E. L. Cowen, E. A. Gardner, & M. Zax (Eds.), *Emergent approaches to mental health problems* (pp. 214–236). New York: Appleton-Century-Crofts.

Spielberger, C. D., & Iscoe, I. (1970). The current status of training in community psychology. In I. Iscoe & C. D. Spielberger (Eds.), *Community psychology: Perspectives in training and research* (pp. 227–246). New York: Appleton-Century-Crofts.

Spielberger, C. D., & Iscoe, I. (1972). Graduate education in community psychology. In S. E. Golann & C. Eisdorfer (Eds.), *Handbook of community mental health* (pp. 909–920). New York: Appleton-Century-Crofts.

Spielberger, C. D., & Iscoe, I. (1977). Community psychology in transition: Reflections on the Austin Conference. In I. Iscoe, B. L. Bloom & C. D. Spielberger (Eds.), *Community psychology in transition* (pp. 315–327). Washington, DC: Hemisphere Publishing Co.

Spielberger, C. D., Piacente, B. S., & Hobfoll, S. E. (1976). Program evaluation in community psychology. *American Journal of Community Psychology*, 4, 393–404.

Spokane, A. R., & Oliver, L. W. (1983). The outcomes of vocational interventions. In S. H. Osipow & W. B. Walsh (Eds.), *Handbook of vocational psychology* (pp. 99–136). Hillsdale, NJ: Erlbaum.

Stahl, R. S. (1977). *The status of precollege psychology in Mississippi: The final report of a survey in 1975-76*. ERIC Document Reproduction Service No. ED ISS 091.

Stapp, J. (1983). *Summary report of 1982–1983 survey of graduate departments of psychology*. Washington, DC: American Psychological Association.

Stapp, J., & Fulcher, R. (1981). The employment of APA members. *American Psychologist*, 36, 1263–1314.

Stapp, J. & Fulcher, R. (1982). The employment of 1979 and 1980 doctoral recipients. *American Psychologist*, 37, 1159–1185.

Stapp, J., Fulcher, R., Nelson, S. D., Pallak, M. S., & Wicheriski, M. (1981). The employment of recent doctorate recipients in psychology, 1975 through 1978. *American Psychologist*, 36, 1211–1254.

Steadman, H. J., & Braff, J. (1983). Defendants not guilty by reason of insanity. In J. Monahan & H. J. Steadman (Eds.), *Mentally disordered offenders: Perspectives from law and social science* (pp. 109–129). New York: Plenum.

Steadman, H. J., Cocozza, J. J., & Melick, M. E. (1978). Explaining the increased arrest rate among mental patients: The changing clientele of state hospitals. *American Journal of Psychiatry*, 135, 816–820.

Steadman, H. J., Keitner, L., Braff, J., & Arvanites, T. M. (1983). Factors associated with a successful insanity plea. *American Journal of Psychiatry*, 140, 401–405.

Stenmark, D. E. (1981, August). *End of the beginning or beginning of the end?* Division 27 Presidential Address presented at the meeting of the American Psychological Association, Los Angeles.

Stenmark, D. E., Taulbee, E. S., & Wright, H. W. (1967). *Community mental health: Comprehensive annotated and indexed bibliography.* Unpublished manuscript, Veterans Administration Hospital, Tuscaloosa, AL.

Stephan, D., & Tully, J. C. (1977). The influence of physical attractiveness of a plaintiff on the decisions of simulated jurors. *Journal of Social Psychology, 101,* 147–150.

Sternbach, R. A. (1974). *Pain patients: Traits and treatment.* New York: Academic Press.

Stigall, T. T. (1983). Licensing and certification. In B. D. Sales (Ed.), *Professional psychologist's handbook* (pp. 285 - 337). New York: Plenum.

Stokey, E., & Zeckhauser, R. A. (1978). *A primer for policy analysis.* New York: Norton.

Stokols, D. (1977). Origins and directions of environment-behavior research. In D. Stokols (Ed.), *Perspectives on environment and behavior: Theory, research, and application* (pp. 5–36). New York: Plenum.

Stokols, D. (1978). Environmental psychology. *Annual Review of Psychology, 29,* 253–295.

Stone, G. C., Cohen, F., & Adler, N. E. (Eds.). (1979). *Health psychology.* San Francisco: Jossey-Bass.

Stricker, G., Claiborn, W. L., & Bent, R. J. (1982). Peer review: An overview. *Professional Psychology, 13,* 5–8.

Strodtbeck, F. L., & Hook, L. H. (1961). The social dimensions of a twelve-man jury table. *Sociometry, 34,* 397–415.

Strodtbeck, F. L., James, R. M., & Hawkins, C. (1957). Social status in jury deliberations. *American Sociological Review, 22,* 713–719.

Strodtbeck, F. L., & Mann, R. (1956). Sex role differentiation in jury deliberations. *Sociometry, 29,* 3–11.

Strong, S. R. (1968). Counseling: An interpersonal influence process. *Journal of Counseling Psychology, 15,* 215–224.

Strong, S. R. (1978). Social psychological approach to psychotherapy research. In S. L. Garfield & A. C. Begin (Eds.), *Handbook of psychotherapy and behavior change* (2nd ed., pp. 101–135). New York: Wiley.

Strongman, K. T. (1973). *The psychology of emotion.* New York: Wiley.

Strother, C. R. (1956). *Psychology and mental health.* (Stanford Conference). Washington, DC: American Psychological Association.

Stunkard, A. J., & Penick, S. B. (1979). Behavior modification in the treatment of obesity. *Archives of General Psychiatry, 36,* 801–806.

Sue, D. W., Bernier, J. E., Durran, A., Feinberg, L., Pedersen, P., & Smith, E. J. (1982). Cross-cultural counseling competencies. *The Counseling Psychologist, 10(2),* 45–52.

Suggs, D., & Sales, B. D. (1978). Using communication cues to evaluate prospective jurors during the voir dire. *Arizona Law Review, 20,* 629–642.

Suggs, D., & Sales, B. D. (1981). Juror self-disclosure during the voir dire: A social science analysis. *Indiana Law Journal, 56,* 749–760.

Super, D. E. (1942). *The dynamics of vocational development.* New York: Harper.

Super, D. E. (1957). *The psychology of careers.* New York: Harper.

Sussman, E. D., & Morris, D. F. (1971). Investigation of factors affecting driver alertness. *JSAS Catalog of Selected Documents in Psychology, 1,* 30.

Symonds, P. M. (1942). The school psychologist—1942. *Journal of Consulting Psychology, 6,* 173–176.

Syverson, P. D. (1982). Two decades of doctorates in psychology. *American Psychologist, 37,* 1203–1212.

Task Force on Education and Credentialing (1983, June). *Draft report to the APA Board of Directors and the Council of Representatives.* Washington, DC: APA.

Taylor, D. A. (1976). State analysis of reaction time. *Psychology Bulletin, 83,* 161–191.

Taylor, F. V. (1957). Psychology and the design of machines. *American Psychologist, 12,* 249–258.

Taylor, F. W. (1911). *The principles of scientific management.* New York: Harper.

Taylor, R. B. (1983). Conjoining environmental psychology and personality and social psychology: Natural marriage or shotgun marriage? In N. R. Feimer & E. S. Geller (Eds.), *Environmental psychology: Directions and perspectives* (pp. 24–66). New York: Pergamon Press.

Taylor, R. B., Gottfredson, S. D., & Brower, S. (1980). The defensibility of defensible space. In T. Hirschi & M. Gottfredson (Eds.), *Understanding crime* (pp. 53–71). Beverly Hills, CA: Sage Publications.

Taylor, R. B., & Shumaker, S. A. (1982, June). *Community crime prevention in review.* Paper presented at the meeting of the Law and Society Association, Toronto.

Tennov, D. (1975). *Psychotherapy: The hazardous cure.* New York: Abelard Schuman Thomas Y. Crowell.

The insanity defense: ABA and APA proposals for change. (1983). *Mental Disability Law Reporter, 7,* 136–147, 210–211.

Thibaut, J., & Walker, L. (1975). *Procedural justice: A psychological analysis.* Hillsdale, NJ: Erlbaum.

Thomas, A., Birik, H. G., Chess, S., Hertzig, M. E., & Korn, S. (1963). *Behavioral individuality in early childhood.* New York: New York University Press.

Thompson, A. S., & Super, D. E. (Eds.). (1964). *The professional preparation of counseling psychologists.* New York: Teachers College, Columbia University.

Thoresen, C. E. (1980). Reflections on chronic health, self-control, and human ethology. *The Counseling Psychologist, 8(4),* 48–58.

Thoresen, C. E., & Mahoney, M. J. (1974). *Behavioral self-control.* New York: Holt, Rinehart & Winston.

Thornberry, T. P. (1973). Race, socioeconomic status, and sentencing in the juvenile justice system. *Journal of Criminal Law & Criminology, 64,* 90–98.

Tiemann, P. W., & Markle, S. M. (1978). *Analyzing instructional contents: A guide to instruction and evaluation.* Champaign, IL: Stipes.

Toomer, J. (1982). Counseling psychologists in business and industry. *The Counseling Psychologist, 10(3),* 9–18.

Touchton, J. G., Wertheimer, L. C., & Cornfeld, J. L. (1977). Career planning and decision-making: A developmental approach to the classroom. *The Counseling Psychologist, 6(4),* 44–47.

Toves, C., Schill, T., & Ramanalah, N. (1981). Sex difference, internal-external control, and vulnerability to life stress. *Psychological Reports, 49,* 508.

Trachtman, G. M. (1981). On such a full sea. In J. E. Ysseldyke & R. Weinberg (Eds.), The future training and practice in school psychology: Proceedings of the Spring Hill Symposium (special issue). *School Psychology Review, 10,* 138–181.

Troutman, C. M., & Shanteau, J. (1976). Do consumers evaluate products by adding or averaging attribute information? *Journal of Consumer Research, 3,* 101–106.

Truax, C. B., & Carkhuff, R. R. (1967). *Toward effective counseling and psychotherapy: Training and practice.* Chicago: Aldine.

Twedt, D. W. (1964). How important to marketing strategy is the "heavy user"? *Journal of Marketing, 28,* 72.

Ulmer, S. (1973). Social background as an indicator to the votes of Supreme Court justices in criminal cases: 1947–1956 terms. *American Journal of Political Science, 17,* 622–630.

Uniform guidelines on employee selection procedures. (1978, August). Federal Register, 43 (166), pp. 38296–38309.

U. S. Employment Service. (1977). *Dictionary of Occupational Titles.* Washington, DC: U. S. Government Printing Office.

Utgaard, S. B., & Dawis, R. V. (1970). The most frequently used training techniques. *Training and Development Journal, 24,* 40–43.

Van Cott, H. P., & Kincade, R. G. (Eds.). (1972). *Human engineering guide to equipment design.* Washington, DC: U. S. Government Printing Office.

VandenBos, G. R., Stapp, J., & Pallak, M. S. (Eds.). (1981). Human resources in psychology (special issue). *American Psychologist, 36,* No. 11.

Vanderzell, J. H. (1966). The jury as a community cross section. *Western Political Science Quarterly, 19,* 136–149.

Varni, J. W. (1980). Behavior therapy in the management of home and school behavior problems with a 4½ year old hemophilic child. *Journal of Pediatric Psychology, 5,* 17–23.

Verbrugge, L. M., & Taylor, R. B. (1980). Consequences of metropolitan population density. *Urban Affairs Quarterly, 16,* 135–160.

Vidmar, N. (1972). Effects of decision alternatives on the verdicts and social perceptions of simulated jurors. *Journal of Personality and Social Psychology, 22,* 211–218.

Virginia Academy of Clinical Psychologists v. Blue Shield of Virginia, 624 F-2nd 476 (4th Circuit, 1980) *Cert. denied,* 450 U. S. 916 (1981).

Vroom, V. H. (1964). *Work and motivation.* New York: Wiley.

Wade, T. C., & Baker, T. B. (1977). Opinions and use of psychological tests: A survey of clinical psychologists. *American Psychologist, 32,* 874–882.

Walfish, S., Polifka, J. A., & Stenmark, D. E. (1984). An evaluation of skill acquisition in community psychology training. *American Journal of Community Psychology, 12,* 165–174.

Walker, E., & McKeachie, W. (1967). *Some thoughts about teaching the beginning course in psychology.* Belmont, CA: Brooks/Cole.

Walker, R. E., Nicolay, R. C., & Stearns, C. R. (1965). Comparative accuracy of recognizing American and international road signs. *Journal of Applied Psychology, 49,* 322–325.

460 Applied Specialties in Psychology

Wallace, S. R. (1965). Criteria for what? *American Psychologist, 20,* 411–417.

Waller, I., & Okihiro, N. (1978). *Burglary: The victim and the public.* Toronto: University of Toronto Press.

Wallin, J. E. W. (1942). The "school psychologist" in retrospect. *Journal of Consulting Psychology, 6,* 309– 312.

Wallin, J. E. W., & Ferguson, D. G. (1967). The development of school psychological services. In J. F. Magary (Ed.), *School psychological services in theory and practice* (pp. 1–29). Englewood Cliffs, NJ: Prentice-Hall.

Wanous, J. P. (1974). A causal correlational analysis of the job satisfaction and performance relationship. *Journal of Applied Psychology, 59,* 139–144.

Wanous, J. P., & Zwany, A. (1977). A cross sectional test of need hierarchy theory. *Organizational Behavior and Human Performance, 18,* 78–97.

Washington v. Davis, 426 U. S. 299 (1976).

Watson, G. (1931). The demand for psychological counselors in education. *Mental Hygiene, 15,* 542–549.

Watson, J. B., & Raynor, R. (1920). Conditioned emotional reactions. *Journal of Experimental Psychology, 3,* 1–14.

Watson, R. I. (1953). A brief history of clinical psychology. *Psychological Bulletin, 50,* 321–346.

Wechsler, D. (1974). *Manual for the Wechsler Intelligence Scale for Children–revised.* New York: The Psychological Corporation.

Weiss, S. M. (1982). Health psychology: The time is now. *Health Psychology, 1,* 81–91.

Weitz, S. (Ed.). (1974). *Nonverbal communication.* New York: Oxford University Press.

Welford, A. T. (1976). *Skilled performance: Perceptual and motor skills.* Glenview, IL: Scott, Foresman.

Wells, G. (Ed.). (1980). On eyewitness behavior (special issue). *Law and Human Behavior, 4,* No. 4.

Wells, W. D. (1975). Psychographics: A critical review. *Journal of Marketing Research, 12,* 196–213.

Westbrook, B. W., & Parry-Hill, J. W., Jr. (1973). The measurement of cognitive vocational maturity. *Journal of Vocational Behavior, 3,* 239–252.

Wexler, D. B. (1981). *Mental health law: The major issues.* New York: Plenum.

White, K. M., Marcuella, H., & Oresick, R. (1979). Psychology in the high school. *Teaching of Psychology, 6,* 39–42.

White, M. A. (1978). Identifying a school's real agenda: Nine steps. *Journal of School Psychology, 16,* 292–300.

White, M. A., & Harris, M. W. (1961). *The school psychologist.* New York: Harper.

White, R. W. (1973). The concept of healthy personality: What do we really mean? *The Counseling Psychologist, 4(2),* 3–12.

Whiteley, J. M. (1980). *The history of counseling psychology.* Monterey, CA: Brooks/Cole.

Whiteley, J. M. (1982). *Character development in college students.* Schenectady, NY: Character Research.

Wickelgren, W. A. (1979). *Cognitive psychology.* Englewood Cliffs, NJ: Prentice-Hall.

Wickens, C. D., Mountford, S. J., & Shreiner, W. (1981). Multiple resources, task-hemispheric integrity, and individual differences in time-sharing. *Human Factors, 23,* 211–229.

Wicker, A. W., & Kirmeyer, S. L. (1976). From church to laboratory to national park. In S. Wapner, S. B. Cohen, & B. Kaplan (Eds.), *Experiencing the environment* (pp. 157–185). New York: Plenum.

Wiener, E. L. (Ed.). (1980). Air traffic control (special issue). *Human Factors, 22,* No. 5.

Wilkie, W. L., & Pessemier, E. A. (1973). Issues in marketing's use of multi-attribute attitude models. *Journal of Marketing Research, 10,* 428–441.

Williams, R. L., & Long, J. D. (1975). *Toward a self-managed life-style.* Boston: Houghton Mifflin.

Williges, R. C. (1982). Applying the human information processing approach to human/computer interactions. In W. C. Howell & E. Fleishman (Eds.), *Human performance and productivity* (Vol. 2, pp. 83–119). Hillsdale, NJ: Erlbaum.

Wilson, G. T., & Franks, C. M. (Eds.). (1982). *Contemporary behavior therapy: Conceptual and empirical foundations.* New York: Guilford.

Wind, Y. (1978). Issues and advances in segmentation research. *Journal of Marketing Research, 15,* 317–337.

Wing, J. F. (1965). Upper thermal tolerance limits for unimpaired mental performance. *Aerospace Medicine, 36,* 960–964.

Winkel, G. H. (1981, August). *The psychologist as form-giver: Rebuilding Bellevue Hospital.* Paper presented at the annual meeting of the American Psychological Association, Los Angeles.

Wohl, J. G. (1981). Force management decision requirements for Air Force tactical command and control. *IEE Transactions on systems, man, and cybernetics* (SMC-11, pp. 618–639).

Wolfe, D., Buxton, C., Cofer, C., Gustad, J., MacLeod, R., & McKeachie, W. (1952). *Improving undergraduate instruction in psychology.* New York: MacMillan.

Wolpe, J. (1958). *Psychotherapy by reciprocal inhibition.* Stanford, CA: Stanford University Press.

Wolpe, J., & Lazarus, A. (1966). *Behavior theory technique: A guide to the treatment of neurosis.* Elmsford, NY: Pergamon Press.

Wolpert, H. W. (1982). The use of cognitive response measures in Ford Motor Company commercial pre-tests. In J. Chasin (Ed.), *Straight talk about attitude research* (pp. 137–144). Chicago: American Marketing Association.

Woods, K. M., & McNamara, J. R. (1980). Confidentiality: Its effect on interviewer behavior. *Professional Psychology, 11,* 714–721.

Woodson, W. E. (1981). *Human factors design handbook.* New York: McGraw-Hill.

Worchel, S., & Teddlie, C. (1976). The experience of crowding: A two-factor theory. *Journal of Personality and Social Psychology, 34,* 30–40.

Wright, L. (1976). Psychology as a health profession. *Clinical Psychologist, 29(2),* 16–19.

Wright, L. (1977). Conceptualizing and defining psychosomatic disorders. *American Psychologist, 32,,* 625–628.

Wright, P. L. (1973). The cognitive processes mediating acceptance of advertising. *Journal of Marketing Research, 10,* 53–62.

Wright, P. L. (1980). Message-evoked thoughts: Persuasion research using thought verbalizations. *Journal of Consumer Research*, 7, 151–175.

Wright, P. L., & Weitz, B. A. (1977). Time horizon effects on product evaluation strategies. *Journal of Marketing Research*, 14, 429–443.

Yamamoto, K. (1968). *The college student and his culture.* Boston: Houghton Mifflin.

Young, S., Ott, L., & Feigen, B. (1978). Some practical considerations in market segmentation. *Journal of Marketing Research*, 15, 405–412.

Youngberg v. Romeo, 102 S. Ct. 2452 (1982).

Zamostny, K. P., Corrigan, J. D., & Eggert, M. A. (1981). Replication and extension of social influence processes in counseling: A field study. *Journal of Counseling Psychology*, 28, 481–489.

Zaro, J. S., Batchelor, W. F., Ginsberg, M. R., & Pallak, M. (1982). Psychology and the JCAH: Reflections on a decade of struggle. *American Psychologist*, 37, 1342–1349.

Zeisel, H. (1971). . . . And then there were none: The diminution of the federal jury. *University of Chicago Law Review*, 38, 710–724.

Zeisel, H., & Diamond, S. S. (1974). Convincing empirical evidence on the six member jury. *University of Chicago Law Review*, 41, 281–295.

Zeisel, H., & Diamond, S. (1978). The effect of peremptory challenges on the jury and verdict. *Stanford Law Review*, 30, 491–531.

Zeiss, M. (1980). Aversiveness versus change in the assessment of life stress. *Journal of Psychosomatic Research*, 24, 15–19.

Zunker, V. G. (1981). *Career counseling.* Monterey, CA: Brooks/Cole.

SUBJECT INDEX

AUTHOR INDEX

Primary source is set in italics.

Cohen, J. B., 294, *430*
Cohen, L. D., 39, *430*
Cohen, R., 146, *447*
Cohen, R. Y., 122, *454*
Cohen, S., 315, 317, *430*
Cohen, Y. A., 129, *430*
Collins, A. M., 290, *430*
Comtois, R. J., 146, *430*
Conti, A. P., 147, *430*
Cooke, G., 361, 369, *430*
Cooper, S., 80, *426*
Copeland, W. D., 148, *430*
Cornell, E. L., 134, *430*
Cornfeld, J. L., 62, *458*
Cornish, W. R., 354, *454*
Corrigan, J. D., 53, 54, *430*, *462*
Cowen, E. L., 80, *146*, *430*, *436*
Cox, V. C., 322, *430*, *446*, *449*, *450*
Craighead, W. E., 146, *431*
Craik, F. I. M., 303, *431*
Craik, K. H., 310, *431*
Creer, T. L., 121, *451*
Criss, M. L., 361, 362, 369, *431*
Crites, J. O., 57, 58, *431*
Crockett, W. H., 230, *428*
Crosson, R. F., 353, *431*
Cummings, L. L., 230, *454*
Cummings, N. A., 120, *431*

Darrow, C., 62, 71, 334, *431*, *444*
D'Atri, D. A., 322, *431*
Davidson, K., 137, *453*
Davis, F., 354, *431*
Davis, G. G., 319, *426*
Davis, H. G., 350, *431*
Davis, J. H., 350, *442*
Davis, M., 64, *431*
Davis, R. V., 227, *459*
Deffenbacher, J. L., 56, *431*
Degan, J., 247, 249, *426*
Dekraai, M. B., 341, 342, 407, *422*, *431*
Dell, D. M., 53, 54, *430*
DeMarche, D. F., 78, *452*
Dembo, T., 310, *425*
Dewar, R., 258, 259, *432*, *445*
Diamond, S. S., 334, 336, 337, 349, 352, 357, *432*, *462*

Dickson, W. J., 210, *452*
Dixon, D. N., 69, *443*
Dominowski, R. L., 260, *428*
Dorken, H., 341, *432*
Drake, E. A., 147, *432*
Drum, D. J., 63, *432*
Dunnette, M. D., 211, 218, 226, 231, 238, *429*, *432*, *451*
Durham, R., 106, *454*
Durran, A., 69, *457*
Dworkin, B., 112, *432*
Dwyer, B. J., 152, *432*

Ebbesen, E. B., 336, 337, 358, *432*, *443*
Edney, J. J., 325, *432*
Egan, G., 52, 72, *432*
Eggert, M. A., 54, *462*
Einhorn, H. J., 226, *432*
Eisdorfer, C., 84, *424*
Eisenberg, A. M., 354, *433*
Ekman, P., 354, *433*
Ellis, A., 35, *433*
Ells, J. G., 258, *432*
Elwork, A., 331, 334, 336, 347, 348, 350, 370, *433*, *453*
Engel, G. L., 107, *433*
Engel, J. E., 280, 300, *433*
Epstein, L. H., 112, 120, *427*, *433*
Erikson, E. H., 61, 130, *433*
Eshelman, E. R., 64, *431*
Evans, G. W., 315, 317, *430*
Everett, P. B., 325, *436*
Ewalt, J., 78, *433*
Eysenck, H. J., 40, 41, *433*

Fagan, T., 151, *433*
Fairweather, G. W., 318, *433*
Fanger, P. O., 271, *433*
Farling, W. H., 151, *433*
Farr, J. L., 220, 238, *443*
Farrington, D. D., 323, *433*
Feigen, B., 303, *462*
Feinberg, L., 69, *457*
Feld, S., 78, *437*
Feldman, S., 336, *433*
Felix, R. H., 78, *434*
Festinger, L., 309, *434*